Standard	Key Elements of the Standard	Chapter and Topic
4: Using Developmentally Effective Approaches to Connect with Children and Families	4a: Understanding positive relationships and supportive interactions as the foundation of their work with children 4b: Knowing and understanding effective strategies and tools for early education 4c: Using a broad repertoire of developmentally appropriate teaching/learning approaches 4d: Reflecting on their own practice to promote positive outcomes for each child	1: Knowledge of Children: Developmentally Appropriate Practice (DAP), p. 8 2: Understand Content and Methods, p. 28 3: Designing an Integrated Study, p. 64 4: Teaching the Large Motor Curriculum, p. 101 4: Planning Large Motor Curriculum, p. 111 5: Teaching the Fine Motor Curriculum, p. 133 5: Planning Fine Motor Curriculum, p. 140 6: Teaching Sensory Development Curriculum, p. 162 6: Planning Sensory Curriculum, p. 168 7: Teaching Language, p. 200 7: Planning Language Curriculum, p. 208 8: Teaching Literacy, p. 227 8: Planning Literacy Curriculum, p. 242 9: Teaching Literature, p. 264 9: Planning Literature Curriculum, p. 274 10: Teaching Art, p. 302 10: Planning Art Curriculum, p. 316 11: Teaching Music, p. 340 11: Planning Music Curriculum, p. 352 12: Teaching Creative Movement, p. 370 12: Planning Creative Movement Curriculum, p. 378 13: Teaching Math, p. 404 13: Planning Math Curriculum, p. 415 14: Teaching Science, p. 434 14: Planning Science Curriculum, p. 440 15: Teaching Social Studies, p. 465 15: Planning Social Studies Curriculum, p. 470
5: Using Content Knowledge to Build Meaningful Curriculum	5a: Understanding content knowledge and resources in academic disciplines 5b: Knowing and using the central concepts, inquiry tools, and structures of content areas or academic disciplines 5c: Using their own knowledge, appropriate early learning standards, and other resources to design, implement, and evaluate meaningful, challenging curricula for each child	1: Content Standards, p. 12 2: Know Local and National Standards, p. 36 3: Why Integrated Curriculum?, p. 58 3: Models of Integrated Curriculum, p. 58 3: Designing an Integrated Study, p. 64 4: What Is Large Motor Curriculum in Early Childhood?, p. 91 4: Standards for Large Motor Curriculum, p. 99 5: What Is Fine Motor Curriculum in Early Childhood?, p. 129 5: Standards for Fine Motor Curriculum, p. 133 6: What Is Sensory Curriculum in Early Childhood?, p. 160 6: Standards for Sensory Development Curriculum, p. 161 7: What Is Language Curriculum in Early Childhood?, p. 193 7: Standards for Language Curriculum, p. 198 8: What Is Literacy Curriculum in Early Childhood?, p. 225 8: Standards for Literacy Curriculum, p. 227 9: What Is Literature Curriculum in Early Childhood?, p. 256 9: Standards for Literature Curriculum, p. 263 10: What Is Art Curriculum in Early Childhood?, p. 297 10: Standards for Visual Art and Aesthetics Curriculum, p. 300 11: What Is Music Curriculum in Early Childhood?, p. 334 11: Standards for Music Curriculum, p. 338 12: What Is Creative Movement Curriculum in Early Childhood?, p. 365 12: Standards for Creative Movement Curriculum, p. 368 13: What Is Math Curriculum in Early Childhood?, p. 397 13: Standards for Math Curriculum, p. 404 14: What Is Science Curriculum in Early Childhood?, p. 429 14: Standards for Science Curriculum, p. 433 15: What Is Social Studies Curriculum in Early Childhood?, p. 456 15: Standards for Social Studies Curriculum, p. 462
6: Becoming a Professional	6a: Identifying and involving oneself with the early childhood field 6b: Knowing about and upholding ethical standards and other professional guidelines 6c: Engaging in continuous, collaborative learning to inform practice 6d: Integrating knowledgeable, reflective, and critical perspectives on early education 6e: Engaging in informed advocacy for children and the profession	1: What Is Unique About Early Childhood Education?, p. 6 Classroom scenarios depict reflective practice and professionalism.

The Standards and Key Elements are from NAEYC. "NAEYC Standards for Early Childhood Professional Preparation Programs." Position statement. Washington, DC: Author. Reprinted with permission from the National Association for the Education of Young Children (NAEYC). Copyright © 2009 NAEYC. Full text of all NAEYC position statements is available at www.naeyc.org/positionstatements. These correlations are suggested by the authors.

Meaningful Curriculum
for Young Children

EVA MORAVCIK

Honolulu Community College

SHERRY NOLTE

Honolulu Community College

STEPHANIE FEENEY

University of Hawai'i at Mānoa

PEARSON

Boston   Columbus   Indianapolis   New York   San Francisco   Upper Saddle River
Amsterdam   Cape Town   Dubai   London   Madrid   Milan   Munich   Paris   Montreal   Toronto
Delhi   Mexico City   São Paulo   Sydney   Hong Kong   Seoul   Singapore   Taipei   Tokyo

Vice President and Editorial Director:
Jeffery W. Johnston
Senior Acquisitions Editor: Julie Peters
Development Editor: Bryce Bell
Editorial Assistant: Andrea Hall
Vice President, Director of Marketing:
Margaret Waples
Senior Marketing Manager: Christopher D.
Barry
Senior Managing Editor: Pamela D. Bennett
Senior Project Manager: Linda Hillis Bayma
Senior Operations Supervisor: Matthew
Ottenweller

Senior Art Director: Diane C. Lorenzo
Text and Cover Designer: Candace Rowley
Cover Image: Jeff Reese
Media Project Manager: Rebecca Norsic
Full-Service Project Management:
Lynn Steines, S4Carlisle Publishing Services
Composition: S4Carlisle Publishing Services
Printer/Binder: R.R. Donnelley & Sons
Company
Cover Printer: Lehigh Phoenix/Hagerstown
Text Font: ITC Garamond

Credits and acknowledgments for materials borrowed from other sources and reproduced, with permission, in this textbook appear on appropriate page within text, or below.

The Standards and Key Elements in the Learning Outcomes section of each chapter are from NAEYC. "NAEYC Standards for Early Childhood Professional Preparation Programs." Position Statement. Washington, DC: Author. Reprinted with permission from the National Association for the Education of Young Children (NAEYC). Copyright © 2009 NAEYC. Full text of all NAEYC position statements is available at www.naeyc.org/positionstatements

Every effort has been made to provide accurate and current Internet information in this book. However, the Internet and information posted on it are constantly changing, so it is inevitable that some of the Internet addresses listed in this textbook will change.

Photo Credits: All photos by Jeff Reese

Library of Congress Cataloging-in-Publication Data

Moravcik, Eva.
Meaningful curriculum for young children/Eva Moravcik, Sherry Nolte, Stephanie Feeney.
p. cm.
Includes index.
ISBN-13: 978-0-13-502690-8
ISBN-10: 0-13-502690-3
1. Early childhood education—Curricula—United States. 2. Curriculum planning—United States. I. Nolte,
Sherry. II. Feeney, Stephanie. III. Title.
LB1139.4.M67 2013
372.19—dc23
2011040450

10 9 8 7 6 5 4 3 2 1

ISBN-13: 978-0-13-502690-8
ISBN-10:   0-13-502690-3

To the children we have taught and who have taught us.

Who We Are

When we read a book, we like to know about the authors. We want to understand their experience, background, and point of view. Though the authors of this book have different backgrounds and experience, each of us comes to early childhood curriculum with a very similar point of view. We have all long held a strong commitment to programs for children that are nurturing and humane and support all aspects of their development.

Eva, the lead author, is a professor of early childhood education at Honolulu Community College. In addition to teaching college classes, her work includes daily contact with children, families, and college students at the Leeward Community College Children's Center. Much of *Meaningful Curriculum for Young Children* grows out of her 20-plus years of creating curriculum and teaching teachers about it. Her daily work with children, family, staff, and college students provides her with grounding in the reality of life in a program for young children.

Sherry also teaches at Honolulu Community College. She currently supervises practicum students in community preschools, and teaches classes on preschool curriculum, infants and toddlers, child development, and child guidance.

Stephanie is recently retired from the University of Hawai'i at Mānoa, where she was professor of early childhood education for many years. She and Eva collaborated on the development of a conceptual framework for teaching social studies to young children and an accompanying curriculum. Stephanie is also the lead author on an introduction to early childhood education text, *Who Am I in the Lives of Children?* along with Eva and Sherry, has done extensive work on the Code of Ethical Conduct with NAEYC members and staff, and is the author of a new book, *Professionalism in Early Childhood Education*.

Stephanie Feeney, Eva Moravcik, Sherry Nolte

Preface

This book was written to help you, a student studying to be an early childhood teacher, develop knowledge of curriculum and an understanding about what makes learning experiences meaningful for young children. We want to share our conviction that young children are entitled to curriculum that has intellectual integrity and our belief that, at any age, real experience is essential for real learning. We want to communicate our deeply held belief that early childhood curriculum should be a joyful experience for both children and their teachers. Finally, even though this is a textbook, we have strived to make it engaging to read and to provide you with lots of practical ideas.

The book's focus is on curriculum for children in the preschool and kindergarten years, though much is valid for both children in the primary grades and toddlers. If you are training to work with children under the age of 5, you will probably take one or two early childhood curriculum courses. *Meaningful Curriculum for Young Children* is designed for these courses. If you are training to be an elementary teacher, it is likely that you will take many elementary curriculum methods courses that touch lightly on curriculum for young children. This book is designed to help you to understand the similarities and differences between curriculum in preschool and kindergarten and curriculum in the primary grades. We assume that you know what young children are like, how they develop, and what constitutes an appropriate early childhood program for young children. If you do not have this background, you will find it useful to read a basic child development text and/or early childhood foundations text.

The Approach of This Book

The cornerstone of this book and our work with children is what we refer to as a *child-centered* approach to early childhood education. This approach has its roots in a long tradition of humanistic and progressive education and the unique history and philosophy of early childhood education. Our ideas have been profoundly shaped by educators, psychologists, and philosophers who have advocated child-centered educational practice, including Friedrich Froebel, Maria Montessori, John Dewey, Lucy Sprague Mitchell, Erik Erikson, Lev Vygotsky, Jean Piaget, Abraham Maslow, Carl Rogers, Sylvia Ashton-Warner, John Holt, A. S. Neill, Barbara Biber, Howard Gardner, James L. Hymes, and Loris Malaguzzi.

We believe that curriculum is about children, not assessment, and that every child is worthy of our respect. We know that each child comes with strengths and that the most effective curriculum is built upon those strengths. We trust children to learn through their most natural activity, play, and the serious inquiry that is a part of play. We reaffirm the tenets of John Dewey, who said that school is not preparation for life, but *is* the life of the child. Finally, we are committed, along with Loris Malaguzzi and the educators of Reggio Emilia, to education in which there is "Nothing without joy!"

The Book's Structure and Features

Meaningful Curriculum for Young Children has five parts, each with an introduction and three chapters.

Part Structure

The first part, *Understanding Curriculum,* provides you with a brief background about early childhood curriculum, a chapter on planning, and a chapter on integrated curriculum. Each of the subsequent parts addresses curriculum in various chapters for the following domains:

- Physical Development (Large Motor, Fine Motor, Sensory)
- Communication (Language, Literacy, and Literature)
- Creative Arts (Art, Music, Creative Movement)
- Inquiry (Math, Science, and Social Studies)

Chapter Structure

Each of the curriculum chapters discusses:

- the subject area for young children
- why the subject area is important
- children's development in the subject area
- early learning standards that apply
- how a learning environment supports children's learning this subject area
- your role in teaching the subject
- activities for teaching
- examples of plans (simple and detailed activity plans, weekly plans, and integrated study plans)
- things to consider when teaching children with special needs or children in the primary grades

Appendix A provides you with forms that you can use for planning.

FIGURE 9.3 Simple Literature Activity Plan

This Is The Way We Look at Books!

Objectives:	Follow a story being read and learn to use a book.
Standard:	Domain III, Standard 5
What you need:	Book—*Barnyard Banter* and other simple books
How to teach:	1. Invite 2–3 children to the library area—ask them to sit. 2. Show the book and read the title. 3. Read the book and invite children to point to the animals and repeat words. Point out how you are holding the book and turning the pages. 4. Invite a child to hold the book and turn the pages. 5. Ask the child to put the book back on the shelf—repeat with another book.
How to assess:	Look/listen for children attending to the story; coming back to the library area later; looking at books without damaging them.

▲ SIMPLE ACTIVITY PLAN

Brief overview of a field-tested plan consisting of the objectives of a learning activity, materials needed, how to teach it (the teacher's role), and how to assess children's learning and development.

FIGURE 9.4 Detailed Literature Activity Plan

Activity:	**This Is The Way We Look at Books!** (A guided book reading experience.)
Literature Focus	
WHO It's For:	This activity was planned for the *Grasshoppers* (eight 3-year-olds), 2–3 at a time.
Rationale:	None of the *Grasshoppers* have ever attended preschool before. Last week they were not attentive during story time and did not seem interested in books. Two books were damaged by children.
Literature Objectives:	*By participating in this activity the children will…* • Develop the ability to follow a story being read aloud by a teacher. • Learn to hold a book, turn the pages, and return the book to the library shelf. • Acquire a disposition to listen to stories read aloud.
Preschool Content Standard:	Domain III Standard 5: Enjoy and understand books.
HOW to Prepare	*What you need:* Library area, library shelf, pillows, books including *Barnyard Banter* by Denise Fleming *Set up:* Make sure all the books are right-side up on the shelf and facing forward
HOW to Teach	*Introduction:* Invite 2–3 children to come to the library area and cuddle close on your lap or beside you Show the book and say something like, "I wanted to read you *Barnyard Banter.* I like the rooster on the cover." *Teaching steps:* 1. Read the first pages of the book and invite children to point to the animals and repeat words. 2. Turn a page and say something like, "I sure do like this book. I have to turn the page carefully so it won't tear." 3. Invite a child to hold the book and turn the pages, saying something like, "Would you like to hold the book so carefully and turn the page?" 4. Continue reading and comment on how the child is turning the pages so carefully. 5. Invite the second child to take a turn and continue reading, commenting on how the child is taking care of the book. 6. When the book is done, invite a child to put the book back on the shelf—ask him/her to make sure the rooster is in front so we can see it.
Closure:	If children continue to be interested, repeat with another book. Otherwise, comment that you really enjoyed reading the book with them and thank children for taking such good care of the books.

HOW to Assess and Document

Objectives	Evidence of Learning Children might …	How to Document This Evidence
Develop the ability to follow a story being read aloud by a teacher.	Be attentive to story being read and ask questions or make comments about it.	Anecdotal observations, annotated photograph
Learn to hold a book, turn the pages, and return a book to the library shelf.	Independently go to the library and look at books appropriately without tearing pages or leaving the book on the floor.	
Acquire a disposition to listen to stories read aloud.	Come to story time quickly and willingly. Ask the teacher to read another story.	

EVALUATION (Things to remember for next time)

Play a game in which you put the book on the shelf the wrong way and the child can correct you. This arose spontaneously with the last pair of children and it was very much enjoyed.

▲ DETAILED ACTIVITY PLAN

More detailed field-tested plan that indicates WHO the plan is for, the rationale, the objectives in a particular domain, the standards associated with it; HOW to prepare for it; HOW to teach it (introduction, teaching steps, closure); HOW to assess and document the learning and development; and finally, an evaluation (what to remember for next time).

FIGURE 4.8 A Study of Pets Sunburst

▲ MAPS OR "SUNBURSTS" OF INTEGRATED STUDIES

A colorful web showing content areas that are integrated into an overall topic of study. Again, content areas are highlighted.

FIGURE 9.5 A Week's Plan: A Study of Water—Week #6

Objectives: To help children to: understand water has different forms (solid, liquid, and gas) that behave in predictable ways; learn about how people use water in different ways (to clean, to cook, to play, to work, etc.).

	Monday	Tuesday	Wednesday	Thursday	Friday
Story 8:30–8:50	*A Drop of Water* by Walter Wick		*Water* by Frank Asch	*Night in the Country* by Cynthia Rylant	*Come On Rain* Karen Hess
Outdoor Activities 9:00–10:00 *Purpose:* *to help children …*	Painting With Water on Sidewalk Learn about the properties of water. Engage in science inquiry.		Water Table Experiments and Painting with Water Learn about the properties of water. Engage in science inquiry.	Tricycle Wash Develop understanding of some of the uses of water.	Water Table Experiments and Painting with Water Learn about the properties of water. Engage in science inquiry.
Small Group (Monsters) 10:00–10:20 *Purpose:* *to help children …*	Cooking Pasta Understand one of the ways that water changes things. Engage in science inquiry.		Lili's Dad—Ocean/Marine Biologist Visit Develop awareness of the ocean and animals that live in it. Become aware that some people have jobs involving water.	Ureshima Taro Develop appreciation for and awareness of literature from different cultures.	Story Time at Library Develop interest in books and literature. Become aware of the community.
Small Group (Plowers) 10:00–10:10 *Purpose:* *to help children …*	Water Drawing Learn about the properties of water. Engage in science inquiry—observing how water evaporates.		Ice Exploration I (Water and ice cubes in a cup) Learn about the properties of water. Engage in science inquiry—observing how ice melts.	Ice Exploration II (Crushed ice and ice block) Learn about the properties of water. Engage in science inquiry—observing how ice melts.	
Indoor Special Activities 10:20–11:30 *Purpose:* *to help children …*	Liquid Watercolors Express ideas and feelings using watercolors. Learn about art elements and techniques.		Tissue Paper Collage Create and express ideas through using the medium of collage. Develop awareness of artistic design.	Wet Paper Painting Learn a new art technique. Create and express ideas through using the medium of paint.	Wet Paper Painting Learn a new art technique. Create and express ideas through using the medium of paint.
Circle Time 11:30–11:45 *Purpose:* *to help children …*	Roll That Pumpkin Bring closure to Halloween. Develop the ability to express feelings and ideas through music.		Row Your Boat Develop the ability to express feelings and ideas through music and movement. Develop physical control and body awareness.	Ame Furi Develop the ability to express feelings and ideas through music and movement. Learn words from a different language and learn how different cultures express ideas about rain.	Row Your Boat Develop the ability to express feelings and ideas through music and movement. Develop physical control and body awareness.

(Tuesday column: ELECTION DAY NO SCHOOL)

▲ WEEKLY PLAN

A 5-day plan showing various activities with the content area (literature, science, etc.) highlighted to show students how the content area is included every day in an overall weekly plan.

Try It Out!

Play with a sensory material (sand, water, or dough) with a young child. Notice how s/he plays with it. As you play, talk about the sensory aspects of the experience. What can you conclude about the value of this play to the child?

◄ TRY IT OUT!

Brief boxes sprinkled throughout that encourage students to be metacognitive about their own learning and teaching of particular things, as well as supporting children as they develop and learn.

CLASSROOM SCENARIOS ►

Many scenarios, including interactions between children and a teacher and descriptions of developmentally appropriate teaching and learning, are presented throughout the book.

During the first few weeks of school, Matty's teachers observe his growing fine motor abilities. He quickly learns to turn the handles to operate the drinking fountain and the faucet, and he delights in getting drenched in the water. He digs in the sandbox using a shovel in his right hand and pushes the big bulldozer with both hands and manipulates a handle so that it lifts and carries a load of sand. He fingerpaints using his hands and arms—when blue, red, and yellow have turned to muddy brown, he makes circles with his index finger in the paint. The job of light-switcher is his favorite and he flips the light switch somewhat more often than is warranted. Matty has many fine motor skills.

IN PRACTICE ▼

Concrete classroom ideas for implementing curriculum.

IN PRACTICE: Tips for Adding Language to Routines and Transitions	
Arrivals & Departures	Greet children and families as they arrive and again at the close of the day. Consciously model the back-and-forth nature of conversation with children's families while children are listening.
Meals	Always sit with children and talk with them at meals. Sometimes ask children at your table an engaging question unrelated to the meal—"What makes you happy when you go home? What do you want to be for Halloween? If you had a puppy what would you name it?"
Bathroom Routines	Using the toilet, washing hands, and brushing teeth all provide opportunities for conversation and language modeling. Talk with children about what they're doing in the bathroom in addition to talking about the events of the day.
Transitions	If waiting is a part of a transition, use it for a language game—ask a riddle ("I'm thinking of a kind of animal that has a long neck"), say a fingerplay, have children join you in a chant or song. Never just stand there talking to another teacher or scolding children for not being quiet or not standing in line!
	Use language riddles to excuse children when they need to go one or two at a time to the next activity—"I'm thinking of someone whose mom is named Tara, whose dad is named Horacio, and whose sister is named Sienna—yes Cielo you can go!"

REFLECTIONS ▼

Short boxes that pose questions to enourage reflection and deeper thinking about curriculum.

Reflect on your observations of early childhood art environments . . .

Reflect on programs that you have observed. How much time was allowed for art experiences? What kinds of art materials and experiences were available? What kinds of access did children have to them? Was artwork displayed? How did staff talk to children about their creative efforts? What changes do you think could have been made to better support children's artistic development?

NEW! CourseSmart eTextbook Available

CourseSmart is an exciting new choice for students looking to save money. As an alternative to purchasing the printed textbook, students can purchase an electronic version of the same content. With a CourseSmart eTextbook, students can search the text, make notes online, print out reading assignments that incorporate lecture notes, and bookmark important passages for later review. For more information, or to purchase access to the CourseSmart eTextbook, visit www.coursesmart.com.

Instructor Supplements

The following instructor supplements to the textbook are available for download on www.pearsonhighered.com/educators. Simply enter the author, title, or ISBN, and select this textbook. Click on the "Resources" tab to view and download the available supplements detailed next.

Online Instructor's Resource Manual

The Online Instructor's Resource Manual (ISBN 0-13-502664-4) includes chapter overviews and objectives, lists of available PowerPoint® slides, presentation outlines, teaching suggestions for each chapter, and questions for discussion and analysis.

Online Test Bank and MyTest Test Bank

The Test Bank (ISBN 0-13-502694-6) provides a comprehensive and flexible assessment package. The computerized test bank software, MyTest (ISBN 0-13-502661-X) is a powerful assessment generation program that helps instructors easily create and print quizzes and exams. Questions and tests are authored online, allowing ultimate flexibility and the ability to efficiently create and print assessments, any time anywhere. The Pearson MyTest includes a rich library of assessment items that can be edited to fit your needs. Access Pearson MyTest by going to www.pearsonmytest.com to log in, register, or request access.

Online PowerPoint Slides

The PowerPoint Slides (ISBN 0-13-502693-8) highlight key concepts and summarize text content. These guides are designed to provide structure to instructor presentations and give students an organized perspective on each chapter's content.

Online Test Item Files in a Variety of Formats

Available for a variety of learning management systems, the online test item files contain the content of the Test Bank.

MyEducationLab

MyEducationLab

In *Preparing Teachers for a Changing World,* Linda Darling-Hammond and her colleagues point out that grounding teacher education in real classrooms—among real teachers and students and among actual examples of students' and teachers' work—is an important, and perhaps even an essential, part of training teachers for the complexities of teaching in today's classrooms. MyEducationLab is an online learning solution that provides contextualized interactive exercises, simulations, and other resources designed to help you develop the knowledge and skills that teachers need. All of the activities and exercises in MyEducationLab are built around essential learning outcomes for teachers and are mapped to professional teaching standards. Utilizing classroom video, authentic student and teacher artifacts, case studies, and other resources and assessments, the scaffolded learning experiences in MyEducationLab offer you a unique and valuable education tool.

For each topic covered in the course you will find most or all of the following features and resources.

Connection to National Standards

Now it is easier than ever to see how coursework is connected to national standards. Each topic on MyEducationLab lists intended learning outcomes connected to the appropriate national standards. And all of the activities and exercises in MyEducationLab are mapped to the appropriate national standards and learning outcomes as well.

Assignments and Activities

Designed to enhance your understanding of concepts covered in class, these assignable exercises show concepts in action (through videos, cases, and/or student and teacher artifacts). They help you deepen content knowledge and synthesize and apply concepts and strategies you read about in the book. (Correct answers for these assignments are available to the instructor only.)

Building Teaching Skills and Dispositions

These learning units help you practice and strengthen skills that are essential to effective teaching. After presenting the steps involved in a core teaching process, you are given an opportunity to practice applying this skill via videos, student and teacher artifacts, and/or case studies of authentic classrooms. Providing multiple opportunities to practice a single teaching concept, each activity encourages a deeper understanding and application of concepts, as well as the use of critical thinking skills. Feedback for the final quizzes is available to the instructor only.

IRIS Center Resources

The IRIS Center at Vanderbilt University (http://iris.peabody.vanderbilt.edu), funded by the U.S. Department of Education's Office of Special Education Programs (OSEP), develops training enhancement materials for preservice and practicing teachers. The Center works with experts from across the country to create challenge-based interactive modules, case study units, and podcasts that provide research-validated information about working with students in inclusive settings. In your MyEducationLab course we have integrated this content where appropriate.

Teacher Talk

This feature emphasizes the power of teaching through videos of master teachers, who each tell their own compelling stories of why they teach. These videos help you see the bigger picture and consider why the concepts and principles you are learning are important to your career as a teacher. Each of these featured teachers has been awarded the Council of Chief State School Officers' Teachers of the Year award, the oldest and most prestigious award for teachers.

Study Plan Specific to Your Text

A MyEducationLab Study Plan consists of a chapter quiz that presents you with feedback on your answer choices, and then provides you with access to Review, Practice, and Enrichment activities to enhance your understanding of chapter content.

Course Resources

The Course Resources section of MyEducationLab is designed to help you put together an effective lesson plan, prepare for and begin your career, navigate your first year of teaching, and understand key educational standards, policies, and laws.

It includes the following:

- The **Lesson Plan Builder** is an effective and easy-to-use tool that you can use to create, update, and share quality lesson plans. The software also makes it easy to integrate state content standards into any lesson plan.
- The **Preparing a Portfolio** module provides guidelines for creating a high-quality teaching portfolio.
- **Beginning Your Career** offers tips, advice, and other valuable information on:
  - **Resume Writing and Interviewing** includes expert advice on how to write impressive resumes and prepare for job interviews.
  - **Your First Year of Teaching** provides practical tips to set up a first classroom, manage student behavior, and more easily organize for instruction and assessment.
  - **Law and Public Policies** details specific directives and requirements you need to understand under the No Child Left Behind Act and the Individuals with Disabilities Education Improvement Act of 2004.
- **Children's Literature Database**—this resource offers information on thousands of quality literature titles, and the activities provide experience in choosing appropriate literature and integrating the best titles into language arts instruction.
- **RTI.pearsoned.com**—this new tool is a Pearson site dedicated to helping you understand and implement Response to Intervention.

Certification and Licensure

The Certification and Licensure section is designed to help you pass your licensure exam by giving you access to state test requirements, overviews of what tests cover, and sample test items.

The Certification and Licensure section includes the following:

- **State Certification Test Requirements**—here, you can click on a state and will then be taken to a list of state certification tests.
- You can click on the **Licensure Exams** you need to take to find:
  - Basic information about each test
  - Descriptions of what is covered on each test
  - Sample test questions with explanations of correct answers
- **National Evaluation Series™** by Pearson: Here, students can see the tests in the NES, learn what is covered on each exam, and access sample test items with descriptions and rationales of correct answers. You can also purchase interactive online tutorials developed by Pearson Evaluation Systems and the Pearson Teacher Education and Development group.
- **ETS Online Praxis Tutorials**—here you can purchase interactive online tutorials developed by ETS and by the Pearson Teacher Education and Development group. Tutorials are available for the Praxis I exams and for select Praxis II exams.

Visit www.myeducationlab.com for a demonstration of this exciting new online teaching resource.

Acknowledgments

Creating a book is a long and arduous process. It starts with the seed of an idea. The authors plant the seed in the fertile ground of possibility and imagination, but it takes lots of work and lots of help to grow it into a book. So we have lots of people to thank.

First and foremost, we have learned from, been inspired by, and derived great joy from the children we have taught over many years and in many settings, in particular at the Leeward Community College Children's Center in Pearl City, Hawai'i. This book is intended to honor their passion to learn and the serious, joyful play through which they learn. We thank them and we thank their families for having shared them with us. You have given us a gift beyond price.

Jackie Rabang and Steve Bobilin, the talented teachers at LCC Children's Center, bring great gifts to their work with children and adult students. We have strived to reflect Jackie's delight in and insight into children and Steve's creativity and humor in this book.

There would have been no need for the book without our students at Honolulu Community College and the University of Hawai'i at Mānoa. Their questions about curriculum and their struggle to turn the dry words of textbooks into living curriculum for young children pushed us to write. We first created *Meaningful Curriculum for Young Children* for them.

We did not have time to write this book and would have been content to teach our classes with cobbled-together readings had it not been for Julie Peters, our editor. Julie convinced us that writing this book was both important and possible. Her encouragement, support, and not so gentle pushing made this book a reality.

We are immensely grateful to Karen Gavey, who drafted Chapter 10, *Visual Art Curriculum*. Karen is a doctoral student in art education at the University of Hawai'i as well as a friend, art teacher, and colleague. She is also the mother of Lili, who invites us to play and reminds us that real learning is filled with laughter.

Our friend and colleague Lisa Yogi, professor at Honolulu Community College, shared her insights into teaching students using Developmentally Appropriate Practice. We appreciate her thoughtful approach and her generous sharing of resources. Astronomer Don Mickey gave us valuable feedback on Chapter 14, *Science Curriculum*. He helped us correct some of our errors and more importantly reminded us that science is active, playful, and joyful. Ginger Fink, a long-time friend, colleague, and trainer, gave us feedback on the brief sections on teaching children with special needs found in Chapters 4 to 15. We appreciate her input and time, not to mention her unflagging sense of humor. Stacy Rose, musician and folk dancer extraordinaire, reviewed the music chapter, helped us correct a few more errors, and validated our viewpoint that everyone needs music. We thank her for helping us to keep music and dance as active parts of our own lives.

We would also like to thank the reviewers for their insights and comments: LaDonna Atkins, University of Central Oklahoma; Catherine DeRosa, Nashua Community College; Gayle J. Dilling, Olympic College; Lynne M. Firsel, Roosevelt

University; Vickie A. Harris, Somerset Community College; Dawn L. Kolakoski, Hudson Valley Community College; Cynthia Kumfer, Ivy Tech Community College; Jeannie P. McCorkle, Ogeechee Technical College; and Carlise Womack-Wynne, Gainesville State College.

The photographs that help make *Meaningful Curriculum for Young Children* come alive are the work of photographer Jeff Reese. His ability to capture a child's moment of concentration or expression of elation beautifully illustrates the content of the book. Thank you, Jeff.

We thank the directors, teachers, children, and families of the programs from which the photographs were taken: the Leeward Community College Children's Center (Pearl City, Hawai'i), Keiki Hauoli Children's Center (Honolulu, Hawai'i), Helen Gordon Child Development Center (Portland, Oregon), South Coast Head Start (Coos Bay, Oregon), and The Child Study Centre at the University of Alberta (Edmonton, Alberta).

Family and friends support us and love us even when we don't deserve it. For their contributions, including good food, willingness to share space with three writers, computer support, good wine, listening ears, good advice, laughter, and companionship we thank Jeff Reese, David Nolte, Don Mickey, Miles Nolte, Philip Moravcik, Robyn Chun, and Steve, Megan, and Jonah Bobilin.

Eva Moravcik
Sherry Nolte
Stephanie Feeney

Brief Contents

Contents

PART 2 PHYSICAL DEVELOPMENT CURRICULUM

PART 4 ARTS CURRICULUM

PART 5 INQUIRY CURRICULUM

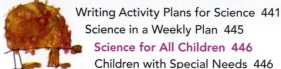

PART 1
Understanding Curriculum

Lively intellectual curiosities turn the world into an exciting laboratory and keep one ever a learner.

LUCY SPRAGUE MITCHELL

This book is written for you, a future or current teacher of young children. It concerns early childhood curriculum (what you teach) and pedagogy (how you teach). Our goal is to help you understand, plan, and implement meaningful and appropriate curriculum for young children.

As an early childhood teacher you will be challenged to design engaging experiences that will result in children constructing an understanding of the world, developing the skills they need, and acquiring attitudes that will lead them to become caring and productive human beings. Nothing will so clearly distinguish you as a professional early childhood educator as your knowledge of what and how young children learn and your ability to help them learn in ways that preserve their zest for learning.

This first part of the book (Chapters 1, 2, and 3) is designed to set the stage for the parts that follow. It provides you with an introduction to early childhood curriculum, and helps you learn how to plan.

In Chapter 1, *Curriculum That Engages Young Children*, we describe what is meant when we talk about curriculum in early childhood education and how it is distinct from curriculum for older children. We look at where early childhood curriculum has come from, discuss where it is today, and point to where it is going. We map out what you need to know and be able to do in order to plan curriculum, explain how curriculum is organized, and make explicit our point of view that:

- learning should be a playful, joyful, and meaningful experience for children.

- all areas of children's development are important.
- planned learning experiences need to reflect and be responsive to children's interests, needs, and learning styles.
- curriculum for young children is not a trivial collection of activities, but instead is serious learning.
- children learn best when curriculum is integrated.

Chapter 2, *Planning, Implementing, and Assessing Curriculum*, describes what planning means in programs for young children. We examine the different kinds of strategies that are used to teach young children and discuss how to choose particular strategies.

Reflect on the meaning of curriculum . . .

What does the word *curriculum* make you think of? What images come into your mind? How do you feel when you hear the word? Make note of your responses and put them away (you might want to tape these notes to the inside back cover of this book). At the end of your study of curriculum, come back and review your notes and see how your perspective has changed.

We provide examples of different kinds of plans and describe what they should include. We take you through a step-by-step process for writing useful, complete, and appropriate activity plans. Because we want you to continue writing plans once you leave the college classroom, we have included examples of simplified planning. We also show how to meaningfully assess and document children's learning.

Finally, in Chapter 3, *Planning Integrated Curriculum*, we give you some background on integrated curriculum and explain why we feel it is the best way to organize the early childhood curriculum. We describe some models of integrated curriculum and show how they are similar to and different from one another. Finally, we provide you with criteria for selecting a topic for an integrated study and show how to design one.

These first three chapters, and the rest of this book, reflect our beliefs about the way people become teachers. Though we rarely specifically state these values this entire book is founded on the belief that:

- you as a learner are worthy of respect and come with unique skills and experiences that will help you to teach.
- like children, you must construct your own knowledge through active engagement.
- like children you will learn best when you are playful, enthusiastic, joyful, and serious about learning.
- curriculum for young children should be engaging, interesting, and worthwhile to both children and their teachers.

The work you are preparing to do is profoundly important to society as a whole and to the young children you will teach—they need and deserve a competent and caring teacher. We hope this book will help you to be that teacher.

Reflect on your hopes and dreams of teaching . . .

Imagine yourself teaching a group of young children. What words describe the teacher you hope to be. Write those words on a sheet of paper and put them up near where you work to remind yourself of your dreams for yourself. Add to them or change them as you learn more about teaching.

"Would you tell me please which way to go from here?"
asked Alice. "That depends a good deal on where you
want to get to," said the cat.

LEWIS CARROLL

chapter one

CURRICULUM THAT ENGAGES YOUNG CHILDREN

What Is Curriculum?

When they speak of *curriculum,* early childhood educators often have in mind different, but related, things. Some are thinking of something very broad—everything the child experiences both in and out of school. This can be called the *umbrella curriculum* (Colbert, 2003). Others are thinking of curriculum models, comprehensive educational approaches that combine theory and practice and address the learning environment, teaching strategies, and teacher support along with curriculum content. The *High/Scope* model (Hohmann, Weikart, & Epstein, 2008), the *Montessori Method,* the *Reggio Emilia* approach (Edwards, Gandini, & Forman, 1998), *Waldorf Education,* and Bank Street College's *Developmental Interaction Approach* (Nager & Shapiro, 2000) are examples of curriculum models. Still others, when they speak of curriculum, mean a document or kit designed by an educator that addresses the whole early education program (e.g., the *Creative Curriculum*) or a content area (e.g., the Breakthrough to Literacy curriculum or the *Second Step* curriculum for social development). These are typically referred to as *packaged* or *commercial curriculum.*

While it is worthwhile to understand the variety of ways that the term *curriculum* is used, the previous definitions will not be particularly helpful to you in learning to design and implement curriculum for the young children with whom you work. In this book we will focus on another view of curriculum—the planned curriculum. We define *planned curriculum* as a teacher or team of teachers using what they know about early childhood curriculum content and teaching strategies to design intentional learning experiences in response to what they know and observe about children.

What Is Unique About Early Childhood Curriculum?

Early childhood educators have long been committed to providing experiences that are meaningful, that engage children, that develop their curiosity, and that support positive attitudes about learning and school. One of the favorite sayings of the educators in the exemplary preschools in Reggio Emilia, Italy, is, "Nothing without joy." Early childhood educators embrace the idea that learning should be a joyful and meaningful experience for children, and this makes us different from many other educators.

Early childhood educators believe that all areas of children's development are important. They believe that planned learning experiences need to reflect and be responsive to children's interests, needs, and learning styles. They understand the critical connections among a child's learning, family, and culture. They know the importance of the teacher's role in designing environments and experiences and in scaffolding children's learning. They understand how play, child choice, and cooperative relationships are important parts of the serious business of learning, and a part of the curriculum. These understandings and beliefs are the underpinning of what is called *developmentally appropriate curriculum*.

What Are the Sources of Early Childhood Curriculum?

All curriculum is based on a vision of society, values, a philosophy, a particular view of learners and teachers, and the ways educators translate this vision into learning experiences. It can originate from three broad sources: (1) beliefs about what is worth knowing, (2) knowledge of learners and their development, and (3) knowledge of subject matter.

Curriculum is also a product of its time. Social and political forces influence educational values and practices. For example, in the United States in the early years of the 20th century, when many immigrants were arriving, a strong curricular emphasis was placed on the acquisition of the English language along with American culture and values. In the years following World War II, curriculum reflected the value that society placed on nuclear families. Today's curriculum mirrors the cultural diversity that is prevalent and more valued today than it was in the past. It echoes society's increasing concerns with young children's readiness for school, educational standards, technology, and the acquisition of basic content, especially literacy. Tomorrow's curriculum will address these and new concerns in ways that we cannot yet anticipate.

In the past, early childhood education stood somewhat apart from vacillating popular points of view regarding curriculum and pedagogy. Many of today's programs have their roots in what can be referred to as the *humanistic* approach to education—an approach that reflects concern for the potential of human beings. The creative thinkers who contributed to this tradition were concerned with issues that included respect for human dignity, the role of education in contributing to all aspects of children's development, the connection between mind and body, the importance of creativity, the value of play, the usefulness of observing children, and the important role of families in children's development. They also saw childhood as a valuable time in its own right, not just as a preparation for adulthood.

You can hear these views in the words of the historical founders of our field:

The proper education of the young does not consist in stuffing their heads with a mass of words, sentences, and ideas dragged together out of various authors, but in opening up their understanding to the outer world, so that a living stream may flow from their own minds, just as leaves, flowers, and fruit spring from the bud on a tree.

John Amos Comenius,
Didactica Magna (The Great Didactic), 1638

Play is the highest expression of human development in childhood for it alone is the free expression of what is in a child's soul.

Friedrich Froebel,
The Education of Man, 1885

While devoted deeply to the growth of ideas and concepts, you have similarly consistently shown that education must plan equally for physical, social, and emotional growth.

James Hymes,
speech to the National Association of Nursery Educators (NANE), 1947

There is an "educational pendulum" that swings between emphasis on the nature and interests of the learner and emphasis on the subject matter to be taught. Each swing reflects a reaction of people to perceptions of the shortcomings of the current educational approach. The swinging pendulum of popular opinion has some important implications for you as an early childhood educator. One is that you must be aware that there will be ongoing shifts in accepted views of curriculum and teaching during your career.

There is greater pressure today than ever before for early childhood educators to address standards and demonstrate the effectiveness of teaching. This offers new challenges, but as we change we always try to remember the history of our field and keep our focus on meaningful learning and the development of "the whole child." Our goal is to help you learn to design curriculum that reflects these historical views and is responsive to the new realities. As you develop your own teaching style, we hope that you will join the long line of educators who put children first.

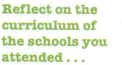

Reflect on the curriculum of the schools you attended . . .

What was taught in the classrooms of your early years? What do you remember most about the curriculum? When were you motivated to learn more? Do any of these experiences influence you today? What are the implications of these experiences for you as an early childhood educator?

Influences on Curriculum Decisions

As you think about curriculum for children, you will decide on the content to be taught, how to organize it, and how to present it. These decisions will be based on your values and beliefs about children and education (and those of the program in which you teach); your assessment of children and knowledge of their families, culture, and community; and your appraisal of whether the content is worthwhile for young children to learn.

Values and Beliefs

What you teach and how you teach reflects your values for society. The children you teach today are potential doctors, politicians, caregivers, artists, teachers,

Reflect on the role of education in shaping the future . . .

Think about what you want the world to be like in the future. What will people need to be like in order for the world you envision to exist? What do children need to learn and experience in school in order to become these people?

parents—people who will make decisions and do work that will affect the lives of others (including your own). What do you want the people of the future to be like? What kinds of knowledge and skills will the children you teach need so they can be productive citizens in society both as it exists now and as it changes in the future? Your answers to these questions will help you to determine your *aims* as an educator—your inspirational ideals and values that frame your educational objectives.

What do you believe about how children learn and what they should be learning? Do you believe children are self-motivated and self-directed learners who will naturally choose what they need to learn? Do you believe that selecting what children will be taught is the responsibility of adults who have more experience and knowledge? Your beliefs about children's motivation and ability to choose worthwhile learning experiences will have an influence on what you teach.

Early childhood educators typically believe in children's inherent ability to learn. They believe that all areas of children's development are important and that play, child-choice, and cooperative relationships are essential parts of the child's educational experience. They value the individuality and dignity of children and families, and appreciate their culture and community. They also believe that adults have a responsibility to select rich and diverse educational experiences for children. In this book we will try to give you the information and skill that you need to teach in ways that reflect these values.

Knowledge of Children: Developmentally Appropriate Practice (DAP)

What you teach and how you teach is based on your knowledge of children. This knowledge enables educators to plan for children at the appropriate level for their age and for their individual needs, backgrounds, and interests. We call this *developmentally appropriate practice* (DAP).

The influential publication *Developmentally Appropriate Practice in Early Childhood Programs* (Copple & Bredekamp, 2009) from the National Association for the Education of Young Children (NAEYC) presents a framework of principles and guidelines for practice that promotes young children's optimal learning and development in early childhood education and care settings. It is grounded both in the research on how young children develop and learn and in what is known about education effectiveness. Although the term *developmentally appropriate practice* and its acronym DAP are widely used and accepted in early childhood education, they are less well known and less accepted in some primary school settings. The terminology may not be universally accepted, but the principles underlying DAP are important and practical to use throughout the early childhood years from birth to age 8.

Where did the term developmentally appropriate practice come from?

The concept of developmentally appropriate practice was created in 1986 by the NAEYC to counteract the growing trend to use age-inappropriate practices with young children. It was revised in 1997 to reflect the complexity of teacher decision making involved in implementing DAP; address issues of diversity (culture, families, special needs); discuss how practice should be assessed and evaluated; and define practices that enhance learning experiences for all children. It was revised again in 2009 to emphasize and include the importance of:

- **Excellence and equity**—providing opportunities for all children to learn.
- **Intentionality and effectiveness** in teaching—having a purpose for educational decisions and the skills needed to explain and implement decisions.
- **Continuity and change**—emphasizing the enduring values of early childhood education's commitment to the whole child; recognition of the value of play; and respect for and responsiveness to individual and cultural diversity and partnerships with families, while recognizing the importance of research and the expanding knowledge base.
- **Joy and learning**—acknowledging that childhood is and should be a time of laughter, love, play, and fun.

What does developmentally appropriate practice say?

Developmentally appropriate practice outlines three dimensions of developmental appropriateness:

- Child development and learning
- The strengths, interests, and needs of each individual child
- The social and cultural contexts in which children live

Knowledge of *child development and learning* refers to research-based information about age-related characteristics. This knowledge allows you to make general predictions about what experiences are likely to best promote children's learning and development. It also provides a framework from which you will prepare the learning environment and plan appropriate experiences that are likely to benefit all the children of a particular age and stage of development.

Knowing *the strengths, interests, and needs of each individual child* means learning about the specific children in your class. This has implications for the way you adapt and are responsive to each child's individual pattern and timing of growth as well as his or her unique personality and learning style. Both the curriculum and adults' interactions with children should be responsive to individual differences in interest, style, and ability.

Knowledge of *the social and cultural context in which children live* refers to the values, expectations, and behavioral and linguistic conventions that shape each child's life at home and in the community. Knowing this helps you to ensure that planned learning experiences are meaningful, relevant to, and respectful of children and their families (Copple & Bredekamp, 2009).

Effective teachers are intentional and thoughtful; this intentionality is a hallmark of developmentally appropriate practice. Teachers begin by thinking about what children of the age they teach are typically like. This knowledge provides a general guide for effective activities, routines, interactions, and curriculum. They then consider each child as an individual within the context of a specific family, community, culture, language, and social group. Finally, they consider the child's past experiences and current circumstances. When you do this, you will see children in your class *as they are* and you will be able to make curriculum decisions that are meaningful and developmentally appropriate for each of them. Figure 1.1 provides a summary of developmentally appropriate practice.

FIGURE 1.1 DAP in a Nutshell

- Meeting children where they are—knowing them well—and enabling them to reach goals that are both challenging and achievable.
- Engaging in teaching practices that are appropriate to children's age and developmental status, being attuned to them as unique individuals and responsive to the social and cultural contexts in which they live.
- Ensuring that goals and experiences are suited to children's learning and development, and challenging them enough to promote progress and interest—not making things "easy."
- Basing practice on knowledge—not on assumptions—of how children learn and develop.

Core Considerations

- **Age/developmental appropriateness**—anticipating and responding to the age/developmental characteristics of children likely to influence the validity of assessment methods.
- **Individual appropriateness**—including making choices and adaptations of assessment methods to get the best information about a particular child.
- **Cultural appropriateness**—considering what will make sense to a child given his or her linguistic and cultural background, as well as interpreting a child's behavior in light of the social and cultural contexts in which he or she lives.
- **Intentionality**—continuously adjusting, changing, and planning for experiences that will promote children's learning and development.

Family, Culture, and Community

What you teach and the way you teach should be respectful of children's families. These families reflect the characteristics and values of their culture and community. As you plan curriculum you might want to ask yourself: What do these families believe is important for children to learn? Are there subjects or activities with which they might be uncomfortable? How can the families and their cultures and this community serve as resources for curriculum?

What's Worth Knowing?

Curriculum has little value if the content isn't worthwhile to the learner. What is worth knowing when you are a young child? Children want to know many things about the world in which they live. They want to know about themselves, about how to get along with others and care for their own needs, about their families and communities, and about the natural and physical aspects of their world. You can see this as you observe a 1-year-old's fascination with water, a 2-year-old's triumphant "Me do it!" a 3-year-old's obsession with trucks, a 4-year-old's passion for firefighters, or a 6-year-old's infatuation for horses.

When we ask our college students to reflect on what they wanted to know when they were young children, their memories are rich and sometimes surprising. They wanted to know about birth and death; the moon and the stars; where rainbows come from and where they go; the nature of God; what makes sand; divorce and conflict; power and authority; the workings of the plumbing and the workings of the mind; the structure of their bodies and the structure of a worm. With few exceptions, they found the answers outside of school.

Children want and need to know complex things about complex topics. But schools often limit curriculum for young children to simple facts to recite: shapes and colors, the alphabet, and numbers. We maintain that for curriculum to be *of worth* to young children it must be based on the genuine **investigation** of a topic that has intellectual significance—in other words, something that is real, that requires real study and thought. In this book we will give you examples of such investigations drawn from real classrooms.

What Do You Need to Know to Plan Early Childhood Curriculum?

Reflect on something you wanted to know when you were a child . . .

Remember a time when you were a child and you really wanted to know something. What did you want to know about? Why was it important to you? What did you do to find out? What did you learn? How was this similar to or different from what you did in school?

You bring some basic knowledge and skills to your work as a teacher. You have physical skills; you know how to take care of yourself and relate to others; you can read, write, and compute; you know things about science and nature, the structure of society, and the arts. You know how to find out the answers to questions. These things will help you to teach—but you need to know more than these basics to be an early childhood educator.

You also need to have the attributes of an educated person—an inquiring mind, an appreciation for culture and the arts, an awareness of others, and an interest in the world around you. In your teaching you will draw on these things, along with specialized knowledge in child development and curriculum.

How Children Learn

Early childhood teachers need to know about young children and how they learn in order to design and implement meaningful and appropriate learning experiences for them. They need to understand that all aspects of development are interdependent. This means that curriculum subjects are not distinct entities, but rather natural parts of the life of the child.

> *The 4-year-old class took a trip to the zoo yesterday. Today, Kurt, Shauna, Max, and Kauri go to the block area. Their teacher suggests that they might build the zoo. They create enclosures around the animals and make a path on which several dollhouse people are placed. Shauna picks up a zebra and puts it in with the lions. Kauri says, "NO! The lions will bite the zebras!" The two argue about the placement of the zebras. The teacher asks the children to think of some ways to put the lions and the zebras together so the zebras won't get hurt. The girls build a nearby enclosure for zebras. Kurt and Max create a wall of blocks that encircles the entire block area. Another child stumbles over it. Max and Kurt yell and the teacher asks, "What could you do so people would know that they should be more careful?" Max goes to the writing center and makes a sign that says ZU! STP! He tapes it to the wall and the teacher suggests that he tell the other children about the sign and what it means.*

These children were engaged in a planned inquiry activity designed to help them build an awareness of a social studies concept (street signs are provided in communities to ensure public safety). But they were also engaged in a satisfying play experience during which they were building motor coordination, using language, developing social problem-solving abilities, and gaining literacy skills.

Try It Out!

Consider the vignette describing children creating a zoo in the block area. Think of three things a teacher could do to support the children's interest and expand their learning.

Your study of child development will inform your teaching. Your knowledge of the theories of Maslow will help you realize that children's basic needs must be met before they are able to engage with learning skills and concepts. You have learned about the theories of Piaget and know that children's thinking and learning differs from that of adults. You know they *construct* concepts when they are actively engaged in working and interacting with people and objects. So you will support their play. You have learned about the theories of Vygotsky and know that children's learning is shaped by their social experiences and by interactions with peers, older children, and adults. So you will be sure to provide *scaffolding* to help children to learn. You also will embrace the children's cultures and will invite their families to participate in activities in your program. You have learned about Gardner's multiple intelligences theory and know that children have unique talents and strengths, so you will strive to identify these strengths and use them to plan effective ways to teach concepts and nurture potential.

You also need to understand how children's modes of learning change throughout the early childhood years. Your teaching should reflect the characteristics of the age and stage of development of the children you teach.

Early Childhood Curriculum

Curriculum includes opportunities for learning that you will provide as choices in your program. It also includes the guided activities that you will implement with individual children and the whole group to help them learn. The planned curriculum will address domains of development (physical, cognitive, language, social, emotional), and at the same time help children develop understanding and skill in one or more subject areas (e.g., math, literature, art). Each subject area in the early childhood curriculum can contribute to all domains of the child's development, but can be seen as primarily emphasizing one or two areas. In this book we will talk about subject areas in clusters that relate to each domain of development. But we keep in mind that subject matter is never neatly divided—children's experience of planned curriculum is always multifaceted.

Teachers of young children need to understand curriculum areas (e.g., what constitutes the curriculum subject and why it is important) and young children's development in relation to the curriculum area (e.g., what you can expect children at a particular age to be able to do and understand). You also need to understand early childhood curriculum content (i.e., what we are trying to teach in each curriculum area).

Content Standards

We are living at a time when standards drive much of what we do in education. States, organizations of curriculum content specialists, and some nations have created *content standards* that provide guidelines for selecting and evaluating curriculum. Teachers in K–12 programs in public schools and state–funded programs for 4-year-olds are almost universally required to address state standards in their teaching. Thoughtfully constructed and well-written standards can help teachers identify what content is most useful and important to students at particular ages and grades.

Every state in the United States and many nations also have early learning standards—content standards for preschool children. These standards reflect what early childhood educators believe is essential knowledge and skills for young children. When these standards are designed to reflect knowledge of how young children learn, they can help you in the complex task of designing curriculum.

Content standards can be useful, but they can also be controversial. There is tension because early childhood educators have found that the ways in which children learn (holistically and self-paced, through integrated activities like play) are not compatible with standards that narrowly define what children should know and be able to do, or that focus only on the subject areas of literacy and math.

It is important to remember that there are many things that content standards do not address. Lilian Katz (2007) suggests that a more appropriate approach would be to look at *standards of experience*. Katz suggests that we should ask ourselves if young children have frequent opportunities to engage in many experiences, such as intellectual engagement, absorbing and challenging activities, taking initiative and accepting responsibilities, experiencing the satisfaction of overcoming obstacles and solving problems, and applying literacy and numeracy skills in purposeful ways.

How Is Early Childhood Curriculum Organized?

Curriculum in early childhood programs can be organized in different ways. You probably remember subject-based curriculum from your elementary school experience. This approach to curriculum focuses on one subject area at a time (math, science, reading) and is organized into discrete blocks of time. Subject-based organization is still typical of teaching in most elementary schools, but it is not the approach that we advocate in developmentally appropriate early childhood programs. In this book we will focus on the *learner-centered* and *integrated* approaches to curriculum that we think are most effective for teaching young children.

Learner-Centered Organization

Learner-centered curriculum is based on the developmental stage, needs, and interests of children. When this approach to curriculum is used, teachers provide some preplanned activities and ensure that children have large blocks of time to play and explore in a planned environment. Teachers make changes in the environment in response to their observations of children.

Some educators believe that all learning experiences should be based on children's interests. They feel that imposing activities that originate from outside sources is counterproductive because children will fail to engage with the content. Planned activities emerge from observations of children and are based on their interests. For this reason this type of organization is often called *emergent curriculum*.

A learner-centered organization is appropriate all or part of the time in early childhood classrooms. It is the best way to plan for infants, toddlers, and young preschoolers. It can also be used with older preschoolers, kindergartners, and primary-age children. But because it is determined by what children bring to the educational experience, it may leave gaps in what is taught and may not be sufficient to provide intellectual challenge and stimulation as children get older.

Integrated Organization

Integrated organization refers to curriculum in which a topic of study provides a focus for the curriculum, serving as an umbrella for different developmental and subject areas. In an integrated study, children investigate a topic in depth over a period of time. The topic forms the hub for curriculum in many different subject areas. Children's interests or the teacher's ideas about what children would enjoy or benefit from can be sources of the topic. *Unit planning, thematic planning, integrated study,* and *project approach* are all forms of integrated organization. They are similar, but each has a somewhat different emphasis.

An integrated approach reflects the idea that children learn holistically. It is mindful of the idea of multiple intelligences—that is, that individuals learn best through their particular strengths or intelligences. Good integrated curriculum provides many different avenues for learning about and exploring a topic. A topic of study can be tailored to fit the learning styles of a group of children and also be made appropriate for the needs of individual children in the group.

Advocates of this approach believe that integrated organization is appropriate and effective, especially for children 4 years and older. For example, a preschool class we know was studying birds. The children had many real experiences with birds in the classroom, in the yard, in the forest, and at the zoo. They hatched eggs and raised quails, painted and drew birds, sang songs about birds, read about birds, played with lifelike models of birds, and created their own books about birds.

We have also seen the integrated approach used effectively with much younger children when the topic was carefully selected, with activities matched to their stage of development. For example, in a toddler classroom we know, the children's activities for several weeks were focused on water. Children *experienced* water in many forms—for washing, playing, drinking. It was a wonderful and appropriate exploration of the nature of water, quite different from a study of water in a kindergarten or 4-year-old class.

An integrated study of a topic contributes to children's growing awareness, skill, and understanding in many areas simultaneously. It provides opportunities for children to have many direct and meaningful experiences with the world. Used thoughtfully, it helps children to understand that learning is connected to life. For these reasons we think that integrated organization is the most effective way to plan curriculum for older preschool, kindergarten, or primary school children. In our experience it also makes teaching more interesting, exciting, and satisfying.

The Process of Designing Curriculum

Young children are learning all the time and from all their experiences, both in and out of school. Early childhood educators need to ask themselves, "How, when, and in what ways do I want to participate in this natural process?" Because children are so interested in the world around them, the choices about the curriculum you provide are almost infinite. Nevertheless, your choices must be thoughtful and appropriate for the children with whom you work.

The first thing to do when designing curriculum for a group of children is to observe them carefully. Based on your observations you can then begin to select content, identify objectives, and decide on teaching and assessment strategies. You can create an environment for this curriculum area—organize space and time, select and create materials. Then you can begin to interact with children in play and planned activities to help them acquire knowledge, skills, and dispositions. Dispositions are tendencies to think, feel, or act in a particular way. Some educators refer to these as *attitudes*. Lilian Katz (2007) defines them as *habits of mind*.

Young children are learning all the time, from all of their experiences. Much of what they learn comes through the routines, relationships, and incidental encounters they have with people, places, and objects. They learn through their own self-directed play. For infants and young toddlers, these are the only ways that they learn. Relationships, learning environments, and routines *are* their curriculum, and continue to provide the foundation of curriculum as they grow older.

This is obvious when you talk to any children about their life in school. Whatever the planned curriculum, you are likely to discover that it is the life of the classroom that is most important—the quality of the snack, the length of time spent outdoors, the teacher, friends, and toys are more important than the quality of the learning experiences. In fact, we know that these things are important even to adult learners.

Relationships, routines, and spontaneous play remain important activities throughout the early childhood years. As children get older, however, teachers can begin to plan a variety of activities to present curriculum content. They can plan to teach through play in a planned learning environment. They also plan to teach concepts and develop skills and attitudes in planned activities led by a teacher.

There are many strategies for teaching every curriculum area. The art of teaching is selecting the teaching strategy that is right both for the child and for the skill or concept being learned. The same activities can be used to teach many different curriculum areas. For example, a child putting together a puzzle of the human body is developing eye-hand coordination and learning to solve problems and interpret symbols, in addition to learning about human physiology. An important part of your job is knowing and being able to articulate how different activities contribute to children's development in different areas.

Final Thoughts

Young children learn by doing, observing, and interacting. They construct and order knowledge through play. You will guide them on this voyage of discovery and help them to understand the world in which they live. As you do so, you support their natural curiosity, develop their love of learning, and help them to become the thinkers and problem solvers of the future.

There are many ways to organize curriculum to ensure that you provide a full range of appropriate activities for the children in your program. No single "right way" prescribes how to think about or teach a particular subject to young children, although some ways are "wrong" because they do not reflect what we know about how children learn.

Your choices about teaching are the way you touch the future. As you learn to be an early childhood educator, you will have opportunities to learn much more about curriculum. In creating this chapter we wanted to give you an overview of curriculum for young children—a framework onto which you could add the practical details you will need to actually teach. We applaud you as you begin this adventure.

At the end of each chapter we identify how the content contributes to your preparation as an early childhood educator. We begin by identifying the learning outcomes. We then suggest some ways you can broaden or deepen your learning. Finally, we suggest some ways that you can demonstrate and document this learning for your professional portfolio.

Learning Outcomes

When you read this chapter, thoughtfully complete activities from the "To Learn More" section, and document this learning as suggested in the "For Your Portfolio" section, you will be making progress in the following *NAEYC Standards for Early Childhood Professional Preparation Programs* (2009):

Standard 1. Promoting Child Development and Learning

Students prepared in early childhood degree programs are grounded in a child development knowledge base. They use their understanding of young children's characteristics and needs and of the multiple interacting influences on children's development and learning to create environments that are healthy, respectful, supportive, and challenging for each child.

The key elements of standard 1 you will have learned about are . . .

1a: Knowing and understanding young children's characteristics and needs

1b: Knowing and understanding the multiple influences on development and learning

Standard 4. Using Developmentally Effective Approaches to Connect with Children and Families

Students prepared in early childhood degree programs understand that teaching and learning with young children is a complex enterprise, and its details vary depending on children's ages, characteristics, and the settings within which teaching and learning occur. They understand and use positive relationships and supportive interactions as the foundation for their work with young children and families. Students know, understand, and use a wide array of developmentally appropriate approaches, instructional strategies, and tools to connect with children and families and positively influence each child's development and learning.

The key elements of standard 4 you will have learned about are . . .

4c: Using a broad repertoire of developmentally appropriate teaching/learning approaches

4d: Reflecting on their own practice to promote positive outcomes for each child

Standard 5. Using Content Knowledge to Build Meaningful Curriculum

Students prepared in early childhood degree programs use their knowledge of academic disciplines to design, implement, and evaluate experiences that promote positive development and learning for each and every young child. Students understand the importance of developmental domains and academic (or content) disciplines in an early childhood curriculum. They know the essential concepts, inquiry tools, and structure of content areas, including academic subjects, and can identify resources to deepen their understanding. Students use their own knowledge and other resources to design, implement, and evaluate meaningful, challenging curricula that promote comprehensive developmental and learning outcomes for every young child.

The key element of standard 5 you will have learned about is . . .

5c: Using their own knowledge, appropriate early learning standards, and other resources to design, implement, and evaluate meaningful, challenging curricula for each child.

To Learn More

Interview an Early Childhood Teacher: Ask the teacher to tell you about his or her view of curriculum. Ask if he or she follows a particular model or program and what he or she uses to plan learning experiences for children. Ask the teacher to explain his or her educational philosophy, values, and beliefs about how children learn. Invite the teacher to tell you how early learning guidelines have had an impact on teaching.

Compare Two Classrooms: Observe two classrooms. Describe the similarities and differences between the two classrooms. Reflect on what the similarities and differences suggest about the different teachers' views of teaching and learning.

Interview Your Grandparent or Someone Your Grandparent's Age: Ask this elder to tell you about his or her early education (preschool, kindergarten, or first grade). Consider how this is the same as or different from your experience and the experience of children today. Explain where you think the educational "pendulum" described in the chapter was when each of you went to school and where you think it is now. Consider how this influenced early childhood programs.

What Was Worth Knowing to You? Write a response to the reflection question on page 11. Use this reflection to talk to peers who are learning to be teachers. What conclusions can you draw from these different responses?

Read More: Select one or more of the books or articles listed in the bibliography for this chapter and read more about this topic.

For Your Portfolio

The previous activities will have helped you to reflect on what you have learned while reading this chapter. Write a formal essay describing what you did and what you learned to document your learning for your professional portfolio.

Bibliography

Bredekamp, S., & Rosegrant, T. (1995). *Reaching potentials: Transforming early childhood curriculum and assessment* (Vol. 2). Washington, DC: NAEYC.

Children's Defense Fund. (1999). *The State of America's Children Yearbook*. Washington, DC: Author.

Colbert, J. (2003, August–September). Understanding curriculum: An umbrella view. *Early Childhood News*, 16–23.

Comenius, J. A. (1967). *Didactica magna* (M. W. Keating, Ed. & Trans.). New York, NY: Russell & Russell. (Original translation published 1896)

Copple, C., & Bredekamp, S. (2009). *Developmentally appropriate practice in early childhood programs*. Washington, DC: NAEYC.

Dodge, D. T., Colker, L., et al. (2010). *The creative curriculum for preschool*. Washington, DC: Teaching Strategies.

Edwards, C. P., Gandini, L., & Forman, G. (1998). *The hundred languages of children: The Reggio Emilia approach*. Greenwich, CT: Ablex Publishing Corp.

Epstein, A. S. (2007). *The intentional teacher*. Washington, DC: NAEYC.

Feeney, S., Galper, A., & Seefeldt, C. (2008). *Continuing issues in early childhood education* (3rd ed.). Boston, MA: Pearson Education.

Feeney, S., Moravcik, E., & Nolte, S. (2013). *Who am I in the lives of children?* (9th ed.). Upper Saddle River, NJ: Pearson.

Froebel, F. (1885). *The education of man*. (J. Jarvis, Trans.). New York, NY: Lovell.

Hohmann, M., Weikart, D. P., & Epstein, A. S. (2008). *Educating young children: Active learning practices for preschool and child care programs* (3rd ed.). Ypsilanti, MI: High/Scope Press.

Hymes, J. L. (1947/2001). Planning ahead for young children. Speech to the National Association for Nursery Education. Reprinted in *Young Children 56*(4), 62–94.

Hyson, M. (2008). *Enthusiastic and engaged learners' approaches to learning in the early childhood classroom*. New York, NY: Teachers College Press.

Kagan, S. L., Scott-Little, C., & Frelow, V. S. (2003). Early learning standards for young children: A survey of the states. *Young Children 58*(5), 58–64.

Katz, L. G. (2007). Standards of experience. *Young Children 62*(3), 94–95.

Kostelnik, M. J., Soderman, A. K., & Whiren, A. P. (2011). *Developmentally appropriate curriculum: Best practices in early childhood education* (5th ed.). Boston, MA: Pearson Education.

Mitchell, A., & David, J. (Eds). (1992). *Explorations with young children*. Mt Rainier, MD: Gryphon House.

Nager, N., & Shapiro, E. K. (Eds.). (2000). *Revisiting a progressive pedagogy: The developmental-interaction Approach*. Albany, NY: State University of New York Press.

National Association for the Education of Young Children. (2009). *NAEYC standards for early childhood professional preparation programs*. www.naeyc.org/files/naeyc/file/positions/ProfPrepStandards09.pdf

National Association for the Education of Young Children & National Association of Early Childhood Specialists in State Departments of Education. (2003). Executive summary early learning standards: Creating conditions for success. *Young Children, 58*(1), 69–70.

Ramsey, P. G. (2004). *Teaching and learning in a diverse world* (3rd ed.). New York, NY: Teachers College Press.

School Readiness Task Force, Good Beginnings Alliance. (2003). *Hawaii preschool content standards: Curriculum guidelines for programs for four-year-olds*. Honolulu, HI: Author.

Seefeldt, C. (Ed.). (2005). *The early childhood curriculum: Current findings in theories and practice* (3rd ed.). New York, NY: Teachers College Press.

Wheatley, K. F. (2003). Promoting the use of content standards: Recommendations for teacher educators. *Young Children, 58*(2), 96–101.

MyEducationLab

Go to Topics 1: History and Theories, 2: Child Development and Learning, and 11: DAP/Teaching Strategies in the MyEducationLab (www.myeducationlab.com) for *Meaningful Curriculum for Young Children*, where you can:

- Find learning outcomes for History and Theories, Child Development and Learning, and DAP/Teaching Strategies along with the national standards that connect to these outcomes.
- Complete Assignments and Activities that can help you more deeply understand the chapter content.
- Apply and practice your understanding of the core teaching skills identified in the chapter with the Building Teaching Skills and Dispositions learning units.
- Listen to experts from the field in Professional Perspectives.
- Check your comprehension on the content covered in the chapter with the Study Plan. Here you will be able to take a chapter quiz, receive feedback on your answers, and then access Review, Practice, and Enrichment activities to enchance your understanding of chapter content.

There is in the act of preparing, the moment you start caring.

WINSTON CHURCHILL

chapter two

PLANNING, IMPLEMENTING, AND ASSESSING CURRICULUM

What is a plan? In everyday life, simply having a predetermined idea of what you are going to do is a plan ("I plan to go dancing this weekend"). But in working with young children, a plan is a written blueprint for teaching. In this chapter we will describe several kinds of planning. Our goal is to help you understand planning and develop the ability to create useful, complete, and appropriate written plans.

Learning about curriculum and learning about planning, teaching, and assessing children go hand in hand. You can't plan until you understand what you're going to teach. But we believe that you need to know how to create plans, how to implement them, and how to assess their effectiveness so you can practice what you are learning about curriculum. For this reason we ask our students to practice writing and implementing plans as a part of the process of learning about curriculum. As you read and reflect on this chapter we hope it helps you to develop the disposition to plan thoughtfully for your work with children.

Why Teachers Plan

By failing to prepare, you are preparing to fail.

BENJAMIN FRANKLIN

While no teacher writes plans for every moment of the day, virtually all teachers create some form of written plan for their work with children. Why? When you first start to teach, your reasons for having plans are much the same as your reasons for following a recipe when you cook—you want a good result! You want to know what you're doing and make sure you have everything you need. You plan in order to avoid unpleasant surprises. You plan as a guide for teaching.

As a student, Eva was hired as an assistant teacher in the campus childcare center. Every week, Kathy, the lead teacher, planned the curriculum and Eva assisted. Eva loved singing songs, reading stories, and playing with children. She had learned to write lesson plans in her college classes, but she didn't enjoy planning lessons. She thought they were phony, boring, and unresponsive to children. And they weren't very much like the weekly calendar that Kathy wrote every week.

When Kathy went on a week's vacation, Eva was left in charge, with Jenny, the aide, to assist. Eva decided that she would not create any plans for the week; instead, she would follow the children's interests. They would have a great time!

Monday morning, Eva walked into the classroom a few minutes before the children arrived. She put out paints at the easel and filled the water table with soapy water. She looked at the art supplies and toys in the cupboards and pulled out a bunch of materials Kathy had never taken out before.

The children dove into the new materials. Soapy water in the water table was a big success, and soon soapy water soaked the carpet. There was glue, sequins, and glitter on the floor. No child was able to put together the new, hard puzzles—they left the pieces all mixed up and some fell under the table. By lunch, manipulative toys were strewn about the classroom, books lay on the floor, and the dishes, dolls, and clothes in the home area were all stuffed in the toy refrigerator. While Eva and Jenny picked up, a child painted on the wall. They had to skip story time and singing to clean up the mess.

This vignette describes an experience that one of the authors had when she did not plan during her first week of being the teacher in charge. In addition to guiding your teaching and avoiding disasters, you will write plans for other reasons: to make sure you have created learning experiences for the children that are responsive to them both as individuals and as a group—their strengths, interests, and needs; to share with families and colleagues; and to meet your professional obligations to address standards and program expectations.

What you plan and the amount of detail you write will vary with your program, training, experience, and personal style of teaching. But, because you are a teacher, you will create written plans.

Kinds of Plans

When early childhood educators use the word *plan,* they usually have one of these meanings in mind.

1. **Activity or lesson plan.** A detailed written outline for a specific learning activity is called an *activity plan* or *lesson plan.* College students write activity/lesson plans as part of the process of learning to teach. Some preschool teachers write plans for activities that need careful sequencing, or when they wish to share them with others. Elementary and special educators call them *lesson plans* and write them often.

2. **Weekly plan.** Regardless of whether they write detailed activity/lesson plans, most teachers write a *weekly plan,* a calendar of activities to be accomplished over the course of a week. Weekly plans are necessarily quite brief. Usually

they include the names of activities and the time slot in which they will take place. They help you to visualize your week, anticipate what you will need, and communicate what will happen to others, but they don't include much detail about how the activities will be taught.

3. **Integrated study plan.** An outline of several weeks of activities, spanning several different content areas (subjects like math, art, or literacy) based on a topic of study is called an *integrated study, a unit plan,* or a *theme.* Like activity/lesson plans and weekly plans, they vary in length, detail, and format.

Elements of a Plan

Whether you are drafting an integrated study, outlining a week, or detailing a specific activity, every written educational plan involves the same essential elements: purpose (why you are teaching), content (what you will teach), methods (how you will teach), and assessment (how you will know whether you achieved your purpose). But educational plans differ in the amount of specific detail they provide.

Every plan has an educational *purpose*, something you are trying to accomplish. Statements of purpose can be called *goals* or *objectives*. Although you may see these words used interchangeably, a distinction can be made between them.

Goals are broad statements of desired ends toward which teaching is directed (e.g., a goal of the early childhood curriculum is to help children become creative thinkers). Goals are generally not accomplished in a single activity. Goal statements are usually found in overall curriculum documents or in the preamble to an integrated study plan. They are not found in activity plans or in weekly plans.

More specific and immediate intended outcomes of activities are called **objectives** (e.g., at the end of this activity children will have developed the ability to make a ball out of clay). Sometimes they are called **learner outcomes.** Activity/lesson plans always have statements of objectives. Weekly plans sometimes include written objectives for the week or for the individual activities. Some teachers have objectives written in a general curriculum plan for the month or year and do not write them down on the weekly calendar.

Young children have little knowledge, possess few skills, play a great deal, and require much care. So it seems to many non-educators that the content of the early childhood curriculum must be extraordinarily simple. However, the content of the early childhood curriculum is complex; understanding it requires intellect and attention. As an early childhood teacher, you will be a scholar whose field of expertise is how children learn.[1]

---

[1]Of the six NAEYC standards for professional early childhood educators, three relate to understanding curriculum and how children learn.

Many strategies or *methods* can be used to deliver curriculum content. One of the pleasures of teaching young children is that there are many different ways to teach. For example, to teach children that *A garden is a place that people create to grow plants*, you might take a trip to a botanical garden, create a garden on your playground, read story books featuring gardens, sing a song about planting flowers in a garden, create a garden with table blocks, make a terrarium, or paint a picture of a nearby garden. One of the challenges of teaching young children is selecting methods that both engage children and help them learn things that are meaningful about the world. Being able to do this requires knowledge of child development and sensitivity to children as individual learners—the core of what is known as *developmentally appropriate practice.*

Assessment of what children have learned is also a part of planned curriculum. How will you know whether children have really learned what you tried to teach? In early childhood settings, especially with children from infancy through kindergarten, assessment is most often done by observing and analyzing what children say and do. Their actions, words, and the work they create (drawings, constructions, etc.) provide you with evidence of children's acquisition of concepts, skills, and dispositions (habits of mind, or tendencies to behave in particular ways, such as curiosity). To make a record of this evidence, teachers write anecdotal records, take photographs, make video recordings, and collect work samples. Examples of several kinds of assessments are included in this chapter. Figure 2.1 shows an example of an anecdotal record; Figure 2.2 shows an annotated work sample; and Figure 2.3 shows an annotated photograph.

This kind of tangible evidence is called *documentation.* Part of the planning process involves thinking about which actions, words, or work will genuinely demonstrate children's learning and what form of documentation will accurately

FIGURE 2.1   **Example of an Anecdotal Record**

Date: 10/18

Anela reached her hand toward Gabrielle at nap time. Gabrielle put her hand into Anela's for just a few seconds. Then she put her blanket into Anela's hand and said, "Here you can hold my blanket, your hand is cold."

Comment: Makes conclusion based on observation.

FIGURE 2.2   **Example of an Annotated Work Sample**

Date: 10/21

Following a trip to a family home near Kahaluu stream, K. created this artwork. Note the images of crayfish to the right of the staircase leading down to the stream. Each has six legs and one has feelers. When questioned, K. explained that the round objects were rocks in the stream.

Comment: Demonstrates awareness of the features of animals as well as geographic awareness.

FIGURE 2.3   Example of an Annotated Photograph

Date: 02/08

After hearing a poem about a "hippo sandwich" ("Recipe for a Hippopotamus Sandwich" by Shel Silverstein) H. drew and painted two pictures of "hippo sandwiches." (See work sample and photograph.)

Comment: Expresses ideas through art.
Art Standard 2: Create and express through a variety of art experiences.*

*From the Hawaii Preschool Content Standards.

capture it. In settings with older children, samples of writing, math, and other academic work also serve as evidence.

Purpose, content, methods, and assessment interact with one another. To achieve a particular purpose (e.g., to learn that gardens are created by people and to communicate what is known), you select the content and methods (visiting and creating a garden and explaining the process). The methods will determine what kind of evidence will be available for you to analyze (e.g., the children's pages from a class-made book about their garden). What you assess depends on your purpose. (Do the class-made book pages include descriptions or drawings of people creating gardens?)

Before You Plan

Whether you are planning for play, to teach a skill or concept, or planning to create an integrated study, there are four things to do before beginning.

1. You need to learn about the children for whom you are planning.
2. You need to know the curriculum content appropriate for the children's age and stage of development, along with effective methods for teaching it.
3. You need to know local and national curriculum standards.
4. You need to have goals.

Learn About Children

Good teachers know about children in general, but they also know the particular children in their class well. You have learned a great deal about children from child development classes you have taken, as well as from your own experience. To learn about the particular children in your class, you will read intake forms, conduct home visits and family interviews, review portfolios from former teachers, and, most importantly, you will make observations. The purpose of the observation skills you learn as a student is to help you become a sensitive and skillful teacher—to inform your planning.

Understand How Children Learn

Why don't we teach young children in the same ways we teach older children and adults? The answer is quite obvious to anyone who has spent time observing young children. They don't learn in the same ways. Knowing how to plan for teaching young children requires that you understand how they learn. A few basic principles guide early childhood planning.

Principle #1: Children learn by doing through play and through concrete, sensory experience. Concepts are learned best when they are directly experienced. Knowledge must be constructed by children from the materials and experiences that are available to them.

Principle #2: Children learn best when they have many direct experiences with the world around them. This involves taking children into the world of people and relationships or bringing these experiences to them. Real experience through trips, visitors, and real-world activities are essential for learning.

Principle #3: Children need to reflect on their actions and experiences in order to develop concepts and understanding of relationships. How does a young child reflect? Children reflect by playing, painting, building, singing, dancing, and discussing their observations and experiences. This is how they *reconstruct* their experiences and *construct* concepts.

Principle #4: Children formulate concepts over time and through repeated experiences. It takes more than one experience to construct a concept. Teachers who understand how children learn are careful to plan so that children can repeat experiences many times. This may be contrary to the strategies of some commercial curriculum guidebooks and the traditional curriculum of many schools, which place a premium on novelty. And it is quite different from the fast pace of today's society. However, it reflects what we know about children and how they learn.

Principle #5: Each child learns in a unique way and at an individual pace. Because children don't all learn the same way, we must teach them in diverse ways. One child might best learn a concept by reading a book, another by singing a song, and others by acting it out. Effective teachers present skills and concepts in diverse ways, knowing that children learn best when they can choose activities that are appropriate and meaningful to them.

Principle #6: Children learn best when adults provide support to help them become more capable. Your job as a teacher is to know many ways to provide support, observe with an open mind and heart, and provide the support needed for each individual child.

Principle #7: Children learn best when there is communication and consistency between home and school. Because young children first experience skills and concepts in their homes, early childhood teaching requires a partnership between the family and the teacher. When you involve families in the curriculum, you make it meaningful.

Know the Individuals

Good teachers observe children all the time. Whether you make written observations or keep mental notes (or do both), you will purposefully watch for a number of things so that you can consciously support children's development through curriculum.

Strengths

Every child has abilities. Thinking about what children are able to do well gives you ideas for what and how to teach them. As you observe each child in your class you will look for these abilities. What can this child do? What does she know? Is he curious, motivated, kind? As you observe each child in your class, you will monitor their acquired knowledge and abilities. New knowledge and skills can be built upon this foundation.

Four-year-old Nathan engages the other children with his ideas and plans. Talking rapidly using a non-standard English dialect, he often directs them in pretend play, trike riding, and building with hollow blocks. Nathan is a leader. He has terrific large motor coordination and strength. He demonstrates creativity.

Interests

Each individual is interested in different things. We all learn best when the learning is inherently interesting. Children learn while doing the things they *like* to do. Knowing their interests can guide you to plan activities that will make children WANT to learn. What activities and tasks are enjoyed by or intrigue the individuals in your group? Which, if any, are avoided—who avoids them? Your plans should reflect these interests.

Nathan loves cars. He knows the names of many different types of cars. In the playground looking out at the parking lot, on walks, and on bus trips he points out and names different models of cars. He draws cars with great detail including hubcaps, tailpipes, and spoilers. On the trikes he pretends to be driving; with hollow blocks he builds cars.

Needs

Just as all children have strengths, all children have needs. As you observe, you will note what is difficult for particular children. Does any child appear to be missing skills or understanding? These are also considerations for planning. However, avoid basing your plans on what children cannot do or do not know. It is discouraging to children (and indeed to us all) to be confronted with deficits. It is far more engaging to start with interests and abilities as a base from which to learn new things.

Nathan has limited interest in books and literacy. Though he is a leader in the class, he rarely participates in group activities. Capitalizing on Nathan's leadership and love of cars, the teachers use Nathan as a resource in a class project making a wooden car that can be ridden. Nathan becomes a highly involved participant in group activities. He reads books on cars and draws and labels plans for the car that the class makes.

Know the Group

Although you may often observe and plan for individual children, you will always plan for the whole class. Good teachers observe their children both as individuals and as a community. Every class of children has a group identity and a group personality. They will have friendships, relationships, and rivalries. Children assume roles in the class that are distinct from their roles in their families—they will be leaders, followers, introverts, extroverts, helpers, rebels, nurturers, clowns, and rascals.

Sometimes, a group is mature and comes with many experiences, lots of language, and skill in relationships. The tenor of such a group will allow you to plan more complex and sophisticated curriculum. At other times, the group will seem much younger and be less experienced. For these children you will need to plan simpler curriculum. What skills and activities are difficult for particular children? Is any child lacking the ability or knowledge needed to participate in school activities? Is any child lacking the disposition to learn, explore, and interact with others? You will use your observations to decide on your next teaching steps—how to engage with children, what activities to plan, how to modify the environment.

Often an intense interest of one or two children will lead to worthwhile curriculum that engages the whole group, as we saw in the example above in which one child's interest in cars led to a successful group project involving building a wooden car. At other times, a child will persistently pursue his or her own interest despite the direction of the class. This happened when one of the children in our class was fascinated by images of Buddha during a group study of food. Part of planning is to recognize and meld the interests of the children into worthwhile curriculum. In this instance, we planned a trip to the Chinatown food markets where we were able to see many statues of Buddha.

Understand Content and Methods

There are many hundreds of different activities that make up curriculum in early childhood programs. The art of planning involves selecting content and teaching strategies that are right for the children (individuals with particular interests, cultures, and abilities) and for the skill or concept being learned. (We use the terms *strategy* and *method* interchangeably to refer to a teaching technique or approach.)

Although there are many methods, four are foundational to early childhood teaching. These can be thought of as existing on a continuum from most **child initiated** (i.e., activities that are selected and directed by a child) to most **teacher directed** (i.e., selected and guided by the teacher).

1. **Play**—activities that are child selected, child directed, and explored independently. The teacher establishes the environment for play.
2. **Scaffolded activities**—activities that involve the engagement of a teacher usually with only one or two children. The teacher responds to the child and may be involved in shaping the direction of the activity.
3. **Small-group activities**—focused, planned, teacher-directed learning activities with 3–10 children. Because the group is small, the teacher can be flexible and responsive to children's interests.
4. **Large-group activities**—teacher-directed, whole-class activities with 10 or more children. Because the group is larger, the teacher must be more directive and in control.

Figure 2.4 lays out some basic activities in each broad curriculum area and suggests the modes (play, teacher-child, small group, large group) that can be effective for teaching.

FIGURE 2.4 Curriculum Activities and Effective Modes for Teaching

	Play in a planned environment—**child directed** (independent/with other children)	Scaffolded—**child directed** (teacher–child)	Small group—**teacher directed**/child inspired (3–10 children)	Large group—**teacher directed** (8+ children)
Language, literature, and literacy			Fingerplays and poems	Fingerplays and poems
	Reading books	Reading books	Reading books	Reading books
		Storytelling	Storytelling	Storytelling
		Discussions	Discussions	Discussions
		Guessing games	Guessing games	Guessing games
	Making books	Making books	Making books	Making books
			Story acting	Story acting
		Story writing	Story writing	
	Puppet play	Puppet play		
			Language experience charts	
	Dramatic play	Dramatic play		
Music and creative movement			Singing	Singing
			Music and singing games	
			Performance	
		Listening and moving to music	Listening and moving to music	Listening and moving to music
		Playing rhythm instruments	Playing rhythm instruments	Playing rhythm instruments
		Composing and improvising songs	Composing and improvising songs	
			Creative movement	Creative movement
Art and aesthetics			Learning trips to plays and concerts, displays, places of beauty	Learning trips to plays and concerts, displays, places of beauty
	Drawing, painting, collage, construction	Drawing, painting, collage, construction	Drawing, painting, collage, construction	Drawing, painting, collage, construction
		Printmaking	Printmaking	Printmaking
	Playdough and clay		Playdough and clay	
		Looking at and discussing works of art	Looking at and discussing works of art	
			Murals	

(continued)

(handwritten annotations: "write book name", "write out activities", "3 for each for group project", and "4" marks in the left and right margins)

29

FIGURE 2.4 Curriculum Activities and Effective Modes for Teaching (continued)

	Play in a planned environment—**child directed** (independent/with other children)	Scaffolded—**child directed** (teacher–child)	Small group—**teacher directed**/child inspired (3–10 children)	Large group—**teacher directed** (8+ children)
Fine motor	Dramatic play			
	Sensory table			
	Sandbox			
		Cooking		
		Caring for pets		
	Puppet play			
			Fingerplays	
	Playdough and clay		Playdough and clay	
	Block play			
	Exploring nature outdoors			
	Puzzles and workjobs (teacher-made games)			
		Woodworking		
		Gardening		
	Manipulative toys			
			Rhythm instruments	
		Stitchery and yarn activities		
		Print making		
		Woodworking		
	Book-making			
	Drawing, painting, collage, construction			
			Sand tray	
			Drawing/writing	
Large motor	Self-selected large motor play (running, walking, jumping, hopping, galloping, skipping, balancing, turning, twisting, rolling, throwing, bouncing, kicking, striking, climbing, swinging, sliding, riding, pulling wheeled vehicles [trikes, etc.])			
	Hollow block play			
			Movement stations	
	Obstacle courses			
			Guided movement	
			Educational gymnastics	
			Active games	
			Walks	
		Gardening		
		Woodworking		

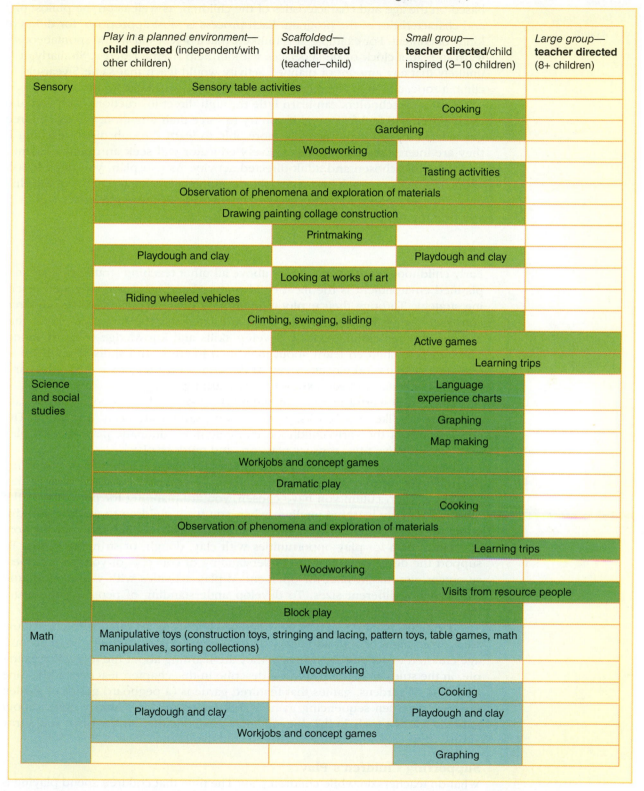

	Play in a planned environment—**child directed** (independent/with other children)	Scaffolded—**child directed** (teacher–child)	Small group—**teacher directed**/child inspired (3–10 children)	Large group—**teacher directed** (8+ children)
Sensory	Sensory table activities	Sensory table activities		
			Cooking	
		Gardening	Gardening	
		Woodworking		
			Tasting activities	
	Observation of phenomena and exploration of materials	Observation of phenomena and exploration of materials	Observation of phenomena and exploration of materials	
	Drawing painting collage construction	Drawing painting collage construction		
		Printmaking		
	Playdough and clay		Playdough and clay	
		Looking at works of art		
	Riding wheeled vehicles			
	Climbing, swinging, sliding	Climbing, swinging, sliding		
		Active games	Active games	Active games
			Learning trips	Learning trips
Science and social studies			Language experience charts	
			Graphing	
			Map making	
	Workjobs and concept games	Workjobs and concept games		
	Dramatic play	Dramatic play		
			Cooking	
	Observation of phenomena and exploration of materials	Observation of phenomena and exploration of materials	Observation of phenomena and exploration of materials	
			Learning trips	Learning trips
		Woodworking		
			Visits from resource people	Visits from resource people
	Block play	Block play		
Math	Manipulative toys (construction toys, stringing and lacing, pattern toys, table games, math manipulatives, sorting collections)	Manipulative toys (construction toys, stringing and lacing, pattern toys, table games, math manipulatives, sorting collections)	Manipulative toys (construction toys, stringing and lacing, pattern toys, table games, math manipulatives, sorting collections)	
		Woodworking		
			Cooking	
	Playdough and clay		Playdough and clay	
	Workjobs and concept games	Workjobs and concept games		
			Graphing	

The relative balance of child-initiated and teacher-directed experiences will vary based on the age and characteristics of the children, as well as on the philosophy and characteristics of the program. Each process is most appropriate for different kinds of content. For example, it is unlikely that a 5-year-old would spontaneously learn to read a clock or tie shoelaces without help from a teacher. Similarly, it is unlikely that any amount of planned activity would teach that same 5-year-old to climb a rope, although she might learn to do so in focused, self-initiated play.

Young preschoolers can learn little through direct instruction. Both you and the children will feel frustrated if you try to force their attention. But as children get older, they gradually become more able to learn through direct teaching if they are interested and motivated. Every educator will seek an optimal balance between child-chosen and adult-directed activity. As you plan, you need to ask yourself which approach best meets the developmental characteristics of the children and your educational purposes. The answers to these questions will help you find the right balance for your group.

Play

Early childhood teachers place play above all other teaching strategies. Play in a planned environment is the most child-centered and most child-initiated teaching strategy. Through their exploration and self-initiated play activities, children construct knowledge and develop skills and interests. The power of play is that it helps children simultaneously develop skills and knowledge of many kinds. Through play children learn about their own interests and skills. They learn to plan and to focus and pay attention. At the same time they enjoy themselves and become motivated to keep exploring and learning.

Play is a powerful learning medium. The tools and "textbooks" of play are play materials like toys, blocks, paint, crayons, sand, water, clay, and wood. The cornerstones of the early childhood curriculum are dramatic play, blocks, play with manipulative toys, sensory play, art, and outdoor play.

Young children need many opportunities for play each day. How and when do you "plan for play"? When you purposefully provide play opportunities that support the curriculum you have chosen, you are planning for play. Play is the most appropriate learning medium when you want children to explore and discover for themselves. For example, to support a child's eye-hand coordination, you might plan for play opportunities with clay, dough, or stringing beads. To support the development of the understanding of concepts of volume and measurement, you might plan for open-ended play activities with water, sand, and containers of different sizes. To develop understanding of people, you ensure that children have lots of time to play with one another.

If you are planning play opportunities while using an integrated curriculum study, you might plan to add dramatic play props related to the topic to encourage children to act out the concepts they are learning about the topic. For example, in the study of gardens that we describe in this chapter, teachers added fine art prints of gardens, games that featured gardens (a pegboard graph of garden flowers, a garden sequencing game, a felt board garden), library books about gardens, garden tools in the dramatic play area, a garden in the yard, and a tray garden with clay objects that children could manipulate.

Supporting Children's Play
What do teachers do while children play? The time that children spend playing is significant for teachers as well as children. There are several things that you do to teach while children play.

Watch and wait. One important teaching strategy while children are playing is to **intentionally wait** and watch without intervening in their play. Children need uninterrupted time to play on their own without adult interference. Intentionally waiting—allowing children time for purposeful play, mindful struggle, and independent discovery—is critical. This means you might let a child build a tall block building, or allow a child to lose a necklace when he puts too many beads on a string. Intentionally waiting is very different from zoning out because you're thinking about your personal life. It's not the same as leaving children on their own to play while you are busy with other tasks or because you don't have enough staff. And it's definitely different from ignoring children's play because you do not think it's important. When you intentionally wait, you know what children are doing and you purposefully choose to let them play and discover on their own. Doing so is a gift to children. Being able to do so is a gift of good teachers.

Observe. Since observation informs good plans, one of the most important things teachers do as children play is observe. Many teachers observe and make notes while children are playing. Others simply observe and write their observations later.

Play. Talented early childhood teachers know how to play. Doing so mindfully helps you build relationships with children and helps children develop play skills. When you play with children, you *model* how to play—how to use toys, how to take on roles, how to support other players. As you playfully interact with children, you might even help them build skills and concepts. However, it takes sensitivity and experience to join children's play without taking it over and interfering.

Acknowledge and encourage. When children are working on a challenging new skill, or when they have accomplished one, you might physically or verbally acknowledge them and encourage them to persevere. A smile, nod, or a simple statement, "You got all the pieces in," lets children know their efforts have been noticed.

Scaffold. The most powerful teaching opportunities arise in play. When you support individual children as they develop a skill or concept during play, it is called *scaffolding*. The term *scaffolding* (coined by Russian psychologist Lev Vygotsky) describes a kind of teaching that often occurs during play. When you scaffold children's learning, you support by helping them *only as much as they need*. As a child acquires a skill or concept, you gradually withdraw your assistance until the child is able to be independent. Vygotsky called the time between when a child is dependent on adults and the time when she or he can be independent the *zone of proximal development* or ZPD (Berk & Winsler, 1995).

You are scaffolding children's learning when you *assist* or "lend a hand," for example, by stabilizing a block structure or holding the string taut as the child cuts it. Assistance need not be physical. Verbally pointing out an alternative to a child who is struggling is another kind of help. You might suggest, "Try looking at the flower first and then drawing." If a child is having trouble stacking blocks you might say, "I see that the big block wobbles when you put it on top of the little block. You might like to use a different block. Maybe it won't wobble so much."

Adjust the challenge. Young children need challenge! Another one of your scaffolding tasks is to be alert to the signs that a child needs a different (harder or easier) challenge. What do these signs look like? The misuse of a toy is sometimes a clue that a different challenge is needed. Often, providing a toy that requires different skills will help. If children destroy or walk away from their work, it is a sign that the challenge may be too great. Substituting simpler materials or processes (e.g., swapping soft dough for stiff clay, or pasting shapes or pictures instead of cutting them out) can ensure that children have appropriate challenges. When a child finishes a project without thought or attention, it may be that the level is wrong. One way to tell if a new challenge is needed is to add a simpler or more difficult variation to an activity. A teacher we know will sometimes challenge children to put together a tray puzzle outside of the tray—when the children easily do this it tells her that they are ready for harder puzzles.

Introduce New Play Materials

When you bring something unfamiliar (a piece of equipment or an activity) into the environment, it needs to be introduced. Introductions can be simple. Present the equipment or activity to the children, demonstrate its use, describe any special ways to use the equipment or do the activity, show where it will be kept or used, and explain when it will be available. Depending on the characteristics of the new experience and the custom in your program, you may do this in a large or small group or with individuals.

Planned Scaffolded Activities

Do you remember learning to drive a car? It's unlikely that you would have developed driving skill by playing with a car. You also probably would not have learned if you had only attended a lecture class on driving. Instead, you learned when you were ready and interested, with the guidance from someone more competent than yourself.

Some complex skills are learned better if they are taught. Skills like playing cat's cradle or putting together a complex puzzle take analysis, demonstration, and practice. To teach children these skills, you will slowly demonstrate while describing what you are doing. Then you will invite children to do it themselves while providing assistance like adjusting their position, narrating their activities, handing them the next piece, or giving a simple direction ("Try turning the piece over").

When you want to help a child acquire a specific concept or skill in the zone of proximal development described by Vygotsky, it is often useful to plan a guided activity in which you work with that child. Planned scaffolded activities permit you to concentrate on a particular child's learning process and participate in a learning dialogue. They allow you to observe and assess a child's knowledge and skill and modify what you do based on the child's response. These activities can be planned to support the development of skills, concepts, and attitudes that you want all the children to develop or the development of the major understandings of a topic in an integrated curriculum.

The smaller the group and the more that time and the environment support self-selected independent activities, the more you will be able to engage in scaffolded activities. This is why low teacher-child ratios and smaller group sizes are used as hallmarks of quality in early childhood settings (Phillips et al., 2000). Well-designed learning centers and large blocks of time for children to work with one another are crucial if you are to have the opportunity to work one on one with children.

Small-Group Activities

Small-group activities enable you to present concepts, facilitate an exchange of ideas between children, and have meaningful personal contact with each child. In

our experience it is a very effective teaching strategy. It reduces waiting time and allows for activities that involve turn-taking, guided peer interaction, manipulation of materials, and quite a lot of teacher assistance.

How many children constitute a small group? This varies with the age of the children. For toddlers, a small group is 2 to 4 children. With preschoolers, a small group may be 5 to 10 children, although fewer is better, especially for 3-year-olds. And with kindergarten and primary grade children, 8 to 12 children is a small group—although again, fewer is better.

In a small-group activity you are able to attend to the way children respond and can evaluate and modify what you do. When you have children with diverse developmental needs (as you do in most classrooms, but always in mixed-age classrooms and those with children who have special needs), you can tailor the length of the small-group time and the kind of activity to match the children in the group. For example, a planned process for naming groups in a class of children ages 2 1/2 through 5 took place in two small groups divided by age. The younger group spent 10 minutes thinking of and naming their group (the Flowers). The older group spent three 15-minute group times on subsequent days brainstorming, negotiating, and voting for their small-group name (the Cloud-Airplanes).

If an adult needs to discuss an activity with the children while it is taking place, then a small group is the best choice. Activities such as "I Spy," planned discussion, acting out stories, creative movement activities, cooking projects, charting activities, and walks in the community work best in small groups.

Small groups that meet together on a regular basis develop an identity of their own. When the children select a name for their group, they further cement feelings of belonging and responsibility. These kinds of regular small-group meetings help children to develop some important self-regulation skills, including the ability to listen and talk in a group, solve problems and make decisions democratically, take leader and follower roles, and accept responsibility for the outcomes of their decisions. For this reason we encourage you to meet regularly in consistent small groups and to allow the groups to name themselves, as took place with the small groups we have used as examples.

Large-Group Activities

Although they are often used in early childhood programs, large-group activities are generally the least effective for teaching and the hardest for teachers to do well. This may account for the fact that children often list them as their least favorite activities in school (Wiltz & Klein, 2001).

In most classrooms children gather together at least once a day for a meeting or circle time. These whole-class gatherings can be valuable when they allow children to share a common experience and build a sense of community. They are appropriate when all children can be active (e.g., by singing a song or engaging in creative movement). Large-group activities are not appropriate if children need to wait quietly, if you need to attend to individual responses (e.g., show and tell), or if you want children to take turns (e.g., in cooking).

With older preschool, kindergarten, and primary school children, large-group activities are effective for group games like dodge ball. In general, the younger the children, the less effective it is to plan experiences for a large group.

Inappropriate Methods

In addition to knowing what methods are appropriate for young children, you also need to be able to identify and avoid inappropriate methods. Your knowledge about how young children learn and your observations of children's responses will help you to know what teaching methods are inappropriate.

You know that young children learn at varying rates, that they are active learners, that they learn through play, and that they need many opportunities to practice skills as they are acquired (Bredekamp & Copple, 2009). Children learn through active engagement and concrete experiences. Therefore, it stands to reason that young children do not benefit from abstract methods of teaching such as worksheets, lectures, and drill on isolated skills. Observe a young child who is required to sit still and complete a worksheet or listen to an adult try to teach a fact out of context. Chances are, you will see a child who is inattentive, unhappy, or disruptive.

These methods do not build understanding and, because they are often aversive, can lead to negative feelings about school. They do not belong in programs for preschool and kindergarten children. Indeed, they have limited utility in programs for primary school children.

Reflect on children's learning . . .

Think of an early childhood program that you know. What did you see children doing as they were learning? How could you tell the children were learning? During what kinds of activities did you sense the children were most engaged?

Know Local and National Standards

Teachers of young children today are required to be *accountable* for their teaching: You need to know what you are supposed to be teaching and you must teach those things. As a professional early childhood educator in the 21st century, you also need to know about early learning guidelines or preschool content standards, which describe either (1) what young children need to know, understand, and be able to do in a variety of learning domains or (2) the learning opportunities that should be provided in early care and education programs.

A variety of professional associations (e.g., National Association for Sport & Physical Education and the National Council of Teachers of Mathematics) have written national standards for most curriculum areas for K–12 education, and some address preschool education. Head Start and almost all states[2] have early learning standards for most curriculum areas. Your program's goals may be based on your state's standards or they may have been developed independently by the staff or a curriculum specialist. These standards help you to know the broad expectations for both you as a teacher and the children you teach.

Good early childhood practices such as creating a rich play environment and providing appropriate teacher-led activities help you to meet standards. But accountability does not simply mean following good practice. It also means you must be able to show how you are teaching to meet the standards. One way to do this is to identify the standards relevant for your plans. We recommend that you keep a copy of your state or program standards close at hand when you write plans.

Objectives

Our plans miscarry because they have no aim. When a man does not know what harbor he is making for, no wind is the right wind.

SENECA, 4 B.C. – 65 A.D.

The starting place for any plan is deciding what you want to teach—the objectives. A plan's objectives describe intended teaching outcomes in terms of the understanding, skills, experiences, attitudes, and dispositions or "habits of mind" (Katz, 1993) that you want children to gain. Since family members and parents often cannot perceive the educational content of the playful activities that form such a large part of the early childhood curriculum, an important part of your professional role is clearly articulating the area of learning and the educational purpose of what you do with children (regardless of whether you have written a plan for it). Being able to do so distinguishes you as a professional and a teacher.

Objectives can be thought of as progressing from simple to complex. In the cognitive domain, simple objectives involve remembering, shown at the bottom of Figure 2.5, which depicts Bloom's Taxonomy of Cognitive Objectives. More complex objectives involve making connections, understanding relationships, evaluating, solving problems, and creating by combining what is known (Anderson & Krathwohl, 2001; Bloom, Mesia, & Krathwohl, 1964), as you see in this figure. If you value helping children to understand concepts and apply them to solve problems and create, then you will identify objectives related to these more complex objectives.

Similar taxonomies have been created for the affective and psychomotor domains (see Figures 2.6 and 2.7). These taxonomies are a little less obvious, but

---

[2] You can find standards for almost every state online. The National Child Care Information and Technical Assistance Center (NCCIC) has links to all state early learning guidelines on its Web site. Availability of standards for other countries vary, but the United Kingdom, Sweden, Singapore, Finland, and New Zealand (among others) have national curriculum standards (in English) that you can view online. Australia and Canada have standards by province or state.

FIGURE 2.5   Bloom's Taxonomy of Cognitive Objectives Revised

Source: From *Learning and Teaching: Bloom's Taxonomy,* by J. S. Atherton, 2009. Available from www.learning andteaching.info/learning/bloomtax.htm. Reprinted with permission.

FIGURE 2.6   Taxonomy of Affective Objectives

Source: From *Learning and Teaching: Bloom's Taxonomy,* by J. S. Atherton, 2009. Available from www.learning andteaching.info/learning/bloomtax.htm. Reprinted with permission.

FIGURE 2.7   Taxonomy of Psychomotor Objectives

Source: From *Learning and Teaching: Bloom's Taxonomy,* by J. S. Atherton, 2009. Available from www.learning andteaching.info/learning/bloomtax.htm. Reprinted with permission.

they help us to generalize the idea that if we want children to be independent and thoughtful, then we need to aim for more complex objectives.

Measurable and Behavioral Objectives

There are different points of view regarding how specific and measurable objectives ought to be. We believe that appropriate objectives include involvement, awareness, and appreciation, as well as concepts, understandings, and skills. For example, we think it is reasonable for a music activity to help children begin to gain some appreciation for music from other cultures. However, since appreciation is not measurable, some educators might reject this objective.

A related form of objective that precisely describes a behavior is called a *behavioral objective*. A behavioral objective describes specific behaviors, the conditions under which they take place, and the criteria for success ("when presented with five sheets of paper with lines drawn down the center, the child will cut at least one sheet of paper along the line"). Behavioral objectives are often used in special education. They leave little room for individual choice, require all children to be at the same place at the end of a lesson, and do not allow for spontaneity or creativity. They are not consistent with the belief that children must construct knowledge from their own active involvement with materials and experiences.

Measurable objectives are useful to help you demonstrate that your teaching has had an effect. And since you may be required to write measurable objectives, it is important to learn how to do so in ways that have integrity (we will provide you with examples). However, in order to be measurable, objectives sometimes focus on trivial, achievable goals. They can lead you to emphasize less important aspects of activities, and you may lose track of important learning that isn't easily observable or measurable.

Some educators make the distinction between these types of objectives by using the term *goals* to describe these important, not easily measured awareness, attitudes, and dispositions. Whatever they are called (and regardless of whether you are allowed to include them in your written plans), it is crucial to remember them. We believe they are the first and most important part of planning.

Learning to Write Objectives

When you first begin to create plans, you may find that writing objectives is challenging. There are many things to consider, and sometimes it's hard to think of the right words. Our college students find it helpful to look at a number of generic "beginnings" for objectives to get started (see Table 2.1 for some examples). If you are required to write measurable objectives, you will select those that can be seen or heard. We have highlighted them in Table 2.1.

Creating Activity/Lesson Plans

An activity or lesson plan is a detailed written design for a single curriculum event. It specifies objectives, lists needed materials, describes teaching procedures, and outlines ways to evaluate success in achieving the objectives. Think

TABLE 2.1 Examples of Beginnings for Objectives

Knowledge	Skill	Attitude	Experience
Learn about . . .	Practice . . .	Develop awareness of . . .	Try . . .
Gain understanding of . . .	Develop skill in . . .	Enjoy . . .	Hear . . .
Describe . . .	Begin to be able to . . .	Develop a disposition to . . .	See
Recognize . . .	Acquire the ability to . . .	Be sensitive to . . .	Taste . . .
Sort . . .	Show . . .	Be respectful of	Touch . . .
Identify/Name . . .	Differentiate . . .	Appreciate . . .	Smell . . .

of an activity or lesson plan as a recipe for teaching. Like a recipe it outlines each essential step, but assumes you know the basics of how to teach. And like a recipe it isn't the whole meal—it is just a part of the educational diet that you will provide to children.

Like many early childhood college teachers, we believe that writing detailed activity/lesson plans is a valuable activity to help you understand how to teach. We will walk you through the process using a detailed activity-planning format (see Figure 2.8) and will provide an example from our own work with children. If you are currently working on writing a plan, you might want to work on yours in tandem with ours. As you gain experience, you will not plan in such detail. But while you are learning the process, you will see that detailed planning is more than a class assignment; it is a strategy for helping you learn to think like a teacher. We will give you a simpler format to use after you are more experienced.

Carefully thinking through the purpose and sequence of an activity helps to ensure success. When your planning is good, you will express yourself clearly to children and feel more comfortable while teaching. Because this process is so valuable, you will practice writing many detailed activity plans during your preparation to become an early childhood teacher. It's helpful to remember that while a plan, like an outline or a recipe, is presented in a linear format, you may actually think about and write a plan in a different way. We will

Reflect on something you planned.

Think back to a time when you planned something in your life—a trip, a party, a project. Reflect on what you did and how you went about organizing the event or activity. What did you do? How did you know that you had succeeded? How did planning or lack of planning impact how it turned out?

FIGURE 2.8   Activity Plan Format—Detailed

Activity:	name, type, and brief description *Primary Curriculum Area Focus*
WHO It's For:	(the child/group for whom you are planning)
WHY This Activity Rationale:	(why you have chosen this activity for these children at this time)
Curriculum Area Objectives:	*By participating in this activity the children will …*
Standard(s):	(state or national)
HOW to Prepare	*What you need:* (materials, equipment, space, time)
	Set up:
HOW to Teach	*Introduction:* (how to begin so children will be interested and know what to do)
	Teaching steps: (what to do and say step by step to provide the experiences that will teach the concepts, develop the skills, and build the attitudes or dispositions that are described in the objectives)
	Closure: (what you will do or say to reinforce/support what children have learned and help them make a transition to another activity)

HOW to Assess and Document (what to look for to identify whether the objectives were met and how to document)

Objectives	Evidence of Learning Children might…	How to Document This Evidence
Objectives from the first part of the plan	Things a child might do or say during the activity if objectives were met Things a child might do or say later during play, routines, or other activities if objectives were met	Observations, work samples, photographs, etc.

describe a typical sequence for planning here, but the way you actually write your plans may be different. As long as you think through all the pieces eventually, it doesn't really matter which part you write down first.

Writing a Plan

Decide What and Explain Why

In the spring of the year in a mixed-age preschool class (19 children, 3 teachers), the 4-year-olds (a group called the Peacocks) were a group who tended not to label items verbally. Many spoke a regional non-standard English dialect. They enjoyed fingerplays and stories. One of the goals of the program was to develop a rich vocabulary in all children.

At the same time, the class was learning about gardens. They had planted a flower and vegetable garden in the yard. The Peacocks were enthusiastic gardeners and especially enjoyed watering plants, digging in the garden with the trowels, and stirring the dirt with the cultivator.

The beginning of a written activity/lesson plan is a brief explanation that sets the stage and helps you to think through what you are going to do with children and why. The first thing you have to do is decide what to plan. To do that, you need to think about your particular circumstances—the children, the setting, the families, and the school. As an example we will use a plan written for a group of 4-year-olds.

Given the situation described above, there are many possible teaching activities—you could read a story about gardens, you could play a guessing game, you could make up fingerplays about gardens. What would you have chosen? (If you are planning along with us, think about each of these areas and write your own plan as we write ours.) The teachers in this class decided to play a "feely box" game (a guessing game in which children feel an item inside a box and without looking guess what it is) using garden tools to help build language. This first part of a plan has four parts:

1. **Activity name and description.** Every teaching activity has a name you can use to talk about it. It can be classified by type—is it a game, a group discussion, a book? If you are writing to share with others (colleagues, families, your college professor), elaborate by briefly describing it.
2. **Primary curriculum content area.** Every activity for young children teaches more than one curriculum area. Although young children learn in integrated ways, identifying and planning for the primary curriculum area is helpful for a number of reasons, especially when you are just learning to plan. When you are clear about the area you are addressing, you are more likely to accomplish your purpose. Although this activity involves science (using the senses to make observations), it is primarily a *language* activity. If your purpose is helping children develop vocabulary, you will want to focus on using new words in context. You will target many of your comments to help children become aware of words; for example, "You called it a shovel—You're right. It IS a lot like a shovel but this kind of shovel is short and has a pointed end. It is for planting seeds, and gardeners call it a trowel." If your purpose had been enhancing children's cognitive ability, you might have invited them to think of why a trowel is needed, "Why do you think they made the trowel so short?"
3. **WHO it's for.** Make a note of the group, age, and number of children for whom you are planning.

41

4. **WHY this activity rationale.** We believe that writing a statement of rationale is one of the most useful things you can do to help yourself become an intentional teacher. The rationale answers the essential teaching question: Why are you planning THIS activity for THESE children at THIS time? It is different from a statement of objectives. Your answer helps to ensure that your activity has some meaningful connection to the children. If you don't have a good answer to this question, you don't really have a good reason for planning this activity.

Figure 2.9 shows the beginning of the plan that one of the teachers wrote.

Identify Objectives and Standards

What do you want to teach? What understanding, skills, experiences, attitudes, and dispositions are the objectives of the activity? In writing objectives, standards can often be your friend. As you look at your state standards or at the standards that national organizations have identified for young children, you may find that someone else has already found just the right words to express what you are trying to accomplish.

The teacher writing the plan for the *Garden Tools Feely Box* decided that she had two language objectives and one objective related to learning through the senses (science). She matched these to her state standards for Communication, Language Development and Literacy, and Cognitive Development: Science. See the plan's objectives and state standards in Figure 2.10.

It is worthwhile to note here that it is better to write a limited number of objectives even though every good activity can teach many things. Limiting the

FIGURE 2.9   Beginning for the Plan *Garden Tools Feely Box*

Primary Curriculum Area: Language

Activity name, type, and brief description: Garden Tools Feely Box, a vocabulary-building game

WHO **It's For:** The Peacocks, eight 4-year-olds

Rationale: As we have been working in the garden, the children have been calling tools and garden objects by different names—some correct and some incorrect.

FIGURE 2.10   Objectives and Standards for the Plan *Garden Tools Feely Box*

Objectives: *By participating in this activity the children will …*

- Learn vocabulary for garden tools such as *trowel, spade, cultivator, watering can, stake, weed fork*.
- Use the sense of touch to make observations.
- Notice and enjoy words.

Standard(s) *HAWAII PRESCHOOL CONTENT STANDARDS**:

Domain III (Communication, Language Development & Literacy) Standard 2: Listen with comprehension to a variety of spoken forms of language. Standard 3: Acquire increasingly rich vocabulary and sentence structure.

Domain IV (Cognitive Development, Science) Standard 1: Increase sensory awareness.

———————

*We will use the Hawaii Preschool Content Standards as placeholders for your state, provincial, or national standards.

number of objectives that you write, especially when you are just learning to write and assess plans, helps you to focus your teaching.

Plan for What You Need

The next step in writing a plan is to begin thinking through what you will need for your activity. Just like when following a recipe, you need to have all the ingredients to make your plan work. Often the difference between a planning success and a failure is having the right materials, equipment, space, and time.

Make a list of the materials you need to prepare, borrow, or buy so that you have them ahead of time. Think about the space and equipment you need, the best time in the schedule for the activity, and how much time to allow. Think about what else is needed. Does anyone need to be called or alerted? Do you need to cut paper or cover the table with newspaper? Plan for it. For the *Garden Tools Feely Box,* the teacher made a list of "ingredients" (see Figure 2.11).

As you think through the steps of the activity and write down the procedures, you may discover that there are additional things you need. You will go back and add these to the ***What you need*** section of your plan. Remember that the children are not a needed material; they should not be listed here.

Plan the Teaching: What You Do

Teaching procedures spell out what you will do and say, and in what order. They are the heart of an activity plan. A teaching plan always includes at least 3 parts—an introduction, teaching steps, and closure. Notice that a teaching plan is ***not*** how you set up the activity (you covered that in the previous section); instead, it is what you will say and do as children are engaged in the activity.

Introduction

The *introduction* describes how you will get children's attention, engage their interest, and let them know what to do. For many activities the introduction can be very simple. Explaining what will happen may be enough for an activity that children are familiar with and that they are predisposed to like ("I brought a game for us to play using some of the tools we've been using in the garden."). For any activity and for almost all young children it is very effective if you begin physically with an experience involving the use of the senses ("You can hold the trowel and see what it feels like."). Another way to introduce an activity is to ask questions that tap into children's prior knowledge ("What tools do you remember using in our garden? What tools do you use in your garden at home? What tools did we see Herman the gardener using?"). This is even more effective if you turn it into a game ("I'm thinking of something that holds water and has a handle that we use in our garden. Can you guess what it is?").

FIGURE 2.11 How to Prepare for the *Garden Tools Feely Box* Activity

What you need:

MATERIALS: Feely box, 4–5 kinds of garden tools (trowel, spade, cultivator, watering can, stake, weed fork, garden gloves) without sharp edges (at least one per child), sturdy tote bag to carry them

TIME: About 10 minutes at small-group time

SPACE: Library area (or any cozy space where children can sit together)

Set up: Gather the tools and put them in the bag. Put together with the feely box.

Think through what children need to understand and be able to do in order to participate in the activity. You may need to introduce an unfamiliar word or concept, or teach a skill. If the activity involves an item that is novel or highly attractive to the children, plan a way for them to get acquainted with it before you begin teaching ("Each person will get a turn to put a hand in the feely box before we start the game."). Skilled teachers know that it is important to give children lots of time for a new experience. In fact, simply introducing an item may be an entire activity. One of the most common mistakes of novice teachers is to introduce many intriguing and exciting objects at one time ("Here are 3 new puppets, a cape to wear, and a magic wand to use in our story."). They are then surprised when children focus on the "things" rather than the content they were planning to teach. The introduction to the *Garden Tools Feely Box* activity can be seen in Figure 2.12.

Teaching Steps

Teaching steps describe what you will do and say to accomplish your objectives. The steps should match the objectives you wrote and should be appropriate to the age and stage of development of the children. The amount of detail can vary. You need at least an outline of the basic steps, simply described, but with enough information that you (or a colleague) will be able to use the plan again at a later date. Beginning teachers, and anyone planning an activity that is particularly complex, should map out what to say and what questions to ask to support the objectives. (See Figure 2.13.)

FIGURE 2.12   Introduction for the *Garden Tools Feely Box* Activity

HOW to Teach   *Introduction:*

- At small-group time, show a trowel and say something like … "I brought a game for us to play using some of the tools we've been using in the garden."
- Ask … "Does anyone know what this tool is called?"
- Listen to children's responses and explain that the word gardeners use is *trowel*. Comment—"I like the word *trowel*—it sounds like *towel* but it looks like a little pointy shovel."
- Bring out the second trowel and let all the children take turns holding it. Explain that in this game you feel a tool inside the feely box and see if you can think of its name.
- Show and name the rest of the tools, encouraging children to think of the names.

FIGURE 2.13   Teaching Steps for the *Garden Tools Feely Box* Activity

HOW to Teach   *Teaching steps:*

1. Put one tool inside the box—leave the rest in the bag.
2. Invite a child to feel the tool inside the box and see if he or she can tell which tool it is.
3. When the child names a tool, open the box and see if he or she is right— celebrate success; if not successful, comment that it was pretty tricky and they'll get to try again.
4. Repeat with all the children, making sure everyone has a success.

Closure

The *closure* of an activity sums up the learning in some way that makes sense for children. It may be a statement you make ("You knew a lot of garden tools.") or it may be a way for children to show something that they know and make a *transition* ("Think of a tool to use in our garden, tell me, then choose a center to play in."). A well-thought out closure and a smooth transition help you to focus children on what they know and are able to do.

For the *Garden Tools Feely Box Activity,* the teacher closed the activity very simply (see Figure 2.14).

Plan for Assessment

What children do and say during and following an activity gives evidence of what they have learned. The last part of a written plan focuses on what to look for in children to indicate that they have gained the knowledge, skill, or attitudes that were described in the objectives, along with ideas for effective ways to document children's learning. (See Figure 2.15.)

In our example, the teacher planned to listen for children using the new vocabulary in the garden or in play. This growth could be documented through anecdotal records. We like to use an anecdotal record form like the sample included in Figure 2.16 to record children's responses.

Implement the Plan

A good plan helps you teach in the same way that a good recipe helps you cook. However, children are not as predictable as flour and salt. The most beautifully planned activity can fail miserably if you are not responsive to the children. If you

FIGURE 2.14 Closure for the *Garden Tools Feely Box* Activity

Closure: After every child has had a success, invite them to help you put tools in the bag. Ask each child to put away a specific tool ("Ezra can you put away the cultivator") and then choose a center for inside time.

FIGURE 2.15 How to Assess and Document the *Garden Tools Feely Box* Activity

HOW to Assess and Document
What to look for to identify if the objectives were met and how to document.

Objectives	Evidence of Learning Children might …	How to Document This Evidence
From the first part of the plan	*Things a child might do or say during the activity if objectives were met; or things a child might do or say later during play, routines, or other activities if objectives were met*	*Observations, work samples, photographs, etc.*
Learn vocabulary for garden tools such as *trowel, spade, cultivator, watering can, stake, weed fork*	• Use garden tool vocabulary in context • Correct teacher when she makes a "mistake" in naming a tool • Label garden tools in drawings	Anecdotal records Drawing samples
Use sense of touch to make observations	• Correctly identify tools by touch	Anecdotal records
Notice and enjoy words	• Ask the name of different objects • Comment on the words (e.g., garden fork has a fork in it)	Anecdotal records

FIGURE 2.16   Anecdotal Record

Primary Domain: Language

Secondary Domain: Social

Date: March 15, 20___

Cara was playing in the pretend area. Aidan picked up the toy trowel. Cara said, "That's <u>my</u> Mommy's trowel not your trowel."

Comment: Uses garden tool vocabulary introduced in the feely box activity.
Defends ideas/needs/rights verbally

went to a lot of trouble to write an activity plan, you may feel committed to using it just the way it's written. Just as a cook must adjust to the tastes of the diners, the characteristics of the ingredients, and the equipment, a teacher must adjust to the children and the circumstances. Experienced teachers know that they will need to make modifications to their plans in response to children's interests and needs. Their teaching resembles a dance in which the children are their partners. They observe and respond to the children—and the children respond to them.

Inexperienced teachers often find it difficult to be flexible in implementing a plan. For example, when one of our students attempted to tell a long, complicated story to a group of 4-year-olds using a Kamishibai (a Japanese storytelling method using poster cards), the children all wanted to examine the cards and did not attend to the long, long story. The novice teacher became flustered by the children's inattention to her story and was unable to incorporate their ideas into her activity or guide the discussion into listening to the story. With more confidence and attention to the children, the discussion could have led to the activity instead of away from it.

Assess and Document Learning

The measure of your success as a curriculum planner and as a teacher is whether children learn and whether their learning matches what you intended to teach. If you have planned well and observed children carefully, you will see evidence that they have gained the knowledge, skill, or attitudes that were described in the objectives. Sometimes you will observe evidence that will tell you that these were not acquired, or that they were acquired incompletely.

In our example, the teacher listened for children using the new vocabulary in the garden or at play. This growth could be documented through anecdotal records (see Figure 2.16). She might also see evidence in work samples (children's drawings, paintings, or other representations) in which children dictate a name for garden tools represented. These could be annotated and collected or photographed to provide documentation of children's learning.

While it is valuable to document children's learning, it is important to make sure that the documentation authentically shows what children have learned. A photograph of a child posing for the camera rarely provides evidence of learning.

Try It Out!

Consider the activity used as an example in this chapter. Brainstorm another way a child might demonstrate his/her acquisition of each objective and a different way that a teacher could document this learning.

Evaluate the Plan

Whether you plan an activity with children or an afternoon at the beach, you evaluate your plan. This is the final element. Ask yourself . . . "Did it go well? Could I have done it better? Should I do it again? Did I accomplish what I intended?" After you have written and implemented a plan, take a few moments (that's probably all you'll have!) to reflect on what you did and how children responded. Reflecting ensures that the learning experience you planned for children also becomes a learning experience for you. Evaluating your planning and implementation is different from assessing whether the children acquired the knowledge, skills, and attitudes you laid out in the objectives.

Sometimes an apparent planning disaster may be the result of overstimulating materials, timing mistakes (not allowing enough time for children to explore materials, or asking children to wait and listen when they need to move and do), poor room arrangement, insufficient opportunities for needed physical activity, or an activity that is too challenging or not challenging enough for the children. Modified and tried again, the plan may prove sound. But if you never think about what happened, you will never be able to figure out what went wrong and make those modifications. However well you plan, you are almost certain to experience a few planning "failures." Don't be discouraged by this. No one is an accomplished veteran the first few times she or he tries. You'll get better with practice! You really will.

It may actually be even harder to evaluate a success. Were the children engaged in the activity because the materials were interesting, because you were responsive to the children, or because Jon was absent today? Evaluate your successes as well as your failures.

It is helpful to note on the plan anything you would add or do differently. Reflecting in this way is usually a requirement for students, but it is good practice for all teachers. Then when you go back to your plans, you will remember what happened last time. Reflecting and evaluating closes the planning circle (see Figure 2.17).

Writing Activity/Lesson Plans in the Real World

When you become a teacher, will you write plans for every activity? It would be impossible and a little silly to spend many hours writing plans for everything you do with children. Written activity plans are useful and may be necessary when clarity and sequence are crucial or where content or procedures are complex or unfamiliar. An activity such as reading a simple, familiar story should be included in a weekly plan, but generally does not require

> **Reflect on planning for children . . .**
>
> Think about a time when you planned an activity for children. What happened? How did having a plan help you? What happened that surprised you? Would you use your plan again? What would you do differently?

FIGURE 2.17 *Garden Tools Feely Box* Activity Evaluation

> **EVALUATION**   The feely box activity was much enjoyed by the children. They were very familiar with *watering can* and quickly began calling the trowel by name. Aidan had difficulty with the stake and insisted that it was not a stake because you can't eat it. The children all wanted to wear the garden glove—it might be a good idea to have a set for working in the garden.

FIGURE 2.18 Activity Plan Format—Simple

Activity Name/Curriculum Area

Objectives:

Standard:

What you need:

How to teach:

How to assess:

FIGURE 2.19 Simple Activity Plan—Example

Activity Name:	Garden Tools Feely Box	**Curriculum Area:**	Language
Objectives:	Children will…		
	• notice and enjoy words		
	• develop vocabulary for garden tools		
Standard(s):	Domain III, Com. St. 2, St. 3; Domain IV, Cog. Sci. 1 St. 1.		
What you need:	Feely box, garden tools, tote bag		
How to teach:	1. Show tool—invite children to guess. Let children take turns holding.		
	2. Show and name all tools; then hide in bag.		
	3. Explain game—feel tool inside box and name.		
	4. Put tool in box (secretly)—invite child to feel and name—open box and see if right.		
	5. Repeat with all the children.		
How to assess:	Listen for children using garden tool vocabulary or commenting on words.		

a detailed written activity plan. Locating the book, reviewing it, and spending a few moments thinking about questions to ask and how to structure a discussion may be enough preparation. However, you should be *able* to write a clear plan for even a simple activity.

When you are a teacher you will write more abbreviated plans than the one presented here. We suggest that you use a simple format that still includes the essential elements (see Figures 2.18 and 2.19). Keep your plans so that they can be easily retrieved and used again—in a digital file, in a notebook, or on 5-by-8-inch cards in file boxes or on metal rings. Digital storage allows you to easily retrieve and revise your plans. However, since technology changes, you may find digital versions unreadable in a few years, so it is wise to always keep a hard copy of your plans.

Creating Weekly Plans

As we have mentioned, most teachers write a *weekly plan,* a calendar of activities to be done over the course of a week. Writing a weekly plan helps you think through what you will do and stay organized. It also helps to keep the teaching team on track. Many teachers post their weekly plans so that families know what's coming up, too. There are different ways to plan activities for each week. Teachers of infants and young toddlers make plans for individual children and for ways to modify the environment. Preschool, kindergarten, and primary grade teachers usually write a weekly calendar.

For most preschool teachers and many kindergarten teachers the schedule of regular daily activities (e.g., story, small group, circle, and outdoor play), and special weekly events (e.g., cooking and field trips), provide a structure for weekly plans. Many also plan ways to modify learning centers each week.

Primary school teachers often use subject areas in lieu of daily "events" to structure the weekly plan. It is common to plan for daily reading, math, and spelling, along with "special" activities that may happen only once a week like art and PE. They frequently use a required curriculum and regularly write elaborate lesson plans that map out details.

As you plan for a week, you will keep in mind the skills and concepts that you want all the children to develop, as well as plans for specific children. You will include routines that are a feature of the week (e.g., cooking or a weekly visit from an adopted grandparent) and activities related to a curriculum focus (e.g., trips, visitors). You will also consider the impact of events in the school, among families, or in the community (e.g., holidays, elections, seasonal activities, bake sales, open house). In addition to planning the activities you will provide, you can also write a short statement of objectives for the week.

Weekly plans vary in the amount of detail included for each activity. Some preschool and primary teachers write an objective or purpose statement for each activity and include it on the plan. Some plan activities for specific children in their group, particularly if the group includes children with special needs. Some include a list of materials to prepare or things to do. An example of a preschool weekly plan (Figure 2.20) is included here. A brief assessment of a weekly plan can be written directly on the plan and kept along with a hard copy.

Integrated Study Plans

Integrated organization refers to curriculum in which a topic of study provides a focus for the curriculum. The topic serves as an umbrella under which different developmental and subject areas are integrated. In an integrated study, children investigate a topic in depth over a period of time. The topic forms the hub for curriculum in many different subject areas. Children's interests or the teacher's ideas about what children would enjoy or benefit from can be sources of the topic. The sample week's plan provided here and the sample activity plan (Figure 2.20) were both from an integrated study of gardens.

Plan as Part of an Integrated Study

We believe that the best curriculum for young children is "integrated" around a topic that engages both children and adults. This does not mean that every learning activity must relate to the integrated study. While the Peacocks in the activity plan example were learning vocabulary, they were also learning about gardens. That same week they also made playdough, played a game called Fire on the Mountain, built with blocks, read books unrelated to gardens, and did many other things.

FIGURE 2.20 Preschool Class Weekly Plan: A Study of Gardens—Week 3

Objectives: To help children to develop a variety of ways to communicate ideas to others (art, words, song, writing) and build a disposition to work together to accomplish things (planting gardens, making dough, etc.).

	Monday	Tuesday	Wednesday	Thursday	Friday
Story 8:30–8:40	*Sunflower* (Bunting)	*The Tiny Seed* (Carle)	*Growing Vegetable Soup* (Ehlert)	*First the Egg* (Seeger)	*And the Good Brown Earth* (Henderson)
Outdoor Activities 9:00–10:00	**Planting Potatoes**	**Washing Garden Pots and Tools**	**Obstacle Course**	**Woodworking: Building a Garden Frame**	**Woodworking: Building a Garden Frame**
Purpose: *to help children to…*	Develop a sense of connection and responsibility for the natural world by caring for a garden.	Appreciate the work required to create a garden. Develop fine motor coordination and strength.	Develop strength and coordination of large muscles.	Develop eye and hand coordination. Develop and use measurement concepts.	Develop eye and hand coordination. Develop and use measurement concepts.
Small Group Striped Caterpillars 10:00–10:20	**Fire On the Mountain!**	**Garden Maps**	**Garden Journal**	***Trip to the Urban Garden*** We leave at 9:00	**In the Garden…Book**
Purpose: *to help children to…*	Develop strength and coordination of large muscles. Acquire behaviors and skills expected in school.	Develop understanding of maps. Begin to learn about art elements and techniques.	Develop a disposition to write. Understand print is talk written down.	Understand that there are different kinds of gardens for different purposes.	Develop a disposition to write. Understand print is talk written down.
Small Group Peacocks 10:00–10:10	***Trip to the Urban Garden*** We leave at 9:00	**Counting and Planting Seeds**	**Reading Jack's Garden**	**Making Playdough**	**Garden Tools Feely Box**
Purpose: *to help children to…*	Understand that there are different kinds of gardens for different purposes.	Learn about the characteristics of plants and gardens. Develop numeracy concepts.	Enjoy and understand books. Acquire literacy skills. Explore print in books.	Learn how materials change when heated, mixed, or cut up. Use language in a variety of ways, such as following steps.	Develop a disposition to notice and enjoy words. Develop vocabulary for garden tools.

	Rock and Sand Wheat Grass Garden	Ink and Watercolor Painting	Cooking Vegetable Soup	Playdough	Garden Collage
Indoor Special Activities 10:20–11:30 **Purpose:** *to help children to…*	Reconstruct ideas about gardens.	Create and express themselves through a variety of art experiences.	Appreciate wholesome food. Develop understanding that food is created by people who cook and grow vegetables.	Increase sensory awareness. Explore physical properties of the world.	Gain aesthetic awareness of plants and gardens. Begin to learn about art elements and techniques.
	Walk around the Chair	**Garden Song**	**Magic Rocks**	**Hoop Jumping**	**Will My Flowers Bloom?**
Circle Time 11:30–11:45 **Purpose:** *to help children to…*	Develop skill in communicating ideas through movement. Develop spatial awareness.	Develop ability to sing tunefully.	Develop skill in communicating ideas through movement. Develop spatial awareness.	Develop a positive sense of self.	Develop the ability to express ideas through music and movement. Learn about the things plants need.
Changes for Indoor Learning Centers	Block area—add smooth stones, people figures, tree blocks.	Dramatic play—add garden tools.	Manipulatives—add garden matching game.	Writing center—garden word cards.	Science—seed comparison.
Changes for Outdoor Zones	Social-dramatic—add gardening boots and hats.	Active play—add wheelbarrows.	Natural elements—shovels and trowels in the sand.	Manipulative-creative—green, yellow, and pink paint at the easels.	

How It Went—What We Changed: The Garden Frame is in place and we will plant morning glories around it next week. The bookmaking activity went really well—check out the book in the library corner. The Urban Garden was a lot of fun—they have a family day on the first Saturday of every month—take your child if you can. Vegetable Soup a big hit—see recipe in this month's newsletter.
Assessment of Objectives: Children communicated with bookmaking, singing, and painting. Garden Frame, Book, and Movement activities worked to build disposition to work together.

When you plan an integrated study, however, it is important to be sure to plan for all areas of curriculum if you can do so with integrity; that is, so that it makes sense and really teaches about both the subject area and the topic of study. In an integrated study, activities are planned in all curriculum areas. However, each of the activities supports learning in more than one curriculum area.

Final Thoughts

The curriculum you plan should reflect your vision for children, for society, and for the future. It should be intellectually engaging both for children and for teachers. The choices you make as you select what you will teach and how you will teach it impact children's lives, your own life, and possibly the larger world. If you take this responsibility seriously, you will be thoughtful and thorough in your planning and use this important part of your work as a way to support all areas of children's development, increase their understanding of the world, build their love of learning, and help them to be the curious, creative, active problem solvers that the world needs.

Learning Outcomes

When you read this chapter, thoughtfully complete activities from the "To Learn More" section, and document this learning as suggested in the "For Your Portfolio" section, you will be making progress in the following *NAEYC Standards for Early Childhood Professional Preparation Programs* (2009):

Standard 3. Observing, Documenting, and Assessing to Support Young Children and Families

Students prepared in early childhood degree programs understand that child observation, documentation, and other forms of assessment are central to the practice of all early childhood professionals. They know about and understand the goals, benefits, and uses of assessment. They know about and use systematic observations, documentation, and other effective assessment strategies in a responsible way, in partnership with families and other professionals, to positively influence the development of every child.

The key elements of standard 3 you will have learned about are . . .

3a: Understanding the goals, benefits, and uses of assessment

3b: Knowing about and using observation, documentation, and other appropriate assessment tools and approaches

3c: Understanding and practicing responsible assessment to promote positive outcomes for each child

Standard 4. Using Developmentally Effective Approaches to Connect with Children and Families

Students prepared in early childhood degree programs understand that teaching and learning with young children is a complex enterprise, and its details vary depending on children's ages, characteristics, and the settings within which teaching and learning occur. They understand and use positive relationships and supportive interactions as the foundation for their work with young children and families. Students know, understand, and use a wide array of developmentally appropriate approaches, instructional strategies, and tools to connect with children and families and positively influence each child's development and learning.

The key elements of standard 4 you will have learned about are . . .

4c: Using a broad repertoire of developmentally appropriate teaching/learning approaches

4d: Reflecting on their own practice to promote positive outcomes for each child

Standard 5. Using Content Knowledge to Build Meaningful Curriculum

Students prepared in early childhood degree programs use their knowledge of academic disciplines to design, implement, and evaluate experiences that promote positive development and learning for each and every young child. Students understand the importance of developmental domains and academic (or content) disciplines in an early childhood curriculum. They know the essential concepts, inquiry tools, and structure of content areas, including academic subjects, and can identify resources to deepen their understanding. Students use their own knowledge and other resources to design, implement, and evaluate meaningful, challenging curricula that promote comprehensive developmental and learning outcomes for every young child.

The key element of standard 5 you will have learned about is . . .

5c: Using their own knowledge, appropriate early learning standards, and other resources to design, implement, and evaluate meaningful, challenging curricula for each child.

To Learn More

Write, Implement, and Assess a Plan: Using the format provided in this chapter, write a plan for an activity in your life unrelated to teaching, such as preparing a meal or running an errand. Think through the objectives, needs, and steps of the activity. Plan for how you will assess your objectives. Implement and assess your plan. Reflect on how having a written plan influenced both what you did and your success.

Have a Conversation with Two Teachers: Talk to two teachers about planning. Find out how often and in what depth they plan. Ask them about how their planning has changed as they have gained experience. Reflect on the similarities and differences between them. If the teachers will share their written plans with you, compare their planning—what elements are present in their plans?

Begin a Plan Collection: Create a binder for the collection of plan examples. At your work or practicum site ask if you can have a copy of a weekly plan and a lesson/activity plan. Create a section for weekly plan examples and another for lesson plan examples. Note on each the age of the children and the type of program.

Add to this collection as you visit or work in different programs.

Create a Documentation Idea List: On your own or with a peer, brainstorm a list of all the ways you could authentically document young children's growth and development. Use this list and add to it as you continue to learn about planning and assessing meaningful curriculum.

Support a Child at Play: In a formal or informal setting, spend some time with a child at play. Use the five support methods described on pages 34–35 (supporting children's play) to engage with the child. Reflect on which method seemed to best suit this child at this time.

Observe a Classroom for Young Children: As you observe the class, consider the different types of learning activities described in this chapter. Make a list of all the learning activities you observe. Reflect on which methods are used most frequently and note how well they appear to support children's learning.

Read More: Select one or more of the books or articles listed in the bibliography for this chapter and read more about this topic.

For Your Portfolio

Write, Implement, and Assess a Plan for Children: Using the format provided in this chapter, write a plan for an activity with children. Think through the objectives, needs, and steps of the activity. Plan for how you will assess your objectives. Implement and assess your plan. Write a reflection on how having a written plan influenced what you did and your success. If the activity was successful, use it to document your proficiency in planning.

The activities listed in the *To Learn More* section will have helped you to reflect on what you have learned while reading this chapter. Write a formal essay describing what you did and what you learned to document your learning for your professional portfolio.

Bibliography

Anderson, L. W., & Krathwohl, D. R. (Eds.). (2001). *A taxonomy for learning, teaching, and assessing: A revision of Bloom's taxonomy of educational objectives*. Boston, MA: Allyn & Bacon.

Baratta-Lorton, M. (1972). *Workjobs*. Menlo Park, CA: Addison Wesley.

Berk, L. E., & Winsler, A. (1995). *Scaffolding children's learning*. Washington, DC: NAEYC.

Biber, B. (1969). *Challenges ahead for early childhood education*. Washington, DC: NAEYC.

Biber, B. (1984). A developmental-interaction approach: Bank Street College of Education. In M. C. Day & R. K. Parker (Eds.), *The preschool in action: Exploring early childhood programs* (2nd ed., pp. 421–460). Boston, MA: Allyn & Bacon.

Bredekamp, S., & Rosegrant, T. (Eds.). (1992). *Reaching potentials: Appropriate curriculum and assessment for young children* (Vol. 1). Washington, DC: NAEYC.

Bredekamp, S., & Rosegrant, T. (Eds.). (1995). *Reaching potentials: Transforming early childhood curriculum & assessment for young children* (Vol. 2). Washington, DC: NAEYC.

Carter, M., & Curtis, D. (1996). *Reflecting children's lives: A handbook for planning child centered curriculum*. St. Paul, MN: Redleaf Press.

Chenfeld, M. B. (1994). *Teaching in the key of life*. Washington, DC: NAEYC.

Copple C., & Bredekamp, S. (2009). *Developmentally appropriate practice in early childhood programs* (3rd ed.). Washington, DC: NAEYC.

Cuffaro, H. K. (1995). *Experimenting with the world*. New York, NY: Teachers College Press.

Dittmann, L. L. (Ed.). (1977). *Curriculum is what happens: Planning is the key*. Washington, DC: NAEYC.

Edwards, C., Gandini, L., & Forman, G. (Eds.). (1998). *The hundred languages of children: The Reggio Emilia approach—advanced reflections* (2nd ed.). Greenwich, CT: Ablex Publishing Corp.

Epstein, A. S. (2007). *The intentional teacher*. Washington, DC: NAEYC.

Feeney, S. (2006). Some thoughts about early childhood curriculum: Which way should we go from here? *Beyond the Journal: Young Children on the Web* (http://www.journal.naeyc.org/btj/200609/FeeneyBTJ)

Feeney, S., Moravcik, E., & Nolte, S. (2013). *Who am I in the lives of children* (9th ed.). Upper Saddle River, NJ: Pearson.

Helm, J., Beneke, S., & Steinheimer, K. (2007). *Windows on learning: Documenting young children's work* (2nd ed.) New York, NY: Teachers College Press.

Hirsch, R. A. (2004). *Early childhood curriculum: Incorporating multiple intelligences, developmentally appropriate practice, and play*. Boston, MA: Allyn & Bacon.

Katz, L. G. (1993). *Dispositions as educational goals*. Urbana, IL: ERIC Clearinghouse on Elementary and Early Childhood Education. ERIC Identifier: ED363454.

Kostelnik, M. J., Soderman, A. K., & Whiren, A. P. (2007). *Developmentally appropriate curriculum: Best practices in early childhood education* (4th ed.). Upper Saddle River, NJ: Pearson.

Moravcik, E., & Feeney, S. (2009). Curriculum in early childhood education: Teaching the whole child. In S. Feeney, A. Galper, & C. Seefeldt, *Continuing issues in early childhood education* (3rd ed.). Upper Saddle River, NJ: Pearson.

National Association for the Education of Young Children. (2009). *NAEYC standards for early childhood professional preparation programs*. www.naeyc.org/files/naeyc/file/positions/ProfPrepStandards09.pdf

Petersen, E. A. (1996). *A practical guide to early childhood planning, methods, and materials*. Boston, MA: Allyn & Bacon.

Phillips D., Mekos, D., Scarr, S., McCartney, K., & Abbott–Shim, M. (2000, Winter). Within and beyond the classroom door: Assessing quality in child care centers. *Early Childhood Research Quarterly, 15*(4), 475–496.

Roopnarine, J. L., & Johnson, J. E. (Eds.). (2008). *Approaches to early childhood education* (5th ed.). Upper Saddle River, NJ: Pearson.

Schickedanz, J., Pergantis, M. L., Kanosky, J., Blaney, A., & Ottinger, J. (1997). *Curriculum in early childhood: A resource guide for preschool and kindergarten teachers*. Boston, MA: Allyn & Bacon.

School Readiness Task Force, Hawai'i Good Beginnings Interdepartmental Council. (2004). *Hawaii preschool content standards: curriculum guidelines for programs for four-year-olds*. Honolulu, HI: Author.

Schwartz, S. L., & Robison, H. F. (1982). *Designing curriculum for early childhood*. Boston, MA: Allyn & Bacon.

Seefeldt, C. (Ed.). (2005). *The early childhood curriculum: Current findings in theories and practice* (3rd ed.). New York, NY: Teachers College Press.

Spodek, B., & Klein, O. (2001). In O. N. Saracho (Ed.), *Yearbook in Early childhood education: Vol. 2. Issues in early childhood curriculum*. New York, NY: Teachers College Press.

Wiltz, N. W., & Klein, E. L. (2001). "What do you do in child care?" Children's perceptions of high and low quality classrooms. *Early Childhood Research Quarterly, 16*(2), 209–236.

Wortham, S. (2005). *Early childhood curriculum: Developmental bases for learning and teaching* (4th ed.). Upper Saddle River, NJ: Pearson.

MyEducationLab

Go to Topics 2: Child Development and Learning, 4: Play, 5: Assessment/Observation, 10: Planning, and 11: DAP/Teaching Strategies in the MyEducationLab (www.myeducationlab.com) for *Meaningful Curriculum for Young Children*, where you can:

- Find learning outcomes for Child Development and Learning, Play, Assessment/Observation, Planning, and DAP/Teaching Strategies along with the national standards that connect to these outcomes.
- Complete Assignments and Activities that can help you more deeply understand the chapter content.

- Apply and practice your understanding of the core teaching skills identified in the chapter with the Building Teaching Skills and Dispositions learning units.
- Listen to experts from the field in Professional Perspectives.
- Check your comprehension on the content covered in the chapter with the Study Plan. Here you will be able to take a chapter quiz, receive feedback on your answers, and then access Review, Practice, and Enrichment activities to enhance your understanding of chapter content.

Relate the school to life, and all studies are of necessity correlated.

JOHN DEWEY, 1900

chapter three

PLANNING INTEGRATED CURRICULUM

What Is Integrated Curriculum?

Integrated curriculum is a way of organizing curriculum around a topic of study. The topic serves as an umbrella under which different developmental and subject areas are included.

You have almost certainly experienced integrated curriculum formally and informally in your life. You experienced integrated curriculum if your third-grade class studied Mexico and you made tortillas (using math, science, and nutrition concepts), learned the Mexican hat dance (developing physical skill while learning about Mexican music), read stories about Mexico and Mexican folklore (developing reading skills, vocabulary, and understanding of literature), and made maps of Mexico. That was a social studies integrated study.

You have experienced an informal and personal integrated study if you have ever gone on a trip and experienced the climate and landscape of a new place (social studies), noted the different plants and animals that lived there (science), learned some phrases that local people used (language), bought a souvenir and calculated how much you had to spend on it (math), visited a museum or gallery (art), and attended a concert or listened to the local radio station (music).

In this chapter we will give you some background on integrated curriculum, describe some models of integrated curriculum that you might hear about, and help you learn how to design an integrated study.

Why Integrated Curriculum?

Most early childhood educators feel integrated curriculum is the optimal way to present learning experiences to young children in the preschool and primary school years. There are some compelling reasons for this.

Good integrated curriculum is relevant and experiential. It involves many subject areas in practical ways. It helps children understand and use knowledge. And it helps them learn to solve problems, think flexibly, and use ideas and skills creatively.

A good integrated study makes learning meaningful. It gives children in-depth experience with a topic that is interesting and can lead to a sense of the power of knowledge and even lifelong interest in a topic. For example, a parent of a 6-year-old reported her daughter coming home and proudly explaining that she had been able to identify an egret to her teacher, saying, "I knew it was an egret because we studied birds in preschool."

Integrated curriculum prepares children for the world of the future. We cannot know what the world 20 years from now will be like. How can you help children learn for a world that is always changing? Although we know that people will continue to need to know how to read, write, and calculate, we can't anticipate the precise knowledge and skills that will be required. However, we can be sure that it will be critical for children to be flexible, self-directed, creative thinkers who excel at problem solving. We know that it will be important for them to have coordinated hands, the capability to communicate well, and the ability to take in information. And we know that many skills related to technology will be different from those used today. How can we teach for the needed abilities and dispositions of the future? One way is through integrated curriculum because it lets children have choices, encourages them to utilize diverse sources of information, and teaches them to think flexibly.

Life is complex and integrated. People need knowledge and skills from all disciplines for each aspect of life—at home, at work, or in school. Whether you are a laborer, a teacher, or a scientist, your work will require you to read, write, count, calculate, communicate with others, use technology, and make wise and economically sound choices. You use these same skills in your home life. And to enrich your life and make it "worth living" so you are able to come to your work refreshed and whole, you need the pleasures of friendship, of the environment, and of music, dance, drama, and art. Your life, everyone's life, is integrated. Integrated curriculum helps children learn how to live an integrated life.

MyEducationLab

Visit the MyEducationLab for *Meaningful Curriculum for Young Children* to enhance your understanding of chapter concepts with a personalized Study Plan. You'll also have the opportunity to hone your teaching skills through video-based Assignments and Activities as well as Building Teaching Skills and Disposition lessons.

Models of Integrated Curriculum

Learning in an integrated way is very natural. We can imagine our Paleolithic ancestors teaching their children about the land, its plants and animals, and the physical skills needed for survival through song, dance, and story, as well as demonstration and practice—an integrated curriculum! However, the first American educator who recognized the importance of integrated curriculum was the educational philosopher John Dewey, who said, "Relate the school to life, and all studies are of necessity correlated" (1900, p. 91). Dewey believed that children learn best in a community in which they engage in activities that involve creative problem solving and responsibilities to others—where learning is not too different from life (Harms & DePencier, 1996). Dewey founded the University of Chicago Laboratory School in 1896 as a place to try out his educational ideas. In his school, work was a carefully designed extension of the familiar life of the home. Projects like crafts and cooking were used as ways to teach practical lessons of reading and arithmetic. In other words, learning was integrated. In Dewey's school a *project* referred to the educational version of the scientific method, the experience of attempting to solve a problem and learning from doing so. In contemporary early childhood education, a project has a slightly different meaning. It refers to an in-depth investigation of a topic undertaken by a class, a group of children, or an individual child.

A number of different approaches to integrated curriculum are used today. All are influenced by Dewey's work.

The Developmental Interaction Approach

One of the most influential models of integrated curriculum, and the one most closely tied to John Dewey, is known as the ***Developmental Interaction Approach*** (sometimes called the *Bank Street Approach*). In New York in 1916, three educators—Harriet Johnson, Caroline Pratt, and Lucy Sprague Mitchell, a friend of Dewey and a strong advocate of progressive education—created a school (now the Bank Street Children's School). Mitchell was deeply committed to young children's learning about their world through direct experiences in their communities. Integrated studies of the community still characterize both the developmental interaction approach at Bank Street Children's School and the curriculum for future educators at Bank Street College.

A developmental interaction classroom is viewed as a representation of society, with social studies and learning trips at the core of the curriculum. Children explore topics they can experience directly in their communities such as the bakery, grocery store, harbor, and public works. Other subject areas are integrated into the exploration of social studies topics. If, for example, the children in a developmental interaction classroom were studying bakeries, they would first take learning trips to different bakeries and then come back to the classroom to work in various ways to represent what they had observed and learned. Follow-up activities might involve reading books about bakeries, cooking, writing, drawing, dramatic play, block building, and would culminate in the creation of a bakery in the classroom or a bake sale. (A description of a bakery study is presented in depth in *Explorations for Young Children* [1992] by Ann Mitchell and Judy David.) A typical study in a developmental interaction classroom lasts for at least a month.

A developmental interaction classroom is set up with centers in which children can make choices about their own learning. Although there are class meetings and group activities facilitated by a teacher, there is also much independent, productive play. Play is an essential part of the developmental interaction approach, especially block building and dramatic play, which allow children to symbolically represent their growing knowledge of the world. These forms of play also provide teachers with insight into how children interpret their experiences.

Educators who advocate the developmental interaction approach stress the importance of the child functioning as a member of the group. Teachers provide children with the experience of living within a democratic community, and are

> **The Developmental Interaction Approach in a Nutshell**
> A study of a social studies topic is selected for a class by the teacher based on his or her knowledge of the children and the learning potential of the topic. The topic is investigated "in-depth," over several weeks through real experiences (learning trips, etc.) and follow-up opportunities to represent learning through play and planned activities (blocks, dramatic play, writing, art, etc.). The community of the classroom is emphasized. A culminating activity ends the study.

expected to be sensitive interpreters and facilitators who respond to the needs and interests of each child. Emphasis is not on understanding "what or how" to teach, but on why each decision is made (Cuffaro, 1995).

The Reggio Emilia Approach

The **Reggio Emilia** approach provides another model of integrated curriculum. This approach takes its name from the small northern Italian city of Reggio Emilia. After World War II, the parents and teachers in the city of Reggio Emilia developed an innovative educational system for young children informed, in part, by Dewey's theories and educational methods. By the 1980s, educators from all over the world were visiting Reggio Emilia to observe the schools and take the ideas from Reggio home.

The focus of the Reggio Emilia curriculum is in-depth project work that emerges from children's intellectual curiosity, social interactions, and interests. These projects may grow out of a *provocation* (a challenge to think and wonder) that the teachers present. For example, a well-known Reggio project arose after teachers "provoked" children's interests by surprising them with the appearance of a life-size giraffe puppet. Following this, children developed an interest in making a portrait of the lion statues in the town plaza. This led to a lengthy learning adventure. Videos about Reggio projects (this one is called *To Make a Portrait of a Lion*) are available from The Learning Materials Workshop in Burlington, Vermont (www .learningmaterialswork.com).

In Reggio programs, teachers view themselves as children's partners in learning; together, they "co-construct" understanding and enjoy discovering with children. Children are encouraged to represent their learning through many "natural languages," or modes of expression, often referred to as "The Hundred Languages of Children" (Edwards, Gandini, & Forman l998). These modes of expression include drawing, painting, working in clay, sculpting, constructing, conversing, and dramatic play. There is no predetermined length of time for a project.

Each Reggio Emilia school has an educational specialist (known as a *pedagogista*) and an art teacher (an *atelierista*). The atelierista works with small groups of children to support them in expressing their knowledge through symbolic representation. Teachers in Reggio programs regard themselves as researchers who conduct systematic study in the classroom by collecting and preparing *documentation* of the children's work for the purpose of better understanding

> **The Reggio Emilia Approach in a Nutshell**
> The teacher, with a group of children, selects an in-depth project that is highly motivating to the children. Many modes or "languages" are used for children to express their growing knowledge symbolically. Strong emphasis is placed on the arts and the learning environment. Teachers collect and prepare documentation of children's projects to share with families and the community.

children, curriculum planning, teacher development, and connecting with families and communities. Photographs of the children working and transcriptions of the children's questions and comments are mounted and displayed with their actual work so that children and parents can examine them.

The Project Approach

The **Project Approach** is an internationally practiced model of integrated curriculum that includes elements of both the Reggio Emilia and the Developmental Interaction Approach (described by Lilian Katz and Sylvia Chard in *Engaging Children's Minds*, 2000). In this approach, a project is defined as an in-depth *investigation* or *study* of a *real-world* topic that is worthwhile and meaningful. Projects typically do not constitute the whole educational program; instead, they are used as one part of the curriculum that may be carried out with an entire class or with small groups of children. In the Project Approach the topic is typically a focused exploration of one thing; for example, children might learn about and make a cardboard box version of a fire engine.

This approach includes a step-by-step process for planning and implementing projects. During *planning,* teachers select a project based on children's interests, the curriculum, and the availability of local resources. Teachers then brainstorm (and represent) their own experience, knowledge, and ideas about the topic in a graphic process called *webbing* (described on page 70).

During **phase 1, the project is begun.** Teachers find out about children's experiences and pre-existing knowledge through stories, discussions, journals, or other activities. Teachers help children develop questions to pursue. These questions will direct the project. A letter about the study is sent to parents, who are encouraged to speak with children and share relevant personal experiences.

During **phase 2, the project is developed.** Fieldwork (learning trips) and visits from experts are provided along with resources (objects, books, magazines, newspapers, music, Web sites) to help investigate the questions that were developed during phase 1. During this phase, children represent their learning in a variety of ways, including constructions, drawing, music, and dramatic play. The initial topic web is added to as a means of documenting the project.

> **The Project Approach in a Nutshell**
> The teacher, with a group of children, selects a learning project that is highly motivating to the particular group. Completing the project requires research to answer specific questions posed by the children or teacher and also entails the development of skills and learning in many developmental areas. The project has three distinct phases: (1) introduction/initial assessment of knowledge; (2) research and representation of learning; and (3) culmination and sharing. The project continues until the children reach a point of completion.

In **phase 3, the project is concluded.** There is no predetermined length of time for a project. When teachers feel the project has reached a natural point of conclusion, they arrange a *culminating event* in which children share what they've learned with others (parents, administrators, other classes, experts). With the teachers' help, children plan and prepare for the event and select appropriate materials and displays as a way of reviewing and evaluating the project.

Emergent Curriculum

A contemporary American version of integrated curriculum, called ***Emergent Curriculum,*** has been described by Elizabeth Jones and John Nimmo (1994) of Pacific Oaks College. In emergent curriculum, integrated studies are based primarily on the interests and passions of children. Interests of teachers and parents may also be included. Emergent curriculum starts with the teacher's observations of children's interests during play, routines, and planned experiences. The choice of topics is viewed as the teacher's responsibility.

Once teachers see an interest emerge, they brainstorm (web) ways to study the topic. In emergent curriculum, webbing is not considered planning. Instead, it is a creative process in which teachers think of many ways to allow children to play with and learn about the topic. A study is typically designed for a small group of children. Plans for activities are then made based on the children's interests, questions, and concerns. The curriculum is called *emergent* because it evolves and changes in ways that were not thought of during the initial webbing process. Since they do not know how the study will progress, flexibility and creativity among teachers is particularly important in emergent curriculum.

Emergent Curriculum Approach in a Nutshell

A curriculum for a child or group of children explores a particular child's or group's understandings and interests. It may be quite small (e.g., band-aids) and fleeting (a day, a week), but more typically lasts for several weeks, as long as the child or children remain interested. The teacher webs ideas for activities, and then designs learning experiences in different subject areas to expand on children's interests.

Unit/Thematic Curriculum

You are probably familiar with the most common version of integrated curriculum widely known as ***Units*** or ***Themes.*** Although you might have to search hard to find a program in your community that follows the Developmental Interaction, Reggio, Emergent Curriculum, or Project Approaches, you need look no further than your neighborhood school for a place where teachers are using a unit approach. Unit/thematic plans have been used for decades and were probably an early incarnation of Dewey's active learning approach to curriculum; for this reason, the approach is sometimes called *Traditional Early Childhood Curriculum* (which is quite different than the subject-based *traditional elementary school curriculum*).

The terms *themes* and *units* are imprecise. Although many teachers use them and many colleges teach about them, we have found no theorist or school associated with unit/thematic planning. And while there are no universally accepted guidelines for them, there are some accepted conventions. In a thematic or unit plan, a curriculum a topic (e.g., sea life) is selected by the teacher as an organizing motif to facilitate planning. Then activities in all or most curriculum areas, related in some way to the topic, are planned and implemented in the classroom. There are wide differences in the ways teachers use a unit/thematic approach. How the topic is chosen, how long the unit lasts, and the kinds of activities tend to follow one of two directions: deep or shallow units/themes.

Deep Units/Themes

We use the words *deep* and *shallow* to describe the different types of thematic curriculum to help explain the differences to our students. It is not universally used terminology. The unit/thematic approach can be *deep,* with attention being paid to providing meaningful and appropriate experiences for the children. Deep and thoughtful thematic curriculum has much in common with the four models we have described. Topics are based on the interests and passions of children and teachers. Thoughtful planning and research are done by teachers. And the foundation for learning is children's opportunity to have real experiences with the world. Because there is important learning and the topic is selected based on children's and teachers' interests, deep units tend to be lengthy (1–3 months), and to involve worthwhile inquiries.

A "Deep" Unit/Theme in a Nutshell

A study is selected for a class by the teacher based on knowledge of the children and the learning potential of the topic. The topic is investigated "in-depth" over 1–3 months through real experiences (learning trips, etc.) and follow-up opportunities to represent learning (blocks, dramatic play, writing, art, etc.). The process for creating the study is not established, but plans are created by the teacher.

Shallow Units/Themes

Unfortunately, units can be *shallow,* giving a surface appearance of integrating curriculum without actually doing so. We use the terms *theme-coating* and *pretend integration* to describe some of the misguided ways we have seen integrated curriculum used.

Shallow units are often dictated by the calendar or an administrator rather than based on the interests of children and teachers (e.g., Fire Prevention, Health and Safety, Shapes Around Me, Responsibility, My Manners). In a shallow unit, the topic may be trivial or "cute" but not worthy of serious exploration (e.g., Mickey Mouse's Birthday, Teddy Bears' Picnic); may not allow for direct experience that leads to real understanding (e.g., dinosaurs, space travel); or may not promote desirable values and worthwhile learning (e.g., pirates, which though real, are certainly not admirable). Sometimes the topic is not developmentally appropriate or meaningful to young children (e.g., St. Patrick's Day, President's Day). Or it may be an attempt to make skills-based curriculum more palatable to the children (e.g., counting dinosaurs or bugs). A whole school or grade level may be "doing" the same theme at the same time; in these situations, individual interests of the children and teachers are not considered at all.

Shallow units are often planned far in advance and repeated each year. The units are usually designed to last for only one or two weeks, so there is little meaningful learning or opportunity for children to explore the topic in depth. The activities that teachers plan in shallow units are often abstract (e.g., worksheets). Plans are often copied from books or the Internet. Shallow unit plans do not serve children, teachers, or our field well. They have brought integrated curriculum under fire for lacking intellectual integrity.

> **A "Shallow" Unit/Thematic Plan in a Nutshell**
> A topic is selected for a class by the teacher or program administrator based on the calendar, tradition, or whim. The topic is used as an organizing motif to facilitate planning over a 1–2 week period. Few (if any) real experiences are provided. The topic is used to provide focus for abstract and unconnected activities (e.g., worksheets, songs, games). Ideas for activities are often derived from books (Theme-a-day!) or the Internet (Patty's Preschool Page).

What's the Difference?

Although these approaches to integrated curriculum have different names and some differences in how they are planned, it is obvious that they have many things in common. Good integrated planning helps children learn about the world through meaningful exploration. Whether it is called a *project,* a *unit,* an *investigation,* or a *study,* all well-designed integrated studies begin with a topic that is of interest to children and teachers. Real experiences with the topic form the foundation of a good integrated curriculum. Teachers plan many ways for children to read about, reflect on, represent, and re-create what they have experienced. The activities are appropriate for both the individuals and the group. While children are engaged in meaningful learning about the topic, they are developing skills in sensing and moving, thinking and problem solving, communicating, creating, and working and playing with others.

The differences are in the history, the terminology, the planning process, the relative emphasis placed on the arts and play, and the extent to which direction comes from the children. Philosophically and practically, and most importantly from the perspective of the children and their families, in every case except the shallow unit plan, these differences are minor.

Designing an Integrated Study

Whatever model of integrated curriculum planning you use, there are some steps you will follow. A worthwhile integrated study is created in a dynamic process that involves observing children, doing initial planning, providing experiences, observing children's responses, and then planning additional opportunities for learning. When you are planning such a study it is important to stay open to possibilities that emerge from children's ideas and interests. A kindergarten teacher we know once planned an integrated study of gardening for her class. A swarm of bees settled in the children's play structure, causing much consternation. After thoughtful deliberation the teacher abandoned her gardening plan and embarked on a study of bees. The children's fear of the bees gave way to fascination as they learned about the social structure of the hive and the production of honey and watched a beekeeper relocate the hive to a site farther away from the classroom.

Plan an Integrated Study

Each of the approaches we have described involves planning. You can begin your planning with goals for children, with awareness of the learning potential of the community in which you live, with the interests of children, with a teacher's interest, or with a topic that you know from experience is of high interest to young children. The approach we present here is one we have used for many years that combines these elements. Planning this way has helped us to provide integrated curriculum that consistently engages children, families, and teachers.

Observe Children

Before you begin to plan it is important to know and observe children. Allow yourself time. It is not necessary to have a study underway at all times. Instead, spend time at the beginning of each school term intensively observing children and getting to know them and their families. Written observations give you data that can be used to inform your planning. Observe children every day and make notes on what you have observed.

Select a Topic

In order to begin integrated planning, you need a topic of study. Meaningful integrated curriculum is based on a well-chosen topic that helps children make connections. Children's lives and their environment—their families, cultures, community, or elements of the local environment—are good sources for the topic. Exploration of these kinds of topics can contribute to children's awareness and understanding of the world and themselves, as well as heightening their sense of uniqueness and pride in their families and community. While these larger goals are being realized, children are exploring, experimenting, discussing experiences, building with blocks, manipulating materials, writing, and cooking.

Is one topic any better or worse than any other topic for the purpose of integrating curriculum? We think so. The best topics for an integrated curriculum study engage children with the investigation of something that is real and important. When you have chosen well there is an almost magical quality to the curriculum. Children are focused, energized, and intensely engaged in the business of learning, and teachers are interested and fully engaged. In order for this to happen, the topic must meet several criteria.

First, it must be of *interest* to children, teachers, and families. For example, when the teacher as well as several mothers of children in a 4-year-old class became pregnant, a curriculum study of babies and birth was a natural focus. The teacher brought in many books, made a sequencing game of fetal development, helped the children compose a simple lullaby, had babies and puppies visit, and took the children on a trip to the local hospital to view the nursery. The children built the hospital in the block area, created a nursery in the dramatic play area, and painted and drew many pictures and wrote many stories about babies. All the children—not just the new big brothers and sisters—learned a great deal about how babies

develop and the ways that families care for infants. They were simultaneously developing fine motor and hand-eye coordination; understanding of letters and numbers; discrimination of size, shape, and color; and a myriad of other skills and understandings.

Next, a topic of study must be *accessible*. By this we mean that you can give children direct and frequent hands-on experience with the topic. If direct experience is not regularly available, the topic—no matter how interesting—will not help young children gain genuine understanding. Frequency must be judged from a child's perspective. Three or four times a week is frequent. Twice a month is not. This is especially important for younger children, but it is true for all young children because this is the way they learn.

We strongly believe that a topic must be *important,* that is, worth knowing about. A good integrated study requires time, effort, and intellectual engagement on the part of children and teachers. It needs to be based on experiences and ideas that are interesting and complex enough to engage both children and adults for a period from several weeks to several months. It's not worth the children's time or yours to study something that is trivial and not worthy of intellectual engagement.

Finally, you should consider whether the topic you choose is the *right size* for the children's age and stage of development: *simple* enough to be understood but *complex* and interesting enough to be explored in some depth. Sometimes teachers choose a topic that is so vague (e.g., change) or so complex (e.g., nature) that it is difficult to find a meaningful focus. A topic should involve concepts and skills that provide the right level of challenge. We call this the "three bears" principle (not too easy, not too hard, just "right").

Many topics can be used for successful integration of subject areas. We have seen teachers of preschoolers plan successful integrated studies of topics such as water, food, trees, animals, insects, family, self, celebration, rain, gardens, and

---

IN PRACTICE: Three Basic Criteria for Topic Selection

The topic is important (worth knowing about when you are 3, 4, or 5)

The topic is interesting and relevant to children *and* teachers

The topic is accessible (you can provide direct, real experience almost every day)

Questions to Ask Before You Decide on the Study Topic

- Is it consistent with the philosophy of the program and values of the families and community?
- Is it the right size? Substantial enough for an in-depth study but not so large and complex that it is impossible for young children to understand

(e.g., insects might be the right size—flies too small—nature too large)

- Can the central concepts in a study of this topic be taught through direct experiences?
- Is a study of this topic realistic in terms of the resources available?
- Can a study of this topic engage the participation, interests, and expertise of children's families?
- Will it help children to understand and appreciate themselves, others, and/or the world?
- Can it generate meaningful activities in all domains of development?

farms. We have seen teachers of older children use these same topics with more depth, and also more complex topics such as the ocean, harbors, grocery stores, hospitals, and bakeries. The In Practice box provides you with some criteria to help you to choose a topic of integrated study.

Write a Rationale for the Study

When you have selected a topic, think through the reasons for your choice. These reasons combine to make the *rationale* for the study. It is helpful to put this in writing. Having a brief written statement of rationale will help you in explaining your curriculum to others and in documenting your work. The rationale should discuss the children's interests, the nature of the group (you will make different choices for a group that is very active, very immature, or very focused), the resources available in the community and among the families of the children, and teacher expertise and interest related to the topic.

In this chapter we will use a study of gardens as an example of integrated curriculum. The teachers of the 3- and 4-year-olds at the Leeward Community College Children's Center, along with Eva and her college students, selected this topic because:

- they had observed children's interest in the plant life on the school playground and in the surrounding community.
- the community was home to several gardens—a native plants garden, an herb garden for a culinary program, a shade house for the propagation of native plants, a children's garden, and a community garden.
- the lilikoi vine that had been planted by the teachers had started to bear fruit and the children were delighting in picking and eating them.
- a back corner of the program yard was unsightly and difficult to supervise. A garden seemed to be a wonderful solution to making good use of the corner.
- the staff and adult students were interested in gardens. One of them actually lived in a community garden.
- one of the adult students had a family member who was able to donate and install the fencing needed to create the garden.

If You Can't Find a Topic

Sometimes teachers despair because a topic isn't immediately apparent or they can't find one that is of interest to *all* the children. If you find yourself in this position there are several options available to you.

1. **Select a topic that is of interest to a few children.** For example, a successful car project that we once used was intensely interesting to several children in the class and it presented intriguing potential to the teacher—soon the entire class was engaged. We have found if a few children are truly interested in a topic AND it excites the teacher, their enthusiasm and interest are contagious.

2. **Narrow a topic.** We recall an occasion when the children didn't seem especially interested in learning about anything in particular, but they did like to eat. Food seemed far too broad a topic. One of the teachers had recently learned to bake bread, and so we chose bread as a topic. It proved to be one of the most fruitful studies we ever undertook.

3. **Expand a topic.** On another occasion a small group of children persistently played ice-cream store during the month before and after the winter break. Although this was a definite passion, we felt that an ice-cream store lacked much depth for a long study. We expanded the topic to look at stores in general (starting of course with the ice-cream store). And as we visited one store after another, a passion for mint chocolate chip ice cream expanded to an understanding and enthusiasm for the stores in our community.

4. **Use the families as resources.** Children's families can be wonderful curriculum resources. They have skills, interests, and knowledge that can serve as a jumping off place for an integrated study. A study of the work of the families at home and in the larger world is almost always successful because important people—the children and their families—are the curriculum focus.

Prepare to Teach

Once you have a wonderful idea for a topic to study, it is tempting to immediately begin to plan what you will do. Creative, enthusiastic teachers are usually brimming with good ideas. You will create a better plan if you take some time to identify the goals of the study; do a little research on the topic and write down the big ideas children can learn; take time to find out what children already know and have experienced; and invite families to participate.

Identify Goals

Why have you selected a study? What is your purpose? An integrated study plan should have a statement of goals, broad statements of desired ends that are not accomplished in a single activity (in contrast to objectives, which are specific and immediate intended outcomes of activities). An integrated study plan should include general goals such as helping children to acquire knowledge, skills, and positive attitudes toward themselves, learning, and other people, as well as specific goals for the topic of study. Consider the following goals for a curriculum study of gardens.

To help children to:

- understand, appreciate, and become familiar with nature in gardens.
- develop a sense of connection to and responsibility for the natural world by caring for a garden.
- begin to learn about the special characteristics of a garden in Hawaii.
- become aware that gardens have significance in Hawaiian and other cultures.
- gain aesthetic awareness of plants and gardens.
- appreciate the work required to create a garden.
- and, as in every integrated study,
  - develop in all domains (physical, social, emotional, cognitive, and creative), and
  - increase knowledge and skills in all content areas (large and fine motor development, language, literacy, math, science, social studies, art, music, and creative movement).

Research the Topic

Once you have selected a topic, it is vital to take some time to learn about it. This is a critical part of the planning process, and one that is often overlooked. Teachers often assume that since they are older and more experienced than children, they do not need to learn anything about a topic in order to teach it. Background reading is often overlooked in the excitement of generating lots of activities. While you do not need to know everything about a topic in order to plan, it is necessary to learn something, particularly if the topic is outside your area of expertise. Children deserve to have accurate information given to them. Even if the topic is something "simple" such as studying "me," you will need to gather information on the children and their families. In our own work in researching topics for integrated curriculum we make use of the information readily available on the Internet, which provides instant access to basic facts and helps us to identify sources for finding out more. The public library and your school library are other important resources to use. Informational books for older children often provide just the right level of background information. Librarians are professionals trained to help you do research. Be sure to ask your librarian for help. Most will be delighted to participate in your study.

Write Big Ideas

Once you have read about the topic, you can identify the important understandings or "big ideas" that you think children can learn through the study. We have used this approach in our teaching for many years. While it takes some time to figure out the big ideas, they provide a clear focus for choosing what and how to teach and lead to deeper and more focused learning.

A list of big ideas will give you a guide for activity choices and will help you to determine if the activities you are designing will actually contribute to children's understanding. We often use a process with students and staff to identify the major understandings for an integrated study. After researching gardens on the Web and reading informational books about gardens (including *Planting a Small Garden* by Philip Clayton, *A Child's Garden* by Molly Dannenmaier, *Plants for Tropical Landscapes: A Gardener's Guide* by Fred Rauch and Paul Weissich, *Gardening with Children* by Monika Hanneman, and *Roots, Shoots, Buckets & Boots* by Sharon Lovejoy), the teachers and adult students at the LCC Children's Center jotted down on slips of paper all the words they could think of related to gardens. They then sorted the words into five piles and assigned a category to each pile. The papers were sorted several different ways and the content was considered. These were the results:

- A place to grow plants
- Different kinds of gardens for different purposes
- Different kinds of gardens in different places
- A home for animals
- Gardeners

The teachers then conferred about what they wanted children to know about each category and wrote a statement of major understandings ("big ideas").

Big Ideas for a curriculum study of gardens:

- A garden is a place that people create to grow plants.
- There are different kinds of gardens for different purposes—to grow food, to enjoy for its beauty, for helping people learn.

- There are different kinds of gardens in different places: hot and dry places, warm and wet places, cold places.
- A garden is a home for wild and tame creatures. Some of them help the plants to grow.
- People who create and care for gardens are called gardeners. They . . .
  - make sure the plants and animals in the garden have what they need—sun, water, nutrients, shade, soil, space, protection.
  - use special tools and materials to make and care for the garden.
  - make the garden beautiful with plants and decorative objects.
  - cultivate and harvest plants.

We write "big ideas" in simple language that a child might use or understand. The point of this activity is not to think of words that are *taught*—instead, they should help you enable children to *construct* these understandings for themselves.

Assess What Children Know and Generate Questions for Inquiry

What do the children understand, and what have they experienced? When you work with young children, it's easy to assume that you know the answers to these questions. But often such assumptions are incorrect. Some teachers begin a study by interviewing the children, asking them: "What do you know about this topic?" Articulate older 4- and 5-year-olds can answer this question and tell you some things. You may be surprised to find out that they know quite a lot. But 3-year-olds, younger 4-year-olds, and children who are less verbal are likely to answer such a question with a blank stare. You will learn more about what they know by observing their play, listening to their informal conversations, and being attentive to their responses to stories and songs.

Along with asking children about what they know, many teachers ask children what they would like to learn. This procedure is called K-W-L, which stands for "What do you KNOW? What do you WANT to know? What did you LEARN?" Again, this will be a more productive question with older preschoolers and kindergartners. Teachers of older children often use this process to guide the design of a study. While it is a good starting place for planning, it must be supplemented with observation of children, reflection, and research. Preschoolers are more able to identify what they know than to identify questions for investigation. Inquiry questions will emerge as they investigate a topic.

Survey Families

You will find out more about what children know and have experienced by asking the people who know them the best—their families. One of the first things you should do with any study is to let families know about it. At the same time you can invite them to share their child's prior experience with the topic and give them an opportunity to participate. An example of a family survey is found in Figure 3.1.

Brainstorm Activities—Webbing

The next step is to generate ideas for activities that will help children develop the major understandings you have identified. For many years we have used a system called *mind-mapping* (a technique popularized by Tony Buzan in the 1970s) to begin our planning. In a mind-map you place a topic in a circle in the center of a piece of chart paper and draw lines radiating outward to map ideas related to the topic. Educators often brainstorm using similar charts, which are referred to as *webs* or *curriculum maps*. The process of mind-mapping or webbing is useful because it

FIGURE 3.1 Family Garden Survey

We're studying gardens. We'd like to know about your child's experiences with gardens and we want to involve your family in our study. What can you do? Please complete the survey and return it with the ways you'd like to be involved checked off.

Name: _____

What kind of real-life experience does your child have with gardens? (For example, with home gardens, with family and friends, in your neighborhood, in the community, on a family vacation.) Please let us know about any experiences that were important to your child.

Does anyone in your family or among your friends have a garden of any kind? Please describe it.

Do you have gardening expertise? (check any that apply)

- ☐ Information—Do you know something about gardens? Are you a gardener? Could you come and tell the children what you know? If it's too technical for children, could you share it with the teachers?
- ☐ Skills—Do you have a garden-related skill like creating compost, planting, cooking vegetables, flower arranging, painting, or photographing gardens? Could you show us your skill or bring us pictures of you doing it?
- ☐ Use—Do you use garden products in an interesting way like making dried flower arrangements? Could you come and demonstrate this at school?
- ☐ School—there are lots of activities we're doing at school—creating a garden, reading stories, cooking, painting, singing. Would you like to share a garden-related story or song with us?
- ☐ Sharing—do you have garden artifacts or a garden story? Did you have a garden when you were a child? Do you have garden tools? Did you ever go to a special garden? Do you have garden-related ornaments in your house? Come show and tell us about them.
- ☐ Creating a garden—we'll be making a garden in our yard and we'll need lots of adult help to get it started—Please join us on March 7th.
- ☐ Trips—we'll be taking garden trips. Please sign up to join us.
- ☐ I have another idea! –I'd like to:

allows you to add ideas as they arise without being concerned about their order or initial organization. When the map is completed, you can examine each item to see how it fits into the whole plan. See Figure 3.2 for a Garden Activities web.

In our own planning we begin by brainstorming trips and resource visitors because these external resources may determine the direction of the plan and other activities that we will use. Ideas for additional activities are then webbed. We like to make a second web using some of the new vocabulary, especially "rare words" that will be introduced and used during the study. In Appendix A, you will find a blank "web" to use to brainstorm activity ideas for an integrated study.

The activities you initially web are just the beginning. As you explore the topic with children, you will plan additional activities and discard some you generated at the beginning because they seem less feasible or appropriate as you get involved in the study. Your initial web is the starting place.

Enrich the Environment

Following the initial planning process, you will begin to gather and create the resources you need to teach. At this time you will reassess the pictures, puppets, dramatic play and block props, games, puzzles, and toys that are available and select some that

Try It Out!

Create a web of activities for an integrated study of a topic you think young children might find interesting, such as Insects, Family, Pets, or Food. Try to think of ways children can have real experiences with the topic and activities through which they can express what they know through art, building with blocks, dramatic play, and creating books.

FIGURE 3.2 **Garden Activities Web**

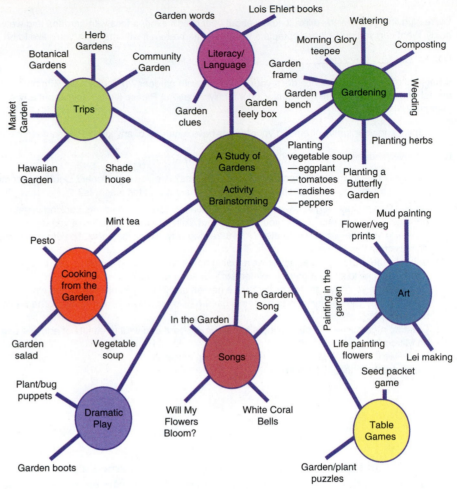

will help children make connections to the topic. You will make a trip to the library to gather good children's literature on the topic. Be sure to ask a librarian to help you to find good resources. Your local museum or art gallery may have prints, posters, or artifacts that can be borrowed to enrich the learning environment.

A good curriculum study is present in almost every classroom center. For example, in the garden curriculum the teachers at the LCC Children's Center added many items to the environment including terrariums, garden beds, a large garden, houseplants, garden puzzles and workjobs, cloth to use in the block area, art prints of plants and gardens, large plush flowers and insects to use in the dramatic play area, garden artifacts for examining, garden boots, informational and story books about gardens, and garden-related words in the writing center.

Sketch Out a Plan for Teaching

Once you have goals, major understandings, and a web of activity ideas you have generated, you are ready to organize them for teaching. Because creating an integrated study is a big job, it's a good idea to begin writing a simple guide for reference as you work. The outline for an integrated study in Figure 3.3 suggests some things to include. Remember that you will continue to observe children

FIGURE 3.3 Integrated Study Outline

1. **Topic:** the focus of the study

2. **Children:** age and characteristics of the children for whom you are planning

3. **Rationale:** why this topic was chosen for these children at this time

4. **Goals:** 3–6 broad statements of desired ends—the attitudes, skills, abilities, and experiences that children are intended to gain by participating in this study

5. **Major understandings:** 4–6 important ideas you intend children to construct by participating in this study, worded as children might understand them, not as objectives

6. **Resources:** books, articles, and other resources you will use to guide your development of the study

7. **Environment additions:** a list of materials to add to each learning center to support awareness of the theme and the development of the big ideas; be sure to include ideas for blocks, dramatic play, manipulative toys, puzzles and games, art, writing center, library, science area, and outdoors

8. **Trips:** a list of learning trips to give children real experience related to the theme

9. Ideas for **Activities:**

   A. *Introductory activities*: how you will introduce the study to children, including the activities that will build *awareness* of the topic

   B. *Activities to build understanding*: a list of activities to encourage exploration, support the development of the major understanding, and build skills

   C. *Culminating activities*: activities to help children *express* and *generalize* what they have learned, including how you will bring closure to the study

10. **Assessment:** activities and work that will demonstrate children's understanding of the big ideas, and ideas for documentation through observation, photography, or the collection of work samples

and plan for each week as you go along. The children's responses, teacher's new insights, families' input, and the serendipitous opportunities that you discover will be added to the integrated plan. You will not be finished with your integrated plan until close to the end of the study.

Implement the Study

Once the initial plans are in place and you have started to make your environment reflect the topic, you can begin implementing activities. The introductory activities should give children awareness of the topic through real experiences and books. They provide the input children need in order to construct understanding of the content.

In preschool we usually select a hands-on introduction to a topic. At the LCC Children's Center, teachers introduced the study of gardens by going to the place in the yard where the garden was to be created and asking the children what they thought would be needed to create the garden. They took a walk to look at the many gardens around the school. During the first weeks they enriched the environment with fine art prints that included plants and gardens, puzzles and workjobs (teacher-made games) featuring gardens, toys and puppets for the dramatic play and block areas, and many books about gardens. They constructed an aqueduct to carry water to the back corner of the yard and added watering the garden to the jobs that children did each day. During the third week they went on a trip to the local community garden that included a special children's garden.

After the initial input, activities to help children build and demonstrate their understanding are implemented. Blocks, art media, dramatic play, music, and book making are all excellent ways for children to construct their understanding and to demonstrate what they are learning. This is a good time for children to have input and discuss their ideas about the topic.

While you are implementing the middle section of the plan, it is important to remain open to changes in children's interests and to fortuitous events. For example, the interest that the children showed in the garden convinced the teachers to build a platform and trellis for morning glories and a garden bench (both with the children) so the children could sit and enjoy their garden.

The activities in a good integrated study can address every curriculum area and help you to teach every content standard. However, they are not the only things that happen in your classroom. Children will continue to read books, sing songs, create art, engage in physical activities, and learn about many things other than your topic of study. As you can see from the week's plan, not all the planned activities during the garden study were about gardens. Trying to fit every activity into a study topic is unnecessary. (See A Week's Plan in Figure 3.4).

Early in the study of gardens the teachers invited families to participate. Over the 3-month course of the study, families helped to create the garden, created a collection of garden boots and tools, donated materials for dramatic play, went on trips to many gardens, donated plants, cooked with the children, came in to read stories, and loaned artifacts from their cultures.

An integrated study has a life span of its own. You may find that children's interest in the topic deepens, as we saw in the study of gardens. The initial plan for 8 weeks of study extended to the end of the school year—3 months. Several families reported that they started gardens at home following the study. You may find that the study links to another topic, as we saw when a study of water led to a study of the ocean.

Eventually you will draw your study to a close. When you are ready to move on to a new topic it is important to plan closure for the children, families, and the teaching team. A class book or newsletter explaining what was learned, a documentation panel, a scrapbook or video that visibly shows the outcome of the study, or a social event during which children's work and learning are shared with others are good ways to both assess the study and bring it to an end. The study of gardens was brought to a close by inviting families to the school for a potluck dinner with individual garden tours (see Figure 3.5 for a guide made for the children's garden tour) conducted by the children. During the evening, children's work and documentation panels of the study were displayed, showing children engaged in the many activities.

Assess the Study

Like any other plan, an integrated study needs to be evaluated. You will assess the study in terms of children's learning, its effectiveness in bringing your classroom community together, and its success in engaging families.

FIGURE 3.4   A Week's Plan: Gardens—Week #7

Objectives: to help children understand that people who create and care for gardens are called gardeners and build appreciation for the beauty of plants and the work involved in creating a garden.

	Monday	Tuesday	Wednesday	Thursday	Friday
Story	*Bug Safari* (Barner)	*And the Good Brown Earth* (Henderson)	*Ten Red Apples* (Hutchins)	*Flora's Surprise* (Gliori)	*Butterfly House* (Bunting)
Outdoor Activities **Purpose:** *to help children to…*	**Caterpillar Crawl** Develop strength and coordination of the torso and the ability to work with others.	**Hoops and Balls** Develop object control skill.	**Hopscotch** Develop balance, coordination and hopping skill.	**Planting Flowers** Understand how flowers are planted in gardens. Gain appreciation for the beauty of plants.	**Butterfly Garden** Learn that plants and animals in a garden interact.
Small Group 1 **Purpose:** *to help children to…*	**Transplant Morning Glory Plants** Develop understanding of how gardeners plant and care for a garden.	**Parts of a Plant Exploration** Learn about the names and characteristics of plants.	**Writing a Garden Poem** Develop the ability to create and appreciate poetry and use poetic language.	**What's Missing in the Garden?** Develop memory and build vocabulary.	**Seed Sorting** Sort and classify seeds by common characteristics.
Small Group 2 **Purpose:** *to help children to…*	**Matching Garden Pictures** Build the ability to match identical images and acquire awareness of the ways in which print can be used.	**Fingerpainting** Develop awareness of art elements and techniques and build sensitivity to color, texture, and temperature.	**Dirt Inquiry** Investigate the properties of dirt and acquire inquiry skills (observation, questioning, hypothesizing).	**Clay** Develop fine motor skill and strength, sensory awareness, and the ability to create using diverse media.	**Clay** Develop fine motor skill and strength, sensory awareness, and the ability to create using diverse media.
Indoor Special Activities **Purpose:** *to help children to…*	**Leaf Printing** Learn about art elements and techniques (printing). Build awareness of the structure and beauty of plants.	**Pipe Cleaner Garden Sculpture** Create using 3-dimensional media. Reconstruct ideas relating to gardens.	**Tissue Paper Garden Collage** Create and express ideas using collage. Reconstruct ideas relating to gardens.	**Tissue Paper Garden Collage** Create and express ideas using collage. Reconstruct ideas relating to gardens.	**Garden Ink and Watercolor Wash** Create and express ideas using the medium of drawing and paint. Reconstruct ideas relating to gardens.
Circle Time **Purpose:** *to help children to develop…*	**"Flowers, Fruits and Vegetables Grow" Song/Game** The ability to sing tunefully and improvise words to songs. Awareness of the tasks of gardeners.	**"In the Garden" Song** The ability to sing tunefully. Awareness of the structure of gardens.	**"Went to the Ocean" Song** Awareness of music elements related to rhythm.	**Flowers in the Flower Garden** The ability to sing tunefully. Awareness of flowers people grow in gardens.	**Garden Fingerplays and Songs** The ability to sing tunefully. Awareness of gardens.

FIGURE 3.5 **Garden Guide for the Garden Tour**

1) long squash

2) morning glories

3) eggplant

4) cucumbers

5) basil

6) lavender

7) french marigolds

8) pineapple mint

(continued)

FIGURE 3.5 **Garden Guide for the Garden Tour** (continued)

9) manoa lettuce

10) tomatoes

11) wonder stone

Assess Children's Learning

As you implement a study you can assess children's learning. To evaluate whether children have acquired the major understandings you have targeted, you can observe their play as it pertains to the study or have children discuss the topic, dictate stories, or write in their journals. Children who make representational drawings may spontaneously, or upon request, draw pictures that demonstrate their understanding. For example, during the study of gardens the 3- to 5-year-old children were provided with many different kinds of art media. Their drawings, sculptures, and collages provided visible proof of the internalization of concepts relating to gardens (see Work Sample 3.1 *Sunflower with Seeds Underground*; Work Sample 3.2 *Map of the Garden*; Work Sample 3.3 *The Garden Sprouts, Stones, Eggplant, and the Garden Gate;* Work Sample 3.4 *A Snail in the Garden;* Work Sample 3.5 *Protea Still Life*). Photographs and videos of the children engaged in learning activities also make valuable documentation of the learning that is taking place.

Work Sample 3.1 **Sunflower with Seeds Underground**—by a 4-year-old
BIG IDEA: Gardeners make sure the plants and animals in the garden have what they need—sun, water, nutrients, shade, soil, space, protection.

Work Sample 3.2 **Map of the Garden**—by a 5-year-old
BIG IDEA: A garden is a place that people create to grow plants.

Work Sample 3.3 **The Garden Sprouts, Stones, Eggplant, and the Garden Gate**—by a 3-year-old
BIG IDEA: There are different kinds of gardens.

Work Sample 3.4 **A Snail in the Garden**—by a 3-year-old
BIG IDEA: A garden is a home for wild and tame creatures.

Work Sample 3.5 **Protea Still Life**—by a 4-year-old
BIG IDEA: There are different kinds of gardens for different purposes: to enjoy for their beauty.

Evaluate, Document, and Preserve the Study

How do you evaluate an integrated study? What constitutes success? Were your goals met? Photographs, work samples, and observations can show you what children learned. They can be put together into curriculum documentation panels. These serve as an evaluation of the study and document children's learning. In addition they make children's learning visible to families and community members.

When you are finished teaching, put the plans and materials you have created especially for this study in a resource box so you can easily store and retrieve them. Cardboard banker's boxes or lidded plastic storage boxes work well for this purpose. It may be some time before you use the resource box again, but when you do, the materials will be there. You will make changes based on new ideas, interests, materials, children, and families, but you will not have to start over again from scratch.

For our own documentation when we are teaching children we create a sunburst, a graphic expansion of the original mind-map to show everything that was planned during the study. Figure 3.6 shows the sunburst for the garden study.

FIGURE 3.6 **A Study of Gardens Sunburst**

Science
Hot and Dry Terrariums
Stroll Through the Garden
Garden Bug Hunt
Leaf/Flower ID Game
Examine and Identify
Leaves
Planting
Dirt Inquiry
Parts of a Plant
Exploration
Creating a Butterfly
Garden
Worm Composting

Social Studies
Planting
Garden Maps
Garden Prediction Chart
Harvesting
Placing Wonder Stone
and Garden Bench
Transplanting
Creating an Aqueduct
Block Garden
Building a Garden
Frame and Platform
Building a Worm Box
Building a
Garden Bench

Math
Flowers in the Garden
3-D Graph
Matching Garden
Pictures Workjob
Felt Garden Graph
Flower Matching Game

Music and Movement
Will My Flowers
Bloom?
In the Garden
Hokey Pokey in
the Garden
Foster Garden Magic
Rocks
Flowers, Fruits, and Vegetables
Grow
Flowers in the Flower Garden (chant)
Plants That in the
Garden Grow

Fine Motor and Sensory
Dirt in the Water Table
Planting Lettuce and Carrot Seedlings
Smelling and Planting Herbs
Washing Garden Tools
Seed Pouring
Seed Transfer Game

Large Motor
Garden Yoga
Caterpillar Crawl
Digging in the Garden
Watering Plants
Wheelbarrow
Watering Plants

Art and Aesthetics
Gardenscapes and
Creating Props for
Gardenscapes
Tissue Paper
Garden Collage
Tissue Paper
Terrarium
Leaf Printing
Nature Collage
Garden Bug Drawing
Nature Bracelets
Garden Collage
Leaf Rubbing
Ink and Watercolor Garden
Pictures
Soil Painting
Pipe Cleaner Garden Sculpture
Garden Still Life
Mud Fingerpainting
Rock and Sand Wheat Grass
Garden
Drawing in the Garden

Literacy and Literature
Plant Name Matching Workjob
In Our Garden ... Class Book
Terrarium Book
Creating a Garden Tour Guide
In Foster Gardens ... Class Book
Garden Bugs Class Book
"First The Seed, Then
The ..." Book
The Carrot Seed
The Very Enormous Carrot
Garden Poem
Oliver's Fruit Salad
Jack's Garden
Journal: How to Plant

Language
What Garden Objects Are
Missing?
Planting Salad Greens
Discussion
Garden Discussion
Tree Discussion
Garden Fingerplays
The Plants We Know Discussion
How Will We Water Our Garden?
Discussion
Garden Guessing Game
Garden Clues

Family Involvement
Garden Tour
Fencing the Garden
Field Trips to: Pearl
City Urban Garden,
Foster Botanical
Garden

Trips
Pearl City Urban Garden
Hawaiian Garden
Foster Botanical Garden
Tree Walk
Mountain Apple Picking Walk
Walk to the Greenhouse
Cafeteria Garden

Cooking
Lettuce and Tomato Salad
Pesto with French Bread
Tree Fruit Salad
Aunty Yumi's Eggplant Parmesan
Pineapple Mint-Infused Juice
Hawaiian Fruit Salad

Big Idea 1
A garden is a place that
people create to grow plants.

Big Idea 2
There are different
kinds of gardens for
different purposes: to
grow food, to enjoy
for their beauty, for
helping people learn.

Big Idea 3
There are different
kinds of gardens in
different places: hot
and dry places; warm
and wet places; cold
places.

Big Idea 4
A garden is a home for
wild and tame creatures.
Some of them help the
plants to grow.

Big Idea 5
People who create
and care for gardens
are called gardeners.
They …
make sure the plants and
animals in the garden
have what they need:
sun, water, nutrients,
shade, soil, space,
protection.
use special tools and
materials to make and
care for the garden.
make the garden beautiful
with plants and decorative
objects.
cultivate and harvest
plants.

**A Study of
Gardens**

Spring 2009

Final Thoughts

Life is an integrated process. Formally in our vocation and informally in our homes and in our avocations we learn, work, create, and interact around topics that have interest and meaning to us. Providing integrated curriculum to young children is a way to make this important way of living a way of learning.

Learning Outcomes

When you read this chapter, thoughtfully complete activities from the "To Learn More" section, and document this learning as suggested in the "For Your Portfolio" section, you will be making progress in the following *NAEYC Standards for Early Childhood Professional Preparation Program* (2009):

Standard 2. Building Family and Community Relationships

Students prepared in early childhood degree programs understand that successful early childhood education depends upon partnerships with children's families and communities. They know about, understand, and value the importance and complex characteristics of children's families and communities. They use this understanding to create respectful, reciprocal relationships that support and empower families and to involve all families in their children's development and learning.

The key element of standard 2 you will have learned about is . . .

2c: Involving families and communities in their children's development and learning.

Standard 3. Observing, Documenting, and Assessing to Support Young Children and Families

Students prepared in early childhood degree programs understand that child observation, documentation, and other forms of assessment are central to the practice of all early childhood professionals. They know about and understand the goals, benefits, and uses of assessment. They know about and use systematic observations, documentation, and other effective assessment strategies in a responsible way, in partnership with families and other professionals, to positively influence the development of every child.

The key element of standard 3 you will have learned about is . . .

3b: Knowing about and using observation, documentation, and other appropriate assessment tools and approaches

Standard 4. Using Developmentally Effective Approaches to Connect with Children and Families

Students prepared in early childhood degree programs understand that teaching and learning with young children is a complex enterprise, and its details vary depending on children's ages, characteristics, and the settings within which teaching and learning occur. They understand and use positive relationships and supportive interactions as the foundation for their work with young children and families. Students know, understand, and use a wide array of developmentally appropriate approaches, instructional strategies, and tools to connect with children and families and positively influence each child's development and learning.

The key elements of standard 4 you will have learned about are . . .

4b: Knowing and understanding effective strategies and tools for early education

4c: Using a broad repertoire of developmentally appropriate teaching/learning approaches

Standard 5. Using Content Knowledge to Build Meaningful Curriculum

Students prepared in early childhood degree programs use their knowledge of academic disciplines to design, implement, and evaluate experiences that promote positive development and learning for each and every young child. Students understand the importance of developmental domains and academic (or content) disciplines in an early childhood curriculum. They know the essential concepts, inquiry tools, and structure of content areas, including academic subjects, and can identify resources to deepen their understanding. Students use their own knowledge and other resources to design, implement, and evaluate meaningful, challenging curricula that promote comprehensive developmental and learning outcomes for every young child.

The key elements of standard 5 you will have learned about are . . .

5a: Understanding content knowledge and resources in academic disciplines

5b: Knowing and using the central concepts, inquiry tools, and structures of content areas or academic disciplines

5c: Using their own knowledge, appropriate early learning standards, and other resources to design, implement, and evaluate meaningful, challenging curricula for each child.

To Learn More

Visit a Classroom: Go to a school where teachers use an integrated curriculum approach. Observe a classroom and see how the topic of study has been added to the environment. Talk to the teacher about how he or she plans for integrated curriculum and brings the topic to life. Ask if a particular model of integrated curriculum is followed. If possible, talk to a child about his/her experience with the topic. If the teacher shares a plan, add it to your collection.

Investigate Web Sites Related to Integrated Curriculum Models: For example:

1. Developmental Interaction Approach
   - Bank Street: www.bankstreet.edu/sfc/curriculum.html, www.bankstreet.edu/sfc/developmental_interaction .html

2. Reggio Emilia Approach
   - The Reggio Emilia Approach to Education: www .reggioemiliaapproach.net/
   - North American Reggio Emilia Alliance: www .reggioalliance.org

3. Project Approach
   - The Project Approach: www.projectapproach.org/
   - Illinois Projects in Practice: illinoispip.org/

Observe a Group of Children: Observe a group of young children for a morning. Pay attention to the things that seem to interest them. Reflect on what you observed, and make a list of topics for integrated study that would be suitable and interesting for this group. Select one that is appropriate according to the list of criteria on page 66. Write a rationale statement for an integrated study of this topic for these children. If possible, share the list with the teacher and listen to her/his feedback on your ideas.

Research a Study: On your own or with one or two peers select an integrated study topic that meets the criteria on page 66. Go to the library or the Internet to get background information on the topic. Read the background information and identify 5–8 "big ideas" that would be important to teach through an integrated study of this topic. Rewrite the big ideas simply in words that a 3- to 5-year-old could understand.

Create a Web for a Study: On your own or with one or two peers brainstorm a web of activities for an integrated study topic that meets the criteria on page 66. Begin by identifying the trips and other real experiences with the topic that you would provide. Add in other activities. Use the form in Appendix A to record your ideas.

Read More: Select one or more of the books or articles listed in the bibliography for this chapter and read more about this topic.

For Your Portfolio

The activities listed in the *To Learn More* section will have helped you to reflect on what you have learned while reading this chapter. Include a copy of your activity web, big ideas, or rationale statement as evidence of your competence.

Write a formal essay describing what you read and what you learned to document your learning for your professional portfolio.

Bibliography

Association for Supervision and Curriculum Development. (2002). *Overview of curriculum integration.* Alexandria, VA: Author.

Berk, L. E., & Winsler, A. (1995). *Scaffolding children's learning.* Washington, DC: NAEYC.

Biber, B. (1984). A developmental-interaction approach: Bank Street College of Education. In M. C. Day & R. K. Parker (Eds.), *The preschool in action: Exploring early childhood programs* (2nd ed., pp. 421–460). Boston, MA: Allyn & Bacon.

Bloom, B. S., Mesia, B. B., & Krathwohl, D. (1964). *Taxonomy of educational objectives* (2 Vols: The affective domain and the cognitive domain). New York, NY: David McKay.

Bredekamp, S., & Copple, C. (2009). *Developmentally appropriate practice in early childhood programs* (Rev. ed.). Washington, DC: NAEYC.

Bredekamp, S., & Rosegrant, T. (Eds.). (1992). *Reaching potentials: Appropriate curriculum and assessment for young children* (Vol. 1). Washington, DC: NAEYC.

Bredekamp, S., & Rosegrant, T. (Eds.). (1995). *Reaching potentials: Transforming early childhood curriculum & assessment for young children* (Vol. 2). Washington, DC: NAEYC.

Buzan, T., & Buzan, B. (1996). The mind map book: How to use radiant thinking to maximize your brain's untapped potential. New York, NY: Plume Publishing.

Carter, M., & Curtis, D. (1996). *Reflecting children's lives, a handbook for planning child centered curriculum.* St. Paul, MN: Redleaf Press.

Carter, M., & Curtis, D. (1996). *Spreading the news: Sharing the stories of early childhood education.* St. Paul, MN: Redleaf Press.

Cuffaro, H. K. (1995). *Experimenting with the world.* New York, NY: Teachers College Press.

Dewey J. (1900). *The school and society.* Chicago, IL: University of Chicago Press.

Edwards, C., Gandini, L., & Forman, G. (1998). *The hundred languages of children* (2nd ed.). Norwood, NJ: Ablex.

Epstein, A. S. (2007). *The intentional teacher.* Washington, DC: NAEYC.

Feeney, S. (2006). Some thoughts about early childhood curriculum: Which way should we go from here? *Beyond the Journal: Young Children on the Web.* http://www.journal.naeyc.org/btj/200609/FeeneyBTJ

Feeney, S., & Moravcik, E. (1995). *Discovering me and my world.* Circle Pines, MN: American Guidance Service.

Feeney, S., Moravcik, E., & Nolte, S. (2013). *Who am I in the lives of children?* (9th ed.). Upper Saddle River, NJ: Pearson.

Goffin, S. G. (2001). *Curriculum models and early childhood education: Appraising the relationship* (2nd ed.). Upper Saddle River, NJ: Merrill/Prentice Hall.

Harlan, J. D., & Rivkin, M. S. (2007). *Science experiences for the early childhood years: An integrated affective approach* (9th ed.). Upper Saddle River, NJ: Merrill/Prentice Hall.

Harms, W., & DePencier, I. (1996). *Experiencing education: 100 years of learning at the University of Chicago Laboratory Schools.* Chicago, IL: The University of Chicago Laboratory Schools.

Helm, J. H., & Katz, L. (2001). *Young investigators: The project approach in the early years.* New York, NY: Teachers College Press.

Hendrick, J. (Ed.). (2004). *Next steps toward teaching the Reggio Way* (2nd ed.). Upper Saddle River, NJ: Merrill/Prentice Hall.

Hirsch, R. A. (2004). *Early childhood curriculum: Incorporating multiple intelligences, developmentally appropriate practice, and play.* Boston, MA: Allyn & Bacon.

Jones, E., & Nimmo, J. (1994). *Emergent curriculum.* Washington, DC: NAEYC.

Katz, L. G. (1993). *Dispositions as educational goals.* Urbana, IL: ERIC Clearinghouse on Elementary and Early Childhood Education. ERIC Identifier: ED363454.

Katz, L. G., & Chard, S. C. (2000). *Engaging children's minds: The project approach.* Norwood, NJ: Ablex.

Kostelnik, M. J., Soderman, A. K., & Whiren, A. P. (2007). *Developmentally appropriate curriculum: Best practices in early childhood education* (4th ed.). Upper Saddle River, NJ: Pearson.

Krogh, S. (1994). *The integrated early childhood curriculum.* New York, NY: McGraw-Hill.

Mitchell, A., & David, J. (Eds.). (1992). *Explorations with young children.* Mt. Rainier, MD: Gryphon House.

Moravcik, E., & Feeney, S. (2009). Curriculum in early childhood education: Teaching the whole child. In S. Feeney, A. Galper, & C. Seefeldt (Eds.), *Continuing issues in early childhood education* (3rd ed.). Upper Saddle River, NJ: Pearson.

National Association for the Education of Young Children. (2009). *NAEYC standards for early childhood professional preparation programs.* www.naeyc.org/files/naeyc/file/positions/ProfPrepStandards09.pdf

Petersen, E. A. (1996). *A practical guide to early childhood planning, methods, and materials.* Boston, MA: Allyn & Bacon.

Roopnarine, J. L., & Johnson, J. E. (Eds.). (2008). *Approaches to early childhood education* (5th ed.). Upper Saddle River, NJ: Pearson.

Schickedanz, J., Pergantis, M. L., Kanosky, J., Blaney, A., & Ottinger, J. (1997). *Curriculum in early childhood: A resource guide for preschool and kindergarten teachers.* Boston, MA: Allyn & Bacon.

Seefeldt, C. (Ed.). (2005). *The early childhood curriculum: Current findings in theories and practice* (3rd ed.). New York, NY: Teachers College Press.

Spodek, B., & Klein, O. (2001). In O. N. Saracho (Ed.), *Yearbook in early childhood education: Vol. 2. Issues in early childhood curriculum.* New York, NY: Teachers College Press.

Wortham, S. (2009). *Early childhood curriculum: Developmental bases for learning and teaching* (5th ed.). Upper Saddle River, NJ: Pearson.

MyEducationLab

Go to Topics 8: Program Models/Approaches, 10: Planning, and 11: DAP/Teaching Strategies in the MyEducationLab (www.myeducationlab.com) for *Meaningful Curriculum for Young Children,* where you can:

- Find learning outcomes for Program Models/Approaches, Planning, and DAP/Teaching Strategies along with the national standards that connect to these outcomes.
- Complete Assignments and Activities that can help you more deeply understand the chapter content.
- Apply and practice your understanding of the core teaching skills identified in the chapter with the Building Teaching Skills and Dispositions learning units.
- Listen to experts from the field in Professional Perspectives.
- Check your comprehension on the content covered in the chapter with the Study Plan. Here you will be able to take a chapter quiz, receive feedback on your answers, and then access Review, Practice, and Enrichment activities to enhance your understanding of chapter content.

Schickedanz, J., Pergantis, M. L., Kanosky, J., Blaney, A., & Ottinger, J. (1997). *Curriculum in early childhood: A resource guide for preschool and kindergarten teachers.* Boston, MA: Allyn & Bacon.

Seefeldt, C. (Ed.). (2005). *The early childhood curriculum: Current findings in theories and practice* (3rd ed.). New York, NY: Teachers College Press.

Spodek, B., & Klein, O. (2001). In O. N. Saracho (Ed.), *Yearbook in early childhood education: Vol. 2. Issues in early childhood curriculum.* New York, NY: Teachers College Press.

Wortham, S. (2009). *Early childhood curriculum: Developmental bases for learning and teaching* (5th ed.). Upper Saddle River, NJ: Pearson.

MyEducationLab

Go to Topics 8: Program Models/Approaches, 10: Planning, and 11: DAP/Teaching Strategies in the MyEducationLab (www.myeducationlab.com) for *Meaningful Curriculum for Young Children,* where you can:

- Find learning outcomes for Program Models/ Approaches, Planning, and DAP/Teaching Strategies along with the national standards that connect to these outcomes.
- Complete Assignments and Activities that can help you more deeply understand the chapter content.
- Apply and practice your understanding of the core teaching skills identified in the chapter with the Building Teaching Skills and Dispositions learning units.
- Listen to experts from the field in Professional Perspectives.
- Check your comprehension on the content covered in the chapter with the Study Plan. Here you will be able to take a chapter quiz, receive feedback on your answers, and then access Review, Practice, and Enrichment activities to enhance your understanding of chapter content.

PART 2
Physical Development Curriculum

And look at your body . . . what a wonder it is! Your legs, your arms, your cunning fingers, the way they move.

PABLO CASALS

The body is a young child's connection to the world. Unlike other animals, human beings are completely helpless at birth and spend years gaining full command of their bodies. In order to develop to their fullest potential, young children need opportunities to move, explore, and manipulate materials. As they gain physical skill, children become increasingly able to care for themselves and move beyond the limits that are imposed by their dependency on others. As they gain the ability to control, care for, and use their bodies, they become more confident and independent. The maintenance of physical well-being is essential to all aspects of development. Having a sensitive, strong, flexible, coordinated, healthy body allows a child to function competently in the world. It is essential for learning and development to occur.

Sensory and motor development are prerequisites to many areas of competence. In order to learn to read and write, children must first develop the ability to make fine visual and auditory discriminations. Writing requires fine motor skill that emerges from years of practice controlling the muscles of the fingers and hands. To appreciate the order and beauty of the world, children must have the ability to perceive it. To translate ideas and feelings into words or art, children must first have a foundation of many real experiences.

In these chapters, we discuss curriculum to support children's *large motor* (sometimes referred to as gross motor or large muscle), *fine motor* (sometimes referred to as small muscle), and *sensory* development.

Principles That Influence Physical Development Curriculum

There's a lot to know about physical development that is important in teaching young children. We're going to look at how child development can guide you in providing a program that is appropriate to the age and stage of the children you teach. While there is theory related to each area of physical development curriculum, there are five over-arching principles that are important in all of them.

Principle #1: Genetic and other inborn characteristics determine a major portion of a child's development. This means we can't rush children into achieving developmental milestones. We can't make children walk early by putting them in walkers, or skip before their nerves and muscles are developed and integrated. Many motor tasks are dependent on development that is timed by an internal clock; we can't make it go faster.

Principle #2: Children's development is influenced by environmental variables. In other words, normal development can be slowed down if children do not have adequate nutrition, rest, protection, health care, nurture, and experience. If we don't make sure that children have good care and lots of opportunities to experience the world and play, they will not live up to their physical potential. In early childhood programs, this influences how we work with **families,** the way we structure our **environment** and **schedule,** and the **activities** we plan.

Principle #3: Physical development follows a predictable sequence. In other words, although each child follows his or her own biological clock, there are some characteristics and events (milestones) that you can anticipate because of where the child is. The characteristics are:

The Cephalocaudal Principle: Development proceeds from the top downward. Head and trunk control precede leg control (not of too much relevance in the preschool years).

The Proximodistal Law: Development proceeds from near to far. Control of the large muscles at the center of the body (shoulders, arms, legs, trunk, neck) will be established before development of the small muscles at the extremities (hands, feet, and face).

Principle #4: Development is cumulative. In other words, prior levels of size, complexity, and control must be in place before new ones can occur. This means that we must build on what children can already do.

Principle #5: Rates of development vary. In other words, each child is unique and will not necessarily be at the same place as any other child of the same age. This means that our programs must be very flexible, with opportunities for a wide range of skill development.

The work of Arnold Gesell and his associates, begun in the 1930s, provides much of the information about physical development currently used by early childhood teachers. Gesell believed that inheritance and maturation determined a major portion of an individual's development, but that environmental factors could influence it positively or negatively. For normal growth and maturation to proceed, children must have adequate nutrition, affectionate human contact, and regular opportunities to exercise. Children need protection from disease, injury, and environmental hazards. Day-to-day care needs to be supplemented by periodic medical examinations to make sure that a child's growth patterns are normal and his or her health is good.

Because physical development follows a predictable sequence, you will be able to plan activities that help children move on to the appropriate next steps. The infant develops head control and reaching and grasping skills before sitting and walking. The large muscles closest to the center of the body grow and develop coordinated functions before the small muscles of the hands and fingers. Because mastery of the muscles of legs, arms, and torso must be accomplished first, good early childhood educators provide many opportunities for active movement. Growing mastery makes large muscle activity enjoyable to young children, and it is a feature of much of their play. They gradually go on to develop small muscle control. The arms, legs, and trunk must work in concert before a child can pump on a swing; and scissors cannot be used until coordination and strength of the hand is well developed.

You have a vital role to play in supporting physical development. Many of the skills that young children need to develop are available as part of the daily activities and routines of an early childhood program. Children need regular opportunities to use their senses and to exercise their large muscles. You need to plan for these things as thoughtfully as you plan any other aspect of the daily program for children, and you need to be attentive to the balance and scope of physical experiences.

Daily routines offer an avenue for physical development. Children involved in self-help activities are mastering essential physical skills. To realize this, you need only observe the delight on the face of a 2-year-old who has used the toilet unassisted for the first time; the struggle of a 3-year-old attempting to button a shirt; or a 4-year-old laboriously cutting the vegetables for a cooking project. You will see that these children are involved in challenging, serious work that will eventually result in gratification and mastery.

In supporting physical development, your first important role is to carefully observe your group of children, taking note of the range of physical skills, attitudes toward physical tasks, areas of strength, and areas in which more practice is needed. Your second important role is to plan a well-rounded program. This includes designing the learning environment to support sensory exploration and large and small muscle activity, providing interesting activities, and communicating with children to encourage their involvement. It is also important to be able to clearly articulate to families, administrators, and other staff members the rationale for the physical development components of your daily program.

Planning is also important. In the three chapters that follow, we will help you understand how to plan for large motor, fine motor, and sensory development curriculum.

A sound mind in a sound body is a short but full description of a happy state in this world.

JOHN LOCKE

chapter four

LARGE MOTOR CURRICULUM
Moving and Learning

Each day we move through our lives, using our legs and arms at home, at work, and at play. But our bodies are more than structures that house and care for our needs. They are the manifestations of who we are. In this chapter we will provide you with information that will help you understand and plan curriculum for young children's large motor development. The curriculum designed to help children gain and maintain physical skills and abilities is often called the *Large Motor* or *Movement* curriculum in preschool settings, and *Physical Education* in primary school settings. Part of your job as an early childhood teacher is to plan a well-rounded program that includes large motor development. To do so, you need to know about children's motor development in general, understand your group of children in particular, and be knowledgeable about teaching strategies to help children learn and grow in this area. It is also necessary to be able to clearly articulate to families, administrators, and other staff members the rationale for the large motor components of your daily program.

Why Large Motor Curriculum?

With few exceptions, preschoolers, kindergartners, and primary school children come to school able to move with skill. They have developed abilities and strengths through their interactions with their families and through play. Why then is the large motor curriculum important in early childhood programs? There are a number of reasons.

The most important reason is that **physical activity is essential for health.** In the past it was assumed that physical inactivity and its attendant health problems—obesity, diabetes, high blood pressure, cancer—were of concern only in adults. Today these are also problems in children, including children under the age of 6 (CDC, 2000; de Onis & Blössner, 2000; Dietz, 2001). Most children today live in social and physical environments that make it easy to be sedentary and inconvenient to be active. Most communities are centered around cars. Walking is discouraged, and it is difficult for children to play with others without a chauffeuring adult. Concerns about safety limit outside play, and even young children engage in sedentary activities like watching television and playing computer games instead.

Elementary schools have reduced the amount of time children spend at recess and in physical education classes. There is a shortage of close-to-home parks and recreation centers. Because of this, early childhood teachers in the twenty-first century have a heightened responsibility to ensure that young children have opportunities to be active in school.

Another reason is that **children's first teachers and schools establish feelings and expectations about exercise and physical activity.** Far more important than developing their large motor skill, you can help children develop a sense of enthusiasm and joy for vigorous physical activity.

Physical skill contributes to academic learning. It was once assumed that academic and physical skills had little to do with one another. Today we know that brain and body develop together. Large motor activities let children experience concepts that would otherwise be abstract (e.g., high, low, twist, turn) and present them with problems to be solved. The attention span and concentration that children bring to academic and creative endeavors is greatly enhanced as they use their bodies in challenging physical movement (Sothern et al., 1999).

Physical ability influences self-concept. A sense of physical competence contributes to self-esteem and self-confidence. Children feel capable if they can walk without getting tired, run quickly in play, or jump across a stream. Feeling capable helps them to feel good about themselves (Sanders, 2002). **Exercise promotes positive mental health.** Being physically active reduces stress, anxiety, and depression. By participating in regular physical activity, children gain a wide array of mental health benefits (Sanders, 2002).

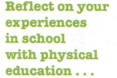

Reflect on your experiences in school with physical education . . .

How was physical education taught in the schools of your childhood? What do you remember most vividly? Did these experiences influence your activities as an adult? Is there anything that you learned that you use in your life today?

Understanding Large Motor Development

Babies are born unable to stand upright or move from place to place on their own. Developing strength and control over the muscles in legs, arms, and torso is one of their first and most pressing learning tasks. Over the course of only 36 months, newborns who are unable to lift their heads or roll over develop into toddlers who have the ability to walk, run, jump, climb stairs, and ride a trike. To become physically competent, children must develop the basic attributes that support development of the body: strength, balance, flexibility, coordination, and agility.

Strength is the physical energy available for movement or resistance. *Stamina* or endurance is the capacity for the sustained use of strength or physical energy. Older children generally are stronger and have greater and more predictable endurance. Strength and stamina increase as children exert energy and effort for prolonged periods of time in challenging activities like walking, running, group games, and riding trikes.

Balance is stimulated through activities such as climbing, running, jumping, and rolling. Such activities help children to develop the ability to identify their position in space and control their physical motions: This ability is called *kinesthetic awareness*. Swinging, turning somersaults, walking on a beam, and jumping on a trampoline are skills that are dependent on kinesthetic awareness and control.

Flexibility refers to the ease and range of movement. Physical suppleness lessens with age as the muscle system becomes less elastic. An infant easily brings toes to mouth, but this flexibility wanes as children get older. One of the goals of the physical development curriculum is to help children retain flexibility while they develop muscular strength.

Coordination involves being able to move different body parts in relation to one another. A child pumping a swing pulls arms and legs forward and backward in unison. A baby crawling or a young child climbing on a jungle gym moves arms and legs in opposition. Initially, young children learn to coordinate their actions by experimenting with, imitating, and exploring movement to gain control. Repetition then internalizes a new skill. Regular opportunities for children to move freely encourage experimentation and practice.

Agility refers to the ability to stop abruptly and change directions. It requires flexibility, strength, coordination, and a well-developed kinesthetic sense. As children gain speed, grace, and precision, they feel a sense of mastery. Much of the pleasure children find in large muscle play stems from enjoyment of their growing agility. Like other areas of physical development, the development of agility requires ample opportunities for children to use their bodies in ways that are challenging and that lead to success.

Milestones of Large Motor Development

In order to plan well for children's large motor development, you need to understand when and in what order large motor skills typically are learned. Then you can anticipate the sequence and general timing of large motor development in young children. However, individual timing varies. If children have not accomplished a skill at the typical age, it does not necessarily mean that they are experiencing a delay (just as accomplishing a skill sooner does not necessarily suggest that they are gifted). Table 4.1 provides you with a quick, though by no means complete, snapshot of the milestones of large motor development.

What Is Large Motor Curriculum in Early Childhood?

The City Children's Center is a small program for preschool children. The Green Room has twenty 4- and 5-year-olds: nine girls and eleven boys. The center has a large yard. There is a big grassy area for running, a trike path, a superstructure with three slides, trees for shade, and lots of equipment. In

TABLE 4.1 Milestones of Large Motor Development

Age	Developmental Milestones
3–4 years	**Locomotor Skills** Walks—forward and backward Runs (smoother and more controlled than a toddler) Vertical jumps (without crouch) Standing long jumps Hops one to three steps Gallops **Non-Locomotor Skills** Balances on one foot briefly **Object Control Skills** Throws overhand without a backswing Catches passively with arms fully extended Bounces a ball with little control Kicks without backswing Pedals and steers tricycles
4–5 years	**Locomotor Skills** Mature Walk—legs close together, toes point forward, arms swing in opposition to legs, steps even, heel strike followed by ball of foot Mature run-leg-arm coordination, true "flight," changes direction/stops quickly Gallops and slides Walks awkwardly on balance beam Climbs up and down stairs and climbing structure unassisted, alternating feet **Non-Locomotor Skills** Balances on one foot for several seconds **Object Control Skills** Throws ball overhand with torso rotation Catches balls with hands and fingers at face height Kicks with backswing Rides tricycle rapidly, steers smoothly
5–6 years	**Locomotor Skills** Walks backward with heel-toe pattern Walks securely, alternating feet on balance beam Vertical jumps Hops 10 times in succession Descends steps with alternating feet Runs, gallops with speed and fluidity Mature standing long jump Turns somersaults **Non-Locomotor Skills** Throws ball overhand with backswing and forward step on same side as throwing arm

TABLE 4.1   **Milestones of Large Motor Development (continued)**

Age	Developmental Milestones

6–8 years	Object Control Skills
	    Dribbles standing still
	    Rides bicycle with training wheels
	
	Locomotor Skills
	    Skips (coordination of a step forward with a hop)
	    Runs quickly
	    Mature overhand throw
	    • Long step forward with opposite leg
	    • Trunk rotation
	    • Backswing with a whipping action into the throw
	Object Control Skills
	    Jumps rope
	    Bats a ball
	    Dodges ball
	    Rides a small bicycle without training wheels
	    Mature catch
	    • Waits with arms at sides, elbows flexed
	    • Adjusts to incoming object
	    • Flexes elbows to absorb momentum
	    Dribbles while moving

their city the weather is warm and pleasant most of the year. Because of this, very little room has been provided for indoor active play.

The class is divided into two small groups who named themselves Dragons and Sharks. Niko (who is 5) and his sister Estella (who just turned 4) are in the Dragons group. Both children are active and tell their parents that at school, they like playing outside the best.

Along with his friends Tyler and Corey, Niko loves to build with the big hollow blocks outside. The boys create buildings and vehicles. Inside, he loves to build with the unit blocks. Most of the other children prefer to ride trikes, play with balls, run, and climb on the superstructure (the play structure with ladders, slides, and platforms).

Estella plays actively both outdoors and inside. She loves to hang upside down with Vivian and Keisha on the chain ladder of the superstructure. She rides trikes with Kaitlyn and Nadia. Indoors she likes to dress up and pretend with Madeline and Jessie.

Without your encouragement, planning, or teaching, most young children in your class will be physically active. What turns this normal activity into curriculum? In large part it is your understanding of the skills they are acquiring, your knowledge of how to support them, and your ability to clearly articulate what it is they are learning. Understanding the large motor skills that young children are learning will aid you in becoming a better teacher, enable you to explain the curriculum to others, and help you to enjoy and appreciate this aspect of the curriculum.

Large Motor Skills

Early childhood is the time when fundamental or basic movement skills are developing. These skills include common motor activities that have specific movement patterns such as walking or running. Movement that transports you from one place to another is called *locomotor*. Movement that involves bending, balancing, and twisting while you stay in one spot is called *non-locomotor*. Fundamental movement skills form the foundation for the more advanced and specific movement activities that children will learn as they get older, such as sports, active games, gymnastics, and dance. Another category of large motor skills developed during early childhood years is called *object control skills,* which involve the use of arms, hands, and feet to move objects like balls. Knowing about locomotor, non-locomotor, and object control skills will help you understand and plan for the children you teach.

Locomotor Skills

Walking, running, hopping, and jumping are called *fundamental locomotor skills.* They are the building blocks of more complex skills.

Walking

For transportation, health, learning, and recreation, walking is perhaps the most important form of physical activity for human beings. Walking helps children build bones and muscles, maintain healthy weight, reduce stress, increase flexibility and stamina, concentrate, have a positive self-image, sleep better, learn about the world, and develop healthy habits. Helping children to love walking gives them lifetime benefits.

Almost all children begin to walk around their first birthday. The achievement of walking is one of the most notable milestones of development. It is the first fundamental locomotor skill to appear. Although we celebrate a child's initial walk, we seldom give much consideration to how children walk and how that walk changes as children mature.

In order to walk, children must have sufficient leg strength to support their body weight. They must have stamina (energy and strength) to transport themselves over distance and flexibility to adapt to different surfaces. They must be able to stay balanced as they walk (requiring a brief moment on one foot). When children walk along a line or on a balance beam they are using *dynamic balance.*

Initially infants walk with small, quick, rigid steps. They place their feet wide apart for stability. Their walk is flat-footed, they point their toes outward, and they carry their arms high without swinging them (called a *high guard stance*). Gradually this gait changes to a more adult-style walk in which legs are closer together and, at each step, the heel strikes the ground followed by the ball of the foot. Arms swing in opposition to the movement of the legs. Steps are even and the stride is long.

Most children achieve a proficient walk by age 3. As children become skilled walkers they learn to vary their walk (e.g., stomping, marching, tip-toe walking, walking backwards, or sideways). Children's coordination in walking improves in obvious ways until age 5. After that changes are subtle.

Running

Running is locomotion characterized by a short phase during which the body is propelled forward into "flight" (both feet leaving the ground simultaneously).

Children cannot run until they have acquired enough leg strength to propel themselves through the air and handle the force of landing and enough coordination to control rapidly moving legs. Most children run for the first time 6 months to a year after they start to walk.

Like walking, an immature run is "flat footed" with toes pointed out. When first running, children use a wide base of support (legs far apart), and their arms are held high. There is no "flight" phase in children's early running. They stand nearly upright without leaning forward. An immature running stride is short and the knee opposite the leg that strides forward bends only slightly. The swing of the arms is rigid. Predictably, an immature run is slow—though it may not seem so if you are chasing a determined toddler.

As a child matures, the stride lengthens, feet are held closer together, toes point forward, and the child leans forward. True flight occurs—both feet leave the ground. A mature run typically occurs by age 4 in boys and by age 5 in girls.

Jumping

Jumping refers to diverse movements in which a person pushes his or her body into the air using leg force and then lands on one or both feet. Jumping is challenging for young children because it requires leg strength AND control both in the air and upon landing. Because of this, jumping is more difficult than walking or running. A jump includes four phases—preparatory, takeoff, flight, and landing.

An exaggerated step down from a higher level at about 18 months of age is sometimes considered the first jump (Payne & Isaacs, 2007). However, the first true jump, a *leap,* occurs at about age 2 when the child propels herself or himself forward and upward with one foot and lands on the other, similar to running. In addition to leaping, children develop skill in several types of jumps in early childhood.

The goal of a *vertical jump* is to achieve height and reach a target with the arms. In a skillful vertical jump, knees are bent in a crouch, arms are lowered, and elbows are slightly flexed. As the legs straighten, the arms swing up and the body stretches, extends, and is propelled into vertical flight. This involves a two-foot takeoff and the child lands on the balls of both feet with knees flexed to absorb the force of the impact. Most children do not achieve mastery of a vertical jump until age 5 (Gabbard, 2004).

The goal of a *standing long jump* is to achieve distance. It is more difficult for young children. A skillful standing long jump starts with a deep crouch and a forward lean. The arms are swung backward and then forward with force. Both feet simultaneously leave the ground. The body stretches during the flight portion of the jump and the child lands on both feet. Most children do not gain proficiency at a standing long jump until age 6 (Gabbard, 2004). During the preschool and kindergarten years children take off and land on only one foot. As a result the jump is more vertical than horizontal.

Hopping (a jump with a one-foot take-off and landing) is the most difficult basic jump. It requires more strength and better balance than other jumps, as well as greater control to create the rhythmic movement typical of sustained hopping.

It involves both arms and legs. Although adults rarely hop in everyday life, it is an important skill for later sports and dance activities.

Initially children hop in place, move their arms very little, and hold them at shoulder height. Immature hopping is jerky and there is little elevation. As balance, strength, and coordination improve, hopping becomes smoother and more rhythmical and arms are swung to assist projection.

Hopping requires the prerequisite static balance skill of standing on one foot. This does not usually appear until 2 1/2 years of age. By 3 1/2 years of age, most children can hop one to three times (Gabbard, 2004). By 5 years of age, the ability to hop 10 times in succession is typical. In general girls demonstrate hopping skills 6 months before boys (Payne & Isaacs, 1995).

Combined Locomotor Skills

Galloping, sliding, and skipping are skills that combine basic locomotor movements. They are normally not mastered until the end of the early childhood years. These combined locomotor skills are learned in early childhood and are later used in sports and dance.

Galloping is usually the first combined locomotor skill to emerge. A galloping pattern joins a walking step and a leap in an uneven rhythm. A gallop involves a slight forward lean with the leading leg and foot thrusting ahead and supporting body weight, after which the trailing foot quickly closes behind and takes the weight. The same leg is always in the lead and arms swing freely from the shoulder. A gallop typically emerges shortly after running (around age 2).

Similar to galloping, *sliding* is an asymmetric, rhythmically uneven movement with one leg leading and the other foot trailing. Sliding, however, is a sideways motion. It is more complicated than galloping because the child is not facing the direction of the intended movement. In sliding, the first step is a slow glide and the second is a quick closing step. Weight shifts from one foot to the other. *Skipping* is typically the last of the three combined locomotor skills to be mastered (between ages 6 and 7). A skipping pattern involves stepping forward on one foot, and quickly hopping on the same foot. This pattern is then repeated with the opposite foot. The alternating step-hop, step-hop pattern requires timing and balance as well as strength and coordination. Mature skipping is well coordinated and continuous. Because girls tend to hop earlier, it is not surprising that they usually skip before boys.

Climbing

Climbing is an outgrowth of creeping (the movement of a baby on hands and knees). It involves ascending and descending on equipment such as ladders, climbing frames, ropes, and stairs using the hands and feet. Initially a child steps up or down with the same foot at each step sometimes called *marking time*.

Proficiency in climbing is typically achieved by age 6 (Gabbard, 2004). Children regress to the immature pattern when a climbing challenge is difficult or frightening.

Non-Locomotor Skills

Movements that are performed in place while standing, kneeling, sitting, lying down, or moving from one of these positions to another are called *non-locomotor motions*. They are sometimes referred to as *axial* or *stability* movements. All non-locomotor motions require balance, coordination, and flexibility (a joint's range of motion). You will be better able to plan for non-locomotor skill development when you know what these skills involve.

Bending and Stretching

When you raise your arms to yawn or reach out to touch your toes, you are *stretching*. Stretching can be a form of exercise in which a specific muscle group is elongated to improve the muscle's elasticity and *tone* (the involuntary partial contraction of healthy muscles). *Bending* brings two adjacent parts of the body together. Joints in the legs, feet, arms, hands, and spine help you to bend. Bending and stretching go together—after you have bent, you stretch back again. For this reason, bending and stretching activities are often explored as contrasts. Healthy young children are generally flexible; they bend and stretch with ease.

Balancing and Transferring Weight

When your center of gravity is over a base of support, you are *balancing*. Balance that occurs in a stationary position (e.g., standing on one or two feet) is called *static balance*. Balance that occurs during a locomotor activity like walking or running is called *dynamic balance*. A wide base of support makes balancing easier than a narrow base—standing on two feet widely spaced is much easier than standing either on one foot or on both feet held together. Children under the age of 5 usually cannot balance on one foot. Static balance is related to visual perceptual ability: It is more easily accomplished when you gaze at a stable object. Balance abilities improve with age, particularly between ages 5 and 7 (Cratty, 1986).

Rocking, Swaying, and Swinging

In *rocking and swaying,* the body's weight is transferred from one body part to another (from foot to foot or leg to leg when standing, from one buttock to the other when seated). *Swaying* is a slow, relaxed, sustained motion. *Rocking* is more forceful and involves greater speed and tension. Control in rocking and swaying is developed as the two are contrasted with one another. *Swinging* involves moving head, torso, arms, legs, or the whole body in an arc around a stationary base like the neck, feet, or shoulders.

Turning, Twisting, and Dodging

Turning involves rotating to shift where weight is placed. Turns can be made with the whole body or with the head or torso in isolation. They are made in a clockwise (right) or counterclockwise (left) direction. *Twisting,* unlike turning, rotates only part of the body. Many body parts can twist—neck, trunk, arms, legs, wrists, ankles, shoulders, and hips.

Dodging engages the whole body to shift quickly to avoid an object or person. Dodging combines non-locomotor skills such as bending, stretching, twisting and turning. Like combined locomotor skills (skipping, galloping, etc.), dodging is more difficult than the individual skills and is achieved later in the early childhood years.

Object Control Skills

Once children develop upright locomotion skills, they can control objects in their environment. *Object control skills* is a term used to describe two sets of abilities. One set entails skills in which force is applied to an object in order to project it; for example, throwing and kicking. The other set concerns the action of bringing an airborne object under control, in other words, catching.

Rolling and Intercepting

Rolling involves pushing an object away from the body along the ground using the hands. *Intercepting* or *capturing* entails stopping a rolled object. Rolling and capturing are precursor skills for throwing and catching.

Rolling is used in a number of games, usually with the goal of knocking over targets (bowling) or pushing other objects out of a space (shuffleboard, curling). Young children first learn to handle balls by rolling them while seated, and they first learn to catch by capturing a rolled ball with legs spread wide apart. At first, capturing is accomplished by stopping a ball with the legs, but with practice, a child learns to capture a ball against the floor using only the hands and then to capture a ball while standing.

Throwing

Throwing is a complex skill with distinct developmental stages. There are several kinds of throwing patterns: underhand, overhand or overarm, one-arm, two-arm, and sidearm. During the infant-toddler stage, throwing and dropping are very similar—toddlers throw objects down. They progress to a two-hand underhand throw, then to a one-hand underhand throw, and finally to a one-handed overarm throw.

One-handed overarm throwing has been studied extensively. Four developmental stages in overarm throwing have been identified. In the first stage (2–3 years), the child faces the direction of the throw, weight does not shift, feet and body remain stationary, the elbow straightens, and the arm thrusts the object forward. In the second stage (3–5 years), the upper torso rotates away from the throw, the child takes a short forward step on the same side as the throwing arm, and the throw is dominated by arm and elbow movement. In stage 3 (5–6 years), the child takes a short forward step on the opposite side of the throwing arm, the arm is flexed in a backswing and follows the throw forward and downward, and the body leans into the throw. In the final stage (6 1/2 years and older), the child takes a long step with the opposite leg, the trunk rotates away from and then toward the throw, and the arm swings in a downward backswing then forward into the throw. Boys typically develop throwing skill at a significantly earlier age than girls (5 1/2 years for boys versus 8 1/2 for girls).

Catching

Catching—bringing an airborne object under control with the hands and arms—is a complex movement pattern. Although throwing and catching are clearly related in function, they are very different skills that develop at different stages. Catching requires the child to visually judge speed and direction, as well as time the movement of his or her body in anticipation of the position of the moving object. While children develop throwing ability during the preschool years, they typically develop mature ability to catch with two hands between 6 and 8 years of age (Gabbard, 2004).

Many variables affect children's ability to catch a ball. The size and weight of the ball, the color of the ball and the color of the background, the speed and angle at which the ball is thrown, and instruction all have been shown to influence this skill.

A toddler's first attempts to catch an aerial ball with two hands are passive. The catcher faces the thrower and holds arms outstretched with palms up to trap the ball against his/her body. The catcher watches the thrower rather than the ball and makes no attempt to move to receive the ball. The child reacts after the ball has arrived rather than before.

As a child gains greater skill, usually between 4 and 6 years of age, attempts are made to adjust hands and arms to the ball's flight. Palms face one another, elbows are bent, and hands are held at face height. When the ball is caught, it is hugged against the body. At this stage children are often fearful of being hit and turn away, lean back, or close their eyes.

At the most advanced level of two-handed catching, the waiting catcher stands with a relaxed posture, arms at sides and elbows flexed. As the object is thrown, feet, arms, and trunk move to adjust to the incoming object. The mature catcher "gives with the catch," flexing elbows to absorb the momentum (the force) of the object being caught. This advanced level is not reached until around 8 years of age (Payne & Isaacs, 1995).

Striking

Striking an object with a part of the body or an implement is another object control skill. Hands, feet, and head are all used for striking, as are implements (paddles, racquets, bats). Striking develops in a similar sequence to throwing. Initially the child uses an overhand chop and then progresses slowly to achieve a sidearm or underhand strike. As the child becomes more mature, there is increased use of a forward step and more range of motion during the swing.

Bouncing a ball in a downward direction and catching it again is a striking skill. *Dribbling* is the term used to describe the ability to bounce a ball three or four consecutive times. Children can develop the ability to bounce a ball using two hands as early as 2 years of age. At this stage they have little control. Dribbling with one hand while stationary is not usually accomplished until age 5 or 6. Dribbling while moving is a much more complex skill.

Kicking, striking an object with the foot, requires many of the balance skills needed for walking or running. The child must be able to balance momentarily on one foot and impart force to the object with the other foot. Initially, when a child kicks, there is little upper body movement and the arms are held out to the sides for balance. As kicking skill develops, the child acquires more backswing and follow through.

Footedness

Just as children begin to display hand preference in early childhood, they also develop a foot preference. The preferred foot is used to manipulate an object when kicking or stamping a target. The development of footedness follows a similar pattern to the development of hand preference. In early childhood, many children exhibit mixed foot dominance. By later childhood, approximately 80% of children show a right foot preference. In footedness, the dominant foot generally leads in mobility tasks (like kicking) while the non-dominant foot leads in stabilization tasks (Gabbard, 2004).

Standards for Large Motor Curriculum

What should you try to accomplish in the large motor curriculum? What goals should you have for young children? In addition to your knowledge of child development, content standards and

Reflect on your favorite large motor activity . . .

Think about your favorite large motor activity—walking, jogging, swimming, tennis, dancing, backpacking, and so on. What makes the activity enjoyable to you? How did you learn to do this activity? How did you feel while you were learning? How do you think you could best bring different kinds of large motor experiences to young children? What can you do to help them develop positive attitudes about physical activities?

guidelines developed by national organizations, states, and individual programs can help you to identify goals for the large motor curriculum. These, in turn, help you to select activities.

Head Start[1] (see Figure 4.1) and almost all states have standards for large motor curriculum. The National Association for Sport and Physical Education (NASPE) has developed Physical Education standards for children in K–12 programs (see Figure 4.2) and a position statement on Appropriate Practices in Movement Programs for Young Children Ages 3–5. These standards present the expectation that teachers provide opportunities for development and/or that children develop:

- overall physical ability (strength, stamina, and flexibility).
- locomotor skill (proficiency, control, and balance in walking, climbing, running, jumping, hopping, skipping, marching, and galloping).
- object control skills (coordinating throwing, catching, kicking, bouncing balls, and using the slide and swing).
- a disposition to participate actively in games, play, and other forms of exercise that enhance physical fitness.

Your program's goals may be based on state or national standards, or they may have been developed independently by your staff or a curriculum specialist. However, it is likely that they will include some version of these goals.

FIGURE 4.1   Head Start Child Outcomes for Gross Motor Skills

○ Shows increasing levels of proficiency, control, and balance in walking, climbing, running, jumping, hopping, skipping, marching, and galloping.

○ Demonstrates increasing abilities to coordinate movements in throwing, catching, kicking, bouncing balls, and using the slide and swing.

Source: Administration for Children and Families, Head Start Bureau, www.hsnrc.org/cdi/child-outcomes.cfm

FIGURE 4.2   National Association for Sport and Physical Education (NASPE) K–12 Standards

Standard 1: Demonstrates competency in motor skills and movement patterns needed to perform a variety of physical activities.

Standard 2: Demonstrates understanding of movement concepts, principles, strategies, and tactics as they apply to the learning and performance of physical activities.

Standard 3: Participates regularly in physical activity.

Standard 4: Achieves and maintains a health-enhancing level of physical fitness.

Standard 5: Exhibits responsible personal and social behavior that respects self and others in physical activity settings.

Standard 6: Values physical activity for health, enjoyment, challenge, self-expression, and/or social interaction.

Source: © 2004, National Association for Sport and Physical Education, www.naspeinfo.org. Used with permission.

---

[1] National organizations concerned with curriculum often fail to include standards or outcome statements specifically for children under five. For this reason we include the Head Start Child Outcome statements related to large motor curriculum as well as a summary that reflects most state early learning guidelines.

Teaching the Large Motor Curriculum

Large motor activities seem so natural for children that it is easy to consider planning unnecessary. However, early childhood teachers have a vital role to play in supporting children's large motor development. Young children develop large motor skills both in active play and through teacher-led activities so your tasks are to:

1. **organize the environment** to inspire diverse kinds of active play for all children.
2. **design a schedule** that allows children ample time for self-selected vigorous physical play and includes time for structured large motor activities.
3. **guide and encourage children** as they play and participate.
4. **plan and implement** structured large motor activities.

As you can see in Table 4.2, there are many modes of activity that are effective for developing large motor skills since it is important to provide both self-selected and structured teacher-directed activities.

Large Motor Learning Through Play in a Planned Environment

Learning to move means being able to run, jump, skip, and climb. Large motor curriculum requires lots of space. Such space is generally not available, or even desirable, in a classroom where large open spaces invite noise and running. Instead, the large motor curriculum must take place in an open space away from the classroom—and a well-equipped, well-designed play yard and/or large motor learning room is the most valuable teaching tool you have. You may not have an ideal environment, but you can maximize the environment that is available.

The Outdoor Environment

Every program for young children needs an outdoor area for active play—space for running, jumping, and exploring different ways to move. Just as the buildings that house programs vary, so do outdoor spaces. An ideal outdoor large motor learning environment for young children includes large flat areas for running and active play, a hill for climbing and rolling, paved paths for riding trikes and pulling wagons, dirt and sand for digging, and a safe, age-appropriate and challenging structure for climbing. Unfortunately, only a few programs have such an ideal outdoor learning environment.

Regardless of whether your outdoor space is an ideal playground designed by an expert, an old-fashioned schoolyard, a field, a rooftop, or a nearby city park, you will need to make sure that it supports safe, active play. Minimally it should be safe[2], include space for running and playing (most guidelines suggest 75 sq. ft. per child), have paved surfaces for bouncing balls and riding trikes, and contain appropriate materials and equipment that you can thoughtfully arrange to provide interesting challenges to children. In a worst case scenario where you have no play yard for running and climbing outdoors or the weather conditions make such play hazardous, you will need to find alternatives. Play in an indoor large motor classroom or trips to a public playground may have to be part of your scheduled day.

---

[2] The Consumer Product Safety Commission (CPSC) has an online handbook that describes critical safety features of playgrounds available at www.cpsc.gov/cpscpub/pubs/325.pdf

TABLE 4.2 Teaching Strategies for Large Motor Curriculum

	Use These Strategies to Help Children Develop:	Play in a Planned Environment — Child Directed (independent/with other children)	Scaffolded Interactions — Child Directed (teacher–child or child–child)	Small Group — Teacher Directed/Child Inspired (3–10 children)	Large Group — Teacher Directed (8+ children)
Locomotor Skills	Walking	Play in a well-equipped and well-designed environment	Obstacle Courses or Activity Stations designed to support the particular skill(s)	Walks in the Community	
	Running				
	Leaping			Guided Movement / Active Games	
	Vertical Jump			Guided Movement / Active Games / Activity Stations / Obstacle Courses / Circle Games and Folk Dance	Guided Movement / Active Games
	Standing Jump				
	Hopping				
	Galloping, Sliding, Skipping				Guided Movement / Active Games / Circle Games and Folk Dance
	Climbing				
Non-Locomotor Skills	Balancing and Transferring Weight		Obstacle Courses / Activity Stations / Listening to and Moving to Music	Guided Movement / Active Games / Obstacle Courses / Activity Stations / Circle Games and Folk Dance	
	Rocking, Swaying, Swinging				
	Bending and Stretching			Guided Movement / Active Games / Circle Games and Folk Dance / Simple Yoga	
	Twisting, Turning, and Dodging				
Object Control Skills	Rolling, Throwing, and Catching	Self-selected play with balls		Active Games	
	Bouncing and Dribbling				
	Striking	Self-selected play with bats and racquets			
	Kicking	Self-selected play with balls			
	Pulling, Pushing, and Pedaling	Self-selected play with wheeled vehicles (trikes, scooters, and wagons)			
	Lifting and Carrying	Self-selected play with hollow blocks	Woodworking and Gardening		

The Active Play Zone

The entire outdoor learning environment contributes to large motor development. Within it, the *active play zone* is the primary location for large motor curriculum. A well-designed active play zone includes big areas where children can safely run, engage in other locomotor activity, and play games, as well as hard surfaced areas for balls and wheeled vehicles. It includes equipment for climbing, balancing, riding, swinging, sliding, and crawling. While you have little control over the size, composition, and fixed equipment in the active play zone in your program, you can ensure that it is free of hazards each day by removing broken glass, protruding roots, damaged toys, cigarette butts, and similar dangers before children play.

You can also establish *visual boundaries* to keep children from walking through areas where others are playing games, climbing, walking balance beams, riding trikes, sliding, or swinging. Traffic cones, recycled gallon jugs filled with water or sand, used tires (usually available for free at a tire store), or potted plants can be used to set off these sections.

Equipment refers to large, expensive, and relatively permanent items such as sets of hollow blocks and climbing structures. Large motor equipment includes items that are permanently affixed like sandboxes, slides, and swings, and movable equipment such as trikes, wagons, and standing basketball hoops.

The most important and versatile piece of equipment for large motor development is a well-designed and constructed *"superstructure"* for climbing. Superstructures provide physical challenges and a place to see things from a different perspective. There are many kinds of superstructures. However, by definition, they always include a variety of ways to climb up and different ways to descend.

If your program does not have a superstructure, then recycled materials can be used to build some substitutes. Wooden shipping crates with securely attached boards or ladders can be used to fashion small climbing structures (be sure to use appropriate cushioning material underneath). It is critical to look at the CPSC guidelines in creating such a structure so that you know how to ensure children's safety.

Climbers (such as arch climbers), slides, swings, merry-go-rounds, see-saws, and spring rockers are other pieces of *fixed equipment* that you may have on your playground. Children enjoy all of these pieces, and each contributes to aspects of large motor development. In general, only a few children at a time can play on any one of these pieces of equipment, and all require maintenance and attentive supervision. If your play yard has any fixed equipment, be sure to check the CPSC guidelines to make sure it is safe. A simplified checklist from the CPSC is included in Figure 4.3.

Every active play zone also requires movable equipment, called *loose parts* by playground experts. Loose parts make a playground dynamic and responsive. With larger and heavier loose parts (e.g., balance beams, tunnels, tumbling mats, parachutes, free-standing basketball hoops, sand and water tables, rocking boats), the teacher arranges portable equipment to create appropriate challenges such as obstacle courses and movement stations.

You can create loose parts out of recycled materials. Logs, boards, boulders, stumps, truck tires, crates, large sturdy boxes, thick ropes, cargo nets, and cable

FIGURE 4.3 Public Playground Safety Checklist CPSC Document #327

○ Make sure surfaces around playground equipment have at least 12 inches of wood chips, mulch, sand, or pea gravel, or are mats made of safety-tested rubber or rubber-like materials.

○ Check that protective surfacing extends at least 6 feet in all directions from play equipment. For swings, be sure surfacing extends, in back and front, twice the height of the suspending bar.

○ Make sure play structures more than 30 inches high are spaced at least 9 feet apart.

○ Check for dangerous hardware, like open "S" hooks or protruding bolt ends.

○ Make sure spaces that could trap children, such as openings in guardrails or between ladder rungs, measure less than 3.5 inches or more than 9 inches.

○ Check for sharp points or edges in equipment.

○ Look out for tripping hazards, like exposed concrete footings, tree stumps, and rocks.

○ Make sure elevated surfaces, like platforms and ramps, have guardrails to prevent falls.

○ Check playgrounds regularly to see that equipment and surfacing are in good condition.

○ Carefully supervise children on playgrounds to make sure they're safe.

Source: U.S. Consumer Product Safety Commission (2008).

spools are among the many items that we have seen teachers use effectively. Be sure to evaluate for safety before using.

Smaller, lighter materials are also essential. They include things to ride and pull like trikes, scooters, and wagons; different kinds of balls to throw, catch, bat, and kick; things to strike with like bats; and materials to build with such as hollow blocks. These materials will be used in teacher-guided activities and also for self-selected play when children create their own challenges.

Indoor Physical Activity Areas

If outdoor space is limited or if the climate dictates that children spend long periods of time indoors, you still need to find ways to provide children with large motor activity on a daily basis. There are several ways to create indoor large motor activity areas.

Ideally, programs have a *Dedicated Large Motor Room,* a space near the classrooms that is available all day. A large motor room needs to be spacious and free of obstacles, and furnished with equipment and materials. In less ideal circumstances a *Temporary Large Motor Activity Space* (a room, hallway, or cafeteria) should be available for an hour or two during the day, with equipment and materials stored nearby.

There are different ways to use an indoor large motor area. At times you will set up *activity stations* around the perimeter of the room. At other times you might set up the space with an activity for all the children to develop a specific skill at the same time (for example, jumping in and out of hoops or throwing bean bags into boxes). The space can also be used for a directed movement activity.

Another alternative is a *classroom movement center.* Because it requires a lot of space and presents safety, noise, and supervision challenges, a classroom movement center is not ideal.

Large Motor Curriculum Throughout the Learning Environment

The outdoor active play zone and an indoor physical activity room are the dedicated spaces for large motor development. However, play in the sensory, hollow block, and woodworking areas also provide opportunities for large motor development. Table 4.3 gives a quick overview of things you should think about as you design an environment for large motor curriculum.

A Schedule for Large Motor Curriculum

To develop strong, flexible, healthy, competent bodies, children need blocks of time for unstructured large motor play several times a day. While there is no universal standard for how often and how long children should have for large motor play, the National Association for Sport and Physical Education (NASPE) recommends that preschoolers engage in unstructured physical activity whenever possible, and advises that they should not be sedentary for more than one hour at a time (NASPE, 2004). The Council on Physical Education for Children (COPEC) recommends 30 to 60 minutes daily. We believe that preschool children should have significant blocks of time (45 minutes to an hour) daily for vigorous physical activity, in both the morning and the afternoon.

In addition to providing time for unstructured large motor play, all programs for young children should include guided large motor activity. The NASPE recommends daily structured physical activity for preschool children and suggests structured physical education totaling 150 minutes per week for elementary schoolchildren.

Your Role in Teaching Large Motor Curriculum

From your own observations, you know that almost all young children enjoy physically active play. But you may have also noticed that a few avoid active play and physical challenges. In any class of young children you will have both. Your job is to support large motor learning for them all. You can do this by providing opportunities for active play as well as structured large motor activities. In addition, there are three important ways that you can support children's large motor learning.

TABLE 4.3 **Environment Areas That Support Large Motor Curriculum**

Center/Area/Zone	How It Supports Development	What to Provide	Important Requirements
Sensory Area/Natural Elements Zone	Suits a wide range of developmental stages and abilities. Provides opportunities for developing coordination and strength of the arms and shoulders.	• Sensory (sand/water) table • Sandbox • Tools and materials to scoop and pour—water, sand, etc.	To enhance large motor development, be sure to include large tools (e.g., rakes, shovels, brooms) and buckets for transporting sand and water.
Hollow Block Area	Both building and dramatic play with hollow blocks support development of coordination, control, and arms, torso, and leg strength. Cleanup builds motor strength.	• A set of hollow blocks • Space for play • Shelves marked for storage	Wooden hollow blocks are heavy and make greater large motor demands; light plastic, softwood blocks are not nearly as effective in building muscle strength.
Woodworking Area	Woodworking tools and projects require and build large motor strength and coordination.	• Woodworking bench and tools	Teacher must supervise well and engage children in woodworking projects.

Modeling Attitude

Demonstrating a *positive attitude* toward physical activity and participating in it yourself is one of the most important parts of teaching the large motor curriculum. In *Developmentally Appropriate Practice* (2009), Copple and Bredekamp describe this aspect of effective gross motor development curriculum: "Adults teach children the pleasure and importance of physical activity . . .". You don't teach pleasure by talking, but you can demonstrate it and you can share it. When you arrive at school in your walking shoes or on your bike, when you climb to the top of the superstructure and slide down during outdoor playtime, when you dance with the children instead of watching them when you play a CD, you are providing a model of an active adult. If you perceive physical activity as hard, unpleasant, or boring, you are likely to transmit your attitudes to children. By demonstrating appreciation and joy in physical activity, you will help the young children you teach to also feel this way.

Try It Out!

Find a large motor activity that you enjoyed in the past or that you have thought about trying. On your own or with a friend, try it out. Do it regularly for a few weeks. Notice how adding a large motor activity to your life influences how you feel.

Participating

Children need someone to toss a ball or to play follow the leader with them, to hold hands and sing Ring-Around-the Rosie, to be the first to walk the balance beam, or to be a strong link in a game of Red-Rover. As you participate in children's activities, you *model skills*, a teaching strategy that is far more powerful than verbal instruction. Most of all, by *playing with children,* you provide a powerful demonstration that being active is natural and pleasurable.

Encouraging All Children

It seems obvious that *all* children deserve encouragement as well as the opportunity to participate in large motor activity. However, it is not uncommon for adults to encourage some children more than others. Boys may be supported more than girls. Physically skilled children may be noticed and praised more than those who are awkward. Eager children may be applauded more than those who are reluctant. And if a child is ignored, discouraged, or criticized, it is unlikely that he or she will acquire a positive attitude toward physical activity.

How do you encourage children's engagement in physical activities? Real encouragement relates to the individual's accomplishment. It does not compare children or imply everyone should be able to do the same thing. Saying "Sam, that's the highest I've ever seen you climb. You're becoming a very strong person" rather than "Look how high Sam can climb" avoids comparison and competition between children. It does not suggest that others should attempt to please you, nor does it make them give up because they cannot achieve the standard you have set.

Children can also be discouraged from physical activity if you are overly concerned about safety. Keeping children safe is critical, but if children are willing to attempt a challenge in a safe environment, they can usually manage it. Occasionally a challenge will be beyond a child's capabilities, and you will need to provide assistance. If a child climbs onto something and is not able to reverse the process, you can give instructions and encouragement, as in "Put your foot on the bar and move your hand down a little bit—now you can step safely" or you can lift the child back to the ground without admonishing the failed attempt.

FIGURE 4.4 Examples of Effective Activities That Support Young Children's Development of Large Motor Skills

Play in a Planned Environment **Child Directed** (independent/with peers) *Usually spontaneous*	One-to-One/Scaffolded **Child Directed** (teacher–child) *Usually spontaneous*	**Small Group** **Teacher Directed/** **Child Inspired** (3–10 children) *Usually planned*	**Large Group** **Teacher Directed** (8+ children) *Usually planned*
Self-selected large motor play *running, walking, jumping, hopping, galloping, skipping, balancing, turning, twisting, rolling, throwing, bouncing, kicking, striking, climbing, swinging, sliding, riding, pulling wheeled vehicles (trikes, etc.)* Set up environment with open space, provide interesting equipment, check for safety, allow ample time for activity several times a day. Observe, modify the environment, narrate children's activity, suggest challenges, guide learning.			
Hollow block play Set up the hollow block area with sheltered space, large hollow wooden blocks and planks, shelves for storage, props (like hats and cloth); allow as a choice with other self-selected large motor play. Observe, modify the center, narrate children's activity, suggest challenges, guide learning.			
	Movement stations Set up 1 station for each 3 children with equipment for a different activity/skill at each. Emphasize similar skills or practice diverse skills. Observe, modify the stations, narrate children's achievements, suggest challenges, guide learning.		
Obstacle courses Set up a sequence of challenges with uncluttered large spaces so children can move through the obstacle course without being rushed. Start simply and add greater complexity. Observe, modify, narrate children's achievements, suggest challenges, guide learning. Encourage children to think of new ideas for creating challenges.			
		Guided movement Plan activities in which all the children in a group participate individually at the same time. Give movement instructions. Observe, acknowledge, encourage, assist, and challenge. Start with a simple short activity. Gradually add more complexity and time.	
		Educational gymnastics Plan activities in which children try simple yoga and exercises like walking a beam, rolling, or standing on one foot.	
		Active games Teach simple games that actively involve all the children most of the time, focus on playing rather than winning, and do not eliminate children.	
		Walks Walk regularly as an activity and as transportation to the park, store, or neighborhood.	
	Gardening With individuals or a small group, plant, water, and weed the garden. Add large motor challenges by inviting children to carry buckets, dig soil, rake, and hoe.		
	Woodworking With individuals or a small group, practice using tools. Select a simple project to work on together. Encourage children to plan their own projects. Plan larger projects to build large motor skill.		

And children need to be sufficiently self directed to work without a great deal of supervision.

Stations can be set up in a sequence as in an *obstacle course.* In order for obstacle courses to work well for young children, it is important to have a relaxed attitude. Children need to be able to work at their own pace without being rushed. As you plan an obstacle course, be sure to carefully think about the challenges each part represents to make sure it helps children achieve new skills. Obstacle courses work in the outdoor environment (in the active play zone) and indoors if you have space that is uncluttered and relatively large. Start simply. Once children understand how an obstacle course works, they will be ready for greater complexity and can even help think of new ideas for creating obstacle course challenges.

Guided Movement

Another way to structure large motor activities is to design activities in which all the children in a group participate individually but at the same time. Sessions can involve movement instructions ("Show me a way to move across the carpet using your feet and hands") or equipment ("Go in and out of a hoop; then move around the hoop in as many different ways as you can think of").

While the children follow the instructions, you can observe and move from child to child, offering acknowledgement, encouragement, assistance, and new challenges (e.g., "Can you think of a way to do it with three body parts touching the ground?"). This strategy is related to guided movement.

Movement sessions work well when the group is relatively small, the environment uncluttered and relatively large, and there is enough equipment for all the children to participate at the same time. These sessions require that children have the ability to follow directions and to work somewhat independently. Such skills develop with experience and time. The first time you bring children together to work on their own, plan a very simple activity that lasts only a few minutes. Gradually add more complexity and time.

Educational gymnastics (also called *non-traditional, developmental* or *creative gymnastics*) refers to simple balance and weight transfer activities. These are often incorporated in guided movement sessions. Unlike traditional gymnastics for older children it does not involve "stunts" or rating. Child-oriented yoga such as the cobra pose or the cat stretch and exercises such as rolling are considered educational gymnastics.

IN PRACTICE: Ideas for Movement Stations

For developing skill in . . .	provide . . .
• walking and changing direction	• a course of traffic cones
• jumping	• a set of spots or hoops in a path
• climbing skill	• a portable climber and slide on a thick tumbling mat
• dynamic balance	• a balance beam
• throwing skill	• bean bags and a target
• kicking skill	• balls and a goal
• striking skill	• racquets and soft balls

Active Games

Games may be one of the first things you think of when you remember physical education. Active games can give children ways to use many fundamental motor skills. However, care needs to be taken in selecting and teaching games to young children. Some games do not actively involve all the children or they eliminate children with limited skills (the ones who most need to play!). They often have complex rules that young children are unable to remember and follow. Games are appropriate when they involve most of the children most of the time, and if they build all children's skills and are enjoyed by them. Games are not appropriate for young children when only one or two children are active during the game (as in traditional Duck Duck Goose), when children are eliminated from play (like Musical Chairs or Dodge Ball), when there is a focus on winners and losers, or when rules or structure are the primary focus (e.g., baseball).

Cooperative games are alternatives to traditional games that are more appropriate for young children. These give children opportunities to experience playing games in which everyone participates without competition and with minimal rules. Cooperative games promote the idea that when everyone works together, everyone wins. (See the In Practice box.)

IN PRACTICE: Cooperative Games

Group Games

Animal Families: It's feeding time on the farm and the animals need to find their families for supper. Whisper the name of an animal (duck, cow, sheep, pig) in each child's ear. When you say, "Animals, find your families," children make their animal's sounds and try to find the other members of their families by the sounds. When families are found, do it again or go on to a new activity. Have older children close their eyes or wear blindfolds and locate their family through sound only.

Bean Bag Freeze: To the beat of a drum, children walk around the room balancing bean bags on their heads. If a bean bag falls off, then the child must freeze until another child can carefully crouch down, pick up the bean bag, and return it. When everyone is frozen, the game is over.

Big Turtle: A group of children get on their hands and knees and a teacher places a "shell" on their backs. The shell can be a gym mat, a blanket, or sleeping mats. The big turtle attempts to move around without losing its shell (an obstacle course can be made for the turtle).

Colored Shape Run: Children sit in a circle. Each child holds a colored shape (4–5 colors, 3–5 shapes so that about one third of children have same shape or same color). The teacher calls out the name of a color or shape ("*TRIANGLES!*") and all the children holding that shape or color run as fast as they can in one direction around the circle and back to their own space. A child then gets to call out another shape or color until all shapes or all colors are called.

Cooperative Musical Chairs: No one is eliminated. Each person finds a chair when the music stops for as long as interest holds. *Variations:* ***Musical Hoops:*** All children have their own hoop—start by standing in the hoops. When the music starts, walk (or another locomotor direction) around all the hoops. As children move, remove some hoops. When the music stops, children jump into any hoop. Encourage children to invite others inside their hoops, and point out the different ways children are able to include other people in their hoops. Continue to remove hoops and encourage sharing of space. ***Musical Laps:*** When the music stops, everyone must find a chair or a lap to sit in if there is no chair. Each time the music stops, one chair is eliminated and the pileup on the laps is greater. (This works best with smaller groups if children are young.)

Fire on the Mountain: In pairs, children sit one behind the other to form two circles: an inner circle and an outer circle. The inner circle is trees; the outer circle is fire fighters. The teacher is the fire chief who calls "Fire on the Mountain Walk, Walk, Walk" (or another locomotor direction). The trees pretend to be burning while the fire fighters walk around the circle and pretend to spray the trees with their hoses. When the fire chief calls "Fire is out!" the fire fighters sit down behind a tree. Then the trees stand up and they become the fire fighters.

The Big Wind Blows: The group holds the edges of a parachute and lifts it up to billow. They chant, "Blow, blow, the big wind blows, Who oh who does the big wind blow?" The teacher calls out categories, "Everybody wearing red." Those children run underneath the parachute and across to find a place to hold on the other side.

Partner Games

Balloons in the Air: Give pairs of children a balloon. Have partners try to keep their balloon in the air by hitting it, blowing it, or catching it in a big scarf or piece of cloth that both children hold.

Musical Partners: Partners walk around the room back to back as music plays. When the music stops, switch partners.

Obstacle Course: Children create an obstacle course with their bodies by making tunnels, bridges, and rocks. One partner closes his or her eyes and the other leads the "blind" partner through an obstacle maze. Then they switch and other children take turns.

Person to Person: Have children walk around in the circle in a random fashion. Play the drum to a walking beat. With a hard beat, say, "Person to person" and ask children to find a partner near them. Then say the name of a body part such as "Knee to knee." Children touch knees and then continue walking and do the activity again.

Stand Up: Partners sit back to back with elbows linked. They try to get up without letting go. This can also be done with three or four friends.

Stick Together: Ask partners to pretend they have sticky bodies and when you name a body part, you want them to stick their body parts together and move in ways you direct. Give instructions that require cooperation. "Your hands are stuck together. Walk with sticky hands. Your elbows are stuck together, jump with sticky elbows. Your legs are stuck together, march with stuck legs." After a couple of directions, have children change partners.

Sources: Orlick 1978; Sobel 1984; ideas were also learned from Hawaii physical education teachers Jewel Toyama, Lisa Hockenberger, and Pamela Jenkins.

Community Walks

One of the simplest and best ways to promote fitness as a part of daily life is to incorporate a walk in your community as both an activity and a method of transportation. Walking is a great way to get to the park or the neighborhood store, view a construction site, or look at the neighborhood. When you walk in your neighborhood on a regular basis, children become familiar with their community. Members of the community come to know the children as well.

How far should you walk with young children? While the development of walking as a skill has been studied in depth, there are no definitive guidelines for walking distances with young children. We know that with experience a group of 3-year-olds can easily walk four or five blocks; a class of 4-year-olds can hike a mile; and a class of kindergartners can walk twice as far. The terrain, weather, safety, staffing, and the health and prior experience of the children will influence how long a walk you attempt.

Planning Large Motor Curriculum

Creating an environment for active play and ensuring that there is adequate time for children to use it is a critical part of the large motor curriculum. However, it is also important to plan structured large motor activities. You plan large motor activities to teach particular children certain skills; introduce the group to new ways of moving and then give time to practice them; make sure you are addressing a program goal or standard for large motor curriculum; and involve large motor skill development in an integrated curriculum study.

Writing Large Motor Curriculum Plans

Estella and Madeline are friends in the Dragon group at The City Children's Center. Georgia is their teacher. The girls are bonded through vivid imaginations, verbal precocity, and a love of music and pretend play. Since they became friends, they are happy when they are together and sad when parted.

The girls have different large motor strengths. Four-year-old Estella is a coordinated, active child who runs, climbs, slides, rides trikes, pulls wagons, and loves to go on long walks. She seems physically fearless and will sometimes take risks that are beyond her skill level. She sometimes falls off the low balance beam when she runs along the narrow board.

Madeline is nearly a year older. Madeline is cooperative, quiet, reserved, and avoids vigorous activities. She is able to run, jump, skip, and gallop, but does so infrequently, awkwardly, and without enthusiasm. She prefers to be an observer during structured physical activities. Madeline loves music and often brings CDs to share. Recently she brought in a CD with lively "swing dance" music.

To plan large motor curriculum, you need to observe the children so that you know each as an individual. Children like Estella develop physical competence from their self-directed play (she has what Howard Gardner calls *bodily-kinesethetic intelligence*), while others, like Madeline, need support to do so. By knowing the children, you can plan both for those who are skilled and for those who are reluctant. All children, not just those who are physically competent, will participate if you minimize competition and incorporate their interests in designing structured activities.

Look at strengths and look at needs. Starting with what children do well helps you to plan for success. Madeline has large motor skills, but does not have a desire to participate in large motor activities. Estella has many physical skills and is very active.

Look at interests. Children engage in vigorous physical activities doing the things they *like* to do. Madeline and Estella love music, imagination, pretend play, and one another. Their interests can guide you to plan activities that will make them WANT to engage in large motor activities and build large motor skills. Activities that incorporate imagination and pretend play as well as challenge them to use and expand their large motor skills might be successful for both children. To help you in writing your plans, Table 4.4 provides some common objectives for the preschool large motor curriculum.

Figure 4.5 shows the large motor development plan Georgia created that provides a worthwhile activity for the whole group while also taking advantage of Estella's skill and building Madeline's disposition to be physically active.

Because she is an experienced teacher, Georgia's short plan leaves out many details. It would not be enough to guide a beginning teacher. The detailed version in Figure 4.6 gives you a better idea of what she planned to do.

Large Motor Curriculum in a Weekly Plan

We believe that children need blocks of time for unstructured large motor play several times a day as well as guided large motor activity daily. In the Week's

TABLE 4.4   Some Typical Objectives for Large Motor Curriculum

Stage and Objectives	Overall Physical Ability (strength, stamina, and flexibility)	Locomotor Skills	Non-Locomotor Skills	Jumping	Climbing	Object Control Skills
Younger preschoolers 3- to 4-year-olds *The ability to . . .*	Walk several blocks without assistance easily.	Walk smoothly and with control—some toe-walking. Run with increasing coordination.	Move body parts in isolation. Balance on one foot. Walk on a line without watching feet. Walk backward.	Jump over low objects. Jump in place with two feet together. Broad jump about 1 foot.	Climb stairs with alternating feet, holding on to handrail. Climb up slide and come down.	Throw ball overhand. Catch with arms fully extended. Peddle and steer tricycle.
Older preschoolers and kindergartners 4- to 5-year-olds *The ability to . . .*	Walk a mile without assistance.	Use heel-toe walk. Run with leg-arm coordination, change direction while moving, and stop quickly. Gallop. Walk backward with heel-toe pattern. Skip (beginning).	Balance on one foot. Walk on balance beam. Turn somersaults.	Jump skillfully over higher objects. Broad jump about 2 feet.	Climb jungle gym skillfully. Climb stairs with alternating feet. Descend steps with alternating feet.	Throw ball overhand. Catch ball with hands. Ride tricycle rapidly, steer smoothly, ride bicycle with training wheels.

Plan example included in Figure 4.7, you will see that two songs with movement are repeated. In addition, parachute play (with a focus on moving as a group) is offered. These activities allow children to develop creative movement skills. Activities that involve creative movement are highlighted.

Large Motor Curriculum in an Integrated Study

Because children learn physically, large motor curriculum is a valuable part of every integrated study. In the sunburst graphic of *A Study of Pets,* large motor activities appear in the section on creative movement and drama, music, and physical development. All of the large motor activities in the study are highlighted in Figure 4.8.

In addition because an integrated study becomes a part of the life of the classroom, children naturally bring the content into their creative movement. When creative movement activities were planned, teachers and the children themselves often suggested movement that reflected these experiences.

FIGURE 4.5 Simple Large Motor Activity Plan

Move Around Hoops

Objectives:	Develop ability to move body parts in isolation and a disposition to engage in vigorous physical activity
Standard:	Domain I (Physical) Standard 5
What you need:	• CD Player and CD *Philadelphia Chickens* (Track 1) • 15 hoops

How to teach:	1. Ask children to sit in hoops, show Madeline's CD.
	 2. Play CD, invite children to listen and …
	    • Isolate—hands or feet ONLY jump and dance. Jump/dance with ONE foot in hoop, both feet IN hoop.
	    • Whole Body—make body jump or dance in the hoop. Dance with a friend around hoop, etc.
	 3. Acknowledge Madeline, ask children to pick up a hoop and hop to teacher.

How to assess:	Look for children making hands/feet jump and dance without moving the rest of their bodies and dance or jump with one foot in the hoop, etc. Document with photos and anecdotals.

Large Motor Curriculum for All Children

Much of our focus in this chapter has been on the large motor program that is provided in preschool programs for typically developing preschoolers. However, all children need and benefit from daily large motor development opportunities, both teacher led and freely chosen.

Children with Special Needs

Willy, one of the 4-year-olds in the Dragons Group, has cerebral palsy. He has limited use of the right side of his body, but is able to walk using a walker. He loves to ride trikes, which he moves by pushing with his left foot. Though Willy cannot yet run, jump, or climb, he is actively included in the large motor curriculum. Willy is creative in finding ways to be a full participant, and the teachers and children in the class enjoy thinking of ways to overcome barriers. They change the way games are played and create new roles for Willy.

It may seem challenging to include children with special needs in the large motor activities that you plan for your typically developing class. But it is often easier than you think. Even children with physical disabilities thrive on physical activity. When you assume that they want to participate and are creative in finding ways to include them, they will be full, if different, participants in the large motor curriculum.

A child with a physical disability like Willy enjoys large motor play just like the others in the class. The benefits he derives from having opportunities for large motor play, peers to play with, and teachers who support him are probably greater than for the rest of the children. Like the teachers in the preceding example, you need to remove barriers and include all the children in finding ways to make Willy a full participant. It is not difficult. The children are likely

FIGURE 4.6 Detailed Large Motor Activity Plan

Activity: Move Around Hoops   **Large Motor Curriculum Focus**

A guided movement activity in which children work with a hoop to build coordination.

WHO It's For: This activity was planned for the *Dragons* (ten 4-year-olds).

WHY This Activity

Rationale: Most of the *Dragons* (especially Madeline and Estella) enjoy music. Building coordination, comfort with movement, and enthusiasm for vigorous activity is a goal for all the children, especially for Madeline.

Large Motor Objectives: *By participating in this activity the children will …*

- Develop the ability to move body parts in isolation.
- Develop a disposition to engage in vigorous physical activity.

Preschool Content Standard: Domain I (Physical) Standard 5: Develop strength and coordination of large muscles.

Indicator: Control body in movement activities.

HOW to Prepare   *What you need:*

- CD Player and CD *Philadelphia Chickens* (Track 1)
- 15 hoops
- large carpeted area

Set up:
Before the children come push back table and check sound level.

HOW to Teach   *Introduction:*
As children come for small group, invite them to sit in one of the hoops. Show them the cover of the CD and say something like: "Madeline brought her favorite CD to share with us. The music makes me feel like jumping and dancing."

Teaching steps:

1. Invite children to listen to the music and make their hands jump and dance while they sit in their hoop. Say, "I wonder if you can make your hands jump and dance." Play the CD for a verse of the first track. Stop the CD.
2. Repeat with feet while sitting in the hoop. Demonstrate/instruct if necessary.
3. Invite children to dance or jump with one foot in the hoop, then with both feet out of the hoop.
4. Invite children to stand and jump or dance in the hoop.
5. Other things to try—dance with a friend around the hoop, march to the music around the hoop, tiptoe to the music around the hoop, lie on your back and make your legs dance in the air, invite children to think of another way.

Closure:
At the end, comment (e.g., "Madeline's music was good for dancing and jumping."). Have children bring hoops while hopping.

HOW to Assess and Document

Objectives	Evidence of Learning Children might …	How to Document This Evidence
Develop the ability to move body parts in isolation.	Make body parts jump and dance without moving the rest of their bodies. Dance or jump with one foot in the hoop, then with both feet out of the hoop.	Anecdotal observations and photographs
Develop a disposition to engage in vigorous physical activity.	Participate willingly throughout the activity and ask to do it again.	

EVALUATION (Things to remember for next time)

Using *Philadelphia Chickens* was very successful! It got Madeline moving—and the rest of the children as well. More work is needed on using hoops. Could do a whole session on in the hoop/out of the hoop.

FIGURE 4.7 A Week's Plan: Water—Week #3

Objectives: To help children to experience water in a variety of natural and manmade settings and understand that water comes from different sources—rain from the sky, streams, lakes, springs, the ocean—and to build physical, communication, creative, and inquiry skills and understanding.

	Monday	Tuesday	Wednesday	Thursday	Friday
Story 8:50–9:00		*Deep in the Swamp* (Bateman)	*Where the Forest Meets the Sea* (Baker)	*Water* (Asch)	*Who Sank the Boat?* (Allen)
Outdoor Activities 9:00–10:00 **Purpose:** *to help children …*	Field Trip Hike to Kahaluu Stream — *Purpose: to experience and learn about natural sources of water and develop physical stamina*	**Stream in the Sand** Reconstruct what was experienced on the field trip. Acquire large motor coordination and strength.	**Measuring Cups in the Water Table** Develop and use measurement concepts.	**Ice in the Water Table** Increase sensory awareness. Learn that water has different forms.	**Dripping Bottle** Engage in scientific inquiry. Develop large motor coordination.
Small Group Swimming Penguins 10:00–10:20 **Purpose:** *to help children …*		**Validate Prediction Chart** Develop inquiry skills and disposition to reflect on experience. Acquire concepts of print.	**Journal** Develop interest in writing. Express themselves through art.	**Using Instruments with *Ame Ga Furu* and Other Rain Songs** Develop creative expression through music. Learn about water in the lives of people from diverse cultures.	**Sink and Float** Engage in scientific inquiry. Learn about the properties of water.
Small Group Rainbow Flowers 10:00–10:10 **Purpose:** *to help children …*		**Big Ball Ramp Rolling** Understand that water has different forms—and each form of water behaves in predictable ways. Develop large motor coordination.	**Ball Rolling with PVC Pipes** Build on concepts developed in big ball ramp rolling activity. Develop large motor coordination.	**Will It Dissolve? Demonstration** Engage in scientific inquiry. Explore and identify characteristics of water. Develop vocabulary.	**Build an Aqueduct** Build on concepts developed in big ball ramp rolling activities. Develop large motor coordination.
Indoor Special Activities 10:20–11:30 **Purpose:** *to help children …*		**Ink and Watercolor Wash—Focus on Stream** Create and express themselves through a variety of art experiences.	**Ink and Watercolor Wash—Focus on Stream** Create and express themselves through a variety of art experiences.	**Making Oatmeal Cookies** Increase sensory awareness. Develop and use measurement concepts.	**Blow Painting** Create and express themselves through a variety of art experiences.
Circle Time 11:30–11:45 **Purpose:** *to help children …*		*Five Little Speckled Frogs* Develop creative expression through music. Develop large motor agility.	*Walk Around the Chair* Develop creative expression through music. Develop large motor control.	*Five Little Speckled Frogs* Develop creative expression through music. Develop large motor agility.	*Little Sally Saucer* Develop creative expression through music. Develop large motor control.

to be far more open and accepting than you anticipate. However, it takes vision and an open mind to see Willy as just another child who has gifts and strengths as well as needs. Though Willy is not his real name, Willy (like all the children with special needs we use as examples in this book) was a real boy in one of our classes. Willy thrived in preschool. By the end of his time with us, he walked without a walker and managed most physical tasks with little assistance. He went on to be fully integrated in his elementary school. Recently we spotted him, now a teenager, waiting at the bus stop with his skateboard.

You can use additional strategies to include children with other disabilities. For a child with a developmental delay, you might need to make directions and activities simpler. For a child with autism, you might need to physically guide the child through activities as movements are being learned. A child with a language disability might need physical and visual cues. But all children, regardless of ability, have the right to large motor activity.

Children in the Primary Grades

It seems self-evident that primary age children also need periods of directed physical activity as well as free play each day. Even though they may take dance lessons, play organized sports, and ride bicycles, the general physical condition of many children today suggests that they do not get regular large muscle exercise and have not become skilled at organized games or sports. In many schools, large motor activity is confined to short "recess" periods. In some states no provision at all is made for regular physical development activities for primary school children (Javernick, 1988).

What about recess for children in kindergarten and the primary grades? Many children today, even kindergartners, have no recess. Children who are poor, African American, and those who score poorly on standardized tests are more likely to attend schools without opportunities for recess (Jarett & Waite-Stupianski, 2009). In light of the growing epidemic of childhood obesity and diabetes, campaigns have been launched to "rescue recess" in public schools. These efforts are supported by numerous organizations (American Academy of Pediatrics, National Association of Elementary School Principals, National Association for the Education of Young Children, American Association for the Child's Right to Play, National Association of Early Childhood Specialists in State Departments of Education, American School Health Association, The National Association for Sport and Physical Education). There is no universal standard for the frequency and duration of recess for young elementary school children. NASPE recommends a daily recess of at least 20 minutes, and no more than two hours of sedentary activity at a time (NASPE, 2004). The American School Health Association recommends a recess of at least 15 minutes several times a day.

If you teach children in the primary grades, strive to make physical activities an integrated and pleasurable part of school life. Needless to say, if you deny physical activity ("No recess!") or impose it as a punishment ("Take a lap!"), it is damaging to children's attitudes toward physical activity and school in general. No thoughtful, well-trained teacher of young children would do this.

If no formal physical education program is provided, you can still include large motor activity in your primary school classroom. Children will enjoy and benefit from calisthenics done to music, guided movement or yoga sessions, and a chance to play on obstacle courses and climbing structures. Organized cooperative games (like those described in this chapter) have appeal and can be played with primary age children. Young children benefit from skill practice

FIGURE 4.8   A Study of Pets Sunburst

Social Studies

KWL: What Do You Know about Pets? What Do You Want to Learn about Pets? (Introductory Activity)

Brainstorming: What New Pet Shall We Get for Our Classroom? What Would It Need?

Dramatic Play: Groomer's Salon

Selecting Pet Names

Prediction Chart: Field Trip to the Humane Society

Science

Baby-Adult Animal Matching Game

Visiting Dog: Observation

Animal Food Guessing Game

Pet Ear Hearing Game

Puppy Growth Sequencing Game

Trips

Pets and Plants to Buy Fish

Walk to See Pet Spider

Foodland to Buy Pet Food

Humane Society

Visitors: Dogs (Introductory Activity), cat, tortoise, cockatiel, therapy dog and handler

Math

Our Pets—graph

Pets/Not Pets

Dog Counting

Pets on Dots Game

Pet Number Collage

Literature

Reading Pet Books (see bibliography)

Fingerplays: My Little Kitty, Five Little Puppies

Large Motor Activities

Pet Circle Game

Game Cat, Cat—Dog!

Pet Relay Game

Run, Pet, Run! Game

Literacy

Games: Pet Names

Child-Authored Books

Pets

Humane Society

The Pet Book (Culminating Activity)

Journal:

My Favorite Pet

What Kind of Fish Should We Get?

What Pets Need

What I Learned About Pets (Culminating Activity)

Fine Motor Activities

Birdseed Table

Puppy Pick-up

Pet Puzzles

Language

Pet Clues

Puppet Pets

Planning for Classroom Fish Tank

Pet Feely Box

Thinking of Pet Names

Art

Life Drawing: Cockatiel, Dog, Rat, Rabbit, Tortoise

Ink and Watercolor Wash—Fish and Tortoise

Tissue Paper Collage—Fish

Life Painting Cockatiels, Fish,

Pet Mural (Culminating Activity)

Creative Movement

Pets Around the Chair

Pet Magic Rocks

Fish (Creative Movement)

Little Bird, Little Bird

Dog Movement

Moving Like a Pet

Music

The Pets

How Much Is That Doggie in the Window?

I Found a Little Dog

Walk Around the Chair: Pets

Little Bird, Little Bird

Did You Ever See the Fishes?

Bingo

The Pets in the House

Creating a Pet Song (Culminating Activity)

A Study of Pets

Big Idea — A pet is an animal kept for company at a person's home, school, or workplace.

Big Idea — There are different kinds of pets with different characteristics and needs.

Big Idea — Some animals are pets. Other animals cannot be pets. They are too large, dangerous, or destructive.

Big Idea — Pets are living creatures that are born, live, grow, and die.

Big Idea — Pets are cared for by a special doctor called a veterinarian.

Big Idea — Pets are cared for by their owners.

Big Idea — Each type of pet has a special type of food.

Big Idea — Some pets have jobs—therapy pets and service animals.

(throwing, kicking and catching balls, jumping, running relays) if it is conducted in a spirit of play and their effort is appreciated as much as success. Field trips can provide exercise in the form of walking and climbing. An occasional teacher-led jog can be a playful deviation from the usual routine. You support physical development when you go beyond the physical education class and recess time mentality and build physical activity into your daily schedule with children.

Final Thoughts

Children's connector to the world—their bodies—grow and develop as they have opportunities to move, explore, and manipulate materials. It is satisfying and exciting to contribute to children's physical development. Whether you are providing an 8-month-old with the encouragement and opportunity to pull up and take her first steps, giving a hand to a 2-year-old risking a first, cautious climb up the superstructure, providing a preschooler with a new ball, or teaching 6-year-olds how to do a simple folk dance, you are making an important contribution to their growth into healthy human beings who will live longer with greater zest for life.

Learning Outcomes

When you read this chapter, thoughtfully complete activities from the "To Learn More" section, and document this learning as suggested in the "For Your Portfolio" section, you will be making progress in the following *NAEYC Standards for Early Childhood Professional Preparation Programs* (2009):

Standard 1. Promoting Child Development and Learning

Students prepared in early childhood degree programs are grounded in a child development knowledge base. They use their understanding of young children's characteristics and needs and of the multiple interacting influences on children's development and learning to create environments that are healthy, respectful, supportive, and challenging for each child.

The key elements of standard 1 you will have learned about are . . .

1a: Knowing and understanding young children's characteristics and needs

1c: Using developmental knowledge to create healthy, respectful, supportive, and challenging learning environments

Standard 4. Using Developmentally Effective Approaches to Connect with Children and Families

Students prepared in early childhood degree programs understand that teaching and learning with young children is a complex enterprise, and its details vary depending on children's ages, characteristics, and the settings within which teaching and learning occur. They understand and use positive relationships and supportive interactions as the foundation for their work with young children and families. Students know, understand, and use a wide array of developmentally appropriate approaches, instructional strategies, and tools to connect with children and families and positively influence each child's development and learning.

The key elements of standard 4 you will have learned about are . . .

4a: Understanding positive relationships and supportive interactions as the foundation of their work with children

4b: Knowing and understanding effective strategies and tools for early education

4c: Using a broad repertoire of developmentally appropriate teaching/learning approaches

4d: Reflecting on their own practice to promote positive outcomes for each child

Standard 5. Using Content Knowledge to Build Meaningful Curriculum

Students prepared in early childhood degree programs use their knowledge of academic disciplines to design, implement, and evaluate experiences that promote positive development and learning for each and every young child. Students understand the importance of developmental domains and academic (or content) disciplines in an early childhood curriculum. They know the essential concepts, inquiry tools, and structure of content areas, including academic subjects, and can identify resources to deepen their understanding. Students use their own knowledge and other resources to design, implement, and evaluate meaningful, challenging curricula that promote comprehensive developmental and learning outcomes for every young child.

The key elements of standard 5 you will have learned about are . . .

5a: Understanding content knowledge and resources in academic disciplines

5b: Knowing and using the central concepts, inquiry tools, and structures of content areas or academic disciplines

5c: Using their own knowledge, appropriate early learning standards, and other resources to design, implement, and evaluate meaningful, challenging curricula for each child

To Learn More

Observe a Program: For a morning, observe a program and see how the staff structures the environment and program to support children's large motor development. Notice both the play opportunities and the planned group activities. Look at the plans and see how the planning reflects what you observed. Interview a teacher to learn what he or she thinks about large motor curriculum.

Observe a Child: For a morning, observe a child in a classroom, with a focus on the child's large motor activity. Notice how the child engages with the planned activities and how he or she constructs his or her own opportunities for learning. Notice the extent to which the child's activity and the planned curriculum seem to match. Observe to see how staff support the child's large motor learning.

Observe a Master Teacher: Spend a morning with an early childhood educator who is experienced and has a curriculum leadership role in a program. (This teacher may be called the "lead," "head," or "mentor" teacher.) Then interview the educator about how he or she plans for and provides large motor curriculum.

Observe a Large Motor Activity: Observe a teacher leading a planned large motor activity. Interview the teacher to find out the objectives for the activity. Reflect on any differences between what you saw and the focus of the plan.

Compare Two Programs: Observe large motor experiences in two early childhood programs. Compare the ways that the two address large motor curriculum—their similarities and differences. Reflect on which program seems to best support children's learning and why. What implications does this comparison have for your future work with young children?

Compare Two Ages: Observe two classrooms, one preschool and one for primary school children. Report on how each supports children's large motor learning. Talk to the staff about how they make their curriculum choices. Notice how development influences curriculum choices.

Explore Resources: Read one of the books from the bibliography or one of the online resources listed here and write a review of it for your classmates.

Promising Practices: Head Start Body Start National Center for Physical Development and Outdoor Play (HSBS), resources to provide the context and next steps for creating high quality play spaces, activities and experiences for young children and their families. www.aahperd.org/headstartbodystart/toolbox/best Practices/promisingpractices.cfm

PE Central: Information for those providing movement programs for young children. www.pecentral.org/preschool/preschoolindex.html

Recess and the Importance of Play: A Position Statement on Young Children and Recess. National Association of Early Childhood Specialists in State Departments of Education www.peacefulplaygrounds.com/pdf/right-to-recess/recess-importance-of-play.pdf

Recess in Elementary Schools: Council on Physical Education for Children, A Position Paper from the National Association for Sport and Physical Education www.cde.state.co.us/cdenutritran/download/pdf/WPRecessinElementarySchoolsCOPEC.pdf

Right to Recess Campaign: www.peacefulplaygrounds.com/right-to-recess.htm

The State of Play: A Gallup survey of principals on school recess. www.peacefulplaygrounds.com/pdf/right-to-recess/state-of-play.pdf

For Your Portfolio

Design a Large Motor Environment: Design and draw a floor plan for a classroom and play yard that would promote children's large motor learning. Share your plan with an early childhood educator, discussing what you included and why. Ask for and consider the educator's feedback and suggestions. Set up a large motor activity center in a real classroom or play yard utilizing as many of your ideas as possible, and let children use it. For your portfolio, include the floor plan, photographs or video of children using the area, and a reflection on what you learned by doing this project.

Plan and Implement a Large Motor Activity: Observe a group of children for a morning, focusing on their large motor interest and skill. Based on what you observed, write and implement a large motor activity using the model shown in this chapter. Collect evidence of children's responses in the form of anecdotal observations, photographs, or video recordings. Reflect on how children responded and what they appear to have learned. What worked? What might you do differently next time? How might you expand on this experience for children? For your portfolio, include the plan, a photograph, and a reflection on what you learned about yourself, children, planning, and teaching.

Create a Large Motor Learning Material: Design and make a large motor learning material to support the development of a particular child or group of children. Introduce it to the child or children and observe how it is used. Reflect on how the children responded and how you felt about what you did. What worked? What might you do differently next time? How might you expand on this experience for children? For your portfolio, include a photograph of a child using the material and a reflection on what you learned about yourself, children, learning materials, and teaching.

Bibliography

American School Health Association. (2005). *Resolution: Elementary schools should provide daily recesses in addition to planned physical education for all students*. Kent, OH: American School Health Association.

Barros, R. M., Silver, E. J., & Stein, R. E. K. (2009). School recess and group classroom behavior in pediatrics. *Journal of the American Academy of Pediatrics, 123,* 431–436.

Berger, K. S. (2008). *The developing person through childhood and adolescence* (7th ed.). New York, NY: Worth.

Berk, L. E. (2012). *Infants and children: Prenatal through middle childhood* (7th ed.). Upper Saddle River, NJ: Pearson.

Black, J., Puckett, M., Wittmer, D. S., & Petersen S. H. (2008). *The young child: Development from prebirth through age eight* (5th ed.). Upper Saddle River, NJ: Pearson.

Bredekamp, S., & Rosegrant, T. (1995). *Reaching potentials: Transforming early childhood curriculum and assessment* (Vol. 2). Washington, DC: NAEYC.

CDC (Centers for Disease Control and Prevention). (2000). *Promoting better health for young people through physical activity and sports: A report to the President from the Secretary of Health and Human Services and Secretary of Education*. Atlanta, GA: U.S. Department of Health and Human Services, CDC National Center for Chronic Disease Prevention and Health Promotion.

Chun, R. S. B. (1994). *Capturing childhood's magic: Creating outdoor play environments for Hawaii's young children*. Manoa, HI: University of Hawaii at Manoa.

Copple, C., & Bredekamp, S. (Eds.). (2009). *Developmentally appropriate practice* (3rd ed.). Washington, DC: NAEYC.

Council on Physical Education for Children (COPEC). (2000). *Appropriate practices in movement programs for young children ages 3–5: A position statement of the National Association for Sport and Physical Education (NASPE)*. Reston, VA: American Alliance for Health, Physical Education, Recreation & Dance.

Cratty, B. J. (1986). *Perceptual and motor development in infants and children* (3rd ed.). Englewood Cliffs, NJ: Prentice-Hall.

Curtis, S. R. (1982). *The joy of movement in early childhood*. New York, NY: Teachers College Press.

de Onis, M., & Blössner, M. (2000, October). Prevalence and trends of overweight among preschool children in developing countries. *American Journal of Clinical Nutrition, 72*(4), 1032–1039.

Dietz, W. H. (2001). The obesity epidemic in young children. *The British Medical Journal, 322*(7282), 313.

Epstein, A. S. (2007). *The intentional teacher*. Washington, DC: NAEYC.

Feeney, S., Moravcik, E., & Nolte, S. (2013). *Who am I in the lives of children?* (9th ed.). Upper Saddle River, NJ: Pearson.

Frost, J. L. (1992). *Play and playscapes*. Albany, NY: Delmar.

Gabbard, C. P. (2004). *Lifelong motor development* (4th ed.). San Francisco, CA: Benjamin Cummings/Pearson.

Gallahue, D. L., & Donnelly, F. C. (2007). *Developmental physical education for all children* (4th ed.). Champaign, IL: Human Kinetics.

Gearheart, B. R., & Gearheart, C. J. (1989). *Learning disabilities: Educational strategies*. New York, NY: Merrill/Macmillan.

Haywood, K. M., & Getchell, N. (2008). *Life span motor development* (5th ed.). Champaign, IL: Human Kinetics.

Head Start Resource Center. (2010). *The Head Start child development and early learning framework: Promoting positive outcomes in early childhood programs serving children 3–5 years old*. Washington DC: Office of Head Start, Administration for Children and Families, U.S. Department of Health and Human Services.

Jarett, O., & Waite-Stupianski, S. (2009). Recess—It's indispensable! *Young Children, 64*(5), 66–69.

Javernick, E. (1988). Johnny's not jumping: Can we help obese children? *Young Children 43*(2), 18–23.

Miller, K. (1985). *Ages and stages: Developmental descriptions and activities birth through eight years*. Chelsea, MA: Telshare Publishing Co.

Miller, K. (1989). *The outside play and learning book: Activities for young children*. Mount Rainier, MD: Gryphon House.

National Association for the Education of Young Children. (2009). *NAEYC standards for early childhood professional preparation programs*. www.naeyc.org/files/naeyc/file/positions/ProfPrepStandards09.pdf

National Association for Sport and Physical Education. (2004). *Moving into the future: National standards for physical education* (2nd ed.). Reston, VA: American Alliance for Health, Physical Education, Recreation & Dance.

Orlick, T. (1978). *The cooperative sports and games book*. New York, NY: Pantheon Books.

Orlick, T. (1982). *The second cooperative sports and games book*. New York, NY: Pantheon Books.

Palmer, H. (2001). The music, movement, and learning connection. *Young Children, 56*(5), 13–17.

Pangrazi, R., & Beighle, A. (2010). *Dynamic physical education for elementary school children* (16th ed.). San Francisco, CA: Benjamin Cummings/Pearson.

Papalia, D. E., Feldman, S., & Olds, S. J. (2007). *A child's world: Infancy through adolescence* (11th ed.). New York, NY: McGraw-Hill.

Parsad, B., & Lewis, L. (2006). *Calories in/Calories out: Food and exercise in*. Washington, DC: National Center for Educational Statistics.

Payne, V. G., & Isaacs, L. D. (2007). *Human motor development: A lifespan approach* (7th ed.). New York, NY: McGraw-Hill.

Pica, R. (2004). *Experiences in movement* (3rd ed.). Albany, NY: Delmar.

Riggs, M. L. (1980). *Jump to joy*. Englewood Cliffs, NJ: Prentice-Hall.

Rowen, B. (1982). *Learning through movement*. New York, NY: Teachers College Press.

Sanders, S. W. (2002). *Active for life: Developmentally appropriate movement programs for young children*. Washington, DC: NAEYC.

School Readiness Task Force, Good Beginnings Alliance. (2003). *Hawaii preschool content standards: Curriculum guidelines for programs for four-year-olds*. Honolulu, HI: Author.

Seefeldt, C. (Ed.). (2005). *The early childhood curriculum: Current findings in theories and practice* (3rd ed.). New York, NY: Teachers College Press.

Sobel, J. (1984). *Everybody wins: 393 noncompetitive games for young children*. New York, NY: Walker.

Sothern, M. S., Loftin, M., Suskind, R. M., Udall, J. N., & Blecker, U. (1999). The health benefits of physical activity in children and adolescents: Implications for chronic disease prevention. *European Journal of Pediatrics, 158*, 271–274.

Stinson, W. J. (Ed.). (1990). *Moving and learning for the young child*. Reston, VA: American Alliance for Health, Physical Education, Recreation, and Dance.

Torbert, M. (1980). *Follow me: A handbook of movement activities for children*. Englewood Cliffs, NJ: Prentice-Hall.

U.S. Consumer Product Safety Commission. (2008). *Public playground safety handbook*. Bethesda, MD: Author.

Witkin, K. (1977). *To move to learn*. Philadelphia, PA: Temple University Press.

MyEducationLab

Go to Topics 2: Child Development and Learning, 6: Environments, and 9: Content Areas/Lessons and Activities in the MyEducationLab (www.myeducationlab.com) for *Meaningful Curriculum for Young Children,* where you can:

- Find learning outcomes for Child Development and Learning, Environments, and Content Areas/Lessons and Activities along with the national standards that connect to these outcomes.
- Complete Assignments and Activities that can help you more deeply understand the chapter content.
- Apply and practice your understanding of the core teaching skills identified in the chapter with the Building Teaching Skills and Dispositions learning units.
- Listen to experts from the field in Professional Perspectives.

- Examine challenging situations and cases presented in the IRIS Center Resources.
- Check your comprehension on the content covered in the chapter with the Study Plan. Here you will be able to take a chapter quiz, receive feedback on your answers, and then access Review, Practice, and Enrichment activities to enhance your understanding of chapter content.

Go to the Course Resources section in MyEducationLab, where you can:

- Use the Online Lesson Plan Builder to practice lesson planning and integrating national and state standards into your planning.

Often the hands will solve a mystery that the intellect has struggled with in vain.

CARL G. JUNG

chapter five

FINE MOTOR CURRICULUM
Manipulating and Coordinating

This morning you woke up. You got ready for your day. You washed. You dressed. You ate breakfast. You used tools—a fork, a toothbrush, a zipper, a comb. Then you began your work or play. You used machines—a computer, a stove, a car. Like your fellow human beings, you are a tool-using animal. From the time you wake until you go to sleep, you coordinate your hands to accomplish the vast array of tasks that make up your daily life. You are a master of fine motor skills.

Fine motor strength and coordination develop during the early childhood years, with the brain, nerves, and muscles maturing together. The skillful use of hands goes by a number of names, including *fine motor* or *small muscle skill, eye-hand* or *hand-eye coordination,* and *manipulative skills.* We use all of these terms, but primarily *fine motor* development and curriculum.

Our goal in this chapter is to help you understand and value young children's fine motor development so that you will purposefully provide appropriate materials and curriculum to support it. We also want to help you develop a repertoire of engaging teaching strategies appropriate for young children.

Why Fine Motor Curriculum?

It is the start of a new school year, and 3-year-old Matty has come to school for the first time. At orientation Matty rode the trikes, climbed the superstructure, threw balls, sat through circle time, listened to a story, and enjoyed the snack of crackers and juice.

On his first day on his own at school Matty enjoys outside time. He laughs as he rides a trike and grins with delight as he climbs the superstructure again. But during inside time another child builds a tower of blocks and Matty knocks them down. A teacher asks Matty to help to pick them up—Matty has difficulty picking up the blocks and cries. Matty takes a puzzle from the shelf. He dumps it onto the table and walks away. A teacher brings him back to help her to put the pieces back—Matty shoves the pieces onto the frame. At lunch time Matty forgoes the fork and spoon at his place and uses his hands to shovel food into his mouth. Matty calls for help when he goes to use the bathroom—he can't manage the zipper on his trousers. He emerges from the bathroom with pants unzipped and hands unwashed. Matty has many fine motor skills to acquire and encounters many challenges.

Fine motor skills are necessary for day-to-day life in the classroom and in the world. Because of this, fine motor curriculum is included in every program for young children, particularly in preschool programs. Sometimes it is included mindfully, by teachers who understand the value and sequence of the manipulative skills young children are learning. Sometimes it is integrated purposefully into other curricula. And often it is included haphazardly, as a by-product of play and other activities. In schools for primary children, it is often ignored unless a child is experiencing difficulty.

As you can see in the vignette above, it is evident that Matty and all **young children need to develop manipulative skills.** It is worthwhile to reflect on why fine motor activities in early childhood programs are considered important.

Fine motor skills work in concert with brain development. As fine motor skills develop, neural pathways spread, making the brain more complex and flexible. There is research to suggest that children's **fine motor skills relate to cognitive skills and knowledge.** In the early childhood longitudinal study, *America's Kindergartners,* the authors report, "Fine motor skills (i.e., visual motor) can predict reading, mathematics and general school achievement, and such perceptual skills may be more predictive than even cognitive skills for later success in reading comprehension" (West, Denton, & Germino-Hausken, 2000).

Fine motor curriculum is important because **fine motor skills are needed to use the tools for every area of life and learning:** self-care, play, understanding, creating, and communicating. In particular, the ability to hold and manipulate pens and pencils as well as to use both hands together to cut with scissors are needed and valued in later schooling. These skills take a great deal of practice before they are easily and quickly accessible. Manipulative skills are built through simple activities such as playing with playdough; stringing beads; and using paintbrushes, crayons, and tongs.

Finally, **self-esteem and positive attitudes toward learning are enhanced as a child develops mastery of the fine motor skills** that increase independence. In the primary school years, children who have difficulty in academic arenas particularly benefit when they have fine motor accomplishments.

Reflect on your fine motor skills and abilities . . .

What talents related to fine motor skills have you developed (such as playing the piano, cooking, sewing, auto mechanics, calligraphy, typing, drawing, knitting)? Think about the kinds of motions that are involved in them. How did you become proficient in these skills? How long did it take? Was it hard or easy to develop? What implications might your experiences have for your work with young children?

MyEducationLab

Visit the MyEducationLab for *Meaningful Curriculum for Young Children* to enhance your understanding of chapter concepts with a personalized Study Plan. You'll also have the opportunity to hone your teaching skills through video-based Assignments and Activities, IRIS Center Resources, and Building Teaching Skills and Disposition lessons.

Understanding Fine Motor Development

The ability to use the hand with dexterity and skill has reached its highest level in humans.

CHARLANE PEHOSKI

Learning to coordinate the hands and fingers begins when babies in their cribs reach out to feel, grasp, and manipulate objects within their reach. Those initial impulses eventually lead to the competent use of tools. Spoons, crayons, hammers, and keyboards are all tools that need to be manipulated by the hands and fingers. Planned activities in early childhood programs can make an important contribution to this area of development.

Milestones of Fine Motor Development

In order to plan fine motor curriculum, you need to understand and be able to anticipate the sequence and general timing of fine motor development in young children. Individual timing varies. If children have not accomplished a skill at the typical age, it does not necessarily mean that they are experiencing a delay (just as accomplishing it sooner does not necessarily suggest that they are gifted). Table 5.1 provides you with a quick, though by no means complete, snapshot of the milestones of fine motor development.

TABLE 5.1 Milestones of Fine Motor Development

Age	Developmental Milestones
Birth–4 months	Grasps reflexively; is unable to purposefully release objects Squeezes and holds objects in a closed fist Reaches for objects (3 months)—arms and hands move together to bat at objects
4–6 months	Reaches with one hand Grasps and holds objects—releases voluntarily Picks up small items
6–12 months	Pinches and holds small objects between thumb and forefingers in pincer grasp Transfers objects from one hand to the other Finds object visually, reaches for it, watches hands Makes marks with crayons and markers Stacks rings and blocks Turns pages of board or cloth book Rolls a ball
1–2 years	Uses both arms equally Moves fingers independently Pokes and points Uses crayons or markers with whole arm movement Holds crayon in closed fist with thumb pointing up (*palmer-supinate grasp*) Progresses from circular to horizontal or vertical scribbles Initiates activity with one hand, but frequently alternates hands Takes off shoes and socks Feeds self with fingers Uses spoon Uses cup Drops and picks up objects Plays pat-a-cake Dumps objects from containers Builds tower of cubes (2 at first, later 3–4)

(continued)

127

TABLE 5.1 Milestones of Fine Motor Development (continued)

Age	Developmental Milestones
2–3 years	Initiates hand use, with movement from the elbow
	Holds crayon or marker with fingers pointing toward the paper (*pronated grasp*)
	Imitates a shape after watching someone else draw it; by age 3 copies a shape from a picture
	Uses both hands to open/close scissors; by age 3 snips paper with scissors in one hand and cuts paper into 2 pieces
	Leads activities with one hand, with the other hand assisting
	Strings large beads
	Places large pegs in board
	Opens door by turning knob
	Puts on and removes simple items of clothing
	Zips and unzips large zippers
	Manages spoon and cup
	Turns pages of book 2–3 at a time
3–4 years	Holds crayons/markers with 3 fingers (*static tripod grasp*)
	Moves scissors in forward direction to cut straight line; by age 4 cuts simple curves with assist hand turning paper
	Has strong preference for lead hand, with some switching; assist hand stabilizes paper
	Puts together 3–6 piece puzzles
	Handles books efficiently
	Builds tower of 8–10 cubes
	Fastens and unfastens large buttons
	Dresses and undresses with assistance
	Uses fork and spoon
	Serves self food without assistance
4–6 years	Has refined wrist and finger movement and decreased elbow and shoulder movement
	Copies crosses, diagonal lines, squares; uses small precise finger movement when drawing
	Uses mature tripod grasp; by age 6 copies numerals and letters
	Holds scissors in a thumbs-up position; makes small, precise cuts; cuts out simple straight-line shapes like rectangles and triangles
	Shows consistent hand preference—skill of dominant hand exceeds that of non-dominant hand
	Dresses and undresses without assistance
	Is proficient in using fork and spoon; by age 6 uses a knife to cut soft food
6–8 years	Masters printing
	Is able to begin learning to play musical instruments and use a keyboard
	Makes models
	Does crafts
	Ties shoes (about age 6)

What Is Fine Motor Curriculum in Early Childhood?

Can you imagine a typically developing child who does not strive to achieve fine motor competence? Young children have an innate desire to manipulate objects. They want to push buttons, pull strings, and pick up and investigate toys. So without encouragement, planning, or teaching, most young children in your class will work on the development of fine motor ability. Is this curriculum? Your knowledge of fine motor skills and how they develop, your expertise in providing materials and activities that build the skills, and your ability to clearly articulate the importance of fine motor activities will turn children's natural play into an important part of the planned curriculum. Understanding fine motor skills will help you be a better teacher and will aid you in explaining the curriculum to others. As you gain this understanding, you will enjoy and appreciate the fine motor curriculum.

Fine Motor Skills

The term *fine motor skills* refers to coordinated activities that involve the fingers, hands, and wrists, as well as the forearms. As an able adult you use these skills without thinking. It is easier to appreciate their complexity if you stop and consider what is involved in fine motor activity.

There are 27 bones in each hand and wrist. Ligaments connect one bone to another, and tendons connect the muscles to the bones. Most of the muscles that operate the hand are in the forearm. The tendons run from the muscles through the wrist to the bones in the hand. Blood vessels and nerves pass through a narrow passage on the inside of the wrist called the *carpel tunnel*. The palm of the hand makes a hollow cavity that changes its shape during grasping in response to the object to be grasped. The muscles in the palm are called *arches*. They run in different directions: across, lengthwise, and sideways. These muscles need to be developed so that hands have the strength for fine motor tasks. One of the reasons that crawling is important for infants is that it strengthens the arches of the hands.

When you clench your fist, the muscles in your forearm change shape. And when you straighten or stretch your fingers, the tendons on the back of your hand move. All of these bones, muscles, tendons, and nerves must work together each time you use your hands.

Fine motor skills like writing, cutting, and keyboarding consist of smaller component abilities and characteristics. Understanding these components helps you to plan fine motor curriculum for children.

Grasp

The first fine motor skill a child develops is the ability to grasp. Grasping begins as a whole hand reflex called the *palmer grasp reflex*. Babies clamp their fingers around anything placed in their palms and have difficulty letting go. This reflexive grasp usually disappears around 4 or 5 months of age and a purposeful grasp begins to develop in its place. When the reflexive grasp disappears, it is replaced by whole hand grasping that enables a baby to deliberately pick up a toy or pull her mother's hair. This grasp goes through a number of changes, each of which are described with a variety of interesting names including *scissors closure* (when an object is held between the thumb and side of the index finger) and *three jaw chuck* (when an object is held at the pads of the index and middle fingers, as well as the pad of the thumb). By about 1 year of age, a precise grasp between thumb and forefingers called the *pincer grasp* appears (Edwards, Buckland, & McCoy-Powlen, 2002).

In early childhood programs children are learning to modify their grasp, acquiring strength (called *grip strength*), and learning to control force used so that they can accomplish tasks and use tools. Carrying a bucket requires a different grasp and different grip strength than holding a spoon or picking up a pea. There are different types of grasps named for the way the hand is used. In a *handshake* grasp, the object being held rests firmly against the palm and all fingers. In a *pinch* grasp, the fingers are on one side of an object, and the thumb is on the other. Typically, an object lifted does not touch the palm. A *support* grasp involves holding something with all of the fingers curled into the palm, such as the handle of a bucket. In a *pencil* grasp, the thumb and fingers work together to hold and move a pencil. Dexterity, strength, and control must all be developed for grasp to be effective.

Grasp undergoes transformation as children learn to write, paint, draw, cut, or maneuver a computer mouse. The development of the grasp used for writing/drawing (called *graphomotor* ability) typically, though not always, develops in the following sequence (see also Figure 5.1).

- Between 1 and 2 years, children use the whole arm to manipulate a drawing tool, holding it in a closed fist with thumb pointing up (called the *hammer* or *palmer-supinate* grasp).
- Next, the tool is held with fingers pointing toward the paper (called a *pronated* grasp).
- A modified mature grasp called *static tripod* typically develops after age 3.
- Between the ages of 4 and 5, most children come to hold writing/drawing implements pinched between thumb and index fingers, resting on their middle finger like most adults (called a *dynamic tripod, mature,* or *efficient* pencil grasp).

From this point onward, writing/drawing is characterized by refined wrist and finger movement with decreased elbow and shoulder movement. And by

FIGURE 5.1 Illustrations of Grasp

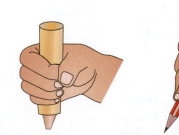 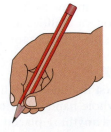

Palmer-supinate grasp   Pronated grasp   Static tripod grasp   Dynamic tripod/mature grasp

age 5 most children are capable of staying within the lines as well as copying crosses, diagonal lines, and squares. The complex refinements required for handwriting proceed once this grasp has been developed.

Eye-Hand Coordination

Eye-hand (also called hand-eye) coordination is the ability to use visual information to control, guide, and direct the hands to accomplish a task, such as drawing or catching a ball. Most hand movements require visual input to be effective. For example, when children are learning to draw, they follow the position of the hand holding the drawing tool visually as they make lines on the paper. As infants explore their world, they develop eye-hand coordination in conjunction with reaching and grasping. A child inserting a puzzle piece into a puzzle tray or a peg into a pegboard is using eye-hand coordination.

Finger Dexterity

Quickly moving your fingertips to tap or press a surface or pick up small objects is called *finger dexterity*. This action is the result of a complex neuromuscular process orchestrated by the brain, nervous system, and muscles of the hand, allowing an abrupt transition from motion (tap) to static force (push). If the transition is not well timed and executed, force will be misdirected and quick precise action like picking up a small bead will be impossible. It takes young children years to develop fine finger muscle coordination and skills such as precision pinching or manipulation (Venkadesan & Valero-Cuevas. 2008).

In-Hand Manipulation

One of the most complex fine motor skills, called *in-hand manipulation,* involves positioning an object within one hand (without using the other hand) for an activity. For example, when you pick up a pen and move it into position with your fingers for writing, you are using in-hand manipulation. Many daily activities involve in-hand manipulation: positioning a crayon, adjusting the paper when cutting with scissors, fastening buttons, tying shoelaces, and using a knife and fork.

In-hand manipulation includes the ability to:

1. pick up objects with the thumb and index finger and then transfer objects into the palm (as you do when you pick up and hold a small object in your hand).
2. transfer objects from the palm to the tips of the thumb and index finger (as you do when you put a coin held in your hand into a piggy bank).
3. rotate fingers to manipulate objects to do tasks (as you do when you remove a jar lid or flip a pencil over to erase).
4. shift objects using fingertips (as you do when you separate two sheets of paper).

Children who have difficulty with in-hand manipulation have difficulty with many everyday activities.

Hand Coordination

In order to clap your hands, eat with a fork and knife, string beads, cut with scissors, rotate the handle of an eggbeater, sew or knit, play an instrument, pour a liquid, tie a shoelace, catch a ball, or even wash your hands, movement in both hands has to be finely coordinated. Coordination between your two hands (called *bimanual* or *bilateral coordination*) seems effortless and automatic, but it is learned and requires a lot of practice. In bimanual coordination, the dominant hand usually serves as the "lead" hand (the one that does the work), while the non-dominant hand serves as the "assist" or guide hand (the one that stabilizes the work). Since hand dominance is not well established for many young children, this may influence the growth of bimanual coordination.

The progression of development in using scissors helps to illustrate how bimanual coordination develops. At 2 years, children must use both hands to open and close scissors. By 3 years, most can hold paper in one hand and snip it with the scissors or cut it into two pieces with the other, but still cannot coordinate both hands in order to cut along a line. By age 4, children typically can move the scissors in a forward direction and guide the paper with the assist hand turning the paper so as to cut along a straight line or along simple curves. By 5 years, most children make smaller, more precise cuts and are able to turn the paper with the guide hand to cut out simple straight-edged shapes. At this age, children hold scissors in a thumbs-up position perpendicular to the floor. By age 6, most children hold scissors in a mature fashion, moving the paper with the assist hand so that the lead hand can cut with some accuracy.

Hand Preference

Hand preference (also known as *handedness* and *hand dominance*) is a fine motor attribute rather than a fine motor skill. Early childhood educators should be attentive to children's hand preference for a number of reasons. Established hand dominance supports efficient and smooth coordination of bimanual activities. Some tasks require different teaching techniques (right-handers write away from their bodies and pull the pencil, whereas left-handers must write toward their bodies and push the pencil) or equipment (scissors, desks). If you know children's hand preferences, you are better able to help them to succeed at fine motor tasks.

The vast majority of people (80% to 90%) are right handed. The remaining 10% to 20% include people who have strong left hand dominance (7% to 10%), those who are ambidextrous (a very small percentage of the population who use either hand for any task), and those who have mixed dominance (Henderson & Pehoski, 2005).

Around 2 years of age, hand preference emerges, although children frequently alternate hands. By age 3, one hand will often lead activities and the other hand assist. Even though some switching will continue, by age 4, a strong preference for a lead and dominant hand is clear. And between 4 and 6 years, hand preference will be consistent and the roles of lead and assist hands will become established. The skill of the dominant hand will exceed that of the non-dominant hand. Today it is not considered appropriate to try to change children's hand preference. Such efforts are largely futile, as true hand dominance appears to be inborn.

FIGURE 5.2 Head Start Child Development and Early Learning Framework: Fine Motor Skills

The control of small muscles for such purposes as using utensils, self-care, building, and exploring.
○ Develops hand strength and dexterity.
○ Develops eye-hand coordination to use everyday tools, such as pitchers for pouring or utensils for eating.
○ Manipulates a range of objects, such as blocks or books.
○ Manipulates writing, drawing, and art tools.

Source: Administration for Children and Families, Head Start Bureau, www.hsnrc.org/cdi/child-outcomes.cfm

Standards for Fine Motor Curriculum

What are the goals of your program for children's fine motor skill development? What state standards apply? There are no national educational organizations devoted to fine motor development (although they are mentioned in passing by organizations devoted to large motor development). Thus there are no national standards for fine motor curriculum. But Head Start and almost all U.S. states have standards for fine motor curriculum. These standards typically lay out the expectation that teachers provide opportunities for development and/or that children develop:

- strength, dexterity, and control
- eye-hand coordination
- ability to write, draw, and paint

Your program's goals may be based on state or Head Start standards, or they may have been developed independently by your staff or a curriculum specialist. However, it is likely that they will include some version of the goals shown in Figure 5.2.

Teaching the Fine Motor Curriculum

Young children need many opportunities to develop fine motor coordination and control. These early years of repetitious small muscle practice are essential for the development of the skill level that enables adults to do things like sewing, writing, drawing, and using a computer. To teach this important aspect of the curriculum you will:

1. **organize the environment** to inspire fine motor play for all children.
2. **design a schedule** that allows children ample time for self-selected fine motor play as well as teacher-planned and -guided fine motor activities.
3. **guide and encourage children** as they play.
4. **plan and implement structured fine motor activities.**

Fine Motor Learning Through Play in a Planned Environment

As you set up a learning environment, you will purposefully and thoughtfully include many opportunities for children to develop fine motor skill and strength. Every program for young children needs to have toys and materials that build

small muscle skills. In a learning center classroom, every area includes fine motor activities. In this chapter we highlight two areas that particularly enhance fine motor development: the indoor *manipulatives* area and the outdoor *woodworking* area.

The Manipulatives Area

The manipulatives area (sometimes called *Toys & Games*) is the center in the classroom that most obviously supports the fine motor curriculum. Manipulative toys contribute to all aspects of fine motor development: eye-hand coordination; finger dexterity; in-hand manipulation; bimanual coordination; and grasp accuracy, strength, and control.

As you set up the manipulatives area, be sure to include four distinct types of manipulative toys:

- building/construction toys
- puzzles/fit-together toys
- collections
- games

If you have space, it is useful to place manipulative toys in two areas: one for construction toys that inspire noisier group play, and another for puzzles, collections, and games that require greater concentration and tend to be used by children either alone or in pairs.

Because manipulative toys have many pieces that are easy to lose or mix up, storage is especially important. An organized and clearly marked manipulatives area with bins or baskets to hold small pieces invites children to play productively. Children can use the materials on tables or on a carpet. Attractive place mats or small carpet pieces can define individual workspaces.

Building and Construction Toys

Using table blocks, Legos, Duplos, Bristle Blocks, Zoobz, log builders, and Tinkertoys strengthens children's coordination and manipulation abilities. All of these toys are open ended and contain many pieces.

The size of pieces and the strength and dexterity required to make them fit together should match the fine motor ability of the children. The youngest preschoolers need construction toys like Bristle Blocks and Duplos that have larger pieces that are easy to put together. Older preschoolers and kindergartners can use smaller construction toys that require more strength and a more delicate touch such as Legos and Zoobz. Primary school age children need greater challenge, and they especially benefit from construction toys that take skill and concentration to connect such as Lincoln Logs, K'nex, and Tinkertoys. If you see a child struggling or giving up, it probably means that the toy is too difficult. If a building toy is misused, this is generally a sign that it is too easy, too hard, or too familiar for the children and a different challenge is needed.

There are many diverse and appealing building toys to choose from. A new set will inspire children to create, play, and develop and practice skills. To ensure enthusiasm and productive play with building and construction toys, it is important to introduce them to children and to exchange or "rotate" one set for another every week or two.

Math manipulatives (e.g., Cuisenaire rods and Unifix cubes) are similar to building toys and build the same fine motor skills. They are often placed in a manipulatives area. In some kindergarten and primary classrooms, math manipulatives have their own center, and in others, they are brought out specifically for a math lesson. We believe that both uses are appropriate.

Puzzles, Beads, and Fit-Together Toys

Closed-ended materials that are designed to be taken apart and put together in one or two ways are classic toys for building fine motor skill. These materials are designed to be used by one child alone. Large wooden beads to be strung on a lace and lacing shapes are classic fine motor toys that fit in this category. Knobbed puzzles, 1- to 2-inch beads, and simpler shaped toys with fewer pieces will be easier for younger or less skilled children to use, whereas ½-inch beads, layered frame puzzles, simple jigsaw puzzles, and more elaborate fit-togethers like the Arcobaleno (a wooden toy from Italy pictured on page 134) will challenge more competent children. Be sure to include a variety of different levels of difficulty (including some that seem a little too easy and some that seem a little too hard) so that every child has an appropriate challenge.

Montessori sensorial materials (e.g., the pink tower, wide stair, and knobless cylinders) are similar to fit-together toys. They build fine motor skills and are sometimes used in manipulatives areas in non-Montessori classrooms. In Montessori classrooms, sensorial materials are allotted their own area.

Collections

Collections of materials such as buttons, shells, seeds, bottle caps and lids, keys, or pebbles provide real-life fine motor challenges as children pick up, sort, and arrange the materials. Safe recycled materials, items that reflect the place where you teach (e.g., shells, rocks, pine cones), or items from the children's families and cultures (e.g., beads, noodles, marbles, or folk toys) can be used to provide activities to develop grasp and eye-hand coordination. Sorting trays (from educational supply catalogues) or egg cartons, ice-cube trays, muffin pans, coin trays, etc. and small tongs and tweezers help children to develop fine motor control.

Games

Manufactured games (such as pegboards, lottos, geoboards, and board games) and those made by the teacher, often called *workjobs,* help children develop fine motor skills. Teacher-made games are particularly loved by children, perhaps because they communicate in a very concrete way that you care about and notice what they like. (See the In Practice box for ideas for simple games you can make.) *Montessori practical life materials* (e.g., dressing frames, pouring, sewing, cutting, spooning, tong and tweezer jobs) are similar to teacher-made games.

The Woodworking Area

A woodworking area is especially valuable for the development of fine motor strength and coordination. Woodworking often appeals to children who shy away from less robust fine motor play. For safety's sake, woodworking requires excellent teacher-child ratios (a teacher must be nearby whenever the center is in use). In some classrooms, limited woodworking tools (hammers and nails) are

Transfer Games	Create a game in which children move small items from one container to another using fingers, tongs, or tweezers. Small wooden beads work especially well with tweezers. Items can be related to an integrated study (e.g., for the Garden Study, transferring seeds from one flowerpot to another). A variation is to transfer water from one container to another using an eyedropper, nasal aspirator, or a syringe.
Sorting Games	Provide an assortment of small, related objects (e.g., buttons, shells) and a sorting tray (a muffin tin, ice-cube tray, or the plastic liner from a box of chocolates). Children sort similar items (e.g., all the four-hole buttons, all the white shells) into the different spaces. Items can be related to an integrated study (e.g., seeds for the Garden Study).
Homemade Puzzles	Create a puzzle just for your class. Use a picture or print (these can be related to an integrated study topic). Two ways to do this: • Tongue depressor puzzles. Glue a picture across a row of wooden tongue depressors. When the glue is dry, slice between the tongue depressors with a sharp knife. Store the puzzle in a clean, smooth-edged can covered with contact paper. • Make two copies of a photograph or art print. Cut one of the copies into pieces (bigger for younger or less experienced children). Laminate both the intact and the cut up pieces.
Clothespin Games	Cover a box or a large coffee can with contact paper. Along the open edge attach pictures (small stickers work well) or symbols that children will recognize (can be related to an integrated study topic; e.g., for a study of Family, a small photo of each child's family). Attach a corresponding symbol or picture to each clothespin. Children pinch the clothespin and attach it to the matching symbol. Variation— use a cardboard circle with pie-like segments and place a picture or symbol in each segment.
Pouring Games	Place different sizes of containers and one or more pitchers in a plastic washtub. Provide something to pour (water, rice, salt, sand). With clear containers, paint lines at varying levels so children can practice pouring up to the line.

available every day and other tools are restricted to days when an extra teacher is present. In others, the woodworking center is made available only on days when there is a volunteer in the classroom to augment the number of teachers available.

Teachers are often uncomfortable with woodworking, and it's important to overcome any concerns you might have. Begin by learning about woodworking—by reading a book (see resources such as Skeen et al., 1984), by taking a class, or by inviting someone who is familiar with woodworking materials into your program to teach you and the children how to use them. Gaining such confidence will enable you to bring a valuable experience to children.

A woodworking area requires a special workbench and proper tools—not pretend, child-sized tools that are usually of poor quality and therefore hazardous (see the In Practice box on page 137). Like any other learning material, children will gain skills and use the materials more safely and productively if they have repeated opportunities to use them.

A sturdy workbench (including vise) and a platform for shorter children

A sawing table that children can kneel on

C Clamps or a small bar clamp

Teacher's safety glasses (not goggles)

Two additional pairs of protective safety glasses (not goggles) for children (attach with an adjustable non-elastic glasses strap to make them fit snugly)

Two lightweight hammers

A regular adult hammer

A hack saw and extra blades

A small cross-cut saw

Two bit braces for drilling and screws, and drill bits, auger bits, and Phillips bits

A good flat-head screwdriver

Two Phillips screwdrivers

A rasp and file

A 25" tape measure

A speed square (to make lines on wood)

Various screws, nails, and glue

Sandpaper

Pencils

Soft untreated wood such as pine or fir (never particle board because of hazardous chemicals)

Fine Motor Materials Throughout the Learning Environment

You are certain to support fine motor development in the manipulatives and woodworking areas. However, the sensory, block, writing, dramatic play, and art areas and the outdoor play environment also include many opportunities for fine motor development. Table 5.2 gives a quick overview of things you can do as you design an environment for fine motor curriculum.

Introducing Fine Motor Equipment

When you bring a new piece of fine motor equipment into the environment, it needs to be introduced. Introductions can be simple. Present the equipment or activity to the children, demonstrate its use, describe any special ways to use it, show where it will be kept, and explain when it will be available. Depending on the characteristics of the new experience and the custom in your program, you may do this in a large or small group or with individuals.

A Word About Tables, Chairs, and Easels

It is important for the development of pencil grasp that worktables and chairs be proportioned to the children. If chairs are too high and the children's heels do not touch the floor, they will be unable to counterbalance themselves as their arm moves across the paper. If the table surface is too high, the upper arm will not be able to control the fingers (Henderson & Pehoski, 2005). Children should be able to sit comfortably in a chair, with feet flat on the floor and trunk supported in an aligned, upright position. The table should be proportioned to the chair so that children's arms can rest comfortably on the tabletop.

Drawing and doing activities on a vertical surface like an easel or chalkboard helps to develop children's arm and hand skills and is considered especially valuable for children who are left handed (Holder, 2003). Easels should be sized so that children can reach the top of the easel. Standing at the easel rather than sitting promotes better fine motor control.

TABLE 5.2   Environment Areas That Support Fine Motor Curriculum

Center/Area/Zone	How It Supports Development	What to Provide	Important Requirements
Sensory Area	Suits a wide range of developmental stages and abilities. Provides opportunities for developing bimanual coordination.	Sensory (sand/water) table Sandbox Tools and materials to scoop and pour—water, sand, etc. Use diverse materials to add challenge (e.g., soapy water, bird seed, aquarium gravel, oatmeal, flour). Add diverse tools appropriate to the materials that require different kinds of fine motor skills (e.g., pitchers, eggbeaters, scoops, turkey basters, waterwheels, measuring cups, sieves, sifters).	To encourage coordinated use of hands, be sure to have eggbeaters, sifters, turkey basters, pitchers, and cups.
Writing Area	All aspects of fine motor development are required for writing, drawing, cutting, folding paper, and creating books.	Tables and chairs, writing implements (pencils, markers, crayons) Cutting and fastening tools (scissors, tape, string, staplers, and hole punches) Things to cut and trace Keyboards: computers, typewriters	Make sure chairs and tables are the right height and children's heels touch the floor so they can counterbalance themselves as their arm moves across the paper.
Unit Block Area	Supports development of eye-hand coordination, control, and hand and wrist strength. Clean-up builds motor strength.	A set of hardwood unit blocks Space for play Shelves marked for storage Props	Unit blocks are fairly heavy. Light plastic, softwood blocks, and table blocks are not effective in building muscle strength. Materials that require delicate touch—table blocks, plastic figures, doll house furniture, small fabric and carpet squares, tiles, stones, tree blocks.
Art Area	Builds all aspects of fine motor development. Doing activities on a vertical surface like an easel or chalkboard helps to develop children's arm and hand skills and is considered especially valuable for children who are left handed.	Work tables and chairs sized to the children Easels Art supplies	Keep chairs away from easels to promote standing.
Dramatic Play Area	As children pretend, they manipulate clothes, tools, and dolls and provide opportunities for grasping and manipulating.	Simple child-sized furniture, dress-up clothes and props Add props/garments that encourage "just-within-reach" skills (geared to children), e.g., big buttons to button, knobs to twist, zippers to zip, keyboards to pretend with, handles to turn, dolls to dress.	Clothes and fasteners should be big enough and simple enough for children to manage independently.

Center/Area/Zone	How It Supports Development	What to Provide	Important Requirements
Natural Elements Zone	As children tend living creatures and play with natural materials, they develop small muscle skill and strength.	Outdoor environment with plants, dirt, trees, grass, and the creatures that inhabit them, garden, bird feeder, pets (see science) Mud and sand in which to dig and water for pouring also support	To make the natural elements zone support fine motor development, it is important to have easily accessed tools—shovels, buckets, scoops, sifters, pots and pans, pitchers, bowls, and cups near at hand.

A Schedule for Fine Motor Curriculum

In addition to adequate materials, sufficient time is needed for children to develop the use of their hands and fingers. The time spent is valuable and children are not "just playing." Children's obvious delight in fine motor activity is a good indicator of their interest and need for frequent and prolonged practice through play. Daily choice times of at least an hour should include access to manipulatives and other materials that support fine motor development.

The "routine" parts of the day are also critical for the development of fine motor skill. These skills have much to do with self-care. As children learn to serve their own food, pour their own beverages, use the water fountain, brush their teeth, wipe the table, put on their shoes, spread out their blankets, and fasten their clothes, they are not only gaining independence but also practicing small muscle skills. The challenge of opening a lunchbox or thermos points out the real-life significance of fine motor development.

Try It Out!

Sit at a child-sized table and write or draw for 15 or 20 minutes. Notice how your neck, hands, and back feel. Try placing a small chair at a big table and writing or drawing again for 15 minutes. How does having a chair and table that is the wrong size for you influence how you write or draw and how you feel about writing or drawing?

Your Role in Teaching Fine Motor Curriculum

You may use observations to plan an activity with thought, materials, time, and well-considered instructional steps. But there is some teaching that cannot be planned. For most fine motor curriculum you will scaffold: You will respond in the moment, with acknowledgement, assistance, or by providing a new challenge.

You can also support children who are experiencing frustration by directing them to experiences that will build skills for more challenging small motor tasks. The child who hasn't yet mastered scissors needs

plenty of experience with dough and clay to build strength, and tools like tongs, which require similar motor action. Some complex fine motor skills must be taught. Skills like cracking an egg, playing cat's cradle, or tying shoes take analysis, demonstration, and lots of practice. When you observe a child struggling to learn these skills, teach by slowly demonstrating while describing what you are doing. Then invite children to do the task themselves while providing assistance like adjusting their position, narrating their activities, handing them the next piece, or giving a simple direction ("Try turning the piece over").

There are many strategies to teach every curriculum area. The art of teaching involves selecting the teaching strategy that is right for the child and for the skill or concept being learned. In fine motor curriculum you can choose from among many different activities (see Table 5.3). However, as you can see, play in a planned environment and scaffolded activities are the most effective for developing fine motor skills. Small-group activities (art, cooking, music, puppet play, and group book-making) also can support fine motor development when children have ample opportunity to cut, knead, pour, stir, paint, glue, saw, crack the eggs, etc. A demonstration does not help children develop fine motor skills. Very few large-group activities are effective for fine motor curriculum. Two notable exceptions, playing musical instruments and fingerplays, lend themselves well to both large-group experience AND fine motor skill development.

Planning Fine Motor Curriculum

Since so much of fine motor curriculum is taught through play and spontaneous interactions in a planned environment, when should you plan fine motor activities for young children? Plan fine motor activities when you want to: teach a specific skill to a particular child or group of children; make sure you are addressing a particular program goal or state standard; or involve fine motor skill development in an integrated curriculum study.

Writing Fine Motor Curriculum Plans

During the first few weeks of school, Matty's teachers observe his growing fine motor abilities. He quickly learns to turn the handles to operate the drinking fountain and the faucet, and he delights in getting drenched in the water. He digs in the sandbox using a shovel in his right hand and pushes the big bulldozer with both hands and manipulates a handle so that it lifts and carries a load of sand. He fingerpaints using his hands and arms—when blue, red, and yellow have turned to muddy brown, he makes circles with his index finger in the paint. The job of light-switcher is his favorite and he flips the light switch somewhat more often than is warranted. Matty has many fine motor skills.

Look at strengths and look at needs. Thinking about what children are able to do well may point to what you need to plan to work on next. Since Matty can turn handles (grasp and strength), push buttons, flip switches, and use his index

TABLE 5.3 Teaching Strategies for Fine Motor Curriculum

Use These Strategies to Help Children Develop:	*Play in a Planned Environment* **Child Directed** (independent/ with other children)	*Scaffolded Interactions* **Child Directed** (teacher–child or child–child)	*Small Group* **Teacher Directed/ Child Inspired** (3–10 children)	*Large Group* **Teacher Directed** (8+ children)
Self-Help Skills	Dramatic Play Sensory Table Sandbox	Dramatic Play Cooking Sandbox Caring for Pets Daily Living Routines (e.g., dressing, toothbrushing)	Dramatic Play Cooking Daily Living Routines (e.g., table setting)	
Strength and Dexterity for Using Tools	Puppet Play Playdough and Clay Sensory Table Block Play Exploring Nature Outdoors	Puppet Play Playdough and Clay Block Play Puzzles Woodworking Gardening	Fingerplays Puppet Play Block Play Gardening	Fingerplays
Eye-Hand Coordination	Puzzles Fit-Together Toys Construction Toys Stringing and Lacing Pattern Toys Sorting Collections Table Games Math Manipulatives Sensory Table Block Play Exploring Nature Outdoors	Puzzles Fit-Together Toys Construction Toys Stringing and Lacing Pattern Toys Sorting Collections Table Games Math Manipulatives Stitchery and Yarn Activities Print-making Rhythm Instruments Block Play Woodworking	Table Games Fingerplays Rhythm Instruments Print-making Block Play Math Manipulatives Stitchery and Yarn Activities	Fingerplays Rhythm Instruments
Graphomotor (writing and drawing) Ability	Book-making Drawing Painting Collage Construction	Book-making Drawing Painting Collage Construction Sand Tray	Book-making Drawing Painting Collage Construction Sand Tray Drawing/ Writing Murals	

finger in isolation (finger dexterity), and he can use both hands together to push (bimanual coordination), you can tell that he has a number of fine motor abilities. Since he has difficulty using spoons and forks, doing up his pants, and carrying heavy blocks, you know he has some needs.

Look at interests. Children use their fine motor abilities doing the things they *like* to do. Matty likes water play; he is interested in big trucks; he has a fascination for mechanical things; and he likes to have an effect—on paint, on the lights, on the faucet. Matty's interests can guide you to plan activities that will make him WANT to practice fine motor skills and build fine motor strength.

Along with Matty, seven other 3-year-olds and ten 4-year-olds share the classroom. Among the other 3-year-olds, William loves airplanes and pretends the shovels in the sandbox are planes. He is beginning to write his name. Lili creates detailed paintings, engages in lots of dramatic play, and loves stories. Ira builds with manipulative toys, loves trikes, and often fights with Matty. Kristi cries a lot, looks at books, and likes to cook. Lani does the hardest puzzles, strings beads, draws pictures of her family, and avoids messy play. Ezra builds with Lego and loves books. Aidan pretends to be a dog all the time—he loves puzzles, water, and manipulatives, and will not use pens, paintbrushes, or crayons at any time.

Look at the group. Although you will observe and plan for individual children, the plans you make will be for activities open to all the children in your class. It may be easy to see that Matty would benefit from an activity filling buckets from the faucet and carting them across the yard to the garden, but would Lani do it? Would it meet Aidan's needs?

To assist you in writing plans for fine motor activities, you may wish to look over the examples of fine motor objectives included in Table 5.4.

TABLE 5.4   Some Typical Objectives for Fine Motor Curriculum

Develop Appropriate to Age	Self-Help Skills	Strength and Dexterity for Using Tools	Eye-Hand Coordination	Graphomotor (writing and drawing) Ability
Younger preschoolers 3- to 4-year-olds *The ability to . . .*	Feed self using a spoon. Drink from a cup with a handle with one hand. Pour from a small pitcher. Unwrap food. Button front/side buttons. Untie and remove shoes. Put on socks and shoes (shoes may be on wrong feet). Put on pants with assistance. Remove pullover garments (T-shirts, etc.).	Use scissors to cut a piece of paper into 2 pieces. Use fork and spoon. Hammer with assistance. Manipulate clay and dough—squeeze, pound, make balls, snakes, and other shapes.	Open and close bottles and jars. Put together 3–6 piece puzzles. Build tower of 4–5 blocks. String 1" diameter beads. Make horizontal rows and vertical stacks of blocks.	Use large crayons, brushes, and pens with ease. Use writing/drawing implement in lead hand and stabilize paper with assist hand. Make lines and circles deliberately in drawing.

TABLE 5.4 Some Typical Objectives for Fine Motor Curriculum (continued)

Develop Appropriate to Age	Self-Help Skills	Strength and Dexterity for Using Tools	Eye-Hand Coordination	Graphomotor (writing and drawing) Ability
	Turn faucets on and off. Wash and dry hands with supervision. Brush teeth (not thoroughly). Wipe nose independently. Use toilet independently and attempt to wipe self.			
Older preschoolers and kindergartners 4- to 5-year-olds *The ability to . . .*	Feed self using a fork or spoon with few spills. Use knife for spreading and cutting soft foods. Serve self food from communal bowl. Pour from a large pitcher or carton. Use napkin. Set table without help. Dress with little assistance. Snap, zip, button and unbutton. Put shoes on correct feet and independently manage Velcro fasteners. Wash and dry hands without supervision. Dispose of paper towels. Thoroughly brush teeth. Use toilet independently.	Use tongs and tweezers to transfer objects. Cut with scissors following a line. Use knife to spread/cut soft food. Use a power grasp on tools (hammer, toothbrush, spoon) independently. Use saw and bit-brace (hand drill) with assistance. Manipulate clay and dough to make tiny 1/8″ balls. Carry sandpails filled with water/sand.	Create bridges, enclosures, and patterns with blocks. Put together 10+ piece puzzles. String small (1/2″ diameter) beads.	Position crayon or pencil appropriately in the hand. Use thin crayons, brushes, and pens with tripod grip. Describe and then deliberately draw representations. Write a few numerals and letters or numeral- and letter-like characters. Print name on paper without lines.
Primary school-age children 6- to 8-year-olds *The ability to . . .*	Cut meat with a knife. Carry a glass of liquid without spilling. Make a sandwich. Dress independently. Tie bows on shoes. Wash hands, brush teeth without reminders.	Turn paper with assist hand to accurately cut shapes using scissors. Sculpt and mold with clay. Use simple woodworking tools (hammer, saw, hand-drill) with supervision and instruction.	Put together 50-piece puzzles. Quickly manipulate/rotate objects in play (e.g., tops, pegs, coins, cards).	Use dynamic tripod grip. Print on line with progressively smaller print, at progressively greater speed. Legibly write upper and lower case manuscript letters and begin to write the cursive alphabet.

FIGURE 5.3   Simple Fine Motor Activity Plan

Water Moving Machines (fine motor focus)

Objectives:	Develop strength in the arches of the hands and increase eye-hand coordination.
Standard:	Domain I (Physical) Standard 4
What you need:	Water table, water aprons, turkey basters, several lengths of clear plastic tubing, waterwheels.
How to teach:	Show basters, tubing, and waterwheels. Ask: "Can you get the water to make the waterwheel go around?" Encourage children to use the baster with the tubing. Demonstrate/instruct if necessary.
How to assess:	Look for children squeezing basters and other objects/materials (dough, scissors), inserting basters and other objects. Document with observations/ photos.

Another part of the art of teaching is to select an activity that can help you meet your goals for children and that will engage many children in your group. When you have a repertoire of appropriate activities, you can choose one that is right for these children from among them. Table 5.4 gives some examples of appropriate activities that you might plan to support fine motor development in young children.

Figure 5.3 shows an example of a plan created for this group of children to build their fine motor skills.

Because Matty's teachers are experienced, the simple plan leaves out many details. It would not be enough to guide a beginning teacher. The detailed version in Figure 5.4 gives you a better idea of what the teachers planned to do.

Fine Motor Curriculum in a Weekly Plan

Children need blocks of time for unstructured motor play that includes fine motor activity. In the example included in Figure 5.5 you will see that there are several large blocks of time each morning during which fine motor activities are provided.

Fine Motor Curriculum in an Integrated Study

As you know, we believe that the best curriculum for young children is integrated around a topic that engages children and adults. This does not mean that every learning activity provided must relate to the integrated study. While the Peacocks in the plan above were enjoying water play with turkey basters, tubing, and waterwheels, they were also learning about Gardens.

For the study of Family included here (see Figure 5.6), only six activities were specifically planned as part of the fine motor curriculum. However, all of the cooking, art, math, and sensory activities, most of the social studies activities, and some language and literacy activities also developed fine motor coordination, strength, and/or graphomotor ability. Activities that were a part of the fine motor curriculum are highlighted on the Family Study sunburst.

FIGURE 5.4 Detailed Fine Motor Activity Plan

Activity: Water Moving Machines   **Fine Motor Curriculum Focus**

Children play with turkey basters, cups, lengths of tubing, and waterwheels at the water table.

WHO It's For: This activity was planned for the *Peacocks* (eight 3-year-olds). Up to four children at a time can comfortably play.

WHY This Activity

Rationale: Most of the *Peacocks* (especially Matty and Aidan) enjoy waterplay. Hand strength and eye-hand coordination are goals for all the children and especially for these two.

Fine Motor Objectives: *By participating in this activity the children will…*

- Develop strength in the arches of their hands by squeezing basters.
- Increase eye-hand coordination while inserting the tips of basters into tubing and directing tubing onto waterwheels.

Other objectives:
Increase sensory awareness, problem solving, and cooperation.

Preschool Content Standard: Domain I (Physical) Standard 4: Develop strength and coordination of small muscles.

Indicators:
- Participate and demonstrate increasing skill in activities that require small muscle strength.
- Show beginning control of tools.

HOW to Prepare   *What you need:*

Water table and water aprons, 4 turkey basters, several lengths of clear plastic tubing, 2 waterwheels

Time: After nap 2–3

Space: Outside at the water table next to the spigot

Set up: Before the children come outside, fill water table and place basters, tubing, and waterwheels in it. Close shelf with other water toys.

HOW to Teach   *Introduction:*

As children come outside, invite them to play at the water table. Show them the basters, tubing, and waterwheels and say something like: "Can you get the water to make the waterwheel go around?" or "I wonder how to get the water through the tubing?"

Teaching steps:

Stay close and watch as the children play. Offer support as needed. Encourage children to insert the tip of the baster into the tubing and squeeze to "blast" water through the tubing. Encourage pairs to work together. Demonstrate/instruct if necessary.

Closure:

As children finish, comment on what they did (e.g., "You made the wheel go round fast. I saw you get the water to go through the tubing.")

HOW to Assess and Document

Objectives	Evidence of Learning Children might …	How to Document This Evidence
Develop strength in the arches of the hands.	Squeezing the baster to make water shoot through the tubing. Squeezing other objects/materials (dough, scissors).	Anecdotal observations and photographs
Increase eye-hand coordination.	Children insert the tips of the basters into tubing. Children direct tubing. Children show increased ability to insert laces into beads.	Anecdotal observations and photographs

EVALUATION (Things to remember for next time)

Shooting the water out of the tubing was extremely engaging. More supervision was required than anticipated. More waterwheels would have been helpful. Most children wanted to play and several children got wet. Lani cried. Bring rain ponchos next time.

FIGURE 5.5 A Week's Plan: Gardens—Week #10

Objectives: To help children learn about the work that is involved in creating and maintaining a garden.

Big Ideas: There are different kinds of gardens for different purposes: to grow food, to enjoy for beauty, and for helping people to learn. People who create and care for gardens are called gardeners. They make sure the plants and animals in the garden have what they need—sun, water, nutrients, shade, soil, space, protection; use special tools and materials to make and care for a garden; make the garden beautiful with plants and decorative objects; and cultivate and harvest plants.

	Monday	Tuesday	Wednesday	Thursday	Friday
Outdoor Activities 9:00–10:00 **Purpose:** *to help children …*	**Smelling and Planting Herbs** Learn about plants that people grow in gardens. Increase sensory awareness.	**Harvesting Lettuce** Appreciate the work required to maintain a garden. Develop connections between gardens and food.	**Cornstarch Goop** Increase sensory awareness. Explore physical properties of the world.	**Planting Ferns and Placing Wonder Stone** Gain aesthetic awareness of plants and gardens. Learn about the different plants grown in gardens.	**Harvesting Basil** Appreciate the work required to maintain a garden. Develop connections between gardens and food.
Small Group 1 Striped Caterpillars 10:00–10:20 **Purpose:** *to help children …*	**Validate Trip Predictions** Compare predictions made before the field trip to what was experienced—the development of inquiry skills.	**In Foster Gardens Book** Build understanding of the similarities and differences between gardens. Develop literacy understanding by authoring a book.	**In Foster Gardens Book** **Garden Bugs Book** Build understanding of the similarities and differences between gardens. Develop literacy understanding by authoring a book.	**Leaf/Flower ID Game** Develop observation skills and knowledge of the different characteristics of leaves and flowers.	**Journals** Develop literacy understanding and the disposition to communicate ideas and feelings in writing.
Small Group 2 Rumpled Peacocks 10:00–10:10 **Purpose:** *to help children …*	**Making New Playdough** Learn how materials change when heated, mixed, or cut up. Develop the ability to use language in a variety of ways.	**Making Cornstarch Goop** Learn how materials change when heated, mixed, or cut up. Use descriptive language.	**Watercolors (outside)** Begin to learn about art elements and techniques.	**Planting Flowers** Appreciate the work required to create a garden and care for it.	**Garden Pretend Play** Develop the ability to symbolize experiences through pretend play relating to gardens.
Indoor Special Activities 10:20–11:30 **Purpose:** *to help children …*	**Examine and Identify Leaves from Foster Gardens** Observe the physical properties of leaves. Learn the characteristics and names of different leaves.	**Leaf Rubbing** Learn about art elements and techniques. Build awareness of the structure and beauty of plants.	**Pen and Paints** Help children create and express themselves through a variety of art experiences.	**Garden Collage** Begin to select different natural materials to represent thoughts or ideas. Gain aesthetic awareness of plants.	**Making Pesto** Develop understanding of the connections between gardens and food. Learn how materials change when heated, mixed, or cut up. Use language in a variety of ways, such as following directions.

FIGURE 5.5 A Week's Plan: Gardens—Week #10 (continued)

	Monday	Tuesday	Wednesday	Thursday	Friday
Lunch Circle Large Group 11:30–11:45	**Garden Finger-plays and Songs**	**Garden Guessing Game**	**Talk About Earth Day/Garden Guessing Game**	***In The Garden* Song**	**Foster Gardens Magic Rocks**
Purpose: *to help children …*	Develop the ability to sing tunefully. Develop awareness of gardens.	Develop vocabulary about plants and gardens.	Develop vocabulary about plants and gardens. Develop an awareness of the natural environment and how it can be protected.	Develop awareness of plants that people grow in gardens. Develop creative expression through music.	Develop creative expression relating to their field trip experiences.

Fine Motor Curriculum for All Children

Fine motor curriculum is a part of every program for young children, and it is an acknowledged and accepted part of programs for preschoolers. However, it is treated somewhat differently in programs that include children with special needs and in programs for primary age children. In programs that include children with disabilities, fine motor curriculum is often included as part of therapy. In the first years of elementary school, fine motor curriculum is rarely addressed unless a child has a problem.

Children with Special Needs

The fine motor curriculum offers joys and challenges to all children. When there are children with special needs in your program, you will need to determine if adaptations should be made to include them in this essential part of your curriculum. As you do so, it is important to make activities for these children as similar as possible to those for other children.

Early childhood educators can support children with disabilities in their struggles for competence and self-sufficiency. All young children, including those with impaired motor control, visual impairments, or limited use of arms and legs need to master fine motor skills. It may take them longer and be a little harder than it is for other children. You may be tempted to protect them from awkwardness and struggle, but it is best not to do too much for them. They need to master skills for themselves,

147

FIGURE 5.6 Study of Families Sunburst

Math
Family Math Game
Family Handprint Game
Family Graph
Family Chores Graph
Family Change Seriation Game
Family Sorting Game
Family Shoe Sequencing Game

Large Motor
Mother May I Game
Making Family Homes
Out of Big Boxes
Family in the Dell Game
Baby Dolls in Strollers
Shopping Carts

Science/Cooking
Cooking Family Favorites
Baking Pumpkin Pie for the Family Potluck

Fine Motor
Family Clothes Pin Workjob
Family Photo Cubby
Decorating
Doll House
Family Block Props
Block Houses
Laundry Folding

Social Studies
All activities in this study are social studies activities.
Mother Child Art Game
Family Birth Stories
Hand Mobiles
Family Photos
Family Quilt
Thanksgiving Dinner Sharing
Family Pictures
Family Tree
Family/Friends Comparison
Family Birthday Calendar
Mapping Family Home and Workplaces

Literacy
Family Birth Stories
Family Photobook
Families Change Stories
Family Names Matching Workjob
Family Letters
Family Adventure Stories
Family Bio Boards
Language Experience
Chart How We Celebrate

Visitors
Family Member Visits (mom and baby, pets, grandparents)
Family Activity Sharing
Cook Family Favorites
Sing Lullabies
Tell Stories
Eat Lunch
Culminating Activity:
Family Potluck

Language
Family Fingerplays
Family Dolls What's Missing?
Families Change Discussion
Family Chores Discussion

Trips
Campus Walks to See Families
Waipahu Cultural Village
Visit to a Family Home

Literature
(see book list)
Carrot Seed Flannelboard
Hush Flannelboard

Music and Creative Movement
Little Red Box
Baby Chicks—Acting Out
Family Lullaby Sharing
Hush Little Baby
We Are Ohana
Under One Sky
House That's Made of Love
Family Puppets
Family in the Dell
Acting Out Family Adventure Stories

Art
Family Mural
Family Pipe Cleaner Sculpture
Family Collage
Family Portraits
Family Quilt Squares
Family Handprints
Family Stick Puppets
Family Picture Frames

Sensory:
Washing Doll Clothes
Baby Doll and Dish Washing
Family Artifacts Feely Box (all cooking activities)

Big ideas

Big idea
There are many different kinds of families with different people in them.

Big idea
Families do things together: have fun and play, work, celebrate.

Big idea
Everyone has a family.

A Study of Families

Big idea
Families take care of each other in different ways: love and support each other, help one another learn and grow.

Big idea
Families change but some things about families stay the same.

Big idea
All families have things that are important to them that they believe in.

and that takes practice. A special education teacher or occupational therapist can help you to make appropriate adaptations for the needs of each child.

Children with physical disabilities will be more self-sufficient if their clothing is adapted to their skills—for example, shirts and skirts fastened with Velcro and zippers with large rings inserted through the tabs so they are easier to manipulate. Some children will be able to balance better while dressing themselves if they do it from a sitting rather than a standing position. Others may be able to function more independently if they are given eating utensils and toothbrushes with extended or thickened handles.

Opportunities for small muscle development can be provided for children with special needs. First, observe the child and consider his or her abilities and then make appropriate adaptations. A child with intellectual disabilities may need more encouragement than other children. A child with visual disabilities needs good lighting conditions and objects in bright colors. Auditory problems will not limit a child from engaging in fine motor activities, but you will need to be certain that the child can understand directions.

Children in the Primary Grades

Most primary grade children know how to print and cut accurately with scissors and knives. Some children of this age will have had experiences with a computer keyboard; others may be skilled as pianists and sculptors.

A classroom filled with tools, materials, games, and activities that develop fine motor skills is essential for these primary school children. Children can be interested in and challenged by mastering the use of a computer, playing a simple tune on a recorder or piano, or learning to weave on a simple loom. Provision of art materials, carpentry tools, and writing and drawing supplies, along with allowing time and space for these activities helps children continue to refine their small muscle abilities.

Handwriting

Handwriting is a complex skill. Although practicing clear handwriting formed a large part of the elementary school curriculum in the past, little actual teaching of handwriting occurs in schools today. Not surprisingly, a disproportionate number of American children have difficulty acquiring handwriting skills (Henderson & Pehoski, 2005).

You may wonder why attention should be paid to handwriting. Don't computers make handwriting unnecessary? Although handwriting is taught less, it is still needed. In fact, computers are often not allowed as a writing tool for children until middle school. Children who are unable to write are often perceived as failures by their teachers and, more importantly, by themselves. Motor patterns used over time become kinesthetic habits, and children who fail to develop these are at a great disadvantage in school. When computers are hailed as the savior of those with poor handwriting, we sometimes forget that both keyboarding and handwriting are graphomotor tasks; and they both require a high degree of fine motor skill.

The implications for early childhood teachers are clear. We must provide fine motor activities that build toward a comfortable and efficient handwriting (and later keyboarding) skill.

A few activities that can do this include:

- drawing/writing with fingers or a stick in a tray of salt or sand
- painting at an easel
- tracing shapes with a pencil
- tearing and pasting paper
- stringing beads
- screwing and unscrewing bottle lids
- transferring solids with tongs, tweezers, and chopsticks
- transferring liquids with a turkey baster and an eyedropper

Final Thoughts

We are tool-using animals, masters of fine motor skills. We must be. To use the tools that we need for work, for learning, for communicating, and for life, we use our amazingly complex hands. It is satisfying and exciting to contribute to children's fine motor development. Whether you are enabling a 2-year-old to control her hands as she experiences the messy thrill of fingerpainting, providing a preschooler with the joyous challenge of putting together a new manipulative toy, or sharing in the triumph of a 6-year-old as he learns to write, you are making an important contribution to their development into individuals who are skilled, able to care for themselves, able to learn, and capable of being independent. It is a wonderful gift.

Learning Outcomes

When you read this chapter, thoughtfully complete activities from the "To Learn More" section, and document this learning as suggested in the "For Your Portfolio" section, you will be making progress in the following *NAEYC Standards for Early Childhood Professional Preparation Programs* (2009):

Standard 1. Promoting Child Development and Learning

Students prepared in early childhood degree programs are grounded in a child development knowledge base. They use their understanding of young children's characteristics and needs and of the multiple interacting influences on children's development and learning to create environments that are healthy, respectful, supportive, and challenging for each child.

The key elements of standard 1 you will have learned about are . . .

1a: Knowing and understanding young children's characteristics and needs

1c: Using developmental knowledge to create healthy, respectful, supportive, and challenging learning environments

Standard 4. Using Developmentally Effective Approaches to Connect with Children and Families

Students prepared in early childhood degree programs understand that teaching and learning with young children is a complex enterprise, and its details vary depending on children's ages, characteristics, and the settings within which teaching and learning occur. They understand and use positive relationships and supportive interactions as the foundation for their work with young children and families. Students know, understand, and use a wide array of developmentally appropriate approaches, instructional strategies, and tools to connect with children and families and positively influence each child's development and learning.

The key elements of standard 4 you will have learned about are . . .

4a: Understanding positive relationships and supportive interactions as the foundation of their work with children

4b: Knowing and understanding effective strategies and tools for early education

4c: Using a broad repertoire of developmentally appropriate teaching/learning approaches

4d: Reflecting on their own practice to promote positive outcomes for each child

Standard 5. Using Content Knowledge to Build Meaningful Curriculum

Students prepared in early childhood degree programs use their knowledge of academic disciplines to design, implement, and evaluate experiences that promote positive development and learning for each and every young child. Students understand the importance of developmental domains and academic (or content) disciplines in an early childhood curriculum. They know the essential concepts, inquiry tools, and structure of content areas, including academic subjects, and can identify resources to deepen their understanding. Students use their own knowledge and other resources to design, implement, and evaluate meaningful, challenging curricula that promote comprehensive developmental and learning outcomes for every young child.

The key elements of standard 5 you will have learned about are . . .

5a: Understanding content knowledge and resources in academic disciplines

5b: Knowing and using the central concepts, inquiry tools, and structures of content areas or academic disciplines

5c: Using their own knowledge, appropriate early learning standards, and other resources to design, implement, and evaluate meaningful, challenging curricula for each child.

To Learn More

Observe a Program: For a morning, observe a program and see how the staff structures the environment and program to support children's fine motor development. Notice both the play opportunities and the planned group activities. Look at the plans and see how the planning reflects what you observed. Interview a teacher to learn what he or she thinks about fine motor curriculum.

Observe a Child: For a morning, observe a child in a classroom, with a focus on the child's fine motor activity. Notice how the child engages with the planned activities and how he or she constructs his or her own opportunities for learning. Notice the extent to which the child's activity and the planned curriculum seem to match. Observe to see how staff support the child's fine motor learning.

Observe a Master Teacher: Spend a morning with an early childhood educator who is experienced and has a curriculum leadership role in a program. (This teacher may be called the "lead," "head," or "mentor" teacher.) Then interview the educator about how he or she plans for and provides fine motor curriculum.

Observe a Fine Motor Activity: Observe a teacher leading a planned fine motor activity. Interview the teacher to find out the objectives for the activity. Reflect on any differences between what you saw and the focus of the plan.

Compare Two Programs: Observe fine motor experiences in two early childhood programs. Compare the ways that the two address fine motor curriculum—their similarities and differences. Reflect on which program seems to best support children's learning and why. What implications does this comparison have for your future work with young children?

Compare Two Ages: Observe two classrooms, one preschool and one for primary school children. Report on how each supports children's fine motor learning. Talk to the staff about how they make their curriculum choices. Notice how development influences curriculum choices.

Explore Resources: Read one of the books or one of the online resources from the bibliography and write a review of it for your classmates.

For Your Portfolio

Design a Fine Motor Environment: Design and draw a floor plan for a classroom and play yard that would promote children's fine motor learning. Share your plan with an early childhood educator, discussing what you included and why. Ask for and consider the educator's feedback and suggestions. Set up a manipulatives center in a real classroom utilizing as many of your ideas as possible, and let children use it. For your portfolio, include the floor plan, photographs or video of children using the area, and a reflection on what you learned by doing this project.

Plan and Implement a Fine Motor Activity: Observe a group of children for a morning, focusing on their fine motor interest and skill. Based on what you observed write and implement a fine motor activity. Collect evidence of children's responses in the form of anecdotal observations, photographs, or video recordings. Reflect on how children responded and what they appear to have learned. What worked? What might you do differently next time? How might you expand on this experience for children? For your portfolio, include the plan, a

photograph, and a reflection on what you learned about yourself, children, planning, and teaching.

Create a Fine Motor Learning Material: Design and make a fine motor learning material to support the development of a particular child or group of children. Introduce it to the child or children and observe how it is used. Reflect on how the children responded and how you felt about what you did. What worked? What might you do differently next time? How might you expand on this experience for children? For your portfolio, include a photograph of a child using the material and a reflection on what you learned about yourself, children, learning materials, and teaching.

Bibliography

Berger, K. S. (2009). *The developing person through childhood and adolescence* (8th ed.). New York, NY: Worth.

Berk, L. E. (2008). *Infants and children: Prenatal through middle childhood* (6th ed.). Boston, MA: Allyn and Bacon.

Black, J., Puckett, M., Wittmer, D. S., & Petersen, S. H. (2008). *The young child: Development from prebirth through age eight* (5th ed.). Upper Saddle River, NJ: Pearson.

Bredekamp, S., & Rosegrant, T. (1995). *Reaching potentials: Transforming early childhood curriculum and assessment* (Vol. 2). Washington, DC: NAEYC.

Bullard, J. (2010). *Creating environments for learning: Birth to age eight.* Englewood Cliffs, NJ: Prentice Hall.

Cratty, B. J. (1986). *Perceptual and motor development in infants and children* (3rd ed.). Englewood Cliffs, NJ: Prentice-Hall.

Department of Occupational Therapy, Melbourne Australia, Royal Children's Hospital. (2005). *Occupational therapy—Kids health information: In-hand manipulation.* www.rch.org.au/emplibrary/ot/InfoSheet_D

Edwards, S. J., Buckland, D. J., & McCoy-Powlen, J. D. (2002). *Developmental and functional hand grasps.* Thorofare, NJ: Slack.

Epstein, A. S. (2007). *The intentional teacher.* Washington, DC: NAEYC.

Feeney, S., Moravcik, E., & Nolte, S. (2009). *Who am I in the lives of children?* (8th ed.). Upper Saddle River, NJ: Pearson.

Gabbard, C. P. (2004). *Lifelong motor development* (4th ed.). San Francisco, CA: Benjamin Cummings/ Pearson.

Head Start Resource Center. (2010). *The Head Start child development and early learning framework: Promoting positive outcomes in early childhood programs serving children 3–5 years old.* Washington DC: Office of Head Start, Administration for Children and Families, U.S. Department of Health and Human Services.

Henderson, A., & Pehoski, C. (Eds.). (2005). *Hand function in the child: Foundations for remediation* (2nd ed.). St. Louis, MO: Mosby.

Hill, D. M. (1977). *Mud, sand, and water.* Washington, DC: NAEYC.

Holder, M. K. (2003). Teaching left-handers how to write. *Handedness Research Institute papers.* www .handedness.org/action/leftwrite.html

Kostelnik, M. J., Soderman, A. K., & Whiren, A. P. (2010). *Developmentally appropriate curriculum* (5th ed.). Upper Saddle River, NJ: Pearson.

National Association for the Education of Young Children. (2009). NAEYC *standards for early childhood professional preparation programs.* www.naeyc.org/ files/naeyc/file/positions/ProfPrepStandards09.pdf

Raver, S. A. (2009). *Early childhood special education— 0 to 8 Years: Strategies for positive outcomes.* Upper Saddle River, NJ: Pearson.

Skeen, P. G., Payne, A., et al. (1984). *Woodworking for young children.* Washington, DC. NAEYC.

Skill Builders Pediatric Occupational Therapy. (2008). *Fine motor development 0 to 6 years.* www .skillbuildersonline.com/

Venkadesan, M., & Valero-Cuevas, F. J. (2008, February 26). Neural control of motion-to-force transitions with the fingertip. *The Journal of Neuroscience, 28*(6), 1366–1373. www.jneurosci.org/cgi/reprint/28/6/1366

West, J., Denton, K. L., & Germino-Hausken, E. (2000). *America's kindergartners.* Washington DC: National Center for Education Statistics.

MyEducationLab

Go to Topics 2: Child Development and Learning, 6: Environments, and 9: Content Areas/Lessons and Activities in the MyEducationLab (www.myeducationlab.com) for *Meaningful Curriculam for Young Children*, where you can:

- Find learning outcomes for Child Development and Learning, Environments, and Content Areas/Lessons and Activities along with the national standards that connect to these outcomes.
- Complete Assignments and Activities that can help you more deeply understand the chapter content.
- Apply and practice your understanding of the core teaching skills identified in the chapter with the Building Teaching Skills and Dispositions learning units.
- Listen to experts from the field in Professional Perspectives.

- Examine challenging situations and cases presented in the IRIS Center Resources.
- Check your comprehension on the content covered in the chapter with the Study Plan. Here you will be able to take a chapter quiz, receive feedback on your answers, and then access Review, Practice, and Enrichment activities to enhance your understanding of chapter content.

Go to the Course Resources section in MyEducationLab, where you can:

- Use the Online Lesson Plan Builder to practice lesson planning and integrating national and state standards into your planning.

The senses are a kind of reason. Taste, touch and smell, hearing and seeing, are not merely a means to sensation, enjoyable or otherwise, but they are also a means to knowledge— and are, indeed, your only actual means to knowledge.

ST. THOMAS AQUINAS

chapter six

SENSORY DEVELOPMENT CURRICULUM

Sensing and Perceiving

At every moment of your life, you are bathed in sensory input.
Sensations of all kinds barrage you. Yet from amongst all of
these sensations—sound, sight, temperature, pressure, aromas,
tastes, awareness of position—you select and attend to what
is important, respond to it, enjoy it or avoid it, and gain information and skill from it. How did you learn to do this? The
way that people perceive and then act on sensory information
(both external and internal) is sometimes called *information
processing.*

   Our goal in this chapter is to help you to understand and
value the educational purpose of young children's sensory exploration so that you will intentionally provide appropriate materials and curriculum to support it. We want you to develop a
repertoire of engaging sensory development strategies to use in
your classroom.

Reflect on sensory experiences you enjoy . . .

Think of a sensory ex-
perience that you especially enjoy
(a hot bath, a walk in the woods,
the feel of sand on your bare feet,
putting up a Christmas tree). What
do you feel or think of as you recall
this experience? What might be
some implications of this memory
for your work with young children?

Why Sensory Development Curriculum?

Children are not born with the ability to fully discriminate sensations, but must
learn to distinguish them. Being able to receive and interpret sensory information
is critical for motor responses (which is why sensory curriculum is most often
placed in the physical development domain), but it is also critical for all kinds
of learning.

All of us learn through our senses, so it is essential to include sensory development in the curriculum. **If a child's ability to receive and use sensory input is impeded, normal development may be delayed.** All good early childhood programs include a strong sensory component. It is the core of the curriculum in programs for infants and toddlers, an integral part of the total curriculum in programs for preschoolers and kindergartners, and a useful component of much curriculum in programs for primary age children.

If children are to gather and use the information that is available to them in the world, they need opportunities to use each of their senses fully. But understanding this can be difficult for adults. By the time children come to your early childhood program, they may have already been taught to avoid some of these sensory avenues to learning. They have been given messages like: "Don't taste, it's dirty." "Don't touch, it's dangerous." "Don't touch, you may break it." So a critical teaching task in the sensory curriculum is to clearly articulate to families, administrators, and other staff members the rationale for the sensory components of your daily program.

The senses are not only the way we learn. **Senses are the source of the appreciation and pleasure we take in the world**. The obvious joy a child shows when rolling down a hill, playing with water, smelling a rose, or rubbing his or her fingers along a soft piece of velvet are observable evidence of the importance of sensory experience.

Understanding Sensory Development

In the sensorimotor period (from birth to 2 years), the senses are the child's primary mode for gathering information and learning. Infants and toddlers learn by experiencing many things—by touching, tasting, and exploring. Young preschoolers are in the transitional stage between the sensorimotor and preoperational modes of learning.

Two related processes are needed for receiving and organizing sensory data. The first is *sensation,* that is, stimulation of the sensory receptors—eyes, ears, skin, etc. The second is *perception,* the process of attending to, discriminating, and interpreting sensation based on past experiences. The brain then *integrates* the information that comes from the senses and uses it in a wide array of physical and cognitive tasks.

The phrase *sensory curriculum* may bring to your mind images of a child playing with fingerpaints or pouring water—activities that involve the sense of touch. But sensory curriculum entails much more than this because *all* of the senses are important in learning about the world. And understanding all of the senses is important for you as a teacher, too.

Visual Perception

The sensory mode we most commonly associate with learning is *sight*. Human beings are highly dependent on vision for gathering information about the world. As adults, we tend to rely on visual information even when other sensory input is available.

From infancy, we use visual information to make judgments. In the past it was thought that newborns were unable to process visual information. Today we know that the visual system of the newborn is quite well developed and the ability to make visual discriminations begins during the first days of life.

Newborns are able to see a nearby object and respond to light (Gabbard, 2004). *Binocular vision* (the ability to use both eyes together to see an object) appears at about 2 months of age.

Although the structures needed to make visual discriminations are in place from birth, they are immature. The neural pathways are not yet developed. They require time, experience, and nurture (good nutrition and care) to mature. Compared to those of adults, infants' eyes are shorter and their corneas are less regular during the first year. So most infants are temporarily farsighted and less able to focus. Because the muscles controlling the eye are not yet strong, it is hard for infants to adjust their focus.

Visual acuity, clearness of vision and the ability to detect details, develops as children mature. *Static visual acuity,* the ability to see detail in stationary objects, develops before *dynamic visual acuity,* the ability to see detail in moving objects (Gabbard, 2004). Dynamic acuity gradually increases during early childhood with a noticeable improvement between 5 and 7 years.

There are other aspects of vision that develop during the early childhood years. *Tracking,* the ability to visually follow moving objects, is evident by 2 months, although it does not reach maturity until puberty. *Perceptual constancy,* the ability to recognize an object when viewed from different angles (e.g., front/back/side), is developed by 4 or 5 months of age. *Depth perception,* the ability to judge how far away an object is from the self, is absent at birth, but is quite well developed by 6 months of age and continues to be refined during the early childhood years. *Spatial orientation,* the ability to recognize an object's orientation in three dimensions, begins to be developed during the preschool years, but is not fully developed until about 8 years of age. The typical reversals that occur in young children's letter formation and identification is related to their immature spatial orientation ability. *Figure-ground perception,* the ability to distinguish an object from its background, develops between 4 and 8 years of age. This ability requires concentration and attention. *Peripheral vision,* the amount of the environment you can see without moving your eyes, does not fully mature until age 5. *Visual motor coordination,* the ability to coordinate visual abilities with body movements, emerges during the first 6 months of life and continues to mature throughout the early childhood years.

Vision, like other senses, requires opportunities for practice. Children develop visual discrimination as they engage in activities that are regularly found in early childhood settings—putting together puzzles, sorting buttons, looking at books, and constructing with blocks.

Auditory Perception

The auditory sense, *hearing,* means to detect, discriminate, and interpret sounds. Hearing begins before a child is born. An interesting recent study has shown that at birth, an infant's cries have the accent or "melody" of the language spoken by their mothers (Mampe et al., 2009). They acquired their "accent" because they have heard it for many months in the womb.

The basic structures needed for hearing are present at birth. However, there are several auditory perception skills that young children must acquire. *Auditory localization,* the ability to locate where sound is coming from, is present in unrefined form at birth (newborns turn their eyes toward a close sound). Within a year,

children begin to localize distant sounds, and by the age of 3 they can effectively determine the direction from which sound is coming. *Auditory discrimination,* the ability to tell the difference between sounds, is also present in crude form at birth. Infants respond differentially to low-pitched and high-pitched sounds; not surprisingly, low pitches are calming. The ability to discriminate sounds grows throughout childhood, and there is a significant difference between the discrimination abilities of a 3-year-old and an 8-year-old. This refinement continues into adolescence. *Auditory figure-ground perception,* the ability to separate irrelevant noises from the primary listening task, has not been as well studied, but is another ability that young children are working on acquiring. Learning to screen the auditory environment—to exclude irrelevant sounds and to attend to what is meaningful—is an important part of language development. In a typical noisy early childhood program, it is easy to become insensitive to subtleties of sound. Sensory curriculum can help children learn to attend to and differentiate among sounds in music, language, and the natural world around them.

Kinesthetic Perception

The *kinesthetic* sense (sometimes called *proprioception*) is awareness of movement and body position. Unlike the other senses, which receive input from outside the body, the kinesthetic sense receives perception from inside the body. Children have kinesthetic experiences when they engage in movements like swinging and rocking and when they are touched and held. To remain upright and to make judgments on how to move, we need to have the ability to discriminate and control our bodies using the kinesthetic sense.

The kinesthetic sense receives input from several different receptors, called the *somatosensory* system. Somatosensory receptors are located in the skin, joints, muscles, and in the inner ear. Sensory input from all are put together in the brain to create awareness of movement and body position.

There are two aspects of kinesthetic perception—kinesthetic *discrimination* (the ability to detect differences or match qualities like weight, force, distance, speed) and kinesthetic *memory* (the ability to reproduce or recognize kinesthetic qualities). These abilities are being developed during the early childhood years, with rapid growth occurring between ages 5 and 8. By age 8, children have acquired kinesthetic discrimination ability similar to that of adults. Kinesthetic memory skill does not reach adult levels until after age 12.

There are several different aspects to kinesthetic discrimination and memory. *Body awareness* is the knowledge of body parts (and the ability to name them), their location and relation to one another, and their capabilities and limitations. Body awareness begins in infancy, before language develops (e.g., "Show me your tummy"). By age 5 or 6, children are aware of and can name all major body parts and by age 7, they are able to name minor parts (e.g., ring finger, heel).

Spatial awareness in the kinesthetic sense refers to the ability to identify one's own location in space and in relation to objects. *Directional awareness* is the conscious understanding of two sides of the body (called *laterality*) and the location of the body with regard to other objects (called *directionality*—e.g., in front, behind, on top).

Vestibular awareness is the ability to establish and maintain balance. Balance is divided into three parts: *postural balance* (the ability to remain erect while sitting or standing), *static balance* (the ability to maintain a desired position without moving), and *dynamic balance* (the ability to maintain balance during a locomotor activity like walking or running).

Tactile Perception

The sense of touch, or *tactile* sense, is the ability to detect and interpret sensation through the skin. By its all-encompassing nature, the skin makes touch a dominant aspect of our lives and a primary mode of learning for young children. We get information about the world from touching things. The tactile sense allows us to make decisions about our comfort and safety.

Cutaneous (skin) receptors perceive touch, temperature, pressure, vibration, and pain. *Tactile localization* (the ability to tell where a tactile sensation occurs on the body) and *tactile discrimination* (the ability to differentiate tactile stimulation) are two abilities that young children acquire.

Infants respond to touch, and touch elicits many reflexes (e.g., grasping, rooting, and the Babinski response). Newborns respond to even mild tactile stimulation. They are most sensitive when touched on their lips, eyelashes, and the soles of their feet.

Young children investigate the world by touching it. Learning about the world through tactile interaction precedes learning about the world visually. By age 4, visual identification of objects is more accurate than tactile identification (Gabbard, 2004). However, skill in tactile localization and discrimination continue to develop. By age 5, the ability to localize and discriminate tactile sensations is well established. By age 8, children are able to make such fine distinctions that they can recreate a pattern that they have felt drawn on their skin. Curriculum in early childhood programs can help children learn to identify and discriminate between tactile sensations so they can make judgments about the world based on properties such as texture, temperature, and pressure.

Olfactory Perception

We make many decisions based on our sense of smell—the *olfactory* sense. We smell bread baking and decide to eat; we smell a rose and bask in the lovely sensation; we smell a dirty diaper and know it is time to change it. Unpleasant aromas give us warnings. Pleasant ones help us recognize people, food, places, and objects we like.

The sense of smell is generated by specialized sensory cells in the nasal cavity. These cells detect very low concentrations of volatile chemicals called *odorants*. Odors are complex. Even easy-to-distinguish smells like the scent of a lemon are composed of many different odorants.

Our ability to discriminate smell is developed during childhood; however, even newborns are highly sensitive to some smells and are able locate their mothers' breast by smell. Very young children have limited olfactory experience and may not be able to make clear judgments based on smells. This is one of the reasons they sometimes drink poisonous substances like ammonia. Preschoolers make many choices based on the smell of things and often reject experiences because of an odor that is unfamiliar or that they judge unpleasant. By the age of 3, children have essentially the same olfactory likes and dislikes as adults (Fox, 2009).

Gustatory Perception

The sense of *taste*, sometimes called *gustation*, is thought of as a "minor" sense, along with smell. Taste is a concrete sense—it is a response to physical contact between taste receptors and soluble molecules, called *tastants*. Reflexes such as sucking, licking, and gagging are elicited by taste.

Taste is often viewed as uninteresting and simple because it provides information about only a few stimulus qualities: sweet, salty, sour, bitter, and *umami* or savory. However, the sense of taste, combined with smell, provides a critical guide to the edibility of food (poisonous or indigestible plants are bitter; fruit is sweet; and salt is appealing). It is interesting to consider the evolutionary advantages that are involved in the ability to perceive taste qualities.

Carbohydrates, an important energy source, are naturally *sweet,* and the taste they elicit is innately pleasant. Infants respond to the taste of sugar with vigorous sucking. Humans and all animals require *salt* to live, because sodium is essential to most physiological processes. Today we eat too much salt, but throughout history, scarcity of salt was a survival issue. Although human newborns do not favor salt the way they do sugar, a preference for salt emerges around 4 to 6 months of age. *Sour* taste is elicited by acids, which can be corrosive. Strong sour tastes, which are associated with high acidity, are almost universally rejected. Rejection of sour taste is normal for most young children. However a few go through a phase when they prefer very sour tastes. *Bitterness* is an innately aversive sensation. It causes babies (and sometimes adults) to gape, thrust out their tongues, and spit up the bitter item. Many toxic substances are bitter. Yet over time, bitter substances like coffee and dark chocolate can come to be enjoyed. *Umami,* also called *savoriness* or *meatiness,* is a newly identified basic taste. Umami is the hearty taste found in meats and other foods (cheese, mushrooms, tomatoes) that have an amino acid called *glutamine,* a protein. Human beings need proteins such as glutamine to grow and repair tissues, so it makes sense that we have a taste receptor for umami.

What Is Sensory Curriculum in Early Childhood?

You may be relieved to know that you do not need to teach young children to identify umami or to understand their somatosensory system. Instead, your task in the sensory development curriculum is to help children become more attuned to all of their senses so they can use them for observing, appreciating, and learning.

The play activities that abound in good early childhood classrooms offer many opportunities for sensory development—taking in information through the senses. Children are developing their senses as they paint; manipulate clay and dough; play in sand, water, and mud; feel the shape, weight, and texture of blocks; observe fish in the aquarium; feel the rabbit's fur and its heart beating; listen to stories; move to music; sort objects by shape, color, and size; and cook, taste, and discuss what they have made. To support the development of the senses, you will provide experiences that use and develop vision, hearing, touch, smell, taste, and the kinesthetic sense. However, it is important to realize that senses are integrated, not isolated.

The "Elephant Groovers" (a group of 3-year-olds) are involved in making banana pancakes. Sheyden touches the flour and salt as he pours it in. Torie smells the banana as she peels it. Emily experiences resistance when she stirs the batter. Keila comments on the bubbles she sees forming as air is beaten in. Their teacher, Jackie, says, "Listen to the sizzle as batter is poured in the pan." And all of the Elephant Groovers eat the finished product with gusto, commenting on its warmth and delicious taste.

Which sense was explored in this activity? Children involved in making pancakes touch and compare the flour and salt, smell the banana as it is mashed, experience resistance when the thick batter is stirred, see the bubbles that form as air is beaten in, hear the sizzle as batter is poured in the pan, and taste the finished product. To separate these sensations would be difficult and unnecessary: Children learn from the entire sensory experience.

Standards for Sensory Development Curriculum

There are no national organizations devoted to sensory development and no national standards for sensory curriculum for children in the primary school years. However, almost all state and Head Start standards address sensory development curriculum. Some place sensory standards in physical development. Others place sensory learning in science curriculum in the cognitive domain. Both placements have validity. When placed in the physical domain, sensory standards usually lay out the expectation that teachers provide opportunities for:

- increased sensory awareness
- experience and exploration with a variety of sensory materials and activities
- increased understanding of the use of eyes, ears, fingers, nose, and mouth, and how the senses work together

When placed in the cognitive domain, sensory standards usually lay out the expectation that teachers provide opportunities for children to:

- use senses to gather information, explore the environment, investigate materials and natural phenomena, and observe processes and relationships

Your program's goals for sensory curriculum may be based on your state standards, or they may have been developed independently by your staff or an education specialist. However, it is likely that they will include some version of the above standards (see Figure 6.1).

FIGURE 6.1   Head Start Child Development and Early Learning Framework Related to Sensory Curriculum

Scientific Skills and Method
- Uses senses and tools, including technology, to gather information, investigate materials, and observe processes and relationships.
- Observes and discusses common properties, differences, and comparisons among objects.

Source: Administration for Children and Families, Head Start Bureau, www.hsnrc.org/cdi/child-outcomes.cfm

Teaching Sensory Development Curriculum

Like the other physical development curriculum areas, sensory exploration is natural for most typically developing children and therefore is easy to overlook. Recognize that you have a vital role to play in supporting children's sensory development. To teach this important area of the curriculum you will:

1. **organize the environment** to inspire sensory exploration.
2. **design a schedule** that allows children ample time for self-selected sensory play and includes time for planned sensory exploration.
3. **guide and encourage children to notice sensation** as they play.
4. **plan and implement guided sensory activities.**

Sensory Learning Through Play in a Planned Environment

A well-equipped preschool or kindergarten class can be a wonderful laboratory for sensory experience. Because you recognize the importance of sensory experiences, one of the things you will do in designing your learning environment is to make sure that it supports development of the senses. What kind of environment does this? First of all, it must be a space that can be used without fear of mess. Obviously, it must have lots to explore with the senses. Fortunately, this is easy to insure. Most early childhood equipment and materials—blocks, manipulative toys, puzzles, books, art materials, dramatic play props, balls, trikes—support sensory exploration. They are supposed to be touched, and they feel good to hold. Often they have beautiful and interesting designs to look at. Many make interesting sounds. Large equipment that is climbed or ridden on stimulates the kinesthetic sense. And although they are rarely designed to be smelled and tasted, it is safe to do so. While almost all classroom areas contribute to development of the senses, two areas in particular are central to the sensory curriculum.

The Sensory Center

If you have space in your classroom, you can have a dedicated center for sensory play. When space is limited, teachers usually provide sensory play experiences in the art or discovery (science) areas, or outdoors.

The heart of a sensory center is a *sensory table,* often called a *water* or *sand table,* although it can hold much more (see the In Practice Box). Since play with these materials can be messy, the center needs space near a sink or on a porch with an easy-to-clean floor. Sensory tables are designed to hold materials that provide tactile experiences. If you do not have one, there are many workable alternatives: plastic dishpans or baby baths on a low table, children's wading pools, plastic or galvanized tubs (available from the hardware or garden supply store). Recycled feed troughs also work well. Along with the sensory table you will need props (bowls, cups, scoops, spoons, buckets, etc.), aprons, and plastic tablecloths or shower curtains to protect clothing and the floor. A place to hang smocks and a dedicated, labeled shelf for storage will also be needed.

To keep young children healthy when playing with water in a sensory table, special precautions need to be taken. Water should be emptied after each group is done playing, and the table and toys should be sanitized. Children with open cuts or sores should not participate in group water play (an individual tub makes a good alternative). Have children wash their hands before and after play in the sensory table.

Salt and flour dough, potter's clay, or other kinds of malleable materials (e.g., plasticene) are important sensory materials. A sturdy table and chairs, along

IN PRACTICE: Ideas for Materials to Use in a Sensory Table

Wet Natural Materials	Props	Dry Natural Materials	Props
Water • Colored water (use food color or easel paint) • Scented water • Warm water • Soapy water • Saltwater Ice • Crushed, cubes, or blocks • Snow Mud, wet sand mixtures • Goop (cornstarch and water) • Flour and water • Flubber (white glue, borax, and water)	• Ladles • Pitchers • Tubing—clear, flexible, and hard PVC • Eyedroppers and basters • Cups • Recycled plastic bottles and containers • Measuring spoons and cups • Hand-operated pumps (found in hand lotion) • Squeeze bottles • Waterwheels • Plastic vehicles, animals, and people • Small objects that float (corks, Styrofoam, ping pong balls) • Eggbeaters and whisks • Tongs • Washcloths and sponges	Sand Dirt Salt Rocks • Aquarium gravel • Pea gravel • Cinder chips Plant products • Sawdust • Cedar chips (animal bedding) • Christmas tree needles • Dried used coffee grounds • Bird seed • Flour/cornmeal • Rice • Oatmeal • Dry beans, peas, popcorn, etc. • Bulk spices/herbs discarded because past "pull" date **Manufactured Materials** • Styrofoam "peanuts" • Shredded paper or paper punch confetti • Fabric or yarn scraps • Buttons, beads, bottle caps Mixture: • "Supersand" (coffee grounds, salt, & cornmeal)	• Ladles • Pitchers • Tubing • Cups • Recycled plastic bottles and containers • Measuring spoons and cups • Plastic animals and people • Stones • Scoops • Sieves • Sifters • Muffin tins • Sticks • Wood pieces • Small sand rakes and combs • Sand wheels • Egg carton

with storage containers, aprons, mats, and tools, will be needed for play with dough or clay.

Another piece of sensory equipment that you may wish to add is a light table, which has a translucent surface with fluorescent light bulbs recessed underneath. The lighted surface provides space for exploring colored transparent materials, building with translucent manipulative toys, and investigating natural materials that are permeable to light. A light table can also be used for watercolor painting, tissue paper collage, and other art activities.

In a large, dedicated sensory area, you can provide games and materials designed for young children to help them to focus on sensory variables. Sound cylinders, color matching games, texture boards, and feely boxes are sensory materials found in many classrooms. You can also create games to develop sensory awareness.

The use of foodstuffs in the sensory table is controversial. Some educators view it as safe, effective, and appealing to children. Others see it as wasteful and disrespectful of families in financial need and those who view food as sacred. For this reason, it is prohibited in Head Start programs. Your choice about whether to use food in this way will be influenced by your own beliefs as well as the dictates of your program and state regulations.

Try It Out!

Play with a sensory material (sand, water, or dough) with a young child. Notice how s/he plays with it. As you play, talk about the sensory aspects of the experience. What can you conclude about the value of this play to the child?

The Natural Elements Zone

The outside learning environment is not simply a space for young children to release pent-up physical energy. It is also a place to explore the natural world both physically and intellectually. The playground zone that best supports sensory exploration is the *natural elements zone.*

The natural elements zone needs plants, dirt, trees, grass, and the creatures that inhabit them. It is a good place to plant a garden, hang a bird feeder, or house a pet. A sandbox, a hill, and a water feature like a pond or fountain might also be placed in the natural elements zone. If your outside play area is a rooftop or parking lot, include natural sensory experiences by adding potted plants, garden boxes, pets, and sand tables (to fill with sand, water, or dirt).

Montessori Sensorial Materials

Some of the materials used in preschools for sensory development were originally designed by Maria Montessori. They are called *sensorial materials* by Montessorians (teachers who are trained in Montessori methods). Montessori's step-by-step, purposeful way of using sensorial materials suggests ways for all early childhood teachers to teach the sensory curriculum.

Montessori identified eight different senses: Visual, Tactile, Baric (pressure or weight), Thermic (temperature), Auditory, Olfactory, Gustatory, and Stereognostic (recognition of three-dimensional objects based on touch). Montessori sensorial materials typically vary in one sensorial dimension. For example, if touch were the focus, a group of fabric pieces all the same color but with different textures might be used. Montessori teachers demonstrate each sensorial material individually to a child to help him/her to focus on the specific sense. The child is then given a closed-ended task that is largely one of organization based on the sensory variable.

The sensorial materials (like all Montessori equipment) are finely crafted and maintained. There are many of them, but we will describe just a few here to give you a snapshot of a particular way of providing sensory curriculum. *Visual materials* like *cylinder blocks* vary in one easy-to-see dimension. Cylinder blocks vary in diameter, circumference, or height. The *pink tower,* ten pink wooden cubes ranging from 1 cm to 10 cm, vary in overall size. The *brown stair,* ten brown rectangular blocks, differ in height. The *color tablets* are sets of colors that range from sharply contrasted pairs of primary colors to 7 shades of 9 colors for children to arrange by gradations in shade and hue. *Tactile materials* are distinguished with the fingers. *Touch boards* and *fabrics* have varying roughness. There are fewer materials for developing awareness of other senses. *Baric tablets* are pieces of wood matched by weight. *Thermic bottles* are pairs of metal containers containing water at various temperatures. Sound cylinders are to be matched or arranged from loud to very soft. *Bells* with different notes are to be contrasted, matched, and arranged from high to low. *Smelling jars* are opaque jars that each contain a ball of cotton moistened with substances of different odors to be matched. *Tasting bottles* contain four tastes to be compared and matched: salt and water, sugar and water, tonic water (bitter), and lemon and water. And for the *Stereognostic sense,* a variety of feely bag and blindfolded sorting tasks are used.

Sensory Materials Throughout the Learning Environment

You are certain to support sensory development in the sensory area and the natural elements zone. However, every area of the classroom includes many opportunities for sensory development.

Materials such as sound cans, sorting boxes, texture boards, pegboards, and puzzles found in the manipulative toys area support the development of sensory discrimination skills. By their very nature, art materials support both the visual and the tactile senses. Materials designed for other curriculum areas are also sensory in nature. The colors in a beautifully illustrated children's book, the different weights and sizes in a set of unit blocks, the sound differences of rhythm instruments, the feel of moving through space on a swing, the cool mush of fingerpaints or clay, the tastes and smells as children cook applesauce—all are sensory highlights of materials that have other purposes. As you provide experiences to children, you can point out their sensory aspects and encourage the children's sensory exploration and involvement.

In addition, you can think about bringing in objects to encourage sensory exploration. A vase of flowers on a table, an interesting piece of driftwood, or a pillow with interesting textures give children a chance to use their senses. Collections of natural objects like rocks, shells, leaves, beans, and seeds give children opportunities to look, touch, and sort.

Table 6.1 gives a quick overview of things you can do as you design an environment for sensory curriculum.

A Schedule for Sensory Curriculum

The time spent in sensory play is valuable. As in all other curriculum areas, sufficient time is needed for children to develop sensory discrimination abilities. Daily choice times of at least an hour should include access to sensory materials. Short (10 to 20 minute) guided small groups should be a regular part of each day. These can include activities planned to enhance all the senses—cooking, music, dancing, tasting, walking—the choices are endless.

TABLE 6.1 Environment Areas That Support Sensory Curriculum

Center/Area/Zone	How It Supports Sensory Development	What to Provide	Important Requirements
Manipulatives Area	Builds visual and tactile perception.	Building and construction toys • Math manipulatives • Puzzles, beads, and fit-together toys • Montessori sensorial materials • Collections of materials such as buttons, shells, seeds • Manufactured games and teacher-made workjobs • Spacious shelf and baskets/bins • Table and chairs or carpeted floor	To encourage sensory awareness, work with children in the area and create sensory challenges—e.g., "Can you find all the ones with a blue dot?"
Art Area	Builds visual and tactile perception.	• Work tables and chairs sized to the children • Easels • Art supplies • Fingerpaints and trays	Be attentive to presentation of art materials. Clean watercolor palettes so that colors are bright and not muddied. Use individual bowls and compartment trays for collage materials. Add scents and salt or sand to give a multi-sensory experience.
Unit Block Area	Builds visual, tactile, and kinesthetic perception.	• A set of hardwood unit blocks • Props for block play • Space for play • Shelves marked for storage	Organization and labeling of the shelves is particularly important for visual perception. Arrange similar blocks together so that the difference in the variables is visible. Never store blocks in a basket or box.
Library	Builds visual perception.	• Book shelf • Pillows or comfortable chairs/sofa • A collection of beautifully illustrated books	Make sure the shelf faces books out so that children can see books to select. Be sure to spend time with children in the library to help them look at books.
Discovery (Science) Area	Builds visual, tactile, auditory, and olfactory perception.	• Tables with space for ongoing explorations • Shelf for storage • Animals, plants, aquariums, and interesting things to investigate	Be sure to allow a wide range of experiments, including things that smell.
Active Play Zone	Builds kinesthetic and visual perception.	• Space to run, jump, and roll • Superstructures, tires, balance beams, trikes and wagons, trampolines, parachutes, tunnels	To make the active play zone support sensory development, it is important to have ways for children to change their level and perspectives.

Your Role in Teaching Sensory Curriculum

You may be wondering how to "teach" sensory curriculum. Unlike large and fine motor development, the sensory curriculum does not have many "skills." In sensory curriculum you are essentially helping children to:

1. be open to and curious about sensations so they can perceive them.
2. compare and contrast sensations that are perceived.
3. use sensory information as a way to learn.

From your own observations, you know that almost all young children enjoy sensory play. But you may have also noticed that a few avoid it. In any class of young children you will have both. Your job is to support sensory learning for all of the children. You will do this by providing opportunities for self-selected sensory play as well as structured sensory activities.

In addition to providing an environment rich in sensory exploration opportunities and planning appropriate sensory activities, you will **model for children.** Model an openness to sensation both with your actions and with your words, for example: "The rose has lovely pink and red petals." "I hear the buzz of the bees." "The yeast smells strong." "Feel the cold, slippery ice." "The lemon has a sour taste." This may require that you hold back your own "yuck" responses. Unless it is truly dangerous, avoid the temptation to tell children that a sensation (aroma, taste, texture, color, etc.) is bad or un-pleasant. Instead, use emotionally neutral words to describe it ("The mouse cage smells like urine; it must be time to change the litter.").

Young children often have strong responses to sensations. They may hold their noses, rub soft paintbrushes against their cheeks, splash in mud, or refuse to touch or taste a new food. You support their developing sensory discrimination skill when you **notice and accept how they respond.** Often, we have learned from our own parents and teachers to see enthusiasm for sensory exploration as messy or naughty. If you have planned a sensory experience and a child refuses to try it, you may feel irritated and perceive them as stubborn. An important way that you support children's sensory learning is by noticing, understanding, and accepting children's responses. You can do this by avoiding negative remarks, making positive comments ("The orange has a sharp smell doesn't it?" "The mud feels good squishing under your feet."), and training yourself to truly accept children's ways of experiencing and expressing feelings about sensory activities.

You can also **help children focus** on sensory aspects of materials and experiences by the ways you call attention to them; for example, you might help children notice the cool, smooth texture of a polished rock by saying things like, "How does it feel in your hands?" "What do you notice when you rub it against your cheek?" "What does it remind you of?"

Reflect on sensory experiences that were a part of school . . .

Think of a sensory experience that you had in school (cooking, exploring a sensory material, looking at something beautiful, making music). What do you feel or think of as you recall this experience? How did it affect your perceptions of school?

Sensory Curriculum Activities

As you can see in Table 6.2 there are many different activities to choose from in sensory development curriculum. However, activities in which children play in a planned environment are the most effective for developing visual, tactile, and kinesthetic awareness. Small-group activities (guided exploration, trips, art, cooking, music, science) can support development in all the senses and are most effective for developing auditory, gustatory, and olfactory awareness. Very few large-group activities are effective for sensory curriculum.

Planning Sensory Curriculum

While much of sensory curriculum occurs as children play in a planned environment, there are times when you will plan structured sensory activities. Plan structured sensory activities when you want to: make sure you are addressing a particular program goal or state standard; build awareness or sensitivity to a particular sense; or involve sensory development in an integrated curriculum study.

Writing Sensory Curriculum Plans

Alan, age 3, loved preschool from his first day. He loved to dig in the sand, he loved to ride trikes, he loved to dance and sing, he loved to paint at the easel, and he LOVED water. In fact, his teacher, Sally, had a hard time keeping him out of the water. In the warm days of early fall, Alan would drench himself with water from the sink, from the water table, and from the hose.

In sharp contrast to Alan was Ivory, also age 3. Ivory also loved preschool—the stories, the teachers, the snacks, and friends were all she talked about at home. But Ivory HATED anything to do with messy play. She would not play in the sand. She would not play with water, dough, or paint. At singing time she put her hands over her ears. She disliked the bathroom—she complained it was smelly. She feared the school rabbit, Sammy, and complained that Sammy was smelly, too.

Children differ in the ways in which they engage with sensory materials. Some, like Alan, come to school as eager sensory explorers. Others, like Ivory, are reluctant to explore using their senses. Teachers often want to analyze why children are different in their responses to sensory activities. They may attribute differences to gender, culture, or race. But some children of both sexes, from all cultures, and of every racial background are like Alan and some are like Ivory. You may assume that the differences come from the family, but this may not be true. Alan's enthusiasm for sensory exploration may or may not have been encouraged in his home. Ivory may or may not have been discouraged from sensory play by her family or caregivers. We don't know why these children are so different. The cause of the differences is not important because your goal for both children is the same. You want Alan and Ivory and all the children in your class to be open to diverse sensations so that they can compare and contrast them and use sensory information to learn about the world.

Your specific objectives for Alan and Ivory will be very different. It's clear that Alan is already an accomplished sensory explorer—that is his strength. He may not yet have the ability to talk about his sensory experiences or make the subtle distinctions that he will use as a young scientist or artist. Ivory also

TABLE 6.2 Sensory Teaching Strategies

Use These Strategies to Help Children Develop:	*Play in a Planned Environment* Child Directed (independent/ with other children)	*Scaffolded Interactions* Child Directed (teacher–child or child–child)	*Small Group* Teacher Directed/ Child Inspired (3–10 children)	*Large Group* Teacher Directed (8+ children)
Visual Perception	Play in all classroom centers, especially Library, Art, Manipulatives, Writing, Science, and Outdoor Natural and Creative zones. Book-making	Interactions in all classroom centers especially Library, Art, Manipulatives, Writing, Science, and Outdoor Natural Areas Pattern Toys Puzzles and Books Woodworking	Guided Exploration Reading Books Art Activities Cooking Daily Living Routines (e.g., table setting) Walks and other trips	Walks and other trips
Auditory Perception	Play in Listening and Music Centers	Puppet Play Rhythm Instruments	Guided Exploration Reading Books and Telling Stories Fingerplays Puppet Play Rhythm Instruments Walks and other trips	Fingerplays Group Music and Movement Walks and other trips
Tactile Perception	In all classroom centers, especially Art, Manipulatives, Dramatic Play, Blocks, Science, and Outdoor Natural and Creative Zones	Playdough and Clay Manipulatives Art activities, especially Collage, Construction, and Stitchery Block Play Woodworking	Guided Exploration Block Play Gardening Table Games Fingerplays Block Play Math Manipulatives Art Activities Sand Tray Walks and other trips	Walks and other trips
Kinesthetic Perception	Outdoor Zones, especially active play and hollow blocks Indoor Centers Dramatic Play, Blocks, Active Play Rooms	Balance Beam Obstacle Course Hollow Block Building Movement Stations Sand Tray	Guided Exploration Block Play Construction Guided Movement Walks and other trips	Guided Movement Walks and other trips
Gustatory Perception	Routines—Lunch and Snack		Guided Exploration Cooking Trips	Trips to restaurants, bakeries, orchards, kitchens
Olfactory Perception	Routines—Lunch and Snack Outdoor play "Smell" bottles	Science Exploration Gardening	Guided Exploration Cooking Gardening Walks and other trips	Walks and other trips

has sensory strengths. She is highly attuned to olfactory sensations. But she may need gentle guidance so she can begin to appreciate and then learn from diverse sensations.

In any class, you will have children like Alan and Ivory. The art of teaching is knowing how to support both of them. Activities that can be messy such as sand, mud, water, clay, and fingerpaints are sometimes rejected by fastidious children, particularly when these activities are available only occasionally for short periods. Reluctant children are more likely to learn to use and enjoy materials if they observe other children enjoying them. It also helps when the use of materials moves in a sequence over several weeks or even months, from structured and contained to more open and unrestricted. For example, fingerpaints might be presented first on a cafeteria tray with individual pieces of paper, small amounts of paint, and protective smocks. Later activities might involve a group mural fingerpainting on the tables in the playground, perhaps with sand and gravel added. Table 6.2 gives some examples of appropriate activities that you might plan to support sensory development in young children.

Figure 6.2 is the plan that Sally created to take advantage of Alan's eagerness to explore the senses, build Ivory's disposition to use hers, and engage the whole class in a worthwhile activity that builds sensory awareness.

Because she is an experienced teacher, Sally's simple plan leaves out many details. It would not be enough to guide a beginning teacher. The detailed version (Figure 6.3) gives you a better idea of what she planned to do.

FIGURE 6.2   Simple Sensory Activity Plan

Textured Shaving Cream Fingerpainting

Objectives:	• Explore and attend to sensation
	• Name familiar tactile sensations
Standard:	Domain IV (Cognitive) Standard 1: Increase sensory awareness.
What you need:	• aprons
	• table covering
	• trays
	• shaving cream
	• paint in 2 colors
	• salt or sand
How to teach:	1. Show shaving cream and salt/sand at morning circle and explain.
	2. At the center, give shaving cream and encourage children to touch it. As children play, describe the experience. Then offer sand/salt or one color to add. Ask questions to encourage exploration.
	3. As children finish, comment on the experience.
How to assess:	Look for children playing with or talking about shaving cream and using words like *wet, soft, slippery*. Document with photos and anecdotals.

FIGURE 6.3 Detailed Sensory Activity Plan

Activity: Textured Shaving Cream Fingerpainting   **Sensory Curriculum Focus**

Children fingerpaint with shaving cream and food color.

WHO It's For: This activity was planned for the *Dancing Dragons* (eight 3-year-olds). Up to four children at a time can comfortably play.

WHY This Activity

Rationale: Most of the *Dancing Dragons* (especially Alan) enjoy fingerpainting. Two (Ivory and Kaitlyn) do not. This activity is designed to support those who already learn through touch to make tactile distinctions. It also is designed to build the disposition to feel comfortable with sensory exploration in those who are reluctant to engage in sensory play.

Sensory Objectives: *By participating in this activity the children will …*

- Explore and attend to tactile, visual, and olfactory sensation (texture, temperature, moisture, color, aroma).
- Name familiar tactile sensations—*wet, soft, slippery.*

Other objectives:

Increase ability to talk about sensory experiences (language), develop self-confidence (social-emotional)

Preschool Content Standard: Domain IV (Cognitive) Standard 1: Increase sensory awareness.

Indicators:
- Explore and experiment using various sensory media in play.
- Begin to identify and discriminate among sensory stimuli.

HOW to Prepare *What you need:*
- Table and 4 chairs
- 8 aprons
- Plastic tablecloth or newspaper
- 8 cafeteria trays
- 1 or two cans of non-menthol shaving cream (lime/lemon scent)
- Squeeze bottles of liquid paint in 2 primary colors
- Salt or sand

Time: Morning activity time

Space: In the sensory area

Set up: Cover the table with a tablecloth or newspaper, hang an apron on each chair, and place a tray at each place.

HOW to Teach *Introduction:*

At morning circle, show shaving cream, tray, paint, and sand/salt. Squirt a little shaving cream on a tray and say something like: "Fingerpainting with shaving cream is available today. It smells good and feels soft. You can use it all by itself or with paint to make it colorful and sand (or salt) to make it feel gritty. There's room for 4 people at the table." If Ivory or Kaitlyn express interest, be sure to choose them first.

Teaching steps:

1. When children arrive, help them put on aprons.
2. Show the shaving cream and say, "You can start with just shaving cream." Squirt some on each tray.
3. Encourage reluctant children to touch the shaving cream with a fingertip, then a thumb, and to then pat it with their hands. As children play, say things like: "It feels soft, slippery, bouncy—it smells lemon-y—it looks like a cloud."
4. Offer sand/salt or one color to add to the shaving cream. Ask questions like: "How does it feel now?" "What happened to the color?" Continue to encourage exploration.

Closure:

As children finish, help them to remove their aprons and comment on what they did (e.g., "You made piles and piles of pink sandy shaving cream."). Send children to the sink to wash their hands. Replace messy trays and aprons with clean ones and invite waiting children to fingerpaint.

(continued)

FIGURE 6.3   Detailed Sensory Activity Plan (continued)

HOW to Assess and Document

Objectives	Evidence of Learning Children might …	How to Document This Evidence
Explore and attend to tactile, visual, and olfactory sensation.	Playing eagerly with shaving cream Talking about the experience (e.g., "It looks like ice cream")	Anecdotal observations Photographs of play with fingerpaint
Name familiar tactile sensations.	Using words like *wet, soft, slippery* to describe the experience	Anecdotal observations

EVALUATION (Things to remember for next time)

Cleanup was a little more difficult than expected. Try outside on a sunny day. Have a change of clothes for Alan.

To assist you in writing plans for sensory activities you may wish to look over the examples of objectives included in Table 6.3.

Sensory Curriculum in a Weekly Plan

Sensory curriculum belongs in your plans for each day with preschoolers. Many planned experiences involve sensory exploration, and for some, it will be the primary purpose of the activity. In the example included here in Figure 6.4, you will see that there are sensory activities planned each day (these are highlighted), although not all of these activities were planned specifically for this reason. Sensory objectives are highlighted and to make the sensory learning more visible to you, we have noted the senses that are primarily involved in each activity. We would not typically include these in the plans we post each week for families.

Sensory Curriculum in an Integrated Study

Because sensory exploration is so integral to young children's ways of being, all integrated studies that are appropriate and successful have sensory curriculum built into them. Each study that you will see as an example in this book—food, bread, gardens, insects, water, stores, birds—has a strong sensory component. And while any study is ongoing, there will be many other sensory activities that can be included.

For the study of food, many activities were specifically planned as part of the sensory curriculum. In addition, all of the trips and the cooking, art and music, science and social studies, large motor and creative movement, and fine motor activities also supported sensory development. Activities that were a part of the sensory development curriculum are highlighted on the Food Study sunburst in Figure 6.5.

Sensory Curriculum for All Children

Sensory development curriculum is a part of every program for young children, and it is an acknowledged and accepted part of programs for preschoolers and infants and toddlers. There are some additional things that you will need to think about if you teach primary age children, or if your program includes children with special needs.

TABLE 6.3 Some Typical Objectives for Sensory Curriculum

Stage and Objectives	Auditory Perception	Tactile Perception	Olfactory Perception	Kinesthetic Perception	Visual Perception	Gustatory Perception
Younger preschoolers 3- to 4-year-olds *The ability to . . .*	Explore and attend to sounds.	Explore and attend to tactile sensation.	Explore and attend to olfactory sensation.	Explore and attend to kinesthetic sensation.	Explore and attend to visual elements, e.g., color, shape.	Explore and attend to flavors in food.
	Differentiate highly dissimilar sounds.	Differentiate highly dissimilar tactile sensations.	Differentiate highly dissimilar aromas.	Name where the body is in space simply (above, below, on top).	Differentiate highly dissimilar colors, shapes, sizes.	Differentiate highly dissimilar tastes.
	Name familiar sounds.	Name familiar tactile sensations.	Name familiar aromas.		Name familiar colors and shapes.	Name familiar tastes.
Older preschoolers and kindergartners 4- to 5-year-olds *The ability to . . .*	Explore, attend to, and show appreciation for sounds.	Explore, attend to, and show appreciation for tactile sensation.	Explore, attend to, and show appreciation for olfactory sensation.	Explore, attend to, and show appreciation for kinesthetic sensation.	Explore, attend to, and show appreciation for visual elements, e.g., color, shape.	Explore, attend to, and show appreciation for flavors in food.
	Differentiate similar sounds.	Differentiate similar tactile sensations.	Differentiate similar aromas.	Discriminate and control body movement.	Differentiate similar colors, shapes, sizes.	Differentiate similar tastes.
	Screen many extraneous or irrelevant sounds.	Screen many extraneous or irrelevant tactile stimuli.	Screen many extraneous or irrelevant aromas.	Identify where the body is in space with greater complexity (behind, beside, inside).	Screen many extraneous or irrelevant visual sensations.	Develop appreciation for a range of tastes.
	Name more usual and note unfamiliar sounds.	Name more unusual and note unfamiliar tactile sensations.	Name more unusual and note unfamiliar aromas.		Name more unusual and note unfamiliar colors and shapes.	Name more unusual and note unfamiliar tastes.
	Use sounds to make decisions.	Use tactile information to make decisions.	Use olfactory information to make decisions.	Use kinesthetic information to make decisions.	Use visual information to make decisions.	Use tastes to make decisions.

(continued)

TABLE 6.3 Some Typical Objectives for Sensory Curriculum (continued)

Stage and Objectives	Auditory Perception	Tactile Perception	Olfactory Perception	Kinesthetic Perception	Visual Perception	Gustatory Perception
Primary school-age children **6- to 8-year-olds** *The ability to . . .*	Explore, attend to, and show appreciation for sounds.	Explore, attend to, and show appreciation for tactile sensation.	Explore, attend to, and show appreciation for olfactory sensation.	Explore, attend to, and show appreciation for kinesthetic sensation.	Explore, attend to, and show appreciation for visual elements, e.g., color, shape.	Explore, attend to, and show appreciation for flavors in food.
	Differentiate between two very similar sounds.	Differentiate between two very similar tactile sensations.	Differentiate between two very similar aromas.	Differentiate kinesthetic sensations and control body movement.	Differentiate between two very similar colors, shapes, or sizes.	Differentiate between two very similar tastes.
	Screen most extraneous or irrelevant sounds.	Screen most extraneous or irrelevant tactile stimuli.	Screen most extraneous or irrelevant aromas.	Identify where the body is in space with greater detail (behind, beside, inside) and make comparisons (e.g., as high as a bird in a nest).	Screen most extraneous or irrelevant visual sensations.	Develop appreciation for a range of tastes.
	Identify and make comparisons between unfamiliar sounds.	Identify and make comparisons between unfamiliar tactile sensations.	Identify and make comparisons between unfamiliar aromas.		Identify and make comparisons between unfamiliar colors and shapes.	Identify and make comparisons between unfamiliar tastes.
	Explain basis for decisions made based on sounds.	Explain basis for decisions made based on tactile information.	Explain basis for decisions made based on olfactory information.	Explain basis for decisions made based on kinesthetic information.	Explain basis for decisions made based on visual information.	Explain basis for decisions made based on tastes.

Children with Special Needs

For almost all children, sensory activities provide success and positive feelings. They are soothing and pleasurable. A few children react very strongly to sensory experiences (Ivory and Alan in the vignette earlier in this chapter were two such children). They may seek out specific sensory experiences and be unable or unwilling to leave them. Or they may find normal sensory experiences frightening or physically uncomfortable (called *sensory defensiveness*).

FIGURE 6.4   A Week's Plan: Food Study—Week #6

Objectives: To help children to understand that there are different kinds of foods that people like to eat and that are needed for health.

	Monday	Tuesday	Wednesday	Thursday	Friday
Story	*Hi Pizza Man*	*Little Red Hen*	*Cat's Cake*	*Pete's a Pizza*	*Everybody Bakes Bread*
Outdoor Activities 9:00–10:00 **Purpose:** *to help children develop …*	**Kitchen Utensils in the Water Table** Increased sensory awareness, fine motor skill, and positive relationships with peers. **Tactile**		**Bean Pouring** Increased sensory awareness, fine motor skill, and experience the concepts of volume and measurement. **Tactile**	**Making Pizza with Malie's Mom** Understanding of diverse families and the foods they enjoy, develop new food and cooking vocabulary, and acquire measurement concepts. **Gustatory & Olfactory**	**Bean Pouring** Increased sensory awareness, fine motor skill, and experience the concepts of volume and measurement. **Tactile**
Small Group Big Cat and Dog Sharks **Purpose:** *to help children develop …*	**What's Missing? (foods)** **Observation** skills and the ability to verbalize what is known. **Visual**	**Cutting and Tasting Tomatoes** Eye-hand coordination, awareness of food, and a sense of independence. **Gustatory & Olfactory**	**What's Missing? (fruit)** **Observation** skills and the ability to verbalize what is known. **Visual**	**Food Words Poetry Making** Awareness of words and the sounds of words, and develop the concept of a poem. **Auditory**	**How to Make Pizza (child-authored recipe)** Awareness that spoken language can be written down and read.
Small Group T-Rex Turtles **Purpose:** *to help children develop …*	**What's Missing? (foods)** **Observation** skills and the ability to verbalize what is known. **Visual**	**Cutting and Tasting Tomatoes** Eye-hand coordination, awareness of food, and a sense of independence. **Gustatory & Olfactory**	**Dancing with Scarves** Creativity, aesthetic awareness, and physical coordination and stamina. **Kinesthetic**	**Feely Food Box** **Sensory awareness** and vocabulary, awareness of the physical properties of foods (e.g., temperature, texture). **Tactile**	***Very Hungry Caterpillar* Art** Ability to create and express with a variety of art media and develop an appreciation for books and an understanding that books are created by people.

(continued)

FIGURE 6.4   A Week's Plan: Food Study–Week #6 (continued)

	Monday	Tuesday	Wednesday	Thursday	Friday
Indoors **Purpose:** *to help children develop …*	**Palette Painting** Ability to create and express with a variety of art media and use art elements of color and design. **Visual**		**Utensil Printing** Ability to create and express with a variety of art media and acquire new vocabulary. **Visual & Tactile**	**Thank You Cards** Awareness that spoken language can be written down and read; acquire concepts of gratitude and appreciation.	**Watercolor Painting** Ability to create and express with a variety of art media and use art elements of color and design. **Visual**
Large Group Circle Time **Purpose:** *to help children develop …*	**Acting Out** *The Carrot Seed* Creativity, vocabulary, and imagination.	**Walk Around the Chair** The ability to create using music and movement. **Kinesthetic**	**Playing Instruments** The ability to use simple instruments appropriately to accompany a song. **Auditory**	**Acting Out** *Hi Pizza Man* Creativity, vocabulary, and imagination.	**Playing Instruments** The ability to use simple instruments appropriately to accompany a song. **Auditory**

Ali started preschool the fall that she turned 3. Right away, the teachers noticed she was different. She didn't talk to children or adults. She often flapped her hands. Every day she painted her hands, face, and body, and immersed her head in water in the sink, fountain, or water table. She cried whenever her feet or hands touched anything gritty or rough like sand. After several months, Ali was diagnosed as having Autism Spectrum Disorder (ASD).

Since sensory input is so vital for learning, you will want to find ways to help all children have positive and successful sensory experiences. To do this, you may at first need to provide gentle guided opportunities to interact with sensory materials.

Ali's teachers educated themselves about ASD. Among other strategies, they used Ali's love of cool, wet, sensory experiences to help her to be calm, develop simple language, and have relationships with other children. They helped Ali to become comfortable with rough tactile experiences by presenting them to her slowly with lots of support. They let her play with soft flour, smooth beans, and crushed ice. Then they moved on to fine salt and sand. Eventually, Ali was able to explore sand and other previously rejected sensory experiences.

Sensory experiences can be especially valuable for children with special needs. They are soothing and can be used at any ability level so children with intellectual disabilities play and explore in the same way as their typically developing peers. Children with visual or auditory disabilities can use their other senses as they play with materials in the sensory table. Since there is no single right way to play with sensory materials, they not only build the ability to perceive but also generate feelings of competency and success.

FIGURE 6.5 Study of Food Sunburst

A Study of Food Fall 2003

Big Idea — Foods have many flavors, tastes, and textures.

Big Idea — People like different foods.

Big Idea — There are many kinds of food to eat.

Big Idea — We need lots of different foods to grow and stay healthy.

Big Idea — We get food from different places.

Big Idea — Some foods are eaten and enjoyed by different families and by people in different places.

Big Idea — Families make food for everyone in the family to eat every day and on special days.

Big Idea — People have jobs growing, making, selling, and serving food.

Sensory
Kitchen Utensils in the Water Table
Lemon Playdough
Pumpkin Scooping
Food Tasting
Flour Sifting
Tapioca Goop
Cornstarch Goop
–also all cooking and science activities

Cooking
Applesauce
Corn on the Cob
Fruit Salad
Fruit Smoothie
Musubi
Orange Juice
Rice
Bread
Brownies
Pizza
Quesadilla
Sugar Cookies
Tuna Fish
Sandwiches
Vegetable Stir Fry

Science
Seed Comparison
Cutting and Tasting Tomatoes
Planting Radishes
Papaya Seed Planting
Fruit Tasting/Juicing
Bread Comparison

Fine Motor
Cutting Vegetables
Shucking Corn
Grinding Corn
Bean Pouring
–also all cooking, art, and sensory activities

Math
Seed and Bean Balance
Graphing Favorite Foods
Bread Graph
Fruit Basket Workjob
Take Your Apple to the Basket Workjob

Large Motor and Creative Movement
The Fruit Bowl Game
Paw Paw Patch
Stretch for Pizza
Baby Chicks Are Crying
Fruit Pantomime
Bread Baking Movement
Good Seed Movement

Literacy
KWL—What Do You Know About Food
Food Words
Food Journals
Trip Books
Baking Language Experience
Seed Letters
Food Poems
Child-Authored Recipes

Art
Seed Collage
Vegetable Printing
Food Pictures Collage
Fruit Printing
Fingerpaint with Seeds
Potato Printing
Cookie Cutter Printing
Still Life Painting

Literature
Reading and *Making Stone Soup*
Hi Pizza Man
Cat's Cake
Eat Up Gemma
Enormous Carrot
Everybody Bakes Bread
Great Big Taro Root
Food Poem Posters
Little Red Hen
Oliver's Fruit Salad
Jake Baked a Cake
Rain Makes Applesauce
To Market To Market

Trips
Campus Herb Garden
Cafeteria
Chinatown
Foodland
Farmer's Market

Music
Come on Let's Go to Market
Wheat Maracas
Aiken Drum
Today Is Monday
Paw Paw Patch
Hawaiian Thanksgiving Song

Language
Food Clues
Cabbage Clues
Feely Food Box
What's Missing?
Discussion—Why We Eat Fruit

Social Studies
Family Cooking
Family Food Stories
Culminating Activity: Family Potluck
Thanksgiving Picture Sharing
Market in the Pretend Area
Hawaiian Thanksgiving Song
Family Cookbook

177

Children in the Primary Grades

If you work with children over the age of 6, you may find that you are confronted with the challenge of encouraging them to continue with sensory exploration as a valid method of learning about the world. Primary age children should continue to have experiences that build sensory awareness and appreciation of the world. It is important to plan experiences for them that employ senses other than the ones traditionally used in schools—looking and listening. They need frequent opportunities to explore and create with art media such as paints, clay, and collage materials. Field trips into natural environments provide a variety of sensory experiences. Visits to view works of art in the community or displays of photographs, prints, sculpture, pottery, and paintings heighten appreciation of beautiful and interesting creations. Gardening and cooking are activities to learn from and to give sensual satisfaction. No eating experience is better than that of the peas from your own patch or the tortillas you make with your classmates as a part of a study of bread. Sensory learning is valuable independent of other educational goals, but it often deepens and enriches other learning experiences. And there is an important aesthetic aspect of sensory development. We live in a world that needs people who can appreciate the beauty and variety of nature, art, and music; the sights, sounds, smells, and flavors of a variety of cultures; and all the other sensory joys that contribute to our humanity.

Final Thoughts

Sensory experiences—perceiving the colors, sounds, tastes, aromas, and textures of the world—are among the greatest of human joys and also comprise the fundamental way we all learn about our world. As an early childhood teacher, one important part of your job is to help the children you teach learn to discriminate sensations so they can receive and interpret sensory information for learning and for joy.

Do this mindfully, and clearly articulate to families, administrators, and other staff members why you are doing so. The end result will be that you will have added richness and learning to the lives of the children you teach and to yourself.

Learning Outcomes

When you read this chapter, thoughtfully complete activities from the "To Learn More" section, and document this learning as suggested in the "For Your Portfolio" section, you will be making progress in the following *NAEYC Standards for Early Childhood Professional Preparation Programs* (2009):

Standard 1. Promoting Child Development and Learning

Students prepared in early childhood degree programs are grounded in a child development knowledge base. They use their understanding of young children's characteristics and needs and of the multiple interacting influences on children's development and learning to create environments that are healthy, respectful, supportive, and challenging for each child.

The key elements of standard 1 you will have learned about are . . .

1a: Knowing and understanding young children's characteristics and needs

1c: Using developmental knowledge to create healthy, respectful, supportive, and challenging learning environments

Standard 4. Using Developmentally Effective Approaches to Connect with Children and Families

Students prepared in early childhood degree programs understand that teaching and learning with young children is a complex enterprise, and its details vary depending on children's ages, characteristics, and the settings within which teaching and learning occur. They understand and use positive relationships and supportive interactions as the foundation for their work with young children and families. Students know, understand, and use a wide array of developmentally appropriate approaches, instructional strategies, and tools to connect with children and families and positively influence each child's development and learning.

The key elements of standard 4 you will have learned about are . . .

4a: Understanding positive relationships and supportive interactions as the foundation of their work with children

4b: Knowing and understanding effective strategies and tools for early education

4c: Using a broad repertoire of developmentally appropriate teaching/learning approaches

4d: Reflecting on their own practice to promote positive outcomes for each child

Standard 5. Using Content Knowledge to Build Meaningful Curriculum

Students prepared in early childhood degree programs use their knowledge of academic disciplines to design, implement, and evaluate experiences that promote positive development and learning for each and every young child. Students understand the importance of developmental domains and academic (or content) disciplines in an early childhood curriculum. They know the essential concepts, inquiry tools, and structure of content areas, including academic subjects, and can identify resources to deepen their understanding. Students use their own knowledge and other resources to design, implement, and evaluate meaningful, challenging curricula that promote comprehensive developmental and learning outcomes for every young child.

The key elements of standard 5 you will have learned about are . . .

5a: Understanding content knowledge and resources in academic disciplines

5b: Knowing and using the central concepts, inquiry tools, and structures of content areas or academic disciplines

5c: Using their own knowledge, appropriate early learning standards, and other resources to design, implement, and evaluate meaningful, challenging curricula for each child.

To Learn More

Observe a Program: For a morning, observe a program and see how the staff structures the environment and program to support children's sensory development. Notice both the play opportunities and the planned group activities. Look at the plans and see how the planning reflects what you observed. Interview a teacher to learn what he or she thinks about sensory curriculum.

Observe a Child: For a morning, observe a child in a classroom, with a focus on the child's sensory activity. Notice how the child engages with the planned activities and how he or she constructs his or her own opportunities for learning. Notice the extent to which the child's activity and the planned curriculum seem to match. Observe to see how staff support the child's sensory exploration.

Observe a Master Teacher: Spend a morning with an early childhood educator who is experienced and has a curriculum leadership role in a program. (This teacher may be called the "lead," "head," or "mentor" teacher.) Then interview the educator about how he or she plans for and provides sensory curriculum.

Observe a Sensory Activity: Observe a teacher leading a planned sensory activity. Interview the teacher to find out the objectives for the activity. Reflect on any differences between what you saw and the focus of the plan.

Compare Two Programs: Observe sensory curriculum experiences in two early childhood programs. Compare the ways that the two address sensory curriculum—their similarities and differences. Reflect on which program seems to best support children's learning and why. What implications does this comparison have for your future work with young children?

Compare Two Ages: Observe two classrooms, one preschool and one for primary school children. Report on how each supports children's sensory exploration.

Talk to the staff about how they make their curriculum choices. Notice how development influences curriculum choices.

Explore Resources: Read one of the books or one of the online resources from the bibliography and write a review of it for your classmates.

For Your Portfolio

Design a Sensory Environment: Design and draw a floor plan for a classroom and play yard that would promote children's sensory learning. Share your plan with an early childhood educator, discussing what you included and why. Ask for and consider the educator's feedback and suggestions. Set up a sensory center in a real classroom or play yard utilizing as many of your ideas as possible, and let children use it. For your portfolio, include the floor plan, photographs or video of children using the area, and a reflection on what you learned by doing this project.

Plan and Implement a Sensory Activity: Observe a group of children for a morning, focusing on their sensory interest and activity. Based on what you observed, write and implement a sensory activity. Collect evidence of children's responses in the form of anecdotal observations, photographs, or video recordings. Reflect on how

children responded and what they appear to have learned. What worked? What might you do differently next time? How might you expand on this experience for children? For your portfolio, include the plan, a photograph, and a reflection on what you learned about yourself, children, planning, and teaching.

Create a Sensory Learning Material: Design and make a sensory learning material to support the development of a particular child or group of children. Introduce it to the child or children and observe how it is used. Reflect on how the children responded and how you felt about what you did. What worked? What might you do differently next time? How might you expand on this experience for children? For your portfolio, include a photograph of a child using the material and a reflection on what you learned about yourself, children, learning materials, and teaching.

Bibliography

Berger, K. S. (2008). *The developing person through childhood and adolescence* (8th ed.). New York, NY: Worth.

Berk, L. E. (2007). *Infants and children: Prenatal through middle childhood* (6th ed.). Boston, MA: Allyn and Bacon.

Black, J., Puckett, M., Wittmer, D. S., & Peterson, S. H. (2008). *The young child: Development from prebirth through age eight* (5th ed.). Upper Saddle River, NJ: Pearson.

Cowart, B. J. (2005). *Taste, our body's gustatory gatekeeper.* New York, NY: Dana Foundation. www.dana.org/news/cerebrum/detail.aspx?id=788

Cratty, B. J. (1986). *Perceptual and motor development in infants and children* (3rd ed.). Englewood Cliffs, NJ: Prentice-Hall.

Feeney, S., Moravcik, E., & Nolte, S. (2013). *Who am I in the lives of children?* (9th ed.). Upper Saddle River, NJ: Pearson.

Fox, K. (2009). *The smell report, an overview of facts and findings.* Oxford, UK: Social Issues Research Centre. www.sirc.org/publik/smell.pdf

Gabbard, C. P. (2004). *Lifelong motor development* (4th ed.). San Francisco, CA: Benjamin Cummings/Pearson.

Head Start Resource Center. (2010). *The Head Start child development and early learning framework: Promoting positive outcomes in early childhood programs serving children 3–5 years old.* Washington, DC: Office of Head Start, Administration for Children and Families, U.S. Department of Health and Human Services.

Hill, D. M. (1977). *Mud, sand, and water.* Washington, DC: NAEYC.

Jacob, T. (2009, December 22). *Smell (Olfaction): A tutorial on the sense of smell.* Cardiff, UK: Cardiff University. www.cf.ac.uk/biosi/staffinfo/jacob/teaching/sensory/olfact1.html

Mampe, B., Friederici, A. D., Christopher, A., & Wermke, K. (2009, November 5). Newborns' cry melody is shaped by their native language. *Current Biology, 19*(23), 1994–1997.

National Association for the Education of Young Children. (2009). NAEYC *standards for early childhood professional preparation programs*. www.naeyc.org/files/naeyc/file/positions/ProfPrepStandards09.pdf

Papalia, D. E., Feldman, S., & Olds, S. J. (2007). *A child's world: Infancy through adolescence* (11th ed.). New York, NY: McGraw-Hill.

Wanamaker, N., Hearn, K., & Richarz, S. (1979). *More than graham crackers*. Washington, DC: NAEYC.

MyEducationLab

Go to MyEducationLab (www.myeducationlab.com) for *Meaningful Curriculum for Young Children*, where you can:

- Check your comprehension on the content covered in the chapter with the Study Plan. Here you will be able to take a chapter quiz, receive feedback on your answers, and then access Review, Practice, and Enrichment activities to enhance your understanding of chapter content.

Go to the Course Resources section in MyEducationLab, where you can:

- Use the Online Lesson Plan Builder to practice lesson planning and integrating national and state standards into your planning.

PART 3
Communication Curriculum

Talking with one another is loving one another.
AFRICAN PROVERB

To understand the world and function in it, individuals need to be able to communicate with others. From birth, people begin learning about communication—the interchange of thoughts, opinions, or information. Relating to others remains a crucial human activity throughout our lives. We learn to communicate in a variety of ways: through non-spoken communication, using body language, facial expressions, and body movements; with sign language, using both hand movements and facial expressions, through spoken communication, using words, and with written communication, using marks or symbols. One of your important jobs as an early childhood teacher will be to encourage children to become skilled communicators—people who can understand and exchange thoughts, feelings, and ideas with others. These skills not only set children on the path for later academic success, but also they allow children to enjoy and participate in rich and meaningful relationships with other people. The goal of the communication curriculum—the focus of this section—is to help children become enthusiastic, competent users of spoken and written language.

There are three communication curriculum areas, *language*, *literacy*, and *literature*. These are often referred to as the *language arts*. In the chapters that follow, you will read about the reasons why the communication curriculum is vital to children's learning in all curricular areas and the ways that it supports growth in every developmental domain.

Language is the foundation for the communication curriculum. Early childhood teachers help children build language skills and abilities in a variety of ways. As you speak to children respectfully and listen to them attentively, you are encouraging language use. When you consciously use interesting words and descriptions in your

daily interactions, you are helping them to build vocabulary and listening skills. When you model using language to mediate problems, communicate information, and share feelings and ideas, you demonstrate the usefulness and value of oral language. Your daily routine will include opportunities to engage in dialog with children as you support their play and encourage their learning. As you sing songs, tell jokes, recite rhymes and poems, and play verbal games with children, you will help them find joy in talking and in using language. A well-planned language curriculum filled with many opportunities for children to engage in communication with others sets the stage for both later learning of oral and spoken language and the development of literacy, the ability to communicate through written language.

Learning to read—to make meaning from the written word—and to write words that have meaning to others is a pivotal skill for young children. Developing skill in understanding and using print is the focus of the *literacy* curriculum. Current research makes it very clear that children who have numerous early literacy experiences are more successful in elementary school. Because early childhood teachers understand the significance of these early literacy experiences, they take time and care to ensure that their classrooms are filled with printed materials that have meaning to young children. In the literacy-rich early childhood classroom, meaningful print is incorporated into every aspect of the classroom day. From the time they arrive, when children can participate in signing in or finding their labeled cubby, through day's end, when they show a family member the class chart of favorite foods, print can be an integral part of the each child's daily experiences. As an early childhood teacher, you will constantly demonstrate to children the value of written language. As you write a note, prepare a list, follow a recipe, or read a story, you are modeling the importance of the written word and setting the stage for literacy learning. You will ensure that your classroom is filled with opportunities for children to use print as an important part of their play, and you will place reading materials and writing tools in accessible places so that children will be encouraged to use them often.

Literature is the third element of the communication curriculum. One of your important jobs will be selecting the books, stories, and poems that you read to children, and making them available for the children to use and enjoy. Sharing literature with young children is one of the most delightful aspects of teaching. As children have opportunities to hear engaging stories and gather useful information from books, they learn to value literature as a source of information and a means of relaxation and pleasure. Children learn a great deal from a rich and thoughtfully planned literature curriculum. They learn about themselves and others like them, as well as those who are different and live far away. They experience suspense and excitement as stories unfold, and they have opportunities to share those experiences with others. This builds social connections and encourages children to develop skills in communicating with others. Through literature, children learn new words and hear less familiar language patterns, thus expanding both their vocabulary and their communication ability. As you thoughtfully select books, display them attractively, and share them in meaning-ful and exciting ways with children, you are setting them on the path to be read-ers throughout their lives.

Communication skills are essential for each child's success both academically and as a member of a family, community, and society. These chapters will help you to develop a communication curriculum that encourages young children to practice these skills in meaningful and joyful ways.

The human mind has not achieved anything
greater than the ability to share feelings and
thoughts through language.

JAMES EARL JONES

chapter seven

LANGUAGE CURRICULUM
Speaking and Listening

Language is a complex, rule-governed system of symbols that allows the communication of an infinite number of ideas. All human beings in every place and from every culture have language that allows communication of feelings, acquisition of information, and exploration of ideas. We have within us a predisposition, a built-in need, to learn language. And every child, unless severely disabled or abusively isolated, learns language without instruction.

Human beings use different kinds of language to communicate with one another. The rise and fall of words spoken aloud (oral or spoken language) is what comes to mind first when you think of language. However, people also communicate using facial expressions, body postures, and gestures. A frown, a wave, a slumped shoulder, and a wink—each conveys meaning. *Sign language,* used in communities of individuals who are deaf or have hearing impairments, is another kind of language. It uses movements of the hands, arms, and body, along with facial expressions to convey information, feelings, and ideas.

Language is essential to the way human beings think. Without language, the complex thinking that makes us human is not possible. As you learn more about how children learn language and how to nurture this learning, you will develop skills that allow you to plan activities and experiences that encourage all children to understand and speak, a critical aspect of becoming successful lifelong learners.

Reflect on yourself as a child . . .

Remember yourself as a young child. Was it easy for you to talk to other people, or did you feel shy or uncomfortable? In which situations or circumstances was it easy for you to communicate? Why? How did your family or teachers support you or discourage you from communicating?

Why Language?

With all the other things you have to do, you may wonder why you need to focus on something that children seem to learn without instruction. Although virtually all typically developing preschool and kindergarten children come to you able to speak and understand their home language, there are compelling reasons for a strong emphasis on language in your classroom.

Language fosters children's ability to think. It helps them organize their experiences in progressively complex ways. Words help them visualize and think about past events and experiences.

Language is key to relationships. To participate in relationships, children must be able to communicate with others. Children with good communication skills relate more successfully to others, and their language grows even more in the relationships they build.

Lamar accidentally broke Nathan's toy car. Nathan threatened Lamar with raised fists and a furious expression. The teacher, Jan, moved quickly. Putting an arm around each boy, she said, "Oh Nathan, your car got broken! You must feel very sad about that. Your face tells me you're mad at Lamar, but I can't let you hit him. Tell him you feel sad your car is broken and mad that he broke your car."

Language helps children identify, express, and manage feelings. Feelings are powerful. By their nature, they are abstract . . . you cannot touch, see, taste, smell, or hear them. When you help children find words for strong feelings like Jan did, you give them a tool not only for expressing feelings but also for understanding and managing them.

Children with strong language skills are more successful in school. Young children with well-developed oral language skills do better in elementary school and in later academic settings than children who have had limited exposure to oral language (Hart & Risley, 2003; Snow, Burns, & Griffin, 1998; Snow & Dickinson, 1991). Perhaps this is because *language is essential for literacy*. It makes sense that in order to read, you must be able to speak and understand language. How could you learn to read if you didn't have understanding of the language you are reading?

There are a number of other ways that oral language skill contributes to literacy learning. When children have conversations and other language experiences, they:

- increase the number of words that they understand (*receptive vocabulary*).
- increase the number of words that they use in speech (*expressive vocabulary*).
- develop the ability to listen to the individual sounds that words make and become aware of the sounds of speech that are translated into written symbols (*phonological awareness*).
- develop background knowledge about the world that helps them to decipher print and gives them something to want to write about.

Finally, **individual families' abilities to help their children learn language vary.** This makes teaching language in school critical for children who live in

MyEducation**Lab**

Visit the MyEducationLab for *Meaningful Curriculum for Young Children* to enhance your understanding of chapter concepts with a personalized Study Plan. You'll also have the opportunity to hone your teaching skills through video-based Assignments and Activities, IRIS Center Resources, and Building Teaching Skills and Disposition lessons.

language-poor homes. Young children whose families are impoverished often are exposed to significantly fewer words than children from families who are more affluent (Dickerson & Tabors, 2002; Hart & Risley, 2003; Snow & Dickinson, 1991). Language-poor families (who may or may not be financially impoverished) are likely to use fewer different words in conversations.

How Young Children Learn Language

Even in the womb, children hear and respond to sounds. During the second trimester of pregnancy, a typically developing fetus has ears and reacts to sounds in the mother's environment. Studies of newborns show that they can discriminate between vocal sounds and that they prefer the sound of their mother's voice to less familiar voices. They also will pay attention to a human voice for much longer than to environmental sounds. Soon after birth, infants intently gaze at the faces and mouths of adults who speak to them, and they begin to make sounds in response to adult speech. When you watch a young infant and adult caregiver engaged in a give-and-take of sounds, it is easy to see that even the youngest children are students of language.

As they get older, infants begin to babble and play with sounds. As they interact with family members and others, they begin to repeat the sounds that they hear and stop using sounds that are not part of their home language. Gradually they learn to use sounds, gestures, and facial expressions to communicate their needs.

Young toddlers begin to put sounds together into recognizable words. They begin to use *holophrases,* single words that communicate a complex idea. A 15-month-old may say, "car." Depending on the situation, he may mean, "I want my toy car." "I see a car." "Where is my car?" or "I want to go in the car." Toddlers also often use *overgeneralized speech,* employing one word for a variety of meanings. *"ju-ju"* may be used for any drink, juice, milk, or water. As they become older, toddlers' vocabularies increase substantially, and by 18 months, many will have a vocabulary of up to 300 words. Toddlers begin putting words together into sentences and are able to express increasingly complicated thoughts. Two-word sentences appear between 18 and 20 months of age and express ideas concerning relationships: "Mommy sock" (possessor-possession), "Cat sleeping" (actor-action), "Drink milk" (action-object), and so on. Next, they create sentences that are short and simple. These *telephraphic sentences* omit function words and endings that contribute little to meaning. "Where Daddy go?" "Me push truck."

Preschoolers continue to rapidly build their vocabulary. As language development proceeds, they join related sentences logically and express ideas concerning time and spatial relationships. They come to understand social expectations for language use and begin to use adult forms of language. As vocabularies expand, the ability to use words increases, and children intuitively acquire many of the rules of language. Many 3-year-olds have a vocabulary of 900–1,000 words (Christie, Enz, & Vukelich, 2011), and that store of words will expand over the preschool years. Some researchers suggest that preschoolers add 2,500 new words per year (Biemiller & Slonim, 2001).

As preschoolers' language becomes more sophisticated, they use it to ask questions, describe needs, and share information. Interestingly, they often switch

Reflect on everyday communication . . .

Think about the skills you use every day to communicate your thoughts and ideas to other people. Identify a simple message you have given today, such as, "The battery on my computer is low." or "Where do you want to eat tonight?" What skills did you need in order to convey this information to someone else? What skills did the other person need to understand your meaning?

from using correct grammar to making mistakes in ways that are consistent with typical usage. For example, they might say "I comed home" instead of "I came home." This is called *overgeneralization,* and it gives us insight into the way that children actively construct their understanding of language.

Milestones of Language Development

Language development follows a predictable sequence. However, every child follows an individual timetable. Some will show language abilities early; others may be listeners who quietly build vocabulary and only later use the words and phrases they have come to understand. The milestones presented in Figure 7.1 provide you with a general guide to the typical sequence of speech and language skill development during the preschool years.

A number of factors can influence the pace and timing of language development. Frequent ear infections or other health difficulties, as well as the amount and type of language used in children's homes, will influence the rate at which milestones are achieved. In addition, milestones of language development are different for children who are learning more than one language (see page 192, English Language Learners).

Theories of Language Development

Child development specialists, linguists, and other professionals who study language acquisition have developed theories about how children learn language. Like the study of child development in other domains, these perspectives are highly influenced by differences in beliefs about whether growth and learning occur as a result of outside influences ("nurture"), inborn traits and characteristics ("nature), or the dynamic interchange between inborn traits and environmental influences ("interactionist").

The Behaviorist Perspective

Based on the work of B. F. Skinner, this perspective assumes that children learn language through external reinforcement. Behaviorists believe that when parents, caregivers, and teachers respond to particular sounds and language patterns that children make and not to others, the children are encouraged to repeat the reinforced sounds and patterns, thus replicating the language of their families and communities. Behaviorists believe all language is learned through imitation of others, rather than by children's internalization of language rules. When you respond to children's language with attention and positive support, you are teaching in a way that corresponds to behaviorists' beliefs.

While behaviorists' theories partially explain how children learn to use words and language, they fail to help us understand how children develop new words or language patterns that they have not heard in the past. For instance, one child we knew noticed a dead lizard and explained, "gecko all done," a phrase he had not heard in this context before, but that expressed the concept clearly.

The Nativist Perspective

Nativists believe that children develop language as a result of innate abilities that are particular to acquiring and using language. In the 1960s, Noam Chomsky, a linguist, focused on children's innate capacity to develop language and to internalize

FIGURE 7.1 Typical Sequence of Language and Skill Development

36 Months

- Use pronouns *I, you, me* correctly
- Uses some plurals and past tenses
- Knows at least three prepositions, usually *in, on, under*
- Knows chief parts of body and can indicate these, if not name them
- Uses 3-word sentences
- Has approximately 900–1,000 spoken words
- Speaks most words intelligibly
- Understands most simple questions dealing with the environment and activities
- Responds accurately to such questions as "What must you do when you are sleepy, hungry, cold, or thirsty?"
- Tells sex, name, age

48 Months

- Knows names of familiar animals
- Uses at least 4 prepositions or can demonstrate understanding of their meaning
- Names common objects in picture books or magazines
- Knows one or more colors
- Repeats 4 digits when they are given slowly
- Repeats words of 4 syllables
- Demonstrates understanding of *over* and *under*
- Uses most vowels and diphthongs* and has the consonants *p, b, m, w, n* well established
- Uses extensive verbalization during activities
- Understands such concepts as *longer, larger,* when a contrast is presented
- Readily follows simple commands even though the stimulus objects are not in sight

60 Months

- Uses many descriptive words spontaneously—both adjectives and adverbs
- Knows common opposites: *big-little, hard-soft, heavy-light,* etc.
- Speaks intelligibly, in spite of articulation errors
- Uses all vowels and the consonants *m, p, b, h, w, k, g, t, d, n, ng, y* (yellow)
- Repeats sentences as long as 9 words
- Defines common objects in terms of use (*hat, shoe, chair*)
- Follows three commands given without interruptions
- Uses fairly long sentences and some compound and some complex sentences
- Uses grammatically correct speech most of the time

*Two adjacent vowel sounds occurring within the same syllable such as cow and boy

Sources: Based on Berk, 2009; Christie, Enz, & Vukelich, 2011; and Santrock, 2010.

and use the rules of grammar. He believed that all individuals are born with a *language acquisition device* (LAD), an inborn ability that allows them to understand and use universal rules of grammar and to develop language. While later theorists challenged the existence of a LAD, contemporary studies of brain development confirm that language development is controlled by particular areas in the brain, and that during the first three years of life, the brain is especially responsive to language stimulation.

If you have noticed that it is easier for very young children to learn language than it is for older children or adults, and if you expect young children to learn language through exposure to adults' speech, then you have confirmed the nativist perspective on language development.

The Social Interactionist Perspective

Interactionists take the viewpoint that children learn language as a result of the interplay between their inborn biological abilities—genetics, brain growth, etc.—and their experiences. Typically developing children are born with the neurologi-

cal structures and cognitive abilities needed to develop language. As they interact with others, they observe and participate in communication. Because they are motivated to engage in these social interactions, they develop language using both their inborn abilities and their increasingly complex language exchanges with the important people in their lives.

Psychologist Lev Vygotsky's work emphasized the importance of social interactions in the development of language. He noted the significant role of older children and adults in supporting children's development of language and other skills. Vygotsky's work highlighted the fact that adults (and more experienced children) provide assistance and support for children as they learn language and communication skills. They interpret, ask questions, expand ideas, and clarify speech. This scaffolding allows children to actively participate in social interactions and provides the support needed for them to build their language and communication abilities.

When you help children to use words to explain an idea, when you rephrase and extend their language to make it clear to others, and when you ask questions to help them clarify or expand their language, you are using strategies from an interactionist perspective.

English Language Learners

Many of the children you teach will come from families for whom English is not the home language. In fact, some population data tells us that in 2010 more than 30% of all school-age children will come from homes in which English is not the primary language (U.S. Citizenship and Immigration Services, 2001). When they enter English-speaking classrooms, they will be learning English as they continue to become proficient in their home language. Children who begin school as non-English speakers are referred to as *English language learners* (ELLs), English as a second language students (ESLs), or emergent bilinguals (EBs).

Sequence of Second Language Development

It is useful to understand how language development occurs for ELLs. Just as children learning a first language differ, ELLs will have individual schedules for their language acquisition; however, the sequence of stages is generally consistent.

When young ELL children arrive at a school where only English is spoken, many respond by *trying to use their home language* to communicate. Some learn quite quickly that this is not effective, and they stop. Others continue speaking their home language for a longer period of time.

As they encounter the frustration of not being understood, ELL children move to the next stage of second language acquisition, *the non-verbal period.* They stop using their first language and seem to intently study the new language. This behavior is sometimes referred to as *spectating* (Tabors, 2008). As they closely observe their peers, they may begin to softly repeat words. This speech is very quiet and not intended to communicate with others. It appears they are *rehearsing* for later communication (Saville-Troike, 1987).

When children first try to use the new language to communicate with others, they use one or two words to communicate a variety of meanings (called *telegraphic* and *formulaic speech*), just like toddlers learning a language. They begin to use some *formulaic* words or phrases that are repeated frequently in particular contexts. They haven't completely mastered the meaning of words and are experimenting with how to use them. With time and practice, ELLs begin to use short phrases of their own; this *productive language* helps them to build relationships with others and become full participants in the life of the classroom.

Children from Diverse Backgrounds

The young children in your classroom will come to you with a variety of language backgrounds. Some will come from families where there has been a great deal of spoken language and verbal communication; others come from families that use few words or communicate less frequently. Some cultures put less emphasis on talking and oral language than do Western cultures, and children from these families may learn to communicate using fewer words and more gestures and nuance. It is important to learn about how each family communicates and to understand the strategies children know and use to relate to both peers and adults. This will allow you to honor the communication conventions of all children's families and to teach children ways to communicate successfully in the school setting.

What Is Language Curriculum in Early Childhood?

Whatever experiences you plan, and whatever happens spontaneously, language is almost constant as you and the children work and play together in the classroom. Language is embedded in almost all aspects of the early childhood curriculum. Even though this is true, there is a separate, intentional part of the curriculum that is called *language.*

You will support children's language learning not through correcting their mistakes or through direct instruction. Instead, you will provide a model and use natural opportunities to expand children's language understanding and skills. In order for this to happen, you must be intentional and work to deliberately create opportunities for language learning that are interesting, meaningful, and enjoyable for young children.

Providing Experience with Language

Whether you are 3 or 23, when you speak, you are using language that you had to learn. As you teach young children, you help them to unconsciously master five aspects of language. Though you may have heard the words *syntax, morphology, semantics, phonology,* and *pragmatics,* you probably never thought that you would be teaching these things to preschoolers. Guess what? Though you will not use these words with the children ("What lovely semantics you're using today!"), you will be teaching these building blocks of language.

Syntax

Syntax is another word for *grammar.* You use grammar every time you speak. Every language has rules about how words link together to make sense. When you say "This is my book!" instead of "Book my this is!" you are using syntax. As children engage with language, they learn to apply rules of grammar that are part of the language they hear. Grammar differs from language to language. For example, a Spanish speaker might say *"mi vestido bonito"* ("my dress pretty"), while an English speaker would say, "my pretty dress."

A language curriculum for young children should offer them many experiences with English syntax. So it's important that you use your "best grammar" when you speak to the children, thus ensuring that they hear how the language is supposed to sound.

Morphology

Rules about the structure of words, how we make plurals, and add suffixes (like *-ed* and *-ing*) and prefixes is called *morphology.* When children say, "I know-ed the ducks" or "I eat-ed some cake," they are demonstrating their understanding of the way English speakers indicate that something happened in the past. When you sing "Five little ducks that I once knew," you are teaching morphology.

As children learn language, they internalize rules and apply them in their speech. Mistakes like *knowed* and *eated* show that they understand rules about past tense and can apply them. With more exposure to language (like singing "Five little ducks" or talking about "the delicious cake we ate"), they learn the many irregular forms of speech in the English language. This is why it's so important to speak clearly and avoid "baby talk" and slang in your speech with children.

Semantics

The meaning of words is called *semantics.* Helping children develop a rich vocabulary (the ability to understand and use many words) is one of your most important tasks as a teacher of language. As children acquire new vocabulary, they develop increasingly complex thinking abilities and refine cognitive categories.

> *"This not a pan," says 3-year-old Jamela, holding up a plate. "This a plate. Use the pan in the stove, not the plate! Put the plate on the table for the Daddy's dinner." At clean-up time, the teacher asks, "Where is the spatula?" Looking around, Jamela finds it and says, "Here's the flipper," and she tucks it into the utensil can.*

Jamela understands characteristics of items and has created categories for them based on how they are used. She labels plates and pans based on their functions. Her receptive vocabulary includes the word *spatula;* she can find it when she hears the word. She does not yet use it in her expressive (speaking) vocabulary. Jamela knows the function of a spatula and is able to categorize it. With additional exposure to the word, it will become part of her expressive language.

Some language specialists suggest that children should encounter and explore at least two to four new words each day (Roskos, Tabors, & Lenhart, 2009). To help children build vocabulary, you must use new and interesting words in spontaneous conversations, intentionally select words to use in planned activities, and provide children with opportunities to hear and use those words in ways that are meaningful.

Phonology

Phonology is the sound structure of the language. In English there are approximately 44 discrete sounds or phonemes. All the words we use in English are made of these sounds. Other languages have different sounds. (That is one of the reasons it's hard to learn another language.) From birth, children are learning to produce the sounds of the language spoken around them.

This ability is strongly related to developing literacy skills. Children have to be able hear the distinct sounds of words to eventually be able read them. Knowing this, you will articulate more clearly when you are in the classroom with children ("Na-ta-lia can you bring me the pit-cher of wa-ter" not "Naduya, cn you bring me da pidcher a wadder").

Pragmatics

You speak in different ways when you're with your friends, when you are in school with your professor, when you visit your doctor, and when you talk to your grandmother. These differences reflect conventions about the social uses of language, called *pragmatics*. As children engage with adults and other children, they learn the many ways to use language in social settings. They begin to understand that the structure and type of language used when talking to family members is different than what is used in school.

One of this text's authors learned about pragmatics when her family moved from Tennessee to Illinois. On her first day in her new school, she responded to a teacher's question with the polite Tennessee reply, "Yes, ma'am." To her great shock and not insignificant embarrassment, she was scolded for being "sassy." The pragmatics of school language in these two locations were different.

Pragmatics includes if and how you make eye contact, when and whether you speak to someone who is respected, and many other things. It is influenced by your culture and experience. As a teacher of young children, you are helping children to learn the pragmatics of school language. As you do, it is critical that you are respectful of the pragmatics that children bring with them from their families.

Teaching Communication Skills

In addition to the five areas of language (syntax, semantics, morphology, phonology, and pragmatics) that you will teach by modeling and interacting with children, there are a number of communication skills you will teach more overtly in planned activities.

Asking and Answering Questions

Have you ever had trouble asking a question? Has anyone ever said to you, "Let me ask that another way," when your answer was not what they wanted or expected? Asking and answering questions is not nearly as simple as it may seem. It requires taking another person's point of view and gathering information to extend their ideas and understanding. Effective teachers encourage children to ask questions and to respond to them appropriately.

Children learn about questions in a number of ways. You model this skill when you frequently ask questions, listen carefully to what children say, and take time to respond to the questions that children pose. Preparing the questions you ask is an important part of your planning process. You can use children's queries as a method of understanding what they know and want to know about a topic. And you build their desire to ask questions by being open and responsive to the questions they ask.

Having Conversations

In order to engage in conversations with others, children need to have a basic understanding about how conversations work. They must know that:

1. conversation goes back and forth between speakers; one listens while the other speaks.
2. conversations have a specific topic that each speaker addresses (if we're talking about apples, you don't suddenly start talking about sheep).
3. each speaker responds to and builds on the other's message.
4. questions are used to help each speaker understand what the other means.

An effective language curriculum will ensure that children have time, opportunity, and motivation to have conversations with adults and with one another.

The Ability to Use Abstract Language

When children first learn to talk, they use language that is specific to a particular situation. They learn to say, "I want milk" at the supper table and "Happy Birthday" at a party. This is sometimes referred to as *contextualized speech;* it happens in the *context* of the situation. As children get older and have more experiences with the world and with language, they learn to talk about ideas and experiences that are not present. This is called *abstract language* or *decontextualized speech*.

Being able to use abstract language is important! Without it you couldn't talk about the past ("When I was a baby I couldn't walk or talk") or the future ("When I get bigger, I'll go to kindergarten like my brother"). You couldn't talk about people or places that are not present ("Mommy went to work. She'll come back after nap."). You couldn't imagine and pretend ("You be the mommy elephant and I'll be the baby elephant. Let's fly to elephant land!").

Using decontextualized speech is a sophisticated process that takes time and experience to learn. Providing children with experiences that invite abstract language encourages symbolic thinking and supports learning in all areas, particularly literacy and language. You are teaching language when you lead a discussion about an upcoming field trip, have a conversation with children about what they did over the weekend, or lead a song about five speckled frogs. You are helping children acquire the skill of using abstract language: the ability to communicate about people, things, and events that are not actually present.

Giving Opportunities to Talk

In order for children to become skilled language users, they need many opportunities to talk with one another and to engage in meaningful conversations with adults. A fundamental element of the language curriculum is providing the time and opportunity for talking with other people.

Teachers do quite a bit of talking in the day-to-day life of the classroom—"please sit quietly," "find your jacket," "it's time to clean up the blocks," "this is a turkey," "thank you for helping"—and these statements model use of language.

However, many teachers pay less attention to talking with children outside of routines. Talking times should be part of planned activities and should be purposefully made a part of interactions throughout the day.

"I brunged these rocks from my home," Elijah tells his teacher, Jen. *"You brought these from home to share with us?"* she asks. *"Where did you find them?"* *"In our yard, I finded them by the swing,"* Elijah explains. *"Are there a lot of rocks in your yard?"* asks Jen. *"We got lots of rocks. My Dad said take 'em."* *"Your Dad said you should bring them to school?"* *"No, he said take them out from by the swing."* *"Oh, your Dad didn't want the rocks near your swings at home. Maybe that was so no one will fall on them and get hurt,"* Jen suggests. *"Yeah!"* Elijah agrees.

Conversations like this can happen at any time during the day or as part of a planned activity. What is important is that the teacher made time to engage the child in a conversation. There was active participation by both Elijah and his teacher, and the conversation was meaningful to the child. Language curriculum includes planned talking times that are structured to encourage all children to participate comfortably in conversations—for example, at a small-group time or when looking at books together. It also requires unstructured time during the day when you and a child can have a conversation, for example, when eating lunch or during learning center time.

Designing Experiences to Talk About

Children are encouraged to talk when they have experiences that are of interest to them and that are relevant to their lives. So, an important part of your role as a teacher is to design engaging learning activities that include opportunities to talk. Cooking, going on a walk, playing a new game, reading a new book, entertaining a visitor, playing with an intriguing new toy, observing an animal, and many other structured experiences, all give children something to talk about. When these are coupled with time and encouragement to talk ("We have flour, sugar, oatmeal, butter, and eggs here—what kind of food do you think we could make? How do you use these ingredients at your house?"), they turn into language curriculum.

Another part of designing experiences for children to talk about is selecting topics of study that engage children and are important to them.

Roberto teaches 4-year-olds. He has noticed the children looking for bugs on the playground and heard them talking about bugs. So he plans a study of bugs. As a part of this study, Roberto brings many bugs into the classroom—caterpillars, a praying mantis, ladybugs, millipedes, cockroaches, crickets, mealworms. He plans a trip to a butterfly garden. He invites an entomologist to come and share a collection of insects. Throughout the study, children talk with excitement about the different insects, the parts of their bodies, and what they eat.

When a study engages children's interests and is filled with content that is important to them, they actively participate in the learning experiences.

Language development is the outgrowth of this as children discuss what they are doing, hear and use new words, and listen to language read from books related to the topic.

Standards for Language Curriculum

There are national and state standards for language. While many states and Head Start have developed standards specific to preschool-age children, national standards are targeted for children from K–12.

FIGURE 7.2   Common Core State Standards: English Language Arts Standards: Kindergarten

CONVENTIONS OF STANDARD ENGLISH

Demonstrate command of the conventions of standard English grammar and usage when writing or speaking.

- Use frequently occurring nouns and verbs.
- Form regular plural nouns orally by adding /s/ or /es/ (e.g., *dog, dogs; wish, wishes*).
- Understand and use question words (interrogatives) (e.g., *who, what, where, when, why, how*).
- Use the most frequently occurring prepositions (e.g., *to, from, in, out, on, off, for, of, by, with*).
- Produce and expand complete sentences in shared language activities.

VOCABULARY ACQUISITION AND USE

Determine or clarify the meaning of unknown and multiple-meaning words and phrases based on kindergarten reading and content.

- Identify new meanings for familiar words and apply them accurately (e.g., knowing *duck* is a bird and learning the verb to *duck*).
- Use the most frequently occurring inflections and affixes (e.g., *-ed, -s, re-, un-, pre-, -ful, -less*) as a clue to the meaning of an unknown word.

With guidance and support from adults, explore word relationships and nuances in word meanings.

- Sort common objects into categories (e.g., shapes, foods) to gain a sense of the concepts the categories represent.
- Demonstrate understanding of frequently occurring verbs and adjectives by relating them to their opposites (antonyms).
- Identify real-life connections between words and their use (e.g., note places at school that are colorful).
- Distinguish shades of meaning among verbs describing the same general action (e.g., *walk, march, strut, prance*) by acting out the meanings.

Use words and phrases acquired through conversations, reading and being read to, and responding to texts.

COMPREHENSION AND COLLABORATION

- Participate in collaborative conversations with diverse partners about *kindergarten topics and texts* with peers and adults in small and larger groups.
  - o Follow agreed-upon rules for discussions (e.g., listening to others and taking turns speaking about the topics and texts under discussion).
  - o Continue a conversation through multiple exchanges.
- Confirm understanding of a text read aloud or information presented orally or through other media by asking and answering questions about key details and requesting clarification if something is not understood.
- Ask and answer questions in order to seek help, get information, or clarify something that is not understood.
  - o Presentation of Knowledge and Ideas
- Describe familiar people, places, things, and events and, with prompting and support, provide additional detail.
- Speak audibly and express thoughts, feelings, and ideas clearly.

Source: Common Core State Standards for English Language Arts (National Governors Association Center for Best Practices, Council of Chief State School Officers, 2010). © Copyright 2010. National Governors Association for Best Practices and Council of Chief State School Officers. All rights reserved.

National Standards

Common Core Standards in the language arts for kindergarten through twelfth grade will be useful to you if you teach in a primary program (see Figure 7.2). They help preschool teachers understand the skills that will be required in elementary school.

Preschool Language Standards

The Head Start Outcomes and your own state preschool early learning guidelines lay out some direction for language curriculum. Head Start outcomes are listed in Figure 7.3. Head Start also includes outcomes specifically for English language development for children who are dual language learners. These standards are listed in Figure 7.4.

Most state standards include the following:

Speaking and Listening

- Shows increasing ability to use language in a variety of ways and in different settings and contexts.
- Listens with understanding to spoken language.
- Participates in progressively more complex conversations.

Language Acquisition

- Uses an increasingly complex vocabulary and sentence structure.
- Shows developing ability to use conventional grammar.

Your program's goals for language curriculum may be based on state or professional guidelines, or they may have been developed independently by your staff or a curriculum specialist. However, it is likely that they will contain content similar to the standards we have described.

FIGURE 7.3 **Head Start Early Learning Framework: Promoting Positive Outcomes for Language Development**

Receptive Language

The ability to comprehend or understand language.

- Attends to language during conversations, songs, stories, or other learning experiences.
- Comprehends increasingly complex and varied vocabulary.
- Comprehends different forms of language, such as questions or exclamations.
- Comprehends different grammatical structures or rules for using language

Expressive Language

The ability to use language.

- Engages in communication and conversation with others.
- Uses language to express ideas and needs.
- Uses increasingly complex and varied vocabulary.
- Uses different forms of language.
- Uses different grammatical structures for a variety of purposes.
- Engages in storytelling.
- Engages in conversations with peers and adults.

Source: Administration for Children and Families, Head Start Bureau, www.hsnrc.org/cdi/child-outcomes.cfm

Receptive English Language Skills

The ability to comprehend or understand the English language.

- Participates with movement and gestures while other children and the teachers dance and sing in English.
- Acknowledges or responds nonverbally to common words or phrases, such as "hello" "good bye" "snack time" "bathroom," when accompanied by adult gestures.
- Points to body parts when asked, "Where is your nose, hand, leg …?"
- Comprehends and responds to increasingly complex and varied English vocabulary, such as "Which stick is the longest?" "Why do you think the caterpillar is hungry?"
- Follows multi-step directions in English with minimal cues or assistance.

Expressive English Language Skills

The ability to speak or use English.

- Repeats word or phrase to self, such as "bus" while group sings the "Wheels on the Bus" or "brush teeth" after lunch.
- Requests items in English, such as "car," "milk," "book," "ball."
- Uses one or two English words, sometimes joined to represent a bigger idea, such as "throwball."
- Uses increasingly complex and varied English vocabulary.
- Constructs sentences, such as "The apple is round." or "I see a fire truck with lights on."

Source: Administration for Children and Families, Head Start Bureau, www.hsnrc.org/cdi/child-outcomes.cfm

Teaching Language

Language is part of every aspect of teaching. It includes a schedule that allows time for informal conversations and planned language experiences, a learning environment with materials that invite discussion, and of course, a variety of planned language activities.

Language Through Play in a Planned Environment

Busy, engaged children talk a lot! The sound of children's voices is the sound of learning. Teachers who value language learning and understand its importance

do not expect children to play quietly. They welcome the sound of laughing and talking.

When you prepare your environment with objects and materials that interest children, you are inviting questions and conversations. If you include a science area that is filled with things to see and do, a library with many books, a writing center with tools for drawing and writing, a block area with props, a manipulative area with games and toys that change regularly, and a sensory table with interesting things to explore, you are sure to encourage children's language.

The Dramatic Play Area

Whether you call it the Home Area, Housekeeping, the Pretend Area, or the Family Center, the dramatic play area of the classroom inspires children to use language. Socio-dramatic play involves recreating familiar scenes such as caring for a baby, fixing a meal, or attending a party. Children use language as they dramatize the familiar characters in these scenes and describe their actions. They use language in the role of the pretend character, "Baby, you eat this food I am giving you," and to direct others about how to play, "OK, now you go to the store to get the baby some more milk."

To enhance children's language, offer a variety of props. Children are inspired to extend their dramatic play and to use increasingly complex language when props suggest interaction. The standard props for dramatic play (telephones, uniforms and caps, fancy dresses, a table with dishes, baby dolls, cooking utensils) all promote dramatic play and encourage children to talk with one another. Props specific to particular topics, such as materials to set up a pretend store or doctor's office, will also encourage language interaction between children.

A Puppet Corner

If space allows, you can offer a *puppet corner*. There's something magical about puppets. They inspire language. Children give voice to ideas and feelings when they use or talk to a puppet.

To set up a puppet corner, you'll need a protected space with two or three sides of shelter. A shelf with something to hold puppets (a wooden puppet rack or an over-the-door shoe organizer) and a small number of puppets that relate to things children are interested in or are learning about are essential. If you place a few related storybooks with the puppets, it will encourage children's dramatizations.

A puppet theater (a standing divider behind which the puppeteer hides) is a nice addition if children are taught to use it. Skillful teachers we know work with children to develop and practice short puppet stories. These can then be presented for other children to see.

A Talking Corner

A great way to inspire conversation is by providing children with a place to go with a friend to get away from the hustle and bustle of the classroom. We have seen creative teachers find myriad ways to do this: refrigerator boxes, wooden packing crates, cardboard storage barrels, a sheet thrown over a table, even a padded claw-foot bathtub. The inside should be smooth and comfortable, and there should be room for just two children inside.

Another idea is to place two chairs in a corner with a nearby shelf filled with "provocative objects" that stimulate children to talk. A prism hung to create a rainbow, a tooth from a shark, a discarded steering wheel . . . many objects are interesting to young children and invite conversation.

The Great Outdoors

Children use language outdoors as well as indoors. Areas where dramatic play occurs such as hollow blocks, the playhouse, and the sandbox are particularly likely to inspire conversations. Teachers who are attentive to language curriculum regularly set up outdoor opportunities for children to read books on a blanket under a tree and engage in dramatic play.

A Schedule for Language Learning

Much of the language curriculum occurs in the play and routines that make up daily life in an early childhood classroom. In order to encourage conversation and language, children and teachers must have time to talk and engage in

Arrivals and Departures	Greet children and families as they arrive and again at the close of the day. Consciously model the back-and-forth nature of conversation with children's families while children are listening.
Meals	Always sit with children and talk with them at meals. Sometimes ask children at your table an engaging question unrelated to the meal—"What makes you happy when you go home? What do you want to be for Halloween? If you had a puppy what would you name it?"
Bathroom Routines	Using the toilet, washing hands, and brushing teeth all provide opportunities for conversation and language modeling. Talk with children about what they're doing in the bathroom in addition to talking about the events of the day.
Transitions	If waiting is a part of a transition, use it for a language game—ask a riddle ("I'm thinking of a kind of animal that has a long neck"), say a fingerplay, have children join you in a chant or song. Never just stand there talking to another teacher or scolding children for not being quiet or not standing in line!
	Use language riddles to excuse children when they need to go one or two at a time to the next activity—"I'm thinking of someone whose mom is named Tara, whose dad is named Horacio, and whose sister is named Sienna—yes Cielo you can go!"

interesting experiences. The regular routines and transitions—eating, toileting, hand washing, moving from playground to classroom—must be talking times—not just tasks to be completed. The In Practice box gives you tips for adding language to routines and transitions.

Small-group times offer children opportunities to learn how to talk with others in a group without having to wait and without being overwhelmed by a large audience. These are also times when you can plan lessons that particularly promote language. We recommend that you include at least one planned small-group experience per day. These experiences can last from 10 to 25 minutes, depending on children's ages.

Circle time is a daily gathering of the whole class (we have also heard it called *rug time, large group,* or *morning meeting*). Large groups can be difficult for children because they often involve a level of inactivity and listening that is beyond their ability. However, skilled teachers plan short (no more than 20 minutes), interesting meetings with opportunities for children to use language in songs, chants, and fingerplays; listen to stories; participate in listening and movement games; and play games with sound and speech. Such activities promote language ability.

Your Role in Teaching Language

Your participation and interaction with children comprise the core of the language curriculum. The way you speak, the way you listen, and the way you encourage language are the most important parts of language teaching in your classroom.

Conversations

Of all the things you do in your daily work with young children, nothing is more important than talking *with* them. Conversations consist of more than giving directions or briefly commenting on a child's work or activity. Real conversation is dialogue: back-and-forth exchanges between speakers. When you express your interest in what children are saying and doing, they will be motivated to respond. This type of conversation, sometimes called *extended discourse,* builds children's language and literacy skills. Create as many opportunities as you can to talk with children about topics that interest them—their pets, their friends, their favorite foods or colors, their families, weekend activities. If you know their interests and discuss them meaningfully, you will be doing a great deal to support their language growth.

Don't be surprised if you find it a little awkward to have conversations when you first start working with children. It's something you have to learn to do and it's something you have to practice. The In Practice box includes some tips for having conversations with young children.

Encourage Children to Talk with One Another

The conversations you have with children are not the only ones that matter. Children learn about language by talking with one another. Knowing this, you can support children by inviting them to converse with one another. As you see them playing side by side at an activity, encourage them to talk, "Can you tell her how you made that farm house for your animals?" "Aaron is interested in birds, and I know you have one at your house. Can you tell him about Tweeter?" Notice and comment when you see children engaged in conversation. "Theo, I saw you and Davis talking together at the sand table. It looked like you were enjoying talking about your sand sculptures."

> **Try It Out!**
>
> Spend some time talking to a child about any topic that interests him or her. Respond to what the child says by clarifying and expanding his or her comments. Try to create a dialog with the child that has five or more back-and-forth conversational interchanges.

IN PRACTICE: Tips for Conversations with Young Children

1. **Get close.** Crouch or sit at the child's eye level. It's easier to hear children's words when you are at their level and physically close to them.

2. **Pay attention.** Show your attention physically as well as verbally with eye contact, smiles, nods, a gentle hand on a shoulder or back. Focus on what the child is saying. Remember this is about the child, not about you.

3. **Listen.** This can be challenging in a room filled with active preschoolers! If you must handle another situation, tell the child you want to listen and will come back; then be sure you return at a calmer moment!

4. **Talk about what is happening.** Narrate what's happening like a "sportscaster." "Emma chose the two square blocks for the base of her structure and Marvie used rectangles." "It took a lot of sand for us to fill this bucket all the way to the top." This gives children opportunities to organize thoughts and ideas before they speak. Be careful to allow time for children to reflect and speak also.

5. **Respond to, clarify, and extend children's language.** This motivates children to continue talking. Clarify what children say, and build on or extend their language. Introduce vocabulary as well as more sophisticated language structures.

6. **Read nonverbal communication.** Notice and put into words what the child is feeling and thinking: "You're really happy." or "That's very exciting." or "It's a little scary."

7. **Don't hurry or interrupt.** If you don't understand, say, "Show me." "Tell me more about that."

Model

Children learn language by hearing it, so it is important that you provide a model of standard language. As an adult, you are able to switch back and forth between standard language usage (sometimes called the *school dialect*) and the informal language of home, but children have not yet acquired that ability. The differences may seem small, but they are important. Children are learning language from you, and in particular, they are learning the language of school from you.

This does not mean that you should correct children's language—in fact, doing so is ineffective and counterproductive. When children's language or pronunciation is corrected, they may become discouraged and reluctant to talk to adults or to engage in conversations with peers (Cazden, 1969). When you hear incorrect word use or a mispronunciation, restate the child's words correctly. "I putted all de blocks in" can be restated without correction: "You put all the blocks on the shelf? Thank you!"

Use Interesting Words

Do you love words? Do you have a large vocabulary? Do you appreciate the way the "just right" word can call up an image? If so, you have a gift to share with children. When you use the words you love in ways that are meaningful, children will learn their meanings and will develop rich vocabularies. If you don't naturally love words or if English is your second language, you may have to work harder to include interesting vocabulary in your speech. Regardless of whether "rare" words come to you easily or you have to work to learn them, as you speak with children be sure to choose words that may be new to them. Use these words in ways that help children understand their meaning.

"You are *curious* about that; you wonder what will happen."

"That's a *tremendous* structure; one of the biggest ones I have seen."

"What an *enchanting* story; I almost forgot I was in the classroom it was so interesting."

"That's a *chimpanzee*. *Chimpanzees* are *apes*. They live in the jungle. They are similar to monkeys but bigger."

Using rare words can be fun for the children and for you as you challenge yourself to think of interesting words. Be careful not to use too many new words at once, or they will be overwhelming for young children. However, frequent "sprinkles" of rich words into your speech will usually capture children's interest. We have found that children who are accustomed to hearing unusual words will often use them appropriately, sometimes surprising us. One 4-year-old we know responded to his teacher's comment about an airplane by saying, "That's not an airplane. It's a fighter jet aircraft, an F-14 Tomcat." Obviously he had experienced a good deal of rich language, especially as related to aircraft!

Show your interest in words and what they mean. For example, when reading a story, wonder aloud about a word's meaning. "'*The wild things roared their terrible roars and gnashed their terrible teeth . . .*' I wonder what 'gnashed' means." When children use an unusual word, ask them to tell you what it means. Encourage children to ask you and other children what words mean and when they do, let them know that you are pleased that they asked.

Ask Open-Ended Questions

Open-ended questions have many correct responses and require more than a single-word answer. They encourage children both to think and to use language to express their ideas. As you ask open-ended questions that involve reasoning

FIGURE 7.5 Examples of Open-Ended Questions

Reasoning

Why did you choose to wear sandals today?

How did you decide which picture to cut out?

Prediction

What might happen if we dropped the ball?

How would this change if we use red instead of blue?

Remembering Past Experiences

What did you see on our nature walk?

What did you enjoy about your weekend?

Comparing

How many things can you name that are smaller than you?

How are the dog and cat alike?

Decision Making

What activities would you like to do today?

How do you think we should set the table today?

Imagining

What would you find if you were exploring on the moon?

What would you do if on Halloween the monsters became real?

Evaluating and Planning

Should we add more flour to the playdough? Why?

What will we need for our pretend bakery?

and explaining, you are helping children to learn to speak and listen. Figure 7.5 offers some examples.

Supporting English Language Learners

The most important practice for supporting young children who are learning to speak English is to show respect for their home language. Reassure families that the ELLs should continue to use their home language and that doing so will not prevent their success in school or with peers. With time, they will develop into dual language speakers who are proficient in both languages. Take time to learn some words and phrases from the children's home languages, and include these phrases regularly in your speech. Find ways to encourage ELLs to use their home language in the classroom. For example, ask them to teach you a song or a game, and use it during Circle Time. Encourage regular family participation and ask families to share ideas with you about music, games, recipes, and other experiences from their culture that you can include in your curriculum.

You will find that many of the practices that are effective for helping all children learn to listen and speak are also useful for supporting English language learners. The In Practice box on page 206 gives you ideas for a number of simple ways to support English Language Learners in the classroom. Observe the children's speech and communication in order to understand where they are in their language development. You will then be able to slightly modify your speech and your teaching practices to include them effectively in the activities and experiences that you plan for all the children in your classroom.

Activities to Promote Language Learning

Although language is a part of almost every activity in the early childhood curriculum, in some activities it is the focus.

Word Games

Most young children enjoy playing with sounds and words. Providing them with varied opportunities to do this builds their listening skills, along with other language abilities. The following activities focus particularly on language skills and vocabulary. As children become more proficient at playing these types of word games, encourage them to give the clues and to lead the other children in the game.

Fill in the Blank is a game in which children complete a sentence. For example: *We wear shoes on our _____. A _____ swims in our aquarium.* Start very simply when you play *Fill in the Blank* so that children can understand and be successful at playing the game. After they have had some practice, the sentences can become more complex and may even have more than one correct response. *A fish has _____ on his body. He also has _____ on his body. Fill in the Blank* can be adapted to a variety of study topics and also works well after reading a story to help children recall certain words or facts.

Clues (sometimes called *Riddles* or *Guess What?*) is a game that encourages children to guess a word as you give increasingly specific clues. This game builds receptive language. For example, *I am an animal. I live in the jungle. I have four legs. I have fur. My fur has stripes. (Tiger)* or *This is a food. Sometimes we eat it at birthday parties. It is made from milk. It is very cold. (Ice cream)*

Opposites is a guessing game in which children guess a clue or fill in the blank with opposites: *I'm thinking of a word that means the opposite of daytime.* Or: *The soup wasn't cold; it was _____.* Learning about opposites is an important cognitive and language skill. It requires that children be able to engage in abstract thinking and have the vocabulary to understand pairs of words with opposed meanings. You can also make a matching game with pairs of cards that have pictures of opposites, e.g., top/bottom; hot/cold; happy/sad; small/big, etc.

Word Pictures is a game in which children think of as many words as they can to describe an object or a picture. For example, bring a large and interesting shell to class and have the children touch and hold it. Then ask each child to share one word that describes the shell. You can make a list of these words to keep track of how many different words the group can think of.

Planned Dramatic Play Scenes also can be used to develop language. While most dramatic play should be spontaneous and child directed, you can enrich children's play and gently guide them to develop mature language through planned dramatic play. This can be a valuable experience for children who do not have the language needed to engage in complex dramatic play.

Interactive Storybook Reading

Language skills are enhanced when children have frequent opportunities to participate in interactive storybook reading. When you read stories to children, they:

- hear many types of language.
- hear new words used in context.
- associate spoken words and sounds with written ones.

IN PRACTICE: Helping Children Plan for Play

1. **Set the scene.** Take children on a field trip, read them a story, or have a visitor come to share about a community role that interests children. For example, pay a visit to your local grocery store or invite a trainer of Assistance Dogs to visit your classroom.

2. **Plan**
   - *Plan the scene.* At circle or small-group time, ask the children if they would like to plan to play. "We had an interesting trip to the market yesterday. Would you like to set up a pretend market here in our classroom?"
   - *Plan the props.* Ask children to think about what you will need for the play scene. As they offer suggestions, write them on chart paper. "Jolie suggested that we'll need play money and Kallie thought we should have a cash register." If the play requires props that are not available in the classroom, ask children to think about where you can find or make what is needed.
   - *Plan the space.* The day before, ask the children to think about how you can set up the area where the play scenes will happen. Older children can create a "map" of the space. Set up the area with the children.

   - *Plan the roles.* On the day, ask children to decide which roles will be used. "We'll need a cashier and someone to set up the produce." Make sure there are roles for all the players. Help the children to think about what people in those roles need to do. Invite the children to choose roles for the first play session. Establish that roles will be traded.

3. **Play**
   - Invite children to play.
   - Observe, and if the play lags or some children seem stuck or confused, offer some ideas and support. "You're shopping at the market? Did you bring your list? Maybe you could tell Trevor what you are shopping for."
   - Model complex language and introduce relevant vocabulary. "I see some milk and some cheese in this section of the market. I wonder if you could add some other dairy products?"
   - Be careful to keep your interventions to a minimum and to remember that the play belongs to the children!

Sources: Based on Bodrova & Leong, 2007; Roskos, Tabors, & Lenhart, 2009.

- practice asking and responding to questions.
- hear and practice decontextualized speech.
- engage in dialogue with others.

Book reading with one or two individuals (as opposed to reading to a group) provides a special opportunity to snuggle up and enjoy being together. This kind of intimate book sharing provides more opportunity to talk about the book. English language learners especially benefit from opportunities to listen to stories read at a pace that they can enjoy and to experience words paired with pictures.

Storytelling

Telling stories is different from reading books. Telling old familiar tales like *The Three Pigs* or the *Shoemaker and the Elves* helps children to understand that stories can be told. Find a simple story you already know well and practice telling it on your own; then share it with children. They will be entranced.

Children also delight when their teachers make up a story about something important and interesting to them. Stories can be about anything: They can be completely made up and magical—about a pretend dragon or a talking turkey, or they can be about familiar people who do something impossible or fun such as *The Day the Butterfly Group Learned to Really Fly*. It can be a little scary, if you are a new teacher, to tell a story without the words of a book to guide you, but with practice, it will become easier.

Children love to tell stories about their own lives. Sometimes these stories are real and other times they are pretend, and sometimes they are a mixture of both. Encourage this storytelling, as it offers opportunities for children to organize their ideas and find ways express them. It is also an excellent time to engage in extended discourse, as you ask questions to help them clarify their thinking, expand their language, and build on their ideas.

Singing

Singing supports children's language and vocabulary development, enhances phonological awareness, and supports auditory memory. Choose some songs with unusual words and pause to wonder about their meaning with the children.

"*Way down yonder in the paw-paw patch.* Hum, that's two unusual words in that song. I wonder what *paw-paw* is? How can we find out? And what's a paw-paw patch?"

Planning Language Curriculum

Even though language is part of every activity, it is important to take time to thoughtfully plan activities that focus on language. To help you with this planning, we have listed some common objectives for the preschool language curriculum in Table 7.1.

Writing Plans for Language

During breakfast, Jackson says to his friend Adrianna, "Hey, this oatmeal is hot!" "Yeah," she replies, "but the milk is cold." Iris, their teacher, says, "The oatmeal is hot; the milk is cold. They have opposite temperatures. I wonder if you can think of some other opposite words. How about the opposite

TABLE 7.1 Some Typical Objectives for the Preschool Language Curriculum

Stage and Objectives	Listening and Comprehension	Speaking	Communication	Vocabulary
Younger preschoolers *The ability to . . .*	• Pay attention to the speech and language of others. • Demonstrate understanding of what people are saying. • Follow 1- or 2-step oral directions.	• Use simple sentences to communicate needs and ideas. • Begin to use conventional grammar, e.g., word order, plurals, tenses. • Ask simple questions.	• Use basic social conventions for conversations: "Hello," "Thank you," "What's your name?" • Engage in short back-and-forth conversations.	• Use pronouns *I, me,* and *you* correctly. • Use simple prepositions, *in, on, under.*
Older preschoolers *The ability to . . .*	• Demonstrate understanding of increasingly complex words and sentences. • Follow 3-step directions. • Listen to stories with understanding and enjoyment.	• Use a variety of nouns, verbs, and descriptive phrases in meaningful ways. • Use increasingly complex sentences. • Tell a simple story.	• Use language to share and gather information, express feelings, and share thoughts and ideas. • Use many words and voice tones appropriate to a variety of situations, e.g., "Are you okay?" to a hurt child, "What do you want to order?" in a restaurant play scene.	• Use adjectives (a *pretty* dress) and adverbs (shouted *loudly*). • Understand and use opposites. • Define objects by their use, e.g., "Shovels are for digging."

of big . . . do you know what that is?" Jackson looks confused, but Adrianna says excitedly, "Little!" "Right," says Iris. "Let's try another one. Jackson, do you know what the opposite of tall is?" He thinks for a minute, and says tentatively, "Short?" "Right. The opposite of tall is short!"

Language curriculum is created both spontaneously in situations where teachers build on what children are saying and through activities that are planned based on the interests and skills that children demonstrate. In the example above, Iris noticed that Adrianna was interested in opposites. She immediately responded by asking Adrianna to name another opposite. Jackson needed a second try, but was able to use the concept correctly. Noticing that opposites are an *interest* as well as something that Adrianna and several of the other children are good at (a *strength*), Iris created a plan to build on this interest. Because she is an experienced teacher, Iris created a short plan to help prepare for this lesson (see Figure 7.6).

Iris's short plan would not be enough of a guide for a beginning teacher. The detailed version, shown in Figure 7.7, gives you a better idea of what she planned to do.

Language in a Weekly Plan

Language learning occurs in every activity and routine. When children are given frequent opportunities for self-selected play in environments that provide a variety of interesting materials, they are encouraged to engage in meaningful language experiences. Language activities must also be planned as part of the daily teacher

FIGURE 7.6 Simple Language Activity Plan

Opposite Word Game

Objectives:	• Use simple opposite word pairs correctly.
	• Use the word *not* in appropriate contexts.
Standard:	HPCS Domain III, Standard 1
What you need:	Twelve cards with pictures of concepts that have easily identifiable opposites; book, *Eric Carle's Opposites*
How to teach:	1. Read *Eric Carle's Opposites*.
	2. Tell children you have a new guessing game to play. Show the cards.
	3. Allow each child to select a card and say, e.g., "The car is in the garage; it is *not* _____ (pause) out of the garage."
	4. Offer prompts as necessary so that everyone will be successful.
	5. After all children have had a turn, remind them that we used *opposites*.
	6. Excuse children by offering each an opposite to guess.
How to assess:	Look/Listen for children using the correct word to correspond with the picture card; discussing opposites in their play and using them correctly; correctly filling in the blank in the word game; and using the word *not* correctly in conversation.

FIGURE 7.7 Detailed Language Activity Plan

Activity:	**Opposite Word Game** (*A fill-in-the-blank and matching card game*)
Curriculum Area:	Language
WHO It's For:	This activity was planned for the *Dancing Dragons* (ten 4-year-olds).
Rationale:	Many of the *Dancing Dragons,* particularly Adrianna and Jackson, have begun to use opposites in their speech and to talk about the idea of opposites. This activity will allow them to hear opposite pairs and receive coaching in identifying opposites.
Language Objectives:	*By participating in this activity, children will:*
	• Use simple opposite word pairs correctly.
	• Use the word *not in appropriate contexts*.
Preschool Content Standard:	Domain III (Communication, Language Development & Literacy) Standard 1: Use language in a variety of ways.
Indicator:	Uses opposites in speech.
HOW to Prepare	*What you need:*
	Twelve cards with pictures of concepts that have easily identifiable opposites, for example, an *empty* glass, a puppy *under* a table, a *tall* building, etc.
	Eric Carle's Opposites
	Set up:
	Do this in small groups; have children seated in a circle so that all can see the cards when they are held up.
HOW to Teach	*Introduction:*
	When children are settled in group, read the *Eric Carle's Opposites*.
	Tell them you have a new word guessing game to play. Say something like, "Yesterday at breakfast Adrianne and Jackson noticed that the oatmeal was hot and the milk was cold. These words are opposites; *cold* is the opposite of *hot*. Today we are going to play a game to try to name words that are opposite to each other."

FIGURE 7.7   Detailed Language Activity Plan (continued)

Teaching steps:

1. Hold up the picture of the tall building and say. "This building is *tall;* it is not _____ "(pause). The children will probably chime in with "short" or "little." "Right, this building is not **short;** it is **tall.** The **opposite** of *short* is *tall.*"

2. Model with a second picture. For example, hold up a picture of a steaming cup of cocoa and say, "This cocoa is _____ (pause). Some children will say "hot"; encourage them by saying, "It is *hot,* it is *not* _____. The **opposite** of *hot* is *cold.*"

3. Allow each child in turn to select a card. Ask the child to hold the card up. Say the sentence with the pictured modifier, e.g., "The car is **in** the garage; it is *not* _____ (pause) **out** of the garage.

4. As children understand, they may be able to answer with sentences with limited or no coaching.

5. Offer prompts as necessary so that everyone will be successful.

6. After all children have had a turn, remind them that we used *opposites.*

7. Read the book, *Eric Carle's Opposites,* encouraging children to guess the opposites as you read the story.

Closure:

Excuse children individually by offering each an opposite to guess, for example, "Jackson, the opposite of top is _____. Okay, you may choose a center."

HOW to Assess and Document

Objectives	Evidence of Learning Children might …	How to Document This Evidence
Use simple opposite words pairs correctly.	• Use the correct opposite word to correspond with the picture card. • Discuss opposites in their play and use them correctly.	Anecdotal observations
Use the word *not* in appropriate contexts	• Correctly fill in the blank in the word game. • Use the word *not* correctly in conversation.	Anecdotal observations, written language transcripts, or audio recording

EVALUATION   (Things to remember for next time)

Make a second set of cards with pictures illustrating the opposite concept. Put these matching cards in the table games area for the children to use independently.

guided activities. In the week's plan, *A Study of Bugs,* shown in Figure 7.8, notice that there are specific activities planned to enhance language development, such as *What Do You Know About Bugs?* (charting activity) and *My House/Your House* (a vocabulary building activity). Other activities, such as cooking, woodworking, and creative movement activities, focus on skill building in other areas, but they also foster language development.

Language in an Integrated Curriculum

An integrated study is an ideal way to build children's language skills because language is a part of almost every classroom activity. A well-planned curriculum includes a variety of opportunities to hear and use vocabulary. An integrated study encourages children to communicate and helps them understand a variety of ways to use language.

In the sunburst *A Study of Bread* (Figure 7.9), you will notice that some activities have been specifically planned to encourage language and listening skills. These are highlighted on the sunburst. All the activities, however, include language in one way or another. For example, the cooking activities introduce

FIGURE 7.8 A Week's Plan: "Bugs"—Week #1

Curriculum Focus: Insects and Similar Creatures
Objectives: To gain knowledge of small, land-based arthropods, gastropods, and annelids (insects, millipedes, spiders, centipedes, snails, slugs, worms, etc.); to develop respect for, interest in, and curiosity about life in general and "bugs" in particular; and to gain inquiry, communication, and physical skills.

	Monday	Tuesday	Wednesday	Thursday	Friday
Story	*The Very Hungry Caterpillar*	*Bugs Are Insects*	*Ant, Ant, Ant*	*The Grouchy Ladybug*	*Anansi The Spider*
Outdoor Activities **Purpose:** *to help children …*	**Stepping Stones** Develop large motor coordination, balance, and self-control.	**Stepping Stones** Develop large motor coordination, balance, and self-control.	**Woodworking** Develop creative industry and practical skills. Develop spatial awareness about shape, form, and structure.	**Woodworking** Develop creative industry and practical skills. Develop spatial awareness about shape, form, and structure.	**Woodworking** Develop creative industry and practical skills. Develop spatial awareness about shape, form, and structure.
Small Group **Purpose:** *to help children …*	**What Do You Know About Bugs? Chart** Develop an interest in communication ideas both verbally and in writing. Communicate ideas about bugs and related topics.	**Caterpillar bookmaking** Develop an interest in meaningful connections between experiences and written communication.	**My house/Your house** A vocabulary building discussion about bugs and where they live. Build vocabulary. Expand understanding about people and their needs. Expand understanding about bugs and their needs.	**Bug Match Game** Increase visual discrimination skills. Build vocabulary, specifically insect names.	**Bug House Project** Learn about collecting and caring for bugs. Learn how to work together. Apply knowledge about buildings and houses.
Indoor Special Activities **Purpose:** *to help children …*	**Caterpillar Drawing** Develop symbolic representation as a means of observation and communication.	**Apple Crisp** Develop and use measurement concepts. Recognize and use symbols.	**Leaf Rubbing** Experience a variety of techniques in art. Explore cause and effect.	**Ink and Watercolors** Develop creative expression through art. Experience a variety of techniques in art.	**Clay** Develop creative expression through art. Develop sensory awareness.
Lunch Circle (large group) **Purpose:** *to help children …*	**Under One Sky** Develop creative expression through music.	**Fuzzy, Fuzzy Caterpillar** Develop creative expression through music.	**Bugs around the Chair** Develop creative expression through music.	**Magic Bugs** Develop creative expression through movement and make-believe.	**I'm Thinking of an Insect** Build listening skills. Increase vocabulary.

Activities that are particularly focused on building language skills are highlighted.

212

FIGURE 7.9 A Study of Bread Sunburst

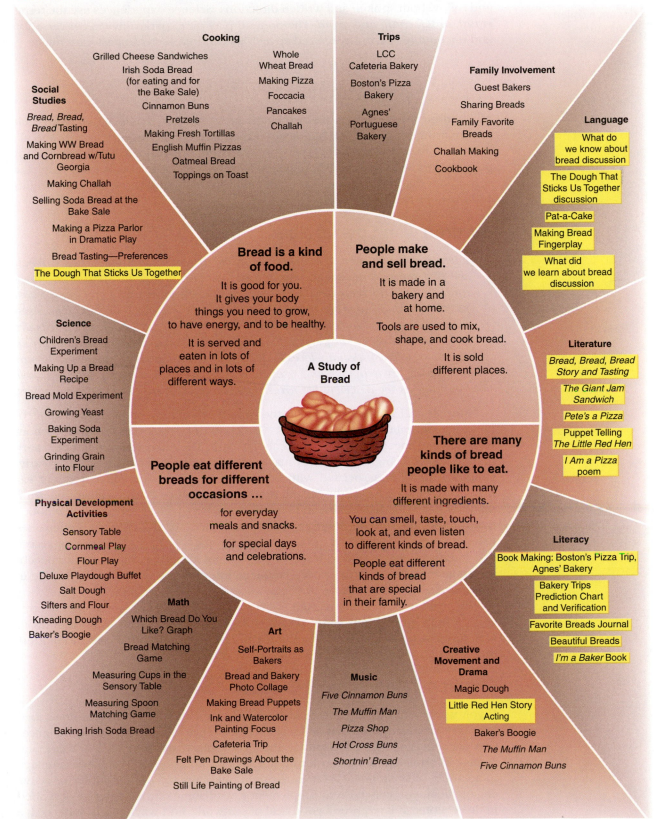

Cooking
Grilled Cheese Sandwiches
Irish Soda Bread (for eating and for the Bake Sale)
Cinnamon Buns
Pretzels
Making Fresh Tortillas
English Muffin Pizzas
Oatmeal Bread
Toppings on Toast

Whole Wheat Bread
Making Pizza
Foccacia
Pancakes
Challah

Trips
LCC Cafeteria Bakery
Boston's Pizza Bakery
Agnes' Portuguese Bakery

Family Involvement
Guest Bakers
Sharing Breads
Family Favorite Breads
Challah Making
Cookbook

Social Studies
Bread, Bread, Bread Tasting
Making WW Bread and Cornbread w/Tutu Georgia
Making Challah
Selling Soda Bread at the Bake Sale
Making a Pizza Parlor in Dramatic Play
Bread Tasting—Preferences
The Dough That Sticks Us Together

Language
What do we know about bread discussion
The Dough That Sticks Us Together discussion
Pat-a-Cake
Making Bread Fingerplay
What did we learn about bread discussion

Science
Children's Bread Experiment
Making Up a Bread Recipe
Bread Mold Experiment
Growing Yeast
Baking Soda Experiment
Grinding Grain into Flour

Literature
Bread, Bread, Bread Story and Tasting
The Giant Jam Sandwich
Pete's a Pizza
Puppet Telling *The Little Red Hen*
I Am a Pizza poem

Physical Development Activities
Sensory Table
Cornmeal Play
Flour Play
Deluxe Playdough Buffet
Salt Dough
Sifters and Flour
Kneading Dough
Baker's Boogie

Literacy
Book Making: Boston's Pizza Trip, Agnes' Bakery
Bakery Trips Prediction Chart and Verification
Favorite Breads Journal
Beautiful Breads
I'm a Baker Book

Math
Which Bread Do You Like? Graph
Bread Matching Game
Measuring Cups in the Sensory Table
Measuring Spoon Matching Game
Baking Irish Soda Bread

Art
Self-Portraits as Bakers
Bread and Bakery Photo Collage
Making Bread Puppets
Ink and Watercolor Painting Focus
Cafeteria Trip
Felt Pen Drawings About the Bake Sale
Still Life Painting of Bread

Music
Five Cinnamon Buns
The Muffin Man
Pizza Shop
Hot Cross Buns
Shortnin' Bread

Creative Movement and Drama
Magic Dough
Little Red Hen Story Acting
Baker's Boogie
The Muffin Man
Five Cinnamon Buns

Bread is a kind of food.
It is good for you. It gives your body things you need to grow, to have energy, and to be healthy.
It is served and eaten in lots of places and in lots of different ways.

People make and sell bread.
It is made in a bakery and at home.
Tools are used to mix, shape, and cook bread.
It is sold different places.

A Study of Bread

People eat different breads for different occasions …
for everyday meals and snacks.
for special days and celebrations.

There are many kinds of bread people like to eat.
It is made with many different ingredients.
You can smell, taste, touch, look at, and even listen to different kinds of bread.
People eat different kinds of bread that are special in their family.

new vocabulary, such as *foccacia*, or *challah*, and encourage children to listen to and follow both spoken and written directions. Science experiences use the terms *equal, proof, chaff,* and *grind*. The pretend play pizza parlor invites conversation and encourages decontextualized speech as children recreate past experience.

Language for All Children

All children will benefit from a rich language curriculum that is in tune with their particular interests and that builds upon their strengths. The experiences and activities we have described for typically developing preschool age children and for preschoolers who are English language learners can be the basis for a language curriculum that meets the needs of all children, including those with disabilities and older primary age children.

Children with Special Needs

> *Jolene is a 4-year-old who has been identified as having a language delay. When she first started preschool 6 months ago, she had almost no spoken language and often did not seem to understand when people spoke with her. Over the past months, her language has blossomed. She speaks mostly in 1- or 2-word phrases, and although it is sometimes hard for others to understand her, her words are becoming clearer as she plays with the other children and participates in group activities. Jolene especially loves to draw and paint. She is always eager to participate in art activities and uses increasingly complex and understandable language as she describes her artwork to her teachers and her family members.*

More than 13 million people in the United States have some kind of speech-language disability (Machado, 2003). Some children may enter your classroom with delayed speech and limited vocabulary use. They may only understand very limited spoken language. Others may not be able to pronounce words clearly. Language delay is associated with a number of factors, including frequent ear infections, hearing loss, other health problems, cognitive delays, autism spectrum disorder, learning disabilities, and limited home language situations. If you notice that a child in your classroom is not meeting many of the language milestones listed on page 191, or if you have concerns about his or her articulation or receptive language skills, talk with the child's family about arranging for a speech-language evaluation. Early speech-language intervention can be very effective in helping young children learn to communicate and use language.

Regardless of whether a child is diagnosed with a delay, the most effective way to help all children learn to talk is to provide them with opportunities to hear and use language in meaningful ways. The early childhood classroom offers ongoing opportunities for every child to learn to communicate.

Children in the Primary Grades

If you work with primary age children, it is likely that you will have a prescribed language arts curriculum that will include a sequence of activities and experiences that encourage children to increase their vocabulary, use language to share and receive information, build conversation strategies, and support the use of language in a variety of situations. If your curriculum offers limited opportunities for active engagement, you may wish to supplement it with some of the strategies described in this chapter. If it requires a good deal of seatwork, find ways to add some active language games and explorations. Be sure to offer numerous conversation opportunities for primary age children who generally enjoy the social aspects of language.

Final Thoughts

Language surrounds us in our homes, in our places of worship, at our sporting events, and in our schools. Learning to use language to communicate with others, to understand the world, and to support reasoning and thinking skills is a primary task of childhood. We hope this chapter has offered you some methods for including language experiences in your classroom in ways that nurture this critical aspect of life and learning.

Learning Outcomes

When you read this chapter, thoughtfully complete selected assignments form the "To Learn More" section, and prepare items from the "For Your Portfolio" section, you will be demonstrating your progress in meeting the following *NAEYC Standards for Early Childhood Professional Preparation Programs* (2009):

Standard 1. Promoting Child Development and Learning

Students prepared in early childhood degree programs are grounded in a child development knowledge base. They use their understanding of young children's characteristics and needs and of the multiple interacting influences on children's development and learning to create environments that are healthy, respectful, supportive, and challenging for each child.

The key elements of standard 1 you will have learned about are . . .

1a: Knowing and understanding young children's characteristics and needs

1b: Knowing and understanding the multiple influences on development and learning

1c: Using developmental knowledge to create healthy, respectful, supportive, and challenging learning environments

Standard 3. Observing, Documenting, and Assessing to Support Young Children and Families

Students prepared in early childhood degree programs understand that child observation, documentation, and other forms of assessment are central to the practice of all early childhood professionals. They know about and understand the goals, benefits, and uses of assessment. They know about and use systematic observations, documentation, and other effective assessment strategies in a responsible way, in partnership with families and other professionals to positively influence the development of every child.

The key elements of standard 3 you will have learned about are . . .

3b: Knowing about and using observation, documentation, and other appropriate assessment tools and approaches

3c: Understanding and practicing responsible assessment to promote positive outcomes for each child

Standard 4. Using Developmentally Effective Approaches to Connect with Children and Families

Students prepared in early childhood degree programs understand that teaching and learning with young children is a complex enterprise, and its details vary depending on children's ages, characteristics, and the settings within which teaching and learning occur. They understand and use positive relationships and supportive interactions as the foundation for their work with young children and families. Students know, understand, and use a wide array of developmentally appropriate approaches, instructional strategies, and tools to connect with children and families and positively influence each child's development and learning.

The key elements of standard 4 you will have learned about are . . .

4b: Knowing and understanding effective strategies and tools for early education

4c: Using a broad repertoire of developmentally appropriate teaching/learning approaches

4d: Reflecting on their own practice to promote positive outcomes for each child

To Learn More

Observe a Program: For a morning, observe a program and see how the staff structures the environment and program to support children's development of language. Notice both the group activities and the language materials planned for the learning centers. Look at the plans and see how the planning reflects what you observed. Interview a teacher to learn what he or she thinks about language curriculum.

Observe a Child: For a morning, observe a child in a classroom, with a focus on the child's activity in language. Notice how the child engages with the experiences offered and how he or she constructs his or her own opportunities for learning. Notice the extent to which the child's learning experiences and the planned curriculum seem to match. Observe to see how staff support the child's language learning.

Observe a Master Teacher: Spend a morning with an early childhood educator who is experienced and has a curriculum leadership role in a program. (This teacher may be called the "lead," "head," or "mentor" teacher.) Then interview the educator about how he or she plans for and provides language curriculum.

Observe Language Activity: Observe a teacher leading a planned language activity. Interview the teacher to find out the objectives for the activity. Reflect on any differences between what you saw and the focus of the plan.

Compare Two Programs: Observe language experiences in two early childhood programs. Compare the ways that the two address language—their similarities and differences. Reflect on which program seems to best support children's learning and why. What implications does this comparison have for your future work with young children?

Compare Two Ages: Observe two classrooms, one preschool and one for primary school children. Report on how each supports children's language learning. Talk to the staff about how they make their curriculum choices. Notice how development influences curriculum choices.

Observe an English Language Learner: With permission from the classroom teacher, observe a child who is learning to speak English as a second language. Record his or her speech as well as non-verbal communications such as gestures and facial expressions. Talk with the teacher about the practices used to help this child learn language and ask how the home culture and language is being included in the classroom.

Explore Resources: Read one of the books from the bibliography and write a review of it for your classmates.

For Your Portfolio

Plan and Implement a Language Activity: Observe a group of children for a morning, focusing on the ways that they express language understanding. Based on what you observed, write and implement a language activity. Collect evidence of children's responses in the form of anecdotal observations, work samples, photographs, or video recordings. Reflect on how children responded and what they appear to have learned. What worked? What might you do differently next time? How might you expand on this experience for children? For your portfolio, include the plan, a work sample or photograph, and a reflection on what you learned about yourself, children, planning, and teaching.

Create a Language Learning Material: Design and make a language learning material to support the development of a particular child or group of children. Introduce it to the child or children and observe how it is used. Reflect on how the children responded and how you felt about what you did. What worked? What might you do differently next time? How might you expand on this experience for children? For your portfolio, include a photograph of a child using the material and a reflection on what you learned about yourself, children, learning materials, and teaching.

Bibliography

Berk, L. E. (2009). *Child development* (8th ed.). Upper Saddle River, NJ: Pearson.

Biemiller, A., & Slonim, N. (2001). Estimating root word vocabulary growth in normative and advantaged populations: Evidence for a common sequence of vocabulary acquisition. *Journal of Educational Psychology, 93*(3), 498–520.

Bodrova, E., & Leong, D. (2007). *Tools of the mind: The Vygotskian approach to early childhood education* (2nd ed.). Upper Saddle River, NJ: Pearson.

Cazden, C. B. (1992). Language development and the preschool environment. In C. B. Cazden (Ed.), *Language in early childhood education* (pp. 3–15). Washington, DC: NAEYC.

Christie, J. F., Enz, B. J., & Vukelich, C. (2011). *Teaching language and literacy: Preschool through the elementary grades* (4th ed.). Upper Saddle River, NJ: Pearson.

Dickerson, D., & Tabors, P. O. (2002). Fostering language and literacy in classrooms and home. *Young Children, 57*(2) 10–18.

Feeney, S., Moravcik, E., & Nolte, S. (2013). *Who am I in the lives of children?* (9th ed.). Upper Saddle River, NJ: Pearson.

Hart, B., & Risley, T. (2003). The early catastrophe: The 30 million word gap. *American Educator, 27*(1) 4–9.

Head Start Resource Center. (2010). *The Head Start child development and early learning framework: Promoting positive outcomes in early childhood programs serving children 3–5 years old.* Washington, DC: Office of Head Start, Administration for Children and Families, U.S. Department of Health and Human Services.

Jalongo, M. (2008). *Learning to listen, listening to learn.* Washington, DC: NAEYC.

Machado, J.M. (2003). *Early childhood experiences in language arts: Emerging literacy.* Albany, NY: Thompson Learning/Delmar.

National Association for the Education of Young Children. (2009). *NAEYC standards for early childhood professional preparation programs.* www.naeyc.org/files/naeyc/file/positions/ProfPrepStandards09.pdf

National Early Literacy Panel. (2009). *Developing early literacy.* Jessup, MD: National Institute for Literacy.

National Governors Association Center for Best Practices (NGA Center), Council of Chief State School Officers (CCSSO). (2010). *Common Core State Standards in English Language Arts.*

Roskos, K., Tabors, P. O., & Lenhart, L. A. (2009). *Oral language and early literacy in preschool.* Newark, DE: International Reading Association.

Santrock, M. (2010). *Child development: An introduction.* (13th ed.). Boston, MA: McGraw-Hill.

Saville-Troike, M. (1987). Bilingual discourse: The negotiation of meaning without a common code. *Linguistics, 25,* 81–106.

Snow, C., Burns, M., & Griffin, P. (Eds.). (1998). *Preventing reading difficulties in young children.* Washington, DC: National Academy Press.

Snow, C., & Dickinson, O. (1991). Skills that aren't basic in a new conception of literacy. In A. P. Jennings (Ed.), *Literate systems and individual lives: Perspectives on literacy and schooling.* Albany, NY: State University of New York Press.

Standards for the English Language Arts. (1996). Newark, DE: International Reading Association, National Council of Teachers of English. www.ncte.org/library/NCTEFiles/Resources/Books/Sample/StandardsDoc.pdf

Tabors, P. O. (2008). *One child, two languages: A guide for early childhood educators of children learning English as a second language.* Baltimore, MD: Paul H. Brookes.

U.S. Citizenship and Immigration Services (formerly the Immigration and Naturalization Service), Census Bureau. (2001). *Immigrants, fiscal year 2001.* Washington, DC: Author.

MyEducationLab

Go to Topics 2: Child Development and Learning, 9: Content Areas/Lessons and Activities, and 13: Cultural & Linguistic Diversity in the MyEducationLab (www.myeducationlab.com) for *Meaningful Curriculum for Young Children,* where you can:

- Find learning outcomes for Child Development and Learning, Content Areas/Lessons and Activities, and Cultural & Linguistics Diversity along with the national standards that connect to these outcomes.
- Complete Assignments and Activities that can help you more deeply understand the chapter content.
- Apply and practice your understanding of the core teaching skills identified in the chapter with the Building Teaching Skills and Dispositions learning units.
- Listen to experts from the field in Professional Perspectives.
- Examine challenging situations and cases presented in the IRIS Center Resources.

- Access video clips of CCSSO National Teachers of the Year award winners responding to the question, "Why Do I Teach?" in the Teacher Talk section.
- Check your comprehension on the content covered in the chapter with the Study Plan. Here you will be able to take a chapter quiz, receive feedback on your answers, and then access Review, Practice, and Enrichment activities to enhance your understanding of chapter content.

Go to the Course Resources section in MyEducationLab, where you can:

- Use the Online Lesson Plan Builder to practice lesson planning and integrating national and state standards into your planning.
- Explore children's literature in the Children's Literature Database to locate books that encourage language development.

Literacy is not a luxury, it is a right and a responsibility. If our world is to meet the challenges of the twenty-first century we must harness the energy and creativity of all our citizens.

PRESIDENT BILL CLINTON

chapter eight

LITERACY CURRICULUM
Exploring and Using Print

You are a literate person. Through the magic of reading and writing, we, the writers of this book, are communicating with you, the reader, over time and distance. As a teacher, as a student, and as a person who lives in the 21st century, you know both the power and necessity of literacy.

You know what literacy means in everyday speech: *the state of being able to read and write.* When educators talk about early literacy, they are referring to something that is related but somewhat different: *the skills that are the foundation for reading and writing.*

As a prospective early childhood educator, you may wonder about what you will be expected to know and do with regard to literacy. You may have heard that young children can't learn reading and writing skills until kindergarten or 1st grade. On the other hand, you may have seen ads guaranteeing that a product or teaching method can teach even infants and toddlers to read. You may question whether you should actively teach children about reading and writing or if it is better to wait until other skills have developed. You may worry that if you don't teach children to be readers and writers in the early years, of if you don't teach these skills in particular ways, they will not be successful as they move into the primary grades.

If you are feeling a bit confused, it's not surprising. There has been significant discussion both in the early childhood field and in the popular press in recent years about the role of early literacy instruction and whether children should be taught reading and writing skills at a young age. Our goal in this chapter is to help you to understand literacy development and learn about how to provide developmentally appropriate early childhood literacy curriculum.

We will describe what is known about the skills children acquire during the early years that help them to become successful readers and writers in primary school. We will outline some teaching strategies that support children's development of literacy skills. With this knowledge, we hope you will become a teacher who can confidently provide activities and experiences that lead children to becoming joyful, competent readers and writers—not just people who are able to read, but people who *want* to do so.

Why Literacy in Early Childhood?

You already know that literacy is critical. It would be virtually impossible to manage modern life, go to school, use a computer, or hold a job without being literate. But it is not nearly as obvious why 3-, 4-, and 5-year-olds need literacy as a component of their education. In the past two decades, a great deal of research has been focused on early literacy. This research provides several compelling reasons for including a strong literacy component in the early childhood curriculum.

1. **Language and literacy are linked to school success.** Increasingly, research supports the fact that language and literacy learning are linked with later school achievement (National Early Literacy Panel, 2009).
2. **Positive early language and literacy experiences make a difference.** Young children who have positive early language and literacy experiences are more likely to become successful readers, writers, and learners than those who do not have access to these early learning opportunities (Strickland & Riley-Ayers, Preschool Policy Brief, 2006).
3. **Important skills for literacy develop during the preschool years.** Researchers are continuing to identify particular early language, reading, and writing skills that seem to be the most important for later success in the primary grades (National Early Literacy Panel, 2009). These "early literacy skills" are not the same as those used in conventional reading and writing. (We will discuss these skills later in this chapter.)

Understanding Literacy Development

Literacy, the ability to make meaning, particularly from print, is a complex set of skills that begins at birth. A baby engaging in an exchange of coo's with her dad; a toddler pointing and asking "Dat?" to a patient and responsive caregiver; a preschooler making lines and letters in the sand with a stick; and a kindergartner pointing out a brand of breakfast cereal in the grocery store are each displaying early literacy skills.

For many years, educators believed that children could only learn to read and write when they had acquired the necessary maturation to learn these complex skills, generally around the age of 6 after their oral language abilities were well established. Parents were told not to teach their children about reading and writing. Children who entered school reading and writing were often scolded (one of the authors of this book was spanked!) because they read and wrote using the "wrong" methods or forms.

However, when educators and researchers realized that some children "taught themselves to read" seemingly without instruction, literacy began to be regarded as *emergent,* a set of skills that develops naturally. It became common to assume that *all* children would learn to read, given positive adults and an environment filled with books.

The last decade has provided significant research that counters both points of view. We now understand that young children are developing skills needed to understand and use written language long before age 6. They are learning literacy skills at the same time they are developing language. However, these literacy skills do not develop in a vacuum. They are the result of interaction between children and adults around print.

Literacy Begins with Language

In order to learn to read and write, children must be able to use language. Hearing children begin learning language even before they are born. An unborn baby is aware of the tones and rhythms of familiar voices. At birth, infants quickly learn to identify and locate voices. They begin experimenting with sounds, and they start to learn to use these sounds to engage adults in beginning "conversations."

As they get older, young toddlers begin to consciously imitate the sounds they hear around them and to use these sounds, coupled with gestures and expressions, to communicate with others. As very young children learn language, they are discovering how to *decode,* to make meaning from verbal symbols. This ability is a core feature of later literacy learning—to decode or make meaning from the written symbols of print.

As they develop and interact with others, children gradually learn to use the word patterns of their home language, moving from conveying meaning in a single word ("ball") to a phrase ("my ball"), to a more conventional sentence ("I want my ball"). As they build these skills, they are paying attention to the sounds and rhythms of oral language. Their vocabularies grow and expand.

Reflect on adult–baby communication . . .

Watch an adult engaging with a young baby. Notice how each uses sound and language to communicate with one another. What is the baby learning about sounds and language? What is the baby learning about symbols? How do you think this might be related to learning to read and write?

Early Literacy Skills

In order for you to support children's development of literacy, it is useful to understand some of the particular skills that are the foundation for learning to understand and use print.

Oral language skill and vocabulary are important for literacy development. As children learn to communicate orally with others, they also are beginning to learn to communicate through reading and writing. Some research suggests that children with larger vocabularies are better able to decode words when learning to read (Strickland & Riley-Ayers, Preschool Policy Brief, 2006). Children who are able to remember and repeat what they hear—for example, a list of words or numbers—have an easier time learning later literacy skills (National Early Literacy Panel, 2009).

Phonological awareness is the recognition that spoken language is composed of smaller units of sound. Children first learn to identify large units or chunks of sound. When children use rhymes such as "*cat, pat, bat, sat,*" they are practicing phonological awareness. As their skills grow, they learn to identify smaller, more discrete parts of speech.

"Tall, tap, tail and Tucker, all begin with my letter," announced 4-year-old Tucker.

Identifying initial sounds, *alliteration,* is a more sophisticated stage of phonological awareness. Later, children will be able to identify distinct syllables within words and eventually will be able to recognize that spoken words are made up of individual sounds called *phonemes*. English has 44 distinct sounds (phonemes) that are made up of one or more letters of the alphabet. *B* as in *ball* is a sound or phoneme, as is *sh* as in *ship*. The word *big* has three phonemes, /b/ /i/ /g/. Children gradually learn that changing any of these units of sound creates a different meaning. This skill is known as ***phonemic awareness.***

/b/i/g	/b/a/g/	t/a/p	/c/o/p
/p/i/g/	/t/a/g/	c/a/p	/m/o/p

Understanding phonemes is a significant early literacy skill because written language is created by using symbols to represent each sound. While most preschoolers will not be able to either write or read the words, it is important for teachers to introduce phonological and phonemic awareness by activities such as playing with sounds through rhymes and chants.

Knowing about the alphabet is another early literacy skill that strongly predicts later school success (National Early Literacy Panel, 2009). For preschool-age children, this means being able to recite the *ABCs*, recognize and name many letters, and associate sounds with written letters. This is called ***alphabetic knowledge.*** This knowledge is built through experiences that are meaningful to children, relevant to their interests and experiences, and presented in ways that are engaging. Having children participate in word and letter drills, non-relevant worksheets, and repetitive alphabet exercises usually lessens literacy learning rather than enhances it (Neuman & Roskos, 2005).

Print knowledge is children's understanding of how printed letters, words, and books work. When infants and young children live, work, and play in homes and classrooms where print is used and referred to, they begin to develop understanding about what print is, why it is important, and some of the rules about print. They come to understand that:

- print and pictures are different.
- print carries meaning.
- print has a stable meaning—each time a word is read, it says the same thing.
- there are different functions for print, such as signs, stories, lists, etc.
- books work in a special way; for example, books have titles written on the cover, you read from front to back, you turn pages one at a time, etc.
- there are some elements of print: groups of letters form words, there are spaces between words, punctuation marks are different from letters, and letters are different from numbers.
- there are rules of print: words are written from left to right and from the top to the bottom of the page.

The foundational skills children need to build literacy are listed in Figure 8.1.

Children's writing skills develop at the same time as their language and early reading skills. Early writing is an important part of learning to read. Research tells us that when children engage in early writing behaviors, they are building skills with print awareness, print conventions, and other important early literacy skills (Newman, Copple, & Bredekamp, 2000).

FIGURE 8.1 Five Key Skills for Developing Literacy

1. Oral Language
2. Vocabulary
3. Phonological Awareness
4. Alphabet Knowledge
5. Understanding of Print

Just as there is a continuum for early language development, there is also a sequence in which young children develop writing skill. Children begin learning about and practicing writing as soon as they are offered writing tools and have enough strength and control of their hands to begin to manipulate them. When provided with writing tools, young toddlers will begin to make marks, experimenting with cause and effect as they use different arm and hand movements and different pressure. With time and increased motor control, children begin to make more deliberate scribbles—marks of all kinds. As their understanding about visual representation increases, children know the difference between drawing and writing and can identify these differences. With continued motor and cognitive development—along with practice, adult support, and appropriate instruction—they progress to creating shapes that look like letters, to copying words and finally to more conventional writing. As they play with writing, they begin to develop the concepts and the skills necessary to progress to more conventional writing.

It is important for you to understand that preschool children develop writing skills at different ages. Some 3-year-olds will start to write discernible letters, while others seem completely oblivious to print. Some 4-year-olds will invent spelling based on the sounds of words, while others are just creating letter-like forms that are not yet legible. These differences are completely normal. When we speak of inviting children to "write" throughout this chapter, we are including all of the various attempts from scribbling to actual print that young children will make on their journey to becoming a writer. Your task is to support children where they are. Figure 8.2 shows examples of these stages.

Significant Differences That Influence Literacy Learning

Children's families and the experiences and values they have provided will significantly influence the ways children relate to literacy learning opportunities. Many children, particularly those from well-resourced families, may come to school having had a variety of experiences with reading and writing that make it easier for them to actively participate in early literacy activities. Other families may have provided less exposure to reading and writing, and these children may need different types of beginning literacy experiences in order to build foundational skills (Snow, Burns, & Griffin, 1998, cited in Bodova McRell report).

English language learners and dual language learners may develop literacy skills in different ways. They benefit from opportunities to learn literacy skills in their home language whenever possible (Slavin & Cheung, 2005).

FIGURE 8.2 Writing Stages and What a Child Does During Each Stage

	Example
Random Marks • Makes marks on paper, uncontrolled scribbles	 Name (appears on left)
Drawing as Writing • Draws pictures to stand for writing • "Reads" pictures • Draws pictures that are usually not recognizable	 Lettuce grows.
Scribble Writing • Makes linear marks, repeats patterns	
Letter-Like Writing • Makes lines and shapes that have characteristics of conventional letters • Distinguishes between drawings and letters or writing	

Random Letters • Writes individual letters and strings of letters and pretends to read them. Letters are usually not related to the words or sounds a child "reads." Letters and scribbles are combined. • Begins to write own name • Commonly makes reversals • Begins to copy words	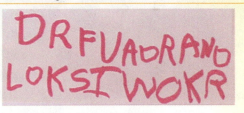 No Crashing!
Invented Spelling • Writes words using their letter sounds, *Mm* for *Mom* • Begins to group letters together to form words and to organize words on the page from left to right • May use some punctuation	Darth Vader and Luke Skywalker
Conventional Writing • Uses increasingly correct spelling and punctuation • Uses conventional organization, left to right, top to bottom, spaces between words.	

Sources: Information in the left column is based on Schickedanz & Casbergue, 2004; Shagoury, 2009.

What Is Literacy Curriculum in Early Childhood?

Like all good early childhood curriculum, literacy should be an integral part of each child's day. It can be included in every early childhood curriculum area. Much of the literacy curriculum in preschool programs grows out of well-designed environments and routines. It includes opportunities for children to:

1. play with print.
2. independently read books for pleasure.
3. play with writing materials in ways that are enjoyable and that make sense to a young child.

However, appropriate literacy curriculum for young children also involves thoughtfully planned, child-sensitive teacher-directed instruction:

- teacher-led activities that focus on word/ letter sounds and print.
- reading books aloud.

You will notice that we have not mentioned some of the activities that you may remember from your primary school days—workbooks and other teacher-directed seatwork. Although these are often used in preschool programs, they are not appropriate for most preschool-age children. In fact, they may do some harm since literacy curriculum that is too difficult, or adult-oriented and boring, can cause children to hate, rather than love reading. Table 8.1 contrasts appropriate and inappropriate literacy curriculum.

TABLE 8.1 Appropriate Preschool Literacy Curriculum Compared to Inappropriate Curriculum

Appropriate Literacy Curriculum for Preschoolers	Inappropriate Literacy Curriculum for Preschoolers
Using print throughout the classroom: cubbies with names, song charts, signs about how to use an activity, labels on shelves and furniture, etc.	Using print only for reading stories and for adult communication, such as parent boards or family newsletters.
Providing daily opportunities to choose from a variety of good books to look at and enjoy in a range of classroom settings.	Keeping books put away except at reading time, and then requiring children to sit quietly at a table to look at a book selected by an adult.
Providing a variety of print materials such as newspapers, magazines, storybooks, printed directions, and reference books.	Providing only beginning readers.
Providing reading and writing materials to use in play, e.g., pencils and paper in the block center for signs, cookbooks and magazines in the dramatic play area, etc.	Having a daily writing period where everyone is required to write the same words.
Modeling meaningful reading and writing, e.g., "This says we will need 75 cents each for our bus trip tomorrow."	Using reading and writing in the classroom without pointing out the ways it is useful.
Playing games to practice hearing discrete sounds such as initial consonants or word ending sounds.	Asking children to circle all the pictures on the worksheet that begin with the same letter.
Writing children's words to describe a painting or drawing they have made (taking dictation).	Asking children to copy the words a teacher has selected.
Inviting children to write their names in meaningful ways, (to sign in, to wait for a turn, to identify their work, etc.).	Requiring children to write their name on a worksheet 10 times.
Playing rhyming and rhythm games in a group activity where it is ok to make mistakes.	Drilling each child in a way that makes children unsuccessful "*Tell me ten words that rhyme with 'cat'*." Completing a worksheet where each separate syllable must be circled.
Allowing children to use invented writing and spelling to make labels, write lists or create stories.	Requiring children to use standard spelling and letter forms.

Standards for Literacy Curriculum

Research on instruction in particular aspects of early literacy learning has made educators aware of the importance of early literacy experiences. This awareness has led national and state organizations to write content standards for literacy (what should be included in the literacy curriculum) and performance standards for learners (what children should know and be able to do at the completion of a particular grade level).

Every state, Head Start, and several national groups have developed guidelines for what young children should know about literacy at various ages, the skills they should acquire, and ways teachers can support this learning. You may be asked to use standards particular to your location or workplace. However, you might also want to look at others. There are four sets of guidelines that we find particularly useful:

- *Starting Out Right: A Guide to Promoting Children's Reading Success*, developed by the National Research Council (Burns, Griffin, & Snow, 1999).
- *A Continuum of Children's Development in Early Reading & Writing*, in *Learning to Read and Write: Developmentally Appropriate Practices for Young Children*. A position statement of the International Reading Association and the National Association for the Education of Young Children, 1998 (Newman, Copple, & Bredekamp, 2000).
- *A Framework for Early Literacy Instruction: Aligning Standards to Developmental Accomplishments and Student Behaviors Revised Edition Pre-K Through Kindergarten* (Bodrova, Leong, Paynter, & Semenov, 2000).
- *The Head Start Child Development and Early Learning Framework: Promoting Positive Outcomes in Early Childhood Programs Serving Children 3–5 Years Old.* (See Figures 8.3 and Figure 8.4.)

While each set of standards/guidelines identifies slightly different goals and practices, all agree that literacy curriculum for children should focus on helping children develop:

- Oral language skills, including vocabulary (some place oral language separately)
- Phonological awareness
- Appreciation for books and other printed materials
- Understanding of the uses of print
- Knowledge about conventions of print and ability to use some conventional print forms
- Alphabet knowledge

Your program's goals may be based on state or professional guidelines, or they may have been developed independently by your staff or a curriculum specialist. However, it is likely that they will contain content similar to those we have described.

Head Start has also developed literacy outcomes specific to children who are English language learners. These are listed in Figure 8.4.

Teaching Literacy

Katie and Shey are in the Pretend Store that they have helped Dana, their teacher, construct after a trip to a nearby market. "We need money," Shey tells Katie. Katie goes to the writing center, gets green construction paper, markers, and scissors. She cuts out six rectangles, makes squiggly marks on each, and then runs back to Shey. "Here," she tells him. "I wrote the money words on these dollars so we can use them." While Katie is working on the pretend money, Shey is busy arranging the groceries in the store. "This one says Cheerios," he says, holding up a box of cereal. "We'll put it here." He stands it on the shelf next to a box of Trix and one of oatmeal. Shey picks up a grocery ad from the newspaper and puts it on the counter next to the pretend groceries. "Now people can see what they need to buy when they come to the store," he tells Katie.

FIGURE 8.3   Head Start Early Learning Framework: Promoting Positive Outcomes for Literacy

Alphabet Knowledge

The names and sounds associated with letters.

- Recognizes that the letters of the alphabet are a special category of visual graphics that can be individually named.
- Recognizes that letters of the alphabet have distinct sound(s) associated with them.
- Attends to the beginning letters and sounds in familiar words.
- Identifies letters and associates correct sounds with letters.

Print Concepts and Conventions

The concepts about print and early decoding (identifying letter-sound relationships).

- Recognizes print in everyday life, such as numbers, letters, one's name, words, and familiar logos and signs.
- Understands that print conveys meaning.
- Understands conventions, such as "print moves from left to right and top to bottom of a page."
- Recognizes words as a unit of print and understands that letters are grouped to form words.
- Recognizes the association between spoken or signed and written words.

Early Writing

The familiarity with writing implements, conventions, and emerging skills to communicate through written representations, symbols, and letters.

- Experiments with writing tools and materials.
- Recognizes that writing is a way of communicating for a variety of purposes, such as giving information, sharing stories, or giving an opinion.
- Uses scribbles, shapes, pictures, and letters to represent objects, stories, experiences, or ideas.
- Copies, traces, or independently writes letters or words.

Source: Administration for Children and Families, Head Start Bureau, www.hsnrc.org/cdi/child-outcomes.cfm

FIGURE 8.4   Head Start Early Learning Framework: Promoting Positive Outcomes for English Language Development

Engagement in English Literacy Activities

Understanding and responding to books, storytelling, and songs presented in English.

- Demonstrates eagerness to participate in songs, rhymes, and stories in English.
- Points to pictures and says the word in English, such as "frog," "baby," "run."
- Learns part of a song or poem in English and repeats it.
- Talks with peers or adults about a story read in English.
- Tells a story in English with a beginning, middle, and end from a book or about a personal experience.

Source: Administration for Children and Families, Head Start Bureau, www.hsnrc.org/cdi/child-outcomes.cfm

Katie and Shey were obviously involved in a literacy activity. Since Dana does not seem to be very involved in the children's activity you might be asking yourself, "Is it teaching?" The answer to your question is **Yes!** Teaching literacy is about helping children find relevant ways to understand and use print. Dana did just that by:

- providing meaningful, real-life experiences with print (the trip to the store, the use of real-life props in the form of cereal boxes and the grocery ad).
- arranging the environment to promote the natural play of children (role play in the pretend store).
- making sure that literacy tools were near at hand for children to use independently (the green construction paper, markers, and scissors).
- ensuring that there was enough time for literacy play to develop.
- allowing children to move freely from the writing center to the dramatic play area.

Additionally, even though you cannot "see" it, this was a planned activity. Dana knew that the trip to the store would inspire dramatic play, so she planned ways to include literacy in that play. The arrangement of the environment and the inclusion of literacy-related props were not accidental. They were a part of Dana's planned literacy curriculum.

Literacy Through Play in a Planned Environment

The environment is one of your most powerful tools for promoting literacy learning. We call a classroom where print is found everywhere a *print-rich environment*. Every classroom area—including learning centers, areas for routines such as meals or toileting, and outside spaces—can include relevant print. Writing supplies can be available in many parts of the classroom. Literacy experiences can be incorporated into daily routines. In this section, we will describe some of the many strategies you can use to include literacy in your learning environment in ways that invite children to engage with print in a meaningful manner.

The Library or Book Center

Every classroom for young children needs to have a classroom library area or book center that offers a relaxing and comfortable place to interact with books. Choose space that is sheltered from classroom traffic so that children will not be interrupted as others engage in noisier activities. The space should be large enough for three to six children to sit comfortably, but small enough to feel cozy and secure.

Furnishings
The library needs special bookshelves. These should display the covers of books so that children can easily see them. Supplemental storage can be provided by including baskets of books. The library should contain comfortable seating (soft couches, chairs, and cushions) so children can snuggle in with a book. An adult-sized chair or sofa makes it easier for adults to share stories and lap reading with children. A listening center, with a small table and chairs and a tape or CD player for listening to recorded stories is a nice addition. And a small private area created from a large box or bin provides a cozy spot for one or two children to enjoy quiet time with a book.

Materials

First and foremost, your library needs to include books! All types of books—picture stories, wordless stories, poetry books, alphabet books, songbooks, child-authored books, informational books—a variety of types should be included. How many books should you include? The International Reading Association recommends that classrooms for young children should have between 5 and 8 books per child—approximately 100 books or more for a class of 18 children. Your program does not need to own all of these books. Regular visits to the public library will allow you to offer children a variety of appropriate choices.

Displaying all of these books at once would be overwhelming for the children. Instead, select books based on the children's interests and literacy levels as well as the current topic of study. Rotate titles regularly to keep children interested, but continue to keep favorite stories available for them to find and enjoy. The number of books available at any given time will depend on the size of your library area. Some experts recommend making available as many books as you have children, plus 5 to 10 more (Bennett-Armistead, Duke, & Moses, 2005). You can include some other materials such as:

- puppets for dramatizing familiar stories
- soft animals for snuggling
- flannelboards with flannelboard story pieces stored in a basket or other open container

Aesthetics

Library areas should be kept uncluttered. Wall displays should be simple, at children's eye level and visually appealing. Some teachers post one or two book covers on the walls; others decorate with a fine art print or book poster, or hang

fabric on the walls. Solid colors and simple patterns produce a calm atmosphere that encourages young children to relax.

The Writing Center

Every early childhood classroom should have a center dedicated to writing. A writing center encourages children to explore and concentrate on using print in ways that are meaningful to them. In the writing center, children can make greeting cards, create books, write words and letters, and experiment with writing tools and papers. Because children see adults using tools such as staplers, hole punchers, and tape dispensers, opportunities to use office supplies are exciting to them and make them feel competent.

Furniture

A small table with space for 3 to 4 chairs is essential in a writing center. It is critical that the table and chairs be sized correctly for the children. Their feet should touch comfortably on the floor and their elbows should rest easily on the table. You will also need a shelf where you can store materials and supplies. In order to encourage children to use the area well, supplies should be visible, accessible, and neatly organized so that it is easy for children to find what is needed for their writing. Some teachers use the end of the shelf to hang chalk or dry erase boards.

Supplies

The writing center needs materials and supplies to encourage children to practice drawing and writing. Rotate some supplies each week to encourage children's continued interest. The In Practice box offers a list of ideas for writing center supplies.

When equipping your writing center, think about the kinds of writing that are relevant for the children in your group and consider adding a chart or individual cards with words that they might need for their writing. For instance, many children enjoy writing letters; for these children a chart listing the words *Dear, Love, To, From, Mom, Dad* would be helpful.

Create cards with individual children's names and pictures and place these in a file box; children can easily find and trace or copy their own and one another's names. As their writing becomes more proficient, add cards with other words for them to use. A box with cut out magazine or catalog pictures can help children think of an idea for a story. Lists of words that children have generated can be posted nearby or placed on index cards for reference. You can also consider ways to relate writing to a particular unit of study, as Dana did in the example. If space is available, include three-dimensional letters that can be used to create words or to match to printed word cards.

Literacy Everywhere

Although it is obvious that literacy learning occurs in the library and writing centers, literacy does not end there. In fact, literacy should be a part of every classroom area. How? The simplest and most common addition to centers is the use of labels. But there is much more you can do.

When children create a structure in the ***block area,*** they often describe it. You can encourage them to make a label for their construction. We like to keep a box of cards with names of types of structures (*airport, store, my house*) for labeling constructions. You can sketch children's block structures and title them with the

---

IN PRACTICE: Writing Center Supplies

- Pencils of many types, thick pencils, #2 thin pencils, colored pencils
- Markers: both thick and thin
- Scissors (be sure they are sharp enough for children to cut with them easily)
- Hole punch
- Tape: scotch, masking, colored
- Glue sticks and small bottles of glue
- Paper: blank, lined, construction, card stock, note cards, wall paper samples, stationery, envelopes
- Pre-made blank books
- Paper folded to resemble greeting cards

- Alphabet chart
- Alphabet stencils
- Sandpaper letters to help children feel the hand movements used in forming each letter
- Stamp pads and stamps, alphabet and other stamps
- Chalk and small chalk boards or dry erase boards or acetate sheets and markers
- One or several picture dictionaries such as *My First Word Book* (Wilkes, 1997) *or My First Dictionary* (Root, 1993)

child's description (*Baylor's Big Block Structure*) and soon children will want to sketch their own work. These sketches can be kept in the block area to refer to like blueprints—another kind of reading. Some teachers photograph block constructions and encourage children to dictate a story about what they created and how they did it; these photographs/stories are then posted in the block area. Books with pictures of many types of buildings, bridges, and roads from your community or from far away can be kept near the block area for reference. Do-it-yourself books for adults also can be stored there, inspiring both building and reading.

Materials typically found in the ***manipulatives*** or ***table toys center*** often have a literacy focus. Purchased or homemade ***games*** with pictures to match, written labels, and written directions all support literacy learning. You can create literacy games (e.g., matching a labeled picture to an unlabeled one or matching letters to related pictures). Games related to favorite children's books also support literacy learning. ***Puzzles*** often include print. A puzzle of a doctor's office may have words written on one or more of the pieces. Some puzzles direct children to focus on matching a piece with a word (e.g., a puzzle with the word *elephant* written on the space for the elephant piece). And of course, there are many alphabet puzzles. Some teachers keep a set of 3-dimensional ***letters*** in the manipulatives center. Sandpaper letters give children a tactile sense of the letter. Magnetic letters and a baking pan encourage active alphabet engagement. Foam, wood, cardboard, and flannel letters encourage manipulation and letter exploration.

The ***science center*** provides a variety of opportunities to include literacy. You can add fiction and non-fiction ***books*** related to science (e.g., insect books next to a bug house, plant books by a plant). ***Label tools*** and the shelf where they are stored (e.g., *magnifier* can be written on both the handle of the magnifying glass and its place on the shelf). Keep ***science journals*** and ***clipboards*** where children can draw or write observations. Post a list of ***science words*** to encourage children to write about what they are doing and seeing. Include ***science flannelboard*** pieces with words, such as the labeled parts of a plant or insect. Display ***charts*** with children's questions and predictions: "What we want to know about how eggs hatch." What will come out of the egg?" Label ongoing science experiments.

> *"Do you want to bring the puppy to see the doctor?" asks Ajit as Willow approaches holding a pet carrier containing a stuffed animal. "Is the puppy sick?" As Willow tells him about her puppy's hurt paw, Ajit scribbles on a pad of paper. "You can sit here," Ajit tells her. "I'll show this to the doctor so she can get you some medicine for your puppy. Sit here," Ajit says. "You can read this magazine if you want to."*

The ***dramatic play*** or ***pretend area*** offers so many ways for children to engage with literacy! A dramatic play area can include items that use *functional print (*print with a purpose). Menus, food containers, grocery store advertisements, magazines and newspapers, signs, calendars, and cookbooks are props that encourage children to interact with print. Their interest in imitating what adults do naturally leads them to engage with print.

Throughout this book we have given you examples of ways to include a topic of study throughout the environment. The dramatic play area is especially appropriate for integrating both a topic and print. You will think of many ways to do this. We offer a few suggestions in the In Practice box.

Young children learn about reading when ***labels, signs and other relevant printed materials*** are part of their classroom environment. In your classroom you have opportunities to create signs, posters, charts, and bulletin boards that invite children to become aware of print.

Study Topic	Related Print Materials
Family/Home	Message pads, magazines and newspapers, catalogs, advertisements, storybooks, toddler books for dolls, cookbooks, calendars, stationery, maps, keyboard
Community: Medical/Vet Office	Magazines, clipboards, prescription pads, charts, books
Community: Fire Station	Telephone, labeled places for gear and supplies, fire safety poster, books
Stores: Grocery, Clothing, Shoes, Pets, Flowers, etc.	Advertisements, coupons, money, phone with order pad, signs, empty containers from products to be sold, printed bags, labeled shelves
Food: Restaurant, bakery, pizza parlor, ice cream store or truck	Menus, signs, cookbooks, recipe charts, order pads and pencils, pretend credit cards

You can label items in the classroom (*fire extinguisher, aquarium, science shelf*, etc.). These labels are most useful if they tell children something important and you find opportunities to use and point them out to children. Areas where children store their work and personal belonging should be clearly labeled with both first and last names. Adding photos, especially for younger children or at the beginning of a school year, gives children an additional clue when looking for their space. In addition to labeled cubbies, we like to provide children's mailboxes, labeled storage shelves for artwork, and family mailboxes.

Walls can contain ***charts*** and ***posters***. Many of these will be created as you discuss topics with children and write down their words. It's important to use the charts you create. Make a point of referring to them ("What was it that we said we needed to make collages? Let's check the chart.") as you work on projects. To avoid clutter and to keep children's interest, remove charts you are not using.

Every early childhood classroom should have an alphabet poster. Hang alphabet posters at children's eye level and refer to them often during activities. As you engage with children in the dramatic play area, you might point to the letter *p* and say, "You are looking for a pan to put the potato in; all those /p/ words begin with this letter, *p*."

Signs identifying classroom areas or giving directions for how to use a specific material can also be included and pointed out to the children. As children experiment with and begin to use writing, encourage them to create signs, hang them, and point them out to others.

Bulletin boards can hold items of interest for both children and families. Look for opportunities to point them out to children. "Keisha, I found an article about caring for dogs in the paper. I put it on the bulletin board so that your family and others with a dog could read about how to take good care of them." Remember that bulletin boards will only be of interest to children and families if you change them regularly and keep them uncluttered.

Find as many ways as you can to ***post children's work,*** both art and written work. Children's work should be labeled with their names. It makes it more meaningful for children and their families if you include a description of the work or transcripts of what children said about it. As children become aware of these labeled descriptions, encourage them to participate in documenting and displaying their work.

Outdoors also can be a place for literacy experiences. How? Add traffic signs to the trike path. Label plants in the garden and shelves in the storage area. Create a place for children to take a break with a basket of books on a mat or blanket in a shady spot. Provide sidewalk chalk or water and brushes to write on pavement.

A Schedule for Literacy Learning

Literacy happens throughout the day in planned activities and through play in an environment prepared for literacy learning. Like learning in all other areas, children develop literacy skills when they have ample opportunities to engage in ***periods of un-interrupted play.*** A schedule that includes large blocks of time (45–90 minutes twice each day in full-day programs) encourages children to immerse themselves deeply into play and provides the most opportunity for them to learn from these experiences.

Daily ***small-group, teacher-led activities*** will often have a literacy component. For example, if you create a graph of the insects you find on the playground, you support math, science, and literacy skills. If you write a group story about the veterinar-ian's visit, children learn about workers in the community while developing literacy knowledge. In addition to ***story time*** once or twice each day, many teachers include a daily independent ***book time*** when children select a book to look at on their own or with a partner.

Large-group activities can also include literacy experiences. *Songs* with ***song charts, rhythm games, interactive stories, oral storytelling, flannelboard,*** and ***puppet stories*** all are good large-group activities that build literacy skills.

Routines and Transitions

Routines and transitions take up much of a young child's day. With only a little effort, these can become literacy activities. ***Looking at books*** provides something worthwhile for children to do during a transition that requires waiting and makes a relaxing way to get ready for nap. Some teachers invite children and the family member who brings them to school to read a book together when they first arrive.

Play sound and ***rhythm games*** during transitions and waiting times. Having a repertoire of ideas that you can use during these times turns wasted time into literacy learning. When the lunch cart is late or the field trip bus can't leave the parking lot due to traffic, begin a rhyming game, clap out rhythm patterns, or ask children to guess a word that you are thinking of that begins with the letter ***B.***

A ***schedule chart*** showing each daily activity in sequence helps children to both feel comfortable about routines and learn about print. A ***toothbrushing*** or ***handwashing chart*** showing the required steps can be posted in the bathroom. A ***job chart*** listing classroom responsibilities with space to add children's names is a powerful way to help children recognize both their own names and those of classmates. A ***menu*** added to the lunch or snack table invites children to see words as they experience tastes, smells, and textures of the food.

Your Role in Teaching Literacy

You will support children's literacy learning and development through the environment you prepare and the activities you provide. As in all other areas of curriculum, you will observe children carefully in order to understand what they know and are able to do with print. When children bring you their scribbled marks to

Try It Out!

Make a list of ways to include rel-evant print in a classroom where you teach or where you have visited. If possible, try to add several of these ideas to the classroom and see how the chil-dren respond.

read, recite the words of a book as they turn the pages, identify a familiar brand of juice, point out the Wal-Mart sign, or ask you to write their names, they are telling you how they are thinking about print. This enables you to develop relevant play and instructional experiences.

Perhaps the most important way you will support children's literacy learning is by responding to them in ways that help them learn to be readers, writers, and creators of meaning.

1. **Acknowledge and celebrate children's attempts** at early reading and writing.

   Ezra brings his teacher, Chas, a paper with many scribbles and some letters. Some letters are written backwards. He says, "Hey! I wrote this for my Mom. Can you read it?" Chas looks carefully at his work and says, "You did a lot of writing, Ezra. Will you read this to me, please?" "It says, 'Hi Mom. I am being good today. I love you. From Ezra.'" He points to the marks as he "reads." Pointing to a mark that looks like a backwards "E," Chas says, "I know this letter." "Yes, it's my name," says Ezra smiling. "Let's put this into your Mom's mailbox so she will be sure to get it when she comes. I know she will feel happy when she reads it. Can you help me find her mailbox?"

Chas supported Ezra's understanding that written words can be read by others. She encouraged his interest in writing and his understanding of several different concepts of print, including identification of the initial letter in his name. She didn't tell him that his writing was unintelligible. This illustrates another important principle of literacy teaching.

2. **Avoid correcting or criticizing children's literacy efforts.**
3. **Point out words and symbols** when you see them and when you see children noticing them. Whether it is the words *KitchenAid* on the classroom mixer, the *Subway* sign seen on a walk, or a logo on a child's shirt, notice them and talk about them with children.
4. **Use print often and obviously.** Point this out to children. "I'm going to write a note to our custodian letting her know that we need more paper towels." Or "Let's start a list of some of the new supplies we want for our art center. Then when we have some more money, we'll know just what to order."
5. **Encourage children to write** notes to others. You can ask them to "pretend write," take an individual child's dictation, or write a note as a group. This works well as a small-group charting activity. "We had a great time when we visited the Bumblebee classroom. Let's work together to create a thank-you chart to tell them what was fun during our visit." Children enjoy creating individual notes to classmates and family members. "There is stationery in the writing center that you could use to write a letter to tell your Granny about the huge building you made this morning. I'll save this photo and we can include it with your letter to her."
6. **Make your use of print apparent** to children and engage them in using it with you. Tell them when you are using reading or writing in a way that is important or meaningful. When you run low on supplies, you might say, "I'm going to leave a note for Ms. Julie to let her know that we need to order some more glue for our art center." Before a cooking project, tell the children, "I'm going to make a list of what we'll need to bake bread tomorrow. Can you help me think of what I need to write down?" On a neighborhood walk, point to a sign on a store and ask, "What do you think this says? Oh, it says they will open at 10:00." Let children see you using written reference materials, "This

tells me that geckos lay eggs," and encourage them to work together to get useful or interesting information from printed resources; for example, "How much does this say that the celery will cost?"

7. **Show your interest in and enthusiasm for reading and writing.** You are a powerful model in children's lives. When they see you using and enjoying print, books, and stories, they are more likely to want to build these skills for themselves.

Activities to Promote Literacy Learning

As you have gathered by now, there are many, many activities that promote literacy learning. In this section we will describe a number of them in some detail. Keep in mind that young children learn best when they have a variety of activities that are playful, engaging, and well suited to their abilities.

Reading Stories

Making time every day to read to children and interact with them as they look at books can be one of the most delightful activities that you will share with children. It is the cornerstone of early literacy teaching. Children need frequent opportunities to hear stories of all types. Children who have had joyful and engaging experiences with books and stories are more likely to become eager readers.

Through stories, children build language skills, including vocabulary and the understanding that language is used differently in individual applications. As you read to children, they come to understand "book language" with words and usage that are quite different from everyday conversations. Research tells us that reading a story to children three or more times is likely to increase their understanding of the story's content. This is particularly true for children who come to school with few prior experiences with book reading (Sénéchal, 2000). Your first job will be selecting books for children to use and enjoy. Next, you must learn to read with enthusiasm and learn to engage children in the story as you read. With regular practice, you will become a skilled story reader and will enjoy this satisfying and teaching opportunity.

Although stories are often read to large groups of children, research shows that young children benefit most from story reading when it is done in small groups of four to six children (Karweit & Wasik, 1996). When you read to a small group, you are able to interact with the children and encourage them to engage with the story during the reading time. Small groups allow all children to easily see and touch the pictures and the print, ask questions, and discuss the story. When you read to children individually or in small groups, you can monitor each child's comprehension, ask questions, and add information to increase understanding of both the story and the printed words.

Dialogic Reading

One method of story reading, *dialogic reading,* was designed to help teachers read to young children in ways that encourage them to become actively involved in the reading process (What Works Clearinghouse, 2007). Dialogic reading involves the use of 4 strategies you can use to increase children's participation and interaction with the story. An easy way to remember these is to think of the word **PEER.**

Prompt   Prompt the child to say something about the book.

Evaluate   Evaluate the child's response; listen and decide how to respond.

Expand   Expand on the child's response; rephrase and add information.

Repeat   Repeat the prompt.

A small group of children is gathered in the reading loft. Yumi has just read the book, Sometimes I'm Bombaloo *by Rachael Vail. She asks, "Why did Katie get so angry?" {Prompt} "She's mad at her baby," shouts Laula. "That's right, Laula." {Evaluate} "She was angry because her baby brother broke her block building." {Expand} "Yeah," says Laula. "What did her brother do that made Katie so angry?" {repeat} Yumi asked. "He banged the blocks on the floor," Laula replied.*

Dialogic reading encourages children to become active storytellers. As they become more familiar with a story, you will talk less and listen more as the child is able to describe increasingly complex aspects of the story.

There are five types of prompts that you can use to encourage a child to talk about a book. Each requires slightly more engagement with the story and more advanced language and reasoning skill than the previous types of prompts. You can remember these by thinking of the acronym **CROWD.**

Completion: Leave a blank at the end of the sentence for the child to complete. "When Katie's brother knocked over her blocks, she felt _____."

Recall: Ask questions about the story . . . the plot, the characters, the sequence of events . . . to encourage children's understanding. "What did Katie's Mommy do after Katie pushed her brother down?"

Open-ended: Encourage the child to tell what is happening in a picture. *Pointing to the picture of Katie's face,* "Tell me what you see in this picture? How do you know what Katie feels now?"

W-: Ask *wh-* questions about the pictures in the books. (*Who, What, Where, Why*) "Why do you think that Katie's Mommy made her go to her room?"

Distancing: Relate pictures and words in the book to the child's own experiences outside the book. "Do you ever get angry with your sister? What does your Mom do when you get mad?"

Dialogic reading is an effective technique for engaging children with books. Studies have shown that it also increases young children's language skills, and is particularly effective for children from low-income families who may have had less experience with storybook reading than children from more privileged circumstances.

Simple Skill-Focused Games and Activities

The early literacy skills described in the section on development provide a good structure for planning simple literacy games and activities. As you gain understanding of literacy teaching, you will begin to make up your own. We have included a few examples in the In Practice box to get you started.

Taking Dictation

In addition to modeling writing and pointing out to children the ways you use writing, you support children's developing writing abilities when you *take dictation,* that is, write down the words that children say.

IN PRACTICE: Games and Activities That Support Literacy

Phonemic Awareness Games and Activities	• **Rhyming** songs, rhymes, games, and stories: *Twinkle-Twinkle Little Star, Green Eggs & Ham, Llama, Llama Red Pajama, Willoughby Wallaby Woo* • **Initial Sound** games: 　"If your name begins with a _R_ sound, you may go to lunch." 　"I'm thinking of someone whose Mommy's name starts with a _Gr_ sound." • **Nonsense Words:** Use these words in rhymes or chants to change the initial sounds: *"Fiddle-dee-diddle-dee-dee" "Riddle-me-middle-mee-mee."* • **Word Sounds:** Ask children to listen for part of a word, for example, *"boa-t."* Ask them to repeat the end sound, _t_, and then think of other words that end with the same sound, *"ca-t" "lo-t" "ea-t."* • **Name Claps:** Clap each sound in children's names and then invite children to choose a partner whose name has the same number of claps.
Alphabet Knowledge Games and Activities	• **Workjobs:** Create games where children match identical letters, match lower to upper case letters, match letters within words, or match letters of initial sounds to pictures of objects or people whose names begin with that sound. • **Letter Hunt:** Show children a letter, and then invite them to go around the classroom and find places where that letter is written. Or, ask children to look for letters that make a particular sound. "I'm thinking about the sound /b/. Let's all try to find one letter somewhere in our classroom that makes that sound." • **Which Letter?** Play a game in which children point to the letter that makes the initial or the ending sound of a word and identify that letter's sound. (It is easier for children to identify initial sounds, so do these first.) • **My Letter:** Hold up each child's name card and ask children to point to the first letter in their name, say it, and then make its sound. "_S_ starts your name, Susan. Can you point to it? Can you make its sound? Let's all make the /s/ sound for _S_usan." • **Activity Letters:** Make picture cards of favorite activities. Label each one. As you dismiss children, ask each to pick their favorite activity, point to and say the first letter, and then tell the letter's sound. • **Alphabet Sequence Guessing Game:** Ask children to think about the alphabet sequence. "I'm thinking of the letter that comes after _G_ and before _I_. What is it?"

There are many occasions for you to take children's dictation, such as when you want to record a title or description of their artwork, a remembered experience, a classroom problem, or their scientific observations. Sometimes, children will come to you because they want you to take their dictation so they can write a letter, create an original story, or re-tell a familiar one. At other times, you will take children's dictation to help them create a book or work as a group to make a chart.

After you have taken dictation, re-read the dictated words slowly, stressing each sound and pointing to indicate each word and sound you are reading. Encourage children to read their own words. "Can you read what you wrote about the caterpillar we found this morning?"

Creating Books

One of our favorite ways to increase children's understanding of print is to create books about their experiences. There are a number of ways to do this.

1. Take photos of children during an activity or experience, write a story about it (with the children or after they have gone home), and then create a book to share.
2. Ask children to tell a story about something important to them or an experience that was memorable; write down their words on the pages of a blank book, and then invite them to illustrate the story.
3. Invite each child to create a page for a book about a topic or an activity, and then bind the pages together to create a book.
4. Invite families to create pages for a class book about their family or a common family experience such as celebrations, pets, or favorite meals.

Creating these books and hearing them read encourages children to learn about conventions of print, features of books (title, author, cover, etc.), permanence of meaning (the written word always says the same thing), and elements of story.

Special Words

We like to offer interested children an opportunity to build a personal collection of words (sometimes called a *word bank)* that are important to them. We call them *special words*. Based on a method first introduced by Sylvia Ashton-Warner in the book *Teacher* (1986), this strategy allows each child to select a word they wish to learn to read and write. The In Practice box describes the steps to follow to use special words with the children in your class. Be sure to refer children back to their special words." Remember you have *Stegosaurus* in your special words. You can use it to help you write it on your picture."

IN PRACTICE: How to Create a Collection of Special Words

You will need: index cards; Sharpie pens or markers; binder rings; single-hole punch.

1. Make a name card for each interested child, punch a hole in the card, and hang it on a binder ring.
2. Invite the child to choose a word that is very important to him/her.
3. Print that word on an index card, making sure that the child can see the letters as they are printed. As you write, say the sound *Mmmmm* (as you write *M*) *aaa* (as you write *O*) *Mmmmm* (as you write *M*) [Mom].
4. Read the word slowly to the child and then invite the child to read it back.
5. Ask the child to trace the word with his/her finger.
6. Punch a hole in the card and place the card on a ring.

7. The next day, bring the card back and invite the child to read it.
8. If the child successfully recalls the word, ask him or her to choose another very important word and write that one on a new card.
9. Punch that card and add it to the first and save it for the next session.
10. If the child does not recall the word, invite him to choose a different word and write it on an index card. Ask the child if you may discard the first word since it is not one he remembers easily.
11. For subsequent sessions, review each card, asking the child to read the word. Keep those that are recalled, and offer to write a new one each time. With children's permission, discard those that are not recalled.

Charts

Charts are effective ways to encourage children to engage with print. They can be used for either small- or large-group activities. You can use charts you have made ahead of time (like song charts) in large groups. But we recommend that when you create charts with the children, you do so in small groups. Following are a few guidelines for charting with children. Make sure that the chart paper is big enough. (We like recycled blueprint paper.) Have extra paper ready in case children's ideas exceed the capacity of a single sheet.

1. Use dark colored fresh markers to write. Use large, clear, conventional print forms.
2. Explain what you are doing and ask a question to get things started. "What are some things that you remember about our trip to the aquarium yesterday? I'm going to write your words on this poster, and after everyone has a turn, I will read each one back to you. Then we will put it up so your families can read your words when they come to pick you up."
3. After you write a child's words, check back to make sure that you have captured their intent. ("I wrote . . . *Swimming Penguins*—is that right?")
4. Illustrate a child's contribution with a quick sketch if possible (don't worry about being a great artist).
5. Be cautious about attributing each child's contribution on the chart; doing so tends to focus on the child rather than the print and can distract children.
6. At the end of the activity and when children are stuck for an idea, read the chart back to the group.
7. Refer to posted charts often.

See the In Practice box for some ideas for creating charts.

Recipes

Almost all young children enjoy food preparation and cooking activities. In addition to being wonderful opportunities for learning math, social studies, science,

IN PRACTICE: Ideas for Creating Charts

- **Song/Chant/Poem Charts:** Print words to favorite songs, chants, or poems. Embellish with a drawing. Point to words (or invite a child to) as you sing/say it with children.
- **Special Event Charts:** After a trip or class visitor, invite each child to tell you something that they recall about the experience. Write their words on the chart and read them back at the end. Post the chart where families and children can see it easily. Refer back to it, noting what children said.
- **Brainstorming Charts:** When you need children to brainstorm ideas (group name, classroom rules,

plans for an activity), create a chart with all of the children's ideas.

- **K/W/L Charts:** These charts allow you to create a place to record what children already know and want to learn about a topic, and, at the end of the study, to review what they feel they have learned. Post K/W/L charts where families can see them and point out children's contributions to their family members. If you replicate the chart in the Family Newsletter, it encourages families to reread them at home with their children.

and nutrition, they are also a good way to engage children in literacy as children read recipes. Recipes can be presented in a variety of ways.

1. *Stations:* On a counter or table, create stations with signs that tell how to complete each step of a food preparation activity.
2. *Charts:* Prepare a step-by-step recipe chart to read and follow as a group.
3. *Books:* Create a recipe book with favorite classroom recipes or use a children's cookbook.
4. *Use directions on the package:* Help children follow instructions on a printed package, for example, to prepare pudding or a packaged muffin mix.

When you create recipe charts, use symbols to help the children follow the directions. Many teachers draw these symbols, but others use images they find on the Internet. If you cover recipe charts or station signs with contact paper, you will be able to save them to use again. Children are usually more proficient in reading a recipe the second or third time, so be sure to repeat food preparation experiences. Leave the recipe up in the classroom for children to see. If the result was really delicious, you may find a child diligently copying it to take home and try again.

Writing Activities

Camari, age 4, handed her teacher a piece of paper on which she had drawn many lines, scribbles, and shapes. Several "C" shapes were included. "I see a lot of lines here," her teacher Mark said to her. Pointing to some wavy lines with circles drawn under them, Camari said, "That's my Uncle's new car." Moving her finger to touch the scribbles above she said, "And this says, 'car.' You can read it." "Yes," Mark said. "I see the 'C' in the word car." "That's just like my name," Camari said excitedly. "I wrote it here."

Camari understands quite a lot about literacy and writing. She knows that words and drawings are different. She understands that print can be read by others. She sees that certain marks consistently are used to write certain words, and she is writing the initial letter of her name, *"C,"* to represent both her name and other words with similar sounds.

You can't learn a language by listening without talking, and you can't learn to read without writing. Children want to write, but their first attempts can be a struggle. Some children will take a while to acquire a comfortable, mature way of holding writing tools. Model ways of holding writing tools without criticizing or shaming children for their immature pencil grips. For example, "When I hold the marker this way, it is easier for me to make the line the way I want it to go." Accept letter reversals, nonconventional writing methods, and invented spelling. Children will not enjoy writing if what they create is consistently critiqued. Instead, help by translating what they wrote for others and by showing your enthusiasm for their developing writing skill. "Your sign says, 'No Crashing.' Shall I write another sign to help everyone know how to read your words?"

You can help children develop writing skill by capitalizing on their inherent interest in print and their desire to be grown up in a number of ways.

1. Encourage children to write their names on their artwork, to sign in each day, and to hold their place for a particular activity. "Here's the sign-up sheet for people who want a turn to make the pizza dough. Write your name here so I know to call you when there is space for you at this table."
2. Invite children to copy words in the environment. "This says 'table.' Do you want to write that word yourself? There are paper and pencils on the writing shelf."
3. Ask children to make signs to communicate important information to others and provide the necessary scaffolding to help them do this successfully. "Let's make a sign to put on your Lego building so that everyone will know you want to save it and show it to your Dad. What shall we write so they will know that? What is the first sound for the word *save?* Yes, *S;* can you make that letter for the sign?"
4. Provide journals (books with unlined pages) and scheduled time for children to write in them. Regular journal time encourages children to write (or dictate) and draw about their experiences. Be sure to read back their words and invite them to do so as well.

Planning Literacy Curriculum

A strong literacy curriculum is much more than a laundry list of activities geared to focus children's attention on print. It goes beyond making books and written materials available. A key feature of meaningful literacy curriculum is a knowledgeable teacher who is attentive to children and uses his or her observations to plan relevant and interesting literacy experiences.

Writing Plans for Literacy

During a study of stores, Serena (the teacher) observed Kelly and Juanita playing in the pretend area. "This says 'Trix'," said Kelly, pointing to the picture of the rabbit on the Trix cereal box. "And this one says, 'cracker'," she said, pointing to the word Triscuit on another box. Juanita brought over an orange juice container. "Yep, this one says 'juice'" she told Kelly, touching the Tropicana word on the carton.

Serena observed that the children were paying attention to the words and pictures on the food containers. She saw that they were beginning to understand that the print on the packages could be read and understood, and that it gave information about the type of food inside of the box. She also noticed that Kelly identified a picture as a word.

Serena planned a matching game to encourage the children to identify a familiar product label, recognize discrete words, and match a label to a word. Because she is an experienced teacher, she wrote a short, almost telegraphic plan as a guide for herself, shown in Figure 8.5.

Serena's short plan would not be enough of a guide for a beginning teacher. The detailed version, shown in Figure 8.6, gives you a better idea of what she planned to do.

Literacy in a Weekly Plan

Literacy learning occurs as children have opportunities for self-selected play in environments that provide a variety of reading and writing tools and materials. Literacy

FIGURE 8.5 Simple Literacy Activity Plan

Food Product Match:	**Literacy**
Objectives:	• Point out differences/similarities between printed words.
	• Match identical words.
	• Identify differences between pictures and print.
Standard:	Domain II, Standard 4
What you need:	Food Product Matching Game (12 cards with labels—4 of each type); game board divided into 3 labeled columns; several food containers; word cards for *Juice, Cereal, Crackers;* basket for cards
How to teach:	1. Show juice carton. Ask, "Does anyone know what this is? How do you know?"
	2. Explain the game. Point out the differences between words and pictures, and point out the product names. Have children find pictures and words.
	3. Pass packages around, and encourage children to find words. Give assistance as needed. Repeat with cereal and crackers.
	4. Give each child a game card. Ask them to figure out what food it is.
	5. Ask each child to find a word that says what's inside.
	6. Ask each child to place a card on the game board. Ask: "How did you know?" Reinforce the point.
How to assess:	Listen for children describing similarities and differences between words and to mention differences between print and pictures.

must also be planned as part of the daily teacher-guided activities. Notice in the week's plan: *Gardens,* shown in Figure 8.7, that some activities such as storybook reading and book making are specifically included to build literacy skills, while others, such as singing songs and cooking, build skills in several areas simultaneously.

Literacy in an Integrated Study

A meaningful study for young children can include literacy throughout the environment and in virtually every type of activity. Figure 8.8, a sunburst for *A Study of Gardens,* highlights activities that were specifically planned to promote literacy learning. Other activities have an additional focus, for example, Planting Lettuce and Carrot Seedlings was planned specifically to encourage fine motor development, a skill directly related to learning to write. In addition, the teacher prepared a step-by-step chart illustrating how to plant the seedlings and encouraged the children to attend to the word and graphic instructions before beginning the activity. Activities like this one that have a literacy element also are highlighted on the sunburst.

Literacy for All Children

Every child, regardless of age or ability, needs and can enjoy literacy experiences. Whether you are planning for toddlers or kindergarteners, children with disabilities, or those with special intellectual gifts, the key is knowing each child's skills, interests, and abilities, and understanding the components and sequences of literacy skill development. Children with differing abilities, including those with developmental delays, can engage in satisfying early literacy experiences when activities are planned with care and attention to their particular learning needs.

FIGURE 8.6 Detailed Literacy Activity Plan

Activity:	**Food Product Match** (A small group/individual matching game)
Curriculum Area:	Literacy
WHO It's For:	Kelly, Juanita, and other children in the *Dancing Bears;* 8 children, age 4.
Rationale:	Kelly and Juanita were pointing out and discussing the labels on products; they noticed product names and symbols, and identified words and pictures as product types.
Objectives:	*By participating in this activity the children will...*

• Point out some differences and similarities between printed words.

• Match identical words.

• Identify differences between pictures and print.

Preschool Content Standard(s):	Domain III (Communication, Language Development & Literacy) Standard 4: Recognize and use symbols.
Indicator:	Identify picture symbols in the environment
HOW to Prepare	*What you need:*

• 15 minutes at small-group time to explain the game and begin it

• The Food Product Matching Game

  1. A set of 12 game cards made with labels from 3 types of familiar foods, for example *juice, cereal,* and *crackers.* (You can easily download copies of these from the Internet.) Paste one label on each card. Make 4 of each type, 12 total.

  2. A game board made of tagboard and divided into 3 even vertical columns.

     Label each column with one of the food types

Juice	Cereal	Crackers

• Food containers for juice, cereal, and crackers—several of each so children don't have to wait very long for a turn.

• Word cards saying *Juice, Cereal, Crackers*

• A basket for the game cards

• Space in the Table Games area to store the game

Set up:

Have containers, board, game cards, and word cards ready near the small group area.

HOW to Teach

Introduction:

When children are settled, show the juice carton and ask, "Does anyone know what this is?" Listen to responses, and then ask, "How do you know?" Tell children they are going to play a game to find words and pictures on food containers that tell what is inside.

Teaching steps:

1. Show the juice container again and ask children to identify what they see on the package and how this tells us what is inside. Respond to ideas by pointing out the differences between the words and pictures, as well as the words for the type of product and the name of the product, e.g., the way the word *Tropicana* looks different from the word *juice.*

2. Show them another juice container and ask who can find a picture of the juice. Ask another child if they can find a word on the juice container.

FIGURE 8.6 Detailed Literacy Activity Plan (continued)

3. Hold up the word card that says *Juice* and say, "This word says *juice*. Can anyone find it on the package?" Pass packages around and encourage children to find the word.

4. Give assistance as needed, e.g., point to '*j*' in the word card and say, "Here's the letter j. It makes a /j/ sound. Can you find this on the package?"

5. Introduce a cracker box and ask what children think is in this package and why. Pass several cracker boxes around and invite children to find some words on the boxes and point to them.

6. Have children find pictures of a cracker and note that the picture is not a word, but is another way for us to know what is inside the box.

7. Show the *cracker* word card. Point out the word and ask children to look for it on the box.

8. Repeat these steps with cereal containers and the *cereal* word card.

9. Give each child one of the product game cards and ask him or her to figure out what kind of food product is pictured; juice, cracker, or cereal.

10. Ask each child to try to find a word on the label that helps them know what is inside of the container.

11. Assist and scaffold as needed to help children distinguish between pictures, logos, and words.

12. Ask each child in turn to place his or her card on the game board.

Closure:

When everyone has had a turn, ask, "How did you know where to put your game card?" Reinforce by pointing out the words on the package tell us the name of the product. Let them know the game will be available in the Table Toys center if they want to play with it. Dismiss children to play.

HOW to Assess and Document

Objectives	Evidence of Learning Children might …	How to Document This Evidence
• Notice some differences and similarities between printed words. • Match identical words. • Identify differences between pictures and print.	• Point out that two different brands of crackers both have the word *cracker* on the label. • Show that the word *Trix* is not the same as the word *cereal*. • Notice that there is a picture of a pirate on the cereal box and refer to it as a picture. • Point to letters that are the same. • Correctly match the game cards to the proper column.	• Observations, work samples, photographs, etc. • Anecdotal records documenting what children say and do during small-group time • Anecdotal records documenting what children say and do as they play with the game during learning centers time • Photos of children placing the game cards onto the game board

EVALUATION (Things to remember for next time)

Follow up by placing food advertisements in the pretend play center and asking the children to find ads with similar names to the food containers.

Children with Special Needs

Jasmine, 4 years old, is an extremely active child. She is constantly moving, running, talking, and wiggling. She rarely chooses any type of table activity and is not able to sit still for a story or small-group activity. Her teachers and her parents agree that it is difficult for her to focus and the family is considering having her tested.

Many preschool teachers have children in their classrooms with behaviors similar to those of Jasmine. Some will eventually be identified as having attention

FIGURE 8.7   A Week's Plan: Gardens—Week #2

	Monday	Tuesday	Wednesday	Thursday	Friday
Story	*First the Seed…*	*Planting a Garden*	*The Carrot Seed*	*The Very Enormous Carrot*	*Jack's Garden*
Outdoor Activities **Purpose:** *to help children…*	**Smelling and Planting Herbs** Identify garden plants. Increase sensory awareness.	**Harvesting Lettuce** Develop understanding of the relationship between food and plants.	**Cornstarch Goop** Increase sensory awareness. Explore physical properties of substances.	**Planting Ferns and Placing Wonder Stone** Gain aesthetic awareness of plants and gardens. Identify characteristics of ferns.	**Harvesting Basil** Develop understanding of the relationship between gardening and food.
Small Group **Purpose:** *to help children…*	**Validate Trip Predictions** Build inquiry skill by comparing predictions to what was experienced. Build literacy skill by referring to a written chart that records children's words.	**In Foster Gardens Book** Build understanding of the similarities and differences between gardens. Develop literacy understanding by authoring a book.	**Garden Bugs Book** Build understanding of the similarities and differences between gardens. Develop literacy understanding by authoring a book.	**Leaf/Flower ID Game** Develop observation skills. Notice differences and similarities between leaves and flowers.	**Journals** Develop literacy understanding. Build a disposition to communicate ideas and feelings in writing.
Indoor Special Activities **Purpose:** *to help children …*	**Examine and Identify Leaves** Observe and identify physical properties of leaves. Learn the characteristics and names of different leaves.	**Leaf Rubbing** Learn about art elements and techniques. Build awareness of the structure and beauty of plants.	**Pen and Paint Drawing** Help children create and express themselves through a variety of art media.	**Garden Collage** Identify different natural materials to use to represent thoughts or ideas. Gain aesthetic awareness.	**Making Pesto** Develop understanding of the connections between gardens and food. Learn how materials change when heated, mixed, or cut up. Use language in a variety of ways. Practice following step-by-step written directions.
Circle Time **Purpose:** *to help children…*	**Garden Fingerplay** **Garden Song** Develop the ability to sing tunefully. Develop awareness of characteristics of gardens.	**Garden Guessing Game** Develop vocabulary about plants and gardens.	**Earth Day Discussion** Develop vocabulary about plants and gardens. Develop awareness of the natural environment and ways to protect it.	**In The Garden Song** Develop awareness of plants that people grow in gardens. Develop creative expression through music. Build literacy skills by seeing words on a chart as they are sung.	**Magic Rocks** Develop creative expression through movement.

Activities that build literacy skills are highlighted.

FIGURE 8.8 A Study of Gardens Sunburst

A Study of Gardens

Spring 2009

Big Idea 1
A garden is a place that people create to grow plants.

Big Idea 2
There are different kinds of gardens for different purposes: to grow food, to enjoy for their beauty, for helping people learn.

Big Idea 3
There are different kinds of gardens in different places: hot and dry places; warm and wet places; cold places.

Big Idea 4
A garden is a home for wild and tame creatures. Some of them help the plants to grow.

Big Idea 5
People who create and care for gardens are called gardeners. They …
make sure the plants and animals in the garden have what they need: sun, water, nutrients, shade, soil, space, protection.
use special tools and materials to make and care for the garden.
make the garden beautiful with plants and decorative objects.
cultivate and harvest plants.

Math
Flowers in the Garden 3-D Graph
Matching Garden Pictures Workjob
Felt Garden Graph
Flower Matching Game

Science
Hot and Dry Terrariums
Stroll Through the Garden
Garden Bug Hunt
Leaf/Flower ID Game
Examine and Identify Leaves
Planting
Dirt Inquiry
Parts of a Plant Exploration
Creating a Butterfly Garden
Worm Composting

Social Studies
Planting
Garden Maps
Garden Prediction Chart
Harvesting
Placing Wonder Stone and Garden Bench
Transplanting
Creating an Aqueduct
Block Garden
Building a Garden Frame and Platform
Building a Worm Box
Building a Garden Bench

Music and Movement
Will My Flowers Bloom?
In the Garden
Hokey Pokey in the Garden
Foster Garden Magic Rocks
Flowers, Fruits, and Vegetables Grow
Flowers in the Flower Garden (chant)
Plants That in the Garden Grow

Fine Motor and Sensory
Dirt in the Water Table
Planting Lettuce and Carrot Seedlings
Smelling and Planting Herbs
Washing Garden Tools
Seed Pouring
Seed Transfer Game

Large Motor
Garden Yoga
Caterpillar Crawl
Digging in the Garden
Watering Plants
Wheelbarrow
Watering Plants

Art and Aesthetics
Gardenscapes and Creating Props for Gardenscapes
Tissue Paper Garden Collage
Tissue Paper Terrarium
Leaf Printing
Nature Collage
Garden Bug Drawing
Nature Bracelets
Garden Collage
Leaf Rubbing
Ink and Watercolor Garden Pictures
Soil Painting
Pipe Cleaner Garden Sculpture
Garden Still Life
Mud Fingerpainting
Rock and Sand Wheat Grass Garden
Drawing in the Garden

Literacy and Literature
Plant Name Matching Workjob
In Our Garden . . . Class Book
Terrarium Book
Creating a Garden Tour Guide
In Foster Gardens . . . Class Book
Garden Bugs Class Book
First The Seed, Then The . . . Book
The Carrot Seed
The Very Enormous Carrot
Garden Poem
Oliver's Fruit Salad
Jack's Garden
Journal: How to Plant

Language
What Garden Objects Are Missing?
Planting Salad Greens Discussion
Garden Discussion
Tree Discussion
Garden Fingerplays
The Plants We Know Discussion
How Will We Water Our Garden? Discussion
Garden Guessing Game
Garden Clues

Family Involvement
Garden Tour
Fencing the Garden
Field Trips to: Pearl City Urban Garden, Foster Botanical Garden

Trips
Pearl City Urban Garden
Hawaiian Garden
Foster Botanical Garden
Tree Walk
Mountain Apple Picking Walk
Walk to the Greenhouse
Cafeteria Garden

Cooking
Lettuce and Tomato Salad
Pesto with French Bread
Tree Fruit Salad
Aunty Yumi's Eggplant Parmesan
Pineapple Mint-Infused Juice
Hawaiian Fruit Salad

deficit disorder. Providing literacy experiences for very active children may at first appear to be a challenge. However, with a bit of innovation, early childhood teachers can adapt many lessons to an active format.

Jasmine's teachers encouraged her to stand near the back of the group during stories or even to stand nearby so that she would be able to listen and still have space to move around without distracting other children. They added written directions and labels to movement games and reviewed them with the children when introducing activities. They developed games and activities that allowed Jasmine to practice literacy skills without having to sit quietly for more than a few minutes at a time.

Literacy activities can be modified to meet the needs of all children. As you add to your repertoire of interesting activities and build skill in determining each child's strengths, interests, and needs, you will find that you can adapt activities to engage the interests of all children in your class.

Children in the Primary Grades

If you work with primary age children, your program will generally have a well-defined curriculum for literacy. If the curriculum includes a teaching philosophy that is consistent with the one presented here, you will include reading and writing opportunities across the curriculum; you will recognize the importance of children's inventive writing and will encourage it. If your program uses a traditional approach, you will want to supplement this with more developmentally appropriate techniques. We have known creative teachers, for example, who offered the required workbooks and readers as a choice for children in addition to a rich, child-oriented literacy curriculum throughout the program. You may be able to win over principals and families when your children not only learn to read and write, but more importantly, want to!

Final Thoughts

Engaging young children in experiences with literacy is one of the most exciting aspects of your work as a teacher. Your careful planning will help to ensure that every child builds these important skills. A skillfully planned and thoughtfully executed literacy curriculum in early childhood programs will lay the foundation for building the abilities children need to thrive in later academic situations and to become competent and fulfilled adults. Your attitude about literacy is as important as your understanding of literacy development and curriculum. When you embrace new learning with excitement and show children the ways that literacy is meaningful in your own life, you are setting them on the path to be the adult readers, writers, and thinkers of tomorrow.

Learning Outcomes

When you read this chapter, thoughtfully complete selected assignments from the "To Learn More" section, and prepare items from the "For Your Portfolio" section, you will be demonstrating your progress in meeting the following *NAEYC Standards for Early Childhood Professional Preparation Programs* (2009):

Standard 1. Promoting Child Development and Learning

Students prepared in early childhood degree programs are grounded in a child development knowledge base. They use their understanding of young children's characteristics and needs and of the multiple interacting influences on children's development and learning to create environments that are healthy, respectful, supportive, and challenging for each child.

The key elements of standard 1 you will have learned about are . . .

1a: Knowing and understanding young children's characteristics and needs

1b: Knowing and understanding the multiple influences on development and learning

1c: Using developmental knowledge to create healthy, respectful, supportive, and challenging learning environments

Standard 3. Observing, Documenting, and Assessing to Support Young Children and Families

Students prepared in early childhood degree programs understand that child observation, documentation, and other forms of assessment are central to the practice of all early childhood professionals. They know about and understand the goals, benefits, and uses of assessment. They know about and use systematic observations, documentation, and other effective assessment strategies in a responsible way, in partnership with families and other professionals to positively influence the development of every child.

The key elements of standard 3 you will have learned about are . . .

3b: Knowing about and using observation, documentation, and other appropriate assessment tools and approaches

3c: Understanding and practicing responsible assessment to promote positive outcomes for each child

Standard 4. Using Developmentally Effective Approaches to Connect with Children and Families

Students prepared in early childhood degree programs understand that teaching and learning with young children is a complex enterprise, and its details vary depending on children's ages, characteristics, and the settings within which teaching and learning occur. They understand and use positive relationships and supportive interactions as the foundation for their work with young children and families. Students know, understand, and use a wide array of developmentally appropriate approaches, instructional strategies, and tools to connect with children and families and positively influence each child's development and learning.

The key elements of standard 4 you will have learned about are . . .

4b: Knowing and understanding effective strategies and tools for early education

4c: Using a broad repertoire of developmentally appropriate teaching/learning approaches

4d: Reflecting on their own practice to promote positive outcomes for each child

To Learn More

Observe a Program: For a morning, observe a program and see how the staff structures the environment and program to support children's development of literacy. Notice both the group activities and the literacy materials planned for the learning centers. Look at the plans and see how the planning reflects what you observed. Interview a teacher to learn what he or she thinks about literacy.

Observe a Child: For a morning, observe a child in a classroom, with a focus on the child's activity in literacy. Notice how the child engages with the experiences offered and how he or she constructs his or her own opportunities for learning. Notice the extent to which the child's learning experiences and the planned curriculum seem to match. Observe to see how staff support the child's literacy learning.

Observe a Master Teacher: Spend a morning with an early childhood educator who is experienced and has a curriculum leadership role in a program. (This teacher may be called the "lead," "head," or "mentor" teacher.) Then interview the educator about how he or she plans for and provides literacy curriculum.

Observe a Literacy Activity: Observe a teacher leading a planned literacy activity. Interview the teacher to find out the objectives for the activity. Reflect on any differences between what you saw and the focus of the plan.

Compare Two Programs: Observe literacy experiences in two early childhood programs. Compare the ways that the two address literacy—their similarities and differences. Reflect on which program seems to best support children's learning and why. What implications does this comparison have for your future work with young children?

Compare Two Ages: Observe two classrooms, one preschool and one for primary school children. Report on how each supports children's literacy learning. Talk to the staff about how they make their curriculum choices. Notice how development influences curriculum choices.

For Your Portfolio

Design a Writing Center: Design and draw a floor plan for a writing center that would promote children's understanding of one or more literacy concepts. Share your plan with an early childhood educator, discussing what you included and why. Ask for and consider the educator's feedback and suggestions. Set up a writing center in a real classroom utilizing as many of your ideas as possible and let children use it. For your portfolio, include the floor plan, photographs of children using the center, samples of work that the children created in the center, and a reflection on what you learned by doing this project.

Plan and Implement a Literacy Activity: Observe a group of children for a morning, focusing on the ways that they express literacy understanding. Based on what you observed, prepare a written activity plan and implement it with the children. Collect evidence of children's responses in the form of anecdotal observations, work samples, photographs, or video recordings. Reflect on how children responded and what they appear to have learned. What worked? What might you do differently next time? How might you expand on this experience for children? For your portfolio, include the plan, a work sample or photograph, and a reflection on what

Explore Resources: Read one of the books from the bibliography and write a review of it for your classmates.

you learned about yourself, children, planning, and teaching.

Plan and Carry Out an Interactive Storybook Reading: Select a story to read to a small group of children. Plan the PEER strategies and CROWD prompts that you will use. If possible, ask a colleague or friend to videotape your story reading or to take notes during the reading. Review the videotape or notes. Reflect on this activity. How did you feel? Which strategies and prompts helped the children engage with the story? What changes would you make the next time? Include this reflection, along with a photograph or copy of the videotape in your portfolio.

Create a Literacy Learning Material: Design and make a literacy learning material to support the development of a particular child or group of children. Introduce it to the child or children, and observe how it is used. Reflect on how the children responded and how you felt about what you did. What worked? What might you do differently next time? How might you expand on this experience for children? For your portfolio, include a photograph of a child using the material and a reflection on what you learned about yourself, children, learning materials, and teaching.

Bibliography

Ashton-Warner, S. (1980). *Teacher*. New York, NY: Simon & Schuster.

Bennet-Armistead, V. S., Duke, N., & Moses, A. (2005). *Literacy and the youngest learner: Best practices for educators of children from birth to five*. New York, NY: Scholastic.

Bodrova, E., & Leong, D. (2007). *Tools of the mind: The Vygotskian approach to early childhood education* (2nd ed.). Upper Saddle River, NJ: Pearson.

Bodrova, E., Leong, D. J., Paynter, D. E., & Semenov, D. (2000). *A framework for early literacy instruction: Aligning standards to developmental accomplishments and student behaviors*. Aurora, CO: Mid-continent Research for Education and Learning.

Bredekamp, S. (2011). *Effective practices in early childhood education: Building a foundation*. Upper Saddle River, NJ: Pearson.

Burns, S., Griffin, P., & Snow, K. E. (1999). *Starting out right: A guide to promoting children's reading success*. Washington, DC: National Research Council, National Academy Press.

Dickerson, D., & Tabors, P. O. (2002). Fostering language and literacy in classrooms and home. *Young Children, 57*(2), 10–18.

Dickinson, D., Golinkoff, R., Hirsh-Pasek, K., & Neuman, S. (2009). *The language of emergent literacy: A response to the National Institute for Literacy*. http://nieer.org/pdf/CommentaryOnNELPreport.pdf

Epstein, A. (2007). *The intentional teacher: Choosing the best strategies for young children's learning*. Washington, DC: NAEYC.

Feeney, S., Moravcik, E., & Nolte, S. (2013). *Who am I in the lives of children?* (9th ed.). Upper Saddle River, NJ: Pearson.

Head Start Resource Center. (2010). *The Head Start child development and early learning framework: Promoting positive outcomes in early childhood programs serving children 3–5 years old.* Washington, DC: Office of Head Start, Administration for Children and Families, U.S. Department of Health and Human Services.

International Reading Association & National Council of Teachers of English. (1996). *NCTE IRA standards for the English language arts.* Retrieved from Standards Doc: www.ncte.org/library/NCTEFiles/Resources/Books/Sample/StandardsDoc.pdf

Karweit, N., & Wasik, B. A. (1996). The effects of story reading programs on the development of disadvantaged preschoolers. *Journal of Students Placed at Risk, 1,* 319–348.

National Association for the Education of Young Children. (2009). *NAEYC standards for early childhood professional preparation programs.* www.naeyc.org/files/naeyc/file/positions/ProfPrepStandards09.pdf

National Early Literacy Panel. (2009). *Developing early literacy.* Jessup, MD: National Institute for Literacy.

Neuman, S. B., & Dickinson, C. (Eds.). (2003). *Handbook of early literacy tesearch.* Boston, MA: The Guilford Press.

Neuman, S. B., & Roskos, K. (2005). Whatever happened to developmentally appropriate practice in early literacy. *Beyond the Journal; Young Children on the Web,* 1-6. www.naeyc.org/files/yc/file/200507/02Neuman.pdf

Newman, S. C., Copple, C., & Bredekamp, S. (2000). *Learning to read and write: Developmentally appropriate practices for young children.* Washington, DC: NAEYC.

Schickedanz, J. (1999). *Much more than ABC's.* Washington, DC: NAEYC.

Schickedanz, J., & Casbergue, R. (2004). *Writing in preschool: Learning to orchestrate meaning and marks.* Newark, DE: International Reading Association.

Sénéchal, M. (2000). The differential effect of storybook reading on preschoolers' acquisition of expressive and receptive vocabulary. *Journal of Child Language, 24,* 123–138.

Shagoury, R. E. (2009). *Raising writers: Understanding and nurturing young children's writing development.* Upper Saddle River, NJ: Pearson.

Slavin, R., & Cheung, A. (2005). A synthesis of research of reading instruction for English language learners. *Review of Educational Research, 75*(2), 247–284.

Snow, C., Burns, M., & Griffin, P. (Eds.). (1998). *Preventing reading difficulties in young children.* Washington, DC: National Academy Press.

Snow, C., & Dickinson, O. (1991). Skills that aren't basic in a new conception of literacy. In A. P. Jennings (Ed.), *Literate systems and individual lives:perspectives on literacy and schooling.* Albany, NY: SUNY.

Standards for the English Language Arts. (1996). Newark, DE: International Reading Association, National Council of Teachers of English. www.ncte.org/library/NCTEFiles/Resources/Books/Sample/StandardsDoc.pdf

Strickland, D., & Riley-Ayers, S. (2006). *Early literacy: Policy and practice in the preschool years.* New Brunswick, NJ: National Institure for Early Childhood Research.

Wasik, B. A., & Bonc, M. A. (2001). Beyond the pages of a book: Interactive book reading and language. *Journal of Educational Psychology, 93*(2), 243–250.

What Works Clearing House. (2007, February 8). *WWC Reports: Dialogic reading.* Retrieved from What Works Clearing House. http://ies.ed.gov/ncee/wwc/reports/early_ed/dial_read

MyEducationLab

Go to Topics 2: Child Development and Learning, and 9: Content Areas/Lessons and Activities in the MyEducationLab (www.myeducationlab.com) for *Meaningful Curriculum for Young Children,* where you can:

- Find learning outcomes for Child Development and Learning and Content Areas/Lessons and Activities along with the national standards that connect to these outcomes.
- Complete Assignments and Activities that can help you more deeply understand the chapter content.
- Apply and practice your understanding of the core teaching skills identified in the chapter with the Building Teaching Skills and Dispositions learning units.
- Listen to experts from the field in Professional Perspectives.

- Examine challenging situations and cases presented in the IRIS Center Resources.
- Check your comprehension on the content covered in the chapter with the Study Plan. Here you will be able to take a chapter quiz, receive feedback on your answers, and then access Review, Practice, and Enrichment activities to enhance your understanding of chapter content.

Go to the Course Resources section in MyEducationLab, where you can:

- Use the Online Lesson Plan Builder to practice lesson planning and integrating national and state standards into your planning.
- Explore children's literature in the Children's Literature Database to find books that promote literacy learning.

Literature is the study of humanity. It is the study of oneself and of the infinite realm of the human heart.

DAISAKU IKEDA

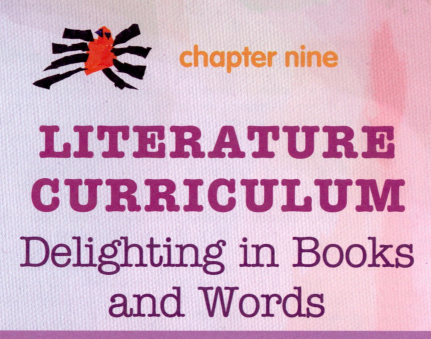

chapter nine

LITERATURE CURRICULUM

Delighting in Books and Words

There is a hushed silence in the classroom as Mary, the teacher in the Sunshine Room, reads Where the Wild Things Are *by Maurice Sendak. The children's eyes follow the book as Mary reads about Max who makes mischief and is sent to bed without his supper.*

As Mary reads the story, her voice changes pitch and volume, rhythm, and cadence. The children are entranced. They roar as the monsters roar their terrible roars. They are silenced when Max orders the monster to be still!

When Mary finishes the story, there is a moment of silence, an intake of breath, and Simeon, age 4 says, "Read it again!"

All of us want to be teachers like Mary, who inspires children to be excited about literature. Becoming such a teacher requires knowledge, skill, commitment, and planning. It takes knowledge of children's literature and understanding of what makes a good book for young children. It takes skill in presenting a book to a group so that children like Simeon are entranced. It takes commitment to going to the library regularly to borrow favorite books and discover new ones. It takes planning to present literature to children every day. Most of all, it requires that you really love children's literature and take joy in sharing it with children. This chapter is designed to help you become a teacher like Mary.

What Is Children's Literature?

Literature is generally thought of as imaginative writing in prose or verse that has lasting value because of its beauty and excellence. Children's literature fits this definition in some ways, and in other ways it does not. Like all quality literature, good children's literature shows craftsmanship, imagination, and excellence. However, literature for children is not entirely contained in books. Oral literature (like nursery rhymes, folktales, fingerplays, poems, songs, and chants) has a significant place in the canon of children's literature. Additionally, although we may refer to *storybooks* and *story time,* children's literature does not consist exclusively of imaginative writing. Non-fiction and other genres are considered part of children's literature. In addition, children's literature is relatively new; time has not yet determined which volumes will endure.

Another difference between literature in general and literature written for children is that most of the time, children's literature is chosen by adults, not young children. Inevitably, it reflects the goals, interests, values, concerns, and taste of parents, publishers, teachers, and librarians, and not children's choices. As a teacher, you will be one of the people who makes literature choices for children. Your goals, values, and taste will influence the books that children in your classroom will have available to experience.

Why Literature?

Books are the tools teachers use to do their jobs. You are becoming a teacher, so you may not think that it is necessary to ask: "Why literature?" Teachers use literature to painlessly provide information, to keep children productively occupied, to teach skills, and to inculcate values. However, there are myriad other reasons to include literature in the curriculum for young children.

Literature builds children's language. Books provide children with a way to hear and understand new words. A book can be turned to again and again; the words and phrases can be reheard, revisited, and gradually understood. The language of literature is slightly different from the language of everyday speech.

It is more thoughtful, poetic, elaborate, precise, and interesting. Children who regularly hear book language have more words available to them, and they develop an ear that can hear the language of books, a necessary prerequisite for reading.

Literature teaches children about the natural and social world. This is obvious in non-fiction (such as Gail Gibbons's books for young children on every topic from apples to zoos). It is also true in fiction set close to home (such as Lois Ehlert's *Planting a Rainbow*) and fiction set in far away places (such as Verna Aardema's *Bringing the Rain to the Kapiti Plain*), as well as in books that use a single concept as a theme (such as Ann Morris's *Bread, Bread, Bread*). Good books for children help them to understand the world in which they live.

Literature helps children understand themselves and other people. Stories help children to understand how and why people behave in the way they do. A story like Molly Bang's *When Sophie Gets Angry . . . Really, Really Angry* can help children understand themselves and their family. A story like Tricia Brown's *Someone Special Just Like You* can build awareness and empathy for people with disabilities. A book provides a window into the world of others that awakens understanding and creates good will.

Good literature teaches values by example. Books like Munro Leaf's *Story of Ferdinand* have within them important messages about right and wrong. Because they are positive and give examples of what to do without preaching or stereotyping, they are far more powerful than setting rules or lecturing children on good behavior.

Literature provides an island of time to reflect and think. Today, at the beginning of the 21st century, many children's lives are filled with noise and activity from the moment they awaken to the time they go to sleep. Books can provide a small oasis where children can escape television, computers, and long hours of school activity and out-of-home care. Everyone needs this kind of stress relief for both physical and mental health.

Literature gives children control. At a time when most entertainment must be plugged in and is managed by adults, literature helps children to connect to something they can control themselves. It helps them to feel capable.

Literature provides pleasure. Have you ever watched young children with books? When a child connects with just the right book, the effect is magical. Eyes are riveted to the page; the book is cuddled close. The child is simultaneously engaged and relaxed. There are many reasons to provide literature to children, but virtually all of them grow out of the pleasure that literature provides.

Literature provides experiences with beauty. Good picture books are works of art. The illustrations give children experience with diverse art styles (e.g., Eric Carle's collages in *The Very Hungry Caterpillar,* Paul Zelinsky's detailed oil paintings in *Rumplestiltskin,* Tomie de Paola's ink and watercolor sketches in *Strega Nona*). The words provide experience with carefully crafted, beautiful language. In a children's book, especially a short book for very young children like Margaret Brown's *Goodnight Moon* or Margaret Chodo-Irving's *Ella Sarah Gets Dressed,* each word must perfectly convey its meaning and feeling.

Children who love books come to love reading. Children who have many positive experiences with literature come to love books. No one learns to read to become proficient at taking tests. Literature is not merely the carrot with which we motivate children to read; in a very real way, the delight of a book is *the most important reason for learning to read.*

Literature and Development

The best, most honest, and most beautiful children's literature may not be perfect for every child. The first thing you need to understand as you begin to share literature as a teacher is the developmental level of the children you teach.

Very young preschoolers (2 1/2- and 3-year-olds) have an attention span that is relatively short for seated activities; they are limited in experience and vocabulary; they are primarily interested in their own experience of the world; and they may not have developed the fine motor skills necessary for turning pages carefully. Oral literature—such as nursery rhymes and fingerplays that are shared in the day-to-day context of play and routine—provides important literature experiences for these children. Books should be durable with heavy pages and hard covers (for a very young or inexperienced group, use board books), relatively short, and concerned with experiences that the child knows or can relate to. It is best if they are written in a straightforward manner and contain easy-to-interpret words and illustrations.

There are predictable social and emotional issues for young preschoolers. They are primarily attached to the important adults in their lives; they are starting to see themselves as separate from their parents; they are learning about friendship but are unlikely to have made a true friend; and they thrive on familiar routines. So a book like *The Runaway Bunny* by Margaret Wise Brown that deals with feelings of anger, love, and security is perfect for them.

Older preschoolers and kindergartners (4- and 5-year-olds) enjoy stories that deal with events and characters that are somewhat beyond their realm of experience. They are much more independent; they are developing true friendships; and they are beginning to show more distinctive personal likes and interests.

While a book like *Where the Wild Things Are* by Maurice Sendak seems to have almost universal appeal because of its illustrations of monsters and its underlying subject matter of power, anger, fear, and belonging, other books appeal to some individuals more than others. Some children are moved and entranced by the moody poetry of *Dawn* by Uri Shulevitz; others enjoy the rhythmic silliness of Beatrice Shenck de Regnier's *May I Bring a Friend?*; and still others enjoy a well-told tale like William Steig's *Sylvester and the Magic Pebble*.

Many children will be fascinated by books that deal with important issues in their lives, such as *Julius Baby of the World* by Kevin Henkes, which deals with the birth of a new baby, or *Charlie Anderson* by Barbara Abercrombie, which includes two children who live in a divorced family.

As children gain more experience with literature, they are able to attend to longer stories with more complex words and plots and more intricate and subtle illustrations. Knowing about children, their interests, their developmental level, their attention span, and the day-to-day events in their lives will help you to pick books that are appropriate and meaningful for your class.

What Is Literature Curriculum in Early Childhood?

Children's literature occupies a singular place in the early childhood curriculum because it is a discipline in and of itself, a subject that non-educators study. While you do not need to be a children's literature expert to do a good job of presenting books to young children, it is interesting to know about the *history* of children's literature. It is useful for you to understand the *genres* of children's literature, and it is important that you have *criteria* for selecting good quality literature to present to the children you teach. Additionally, you need to know how early learning *standards* apply to literature curriculum.

The History of Children's Literature

Until the 19th century, children's literature was not recognized, either academically or by publishers, as a separate or important part of literature. Before there could be children's literature, there had to be:

- a **concept of childhood** and children as different from adults.
- a **literate populace** to read and treasure books.

- **value placed on children** so books would be shared with them.
- the **ability to create books** inexpensively.

The first literature for adults as well as young children consisted of stories and poems committed to memory and told aloud. This ***oral tradition*** was the literature of the common folk; hence it is known as *folktales* or *folklore*. Since it was for everyone—not just children (and remember children were not regarded as being too different from adults)—much of it was bloody, explicit, and scary. Many fine children's books have been constructed from or have been created in the style of ***folktales*** (e.g., James Marshall's *Goldilocks and the Three Bears*), **myths** (sacred stories from a culture that explain the world's origins and powers, such as Gerald McDermott's *Anansi the Spider*), ***fables*** (succinct moral stories of animals, plants, or forces of nature with human characteristics, such as Jerry Pinkney's *The Lion and the Mouse*), and ***legends*** (traditional stories often regarded as true but actually fiction, such as David Wisniewski's *Golem*).

The first *picture book* for children was written in 1658 by Jan Amos Comenius and was titled *Orbus Pictus* (*The World in Pictures*). Comenius believed that children needed interesting material that was different from what was provided for adults. John Newbery (after whom the Newbery Award for children's literature was named) was the first printer to market children's books. His book, *A Little Pretty Pocket-Book: Intended for the Instruction and Amusement of Little Master Tommy and Pretty Miss Polly,* published in 1744, is considered a landmark in children's literature. This book contained several pages of games and amusements. At the top of each page was a letter of the alphabet, followed by an illustration of the activity, a verse describing it, and a small verse with a moral lesson.

> **Try It Out!**
>
> Find one of the old books for children mentioned here and read or reread it. Think about what it says about the author's and society's view of children and childhood at that time.

Over time, books for children became more common. Some of these still are read today. Have you read *Robinson Crusoe* (1762), *Little Women* (1868), *Twenty Thousand Leagues Under the Sea* (1869), *Treasure Island* (1883), *The Wind in the Willows* (1908), or *The Secret Garden* (1910)? If so, you read some of the earliest literature written for children. You will notice that none of these are picture books, although the versions you read probably contained a few illustrations.

When we talk of literature in early childhood today we mean *picture books,* which consist mainly of pictures and very few words. Picture books had to await the technology of the late nineteenth century in order to be produced. The first picture book that matches our 21st century model, *Peter Rabbit,* was written by Beatrix Potter in 1901. Its publication marked the beginning of the era of picture books for young children. Picture books and early childhood education as a field share some common history. Lucy Sprague Mitchell, the founder of the Bank Street College of Education in New York City, promoted picture books for young children. She brought authors and illustrators together and persuaded them to create books for young children that reflected the "here and now" of children's lives. Such well-known classics of children's literature as *Goodnight Moon, Caps for Sale, A Hole is to Dig, The Noisy Book, Mike Mulligan and His Steam Shovel,* and *Angus and the Cat* are the products of this time (Sutherland, 1997).

The changes in picture books over the next decades reflect the changes in society. Each book tells a story of changing views of children, of people, and of the world, from the rollicking silliness of Dr. Seuss (*The Cat in the Hat,* 1959) to the views of inner city life by Ezra Jack Keats (*Whistle for Willie,* 1964), to the lavishly illustrated work of Eric Carle (*Brown Bear, Brown Bear,* 1969), and finally, to the inclusion of minorities and women as full characters (Barbara Cooney's *Miss Rumphius,* 1985, and Juanita Havill's *Jamaica Tag-a-long,* 1990). As you select books for young children, look at when they were written and consider how they reflect their particular time and place.

The Genres of Children's Literature

Part of what creates active, eager readers is the sense of adventure that accompanies making a choice and opening a new book. Part of your job is choosing representatives of the different kinds or genres of literature to share with children. In literature, a *genre* is a category or type of work. In children's literature, *genre* usually refers to the content of the book (e.g., informational vs. fiction) or technique used (e.g., picture books). Although it is certainly possible to read other kinds of books to young children, in early childhood we almost exclusively use picture books and oral literature, so we will only focus on the different content genres used with young children. Each genre serves a different purpose and appeals to different children at different times, supporting their existing interests and helping to build new ones. It's important to know about genres to ensure that you give children experience with them all.

Fiction

Human beings are storytellers—it seems to be a part of who we are: We listen to, like to tell, and learn from stories. So when you think of literature, you probably think of stories, in other words, *fiction.*

What comprises a story for preschool children? It's not just relating events in order. Instead, it is a carefully crafted combination of words and illustrations that encourages children to understand the reasons behind events. A story has

a *setting*—a place and time in which the story takes place (e.g., "Once upon a time, a long time ago, in China"). It has a *plot*—a series of actions that move from the beginning (when the stage is set and a *conflict* or *problem* is introduced) in a related sequence to a logical ending. It has *characters*—with personalities and abilities (the main character is called the *protagonist*). A story has a *theme*—a central idea or message. Finally, a story has a *style*—a unique way of expressing ideas in words and in illustrations.

In a story for young children, it's important that the plot, setting, characters, and style (e.g., words, sentence patterns, imagery, and illustrations) reflect children's understanding and ability to comprehend their world.

- The setting should be well drawn, giving the illusion of reality in time and place.
- The plot should be relatively simple, without a lot of sub-plots and with a definitive ending. It should lead children to understand the reasons behind events.
- The characters should be memorable, believable, and consistent—not stereotyped or unidimensional (all good or all bad). They should behave in ways consistent with their traits.
- The theme or message should be fairly obvious and unambiguous.
- The style should be appropriate to both the story and the characteristics of the children—the younger the children, the clearer and simpler both illustrations and words need to be.

Good fiction for young children can illustrate life, enchant, instill a love of literature, entertain, and bring pleasure. The author's and illustrator's abilities to communicate in ways that create memorable, believable characters help to develop young children's understanding of life's experiences and are what makes a good story for them. The point of a good story need not be made in a heavy-handed manner; stories that preach or minimize the importance of children's feelings or experiences will not be appealing to them.

There are several types of fiction that you will present to children. Fanciful fiction or fantasy, realistic fiction, and folklore are important and belong in your classroom.

Fantasy

Engaging in fantasy is among the most important of childhood activities, so it should come as no surprise that fantasy comprises much of both the literature of childhood and the traditional literature of cultures and nations. Fantasy can be either specially written for children or a retelling of a traditional story.

There are two kinds of fantasy. The first kind involves real things behaving in fantastic ways. In this type of fantasy, characters have personalities very like the children and adults we meet every day, but they have abilities that are amazing. Peggy Rathham's *Officer Buckle and Gloria* is an example of this type of fantasy. The dog Gloria is able to entertainingly act out hazards to the delight of children and the distress of Officer Buckle. Familiarity coupled with pretending is what makes fantasy appealing to children. The realism within the fantasy allows children to put themselves into the story.

Another type of fantasy involves magical realms and beings. This is the fantasy we associate with fairy tales and fairy tale-inspired fiction. In it you will find witches, fairies, giants, magic spells, and monsters. Maurice Sendak's *Outside Over There* is an example of this type of fantasy. But like the more sedate fantasy in which dog-like dogs are able to act, the key in magical fantasy is how it helps children relate to real life.

Fantasy delights because it has its own logic and rules that remain true for the story. Sylvester, the unfortunate donkey in *Sylvester and the Magic Pebble,* finds a pebble that grants wishes when it is held. As a donkey, he can pick up the pebble and wish himself into a boulder to escape from a lion, but as a boulder without hooves, he cannot pick up the magic pebble and transform himself back.

Realistic Fiction

Realistic fiction portrays people, particularly children, with an affectionate, unsentimental voice. The term *here-and-now* fiction was coined by Lucy Sprague Mitchell to describe stories in which realistic children are depicted in everyday situations. Books like Miriam Cohen's *Will I Have A Friend?* and Jane Yolan's *Owl Moon* show the small dramas of everyday life in contemporary settings. The grannies portrayed in Margaret Wild's *Our Granny* are realistic people with real flaws who are beloved by real grandchildren. The children in Gary Soto's *Too Many Tamales* disobey like real children and lose their mama's ring.

Other books realistically portray children's lives from other times or other places. We like to call this kind of stories *there-and-then* stories. Like here-and-now stories, they illuminate children's lives by pointing out the way children in different times and places deal with similar issues and experiences. The children in Alice Mclerran's *Roxaboxen* play pretend in a desert of generations ago, while those in Cynthia Rylant's *When I Was Young in the Mountains* experience day-to-day life in a community from long ago in Appalachia.

In the past, realistic fiction failed to pay adequate attention to minorities, individuals with disabilities, and other groups of children, and, in so doing gave them no one to identify with in the books that they read. We know now that if we are to lead all children to a love of reading, we need to include books that reflect people who are like them. If we are to support the development of children who appreciate the common humanity they share with people who are different from them, they need books that include a range of diverse characters.

Today, a wealth of stories include characters who have disabilities, who are poor, who are ethnically diverse, and who live in families as varied as those of real children. An important characteristic of these books is that the plot is relevant to children and central to the story; it is not just a vehicle for a well-meaning message. Ezra Jack Keats's *Peter's Chair* is about a little boy who does not want to give up being the baby of the family—he happens to be African American and live in an urban setting. Anne Herbert Scott's *On Mother's Lap* depicts a similar theme, only the main characters are Inuit and live in an arctic village. Niki Daly's story of a little girl who damages the fabric her mother bought for a special dress in *Jamela's Dress* transports us to a black township in South Africa where children like the ones in your class play and sometimes make mistakes.

Make sure that the books you choose represent diverse ethnicities, lifestyles, cultures, appearances, race, ages, and activities among people. Mothers should not be cast solely in the role of nurturers. Families should include single parents, same-sex parents, and only children. Minorities should appear in many professions and activities. Girls as well as boys should be adventurous and outgoing, feeling, and creative. Elderly people should be portrayed as attractive and active as well as aged and infirm. People with disabilities should be portrayed as being more like other people than different.

Folklore

Stories based on the oral tradition of folklore are a part of our world heritage that children can begin to enjoy in early childhood. Folktales touch on themes and questions that have universal appeal and similarity, such as magic, good and evil, joy and sorrow, and the origins of the world and the people and animals that inhabit it. Folktales are satisfying in their construction. They have a clear beginning and ending and are concise. They appeal to children's sense of justice and humor. Retellings of familiar fairytales like Susan Jeffer's lushly illustrated European tale *Snow White* and less familiar folktales like Verna Aardema's African tale *Why Mosquitoes Buzz in People's Ears* are an important part of your classroom library.

Informational Books

All children are curious. They explore the world, and they want to know how things work and why things are the way they are. Informational books should be written in understandable, direct language; have aesthetically pleasing words and illustrations; and broaden children's understanding of topics that they are interested in. In order to teach and entertain, these books must be factually accurate, current, and not overgeneralized or filled with half-truths. To enhance interest and not bore, they must be well paced and skillful in their presentation of concepts. Illustrations help to convey more than the words alone can. To be appealing and accurate without being demeaning or insincere is the great challenge of informational books for young children.

Dianna Hutts Aston (*An Egg Is Quiet*), Gail Gibbons (*The Seasons of Arnold's Apple Tree*), George Levenson (*Pumpkin Circle: The Story of a Garden*), and Aliki (*My Five Senses*) are a few of today's authors who have written informational books for young children that are direct, accurate, and appealing.

Informational books can promote a host of instructional goals. Some address scientific, social, and environmental concerns once thought inappropriate or too controversial for the young—concepts like birth, death, sex, racism, aging, war, and pollution. When well written and illustrated, these books can help children to understand aspects of their lives about which they may have vital concern. Others, written to meet a societal demand for curriculum material on a current issue or fad, may be inappropriate for young children. Some seem to suggest that it is children's responsibility to handle the problems that generations of adults have created. These books are often promoted unrealistically as a cure for social ills, for the troubles of today's society or children.

Good literature must provide more than a "band-aid." If books were produced hurriedly to address a short-lived concern, the language used and style of illustration may be sentimental, stereotyped, or carelessly executed. If the subject matter is inappropriate, the books generally treat the subject in a superficial, simplistic, or inaccurate manner. These "band-aid" books that purport to teach children how to avoid sexual abuse or drugs, or how to fix the problems of pollution or the disappearing rainforest do more to alleviate the concerns of adults than to solve the problem or ensure the welfare of children.

Mood and Concept Books

A special category of picture books, called *mood and concept* books, have limited story lines and do not provide a great deal of information—yet they still delight and inform. Mood and concept books sensitize children to ideas, feelings, and awareness. They help to expand the realm of a child's experience. Although they may have a simple story line, it is usually incidental. The point of the book is the concept it brings to light or the feeling it evokes.

Mood Books

We call books that evoke a feeling *mood* books. Mood books encourage children to think and use language. Unlike concept books, they do not attempt to teach a concept. Instead, they heighten children's awareness of the world. Mood books could almost be defined as poems.

There are many kinds of mood books. Uri Schulevitz has illustrated books that evoke the feeling of the first snowflake (*Snow*), raindrop (*Rain Rain Rivers*), and the first finger of sunlight (*Dawn*). Wordless books like Pat Hutchins's *Changes Changes* and her nearly wordless *Rosie's Walk,* as well as Jan Ormerod's beautiful books that depict a child's morning (*Sunlight*) and evening (*Moonlight*) are a part of this category. When you read a book with little plot, few words, and lovely illustrations that makes you want to look at each page carefully, you are likely to be looking at a mood book.

Concept Books

Concept books use organizing frameworks like the alphabet (e.g., Bill Martin Jr.'s *Chicka Chicka Boom Boom*), aesthetic experiences (e.g., Lucy Micklethwaite's *Spot the Cat*), colors (e.g., Leo Lionni's *Little Blue and Little Yellow*), shapes (e.g., *Museum Shapes*), numbers (e.g., Karen Katz's *Counting Kisses*), or ideas (e.g., Ann Morris and Key Heyman's *Loving, Tools,* and *Hats, Hats, Hats*). Concept books provide a sense of joy and wonder in the world when they are well designed and illustrated.

Poetry

Young children have a natural response to rhythm and rhyme, and they often speak in the singsong cadences of Mother Goose. Rhymes and finger games are nearly universal forms of literature passed down from adult to child around the world. Poems and rhymes can be shared as oral literature or in printed collections in your library corner.

Nursery rhymes of all cultures include common themes: animals, unusual or grotesque people, street cries, games, fantasy creatures, clapping and finger play, riddles, tongue twisters, nonsense, counting rhymes, proverbs, and simple verse stories. *Fingerplays,* simple rhymes accompanied by actions and sometimes song, can be traditional (like *The Eency Weency Spider*) or may be by known authors (like Vachel Lindsey's *There Was a Little Turtle*). While both fingerplays and nursery rhymes originated as oral literature, they can be found in book form, some as individual rhymes and some as collections.

Many books for young children are written in the form of poetry. Poetry that is sometimes, but not always, rhythmic and rhymed presents mood and melody in language in a natural and unforced manner. Poetry helps to enhance children's understanding of the world and develops their sensitivity to language. It can inspire and move children, or it can calm them. Poetry is more than rhyming words. Poetry consists of words carefully chosen that remain in memory long after they are gone, words that have music and power. Children are surprisingly interested in hearing poems, and an illustrated anthology of poems for children in the classroom library may become a favorite book. *Tomie dePaola's Book of Poems* and *The Random House Book of Poetry for Children,* edited by Jack Prelutsky, are two good examples. Individual poems illustrated as books like Clement Moore's *The Night Before Christmas* (a particularly appealing version has been illustrated by

Tomie dePaola), many versions of Edward Lear's *The Owl and the Pussycat* (we like the version illustrated by Jan Brett)**,** or Arnold Lobel's illustrations of Kumin's *The Microscope* make a good introduction to poetry. Robert Louis Stevenson's *A Child's Garden of Verses,* Edward Lear's *Book of Nonsense,* and A. A. Milne's collections *When We Were Very Young* and *Now We Are Six* are other good choices to share with young children.

Criteria for Choosing Children's Literature

Not every picture book belongs in your class. Part of your job in teaching literature is to make good choices about which books you will make available and read to children. While there are many diverse opinions on what good children's literature is, there is some general agreement among specialists in children's literature. Good children's books:

Reflect on the books you loved as a child . . .

What books did you love when you were a child? What did you love about them? Why were they important to you? How did you discover those books? When was the last time you read one of them? How have you shared these books with children?

1. **Show respect for children.** They are not condescending (that is, they do not talk down to children). They do not stereotype children (or anyone) by culture, race, age, or ability.
2. **Are executed beautifully.** They are written and illustrated with care and craftsmanship. There is attention to detail. The language used is aesthetically pleasing. The illustrations are created with artistry and use a medium that is appropriate to the content.
3. **Have integrity.** They have honesty and truthfulness within the context of the story. In non-fiction, this means that they are accurate in the facts they present. In fiction, it means that the details are accurate when presenting reality, culturally true in folklore, and consistent and believable in fantasy.
4. **Teach by example.** They instruct without preaching or moralizing. They do not barrage children with *shoulds* and *shouldn'ts*. They encourage children to think for themselves and draw their own conclusions.

Try It Out!

Go to the library and look for some of the books that we have mentioned. See how they meet the criteria for children's literature presented here.

5. **Help children to understand and feel more deeply.** This can mean a deeper appreciation of language, a better understanding of people, or a greater appreciation of the world in which we live.
6. **Interest and delight children.** There are so many wonderful children's books available today. What delights a 3- or 4-year-old? Sometimes, beautiful illustrations; sometimes, the rhythm of words; sometimes, a subject that fascinates. Though there are many other criteria for quality, the one that is most important is whether children want you to read it again.
7. **Do not sell products.** There is a distressing tendency on the part of corporations to market books for children based on movies, TV shows, and products like Cheerios and M&M's. Such books are advertisements, not literature. We believe it is unethical to use them because by doing so, you are tacitly endorsing the movie, show, or product and selling them to children. They should not be in your classroom.

Standards for Literature Curriculum

Like every other curriculum area, there are standards that apply to literature curriculum. Few states have standards for preschool literature curriculum; instead, Head Start and most states combine literature and literacy standards. Similarly,

FIGURE 9.1 Head Start Child Development and Early Learning Framework: Book Appreciation and Knowledge

The interest in books and their characteristics, and the ability to understand and get meaning from stories and information from books and other texts.

- Shows interest in shared reading experiences and looking at books independently.
- Recognizes how books are read, such as front-to-back and one page at a time, and recognizes basic characteristics, such as title, author, and illustrator.
- Asks and answers questions and makes comments about print materials.
- Demonstrates interest in different kinds of literature, such as fiction and non-fiction books and poetry, on a range of topics.

Retells stories or information from books through conversation, artistic works, creative movement, or drama.

Source: Administration for Children and Families, Head Start Bureau, www.hsnrc.org/cdi/child-outcomes.cfm

the National Council of Teachers of English (NCTE) and the International Reading Association (IRA) have jointly created standards for children in grades K–12 that integrate literature standards.

Preschool Literature Standards

Head Start Child Development and Early Learning Framework standards for literature are included in its literacy standards and are called *Book Appreciation and Knowledge*. These standards lay out the expectations that children will show interest in literature, learn how to handle books, and acquire skill in literature related activities like retelling a story. (See Figure 9.1.)

State standards tend to be in synchrony with the Head Start outcomes framework. If your state has separate literature standards, they are likely to read something like this: Preschool programs should provide opportunities for children to:

- listen to a wide variety of age-appropriate literature read aloud.
- value and develop interest in books, songs, rhymes, stories, and reading-related activities.
- relate themes and information in books to their personal experiences.
- acquire knowledge of how to use a book.
- retell a story following the pictures in a book.

Standards for Primary Grades

Common Core Standards in the language arts for kindergarten include standards related to literature (Figure 9.2). They help preschool teachers understand the skills that will be required in elementary school.

Teaching Literature

The best way to help children learn the joy of reading and become motivated to read is by having good books available and reading to children often. Sharing literature with children, supporting them as they come to understand and make literature choices, and observing them as they discover literature is one of the great pleasures of teaching. Children need many opportunities to look at books, to hear stories, and

FIGURE 9.2 **Common Core State Standards: English Language Arts Standards: Related to Literature**

Key Ideas and Details
- With prompting and support, ask and answer questions about key details in a text.
- With prompting and support, retell familiar stories, including key details.
- With prompting and support, identify characters, settings, and major events in a story.

Craft and Structure
- Ask and answer questions about unknown words in a text.
- Recognize common types of texts (e.g., storybooks, poems).
- With prompting and support, name the author and illustrator of a story and define the role of each in telling the story.

Integration of Knowledge and Ideas
- With prompting and support, describe the relationship between illustrations and the story in which they appear (e.g., what moment in a story an illustration depicts).
- With prompting and support, compare and contrast the adventures and experiences of characters in familiar stories.

Range of Reading and Level of Text Complexity
- Actively engage in group reading activities with purpose and understanding.

to see adults using and enjoying books. Nothing is more important than creating the desire to read books. To do this you will make literature a part of your program environment and your formal and informal teaching every day.

Literature Through Play in a Planned Environment

Every program for young children needs to have a good place for reading stories to a group and a comfortable place for children to enjoy books on their own and with an adult. But literature need not be confined to these areas. In many classrooms, teachers spread relevant books throughout the environment. They may have a shelf of science-related books in the science area, a basket of board books next to the cradle in the dramatic play area, a flannelboard with pieces to retell a story in the manipulatives area, a children's dictionary in the writing center, and a blanket and basket of books under a tree in the yard.

A Library Area

Having a good library (sometimes called the *book area*) that is comfortable, quiet, well lit, and stocked with a selection of quality children's books is critical to inspiring children's desire to read and ensuring their acquisition of book-related skills. Without ongoing access to diverse kinds of good books, they will not acquire knowledge of literature and they may not find the books that call to them. For your classroom library, be sure that:

- it is in a cozy, well-lit location sheltered from classroom traffic.
- there are lots and lots of books representing all the genres described in the preceding pages (5 to 8 books per child in the library at one time—i.e., for 6 children, at least 30 books).

- bookshelves display book covers.
- there is comfortable seating for both children and adults (critical so that adults are physically comfortable reading to children one on one).

In addition, if you have space in the area, include:

- a private area for one or two children to enjoy quiet time with a book.
- decorations such as posters and book covers.
- a listening center with headsets for recorded stories.

A Story or Meeting Place

Experienced teachers who are good story readers can easily read to a class of 15 to 20 children. Teachers with less experience have more positive and longer book sharing times if the group is smaller. However, most teachers read stories to a group of children at least once a day.

Where do you read stories to a group of children? Occasionally a classroom will include a small amphitheater or set of stairs that is perfect for story reading. More typically you will use an area of the classroom that serves another function, often the block center.

A story place has special requirements. It needs to have *good lighting* that shines on the page and not in children's eyes so children can see a book's pictures. Young children need to move when they listen to a story, so it's important for there to be *enough space* for wiggly children. It needs to be *sheltered from noise* so children can hear the words. It needs *comfortable seating* and *relatively few distractions* so that children remain attentive to the story. As you design your classroom, keep these needs in mind.

Creative teachers find many ways to limit distractions and signal to children that an area has become the story place. Some hang curtains over shelves or move dividers in front of shelves to keep tempting toys out of small hands. Some set out mats, blankets, carpet squares, or pillows for children to establish boundaries and make sitting more comfortable.

In addition to providing a place for group story reading, you need a way to make it easy for children to see you as you read. Children will be better able to attend and you will be more comfortable if there is a low chair or stool for you to sit on at story time. A nearby chair, table, or easel will be needed to hold props like flannelboards and puppets.

Reading Outdoors

Reading a story outdoors can be a wonderful experience for children and teachers. Sitting in the shade of a tree with a light breeze blowing creates an atmosphere that makes reading a story even more special. Of course, if it's too hot, too cold, too noisy, too windy, too damp, or the ground is rocky or you're plagued by ants, it's not so special.

When you take a story outside, be sure to adequately prepare. Check for hazards, scan the horizon for rain clouds, spread a big blanket in a shady place where there are few rocks, set down a stool and a basket of books, and *then* call the children to enjoy the story.

> **Try It Out!**
>
> Read a few good books to a child under a tree or in a cozy spot nestled on pillows. How did the environment affect the experience?

A Schedule for Literature

Good preschool programs provide large blocks of time each day during which children have free access to literature and teachers can read to one or two children at a time. It is during such times that you will have your best reading experiences as you cuddle up together in a comfy chair and read a favorite story to one or two children.

It is also important to include scheduled story time at least twice in a full day. Story time can last for 10 to 20 minutes depending on the age, experience, and attention of the children. In order for children to fully benefit from being read to, they must first be interested and able to focus. Anxious, uncomfortable, hungry, or overtired children will not be able to lend their attention to a book, so it is better to schedule story time after breakfast or lunch rather than before. If you share a large room with another teacher and class, schedule group story times when the other class is out of the room.

Another way to provide literature time for children is to include reading time (sometimes called DEAR—drop everything and read) in the daily schedule. In many programs, about 10 minutes before nap time is set aside for children and teachers to rest and enjoy books.

Your Role in Teaching Literature

Helping young children to understand and love literature involves choosing books thoughtfully, designing an inviting book area, and creating a schedule for group and independent reading. However, to help young children to understand and love literature you *also* must:

- learn to read to children with skill and responsiveness.
- know how to provide activities based on literature.
- help families make literature a part of their children's lives at home.

Reading to Children

There are different ways of reading to children depending on the age and experience of the children, your purpose, and the type of book you are reading. If you have selected books that are appropriate to the age and interests of the children, you should read the words as the author has written them. This gives children the experience of rich language, one of the most important aspects of literature. Children who are beginning to attend to reading also will develop understanding of the constancy of print. It is usually best to read the text continuously without interruption. This helps children to develop the sense of the story, follow the flow of the book's language, and remain attentive.

With very young and inexperienced children, or non-English speaking children, you may find books that are valuable but are too wordy or too difficult for them to understand. In this case you may just wish to talk about the pictures, convey the story in simpler words, or select alternative books that match your children's needs.

Questions and comments can also serve as a bridge between the child's life and the book, "Little Sal is filling her bucket with blueberries just the way we filled our buckets with crabapples when we went to the farm." One of your most important goals in presenting literature to children is to help them to develop an understanding and love of books. They should never feel pressured by questions about books: If they feel that story time is really quiz time, they may avoid reading altogether.

Reading to a Group
Reading aloud is an art. Reading aloud to a group of young children is a specialized aspect of that art. It includes prosaic and often overlooked skills such as holding a book so everyone can see it and reading a book sideways or upside down. It also involves knowing how to capture the attention of a group of young children, discerning behaviors that signal a potential disruption, and using strategies to manage a group of children. Finally, it involves using acting skills to manipulate your face and voice to communicate the meaning of the words. Thus, reading aloud to young children is an art, and like any art it takes some practice.

Before you read to a group of children, read the book yourself and make sure you are familiar with the story and know how to pronounce all the words. It is also important to be familiar with the illustrations. While you want there to be surprises for children, you don't want to be surprised yourself. Anticipate which words and images may distract children, and be prepared for how you will handle them.

To be able to say the words effectively, you will probably need to practice. Many children's books are written in rhyme, and the words have cadence (a regular and agreeable modulation in the sound of the words). It is important to read the book in a way that emphasizes this. For example reading the story of *The Three Little Pigs* is more effective if your pitch rises on the marked syllables and you emphasize them "I'll **huff** and I'll **puff** and I'll **blow** your house in." It is much less interesting to children if you read in a monotone and without the rhythm.

Be sure to limit distractions: Ask other adults to avoid talking and making noise during the story. Set up the environment with a low chair or stool for you and a place for children to sit in front. A large group benefits from a defined area in a wide "slice of pie" shape (use carpet squares, masking tape, spots, cushions, or a big blanket). Help children settle down and focus by singing a simple song or doing a fingerplay or by saying something about the book (e.g., "This story is about a little green witch and I think it might remind you of another story you know."). Show the book cover and read the title, along with the author's and illustrator's names. Vary how you say this: "written and illustrated by Eric Carle,"

or "Mem Fox wrote the words and Helen Oxenbury painted the pictures," or "the author is Bill Martin Jr. and the illustrator is Lois Ehlert." Remind children of other books you have read by the same author/illustrator—"He wrote *Brown Bear Brown Bear*!"

As you read, hold the book a special way. Using one hand, hold the book in the middle, from the bottom, and rest it on your palm. Support the back of the book with either fingers or thumb, and hold the pages open with the remaining fingers. Face the book forward and low, slightly above children's eye level. Tilt it toward the children (slightly inward and downward) so they can see the pictures and you can see the words. Each time you turn a page, turn the book slightly so all the children can see.

Use a natural voice as you read. Speak clearly and loudly enough for children to hear. Read with expression; match your volume, tempo, facial expression, and gestures to the content of the story. Define new words simply as they arise; for example, "A newt is like a lizard but it sometimes lives in streams and ponds."

Occasionally make a statement or ask a question, for example, "I wonder what will happen when the bears go upstairs. What do you think Goldilocks will do when she wakes up?" Do this sparingly so as not to interrupt the narrative and cause children to lose focus. Respond to children's comments and questions minimally with eye contact, smiles, nods, and brief verbal responses (e.g., "that's right, that's an interesting question"). Avoid having a dialogue with one child during a story because it distracts from the narrative—but be sure to come back to the child's question or observation at the end. We have seen story times fall apart when teachers stopped to have a conversation with one child as the others lost interest.

While you are reading, be observant! Pay attention to children. Notice when they are restless, inattentive, or confused. If children seem distracted, ask an individual or the whole group a focusing question or invite the whole group to stretch or move in a way related to the story (e.g., "Show me *your* ten little fingers and ten little toes") and then continue reading.

Knowing how and when to end is also a book reading skill. Make a comment or return to a question a child asked. "Luke was wondering why the cows wanted blankets. Can anyone think of a reason?" If you are going to read a second or third story (and we encourage you to do so), be sure to give children a chance to wiggle and move in between. A fingerplay or song will help you do this in a controlled way. However, don't read another story if children were unable to stay focused during the previous one. Helping children make a smooth transition to the next activity is a part of your teaching skills repertoire that you will apply when ending story time, as you will with any other activity.

Lap Reading

Reading to one or two children as they sit next to you or on your lap is another art. However, you can be more relaxed reading to one or two children because you don't need to focus on group management.

More personal connection and dialogue is possible when you read to one or two children at a time. While part of the art of group reading is knowing how to defer conversations, part of the art of lap reading is having a dialogue during the story. Comments and questions can help develop understanding by enlarging on events in the books: "I wonder what the Gunniwolf wants. The little girl seems to be going deeper into the jungle. Why do you think the Gunniwolf talks like that?" Such interaction can help you become better attuned to children's needs, feelings, and interests.

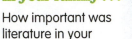

Reflect on the role of literature in your family . . .

How important was literature in your family? Do you remember being read to? What effect did this have on you? How did your family's interest or lack of interest in literature influence your attitudes and values?

Helping Families Provide Literature to Children

An essential part of the literature curriculum is helping families use and choose good books for their children. Few families have spent time learning about good literature for young children. Some may not understand the importance of adults reading to children. In some families, illiteracy is a barrier. If parents cannot read well, they often feel ashamed or embarrassed, which prevents them from attempting to read to children at all. Family literacy programs that combine early childhood and adult literacy education may be available in your community.

You can help children's families to provide good literature to their children. Feature a review of good books for children in your newsletters to families. This can provide a guide for trips to the library. In communities where families are financially able, you may wish to introduce one of the children's book clubs that sell good quality paperbacks for a few dollars.

A simple and effective way to encourage family reading is by making good classroom books available for overnight borrowing. A selection of wordless books and simple repetitive books can help adults for whom reading is difficult. Your careful explanation of how important reading is to children and how special the books are to you will help ensure that they are returned undamaged. Special *book bags* can be used to protect the books as they travel to children's homes and back to school again in the morning. We like to include a journal for families to write down their experience with the book and a small toy related to the story. The establishment of this routine will help children later on when they begin to use public libraries on their own. You can also encourage families to take regular trips to the library with their children to borrow books and to attend library-sponsored story hours. Community organizations are often willing to provide small grants to create a book bag program.

Literature Activities

Literature is enhanced when it is not isolated from other classroom experiences. It can be a launching point for many other kinds of activities. For example, a memorable phrase such as *"I'll huff and I'll puff and I'll blow your house down"* from the traditional story *Three Little Pigs* may be the perfect response when the cardboard box house you created one day in the yard is discovered on its side the next day.

Different Ways to Tell Stories

While reading picture books is the most common way to share literature with children, there are a number of other techniques that delight children and help them to build understanding of literature.

Oral Storytelling

The most personal way to share literature with young children is through oral storytelling. It is flexible because you can do it anywhere without props or a book, and you can adapt the length of the story and the words to your audience and situation. Oral storytelling is creative: Even though you may be retelling a familiar old tale like *The Story of the Three Little Pigs,* you will be presenting it in your own way.

Telling a familiar story without a book or prop requires that you know the story well. In order to be comfortable doing this, you need to reflect on the story, map out its sequence, and identify the elements (both plot and style) that are important. Once you have memorized these basics, you can retell the story with embellishments from your own imagination or based on suggestions from the children.

> **Try It Out!**
>
> Retell a familiar folktale that you know well to one or two children.
> Ask them for their ideas (e.g., What did Red Riding Hood have in her basket?) and include them as you tell the story.

Flannelboards and *puppets* are good props to use in telling stories to very young children because they are simple, easy to focus on, and can be touched and manipulated. They also contribute to the experience of older children who are captivated by their novelty and who enjoy using the materials for their own storytelling.

While flannelboard stories are available for purchase from educational supply companies, we prefer the personal quality of homemade stories. They model the value of doing things yourself, and they quite literally represent your time and love. Children understand and appreciate this. A good flannelboard story is based on a simple story from a book or a traditional tale, rhyme, or song. The focus and sequence of the story should be clear. It should not involve too many pieces or too complex a story. Simple stories like Ruth Crockett Johnson's *The Carrot Seed,* traditional folktales like *The Three Bears,* and nursery rhymes like *Humpty Dumpty* all make good flannelboard stories.

Children love puppets and will be mesmerized by them. Do you wonder what to do with puppets besides letting children play with them (an activity that often degenerates into Punch and Judy-style hitting)? One idea is to use the puppet as the narrator for an oral retelling of a story. For example, a pig or wolf puppet could retell the story of *The Three Little Pigs.* If the story has only one or two characters, you can act out the story with the puppets (*The Very Hungry Caterpillar* works well this way). A capable child can take on a supporting role. Avoid having too many puppets to manipulate or the story will get lost in the task of managing the puppets.

Acting Out Stories

Another way to tell a story is to involve children in acting it out. It is a rare group of young children that does not spontaneously begin to take on the role of the monkeys in Esphyr Slobodkina's *Caps for Sale* after hearing it one or two times. With the addition of a few props and some adult direction, you can introduce a new way to tell a story.

Choose a story that has a number of characters (*Swimmy* by Leo Lionni is a good choice). After reading the story once or twice, plan with children to act it out. Agree on roles, and decide who will take on each one; children can have more than one role as long as the characters don't appear in the same scene. Decide on how the action will occur. ("Here behind the shelf is where the school of little red fish will hide.") Then read the story while the children act it out.

Recorded Stories and Poems

Recordings of stories and poems for children can add an extra dimension to a familiar book. Many of the paperback book clubs for children include inexpensive audio recordings with books. We especially like recordings of authors reading their own work. Sometimes these are very well done. We also recommend the extremely well crafted recordings of Rudyard Kipling's *Just-So Stories* narrated by Danny Glover and Jack Nicholson and accompanied by the music of the South African a cappella chorus Ladysmith Black Mambazo and Bobby McFerrin.

It is vital to remember that no recording, however good, is a substitute for daily reading time. Some recordings are made without aesthetic awareness or respect for children. These are often sold in grocery stores and seem to be the literary equivalent of the candy and junk food displayed at checkout stands.

Similarly, there are many fine video versions of good children's literature, as well as others that do not contribute to children's development. While videotaped books are certainly preferable to typical children's television programming, we do not believe that either deserves a regular role in the classroom. Occasionally, after a child has had exposure to a book, a short film or videotape of the book can add new dimensions and enlarge on his experience. Only the very best of these should be included in your program (e.g., there is a delightful version of Maurice Sendak's *In the Night Kitchen*). They must be thoughtfully conceived and well executed, making use of the talents of accomplished filmmakers, animators, and storytellers.

Literature Extensions

Another way to bring literature to children is through *literature extensions,* sometimes called *story stretcher*s. Literature extensions are activities that use an element from a story as a springboard for further learning. There are many ways to extend literature; some are very simple, such as doing the fingerplay *The Little Seed* after you have read the story *The Tiny Seed*. Others are more complex, like bringing a dog to school to bathe after you read *Harry the Dirty Dog*. Literature extensions are valuable for several reasons.

1. They enhance children's enjoyment of a particular story and build their disposition to spend time with books.
2. They enhance children's understanding of a particular aspect of literature by illuminating an element of the story. For example, acting out *The Carrot Seed* helps build understanding of characterization.
3. They build children's awareness that literature is connected to real life. For example, having the class make and eat tamales after reading *Too Many Tamales* makes the content more real.

4. They provide skill and understanding in curriculum areas besides literature. For example, creating a game in which children match Eric Carle's bug collages to photographs of the real animals helps children gain science awareness.

A good literature extension has a number of characteristics. It has a connection to the story that helps children understand the story better; for example, cooking oatmeal and waiting for it to cool helps children understand why the three bears had to go out for a walk. It has an educational purpose, and builds knowledge, skill, or awareness. Story stretchers are more than fun; for example, creating a worm terrarium as an extension of Doreen Cronin's *Diary of a Worm* helps children learn about worms, whereas eating gummy worms in pudding mud does not. It uses the book as a central part of the activity. It's not a literature extension to put out blue paint after reading Arnold Lobel's *The Great Blueness* unless you talk about how Lobel used blue and then make comparisons between the book and children's work. The In Practice box gives you ideas for a variety of types of literature extensions. Each of these only becomes a literature extension when you help children make a connection to the book, poem, or story.

IN PRACTICE: A Few Ideas for Literature Extensions

Art—Use an art technique that a book illustrator uses—for example, the collage technique of Eric Carle.

Dramatic Play—Set out the props for a story such as *The Little Red Hen* by Paul Galdone.

Large Motor Activities—Create an active game that matches a story, like an obstacle course for *Going on a Bear Hunt* by Helen Oxenbury.

Trips—Go on a trip to see something mentioned in a book, for example, a trip to a pumpkin patch to go with Helen Cooper's *Pumpkin Soup*.

Write a Letter—Write to the living author or illustrator of a favorite book (e.g., Mem Fox, Tomie de Paola, Lois Ehlert), or to one of a book's characters (e.g., Jack from Steven Kellogg's *Jack and the Beanstalk*).

Music—Sing a song that reflects a story, such as Elizabeth Cotton's *Freight Train* or *Freight Train* by Donald Crews.

Food Activities—Cook or taste something mentioned in a story like blueberries for *Blueberries for Sal* by Robert McCloskey *or* cookies for *The Doorbell Rang* by Pat Hutchins.

Games/Workjobs—Make a game based on a story, like a matching game to go with *Goldilocks and the Three Bears* or a seriation game to go with the *Three Little Pigs* stories (James Marshall has created good versions of both).

Learn a Poem, Rhyme, or Fingerplay—Relate the poem, rhyme, or fingerplay to the story, e.g., use *Here Are the Beehives* with Patrica Polacco's *The Bee Tree*.

Write a Group Story—Create your own version of a story; for example, revise *If You Give a Mouse a Cookie* with a different animal and food (e.g., *If You Give a Dog a Dumpling*).

Literature Studies

Literature can also be used as the focus for a series of activities known as a *literature study* or *web*. In a literature study, you teach about literature and a particular story or type of story. For example, you might take Galdone's version of *Goldilocks and the Three Bears* and do several things with it.

1. Expand children's understanding of the story itself by doing interesting activities and using ideas from the story, e.g., put props for the story in the dramatic play area, act out the story as a group, make puppets to retell the story, make porridge to develop an understanding of the word, play games that develop concepts using comparisons of size and qualities used in the story (*small, middle, large—hard, medium, soft—hot, warm, cold*).

2. Discuss the feelings and motivations of the characters—why did Goldilocks go in the house? How did the bears feel when they found the porridge eaten? What else could Goldilocks have done?

3. Read several versions of the story, including some from different cultures/times. Expand children's understanding of literature (read other folktales, compare folktales with 3 characters [3 pigs, 3 bears], read as many other books written/illustrated by Paul Galdone as possible and compare the different books, read "fractured" versions of the story, write a group variation of the story).

Other types of literature studies focus on:

• a particular *author/illustrator* whose work children enjoy.
• a *character* found in many folktales such as the fairy godmother, the big bad wolf, or Anansi.
• a particular *story* that children love such as *Tikki Tikki Tembo*.
• a favorite, familiar *genre* like Mother Goose Rhymes that exist in many different versions.
• a *topic* that occurs over and over in many stories like the constancy of a mother's love or eating pancakes.

Planning Literature Curriculum

You will not write a plan every time you read a story. Scheduling daily story times, creating an environment for enjoying literature, and ensuring that there is adequate time for children to use it are the most important parts of the literature curriculum. However, you will plan literature activities as part of an integrated curriculum and when you want to help children acquire some specific literature skills, concepts, and dispositions.

Writing Literature Plans

Since literature is so valuable for teaching so many curriculum areas, it is easy to overlook planning curriculum for literature learning itself.

At the beginning of the school year in the Grasshoppers Room (young 3-year-olds), Carol, their teacher, carefully chose a selection of books about separation and starting school (Cohen's Will I Have a Friend, *Appelt's* Oh My Baby Little One, *Penn's* The Kissing Hand*) as well as some simple stories*

(Fletcher's Barnyard Banter, *Williams's* More More More Said the Baby, *Tafuri's* Have You Seen My Duckling?, *and Brown's* Goodnight Moon). *Story time was difficult with this very young group. They just didn't seem able to sit still for stories. At the end of the week, she was dismayed to find torn pages in the books.*

Although Carol had planned well for social-emotional development and the typical interests of young 3-year-olds, she had failed to plan for their developing abilities related to literature. Realizing this, she took a step back and thought again about what she wanted the children to learn.

What does Carol, or any teacher, want to develop in young children? What are the skills they need to enjoy books and be responsible members of a classroom community that includes books? What are the concepts that will help them to understand and use literature well?

Perhaps it is easiest to identify dispositions. Every teacher wants children to develop the disposition to:

- *love books* and regard reading as a delightful activity.
- *choose books* as a form of play.
- *go to books* as sources of information, comfort, and inspiration.
- *treasure books* and treat them with care.
- *listen to books* being read and stories told aloud by a teacher in school.

There are some skills that children need in order to develop these dispositions. Children should be able to:

- *get books* from a library shelf or book basket *and return them* right-side up, without damage.
- *hold books so they can be read*—right-side up, face forward, and *look at books*—from front to back, turning one page at a time without tearing pages.
- *attend to a book* and follow a story being read to a group and *participate* in positive ways during group story times (e.g., chiming in with a pattern book, answering questions).

Children also need to understand some things about literature. The very basic understandings include the following:

- *A book is* a special object with interesting words and pictures to experience inside.
- *There is a specific way to use a book* (you look at it on your own or with others—it is not for building with, stepping on, drawing in, tearing, or otherwise manipulating).
- *Pictures in books have meaning*—they represent something and help you understand the words.
- *The story/information/pictures in a book are constant*—no matter who reads it, no matter when—it always stays the same.
- *A book is written and illustrated by people called authors* (who write the words) *and illustrators* (who create the pictures).
- *Books have a beginning, middle, and end.*
- *Some books have a story* in which *characters* have a *problem* that they work to *solve* by the end.

FIGURE 9.3   Simple Literature Activity Plan

This Is The Way We Look at Books!

Objectives:	Follow a story being read and learn to use a book.
Standard:	Domain III, Standard 5
What you need:	Book—*Barnyard Banter* and other simple books
How to teach:	1. Invite 2–3 children to the library area—ask them to sit.
	2. Show the book and read the title.
	3. Read the book and invite children to point to the animals and repeat words. Point out how you are holding the book and turning the pages.
	4. Invite a child to hold the book and turn the pages.
	5. Ask the child to put the book back on the shelf—repeat with another book.
How to assess:	Look/listen for children attending to the story; coming back to the library area later; looking at books without damaging them.

- *Some books have information* that helps you to learn about something. If you want to find something out, you can look in a book.
- There are *words to describe the parts of a book:* cover, spine, title, title page.

So Carol started again and planned the activity described in Figure 9.3 to help the children in her class use and enjoy books.

Because she is an experienced teacher, Carol leaves out many details in her short plan. It would not be enough of a guide for a beginning teacher. The detailed version that follows in Figure 9.4 gives you a better idea of what she planned to do.

Literature in a Weekly Plan

Literature belongs in your class each day and throughout the weekly plan for preschoolers. In the example shown in Figure 9.5, you will see that there is a story planned for every morning. In addition, literature is the focus for small group activities twice in the week. This format does not show the afternoon, when another story time is planned.

Literature in an Integrated Curriculum

Although we appreciate and enjoy the literature studies described earlier in this chapter, we do not feel that they are sufficient or concrete enough to serve as the content for a sustained integrated study with young children.

Our preferred way of employing literature in integrated curriculum is to use it to support the study of a meaningful topic that children want to learn more about. In the sunburst graphic of *A Study of Plants* (Figure 9.6), activities appear in the section on literature. However, literature was also a part of some cooking activities (Pumpkin Soup) and language activities. Literature activities are highlighted.

FIGURE 9.4   Detailed Literature Activity Plan

Activity:	**This Is the Way We Look at Books!** (A guided book reading experience)
Literature Focus	
WHO It's For:	This activity was planned for the *Grasshoppers* (eight 3-year-olds), 2–3 at a time.
Rationale:	None of the *Grasshoppers* have ever attended preschool before. Last week they were not attentive during story time and did not seem interested in books. Two books were damaged by children.
Literature Objectives:	*By participating in this activity the children will ...*

- Develop the ability to follow a story being read aloud by a teacher.
- Learn to hold a book, turn the pages, and return the book to the library shelf.
- Acquire a disposition to listen to stories read aloud.

Preschool Content Standard: Domain III, Standard 5: Enjoy and understand books.

HOW to Prepare

What you need:

Library area, library shelf, pillows, books including *Barnyard Banter* by Denise Fleming

Set up:

Make sure all the books are right-side up on the shelf and facing forward

HOW to Teach

Introduction:

Invite 2–3 children to come to the library area and cuddle close on your lap or beside you

Show the book and say something like, "I wanted to read you *Barnyard Banter*. I like the rooster on the cover."

Teaching steps:

1. Read the first pages of the book and invite children to point to the animals and repeat words.
2. Turn a page and say something like, "I sure do like this book. I have to turn the page carefully so it won't tear."
3. Invite a child to hold the book and turn the pages, saying something like, "Would you like to hold the book so carefully and turn the page?"
4. Continue reading and comment on how the child is turning the pages so carefully.
5. Invite the second child to take a turn and continue reading, commenting on how the child is taking care of the book.
6. When the book is done, invite a child to put the book back on the shelf—ask him/her to make sure the rooster is in front so we can see it.

Closure:

If children continue to be interested, repeat with another book. Otherwise, comment that you really enjoyed reading the book with them and thank children for taking such good care of the books.

HOW to Assess and Document

Objectives	Evidence of Learning Children might...	How to Document This Evidence
Develop the ability to follow a story being read aloud by a teacher.	Be attentive to story being read and ask questions or make comments about it.	Anecdotal observations, annotated photograph
Learn to hold a book, turn the pages, and return a book to the library shelf.	Independently go to the library and look at books appropriately without tearing pages or leaving the book on the floor.	
Acquire a disposition to listen to stories read aloud.	Come to story time quickly and willingly. Ask the teacher to read another story.	

EVALUATION   (Things to remember for next time)

Play a game in which you put the book on the shelf the wrong way and the child can correct you. This arose spontaneously with the last pair of children and it was very much enjoyed.

FIGURE 9.5 A Week's Plan: A Study of Water—Week #6

Objectives: To help children to: understand water has different forms (solid, liquid, and gas) that behave in predictable ways; learn about how people use water in different ways (to clean, to cook, to play, to work, etc.).

	Monday	Tuesday	Wednesday	Thursday	Friday
Story 8:30–8:50	*A Drop of Water* by Walter Wick		*Water* by Frank Asch	*Night in the Country* by Cynthia Rylant	*Come On Rain* Karen Hess
Outdoor Activities 9:00–10:00	Painting with Water on Sidewalk		Water Table Experiments and Painting with Water	Tricycle Wash	Water Table Experiments and Painting with Water
Purpose: *to help children …*	Learn about the properties of water. Engage in science inquiry.		Learn about the properties of water. Engage in science inquiry.	Develop understanding of some of the uses of water.	Learn about the properties of water. Engage in science inquiry.
Small Group (Monsters) 10:00–10:20	Cooking Pasta	ELECTION DAY NO SCHOOL	Lili's Dad—Ocean/Marine Biologist Visit	Urashima Taro	Story Time at Library
Purpose: *to help children …*	Understand one of the ways that water changes things. Engage in science inquiry.		Develop awareness of the ocean and animals that live in it. Become aware that some people have jobs involving water.	Develop appreciation for and awareness of literature from different cultures.	Develop interest in books and literature. Become aware of the community.
Small Group (Flowers) 10:00–10:10	Water Drawing		Ice Exploration I (Water and ice cubes in a cup)	Ice Exploration II (Crushed ice and ice block)	
Purpose: *to help children …*	Learn about the properties of water. Engage in science inquiry—observing how water evaporates.		Learn about the properties of water. Engage in science inquiry—observing how ice melts.	Learn about the properties of water. Engage in science inquiry—observing how ice melts.	
Indoor Special Activities 10:20–11:30	Liquid Watercolors		Tissue Paper Collage	Wet Paper Painting	Wet Paper Painting
Purpose: *to help children …*	Express ideas and feelings using watercolors. Learn about art elements and techniques.		Create and express ideas through using the medium of collage. Develop awareness of artistic design.	Learn a new art technique. Create and express ideas through using the medium of paint.	Learn a new art technique. Create and express ideas through using the medium of paint.
Circle Time 11:30–11:45	Roll That Pumpkin		Row Your Boat	Ame Furi	Row Your Boat
Purpose: *to help children …*	Bring closure to Halloween. Develop the ability to express feelings and ideas through music.		Develop the ability to express feelings and ideas through music and movement. Develop physical control and body awareness.	Develop the ability to express feelings and ideas through music and movement. Learn words from a different language and learn how different cultures express ideas about rain.	Develop the ability to express feelings and ideas through music and movement. Develop physical control and body awareness.

278

FIGURE 9.6   A Study of Plants Sunburst

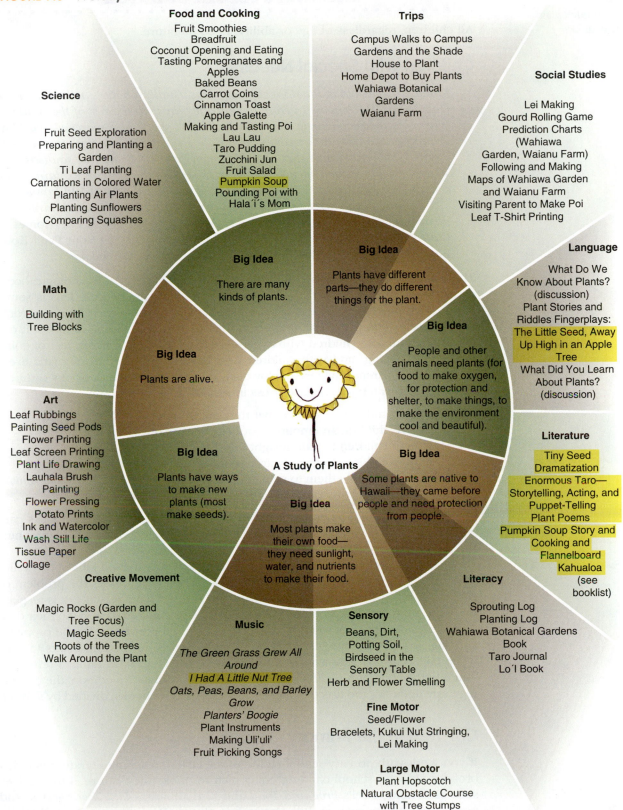

Food and Cooking
Fruit Smoothies
Breadfruit
Coconut Opening and Eating
Tasting Pomegranates and
Apples
Baked Beans
Carrot Coins
Cinnamon Toast
Apple Galette
Making and Tasting Poi
Lau Lau
Taro Pudding
Zucchini Jun
Fruit Salad
Pumpkin Soup
Pounding Poi with
Hala´i´s Mom

Trips
Campus Walks to Campus
Gardens and the Shade
House to Plant
Home Depot to Buy Plants
Wahiawa Botanical
Gardens
Waianu Farm

Social Studies
Lei Making
Gourd Rolling Game
Prediction Charts
(Wahiawa
Garden, Waianu Farm)
Following and Making
Maps of Wahiawa Garden
and Waianu Farm
Visiting Parent to Make Poi
Leaf T-Shirt Printing

Science
Fruit Seed Exploration
Preparing and Planting a
Garden
Ti Leaf Planting
Carnations in Colored Water
Planting Air Plants
Planting Sunflowers
Comparing Squashes

Math
Building with
Tree Blocks

Art
Leaf Rubbings
Painting Seed Pods
Flower Printing
Leaf Screen Printing
Plant Life Drawing
Lauhala Brush
Painting
Flower Pressing
Potato Prints
Ink and Watercolor
Wash Still Life
Tissue Paper
Collage

Creative Movement
Magic Rocks (Garden and
Tree Focus)
Magic Seeds
Roots of the Trees
Walk Around the Plant

Music
*The Green Grass Grew All
Around*
I Had A Little Nut Tree
*Oats, Peas, Beans, and Barley
Grow*
Planters' Boogie
Plant Instruments
Making Uli'uli'
Fruit Picking Songs

Language
What Do We
Know About Plants?
(discussion)
Plant Stories and
Riddles Fingerplays:
The Little Seed, Away
Up High in an Apple
Tree
What Did You Learn
About Plants?
(discussion)

Literature
Tiny Seed
Dramatization
Enormous Taro—
Storytelling, Acting, and
Puppet-Telling
Plant Poems
Pumpkin Soup Story and
Cooking and
Flannelboard
Kahualoa
(see
booklist)

Literacy
Sprouting Log
Planting Log
Wahiawa Botanical Gardens
Book
Taro Journal
Lo´I Book

Sensory
Beans, Dirt,
Potting Soil,
Birdseed in the
Sensory Table
Herb and Flower Smelling

Fine Motor
Seed/Flower
Bracelets, Kukui Nut Stringing,
Lei Making

Large Motor
Plant Hopscotch
Natural Obstacle Course
with Tree Stumps

Big Idea
There are many
kinds of plants.

Big Idea
Plants have different
parts—they do different
things for the plant.

Big Idea
People and other
animals need plants (for
food to make oxygen,
for protection and
shelter, to make things, to
make the environment
cool and beautiful).

Big Idea
Plants are alive.

Big Idea
Plants have ways
to make new
plants (most
make seeds).

Big Idea
Some plants are native to
Hawaii—they came before
people and need protection
from people.

Big Idea
Most plants make
their own food—
they need sunlight,
water, and nutrients
to make their food.

A Study of Plants

Literature for All Children

All children, regardless of age or ability, need literature.

Children with Special Needs

Jamie, a 4-year-old in the Hongos group, was usually a happy, articulate child. One day he didn't come in from the outside play with the rest of the children. When his teacher, Laurie, realized he wasn't there, she searched the playground. She found Jamie wedged behind the shed crying and banging his head against the fence. Jamie was not able to tell Laurie why he was so distressed. When his mother came to pick him up at the end of the day, she explained that she and her husband were getting divorced and they had just told Jamie.

The next day Laurie brought in an armload of books about children and divorce including Charlie Anderson *by Barbara Abercrombie,* Two Homes *by Claire Masurel,* Dinosaurs Divorce *by Marc Brown,* It's Not Your Fault Koko Bear *by Vicki Lansky, and* My Family's Changing *by Pat Thomas.*

There is a long tradition of using books to address a variety of psychological concerns (fears, worries, anxieties, stressful life problems) in children. This is sometimes called *bibliotherapy,* and it is useful for children who have a serious chronic problem (e.g., illness or disability) with which they need to come to terms. It can also be helpful with children who experience fears (e.g., nightmares, fear of going to school, bullying) and with children who have experienced a traumatic event (e.g., death, a parent's military deployment, crime, riot, accident). Books can help children deal with psychological stress in several ways:

1. They help children to realize that they are not alone in their problem.
2. They give children an emotional outlet or stress release.
3. They help children to gain insight into their problems.
4. They help children to gain awareness of options for action.
5. They may also help them to gain appreciation for the good things that remain even when problems exist.

Additionally, bibliotherapy books can help other children in your class gain *empathy* for others and thus can promote their tendency to help rather than hurt those who have problems.

Not all books that appear to provide bibliotherapy do a good job. Good bibliotherapeutic literature is developmentally appropriate: It addresses the problem or concern in a way that the child can understand at his or her age/stage. It is respectful of the child with the problem or concern. It helps children to develop their own understanding, does not suggest that the child should prevent or fix the problem, and suggests useful coping strategies. A good resource for finding books to help when children have problems is *A to Zoo* by Carolyn and John Rima, a reference found in the children's section of most libraries. Now in its 7th edition, the book is regularly updated, and lists the titles of 23,000 children's books, divided by subject.

Children in the Primary Grades

If you work with primary school children, the task of teaching literature is much broader. Primary school children enjoy picture books they can read themselves such as Arnold Lobel's *Frog and Toad* and Else Minarik's *Little Bear* series, and predictable books such as Bill Martin Jr.'s *Brown Bear, Brown Bear.* Because of their greater attention span, they can appreciate listening to longer picture books such as Chris Van Allsberg's *The Polar Express* and chapter books with few pictures like Mary Norton's *The Borrowers,* Laura Ingalls Wilder's *Little House on the Prairie,* and E.B. White's *Charlotte's Web.*

Even after children begin to read, it is essential that you continue to read to them—we lose some children as readers because of current practices in school that emphasize the acquisition of skills and often make reading seem like hard dirty work. Since the development of reading ability varies, reading aloud enables all children, not just the eager readers, to enjoy books. Additionally, reading to primary children provides shared experiences and enables children to enjoy books that are beyond their reading skill, but within their comprehension. We think that reading aloud is so important that we regularly read high-quality children's picture books in our college classes.

Final Thoughts

Sharing literature with young children is one of the greatest gifts you can give both the children and yourself. Being a knowledgeable, skilled, committed professional teacher of literature is easy—if you really love children and books and you are willing to work. We hope you are as eager to do this as the children in your class will be for the literature you will share with them.

Learning Outcomes

When you read this chapter, thoughtfully complete activities from the "To Learn More" section, and document this learning as suggested in the "For Your Portfolio" section, you will be making progress in the following *NAEYC Standards for Early Childhood Professional Preparation Programs* (2009):

Standard 1. Promoting Child Development and Learning

Students prepared in early childhood degree programs are grounded in a child development knowledge base. They use their understanding of young children's characteristics and needs and of the multiple interacting influences on children's development and learning to create environments that are healthy, respectful, supportive, and challenging for each child.

The key elements of standard 1 you will have learned about are . . .

1a: Knowing and understanding young children's characteristics and needs

1c: Using developmental knowledge to create healthy, respectful, supportive, and challenging learning environments

Standard 4. Using Developmentally Effective Approaches to Connect with Children and Families

Students prepared in early childhood degree programs understand that teaching and learning with young children is a complex enterprise, and its details vary depending on children's ages, characteristics, and the settings within which teaching and learning occur. They understand and use positive relationships and supportive interactions as the foundation for their work with young children and families. Students know, understand, and use a wide array of developmentally appropriate approaches, instructional strategies, and tools to connect with children and families and positively influence each child's development and learning.

The key elements of standard 4 you will have learned about are . . .

4a: Understanding positive relationships and supportive interactions as the foundation of their work with children

4b: Knowing and understanding effective strategies and tools for early education

4c: Using a broad repertoire of developmentally appropriate teaching/learning approaches

4d: Reflecting on their own practice to promote positive outcomes for each child

Standard 5. Using Content Knowledge to Build Meaningful Curriculum

Students prepared in early childhood degree programs use their knowledge of academic disciplines to design, implement, and evaluate experiences that promote positive development and learning for each and every young child. Students understand the importance of developmental domains and academic (or content) disciplines in an early childhood curriculum. They know the essential concepts, inquiry tools, and structure of content areas, including academic subjects, and can identify resources to deepen their understanding. Students use their own knowledge and other resources to design, implement, and evaluate meaningful, challenging curricula that promote comprehensive developmental and learning outcomes for every young child.

The key elements of standard 5 you will have learned about are . . .

5a: Understanding content knowledge and resources in academic disciplines

5b: Knowing and using the central concepts, inquiry tools, and structures of content areas or academic disciplines

5c: Using their own knowledge, appropriate early learning standards, and other resources to design, implement, and evaluate meaningful, challenging curricula for each child.

To Learn More

Observe a Program: For a morning, observe a program and see how the staff structures the environment and program to support children's love of literature. Notice both the play opportunities and the planned group activities. Look at the plans and see how the planning reflects what you observed. Interview a teacher to learn how he or she thinks about literature curriculum.

Observe a Child: For a morning, observe a child in a classroom, with a focus on the child's engagement with literature (with and in addition to books). Notice how the child engages with the planned activities and how he or she constructs his or her own opportunities for learning. Notice the extent to which the child's activity and the planned curriculum seem to match. Observe to see how staff support the child's love of literature.

Observe a Master Teacher: Spend a morning with an early childhood educator who is experienced and has a curriculum leadership role in a program. (This teacher may be called the "lead," "head," or "mentor" teacher.) Then interview the educator about how he or she plans for and provides literature curriculum.

Observe Story Time: Observe a teacher conducting story time. Interview the teacher to find out her objectives for story time. Reflect on any differences between what you saw and the objectives.

Compare Two Programs: Observe literature experiences in two early childhood programs. Compare the ways that the two address literature—their similarities and differences. Reflect on which program seems to best support children's love of literature and why. What implications does this comparison have for your future work with young children?

Compare Two Ages: Observe two classrooms, one preschool and one for primary school children. Report on how each supports children's love of literature. Talk to the staff about how they make their curriculum choices. Notice how development influences literature choices.

Explore Resources: Read one of the books from the bibliography or the online resources listed here and write a review for your classmates.

Children's Literature Network: www.childrensliteraturenetwork.org/index.php

Children's Literature Web Guide: people.ucalgary.ca/~dkbrown/index.html

Guide to Research in Children's and Young Adult Literature: www.library.illinois.edu/edx/edkclass.htm

Vandergrift's Children's Literature Page: comminfo.rutgers.edu/professional-development/childlit/ChildrenLit/

For Your Portfolio

Design an Environment for Literature: Design and draw a floor plan for a classroom and play yard that would promote children's love of literature. Share your plan with an early childhood educator, discussing what you included and why. Ask for and consider the educator's feedback and suggestions. Set up a library center in a real classroom utilizing as many of your ideas as possible and let children use it. For your portfolio, include the floor plan, photographs or video of children using the area, and a reflection on what you learned by doing this project.

Plan and Implement a Story Time: Observe a group of children for a morning, focusing on their interest in books and the world/people. Based on what you observed, select some books and plan and implement a story time for these children. Collect evidence of children's responses in the form of anecdotal observations, photographs, or video recordings. Reflect on how children responded and what they appear to have learned. What worked? What might you do differently next time? How might you expand on this experience for children? For your portfolio, include

the plan, a photograph, and a reflection on what you learned about yourself, children, planning, and teaching.

Create a Literature Extension: Plan a literature extension to support the development of a particular child or group of children. Read the book to the child or children and then share the extension. Reflect on how the children responded and how you felt about what you did. What worked? What might you do differently next time? How might you expand on this experience for other children? For your portfolio, include a photograph of a child using the material and a reflection on what you learned about yourself, children, literature, and teaching.

Bibliography

Feeney, S., & Moravcik, E. (2005, September). Children's literature: A window to understanding self and others. *Young Children, 60*(5), 20–28.

Feeney, S., Moravcik, E., & Nolte, S. (2013). *Who am I in the lives of children?* (9th ed.). Upper Saddle River, NJ: Pearson.

Head Start Resource Center. (2010). *The Head Start child development and early learning framework: Promoting positive outcomes in early childhood programs serving children 3–5 years old*. Washington DC: Office of Head Start, Administration for Children and Families, U.S. Department of Health and Human Services.

Hymes, J. L. (1958). *Before the child reads*. Evanston, IL: Row, Peterson, and Co.

Jacobs, L. (Ed.). (1965). *Using literature with young children*. New York, NY: Teachers College Press.

Jalongo, M. R. (2004). *Young children and picture books: Literature from infancy to six*. Washington, DC: NAEYC.

Keifer, B. Z. (1995). *The potential of picturebooks*. Columbus, OH: Pearson.

Lukens, R. J. (2007). *A critical handbook of children's literature* (8th ed.). Boston, MA: Allyn & Bacon.

National Association for the Education of Young Children. (2009). NAEYC *standards for early childhood*

professional preparation programs. www.naeyc.org/files/naeyc/file/positions/ProfPrepStandards09.pdf

National Governors Association Center for Best Practices (NGA Center), Council of Chief State School Officers (CCSSO). (2010). *Common Core State Standards in English Language Arts*.

Nodelman, P. (2008). *The hidden adult: Defining children's literature*. Baltimore, MD: The Johns Hopkins University Press.

Nodelman, P., & Reimer, M. (2003). *The pleasures of children's literature* (3rd ed.). Boston, MA: Allyn & Bacon.

Norton, D. E., & Norton, S. E. (2011). *Through the eyes of a child* (8th ed.). Upper Saddle River, NJ: Pearson.

Raines, S., & Canaday, R. J. (1989). *Story stretchers*. Silver Spring, MD: Gryphon House.

Sawyer, W. E. (2011). *Growing up with literature* (6th ed.). Florence, KY: Wadsworth Publishing.

Sutherland, Z. (1997). *Children and books* (9th ed.). Boston, MA: Allyn & Bacon.

Temple, C., Martinez, M., & Yokota, J. (2011). *Children's books in children's hands* (4th ed.). Upper Saddle River, NJ: Pearson.

Trelease, J. (2006). *The read aloud handbook* (6th ed.). New York, NY: Penguin.

MyEducationLab

Go to Topics 2: Child Development and Learning, and 4: Play in the MyEducationLab (www.myeducationlab.com) for *Meaningful Curriculum for Young Children,* where you can:

- Find learning outcomes for Child Development and Play along with the national standards that connect to these outcomes.

- Complete Assignments and Activities that can help you more deeply understand the chapter content.
- Apply and practice your understanding of the core teaching skills identified in the chapter with the Building Teaching Skills and Dispositions learning units.
- Listen to experts from the field in Professional Perspectives.

- Check your comprehension on the content covered in the chapter with the Study Plan. Here you will be able to take a chapter quiz, receive feedback on your answers, and then access Review, Practice, and Enrichment activities to enhance your understanding of chapter content.

Go to the Course Resources section in MyEducationLab, where you can:

- Use the Online Lesson Plan Builder to practice lesson planning and integrating national and state standards into your planning.
- Explore the Children's Literature Database to find numerous examples of children's literature.

PART 4
Arts Curriculum

Every child is an artist. The problem is how to remain an artist . . .

PABLO PICASSO

In all societies, people create and appreciate art, music, and dance. The fundamental human need to express ideas and feelings through the arts has existed from the dawn of human history. The arts are vital in the development of children who can feel as well as think and who are sensitive and creative. They nurture an awareness of aesthetics (the appreciation of beauty) that can be destroyed in the pervasive grayness of factories, freeways, and institutional buildings.

The next three chapters concern the arts—music, art, and creative movement. The three subjects are grouped together because they all help children recognize and express their feelings, communicate their ideas in new forms, and develop their senses. Although the arts can be a vehicle for all kinds of learning—physical, social, emotional, and cognitive—and while creativity is not confined to the arts, we link the arts with emotional development and creativity because they are especially powerful in fostering these aspects of development.

Experiences in early childhood programs help young children to retain their innate responsiveness to the arts and to develop their natural expressiveness. Through arts experiences, children come to:

- feel good about themselves as individuals.
- develop the ability to observe and respond sensitively.
- develop skill and creativity in art, music, and movement.
- develop a beginning understanding of the arts disciplines.
- become appreciative of music, art, and dance from their own and other cultures, times, and places.

Creativity, or originality, is not confined to artists or to people who have great talent or high intelligence. All people are creative when they put together what they know and build something that is new *to them:* an idea, a process, or a product. The arts are a primary avenue for developing the ability to think and act creatively.

Creativity is easy to see in the arts, but it also occurs in other activities typically found in early childhood programs, such as building with blocks and construction toys, engaging in dramatic play, writing stories, playing with words, solving problems, and inventing games. The creativity of play leaves no lasting product, but is important to recognize and acknowledge. It is also important to keep in mind that children are not always being creative when they are involved in the arts. If they are afraid of not being accepted or feel that their work must meet adult standards, they may make stereotypic "acceptable" products or responses in order to receive approval and praise.

The pre-primary schools of Reggio Emilia are internationally noted for the creative behavior and expression of their children. The philosophy of the Reggio Emilia schools points to some important considerations for early childhood educators in designing curriculum for creativity. Loris Malaguzzi, the founder of the schools, provides the following guidance:

- "Creativity should not be considered a separate mental faculty but characteristic of our way of thinking, knowing, and making choices."
- "Creativity seems to emerge from multiple experiences with a well-supported development of personal resources, including a freedom to venture beyond the known."
- "Creativity seems to express itself through cognitive, affective, and imaginative processes. These come together and support the skills for predicting and arriving at unexpected solutions."
- "The most favorable situation for creativity seems to be interpersonal exchange with negotiation of conflicts and comparison of ideas and actions being the decisive elements."
- "Creativity seems to find its power when adults are less tied to prescriptive teaching methods but instead become observers and interpreters of problematic situations." (Edwards et al., 1993, 70)

Understanding how young children develop helps you to provide a climate that supports creativity, imagination, and self-expression. Satisfying and successful experiences with the arts occur when you understand what you can

reasonably expect of children and when you provide activities that match their needs and abilities. When children's unique expressions are acknowledged, they become aware of their value as individuals and their self-concept is enhanced. For young children, the most important aspects of the arts are the development of awareness, new skills, and feelings of self-worth. In order to support creativity, it is important to give children many choices in their work, to provide a variety of creative materials (some constant and some changing), and to support children's efforts without being too directive.

Neither children nor adults create in a void; creative expression is an outgrowth of other life experiences. Your role is to offer experiences that heighten children's awareness and provide them with inspiration for artistic expression. These may be as simple as carefully examining an apple, visiting a baby, or taking a trip to the beach. Creative expression is also stimulated by experiences with the arts. When children have opportunities to view artwork of many kinds, to listen to music, and to attend dance and drama productions, they begin to understand the potential communication power and joy of the arts.

We often hear our students despair about their ability to make meaningful creative experiences a part of their programs because they do not feel they are talented or creative. It is not necessary to be an artist, musician, or dancer in order to help children have good experiences with the arts. Children are not harsh critics, and they will learn from your participation and enthusiasm. Even if you do not feel that you are talented in the arts, you have a responsibility to include them in your curriculum. You can develop a receptive attitude toward the creative expression of children and toward the arts in general. Every community has resources—artists, educators, reference materials—that can guide you in providing good arts experiences for children.

Reflect on your experiences with the arts in school . . .

What experiences did you have in school with the arts? How did your teachers support or discourage creativity and individuality? How did this affect your feelings about creativity and your ability as an artist, musician, or dancer?

Bibliography

Edwards, L., Gandini, C., & Forman, G. (1993). *The hundred languages of children: The Reggio Emilia approach to early childhood education.* Westport, CT: Ablex Publishing.

Art is the signature of civilizations.

BEVERLY SILLS

chapter ten

VISUAL ART CURRICULUM
Creating with Hand and Eye

Whether you realize it or not, art is part of your daily life. Every day, you see and are enriched by art. You select art to make your home beautiful. There are fine art prints in your doctor's office, and you are calmed by their loveliness as you wait. You view the paintings hanging in your bank and assess the beauty of the art or the skill of artists. Art is even present when you do mundane chores. Did you choose a lovely piece of stationery to write a thank you note for a gift? Did you doodle a flower on the corner of your grocery list? Did you first look at the photos and artwork in this book before you read the words? Even if you do not think of *yourself* as an artist or a person who loves art, you are a *consumer* of the artistic work of others and someone who makes aesthetic choices. Visual art is an important part of your life.

Part of your job as an early childhood teacher is to plan a well-rounded program that includes artistic and aesthetic development (the ability to create and appreciate beauty). To do this, you need to know about children's artistic and aesthetic development in general, understand your group of children in particular, and be aware of teaching strategies to help children learn and grow in this area. You also need to be able to clearly articulate to families, administrators, and other staff members the rationale for art and aesthetic components of your daily program. This chapter will provide you with the information you need to understand and plan the visual art curriculum so you can support your students as they gain a sense of themselves as artists and art appreciators.

Why Art Curriculum?

Art enables us to find ourselves and lose ourselves at the same time.

THOMAS MERTON

Since the time of Pestalozzi and Froebel, art has been a part of the early childhood curriculum. The pervasiveness of visual art makes it obvious how important art is in our society. But why should teachers of young children today be especially attuned to this area of curriculum?

Young children come to us as artists. By the time most young children enter preschool, they are already artists. They make aesthetic judgments in the choices of the toys they play with and the books they look at. Many have developed a repertoire of mark-making skills, and show a keen interest in exploring and experimenting with art media and materials. Preschool art curriculum builds on these existing skills and interests.

Art is an inherent part of being human. The ability to create art is a uniquely human trait. It bridges the gulf of different languages, cultures, and eras, giving insight and providing a common bond with other human beings. It is a universal language (Gee, 2000).

Art is a form of play. The processes involved in creating art are enjoyable, playful, physical, and sensory. As such, art helps meet one of children's basic needs—the need to play. Children are playing as they are creating. They gain satisfaction from their artistic process. As you watch a young child engaged in the joyful pleasure of painting or remember the satisfaction you felt in creating a piece of artwork, it becomes clear that art is valuable in and of itself for the satisfaction it brings. Satisfaction, pride, and joy have been interwoven with the arts since humans began creating art some 70,000 years ago (Cox, 2005).

Art gives children a way to communicate. One of the main reasons for providing art in early childhood programs is to give children an opportunity to express and communicate ideas, knowledge, and feelings (Cox, 2005; Pitri, 2001). Art also gives sensitive teachers a window into children's feelings. Visual art products serve as artifacts that record children's journeys, as you can see in Work Sample 10.1.

Art is a way children come to know about the world. Traditionally, in early childhood education, art was justified as being beneficial to children because it allowed them to release and deal with strong feelings. While this is true (as is obvious from Work Sample 10.1), there is a growing feeling that the arts can do more than this. Art is a powerful tool that children can use to investigate and discover the world around them. Through art they gain cognitive skills as they represent, recreate, and connect experiences. They can use art to communicate their growing knowledge and understanding. You can see this in Work Sample 10.2, in which a child demonstrates his understanding of an insect and uses art to communicate what he's learned.

Art provides children with a connection to their culture. Think about your own family and the special objects that convey your culture, perhaps your grandmother's antique lace tablecloth that she brought with her when she left her native country or a wooden carving made by your grandfather. These works of art have pride of place in your home and in your life. They are beautiful and help you to know who you are. Art connects us all to the past, to the present, and to future cultures. When children have an opportunity to see art, they are

MyEducationLab

Visit the MyEducationLab for *Meaningful Curriculum for Young Children* to enhance your understanding of chapter concepts with a personalized Study Plan. You'll also have the opportunity to hone your teaching skills through video-based Assignments and Activities, IRIS Center Resources, and Building Teaching Skills and Disposition lessons.

During Chinese New Year one of the children brought a lion mask to school. The lion was stored in a closet. Ho'ohila (age 4) approached Eva, "I'm <u>scared</u> of the lion," she said. Eva took out the lion mask and together she and Ho'o examined it and tried it on. "I'm <u>scared</u>," Ho'o repeated. When the lion mask was brought out for group dancing, Ho'o's eyes widened and again she said, "I'm <u>scared</u> of the lion." Eva invited Ho'o to go outside away from the scary lion. Outside they could hear the dance. "I want to peek in the window so I can see the scary lion," Ho'o said. Eva lifted her up to peek. Ho'o laughed and waved. "I see the scary lion." Then Ho'ohila took paper and pen and in rapid succession made a series of pictures and dictated what each represented.

1. Ho'o drew the lion . . .

The same scary lion from my school.

2. . . . then expressed the way she felt . . .

That's me falling.

3. . . . and wished the frightening lion away.

The scary lion is all crossed out from this world.

4. Next she drew the experience of observing the lion . . .

Watching the scary lion.

5. . . . and how scary that felt.

Looking at the lion and that's <u>VERY</u> scary.

6. Then she drew how she might be scarier than a lion . . .

That's me—I have 3 faces and one eye!

7. . . . and envisioned herself turning tables on the lion!

That's me—I'm looking at the lion and saying, "AAAAAAAH!"- I'm scaring him!

8. With the scary lion scared and a vision of herself as powerful, Ho'ohila declared herself unafraid!

The scary lion—<u>I'm not even scared!</u>

Work Sample 10.2

A Cockroach with Golden Wings—At the end of a study of insects, Christian, age 5, took pieces of tissue paper from a basket on the table. On a sheet of cardboard, he carefully placed the pieces of tissue paper, with each piece touching the others: a head, a thorax, and an abdomen. Christian glued the tissue paper down, and then took six strips of green tissue and attached six legs to the abdomen.

learning about the world, their own culture, and the culture of others. When they create art, they are contributing to their own culture—the culture of childhood.

It is important to model and teach about those things that we value. Aesthetic experiences have intrinsic value. They allow appreciation of a moment for itself. Responding to a lovely sunrise, a painting, or a piece of music requires no coercion. Aesthetic enjoyment provides an avenue through which people can find focus and achieve balance and tranquility in an increasingly fast-moving world. If appreciation of beauty is important, then we need to share this with children. Children who learn to love beauty in nature and in the arts are likely to want to protect and nourish these valuable resources.

Providing art and aesthetic experiences for young children reflects our high value for children and childhood. The arts are the best that our culture has to offer. You would not be studying early childhood education if you did not believe that young children need and deserve the best we have to give. In the words of poet Walter de la Mare, "only the rarest kind of best in anything can be good enough for the young" (1942, 9).

Understanding Children's Artistic Development

When can children become artists? When do they start to respond to art? The answers to these questions depend in part on your definition of art itself. Infants as young as 1 year of age begin to experiment with mark-making using whatever tools and materials are available, whether by dragging their fingers through spilt milk, or trailing a stick through sand. Is this art? Babies have long been known to show visual preferences for strongly contrasting images. Is this an aesthetic preference? There are no definitive answers; however, children's art and the development of their graphic activity have been studied for well over a century, and they continue to be an area of significant interest for researchers.

Theories of Artistic Development

During the 20th century, many researchers described stages in artistic development (Gesell, 1946; Kellogg, 1969; Lowenfeld & Brittain, 1964; Luquet, 1927; Read, 1943). And although parallels can be made in different media types, all primarily look at drawing. Researchers differ in the number of stages they include; however, each describes a similar path from primitive mark-making (typically called *scribbling*) to the creation of complex representational images. Presently it is unknown whether artistic development is universal.

Theories generally agree that the process of children's artistic development is complex, social, and fluid or changeable (Cox, 2005). In other words, children don't all make artistic progress in the same way or at the same time. Instead, children's artistic development is like an intricately woven tapestry. Each child's development is influenced by social interactions with peers and teachers. In our experience, there is unevenness in children's artistic development. Children occasionally revert back to a less sophisticated technique after they have moved forward, and they show exploratory activity whenever they try a new medium.

We find it useful to contrast a traditional stage theory such as that described by Viktor Lowenfeld in 1947 (Lowenfeld & Brittain, 1987) with a more contemporary theory or "map" of artistic development such as that proposed by Anna Kindler and Bernard Darras (1997). These theories provide different explanations for children's artistic development and give us two different lenses through which to view it.

Lowenfeld and Brittain

Stage theories are based on the idea that there is a pattern of distinct stages in children's artistic development. Stages have a constant order related to age. Lowenfeld and Brittain's theory describes stages from ages 2 to 18 (we address only those related to early childhood) and closely aligns with Piaget's theory of cognitive development. They suggested that stages often "fuse into one another," and believed that children did not necessarily move from one stage to another at exactly the same time.

Although Lowenfeld and Brittain's stage theory begins with 2-year-olds, infants who are given access to art materials begin to make marks when they are as young as age 1, as you can see in Work Sample 10.3. We will follow Lili's journey of artistic development throughout this chapter. And you will note that she came to each stage many months before those identified as typical.

Stage 1—Scribbling Stage (Ages 2–4)

Although the word *scribble* has a negative meaning in the world of adults it implies careless or worthless writings or drawings), it has quite another connotation in early childhood education in general and among art educators in particular. *Scribble* in early childhood education refers to non-representational mark-making. It may be random or deliberate, and both are considered legitimate forms of artistic expression. Lowenfeld identified scribbling as a very important stage of artistic development. The scribbling stage consists of three substages: (1) *disordered and random* scribbling; (2) *controlled* scribbling; and (3) *named* scribbling (Lowenfeld & Brittain, 1987; Schirrmacher, 1998).

Children who engage in scribbling primarily for kinesthetic pleasure are in the *disordered and random scribbling* substage. During this substage, they use large motor movements to scribble. Often they do not even look at the paper and may scribble off the edges of the page. In Work Sample 10.3, Lili was in this substage.

Controlled scribbling is the substage in which children begin to use smaller marks, as they gain finer control. In the controlled scribbling substage, motions are repeated, and more intricate scribbles such as loops and swirls appear (see Work Sample 10.4). Because children's eye-hand coordination has improved, they tend to keep their scribbles on the page.

In the *named scribbling* substage, children show more concentration and a greater variety of lines. At this stage of artistic development, young children become interested in naming their drawings, even though the drawings are far from representational. You can see in Work Sample 10.5 that Lili had better fine motor control and was beginning to emphasize the placements of the marks. She was aware of and used empty space in her compositions, and she also named her scribbles.

Stage 2—Preschematic Stage (Ages 4–7)

You may be wondering when children finally start making drawings that are recognizable or representational. In the *preschematic stage*, children make their first attempts at representational images. Most children in preschool are in this stage of artistic development or they soon reach it.

Work Sample 10.3 Drawing by a 1-Year-Old—Shortly after her 1st birthday, Lili firmly held a thick red marker in a fist grip in her right hand. On a large sheet of paper, Lili's pen recorded the movement of her arm. She swung the pen over the paper and occasionally when the pen touched the paper left a bright red mark. At the time of this drawing Lili had been walking for 3 weeks.

Work Sample 10.4 Controlled Scribble—Several months after her first drawing, Lili's marks were more varied and concentrated in the center of the paper. They were more controlled.

Work Sample 10.5 Named Scribbles—At age 2, Lili's scribbles became more controlled, and Lili started to describe her drawings, saying, "Look! I making circles!"

Work Sample 10.6 Mandala Face—Lili's first representational image, created when she was 2 years and 9 months old, was of a face made of the circles and lines that she had practiced earlier.

Work Sample 10.7 "Tadpole" Human Figure—Tadpole human figures like this one are typical of young 3-year-olds. They are an extension of mandala faces.

The human figure is usually a child's first representation. There are some typical motifs that you will come to recognize. Human faces are nearly always children's first representational work and are often known as *mandalas* (see Work Sample 10.6). Mandala faces have eyes, mouths, sometimes noses, and little else.

Tadpole figures (people with legs and arms that emerge directly from heads) typically appear soon after mandala faces (see Work Sample 10.7). Both mandalas and tadpole figures are built from the earlier scribbles.

With the gradual addition of torsos and features, and the introduction of subjects other than the human figure, children begin to exhibit personal style that is easily recognizable by family members and teachers. Objects are generally drawn facing forward, and color is used expressively, but not realistically. For example, a 4-year-old may draw her mother's hair with a blue marker even though she knows that her mother's hair is brown (see Work Sample 10.8).

Work Sample 10.8 **Human Figures with Torsos and Detail**—Note fingers, toes, and belly buttons in Lili's drawing of her Mommy and herself at age 4 years and 3 months.

Work Sample 10.9 **Lili's drawing of St. George and a Firebreathing Dragon with a Castle in the Background (age 4 years and 10 months)**—As Lili neared the schematic stage, random scribbles were no longer included in her drawings and she began to create a skyline and baseline. This drawing was completed after a trip to visit her grandparents in Europe where she saw castles and depictions of St. George and the Dragon.

Although children in the preschematic stage are developing their ability to make representational images, these images are often combined with other scribbled marks. It is only as they near the next stage (see Work Sample 10.9) that scribbles are omitted.

Stage 3—Schematic Stage (Ages 7–9)

The final stage that is a part of the early childhood years is the *schematic stage*. During the schematic stage, drawings become more detailed and decorated. Children typically draw a base line at the bottom of the page upon which they draw their objects and figures. A skyline is often drawn at the top of the page. During this stage, children usually draw what they know in 2 dimensions. X-ray drawing also appears, showing interior and exterior views simultaneously. The schematic stage is most often seen in primary school age children.

Kindler and Darras

Art educators and researchers Anna Kindler and Bernard Darras have created a map of artistic development (1997) as an alternative to the stage theories. Kindler and Darras believe that children's art is a semiotic (symbolic) activity, a form of sign language that children use to communicate their ideas, knowledge, and feelings. They observed that children's drawing is often accompanied by language (commentary, description, storytelling), movement, and singing. Although the map of artistic development includes time frames from birth to adult, we will only discuss the early childhood time frame.

Kindler and Darras divide early childhood into five phases, which they call *iconicity levels*. These levels are not viewed as stages; rather, they are seen as describing a range of behaviors and possibilities. Perhaps more significantly, Kindler and Darras believe that children can engage in more than one level at a time.

Iconicity 1

In Iconicity 1, movement is central. Pictorial imagery occurs when marks are left from physical actions. For example, an infant or toddler may make marks by drawing a finger through spilt milk or by dragging a stick through the dirt or sand. The child's focus is on the movement, not on the marks themselves. Lili's first drawing (Work Sample 10.3) is clearly an example of Iconicity 1.

Iconicity 2

In Iconicity 2, there is a dramatic shift from actions that inadvertently cause marks to a focus on the marks themselves. Children begin to produce and repeat predictable graphic forms such as circles. They begin to explore relationships between the graphic forms.

Between the ages of 2-and-a-half and 3, Lili's drawing took a very dramatic turn. She would spend long periods of time covering page after page of similar shapes such as the circles in Work Sample 10.10. She would change the size of the circles and their location on the page as if she were perfecting the shape.

Shortly after working on circular shapes, Lili created many pages covered with lines; Work Sample 10.11 shows a vertical line crossed by several shorter, almost perpendicular horizontal lines. The fine motor skills required to create such drawings were growing more and more advanced.

As shown in Work Samples 10.10 and 10.11, Lili spent a great deal of time perfecting circles and lines; however, she also did this with dots. These three graphic symbols became very important in her artistic development and formed the basis of her future work.

Iconicity 3

During Iconicity 3, children seem to focus on representing actions rather than objects. Sounds and gestures accompany the creation of pictures. For example, a child may say "Vroooooooom" while quickly drawing a wriggly line. Children appear to realize that imaginary actions can be recorded in pictures. These pictures become a form of storytelling, as shown in Lili's Work Sample 10.12.

Iconicity 4

During Iconicity 4, as children come to realize that drawings can convey meaning, their focus changes from the action of drawing to the graphic form (the picture they have drawn). However, the story they tell and the physical movements are still often combined with representational images. These early images often look

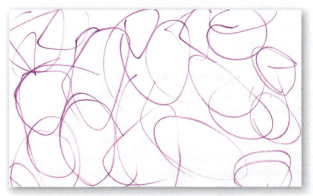

Work Sample 10.10 **Perfecting a Scribble**

Work Sample 10.11 **Lines**

Work Sample 10.12 **Scribbles as Storytelling**—In this rich and intense scribble, Lili, at age 3 years and 4 months, went over and over the lines, making them darker and darker until they shone. As she created the circular scribble, she said with excitement, "I making a moon. Look a moon!" Lili's understanding of the round-ness of the moon was translated into her drawing.

Work Sample 10.13 **Cricket**—Drawing of a cricket by a 4-year-old. Note the human face, ears, and hair.

the same, and the form used for *Mommy, Daddy, dog* (even *bug*) are sometimes very similar (see Work Sample 10.13).

Iconicity 5

In Iconicity 5, children become competent in using symbols, and their drawings can be understood without an explanation (as in Lili's drawing of St. George and the Dragon in Work Sample 10.9). Pictures become more complex and detailed. Spatial organization and elements are considered during the production process. Children continue to narrate as they work.

What Is Art Curriculum in Early Childhood?

Do you remember fingerpainting, cutting construction paper, and drawing with fat crayons? Those familiar activities in which you explored and created using art media are called *studio experiences*. Another aspect of the art curriculum is *aesthetic appreciation experiences*, in which children have opportunities to en-counter, discuss, appreciate, and think about art.

Both are valuable and can be a part of the art curriculum for young children. You need to understand both in order to achieve the curricular goals of helping children to:

- develop creativity and art skills.
- express feelings and ideas through art.
- begin to understand art as a discipline.
- observe and respond sensitively to visual art.
- come to appreciate art from their own time as well as other cultures and eras.
- construct understanding through art.

Approaches to Art Curriculum

Three approaches to teaching art to young children have developed over time: child centered, teacher centered, and art centered (Dixon & Tarr, 1988). At oppo-site ends of the spectrum are child centered and teacher centered.

A *child-centered approach* to teaching art reflects the view that art for young children should be open ended and process oriented. In this approach, adult intervention is avoided because it "is seen as an impediment for artistic development" (Mulcahey, 2009). Children are given free access to paints, clay, markers, and glue, and they are given little instruction in how to use them. Until recently, this viewpoint has been predominant in early childhood education. If you attended a developmentally oriented preschool, this is probably the approach that was used.

In a *teacher-centered approach*, there is a focus on pattern art (often called *craft*, a practice we strongly disagree with—see the note on page 314) and fine motor skill development. In this approach, children copy an adult-made model, or cut out or color duplicated shapes or "patterns." Since the focus is on skill development and following instructions, there is little room for children's creativity or artistic expression. Indeed, using the word *art* to describe this approach is a misnomer. This approach has been predominant in some preschools and many primary schools. If you remember coloring sheets and look-alike projects in your early schooling, this is the approach that was used.

An *art-centered approach* focuses on both art production and art appreciation (Dixon & Tarr, 1988). It encourages children's aesthetic development and art appreciation in addition to developing their skill in using art media. The teacher is a facilitator who provides some instruction and modeling of techniques. The teacher also serves as a guide who helps children learn about art and society by viewing and discussing fine artwork.

The goal of the art-centered approach is to nurture not only children's individual creativity and expression, but also their aesthetic development. There is a careful balance between process and product. The teacher's job in an art-centered approach is to support children in developing the ability to effectively express their ideas and feelings, not to dictate the *content* of children's artwork (the ideas and feelings the child draws, paints, or sculpts).

We prefer the art-centered approach for young children because it supports their artistic development and expression, exposes them to the nature of beauty, and allows them to explore and experience the world through art. It matches our values and belief that young children need time and space to explore media and materials; guided experiences in which teachers model art processes and techniques; and opportunities to learn to appreciate fine art.

One particular art-centered method is called Discipline Based Art Education (DBAE). Created in the 1960s and developed further in the 1980s by the Center for Education in the Arts (Dobbs, 1998; Getty Center for Education in the Arts, 1985), DBAE is a balanced art-centered approach that consists of four specific disciplines: (1) Aesthetics, (2) Criticism, (3) Art History, and (4) Production/Studio (Dobbs, 1998; Getty Center for Education in the Arts, 1985). DBAE concentrates on developing children's abilities in the production, appreciation, and criticism of art through exposure to fine artwork (Dobbs, 1998). The teacher's role is to select content and to teach knowledge, skills, and understandings (Zimmerman & Zimmerman, 2000).

Art Elements: The Building Blocks of Art

Every work of art is composed of visual, graphic, and other sensory *art elements*. Children experience these elements long before they are consciously aware of them or learn to talk about them. Much of the creative process of art for young children is exploration of the elements of art. Both studio art and aesthetic appreciation experiences for young children can be designed to help them become aware of and explore the elements that make up works of art. You will help children to think about art by being aware of and talking with them about these elements. But in order to talk with children about the elements of art you have to be aware of them yourself.

Line

Line is a part of every painting, drawing, collage, print, or sculpture. Line can be described by kind or quality: straight, curved, wandering, wiggling, jagged, broken, zig-zag, heavy, light, wide, thin. Every linear aspect of a piece of art has length, a beginning and an end, and direction (up/down, diagonal, side to side). Lines have relationships with one another and other parts of the work. They can be separate, parallel, or crossed. When children fill their paintings and drawings with many different kinds of lines, as Lili did in Work Sample 10.11, they are exploring this element.

Color

Colors have qualities and can be referred to by either name or hue—red, scarlet, turquoise, magenta. These color names add richness to the experience of color. They can be pure—primary colors (red, blue, yellow), white and black—or mixed. Different colors are considered to have temperature—coolness at the blue end of the spectrum, or warmth at the red end of the spectrum. They have different degrees of intensity or saturation (brightness or dullness) and value (lightness or darkness). Colors change as they mix. They are related to one another (orange is a color that is related to red) and look different when placed next to other colors.

Children who combine colors in painting or coloring with chalk or crayons are exploring the nature of this element. Discovering how colors are created takes much experimentation. A child may mix primary colors inadvertently many times before he or she suddenly experiences the magic of blue and yellow becoming green. The wonder of such a discovery can be dampened by too much teacher intervention.

Shape and Form

Shape (2 dimensions) and form (3 dimensions) in art are more than circles, spheres, squares, cubes, or triangles. Shape and form can be regular and geometric like circles, cylinders, and hexagons, and they can be organic or irregular. Children and artists combine these two. In artwork, shapes can be thought of as filled or empty. In relationship to each other, shapes can be separated by space, connected or overlapping, or enclosed by one another. When the boundaries of a shape or form are completed, it is closed; if the boundary is left uncompleted (like a U or a C), it is open. Shapes can be solid (like a ball) or they can use empty space as part of the form (like a tire).

In Work Samples 10.6, 10.10, and 10.12, Lili was using and exploring a regular, geometric shape (a circle), whereas in the drawings in Work Sample 10.1, Ho'ohila used primarily irregular shapes.

Space

The distance within or between aspects of a piece of artwork is the element known as *space*. The location of a line, shape, or color is part of the work—center, top, bottom, side, left, right. Space can be crowded and full, or sparse or empty, and these distinctions give feelings of freedom or cramped enclosure to the work. The space can have balance with other spaces or forms. Boundaries in a work and ideas like inclusion and exclusion are a part of the spatial qualities of artwork.

Design

Design refers to the organization of a piece of work. All of the elements discussed thus far can be called *elements of design*. Children initially work without a plan or artistic purpose: Their art is sensory and exploratory. Nancy Smith refers to children's approach to paper in painting at this stage as a place "to play, a sort of two-dimensional park" (Smith, 1993). As they gain experience, they become more aware and the elements of design enter their work. There is awareness of the unity of the work or of a division of elements. A planned, organized piece of work can have a concept (like a circular shape) repeated or varied. The way color, line, shape, and form are placed can give the work an actual texture or the impression of texture. Elements are used with an awareness of their relationship to one another, although effects may be unexpected. Symmetry, balance, and alternation are some of the characteristics found in design.

Standards for Visual Art and Aesthetics Curriculum

What should you try to accomplish in the visual art and aesthetic curriculum? What goals should you have for young children? Content standards and guidelines developed by national organizations, states, and individual programs can help you identify goals for the visual art and aesthetic curriculum. These, in turn, can help you select activities.

While there are no national standards for visual arts and aesthetics in preschool programs, Head Start (see Figure 10.1) and almost all states have standards for the arts curriculum. The National Art Education Association has developed standards for children in K–4 programs (see Figure 10.2). Almost all of them lay out the expectation that teachers provide opportunities for children to:

- experience, explore, and enjoy art media.
- develop creativity and expressive and representation skills.
- learn about art elements and techniques.
- reflect on and appreciate the art of others.

The amount of detail prescribed in the standards for different states varies. Some have very general statements, whereas others provide detailed expectations. And as you can see from the preschool standards for Head Start (Figure 10.2) and the national standards for children in kindergarten and primary school (Figure 10.1), there is greater specificity of content in the standards for older children. However, the focus on the development of artistic skills enabling children to be more expressive and to learn about art that is personally meaningful is consistent.

Your program's goals may be based on state or national standards, or they may have been developed independently by your staff or a curriculum specialist. However, it is likely that they will include some version of these goals.

FIGURE 10.1 **Head Start Child Development and Early Learning Framework:
Creative Arts Expression—Art**

The use of a range of media and materials to create drawings, pictures, or other objects.

- Uses different materials and techniques to make art creations.
- Creates artistic works that reflect thoughts, feelings, experiences, or knowledge.
- Discusses one's own artistic creations and those of others.

Source: Administration for Children and Families, Head Start Bureau, www.hsnrc.org/cdi/child-outcomes.cfm

FIGURE 10.2 **National Art Education Association Visual Art Content Standards: K–4**

Standard 1: Understanding and applying media, techniques, and processes
students should
- know the differences between materials, techniques, and processes
- describe how different materials, techniques, and processes cause different responses
- use different media, techniques, and processes to communicate ideas, experiences, and stories
- use art materials and tools in a safe and responsible manner

Standard 2: Using knowledge of structures and functions
students should
- know the differences among visual characteristics and purposes of art in order to convey ideas
- describe how different expressive features and organizational principles cause different responses
- use visual structures and functions of art to communicate ideas

Standard 3: Choosing and evaluating a range of subject matter, symbols, and ideas
students should
- explore and understand prospective content for works of art
- select and use subject matter, symbols, and ideas to communicate meaning

Standard 4: Understanding the visual arts in relation to history and cultures
students should
- know that the visual arts have both a history and specific relationships to various cultures
- identify specific works of art as belonging to particular cultures, times, and places
- demonstrate how history, culture, and the visual arts can influence each other in making and studying works of art

Standard 5: Reflecting upon and assessing the characteristics and merits of their work and the work of others
students should
- understand there are various purposes for creating works of visual art
- describe how people's experiences influence the development of specific artworks
- understand there are different responses to specific artworks

Standard 6: Making connections between visual arts and other disciplines
students should
- understand and use similarities and differences between characteristics of the visual arts and other arts disciplines
- identify connections between the visual arts and other disciplines in the curriculum

Source: Consortium of National Arts Education Associations (1994). Used with permission of the National Art Education Association.

Teaching Art

Providing children with art media, supporting them as they realize artistic possibilities, and observing them as they discover their artistic voice are some of the most rewarding teaching experiences you will have. To do this you will bring art and aesthetic development experiences into your classroom every day.

Art Through Play in a Planned Environment

Your learning environment will influence the art curriculum you are able to present to children. There are enormous variations in the kinds of space that will be available to you for your art program. You might have a purpose-built classroom with a specially designed art studio, tall windows that let in lots of light, and lots of space for ongoing projects. You might have to make do with a shared church basement with little natural light where you have to tidy away art at the end of each day because the room is used each night for meetings. More than likely you will have a conventional classroom with a corner for an art center. Regardless of the space, you can create a beautiful, warm, inviting, and workable space for yourself, the children, and their families.

The Art Area or Studio

The heart of the art curriculum in your classroom will be the art area. Teachers influenced by early childhood programs of Reggio Emilia often call this area a studio or *atelier* (the Italian word for artist's workshop). Because of its importance, the location of the art area needs to be carefully thought out. Ideally, an art studio would be housed in its own room adjacent to the classroom. Since such space is rarely built into early childhood classrooms, you will most likely need to be content with dedicating a corner of your room for art.

Which corner for art? A few built-in features will determine where you place your art area. Art is often messy, so select a part of the classroom where the floor is made of tile or linoleum that is easily cleaned. Access to water and a sink are essential for setting up and cleaning after art experiences, so the art area needs to be near water if at all possible. Artists need to see, so choose an area in which there is good light from either natural (preferable) or artificial sources.

Furnishings in the art area should include one or two child-sized tables with workspace for four or five children and a teacher and one or two easels sized to the children (so children can reach the top of the paper). We prefer children to stand at an easel so that they can utilize the full range of motion of their arms. A place for drying finished work is important. A drying rack with wire shelves is best for this purpose, but a clothesline or clothes rack makes an acceptable substitute. Drying space on a shelf for 3-dimensional work is also needed.

Storage is essential in planning an environment for art. You will need a place to store supplies that only the teacher can access such as packages of construction paper and gallons of paint. If there is enough space and sufficient staff to supervise, you can also provide a shelf of art materials (collage materials, glue, paper, scissors, paint, markers, pens, clay, clayboards) at children's level. A collection of bowls, baskets, and containers for organizing and displaying art materials will also be needed.

The Library

A good and often overlooked area for enhancing children's understanding of and appreciation for art is the library. The illustrators of children's books are artists. Children's picture books contain works of art that are accessible to everyone who has a library card. And you can easily make books available for children to independently enjoy. Be sure to select books that demonstrate diverse kinds of art in their illustrations.

In addition to the art that illustrates children's fiction and non-fiction picture books, there is a growing genre of children's literature specifically designed to help children to see, appreciate, and understand fine art. The work of Lucy Micklethwait (*Spot the Dog, Spot the Cat*), books published by art museums such as the Metropolitan Museum of Art (*Museum ABC* and *Museum 123*), and many others are available in most public libraries and in all museum gift shops.

Art Everywhere

Although children create art in the art area and enjoy looking at illustrations in picture books, art education does not end there. Children learn about art and aesthetics throughout a well-designed classroom—in the way you place the furniture and maintain it.

Go into a classroom and look. Is it clean or dingy? Do colors and patterns coordinate or clash? Are materials stored in clean, attractive baskets and containers, or are they shoved into broken boxes? Are blocks organized and stacked by type, or are they thrown into a box? Are shelf tops uncluttered, or are they piled with mess? Are books well cared for, or does the library contain a torn assortment of garage-sale rejects? Is children's art carefully displayed, or is their art on display several months old and torn? Are there healthy plants and vases of flowers, or are these items dead or absent? In the writing center, do pens work, are pencils sharpened, are crayons whole, and is paper neatly stacked? Are there places for dolls, dishes, and clothes in the dramatic play area, or are materials stuffed into the toy stove and fridge? In other words, does the teacher value, model, and care about art, beauty, and order?

Aesthetic education is supported not only in the overall beauty and order of the classroom, but also through the display of fine art in the classroom. Every teacher needs a collection of art to display in the classroom (start your collection now!). These images can include art prints and postcards. They can be obtained through museum gift shops and online (see Figure 10.3). An inexpensive source

FIGURE 10.3   Sources for Fine Art Prints for the Classroom

Museums
- The Louvre Museum: www.louvre.fr/llv/musee
- Metropolitan Museum of Art, New York: www.metmuseum.org
- Smithosonian American Art Museum: www.si.edu/museums/american-art-museum
- Museum of Modern Art: www.moma.org
- The Getty Museum: www.getty.edu/museum
- The National Gallery of Art, Washington, DC: www.nga.gov

Online Sales of Fine Art Posters
- Art.Com: www.art.com
- artExpression: www.artexpressions.com
- Allposters.com: www.allposters.com

of art prints is calendars. Most art museums have education departments with lending collections for teachers. If you don't live near a museum, you can visit museum sites on the Internet. Some of these museums allow you to download artwork from their collections.

Aesthetic education can also be provided by using art postcards in homemade games, visiting art museums, inviting practicing artists to the classroom to give a demonstration on a particular medium or technique, and using cultural and fine art objects, donated by staff and families, to create a classroom gallery.

The Creative Zone Outdoors

Art education can also be supported in the outdoor environment. The location of your school, whether you must share outdoor space, and the local climate will influence the way you will provide art out of doors and how frequently you can use the space. A well-designed playground will include a creative zone. This is where you will place easels and tables that can be used for a variety of art processes. Woodworking and hollow block building also contribute to artistic and aesthetic growth and can be easily placed in this area outdoors.

Art Supplies

Do you remember how delightful it felt to draw with a new box of crayons? The unbroken, clean colors were alive with possibilities, and they inspired you to draw. Supplies are a critical part of the art curriculum because they have an impact on how children explore art. For this reason, art supplies should be chosen and presented with care. We find that when we provide good quality materials, children use them well, as long as we keep in mind the nature of young children. When you can, choose art supplies that are good quality and avoid gimmicky or cheap materials. Providing quality materials to children not only gives them a very satisfying result, but also says that you value their artistic endeavors.

A Schedule for Art Curriculum

In the not-so-distant past, art was a cornerstone of every young child's school day. Today, academic pressure often pushes art education to the edges of the curriculum. We encourage you to return art to its rightful place and include two types of art in the daily schedule. The first is self-selected and self-directed access to art materials. The second is planned art experiences in which you and children work together. Since art projects can take an extended period of time to complete, have large blocks of time available for art experiences, and be sure to give children opportunities to work on the same project over a few days.

Your Role in Teaching Art

Although children do much of the work of learning to be artists on their own, you have an important role. Like

other areas of development, artistic development needs to be nurtured and supported. When you provide an environment, materials, experiences, and relationships that support creative development and aesthetic appreciation, your classroom will have a *creative climate,* an atmosphere where creative expression is nurtured and creativity can flourish. You will help children find their visual and symbolic "voice," which lets them communicate their thinking and understanding.

Accepting and Appreciating Children's Art

What kind of art do you appreciate? Do you like a young child's scribbles and blobs, or are they hard for you to enjoy? Do you prefer art that is cheerful, with easily recognized symbols? Are you disturbed when a child's work depicts something unpleasant or unseemly? How do you feel about the two self-portraits in Work Sample 10.14—one depicting a sad face and one without conventional features?

One of the most important things you can do as a teacher of art is to learn to accept and appreciate children's art. When you genuinely accept and appreciate the range of children's development and feelings, you will support all of their work. If you reserve appreciation and acknowledgment for work that meets adult standards, you communicate that you are looking for correct rather than creative responses. As you gain understanding of the meaning of children's stages of development in art and are charmed by their fresh, non-stereotyped efforts, you will find it easy to be genuine in your appreciation of their work.

Reflect on your observations of early childhood art environments . . .

Reflect on programs that you have observed. How much time was allowed for art experiences? What kinds of art materials and experiences were available? What kinds of access did children have to them? Was artwork displayed? How did staff talk to children about their creative efforts? What changes do you think could have been made to better support children's artistic development?

Encouraging Children as Artists

How do you show that you accept and appreciate children's work? Indiscriminate or insincere praise is not appropriate. Teachers who respond to each child's work with "That's beautiful!" or "Good Work!" are either tuned out because their praise is meaningless or they turn children into praise-junkies who can't create without constant approval. Instead, show appreciation of children's work by providing verbal and non-verbal acknowledgement. For example, you can comment on effort, "You worked hard," innovation, "You tried it a new way," or technique, "You covered the whole paper."

We believe that it is important to refrain from evaluative responses such as *good, bad, ugly, beautiful,* and *messy* and instead help children to become their own evaluators: "What do you like best about it?" "When you do it again, what

Work Sample 10.14   Two Self-Portraits by 4-Year-Olds

will you do differently?" Children who are encouraged rather than evaluated develop skills that help them create their own standards and meet their own goals. When finished artwork is mounted carefully and prominently displayed in the classroom, it also demonstrates to children (and their families) that you appreciate their work.

Sometimes it is hard to accept it when children do not wish to participate in art. Time, acceptance, and encouragement are needed for some children to discover an interest in art. A long period of disinterest or observation may precede participation. A child may simply be more interested in different activities or alternative ways of being creative. They may not want to attempt art activities because they already feel they cannot measure up to their teacher's or parent's expectations.

Talking with Children About Their Art

You are important in children's process of learning about art. As you support and guide children in using media and teach them technique, you can also model specific art language. As you look at and talk with children about art, remember to discuss color, shape, space, line, form, design, and effect. You might say, "You used hundreds of dots to fill in that shape—it stands out on your paper." You may want to write down all the words you can think of to describe an element of art, for example, for line—*jagged, broken, wide, narrow, short, long, curved, flowing, wavy, zigzag, curly, twisted, straight, upright, leaning, turned.* These kinds of words give you important things to say to children about their work. "You used lots of lines in your work: short narrow ones, wide jagged lines, there are even two wavy lines!" In addition, these descriptions will help children become able to discuss their own work and the work of others.

As children work, it is best, especially at first, to offer only minimal input. Comment on children's effort, innovation, and technique. Avoid asking children *what* they have created. They may have had nothing particular in mind, and the question implies that they should have. Instead, you can ask them if they wish to tell you about what they have done, and accept it if they do not.

Helping Families Understand Their Children's Art

It can be hard for families to accept the messiness and non-productive nature of young children's artistic expression. One of your essential roles is to allow this messiness and to help families to understand the importance of their children's art process. As you explain what their children do and what their work means, you are helping families to understand the development of their child and your work as a teacher.

Displaying children's art in the classroom or hallways can be done with the care of a curator. Work can be displayed using construction paper backing, or with reusable frames or mats. Each piece of art can have the name of the artist and the date displayed next to it. A brief description of the medium, the developmental importance, or the ways in which the art is a part of children's learning can be posted with a display of art. If your school or community has a place for public display, consider joining with other teachers to create an art show. In this way you illustrate the value of children's artistic endeavors.

Carefully packaging children's work for their journey home also conveys a message. One teacher we know uses ribbon to tie children's paintings in a neat roll. To both the families and children, this says: "This work is valuable."

Nurturing Art Appreciation and Skill in Yourself

If you are going to provide a creative climate, you first need to value art and beauty in your own life. While it is not necessary for you to be an artist to help young children enjoy art, it *is* necessary for you to believe that experiences with and participation in art are valuable. Do you do this? It may be that you need to nurture your own love of beauty and appreciation for art.

Begin by reflecting on the role of art in your life. Treat yourself to an afternoon at a gallery or of quiet perusal of art books at your library. Watch a video about art (we enjoy the *Sister Wendy* series that is available in many public libraries). Become aware of the art you enjoy and share it with children.

Are you an artist? You probably have more artistic talent than you realize. Unlocking your own artistic ability is a good way to prepare for sharing art with children. Perhaps you used to draw, paint, or create beautiful craft items. Consider reacquainting yourself with your old hobby. Did you always want to learn? There are community art education classes almost everywhere to help you to unlock your sleeping talent.

Art Activities

What comes to mind when you envision young children engaged in art? Perhaps you see a child painting at an easel or drawing with crayons at a table. If so, you already know about two of the basic processes used in the early childhood art curriculum. Although you will see many different kinds of art activities provided for young children, we identify five basic art processes that serve as the foundation in early childhood art curriculum: drawing, painting, printmaking, collage and construction, and modeling and sculpting.

Drawing

Drawing, creating 2-dimensional visual art with an instrument on a flat surface, is the most basic and perhaps the most important art process for young children. Drawing media typically used in early childhood classrooms include crayons, felt pens, pencils, chalk, and pastels. In the past, crayons were the most common drawing instrument for young children, but today felt-tip markers are often preferred for their vibrant colors and ease of use. Drawings can be permanent on surfaces (known as *supports*) like paper or temporary on a support like a chalkboard. While drawing can involve color, line and shape are the dominant elements of a drawing.

People have drawn since the dawn of time—cave drawings are the first known form of art—so it is unsurprising that virtually all children draw. They draw with their fingers and sticks in sand, dirt, snow, fogged windows, fingerpaint, and flour dropped on the table.

The ability to draw requires the same fine motor control of an instrument as is required for writing (called *grapho-motor skill*). The initial stages of graphic skill (described earlier in this chapter) are also the initial stages of writing. Grapho-motor ability is therefore doubly important—both for artistic and literacy development. Both are ultimately ways to communicate meaning symbolically. As a teacher, your perspective on drawing differs somewhat from your perspective on writing. In drawing, you are focused on helping children to be creative and to aesthetically symbolize what they feel and know. In writing, you help children learn to make specific symbols they will later use to share ideas using words.

Look around an early childhood classroom. Where do you see drawing instruments? Are they in the art center, writing center, and science center? Does

Work Sample 10.15 Observational Drawing of a Monarch Butterfly, Chrysalis, and Caterpillar by a 4-Year-Old

Work Sample 10.16 Observational Drawing of a Crayfish by a 4 1/2-Year-Old

the teacher encourage children to draw both independently and as a group activity? Does the teacher talk with children about their drawings? Are new drawing instruments introduced? Drawing should be a part of the way teachers help young children to communicate their ideas and feelings every day.

Observational (Life) Drawing

Learning to draw is, in part, learning to see. By drawing an object, we learn to see it better. When artists, regardless of age, draw what they can see, they need not rely on memory. Observational, or life drawing is a technique that helps children both to see and to draw. The examples included in Work Samples 10.15 and 10.16 attest to the power of life drawing.

In the past, observational drawing as an activity for children was frowned upon. Educators worried that it might "stifle the pride, the pleasure, the confidence so necessary to the growth of a creative spirit" (Kellogg & O'Dell, 1967, in Cox, 2005). This is no longer believed to be true (Mulcahey, 2009; Pelo, 2007).

In order for observational drawing to be successful, it is important that children have sufficient time to study the object that is to be drawn. The teacher should open a discussion about the object with the children by asking questions such as: "Tell me, what do you see? What shapes do you see? What lines can you see?" A well-thought-out discussion may inspire children to include some of the elements of art and principles of design that they discussed.

> **Try It Out!**
>
> Think of a plant or animal from your home or yard, and draw it.
> Then draw it again while observing it. What differences do you notice? What does this imply for teaching art to children?

Ink and Watercolor Wash

An especially powerful drawing technique that we have used is to combine drawing and painting in a process called *ink and watercolor wash*. For this technique, children draw with a permanent fine-point marker on heavy paper. They then select several hues of liquid watercolors (see watercolors in the section on painting) and paint over the drawings (see Work Samples 10.17 and 10.18).

Painting

Painting is the art of applying a liquid medium, usually colored, to a surface with a tool like a brush or a sponge. While line and form are dominant in drawing, color is the most important element in painting.

There are many different painting techniques to use with young children—easel painting, fingerpainting, palette painting, watercolors, and mural painting.

Work Sample 10.17 Ink and Watercolor Wash (a fish)

Work Sample 10.18 Ink and Watercolor Wash (caterpillar on a crown flower)

Painting with tempera paint (a quick-drying egg-based paint also called *poster paint*) at an easel with a thick brush is the classic early childhood painting experience. Tempera paints are the mainstay for early childhood education, and are used for easel painting, fingerpainting, murals, and other projects.

Holding a brush, like holding a pen or pencil, requires grapho-motor skill. So painting, like drawing, develops the fine motor skills needed for later writing.

Easel Painting

There's a reason that easel painting is the basic early childhood painting experience. Easel painting involves both large (arm and shoulder) and fine (hand and

IN PRACTICE: Drawing Variations

Offer a variety of drawing materials: crayons, chalk, pastels, felt-tipped marking pens, and colored pencils, and demonstrate their use.

Crayons	Chalk
• Unwrap crayons and use them on their sides. Cover paper with wide swipes of color. • Cover light colors with dark and scratch though the top layer with a toothpick. • Crayon resist: Paint over light-colored crayon drawings. • Layer light colors to create colors.	• Use one color, smudge outwards to soften the edges; on top draw with hard lines. • Use chalk on wet paper to enhance color brilliance or dip chalk in water. • Use chalk dipped in milk; this resists rubbing off and increases the brilliance of colors.
Felt-Tipped Marking Pens	**Charcoal**
• Use black pens after drawing or painting to create a black outline. • Use only black pens and create pen-and-ink style drawings. Provide black pens of different widths (ultra-fine to thick).	• Explore charcoal and the shades it can create from dark black to pale gray. • Use charcoal briquettes to draw on the sidewalk to introduce artist's charcoal.
Oil Pastels	
• Use a finger or a soft cloth to blend two colors at the edges to make a third color. • Use a watercolor wash over a white oil pastel drawing.	

wrist) motor skills. Since young children first develop control of their shoulders and arms, painting at an easel is easier and more satisfying than painting at a table; in addition, it also helps to develop children's arm and hand skills. It's important for children to be able to reach the entire surface of the paper when painting. Because it is so valuable, we believe that easel painting should be available every day to children. For everyday use, the primary colors (red, yellow, and blue) as well as black and white are most important since these colors can be mixed to create all other colors. Some teachers prefer giving children the colors that photographers and printers use (turquoise, magenta, and yellow) because these create purer secondary colors (green, purple, and orange) rather than the muddier versions that occur when red, blue, and yellow tempera paints are mixed (see Work Sample 10.19).

Fingerpainting

Fingerpainting is the most natural of painting variations (and some would argue that it is the most basic form of painting). Toddlers and many young 3-year-olds will fingerpaint whenever paint is presented to them (or anything paint-like, including mashed potatoes).

It's easy to see that fingerpainting is a sensory activity, but how does it contribute to artistic development? "Finger-painting invites attention to color, texture, and to movement, as children run their fingers, the palms and backs of their hands, their arms and elbows across paper slick with colored paint" (Pelo, 2007, p. 27). It is easy to call children's attention to the magical ways in which two colors change when fingerpainting.

There are many ways to provide fingerpaint. Commercially prepared fingerpaints can be used, but if none are available, the simplest fingerpaint is tempera paint mixed with a small amount of liquid soap. Children can fingerpaint on large baking trays, directly on a table, or onto an easel. Fingerpaints can also be used on slick paper designed for fingerpainting or heavyweight paper of any kind. However, enthusiastic young children are likely to make holes in any paper.

The nature of fingerpainting is ephemeral; to capture it, you can either photograph it or make a print by placing a piece of paper over the fingerpainting, gently pressing down, then carefully pulling the paper off the paint (a technique called *mono-painting*). Work Sample 10.20 shows an example.

One way to vary the fingerpainting experience is to add texture to the paint by including an ingredient such as salt, sand, or sugar, or a scent such as peppermint. Another variation is to use shaving cream or boiled cornstarch to make a slippery base for the fingerpaint.

Work Sample 10.19 Easel Painting by a 3-Year-Old

Work Sample 10.20 Monoprint Made of a Fingerpainting

Palette Painting

One of our favorite painting experiences is palette painting (see Work Sample 10.21). In palette painting, children are presented with the primary colors (red, yellow, blue/turquoise, magenta), which allows them to create a myriad of colors similar to the process that artists use as they paint. As with watercolor painting, it is essential for children to learn a 3-step process for washing their brush in between colors: (1) wash the brush, bouncing it on the bottom of the water cup; (2) dry the brush on a small sponge; (3) wet the brush and choose a new color. It is also important to clean the water pots regularly. It helps to have a water station with clean water and a basin for the dirty water set up so that children can change their own water when they need to.

Children need extended experience with palette paints as well as many opportunities to experiment with the primary colors before they will create new and exciting secondary and tertiary colors. After children have experimented with mixing the primary colors, you can add white and black so they can make tints (adding white) and shades (adding black).

Work Sample 10.21
Palette Painting—
Self-Portrait by
a 4-Year-Old

Watercolor Painting

Do you remember the joy of opening up a brand new set of watercolors with all 8 colors pure and new? Did the bright colors call out to you . . . *Paint a rainbow! Paint a flower garden!* Watercolor paints can be immensely appealing to young children. You probably also remember a sad day (maybe even the same day) when your watercolors were dirty and mixed—with the yellow, red, and orange buried beneath a muddy coat of brown or black.

Watercolors can be challenging to use, but they also can offer some remarkable results. One of the difficulties young children have with watercolors is their tendency to not wash the brush properly, and then the colors turn muddy brown. Therefore, it is important for you to model using watercolors and especially

---

IN PRACTICE: How to Palette Paint

Palette painting is a technique in which children have primary colors (red, blue, and yellow or cyan, magenta, and yellow), white and black paint in small quantities along with a mixing surface (or palette). It enables children to discover elements of color and to observe how they change.

Children mix the colors that they want for painting. You will need the following materials for each palette:

- Five small containers for the paint (furniture casters work well, as do the lids from baby food jars)
- A cookie sheet or cafeteria tray
- A small sponge

- A small brush
- A cup for water

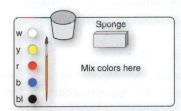

The only instruction that children need to succeed with palette painting is to learn to wash their brushes in the water when they change colors and to dry the brushes on the sponge before using a new color.

Note: Often children focus on color mixing for quite a while and will move on to painting when they have experimented enough. We have observed children explore a single color group for many days. You might ask children to make as many shades of (blue, yellow, red) as they can and discuss how they made them and how they are different. The color swatches can be torn or cut to use for collages. A side benefit of palette painting is that it is a very efficient way to use the paint with little waste.

washing the brush by bouncing it on the bottom of the water cup and drying it on a sponge before getting a new color. This 3-step process is hard for young children to learn. And as with palette painting, it is essential to regularly change the water.

There are two basic types of watercolors: pan paints and liquid watercolors. In our experience, liquid watercolors are the easiest for young children to use. We place about 2 teaspoons of liquid watercolor in furniture casters on a tray with a cup of water and a sponge to wash (similar to the palette painting setup, see the photograph on page 299). To minimize waste and ensure good results with liquid watercolors, we ask children to choose one or two colors at a time.

Pan paints (sets of 4–12 colors and a brush in a plastic or metal case) are more difficult for children to manage. Part of the joy for younger children is to run the brush over all of the paints, mixing them together. Artist quality watercolor pan paints produce good results, but care and attention is required to keep the pan paints bright.

Printmaking

Printing or printmaking involves applying paint or ink to an object and imprinting a surface to make an image, or rubbing a flat textured object beneath a surface. The placement of the object being printed requires use of the element of *space*, the critical artistic element explored in printmaking. Printmaking often evolves out of the process of painting (Striker, 2001) when a child uses his or her hand or brush (or another object) to print rather than paint. There are five printing processes typically used in the early childhood classroom: stamped prints, stencils, embossed prints, mono-prints, and etched prints.

IN PRACTICE: Painting Variations

Painting can be varied by offering different kinds of paints, different shades of paint, and different techniques for painting. Show children some of the following:

Using Brushes	Color Combining
• Make thin and thick lines, splotches and blots, wiggles, smears, drops, loops, twirls, and swirls. Talk about what a brush can do. • Use a variety of objects for brushes: cotton swabs, feather dusters, feathers, brayed bark, straw, fur, grasses.	• Talk about the ways colors affect one another and change as they are mixed. • Provide experiences using limited combinations of colors. • Provide experiences using paint with various shades of a single color.
Fingerpainting	**Watercolors**
• Have a tray and paper. For each painting, use liquid soap, fingerpaint base, and tempera paint (or a commercial fingerpaint). • Have children fingerpaint directly on the trays and make prints by placing paper on the image. • Add textured materials to the paint—salt, sand, sugar. • Make mud fingerpaint.	• Wet the brush, rub the brush in paint, paint, wash the brush and dry it on the sponge, and choose new color. • Wet paper and drop on small amounts of paint, move the paper and let paint flow. Let two colors "marry" and become a new color. • Use dilute food color instead of paint.
	Textures
	• Add sand, sugar, salt, or other substances to the paint to create textures in the paint.

Stamping involves using simple objects such as toilet paper rolls, fruits and vegetables, or sponges dipped into tempera paint, and then stamping them onto paper. This can also be done with body parts such as hands, feet, and fingers, which is much enjoyed by preschoolers. **Stencils** can either be positive or negative shapes. They are created when a shape or object is painted over or when an empty space is painted into. This process results in a print. **Embossed prints** are created when a raised design is created on a piece of cardboard or wood with string or flat objects glued onto a base. The print is made by laying down a piece of paper and rubbing the paper with chalk, crayon, or charcoal. They can be done with 3-dimensional objects by placing materials such as leaves, rocks, fabrics, and shoe soles under paper or by placing fabric over them and rubbing with crayons or chalk to create a print. **Mono-prints** are single prints taken from a fingerpainting as previously discussed or from a wax crayon drawing that is covered with paper and then ironed with a warm iron (needless to say, this should be done by an adult). The final printing process is *etched printing,* in which a child etches a design into a piece of cardboard or Styrofoam with a pencil, rolls a layer of ink on it with a brayer, places paper over the etching, presses down with a clean brayer, and lifts the print.

Collage and Construction

The word *collage* comes from the French verb *coller* ("to paste") and is the process of gluing or otherwise affixing paper, fabric, and other materials to a flat surface (Striker, 2001). Typically, collage in early childhood programs involves assembling and then gluing paper and small flat objects onto a base. Cutting, tearing, and folding skills are often employed in collage making.

Construction as an early childhood art activity is similar to collage, but involves working with 3-dimensional materials (e.g., cardboard, plastic, wood). Woodworking, weaving, stitchery, soft sculpture, and papier-mâchē are other construction techniques. Since the shapes and objects that are being glued are largely provided by the teacher, the art element that children explore most in collage and construction is *space*.

Recycled Collage and Construction

Collage and construction with recycled materials is an ecologically sound art activity that is enjoyed by children and their families. Families can be involved in bringing in materials (boxes, corks, egg cartons, plastic containers, bottle tops, wrapping paper, ribbons, buttons, fabric scraps, yarn, notecards, postcards, etc.). If you have space in the classroom or yard, a collage/construction center can be established to allow children to create collage and construction independently.

Tissue Paper Collage

Tissue paper collage is a collage technique that we find particularly appealing to children. It is most successful when teachers prepare the raw materials carefully by cutting different colors of art tissue into diverse regular and irregular shapes. A paste brush is used to brush dilute glue over the tissue paper on fairly heavy white paper. This activity works best when the teacher demonstrates the technique. (See Work Sample 10.22.)

Modeling and Sculpting

Modeling and sculpting involve molding a soft material or carving a hard one to create a 3-dimensional work of art. Materials used in early childhood modeling and sculpting activities include clay, playdough, commercial oil-based modeling

Work Sample 10.22
Tissue Paper Collage
In the Stream by a
4 1/2-Year-Old

media (plasticene), or other non-toxic alternatives such as air-dry clay. Modeling and sculpting give children experience with the art elements of *shape* and *space*.

Recently, art researchers have begun to study children's development in sculpture. Unlike children's pictorial development, which progresses from scribbling to representation, children begin sculpting 3-dimensionally early and favor modeling upright figures; however, this changes as children grow more familiar with the material, and then they create flat, 2-dimensional shapes (see Work Sample 10.23). Later, children return to modeling upright figures (Golomb, 2004).

Children should be given plenty of time to work with modeling materials, sculpting at first just with their hands. As they become more familiar with the medium, they can be introduced to sculpting tools such as blunt knives, rounded sticks, and lengths of dowels for rolling. Avoid using cookie cutters and similar pattern shapes, as they do not offer a creative experience and therefore limit and prescribe the children's work. Children age 4 and older can begin to learn simple clay work techniques such as pinch pots and coil building.

Work Sample 10.23
Dough Modeling: A Spider (flat sculpture)—Created by Lili, age 4

A Few Cautions

About Craft, Coloring Books, and Pattern Art

At times teachers will make a distinction between work they call "craft" and other work they call "art." Often the "craft" activities consist of look-alike patterns. What is craft? The dictionary defines *craft* as something such as a piece of pottery or carving produced skillfully by hand, especially in a traditional manner. The handwork that we give children to do—clay work, woodwork, stitchery, and paper folding and cutting can legitimately be called *craft* and are worthwhile activities for young children. They are especially appropriate for primary school children who have the fine motor coordination required to learn a craftsman's technique. True craft is a far cry from look-alike coloring books or identical snowmen made with cotton balls.

We believe that creative expression should be a reflection of the child's ideas and abilities. Prepared patterns to be copied by children and coloring books have nothing to do with the development of creativity or self-expression. Many researchers believe that coloring books, ditto sheets, and pattern art are not "art" at all, and should be avoided at all cost (Cox, 2005; Striker, 2001) because they can be destructive to children's feelings of competence and self-worth, may cause children to become dissatisfied with their own creative work, and may reduce creativity. These activities take up valuable time that children should be using to develop other skills, awareness, and ideas. They are not used in good early childhood programs.

The Use of Foods in Art Activities

There is controversy about using food for sensory and artistic experiences, with many programs banning the practice. Remember to be mindful of your program's guidelines when planning art experiences that use foods, and be sensitive to your children's families' beliefs about the appropriate use of food. If it violates family beliefs, or if families are in financial need, it is best to avoid these activities.

Aesthetic Appreciation Activities: Understanding the Nature of Art

Every human being has the potential to develop sensitivity to beauty and the heritage of the arts. In the beginning of this chapter we defined aesthetics as the study of beauty, art, and taste, and the ability to create and appreciate beauty. Malcolm Ross says, "Aesthetic perception involves the capacity to respond to the uniqueness, the singular quality of things—to value individual integrity and to reject the cliché and the stereotype" (1981, p. 158). So, another part of the early childhood art curriculum is to unlock this potential.

In the past, helping children to see the beauty in their world, in their own creative works, and in the works of others was often overlooked in the early childhood art curriculum. Some teachers mistook sharing fine art with presenting a model to be copied. Today we know that providing a range of artwork in diverse media and styles does not provide a model to be copied, but instead opens the door to a range of art possibilities. This understanding is reflected in the many states that include aesthetics in early childhood art standards.

Aesthetics can be included throughout your classroom and interwoven into your curriculum. You support aesthetic development in two ways. One way is by creating an environment that is beautiful and filled with art and natural items that are beautiful. (For example, in an integrated study, one of the first things you should do is find art images to illustrate the topic.) The second is through activities that give children opportunities to interact with fine art as illustrated by the plan in this chapter.

Talking to Children About Fine Art

Having a conversation with a young child about a piece of fine artwork can be simple, yet it can help them to appreciate and have insights about art. When initiating a conversation about fine art, try to keep your questions open ended, when possible, so that a range of answers are acceptable. Remember that in art there are no "wrong" answers. Figure 10.4 shows an example of a conversation Lili, 4, had with her teacher, Karen, about Mary Cassatt's painting "Children Playing on the Beach." (See www.nga.gov/collection/gallery/ggcassattptg/ggcassattptg-52163.html)

FIGURE 10.4 Conversation About "Children Playing on the Beach"

K: Tell me, what do you see?

L: I see a crab hiding in the sand. I see two girls with spades and buckets.

K: What do you like in this picture?

L: I like the sail (points to the white triangle shape in the background).

K: Somebody made this, just like you make art. She was a woman and her name was Mary Cassatt. She made this a long time ago.

L: Is she dead? Does she have a gravestone?

K: Yes, she died a long time ago, and is probably buried in France where she lived.

K: What kind of weather is it?

L: It's daytime, it looks like it's hot.

K: Do you notice anything else?

L: I notice a crab and some sand.

K: What colors do you see?

L: I see blue and sandy colors.

K: Are the colors bright?

L: The sand is bright, but the sea is dark.

K: What do you think the little girls are saying?

L: They are just playing next to each other.

K: How does the painting make you feel?

L: It makes me happy.

K: Do you like the painting?

L: Yes!

Planning Art Curriculum

Kristiana, age 4, sits quietly in the school garden. She looks up at the tall giant sunflowers, planted several weeks ago. The sunflowers sway and dance in the warm breeze. Kristiana spends several minutes alone, breathing in the summer smells and listening intently to the sounds the sunflowers make as they dance in the dappled sunlight. From a distance, Karen, the teacher, observes.

You begin planning for art experiences by providing raw materials and paying attention to children. Karen began this process by giving children time and a place to enjoy nature, by providing them with additional experiences to extend their aesthetic experience, and by joining with them in enjoying the beauty of nature. She knows that simply providing the initial experience is not enough to help children develop aesthetic appreciation or artistic skill. Using the children's own aesthetic experiences helps the teacher to capitalize on this "teachable moment."

The most important thing Karen can do to build children's aesthetic appreciation and artistic ability and disposition is to look and listen for children's own inspiration. One of the National Art Education Association's standards for young children is choosing and evaluating a range of subject matter, symbols, and ideas" (Consortium of National Arts Education Associations, 1994). The Head Start Child Development and Early Learning Framework also supports the importance of children's aesthetic appreciation in its standard: "Discusses one's own artistic creations and those of others." To be confident in artistic production and aesthetic experience, children need to be able to:

- be observant and open to aesthetic experience.
- experiment and explore with basic materials and media.
- be able to describe and discuss their own artwork and the work of others.
- use ideas, knowledge, and personal experiences as subject matter.
- discuss fine artwork and be familiar with art terms.

Writing Art Curriculum Plans

To build on the children's interests and to help them to enjoy an aesthetic experience, Karen planned an activity on appreciating sunflowers for them. Because she is an experienced teacher, she wrote a short, almost telegraphic, plan as a guide for herself (see Figure 10.5).

Karen's short plan would not be enough of a guide for a beginning teacher. The detailed version in Figure 10.6 gives you a better idea of what she planned to do.

Art Curriculum in a Weekly Plan

We have already mentioned that we believe that art should be a part of every school day for young children. This does not mean, however, that each day you need to bring a new and "exciting" art activity. Indeed, we believe that repetition is particularly valuable when planning art. Children benefit greatly by using the same media over a long period of time—it takes many experiences to fully explore the possibilities of the media. Repeated experiences help children to develop skill and their own visual language.

FIGURE 10.5 Simple Art Activity Plan

Appreciating Sunflowers

Objectives:	Observe and discuss art; create art that shows a feeling or idea.
Standard:	Domain V, Art Standard 1; Aesthetic Appreciation, Standard 1
What you need:	Print of "Sunflowers" by Vincent Van Gogh (www.vangoghgallery.com/painting/sunflowerindex.html or www.nationalgallery.org.uk/paintings/vincent-van-gogh-sunflowers)

- Easel and paints—several shades of yellow as well as other colors
- Vase of sunflowers on table near easel

How to teach:

1. Explain: I noticed children looking at sunflowers–show the vase of sunflowers. Ask: "What do you like about sunflowers?" (Start w/ Kristiana.) Listen/summarize.
2. Show print, and invite children to look. Introduce the name of artist. Ask: "What do you think Van Gogh liked about sunflowers?" Listen/summarize.
3. Invite children to talk about shapes, colors, lines.
4. Show paints. Note sunflowery colors. Put a vase of sunflowers on the table near the easel. Invite children to paint.
5. Stay near/talk as children paint. Encourage looking at flowers and print.

How to assess: Look/listen for children describing art/attending/asking questions/discussing their art.

FIGURE 10.6 Detailed Art Activity Plan

Activity:	**Appreciating Sunflowers** (discussion and painting)
Curriculum Area:	Visual Arts and Aesthetics
WHO It's For:	Kristiana and the Airplanes (the 4-year-old group)
Rationale:	All of the children, and Kristiana in particular, frequently go to look at sunflowers in the school garden. Kristiana seems mesmerized by the sunflowers' movement and beauty. This activity is designed to extend her personal aesthetic experience to the small group.
Art Objectives:	*By participating in this activity the children will …*

- Observe and discuss an artist's work ("Sunflowers" by Van Gogh).
- Use tempera paint and brushes to create artwork that communicates a feeling or an idea.

Preschool Content Standard(s):	Domain V, Art Standard 1: Create and express themselves through a variety of art experiences.
Indicator:	Use art materials to explore and extend topics being studied in the classroom. Aesthetic Appreciation, Standard 1: Develop appreciation for natural and cultural beauty and the visual and performing arts.
Indicator:	Look at and respond to works of visual art.
HOW to Prepare	*What you need:*

- 15–20 minutes at small-group time in the art area, followed by 1-hour choice time when the activity will be available
- Print of the painting "Sunflowers" by Vincent Van Gogh (http://www.vangoghgallery.com/painting/sunflowerindex.html or www.nationalgallery.org.uk/paintings/vincent-van-gogh-sunflowers)
- A vase of sunflowers
- An easel
- A variety of paints in paint cups with a brush in each (be sure to have several shades of yellow as well as other colors)
- Table near the easel

Set up:

Set up an easel with the print of Van Gogh's "Sunflowers" in the art area. Place the vase of sunflowers and pots of paint on the table.

(continued)

FIGURE 10.6   Detailed Art Activity Plan (continued)

HOW to Teach

Introduction:

- Meet in the art area. Explain that you noticed children looking at sunflowers in the garden.

- Show the vase of sunflowers and say something like, "I really like sunflowers. I think the yellow petals are beautiful. Kristiana, what do you like about the sunflowers?" Allow Kristiana to share.

- Invite others to share something they like about the sunflowers.

- Listen to what they say, and summarize their comments, emphasizing qualities children mentioned (e.g., "Caleb likes the long green prickly stems. Amanda likes the bright yellow pollen on the inside of some of the flowers.").

Teaching steps:

1. Say something like: "Sometimes artists paint pictures about things that they like."

2. Show the poster and invite children to look at it. Say: "These sunflowers were painted by an artist named Van Gogh" (you may want to use first name and/or talk about name).

3. Ask: "What do you think Van Gogh liked about sunflowers?"

4. Listen and summarize, noting feelings, art techniques, and elements mentioned (e.g., "I think you're right. Van Gogh used so much yellow in the painting that he must have loved the deep golden yellow of the sunflowers" or "Yes, I see the way he made the petals curly, he must have smiled when he saw their curly shapes.").

5. If children are attentive, invite them to tell you about the shapes, colors, and lines that they see. (If they are losing interest, move on quickly to the next part of the activity.)

6. Explain that if they choose to paint today, you have made extra paint in sunflower-y colors for them to use (show the paints). Note that they can choose the paints they would like to use.

Closure:

Put the vase of sunflowers in the middle of the table near the easel. Comment, saying something like: "You are artists just like Van Gogh. You paint with colors and lines and shapes and make paintings that show what you like and how you feel. I wonder if you will paint today." Invite two interested children to paint. Invite the rest to choose another activity. (Note that everyone can have a turn and you will call them when space is available.)

NOTE: Stay near the art area and talk with children as they paint. Encourage them to refer to flowers and print if they appear to be interested.

HOW to Assess and Document

Objectives	Evidence of Learning Children might …	How to Document This Evidence
Observe and discuss an artist's work.	Describe an element of the painting during the discussion. Attend to the discussion. Ask questions. Go and look at the painting during choice time. Point it out to peer, parent, or teacher.	Observations
Use tempera paint and brushes to create artwork that communicates a feeling or an idea.	Paint at the easel and comment on your own work, explaining how the painting feels or the object they are representing.	Sample of painting with annotation of words/dictation

Other Things to Do: • Hang the print on the wall in the classroom near the art area.

• Once paintings are dry, hang them near the print. Post children's words and descriptions to describe the sunflowers, the print, and the flower-inspired paintings.

On Another Day: • Invite children to mix paint colors that they see in the painting and in the real sunflowers.

• Ask children what colors they see and how they would make that color. Have the children mix the paints into the paint pots. When all the colors are mixed, they can be placed at the easel, and children can choose to paint with them if they wish.

EVALUATION This was amazing! Dalton and Kristiana especially produced beautiful, unique sunflower paintings. Van Gogh would have loved them. I had to keep the sunflowers out all day!

In the week's plan example shown in Figure 10.7, you will see that painting with water on a dry surface and wet paper painting are repeated. In addition, easel painting, self-selected drawing, and books with artwork are available daily. This repetition allows children to develop art skills. Activities that involve art and aesthetics are highlighted.

Art in an Integrated Study

Because art provides a means by which children express their growing understanding and also helps children see and know what they are learning, it is an important part of every integrated study. In the sunburst graphic of the study of water presented in Figure 10.8, art is obvious in a few specific activities. But art also is a part of the environment in the form of illustrated books created by children, art prints displayed in the classroom, and children's literature.

In addition, because an integrated study becomes a part of the life of the classroom, children naturally bring it into their art. They went to a stream, the beach, and a water garden, so these experiences were often a part of their art. This process is organic, that is, it grows from the children themselves and does not require the teacher to impose a topic.

Every integrated study can include many art and art appreciation activities. Those described below are ones that we include for every study.

1. *Observational (Life) Drawing.* Providing objects related to the study for children to discuss and then draw. This can be combined with *Ink and Watercolor Wash*. For the study of water, children drew and painted crayfish that they had gathered on the trip to the stream.
2. *Art and Artifacts Display.* Staff and families will have art and artifacts related to any worthwhile topic. These can be examined and discussed, and then placed on display. For the study of water, families sent in special glasses, art prints, and a beautiful plate decorated with a picture of a waterfall.
3. *Fine Art Postcard Games.* Fine art postcards can be turned into games. These can involve a multitude of subject areas from math to geography. For the water study, a game was made in which children had to hunt for different forms of water in fine art postcards. Games can be placed in the manipulatives area in the classroom.
4. *Fine Art Prints.* Fine art prints related to the topic can be displayed throughout the classroom alongside children's artwork. For the water study, these included Japanese prints of mountains, rivers, the ocean, and streams.
5. *Beautifully Illustrated Books.* Art/storybooks related to the topic can be included in the library. For the water study, many, many stories included images of water and these led to many discussions of how artists depict water.

Art for All Children

Art and aesthetics are important for all young children. From the sensory joy of a toddler who is fingerpainting to the thoughtful reflection of a first grader enjoying a statue in a neighborhood park, young children come to art with enthusiasm and

FIGURE 10.7 A Week's Plan: Water—Week #1

Objective: To introduce the study and help children begin to understand that water has unique properties and people need water for different things (to drink, clean, cook, play, work, etc.).

	Monday	Tuesday	Wednesday	Thursday	Friday
Story 8:30–8:50	*Water, Water Everywhere* (Bix and Rauzon)	*Come On, Rain* (Hesse)	*The Storm Book* (Zolotow)	*The Important Book* (Brown)	*Water Dance* (Locker)
Outdoor Activities 9:00–10:00 **Purpose:** *to help children to…*	**Trike Washing** Develop awareness of the uses of water. Build motor coordination and sensory awareness.	**Planting Seeds** Develop awareness of living things and their needs. Enhance sensory awareness and the ability to observe.	**Easel Painting under the Tree** Express ideas and feelings using paint. Learn about art elements and techniques.	**Easel Painting under the Tree** Express ideas and feelings using paint. Learn about art elements and techniques.	**Parachute Play** Learn to work cooperatively as a group. Develop large motor coordination.
Small Group (Monsters) 10:00–10:20 **Purpose:** *to help children to…*	**INTRODUCTION OF THE STUDY** **Drops of Water on a Coin** Observe some of the properties of water.	**Journals: Water** Develop concepts of print. Acquire the ability to express ideas through words and drawings.	**Paintings of Water Discussion and Painting** (*The Great Wave* by Hiroshige and *Water Lilies* by Monet) Observe and discuss art and use paint to create artwork to communicate a feeling or idea.	**Water Measuring Activity** Observe properties of water. Develop and use measurement concepts.	**Drops of Water on a Coin** Observe some of the properties of water.
Small Group (Flowers) 10:00–10:10 **Purpose:** *to help children to…*	**INTRODUCTION OF THE STUDY** **Water on Wax Paper** Observe some of the properties of water.	**Planting Seeds** Develop awareness of living things and their needs. Enhance sensory awareness and the ability to observe.	**Water Pouring** Observe some of the properties of water. Develop coordination and self-control.	**Water Pouring** Observe some of the properties of water. Develop coordination and self-control.	**Sink and Float** Observe some of the properties of water. Explore buoyancy.
Indoor Special Activities 10:20–11:30 **Purpose:** *to help children to…*	**Mixing Mudpaint** Develop creativity. Observe some of the properties of water.	**Clay** Develop sensory awareness. Use art elements of shape, form, and texture.	**Palette Painting** Create and express ideas through the medium of paint. Develop awareness of art element color.		**Clay** Develop sensory awareness. Use art elements of shape, form, and texture.
Circle Time 11:30–11:45 **Purpose:** *to help children to…*	**Songs of the Week:** *Row, Row, Row Your Boat; The Wheel of the Water; Eency Weency Spider* Build a repertoire of songs. Develop ability to express ideas through music. Learn about musical elements. Acquire the ability to work cooperatively as a member of a group.				

320

FIGURE 10.8 A Study of Water Sunburst

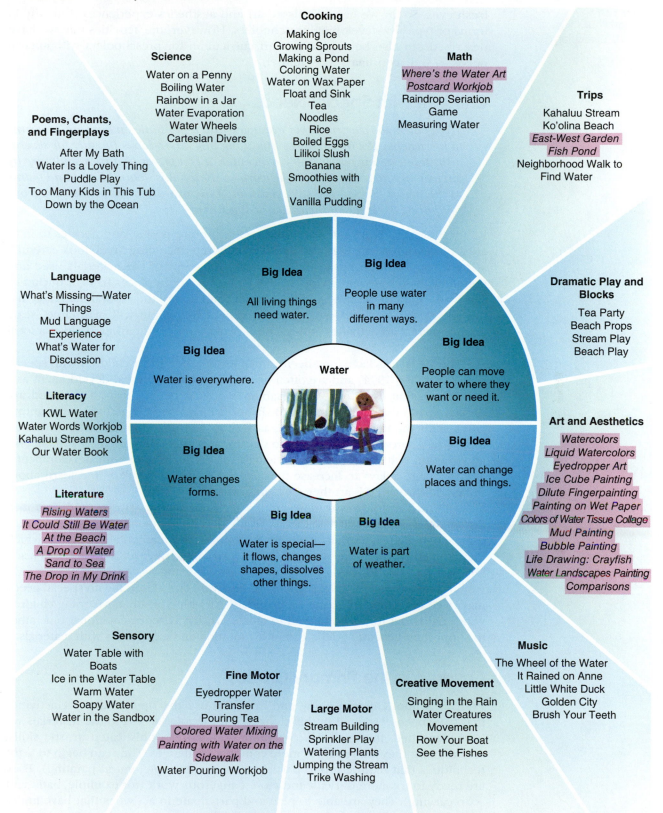

Cooking

Making Ice
Growing Sprouts
Making a Pond
Coloring Water
Water on Wax Paper
Float and Sink
Tea
Noodles
Rice
Boiled Eggs
Lilikoi Slush
Banana
Smoothies with
Ice
Vanilla Pudding

Science

Water on a Penny
Boiling Water
Rainbow in a Jar
Water Evaporation
Water Wheels
Cartesian Divers

Math

*Where's the Water Art
Postcard Workjob*
Raindrop Seriation
Game
Measuring Water

**Poems, Chants,
and Fingerplays**

After My Bath
Water Is a Lovely Thing
Puddle Play
Too Many Kids in This Tub
Down by the Ocean

Trips

Kahaluu Stream
Ko'olina Beach
*East-West Garden
Fish Pond*
Neighborhood Walk to
Find Water

Language

What's Missing—Water
Things
Mud Language
Experience
What's Water for
Discussion

**Dramatic Play and
Blocks**

Tea Party
Beach Props
Stream Play
Beach Play

Literacy

KWL Water
Water Words Workjob
Kahaluu Stream Book
Our Water Book

Art and Aesthetics

*Watercolors
Liquid Watercolors
Eyedropper Art
Ice Cube Painting
Dilute Fingerpainting
Painting on Wet Paper
Colors of Water Tissue Collage
Mud Painting
Bubble Painting
Life Drawing: Crayfish
Water Landscapes Painting
Comparisons*

Literature

*Rising Waters
It Could Still Be Water
At the Beach
A Drop of Water
Sand to Sea
The Drop in My Drink*

Sensory

Water Table with
Boats
Ice in the Water Table
Warm Water
Soapy Water
Water in the Sandbox

Fine Motor

Eyedropper Water
Transfer
Pouring Tea
*Colored Water Mixing
Painting with Water on the
Sidewalk*
Water Pouring Workjob

Large Motor

Stream Building
Sprinkler Play
Watering Plants
Jumping the Stream
Trike Washing

Creative Movement

Singing in the Rain
Water Creatures
Movement
Row Your Boat
See the Fishes

Music

The Wheel of the Water
It Rained on Anne
Little White Duck
Golden City
Brush Your Teeth

Big Idea
All living things
need water.

Big Idea
People use water
in many
different ways.

Big Idea
Water is everywhere.

Big Idea
People can move
water to where they
want or need it.

Water

Big Idea
Water changes
forms.

Big Idea
Water can change
places and things.

Big Idea
Water is special—
it flows, changes
shapes, dissolves
other things.

Big Idea
Water is part
of weather.

fresh eyes. So far we have discussed art and aesthetics experiences primarily in terms of typically developing preschoolers. However, the activities that we have described can also be the basis of art curriculum for preschoolers with special needs as well as primary age children.

Children with Special Needs

Myra enters the classroom her eyes wide and a big smile on her face. She runs to her teacher Robin and gives him a big hug. Myra looks intently for several minutes at a new poster in the art center. It is a poster of a rock sculpture by environmental artist Andy Goldsworthy. Myra holds Robin's hand and points to the poster "rocks" she says smiling. Myra usually talks in just one-word sentences, she is a child with Down syndrome.

Robin observes Myra's interest in the rock sculpture poster, and decides to initiate a discussion at small-group time. The children, including Myra, look carefully at the rock sculpture poster and describe it in terms of the materials used and the elements of line and shape. In the art center Robin places trays, a bucket of sand, and smooth pebbles so that children can explore the natural materials that the artist used, but on a much smaller scale. Later Robin will plan larger scale environmental art activities in the school playground, and farther afield at a local beach or woods.

The visual arts have long been valued as therapeutic for children with special needs (Schiller, 1994) and are often used to support emotional development and skill acquisition. Children with disabilities greatly benefit from a balanced approach to art education, such as DBAE, and gain sensory, cognitive, and manipulative skills through art production, as well as learning about art and increasing their visual perception and ability to discuss artworks (Hurwitz & Day, 2001). An art program rich in aesthetic experiences can help children with developmental and language delays to increase their language and vocabulary and learn about the world through the art they view and discuss.

Although children with developmental delays such as Down syndrome may develop at a slower pace than their typically developing peers, they begin their artistic experiences in a similar manner with a prolonged manipulative stage in which they primarily explore the materials given (Hurwitz & Day, 2001). When you teach children with special needs, it is important to accept and be conscious of each individual child's developmental stage in art. Be aware that children with special needs may need extra time to master art materials. As with typically developing children your goal is not to push children to create art that is representational but rather to support and encourage the child's exploration and expression with materials.

Children in the Primary Grades

Primary school children enjoy and can fully use the open-ended art activities that have been described in this chapter. With regular access to the materials we have described, they will develop more and more sophisticated artistic skills. Additionally, they are ready for more complex challenges. They can begin to learn techniques that require group participation (for example, mural painting). They are ready to try more difficult and more dangerous work (for example, batik and soap carving). They are able to plan and participate in activities that have multi-step processes (for example, pottery). And they are ready to learn more about art history and art criticism.

Unfortunately, you may be placed in a situation where you are allowed little time to give your class of young primary school children these opportunities. We encourage you to stand up for art and to provide creative art experiences whenever you can. It is easy to allow art to become a series of look-alike holiday crafts. However, doing so does not serve children.

Final Thoughts

Art is part of life. It is a part of your life; it is part of children's life. It is important to help children become people who can feel as well as think, who are sensitive to and willing to stand up for a world in which art is valued. Your job as an early childhood teacher is to know about artistic and aesthetic development and to help children become artists and art appreciators. Your job is to help families, administrators, and other staff understand the visual art curriculum. It's an important job.

Learning Outcomes

When you read this chapter, thoughtfully complete activities from the "To Learn More" section, and document this learning as suggested in the "For Your Portfolio" section, you will be making progress in the following *NAEYC Standards for Early Childhood Professional Preparation Programs* (2009):

Standard 1. Promoting Child Development and Learning

Students prepared in early childhood degree programs are grounded in a child development knowledge base. They use their understanding of young children's characteristics and needs and of the multiple interacting influences on children's development and learning to create environments that are healthy, respectful, supportive, and challenging for each child.

The key elements of standard 1 you will have learned about are . . .

1a: Knowing and understanding young children's characteristics and needs

1c: Using developmental knowledge to create healthy, respectful, supportive, and challenging learning environments

Standard 4. Using Developmentally Effective Approaches to Connect with Children and Families

Students prepared in early childhood degree programs understand that teaching and learning with young children is a complex enterprise, and its details vary depending on children's ages, characteristics, and the settings within which teaching and learning occur. They understand and use positive relationships and supportive interactions as the foundation for their work with young children and families. Students know, understand, and use a wide array of developmentally appropriate approaches, instructional strategies, and tools to connect with children and families and positively influence each child's development and learning.

The key elements of standard 4 you will have learned about are . . .

4a: Understanding positive relationships and supportive interactions as the foundation of their work with children

4b: Knowing and understanding effective strategies and tools for early education

4c: Using a broad repertoire of developmentally appropriate teaching/learning approaches

4d: Reflecting on their own practice to promote positive outcomes for each child

Standard 5. Using Content Knowledge to Build Meaningful Curriculum

Students prepared in early childhood degree programs use their knowledge of academic disciplines to design, implement, and evaluate experiences that promote positive development and learning for each and every young child. Students understand the importance of developmental domains and academic (or content) disciplines in an early childhood curriculum. They know the essential concepts, inquiry tools, and structure of content areas, including academic subjects, and can identify resources to deepen their understanding. Students use their own knowledge and other resources to design, implement, and evaluate meaningful, challenging curricula that promote comprehensive developmental and learning outcomes for every young child.

The key elements of standard 5 you will have learned about are . . .

5a: Understanding content knowledge and resources in academic disciplines

5b: Knowing and using the central concepts, inquiry tools, and structures of content areas or academic disciplines

5c: Using their own knowledge, appropriate early learning standards, and other resources to design, implement, and evaluate meaningful, challenging curricula for each child.

To Learn More

Observe a Program: For a morning, observe a program and see how the staff structures the environment and program to support children's artistic development. Notice both the play opportunities and the planned group activities. Look at the plans and see how the planning reflects what you observed. Interview a teacher to learn what he or she thinks about art curriculum.

Observe a Child: For a morning, observe a child in a classroom, with a focus on the child's art activity and aesthetic awareness. Notice how the child engages with the planned activities and how he or she constructs his or her own opportunities for learning. Notice the extent to which the child's activity and the planned curriculum seem to match. Observe to see how staff support the child's art and aesthetic learning.

Observe a Master Teacher: Spend a morning with an early childhood educator who is experienced and has a curriculum leadership role in a program. (This teacher may be called the "lead," "head," or "mentor" teacher.) Then interview the educator about how he or she plans for and provides for art in the curriculum.

Observe an Art Activity: Observe a teacher leading a planned art activity. Interview the teacher to find out the objectives for the activity. Reflect on any differences between what you saw and the focus of the plan.

Compare Two Programs: Observe art experiences in two early childhood programs. Compare the ways that the two address art curriculum—their similarities and differences. Reflect on which program seems to best support children's learning and why. What implications does this comparison have for your future work with young children?

Compare Two Ages: Observe two classrooms, one preschool and one for primary school children. Report on how each supports children's artistic development. Talk to the staff about how they make their curriculum choices. Notice how development influences curriculum choices.

Explore Resources: Read one of the books from the bibliography or review the online resources listed here and write a review of it/them for your classmates.

Children's Museum of the Arts: cmany.org/intro.php?pn=home

National Art Education Association: www.arteducators.org/

Young at Art Children's Museum: www.youngatartmuseum.org/

For Your Portfolio

Design an Art Environment: Design and draw a floor plan for a classroom and play yard that would promote children's art and aesthetic learning. Share your plan with an early childhood educator, discussing what you included and why. Ask for and consider the educator's feedback and suggestions. Set up an art studio in a real classroom or play yard utilizing as many of your ideas as possible and let children use it. For your portfolio, include the floor plan, photographs or video of children using the area, and a reflection on what you learned by doing this project.

Plan and Implement an Art Activity: Observe a group of children for a morning focusing on their artistic interest and skill. Based on what you observed write and implement art activity. Collect evidence of children's response in the form of anecdotal observations, work samples, photographs, or video recordings. Reflect on how children responded and what they appear to have learned. What worked? What might you do differently next time? How might you expand on this experience for children? For your portfolio include the plan, a photograph, and a reflection on what you learned about yourself, children, planning, and teaching.

Create an Aesthetics Learning Material: Design and make an aesthetic awareness learning material to support the development of a particular child or group of children. Introduce it to the child or children and observe how it is used. Reflect on how the children responded and how you felt about what you did. What worked? What might you do differently next time? How might you expand on this experience for children? For your portfolio, include a photograph of a child using the material and a reflection on what you learned about yourself, children, learning materials, and teaching.

Bibliography

Consortium of National Arts Education Associations. (1994). *National standards for arts education: Dance, music, theatre, visual arts: what every young American should know and be able to do in the arts.* Reston, VA: Music Educators National Conference.

Cox, M. (2005). *The pictorial world of the child.* Cambridge, UK: Cambridge University Press.

de la Mare, W., Illus. by D. P. Lathrop. (1942). *Bells and grass.* New York, NY: Viking Press.

Dixon, G. T., & Tarr, P. (1988). Extending art experiences in the preschool classroom. *International Journal of Early Childhood, 20*(1), 27–34.

Dobbs, S. M. (1998). *Learning in and through art—A guide to discipline-based art education.* Los Angeles, CA: The J. Paul Getty Trust.

Feeney, S., & Moravcik, E. (1987). A thing of beauty: Aesthetic development in young children. *Young Children, 42*(6), 7–15.

Feeney, S., Moravcik, E., & Nolte, S. (2013). *Who am I in the lives of children?* (9th ed.). Upper Saddle River, NJ: Pearson.

Gee, K. (2000). *Visual arts as a way of knowing.* York, ME: Galef Institute, Stenhouse Publishers.

Gesell, A. (1946 [1977]). *The child from five to ten.* New York, NY: HarperCollins.

J. P. Getty Trust. (1985). *Beyond creating: The place for art in America's schools.* A Report by the Getty Center for Education in the Arts, April, 1985. Los Angeles, CA: Author.

Golomb. C. (2004). Sculpture: Representational development in a three dimensional medium. In E. Eisner & M. Day (Eds.), *Handbook of research and policy in art education* (pp. 32–39). Mahwah, NJ: Lawrence Erlbaum Associates Inc.

Head Start Resource Center. (2010). *The Head Start child development and early learning framework: Promoting positive outcomes in early childhood programs serving children 3–5 years old.* Washington, DC: Office of Head Start, Administration for Children and Families, U.S. Department of Health and Human Services.

Hurwitz, A., & Day, M. (2001). *Children and their art methods for the elementary school* (7th ed.). Orlando, FL: Harcourt.

Kellogg, R. (1969). *Analyzing children's art.* Palo Alto, CA: National Press Books.

Kellogg, R., & O'Dell, S. (1967). *The psychology of children's art.* New York, NY: CRM Random House.

Kindler, A. M., & Darras, B. (1997). Map of artistic development. In A. Kindler (Ed.), *Child development in art* (pp. 17–44). Reston, VA: National Art Education Association.

Lowenfeld, V. (1947). *Creative and mental growth.* New York, NY: Macmillan Publishing Company.

Lowenfeld, V., & Brittain, W. L. (1964 [1987]). *Creative and mental growth* (8th ed.). New York, NY: Macmillan Publishing Company.

Luquet, G. (1927). *Le dessin enfant.* Paris: Alcan.

Mulcahey, C. (2009). *The story in the picture: Inquiry and artmaking with young children.* New York, NY: Teachers College Press.

National Association for the Education of Young Children. (2010). *NAEYC standards for initial & advance early childhood professional preparation programs.* www.naeyc.org/files/ncate/file/NAEYC%20Initial%20and%20Advanced%20Standards%206_2011-final.pdf

Pelo, A. (2007). *The language of art: Inquiry-based studio practices in early childhood settings.* St. Paul, MN: Redleaf Press.

Pitri, E. (2001). The role of artistic play in problem solving. *Art Education, 54*(3), 46–51.

Read, H. (1943). *Education through art.* London, UK: Faber and Faber.

Rockefeller, D. J. (1977). *Coming to our senses: The significance of the arts for American education.* T. A. E. a. A. Panel. New York, NY: McGraw-Hill.

Ross, M. (1981). *The aesthetic imperative: Relevance and responsibility in art education.* Oxford, UK: Pergamon Press.

Schiller, M. (1994). Give students with special needs something to talk about. *Art Education, 47*(6), 12–15.

Schirrmacher, R. (2008). *Art and creative development for young children* (6th ed.). New York, NY: Delmar Publishers.

Smith, N. R. (1993). *Experience and art teaching children to paint* (2nd ed.). New York, NY: Teachers College Press.

Striker, S. (2001). *Young at art: Teaching toddlers self-expression, problem-solving skills, and an appreciation for art.* New York, NY: Henry Holt and Company.

Zimmerman, E., & Zimmerman, L. (2000). Art education and early childhood education: The young child as creator and meaning maker within a community context. *Young Children, 55*(6): 87–92.

MyEducationLab

Go to Topics 2: Child Development and Learning, and 9: Content Areas/Lessons and Activities in the MyEducationLab (www.myeducationlab.com) for *Meaningful Curriculum for Young Children,* where you can:

- Find learning outcomes for Child Development and Learning and Content Areas/Lessons and Activities along with the national standards that connect to these outcomes.
- Complete Assignments and Activities that can help you more deeply understand the chapter content.
- Apply and practice your understanding of the core teaching skills identified in the chapter with the Building Teaching Skills and Dispositions learning units.
- Listen to experts from the field in Professional Perspectives.

- Examine challenging situations and cases presented in the IRIS Center Resources.
- Check your comprehension on the content covered in the chapter with the Study Plan. Here you will be able to take a chapter quiz, receive feedback on your answers, and then access Review, Practice, and Enrichment activities to enhance your understanding of chapter content.

Go to the Course Resources section in MyEducationLab, where you can:

- Use the Online Lesson Plan Builder to practice lesson planning and integrating national and state standards into your planning.

Where words fail, music speaks.

HANS CHRISTIAN ANDERSEN

chapter eleven

MUSIC CURRICULUM
Creating with Heart and Voice

Before there was history, before there was writing, before there were instruments, perhaps before there was language (Levitin, 2006), there was music. Music is the art form that uses sounds organized by pitch, duration, and relationship to one another. Music is ubiquitous in our days and nights. It wakes us in the morning and soothes us at night; in between, music is our companion as we travel to work or school, it accompanies virtually all forms of entertainment, and it serves as the background for every major event of our lives.

Even before we are born, we experience music—of a heart-beat, of our mother's voice, of the music she listened to. Music is a universal language that transcends borders. It communicates feelings, makes us happy or sad, calm or excited—and can evoke feelings of patriotism, sanctity, love, and empathy. As part of the human family, whatever their age, all young children need music.

Why Music?

The most important reason to provide music in early childhood programs is that **listening to and making music brings pleasure.** Taking pleasure in music is an essential part of being human. Although music leaves no lasting product and its outcome is not immediately measurable on standardized tests, music is valuable for the joy it creates. We will outline other vital reasons to make music part of the early childhood curriculum, but the

Reflect on music in your life . . .

Think about the role of music in your life. Is it an important focus or does it serve as background to your other activities? Do you think of yourself as musical? What music do you like best? When did you start to like it? Who do you share music with? Who shared music with you? What influences the choices you make about music in your life?

fact that all human beings are attuned to and gratified by music is the most fundamental reason that it belongs in your classroom.

Another reason that music is essential in early childhood education is that **music provides a powerful and direct link to emotions.** Although young children are learning language, it is not yet the best way for them to communicate. The language of music helps you to reach children in ways that words cannot. It can calm a tense or angry child, create a mood of happy anticipation, build or defuse energy, and help children make an emotional transition to the classroom.

Sharing music with others is an important way to **be a part of a social group—a culture, a community, a family.** One of the hallmarks of any culture is its music. Even if you love popular music, you probably feel at home when you hear the familiar music of your family and culture, whether it is the precise music of a classical string quartet, the enticing rhythms of salsa, or the moving harmonies of gospel songs. The music you share with children creates a bond. The songs you share become *their* songs, those you and the children have in common. And when you play recordings of the music of their culture, they know they have come to a place that is safe.

Like science, math, and literacy, music is a serious branch of learning. The music you provide helps children begin to **learn about music as a subject** and start to **develop the skills of a musician.** As you will read later in this chapter, there are many things that young children are learning about music when you mindfully provide them with music experiences.

Music helps develop the ability to listen. In order to enjoy and make music, children must first listen. Hearing and listening are different. Hearing is the passive perception of sounds, whereas listening requires deliberate focus. Listening is vitally important in the learning process and is related to attention span and concentration. Music curriculum is a path to building this important ability.

Music can also be **a path to many other kinds of learning.** It is a powerful vehicle for *developing language*. Language used in singing provides experience with new vocabulary ("The song says that Aiken Drum played upon a ladle—have you ever seen a ladle?") and with using words in new ways ("*He'd many a-mile to go that night before he'd reach the town-o!*"). It helps to build literacy skills related to phonemic awareness (*Willoughby wallaby woo*).

Songs can be used as *mnemonic devices* for remembering facts that might not otherwise be easy to recall (do you sing the ABC song to remember whether Q comes before R?). For some people, singing facts in a song can help them to retain large amounts of information (Sacks, 2007).

There is evidence that listening to music has a **positive impact on learning** (Campbell, 2000). And there is research to suggest that children's musical skills (e.g., being able to keep the beat in a song) are linked to *school success* (Weikart, 2003).

Singing and moving together can be one of the few activities that are enjoyable for young children in a group. So it is one of the ways that young children begin to learn to be a participant in a group, and a way they **develop positive school behaviors.**

All children have musical potential. Some children have musical gifts, an early sensitivity to music coupled with a good musical memory and the ability to acquire music skills more easily—what Howard Gardner describes as *musical intelligence*. However, *all* children can learn to make, respond to, and enjoy music. To reach their potential, they need many experiences with a wide variety of music and frequent opportunities to participate in developmentally appropriate music activities.

MyEducationLab

Visit the MyEducationLab for *Meaningful Curriculum for Young Children* to enhance your understanding of chapter concepts with a personalized Study Plan. You'll also have the opportunity to hone your teaching skills through video-based Assignments and Activities, IRIS Center Resources, and Building Teaching Skills and Disposition lessons.

Understanding Musical Development

How do children learn to make music—to sing, to play, to create? A hundred years ago there were no radios, no TVs, few record players, and few musical superstars. But every town had musicians; most homes had pianos, guitars, or fiddles; and almost all people made music. They sang and played with and for each other as entertainment. Singing, like talking, was something that everyone did. No one said, "I can't sing." This is still true in many cultures and many places. But today, in America and in some other societies, many adults, including teachers and parents, are musically mute and passive. They allow experts and machines to make all their music. And because of this, their children become musically mute and passive.

Children need not grow up feeling that music is only created by experts. Young children's musical responses are strong. From the first moments of life, they are soothed by quiet music and respond to a distinct beat and quick tempo with strong, rhythmic movement. Music evokes and describes feelings, and provides an emotional outlet. As they grow, children may come to express feelings of joy or sadness with a song. They may express angry or aggressive feelings in a dance. And as preschoolers, they can come to understand, in simple terms, the elements that make up the discipline of music.

Music is both a cultural and a social experience. People have bonds that are cemented by the music they share (Levitin, 2006). So it is not surprising that the musical culture of the home will have a profound influence on a preschooler's musical expression. Since practically all people listen to music, virtually all children come to you with musical heritage. A child whose family listens to music from their culture will sing and respond to this music, as will a child whose family prefers to listen to popular radio.

On her first day of life, Molly hears music. She sleeps in an incubator in her mother's hospital room. The lights are low and a CD of soft Celtic music is playing. It is comfortingly familiar to Molly; it is the music her mother played throughout her pregnancy. While Molly nurses, her mother croons to her, singing old tunes with new words repeating over and over that Molly is loved and wanted. When her father takes a turn, he too sings songs in praise of Molly. Molly has started a life that will be filled with music.

From birth, children respond to music physically and enthusiastically. Research has shown that infants recognize the music they were exposed to *in utero*. They respond to music that is *consonant* (pleasant with stable, predictable harmonies) rather than music that is *dissonant* (harsh, clashing and unharmonious) (Levitin, 2006).

As an infant, Molly responds to music with smiles and coos—sometimes it is the only thing that can calm her when she is unhappy. Like all babies, she makes music when she cries. In distress, her cries are high pitched. When she is hungry, her cries are lower pitched and have a regular rhythm. And there is music in her happy vocalizations—she "lalls" and "trills" in response to her parents' talking and singing.

Molly loves her "Baa-baa" music box and her elephant rattle. Both her parents sing to her—though sometimes now they sing "Molly is a fussy girl." Molly, unaware of the criticism, stops fussing and vocalizes along with them and moves her body to the song. The familiar CD is played to soothe her to sleep each night.

In many ways, music precedes speech. Crying is a baby's first sound. Pitch, loudness, and rhythm are aspects of a song and a cry that have meaning parents and caregivers come to understand. Infants' first vocalizations are akin to song and are called *lalling* and *trilling*. Favorite toys are often objects that make sounds: rattles, chimes, bells, drums, and music boxes. By 10 months, infants indicate preferences for music by rocking, swaying, kicking, or clapping hands to a favorite tune and becoming quiet for favorite lullabies.

As a toddler, Molly loves to dance. She spins and twirls to lively music played on the boom box. Her mom and dad dance with her. Her favorite song is one made up by her father ("Molly-Moo has lost her shoe") and she sings the chorus often ("Shoe-shoe-shoe—where's my shoe?"). Twice a week she goes to a parent-child play morning and Molly sings simple songs with the other toddlers. At night her favorite CD continues to be her lullaby.

By 18 months, toddlers begin to sing and explore sound. Nursery rhymes and songs are much enjoyed. Toddlers rarely learn to sing whole songs, but will learn melodic fragments (*e-i-e-i-o*)—though they usually sing them with their own words (*ya-ya-yee-yee-o*) and place fragments from different songs together.

Children come to early childhood music experiences from diverse backgrounds. By age 2 they show a preference for music from their culture (i.e., the music they hear in their home). Children's home languages and cultures can enrich your music program when you view them as valuable and welcome them into the classroom.

From age 2, children "dance" with swaying bodies, bending knees, and swinging arms. Two-year-olds sing within a limited vocal range and move to music at their own tempo. Throughout the toddler years, music and movement are almost inextricable. When they listen, sing, or play an instrument, children also must dance.

When she is 3, Molly attends preschool. She likes the other children and enjoys group time when the children gather to sing songs to the accompaniment of the teacher's autoharp. However, separation is hard and although they play soft music at naptime, Molly finds it hard to sleep—it's not her *music. The teacher invites Molly's family to come in and join them at circle time. Molly's dad teaches the class the "Molly-Moo has lost her shoe" song. Soon the whole class is singing the song, substituting other names ("Ralphie-Roo has lost his shoe"). The children invent actions to go with the song.*

Three- and four-year olds have a great deal more physical coordination and language skill than toddlers. Their ability to participate in music activities is much greater. They can reproduce tunes, but cannot easily match their pitch to that of others. For this reason, teachers must learn to match their pitch to that of the children. Like toddlers, they have a limited singing range. Preschoolers typically sing best from about D to A above middle C, the range of the "teasing chant" (Greenberg, 1979). However, there is research to suggest that children can sing with greater range and accuracy if they have a wider experience of music coupled with adults who have greater expectations of their vocal ability (Flowers & Dunne-Sousa, 1990). In other words, if you provide children with more musical experiences, sing with them more, and ask them to sing with you more often, they will have greater musical ability.

Preschoolers are among the most active of song creators, and they often make up repetitive, atonal songs as they go about their daily activities. Movement is often an inspiration for the creation of songs. A child swinging on a swing, riding a trike, or riding a see-saw will often sing to herself to the rhythm of the physical activity ("Swinging, swinging, I am swinging. Swinging, swinging, I am swinging. Up up up, down down down. Swinging, swinging see me swinging"). Preschoolers especially like action songs and musical games (do you remember dancing the *Hokey Pokey*?). Young preschoolers also enjoy playing simple rhythm instruments, although without guidance, little distinction is made between noise making and rhythmic accompaniment. Table 11.1 lists milestones in children's musical development.

TABLE 11.1   Milestones in Children's Musical Development

Age	Typical Musical Characteristics/Milestones
Infant/Toddler (Birth to 3 years)	• Responds to music by listening and moving from birth • Uses objects as sound makers • Experiments with sounds in a musical way (*lalling* and *trilling*) • Responds to music by vocalizing (from 6 months) • Echoes back tones sung by others • Sings for the first time at approximately 18 months • Shows preference for songs from their home culture at age 2
Younger Preschooler (3–4 years)	• Responds particularly to strongly rhythmic music • Moves and sings to music • Sings spontaneously in play • Has comfortable singing range from D to A above middle C • Repeats and requests the same song many times • Joins in when others are singing • Able to match simple tunes • Uses simple rhythm instruments • Responds to music with movement, but at own tempo
Older Preschooler/ Kindergartner (4–6 years)	• Has increased singing range, A below middle C to C# an octave above middle C • Matches pitch and tempo with increased accuracy • Easily participates in group music activities and games • Sings entire songs accurately • Synchronizes movement with music rhythm and tempo • Enjoys focused listening activities • Begins to identify familiar tunes • Adds dynamics to singing • Identifies and uses simple instruments appropriately with guidance
Primary School Child (6–8 years)	• Sings accurately (on pitch/tempo) with sensitivity • Has strong sense of rhythm • Evaluates own musical ability critically • Begins to identify harmony and sing simple "parts" (e.g., rounds) by age 8 • Begins to enjoy rehearsal and performance • Expends serious effort and ability to master musical skills if interested • Uses "real" instruments with instruction (e.g., piano, guitar, violin) and begins to learn notation

By age 4 1/2 or 5, if given opportunity, encouragement, and musical experience, most children sing tunefully in a range that exceeds an octave (Flowers & Dunne-Sousa, 1990), understand basic music concepts (loud/soft, fast/slow), remember songs with several verses, move rhythmically to music, and play simple instruments appropriately. If they have had limited music experience, more time and experience will be needed to develop these skills. Of course, each child is an individual and brings his or her own unique music interest and abilities. And each will take away the knowledge and skill that he or she is capable of understanding and developing.

What Is Music Curriculum in Early Childhood?

Music curriculum for young children can be thought of as experiences with music that we offer rather than concepts about music that we teach. When children are provided appropriate music experiences, they develop musical awareness and understanding (the *elements* of music) and they acquire musical skills and dispositions (the *processes* of a musician). These processes and elements constitute a framework for what children learn in the early childhood music curriculum.

Music Elements

Musical *elements* (rhythm, tone, and form) are the raw materials out of which every piece of music is made. The organization of these elements is what distinguishes music from noise. Even if you have no musical training yourself, you respond to musical elements and intuitively understand them. However, you may not be able to easily identify and talk about what you comprehend. It is useful for you, as a teacher, to have a more formal knowledge of the building blocks of music and to possess the vocabulary to talk about them. You will use these words in your planning, in talking to colleagues, and in sharing with family members.

Although learning about the elements in isolation is not meaningful to young children, they will encounter these elements as they experience music. Sometimes you will mention them as you teach children. As you provide music experiences, talk to the children, and encourage them to listen, you are teaching about musical elements in natural and appropriate ways.

Rhythm

Time and movement in a piece of music is called *rhythm*. Movement in music is powerful both for listening and for music making. It is the part of the music that makes you want to get up and dance. It's what compels young children to move their bodies when you play Cajun, salsa, reggae, or classic rock and roll music in the classroom.

Rhythm includes *beat,* the musical pulse that you respond to by tapping your toes, swaying, or clapping. Beat is sometimes referred to by educators as *steady beat*. Every song has a pattern of strong and weak beats (e.g., the 1st note of each line in *Twinkle, Twinkle Little Star* is a strong beat—you feel it as heavier and more important than the other 3 beats in each line). Next time you sing the song with children, try clapping and saying, "Let's clap the beat of *Twinkle, Twinkle Little Star*."

The notes in a melody and the beat of the song do not always perfectly align. *Melodic rhythm* (sometimes known as *meter*) is the rhythm of the melody in a piece of music or words in a song. When you clap to every syllable of a song as if you were singing it, you are demonstrating the melodic rhythm. When you clap to the words of *Twinkle, Twinkle Little Star,* you are clapping one melodic rhythm. When you clap to the words of *Baa Baa Black Sheep* (the same tune!), you must add additional claps (*have you any wool*) because it has a different melodic rhythm. Melodic rhythm makes many songs instantly recognizable. If you have never noticed that *Twinkle, Twinkle Little Star, Baa Baa Black Sheep,* and the *Alphabet Song* all have the same melody, it's because you were attuned to their different melodic rhythms. Try clapping the *rhythm of the words* with children—make it a game—"Am I clapping *Baa Baa Black Sheep* or *Twinkle, Twinkle?*"

Speed in music is called *tempo*—fastness or slowness. Tempo helps to convey emotion. Most fast songs feel happy, and most slow songs feel sad or ominous. If you sing the last verse of *Puff the Magic Dragon* slowly, you express Puff's sadness as Jackie Paper leaves childhood. When you resume a quicker tempo for the final chorus, you express the hopefulness that the dragon will find another child companion.

The points of silence in a piece of music are called *rests.* They are essential parts of a song, although they are not easily recognized by children. You can distinguish these more easily when they are very distinct, as in the rest that occurs just before the chorus of *The Battle Hymn of the Republic.*

Tone

Whereas rhythm concerns the movement of music, *tone* concerns the sounds you hear. It involves *pitch,* the highness or lowness of a tone, and *melody* or *tune,* the arrangement of notes into a sequence. Tone also involves the way the notes sound. A tone has color or *timbre* (pronounced *tám-ber*), a characteristic sound because of the instrument or voice that made the tone, and *dynamics,* the loudness or softness of the tone.

Pitch is caused by vibration. A longer, thicker string on a bass, a bigger drumhead on a kettle drum, and a taller air column in a bassoon vibrate more slowly, and so these instruments sound lower than a violin, snare drum, or flute. People have given names to different tones (called *notes*—C, D, E, F, F#, etc.). Notes repeat in octaves (groups of 12 notes—8 notes, 4 sharps/flats) that are higher or lower.

Children's vocal cords are shorter than those of adults, and so their voices are about an octave higher than those of most women, and two octaves higher than those of most men. This sometimes makes it hard for adults and children to sing "on pitch" together. It means that you have to start songs at a higher pitch to make it easier for children to sing (remember you can sing the song an octave or two lower). Difference in pitch conveys different moods. *Happy Birthday* trilled on a flute sounds happy; in the low booming voice of a tuba, it sounds melancholic or silly.

Notes strung together make a *melody.* You recognize a melody because you remember the relationship of the tones to one another or the pattern of tones. This pattern is recognizable whether it's played higher or lower, louder or softer, faster or slower. As you sing with children, you can help them to be aware of melody by talking about the tunes you sing: "Does the melody of *ABC* remind you of any other song?"

Difference in *timbre* (for example, between a violin and a flute) is one of the elements to which children first respond in infancy and then strongly respond to throughout early childhood. Timbre communicates emotion. The bright sounds of a flute convey a very different feeling than the mellow timbre of a cello.

Try It Out!

Think of a simple, familiar song you could sing with a preschool age child. Plan several ways to purposefully and playfully introduce some of the musical elements—e.g., *"Now let's clap to the beat!"* Try your ideas out with a child you know.

Dynamics refers to the loudness or softness of tones. Children are very responsive to dynamics. With time, practice, and support, they can learn to control whether they sing a song or play an instrument loudly or softly. This is best accomplished if it is presented as an interesting challenge. It is important to remember that young children are exuberant and loud when they enjoy a song or an instrument, so playing or singing softly can be challenging for them. However, even 3-year-olds can learn to sing rather than shout.

Form

The structure of musical pieces is called *form.* All songs are composed of *phrases,* short but complete musical ideas. The first line of *The Eency Weency Spider* is an example of a phrase. *Repetition* occurs when identical musical phrases are used in a song, as in the first and last lines of *Twinkle, Twinkle Little Star.* A phrase that is obviously different from the ones that came before provides *contrast,* like the third line of *Happy Birthday to You.* When similar phrases occur in a song (like the first two lines of *Shoo Fly*), it is called *variation.* As you play several chords or sing 1-2-3 to establish the pitch and tempo of a song before you start to sing it, you are providing an *introduction.* And when you close a song by singing the last line a little more slowly or with a slightly different tune, it is called *coda.*

The Processes of a Musician

Another part of the music curriculum involves helping young children begin to develop the skills of a musician. Musicians develop numerous technical skills, many of which are beyond the capacity of a young child. The skills that are acquired in early childhood are called *musicianly processes.* These serve as the basis for the activities that we provide in the music curriculum.

Singing

Singing is among the most human of musical activities. People have always sung songs: to calm themselves and their children, to entertain others, to pass the time, to remember and share information, and to have fun. Singing is instantly accessible to anyone with vocal cords. It offers opportunities for children to experience music and to develop musical appreciation and understanding. The best songs for young children to sing are relatively short and simple, contain a distinct rhythm, and have a relatively small vocal range.

Playing Instruments

Playing simple instruments helps young children to acquire musical skills and understanding. Regular experience with instruments gives children the opportunity to construct understanding of the ways that musical sounds are produced. They learn about the nature of sound (tapping wood sounds different from tapping a cymbal) and how their actions influence the music (a hard tap makes a louder sound than a soft tap). It helps them to learn about musical elements like beat and timbre. It also can help them to learn to listen. Children's initial exploration of instruments will almost inevitably result in cacophony (unpleasant noise), similar to the way their first play with blocks may be to make an untidy heap on the floor. As in piling blocks, this musical exploration is a necessary first stage. It may require teacher guidance to help children see the potential of the material and engage in more productive play (i.e., music making as opposed to noise making).

Composing and Improvising

Does composing and improvising sound too sophisticated for young children? When you hear children singing to themselves as they play, that's often what they're doing. Many young children spontaneously create (*compose*) and change (*improvise*) songs to accompany their play. The songs they know from home, learn in school, and hear on TV and radio are incorporated into their repertoire of melodies, phrases, and rhythms that they will use in their own creative music. When you help children think of new words to a familiar song or create an accompaniment with an instrument, they are *improvising*.

When a child or group of children creates a song with new words, melody, and accompaniment, they are *composing*. If you help them think about their songs and preserve their work by taping it or writing it down (see Work Sample 11.1), you are scaffolding their composing so that they can eventually compose music on their own.

Listening and Appreciating

Have you ever known a child who wanted to hear a song sung or a recording played over and over? Were you such a child yourself? Children *appreciate* and enjoy *listening* to music made by others. When you have professional and amateur musicians (even you!) play instruments and sing in the classroom, it helps children to understand that *music is made by real people*. This is important! Imagine learning to use a computer, drive a car, or read a book if you had never seen anyone doing so. Children are not music critics. They will enjoy and benefit from hearing and seeing a family member, teacher, or neighbor singing or playing an instrument. If more accomplished musicians are a part of your school or personal community, be sure to invite them to come to your classroom and make music.

Work Sample 11.1 **Child-Composed Song**

We Like Bugs!
composed by the Dancing Dragons (4- and 5-year-olds)

Chorus: We like bugs! We like bugs! We like bugs! Oh we like bugs!
We like the butterflies! We like the dragonflies
We like the cockroaches! We like stink bugs!

They fly, they run, they eat, they buzz.
They grow chrysalises, they shed their skins.

We like the ladybugs! We like the centipedes!
We like the scorpions, we like praying mantids!

They fight, they bite, they hide under leaves,
They pinch, they inch, and ladybugs fly!

We like walking sticks! We like grasshoppers!
We like spiders! We like bees!

Some taste bad. Some look like fruit.
Some are camouflaged. Some make honey.

Recorded music also can provide important experiences for children. What kind of recorded music should you provide for children to listen to? Children deserve to hear music that is well crafted and that provides a good example of its particular genre. The National Association for Music Education (MENC) states the following in its position statement on music and early childhood education: "Children's learning time is valuable and should not be wasted on experiences with music or activities of trite or questionable quality." They suggest that we include music of "high quality and lasting value, including traditional children's songs, folk songs, classical music, and music from a variety of cultures, styles, and time periods" (MENC, 1991). Unfortunately, music created specifically for classrooms often does not meet this standard. Often they are not good examples of their genre, attempt to barrage children with facts, or coax them into good behavior. Recordings for children should be as enjoyable for adults who like the genre as they are for children. If the music makes you wince (and you usually like the style), it's not good music. We include a list of some of our favorite recordings for children in Table 11.2. There are many more! If your favorite children's recording artists are not included here, it's probably because there just wasn't room to list them.

Choose diverse styles of music along with music from different cultures. Look for music that has withstood the test of time, and be wary of recordings that promise to teach children to read, learn math, behave well, or achieve cardiovascular fitness: Their primary purpose is not musical, and they often aren't very good music (unless the music was written by a musician with understanding of and sensitivity to children, as well as a sense of humor). The resource list at the end of the chapter provides Web sites that include recommendations for recordings of children's music.

Performing

Because the goal of music education is to help children to become comfortable with musical expression, *performance* is the least important part of the music curriculum for young children. Performing for others is another musician's skill. However, it requires the ability to take the perspective of others (the audience) and it can cause anxiety and stress, so formal performance is not appropriate for preschoolers. The MENC position statement asserts: "[Young] Children should not be encumbered with the need to meet performance goals" (1991).

Since preschoolers are generally not self-conscious with people they know well, an appropriate alternative to formal performance is to invite family members to participate in or observe a group music time in the classroom. It may seem to the adults that they are watching children perform, but to the children it will feel like a normal music time.

Standards for Music Curriculum

What are the goals of the music curriculum? Head Start and almost all states have standards for preschool music curriculum, although some states combine all the arts and have standards that do not differentiate art, music, and dance (creative movement). A national consortium of arts education organizations has created music standards for children in grades K–4 that are the same as the standards for K–12, but with age-appropriate indicators.

Preschool Music Standards

Head Start Child Development and Early Learning Framework for music is very simple. It lays out the expectations that children will participate in music activities and experiment with musical instruments. (See Figure 11.1.)

TABLE 11.2   A Few Artists and Their Recordings for Children That We Like

Genre	Artists	Recording
Traditional Folk Music	Pete Seeger	*Birds, Beasts and Little Fishes*
	Ella Jenkins	*Play Your Instruments*
	Raffi	*Singable Songs for the Very Young*
	Sam Hinton	*Whoever Shall Have Some Good Peanuts*
Contemporary Singer/Songwriters	Jack Johnson	*Sing-A-Longs and Lullabies from the Film Curious George*
	Cathy Fink and Marcy Marxer	*Pillow Full Of Dreams*
	Tom Chapin	*Mother Earth*
Blues	Keb Mo	*Big Wide Grin*
	Taj Mahal	*Shake Sugaree*
	Sweet Honey in the Rock	*I Got Shoes*
Rock and Roll	The Sippy Cups	*One Day Soon*
	Eric Herman	*The Kid in the Mirror*
	Sandra Boynton and Michael Ford	*Philadelphia Chicken*
Reggae	Ziggy Marley	*Family Time*
	Bob Marley	*B Is for Bob*
Classical	New York Philharmonic	*Bernstein's Favorites: Children's Classics*
	Anastasi Mavrides	*Classical Child at the Opera*
Celtic	Golden Bough	*Celtic Songs for Children*
	The Clancy Children	*Irish Songs for Children*
World Music	Putamayo	*World Playground*
	Various	*The Rough Guide to World Music for Children*

FIGURE 11.1   Head Start Child Development and Early Learning Framework: *Music*

The use of voice and instruments to create sounds.
- Participates in music activities, such as listening, singing, or performing.
- Experiments with musical instruments.

Source: Administration for Children and Families, Head Start Bureau, www.hsnrc.org/cdi/child-outcomes.cfm

FIGURE 11.2 **Summary of Additional Preschool Music Standards from Different States**

Singing

- Sing expressively—independently and with others.
- Approximate pitch in singing.
- Create and improvise simple songs and rhythmic patterns.

Listening

- Listen to various kinds of music.

Acquiring Musical Knowledge

- Begin to identify music elements and techniques.
- Distinguish between different types of music (loud/soft, fast/slow, happy/sad, etc.).

Appreciating Music

- Demonstrate a preference in music.
- Select and recognize a variety of songs from diverse cultures.
- Respond to different musical styles through movement and play.
- Demonstrate appreciation for different forms of music.

FIGURE 11.3 **National Standards for Arts Education: *Music***

What every K–4 student should know and be able to do in the arts.

Standard 1: Singing, alone and with others, a varied repertoire of music

Standard 2: Performing on instruments, alone and with others, a varied repertoire of music

Standard 3: Improvising melodies, variations, and accompaniments

Standard 4: Composing and arranging music within specified guidelines

Standard 5: Reading and notating music

Standard 6: Listening to, analyzing, and describing music

Standard 7: Evaluating music and music performances

Standard 8: Understanding relationships between music, the other arts, and disciplines outside the arts

Standard 9: Understanding music in relation to history and culture

Source: From *National Standards for Arts Education.* Copyright © 1994 by The National Association for Music Education (MENC). Used with permission.

Participation and using instruments are included in the music standards in almost all states. However, additional expectations are included in most states' standards (though no state includes them all). These are summarized in Figure 11.2.

Primary Grades Music Standards

A Consortium of Music Educators (called the National Committee for Standards in the Arts) has developed music curriculum standards for children in K–4 programs (Figure 11.3). The standards for these grades are identical to those for K–12. However, the indicators (not included here) are differentiated for the primary grades and can be found at the National Association for Music Education (MENC) Web site: (www.menc.org/resources/view/national-standards-for-music-education/).

Teaching Music

Every young child's day should include music. It should be part of the program environment, included in the daily schedule, and part of your interactions with children. Of course, it should also be part of your planning.

Music Through Play in a Planned Environment

Young children learn about all subject areas through play in a planned environment in which they can try on roles, fantasize, and explore new ideas. How is this true for music? Children's play often involves singing, creating sounds, and musical improvisation. They sing or create songs as they play with dolls, dig in the sand, look at books, or paint at the easel. They explore sounds as they run a stick along a fence, tap two blocks together, or run the marbles down a marble runway.

Equipping a Classroom for Music Learning

How does the environment support children's musical play? Young children can make music everywhere, so it is important that every classroom has the raw materials from which the music curriculum can be created. We begin our discussion of the environment by describing the equipment and materials important to the music curriculum.

A Sound System and Recordings

Every early childhood classroom needs a serviceable sound system and a collection of recorded music that includes good children's recordings and other musical genres that reflect children's cultures as well as classical, folk, jazz, and world beat. The recordings you play in the classroom will help children feel at home and will make them aware of musical alternatives.

Should you have music playing all the time? No! Recorded music is so commonplace in our society that it has become audible wallpaper—something that is ignored and unheard. For this reason, we recommend against playing recorded music constantly (or commercial radio at any time). There are a number of public radio stations that have excellent children's music programming as well as a Web site called KPR (Kid's Public Radio) that has 2 music program streams that we believe are worth listening to. However, since you cannot control what is played, we do not recommend that you use them in the classroom.

Instruments for Teachers to Play

Was there a piano in your kindergarten classroom? It was once assumed that every teacher would be able to play piano to accompany children's singing, so a piano was a standard piece of equipment in early childhood classrooms. This is not true today.

However, every teacher should be able to play an instrument (a keyboard or a guitar, autoharp, ukulele, or other easily held instrument such as a banjo, mandolin, or dulcimer) to accompany music activities. You need not be a music expert. Playing a few simple chords on at least one of these instruments is within virtually everyone's ability. We recommend that you take a few lessons or teach yourself with the aid of a book (see Figure 11.4). You'll be glad you did. Even our least musically inclined students report great success once they pick up an instrument and start to play. Tuners are available free online to make tuning relatively easy (www.seventhstring.com/tuner/tuner.html and www.get-tuned.com/online_tuners.php).

Instruments for Children to Play

A collection of simple instruments that children can play is another essential part of the classroom music environment. Good instruments for children are well made, have good tone, and are satisfying and easy to play. Rhythm instruments (non-pitched percussion instruments) are easy and satisfying for children to play.

FIGURE 11.4 **Books to Help You Teach Yourself to Play an Instrument**

Country & Blues Guitar for the Musically Hopeless by Carol McComb
You Can Teach Yourself Autoharp by Meg Peterson
Play Ukulele Today!: A Complete Guide to the Basics by Barret Tagliarino

FIGURE 11.5 **Essential Rhythm Instruments for a Preschool Classroom**

There should be duplicates (or triplicates) of every instrument and enough of one or two types so that all the children can sometimes play the same ones.

- Tone Block
- Hand Drum
- Tambourine
- Maracas
- Triangles and Strikers
- Cow Bell
- Small Cymbals
- Claves
- Sandpaper Blocks
- Rhythm Sticks (a pair for each child)
- Egg Shakers (one for each child)
- Wrist Bells (one for each child)

We strongly believe that young children deserve to have real, good-quality instruments rather than homemade noisemakers. They must fit well in small hands, be sturdy enough to take the enthusiastic handling of many young children, and, of course, they must sound good. A good drum, tone block, or triangle is tuned to a particular pitch and when struck has a sound that rings out (a poorly made one will just thud). Figure 11.5 provides a list of the essential rhythm instruments needed for a preschool classroom.

Good instruments are an investment. They should be stored and handled carefully like any other piece of valuable equipment. Used as dramatic play props, tossed into a box for storage, or left lying on the floor to be stepped on, they will have a short life span. If you treat them in this way you are demonstrating that you think musical instruments need not be treated (or played) with care. We like to store rhythm instruments carefully, with each type housed in its own basket or box out of reach of children. Purposefully make them available when you want to give children an opportunity to explore and play.

Classroom Areas That Inspire Music

A few areas especially inspire children's musical expression. Areas where children are engaged in fantasy play such as dramatic play or blocks motivate musical accompaniment: singing to the baby doll, humming a tune while building with blocks, or representing a character by chanting a refrain (*Fee-Fi-Fo-Fum!*). When children are involved in rhythmic physical activity, they often add song to their play (outdoors in the active play zone, swinging on swings, indoors in the sensory area, or rocking in a rocking chair). Areas where children can be physically or psychologically alone (in a carpet lined crate in the library, in the bathroom, under the play structure) also seem to move children to make music.

A music area?

It is possible to include a music area in a preschool classroom. In fact, you may have been told that it is important to have one. Although we love and appreciate music, as preschool teachers and professors who supervise students in diverse settings, we disagree with the practice of creating a music area similar to the dramatic play or block area.

It may be *because* we love and appreciate music and musical instruments that we feel music centers in preschool classrooms are usually not appropriate. Here is an example of what we often see.

> It is activity time in the Blueberry Room. Children build with blocks, dress up and pretend, do puzzles, look at books, paint at an easel, and play with play-dough. In one corner, they play in the music center. The area is small (there wasn't much space left after placing all the other centers).
>
> In the middle of the floor in the music center there is a beautiful, big "gathering drum." On the shelves there are rhythm sticks, a good-quality tambourine, a xylophone, scarves for dancing, a basket of egg shakers, and music books.
>
> Jamie is joyfully using rhythm sticks to bang on the drum. Alana shakes the tambourine. Marco whips a scarf back and forth as he dances. Sandi, the teacher, watches from the library where she is trying to read to a few children (noise from the music area makes it hard). She smiles because the children are purposefully involved in making music. Sandi returns to the story.
>
> A moment later Alana drops the tambourine (purchase price $20.00) on the floor—it clangs, a fracture appears, and a jingle falls off. Marco steps backwards as he dances and falls onto the drum. At the sound, Sandi leaves the story to go to help. Fortunately, no one was hurt. Unfortunately, in addition to the tambourine being fractured, the head of the gathering drum (purchase price $207.00) is also broken. Suddenly, the equipment budget for two months has been spent.

The essence of learning centers in a preschool classroom is that they are places where children can play independently. Teachers provide appropriate materials, structure, guidance, and supervision. But good-quality musical instruments are not toys. Unlike blocks and sturdy puzzles, they are fragile. The natural and appropriate play of young children is exuberant. They are just learning to control the force of movements like hitting a drum or tambourine. They need space to move and dance to music. The children in the above vignette were behaving well and following the rules of the classroom. The teacher was supervising. But the children gained little from the experience, and the overall impact on the classroom was negative.

We believe most preschool music centers negatively impact the aural (sound) environment. They create an unpleasant atmosphere in which it is hard to concentrate or appreciate music. They fail to provide much music learning and show disrespect for the good-quality instruments that young children deserve to use.

There are other ways to give children the positive exploration experiences that are the intention of teachers who set up music centers. Sound exploration activities can be added. A wide variety of one-on-one teacher-child activities promote music exploration and understanding, but these are guided rather than independent activities. These guided activities require space, and you might have a special corner for them—but not a music center for independent exploration. We will talk about these kinds of activities in the section on music activities (see pages 347–352).

The Library Area

You may be surprised to find the library area listed as one of the classroom areas that supports music development. We place it here for several reasons. Many picture books have been created to illustrate songs. Children are attracted to song picture books. The illustrations help them understand the concepts and lyrics, and make the songs easier to understand and enjoy. There are hundreds of such books available at your local library. They include favorite children's songs like John Langstaff's *Frog Went A Courtin'*, Pete Seeger's *Abiyoyo,* and Simms Taback's *There Was an Old Lady Who Swallowed a Fly*. Familiar adult songs that children enjoy have also been made into picture books (often with accompanying CDs) such as Pete Seeger's *Turn, Turn Turn,* Rodgers & Hammerstein's *My Favorite Things,* and Will Smith's *Just the Two of Us*. Illustrated books with songs that are enjoyed by children but are difficult to sing such as *The Teddy Bears' Picnic* and *This Land is Your Land* are good musical additions to the library. Holiday songs like Ezra Jack Keats's *Little Drummer Boy* and Maxie Baum's *I Have A Little Dreidel* have also been made into appealing picture books.

In addition to housing picture books, the library can be a location for collections of children's songs such as Langstaff's *Songs to Grow On,* Imoto's *Best-Loved Children's Songs from Japan,* and Hall's *Los Pollitos Dicen/The Baby Chicks Sing*. These usually include illustrations and expose children to musical notation. Many teachers place a listening center (a CD player with multiple headsets) in the library, and these can be used for listening to both music and recorded stories.

Music Outdoors

Is there a place for music outdoors? Yes! Music can and should be included in the outdoor environment. The simplest way is to provide space and time for children to run, jump, ride, swing, climb, build, create, and relax. All of these activities may lead to spontaneous singing.

You can bring music experiences outdoors. Hang a tuned wind chime (chimes made with metal tubing in which each piece is in tune so that the resulting sound is music rather than noise) in a tree and nature will become your musician. Play good music on a portable player outside and inspire children to dance with scarves or ribbons. Bring a guitar or autoharp and a blanket outside, and sit under a tree and sing together. Add rhythm instruments and let children play along.

Another way to provide children with the opportunity to explore musical sounds is by adding musical elements to the permanent structures in the yard. Many playground manufacturers have created music features (drums, xylophones, and other musical equipment) that can be added to play yards. These are permanent installations that are expensive, so you can't create them on your own. However, you can inexpensively add sound features to your play yard. On a fence, hang lengths of wood, metal, and plastic pipes (from the hardware store), pans and pots (from the thrift store), and other safe objects (be creative!) and let children explore the sounds these make (hang a canister filled with wooden and metal spoons to use as strikers). Lengths of PVC pipes make whispering tubes through which children can explore sounds as they talk or sing songs to one another.

A Schedule for Music Learning

Music blossoms in a program in which time is allowed both for self-directed play and teacher-guided music. The combination is essential. Daily group music times should be planned into every program. Just as you would not have a day without a story or lunch, you should not have a day without music. They are equally essential.

Your Role in Teaching Music

I don't sing because I'm happy; I'm happy because I sing.

WILLIAM JAMES

Do you love to sing? Are you confident about your ability to share music with others? Do you dread the idea of teaching music? Are you worried that you don't have much to offer children? Or are you somewhere in between? In our experience, teachers seem to be less comfortable teaching music today than they were a generation ago. Of course, there are exceptions.

> *Spring was a musician before she became a preschool teacher, so it was as natural as breathing for her to include music in the classroom. She made up songs during transitions, hummed lullabies at naptime, introduced musical elements using rhythm instruments, sang folk songs and show tunes at group time, and taught herself to accompany them on the ukulele. She encouraged children's families to bring in CDs to listen and dance to. The children in Spring's class sang, made up songs, danced, explored sound, and talked about music.*

If you are like Spring, you intuitively know that your role as a teacher is to bring your love of music into the classroom in many ways. If so, you are lucky. Teaching music in preschool is something that will be a joy for you from the very first day. Or . . . perhaps you are like Jodi, another teacher we know.

> *Jodi had been told by her 1st grade teacher that she sang out of tune. When she was 7, her mother told her she sang like a frog. Jodi had not sung in front of anyone since that day. She joked that the only instrument she played was the radio. Jodi rarely sang with the children, and she knew few songs. Instead she played "easy listening" radio and CDs. Jodi's group times rarely included music. The children in her class were similarly unmusical.*

If you are like Jodi, you have some barriers to overcome. It may give you some comfort to know that many teachers feel just like you. It may make you even happier to know that virtually everyone can make music with young children. What should you do?

Sing!

It's hard to bring music to young children unless you sing with them. You don't have to impress anyone or go on stage. You probably sing a lot better than you think you do. Children will be your most uncritical audience. They will enjoy your singing (they really will!). Sing with children every day, throughout the day—individually in spontaneous activities, during transitions, and during planned group times.

Do you worry that you might be out of tune when you sing? If so, you may lack confidence and become tense. Singing, like any physical activity, is best done if your muscles are relaxed and strong. If you are tense, you won't sound good. When you sing with confidence, you will sound much better.

It's also possible that you have an unconventional voice. There is no one kind of voice that is right for singing! Some people love the raspy voices of Bob Dylan and Susan Tedeschi or the nasal voices of Willie Nelson and Avril Lavigne. Some people hate the sound of trained operatic voices, but others think opera is one of the highest forms of art. What is pleasing to your ear depends a good deal on your expectations and culture. You will enjoy singing a whole lot more if

you learn to appreciate the voice you have instead of wishing you sounded like someone else.

If you have avoided singing for a long time, both your voice and your ear are out of practice. You may have trouble controlling your vocal cords and breathing. You may not know how to listen to the music and adjust your voice to what you hear. The best way to overcome these problems is to sing with other people. As you sing with them, you will strengthen your voice, develop control, and learn to listen and match your pitch to the others' voices. Join a choir or chorus if you can. If you can't, sing along with the radio. No matter what, sing with the children. Just sing.

Be Enthusiastic!

Music should be joyful. When you share music with young children, be enthusiastic! Show you like music by smiling, clapping, tapping your feet, and dancing as you sing or listen to music. When you are enthusiastic, you give a powerful message to children. You are saying, "This is worthwhile. This is something I care about. This is something I enjoy—and you will too." Putting on a CD and instructing children to sing along as you stand by unmoving and unsmiling also gives a message—a bad one.

Be Spontaneous!

Children are naturally spontaneous music makers. You can and should be, too. Spontaneous music making simply means adding music to play and routines. You are a spontaneous music maker if you sing a song you know at an appropriate moment (for example, singing the song *See the Fishes* as you watch the guppies in the class aquarium or the song *Mr. Sun* as the sun peeks out from behind a cloud). Creating new words to suit a situation (e.g., singing "Jenni wore a new hat, a new hat, a new hat. Jenni wore a new hat, to school today"—to the tune of *Mary Wore Her Red Dress*) requires only slightly more creativity.

Another way to be a spontaneous music maker is by making a chant (using 1 to 3 notes sung repetitively and rhythmically) to go with an activity while it is in process. This is akin to the recitative or arioso of an opera (the sung bits in-between the arias). These are not great music—it's just singing what you're doing in the same way that you might talk about it. We have heard teachers chant: "Come to the circle everyone. Now it's time to have some fun!" (repeated until everyone gets there); "Washing, washing, washing hands—bubbles on the top and bubbles in between!" (repeated until the hands are clean); "Stir the cookies up, stir the cookies up, Stir and stir and stir stir stir" (repeated until the dough is mixed); "My turn, your turn, everybody gets a turn" (repeated until everyone gets a turn).

Many teachers create special clapping rhythms to alert children to a transition or to get children's attention (*CLAP*, *CLAP*, clap-clap-clap. *CLAP*, *CLAP*, clap-clap-clap). This is both a management strategy and a way to include music in the life of the classroom.

Accept and Embrace Musical Diversity

Children and their families will come to you with diverse music abilities, experiences, and preferences. One of the most important parts of your role as a teacher of music is to accept and embrace these differences. That means you need to be respectful and positive when a child does not sing in tune, sings loud, or refuses to sing at all. It means that you need to listen with an open, appreciative mind to the songs a child or family sings even if they sound odd to your ears.

Make Good Choices

Another part of your role is to carefully choose songs and recordings to share with children. Choose simple songs with singable melodies and lyrics. Choose a comfortable range for children (approximately middle C to E an octave above). Include diverse styles of music from many cultures. Vary the lyrics of songs so you can sing about the children and their activities and interests. You can learn songs from recordings for children, from other teachers, or from books. The songs you know are a great starting place.

The MENC position statement outlines our responsibility to provide children with diverse, high-quality music—not just what is easily available and most familiar. Remember, children are likely to have had plenty of exposure to TV music (*Barney, Sesame Street,* Disney, Pokemon, etc.) and commercial radio. Your public library has a collection of recorded music that you can borrow for learning and that you can use to extend what you have at school. Look for lively classical music, diverse cultural music, good children's music, and the best of other music genres. Use all recorded music mindfully—to accompany an activity (like creative movement or art), to help children listen to a musical piece, or to create a calm atmosphere at naptime or a meal.

Music Activities: Singing and Beyond

Do you think there are so many music activities that it's hard to know where to begin, or do you wonder what you can possibly do besides sing a song now and then? This section is designed to give you an overview of different kinds of music activities that you can provide for children. Whether you are a music expert or a novice, it is useful to have some categories for thinking about the music activities that you will plan.

Singing Activities

When you think of music in preschool, you probably think of a group of children sitting in a circle around a teacher strumming a guitar. This is usually called *Circle Time* or *Group Time* and it is one of the main ways that music curriculum is delivered in preschool. Group music times can be fun. Everyone participates, a sense of community is built based on the shared experiences, and young children learn how to be a part of a group.

Children are capable of learning more songs than you may expect. So a repertoire of easy-to-sing songs is an important part of your teaching tool kit. You probably already know many songs that are appropriate to sing with children. A valuable teaching resource is a list of songs you know by heart. The In Practice box will give you a start. Add other songs that you know from your own culture and community. You will learn more in classes and workshops, from colleagues, and from the children you teach and their families. These are treasures that you can share.

Different kinds of songs appeal to different children, and they provide varied musical experiences. *Simple, traditional children's songs* like *Are You Sleeping?* and *It's Raining, It's Pouring* are short and easy for children to learn to sing independently. They have limited tonal range, so young children are able to sing them accurately from the start.

Fingerplay songs like *The Eency Weency Spider* and *Where Is Thumbkin?* support children in understanding how a song can express ideas. They provide a bridge between physical expression and verbal and musical expression. There is a difference between fingerplay rhymes (which are said without singing a tune) and fingerplay songs (which involve singing). While both are good teaching tools, fingerplay rhymes don't contribute as much to music learning.

Because fingerplay songs are done while seated, they don't require group coordination and so are more successful for inexperienced children and teachers. Almost any song can be turned into a fingerplay song; and, if you add actions for a group of children that needs to move while singing, you will have more successful group music activities.

Action songs, like *Did You Ever See a Lassie?* or *Che Che Kole,* use whole body movement and may be more challenging than fingerplay songs. Because they involve vigorous action, they are well suited to young children. Children will learn the actions before they learn to sing the song. Once learned, they help to build awareness of the rhythm and form elements of the songs involved.

Similar to action songs, *circle games* and *play-party songs* like *The Hokey Pokey, The Farmer in the Dell,* or *Brown Girl in the Ring* involve whole body movement. Movements are usually prescribed (you put your foot into the center). They require group cooperation and interaction, and are children's first dances (similar to folk dances).

1. Alphabet Song
2. Are You Sleeping?
3. Baa, Baa Black Sheep
4. Bingo
5. Did You Ever See a Lassie?
6. Did You Feed My Cow?
7. Do You Know the Muffin Man?
8. Do-Re-Mi
9. Down by the Bay
10. Eency Weency Spider
11. Farmer in the Dell
12. Green Grass Grows All Around
13. Happy Birthday to You
14. Head, Shoulders, Knees and Toes
15. Here We Go Round the Mulberry Bush
16. Hickory, Dickory, Dock
17. Hokey Pokey
18. Home on the Range
19. I'm a Little Teapot
20. I've Been Working on the Railroad
21. If You're Happy and You Know It
22. It's a Small World
23. It's Raining, It's Pouring
24. Jack and Jill
25. John Jacob Jingleheimer Schmidt
26. Little Bo Peep
27. Little Bunny Foo-Foo
28. London Bridge Is Falling Down
29. Mary Had a Little Lamb
30. Michael Row the Boat Ashore
31. My Bonnie Lies Over the Ocean
32. My Darling Clementine
33. Oh Susanna!
34. Oh, Dear What Can the Matter Be?
35. Old McDonald Had a Farm
36. On Top of Old Smokey
37. Polly Wolly Doodle
38. Pop! Goes the Weasel
39. Puff the Magic Dragon
40. Ring Around the Rosie
41. Rock-a-Bye Baby
42. She'll Be Comin' Round the Mountain
43. Sing a Song of Sixpence
44. Six Little Ducks
45. Skip to My Lou
46. The Wheels on the Bus
47. There Was an Old Lady Who Swallowed a Fly
48. There's a Hole In the Bucket
49. Three Blind Mice
50. Twinkle, Twinkle Little Star
51. Where Is Thumbkin?
52. Where, Oh Where Has My Little Dog Gone?
53. Yankee Doodle

Echo songs and *call and response songs* (sometimes called *song fragments*) are useful because they give children the opportunity to sing short phrases alone. Echo songs (like *My Aunt Came Back* or *Down By the Bay*) invite children to repeat the same words as the teacher and so are easier to sing. Call and response songs (like *John the Rabbit* or *Did You Feed My Cow*) require children to learn and remember a simple pattern and sing their part.

The longest songs we typically sing with young children are called *story songs* (tales sung to tunes). Before writing and books were common, rhymes and melodies helped bards (story singers) to remember the sequence of a story. Story songs have characters and plot just like any story, and they can be shared with young children in a number of ways. Singing a story song can work well if you know the song well and have skill in telling stories without books. If not, there are many beautifully illustrated story song books (like Spier's *The Fox Went Out on a Chilly Night*). Singing these to the children rather than reading them helps children develop music, literature, and literacy skills and sensitivity. Story songs can also be told with props like puppets or flannelboard pieces. Additionally, many story songs are available in recorded form and can be listened to at a listening center.

You can enhance children's understanding and appreciation of a song and integrate music across content areas using *song extensions* just as you might extend a story. Props like puppets or flannelboard pieces can add to children's enjoyment and can help them to visualize the meaning of the lyrics. *Song charts* with words and pictures can give children beginning knowledge of the ways in which songs can be recorded and also build literacy skills. *Modifying* a song to personalize it to a child or the group helps children begin to learn the musician's skills of improvising and composing. *Accompanying* a song using rhythm instruments gives children understanding of the musical uses of instruments and builds understanding of musical elements. *Singing parts* by alternating verses between groups or taking turns singing verse and chorus begins to prepare children for more mature musical experiences and builds social skills.

Instrument Activities

As we have mentioned before, we do not believe in using musical instruments as toys. So you may be wondering how to include instruments in your music curriculum.

A good way to start is by beginning with the *body as an instrument*. Different sounds can be made by clapping, stamping, and slapping hands, feet, and knees. Before you begin to use instruments, you can introduce many music concepts (fast/slow, loud/soft, long phrases/short phrases) by clapping, stamping, or slapping knees, hands, and chest. A simple activity for young children is to clap or stamp *name rhythms*. Initially, you will introduce these (inviting everyone to join in: "Let's clap Ma-ry, Ma-ry, Ma-ry") and as children become familiar with them, you can invite them to make up different ways to create their own name's rhythm ("Jo-nah Chun" *stamp-stamp-clap*).

Using rhythm instruments with young children requires some thought and planning. Before you begin, think about how you will *introduce the instrument*. At first, it is wise to have all the same instruments for all the children. If every child has an identical egg shaker, pair of rhythm sticks, or wrist bell, no one feels left out. Invite children to explore the sound of the instrument. Suggest some different ways to play it (up high/down low, fast/slow, loud/soft). Then sing a familiar song while playing the instrument. That's enough for one day.

When children are familiar with using these instruments, you can begin to introduce the instruments they will have to share. In a small group, bring out the drums, tambourines, triangles, or other instruments and demonstrate how they are played. Let each child have an ample turn to explore. Don't forget to have an interesting task for the children who are waiting.

Another important part of using instruments is to have a plan for how you will *pass out instruments* to avoid arguments, pushing, and grabbing. Some teachers sing a song ("Come on Megan and get a drum, Come on Jonah and get some bells"), others have 2–3 instruments set out on mats and each child then chooses a mat. Avoid having children wait and watch while their favorite instrument is chosen by someone else.

Once everyone can use instruments, there are many things you can do. Rhythm instrument games help children to understand musical elements. *The Mystery Sound Game* helps children to identify different instruments (play the instrument out of sight and have children guess what it is—they are learning about *timbre*). *Fast and Slow* is a game in which children follow along, playing their instruments to match your *tempo* as you play yours. *Stop and Start* is a game in which children play their instruments as you sing a line of a song and stop when you stop (they are learning about *phrases*). *Loud and Soft* is a game in which children explore *dynamics* as they follow along as you gradually increase the volume of your instrument (called a *crescendo*) and then gradually decrease it (called a *decrescendo*). This works well if you have a simple song to accompany such as *Are You Sleeping*?

Older preschoolers who have done all of these activities are ready to use instruments to purposefully *accompany singing*. Talk with children about the song you are going to sing and invite them to think of how an instrument might best highlight the words or melody. This works well with story songs: "What kind of instrument shall we use when the song says, '*Next to come in was a little black bug carrying the water jug*'?"

You will not teach preschoolers how to read conventional musical notation. However, you can use *inventive notation*, a term we use to describe simple symbols you select with children. For example, you might decide that V means "tap the carpet with the rhythm sticks," and that X means "tap them together." You might then "notate" *Skip to My Lou* as XX-VVV, XX-VVV, XXXX-VV-X and write it on chart paper for the children to read.

Listening Activities

Most young children come to school aware of and sensitive to sound. But in a noisy classroom, they often learn to tune out. We know that being able to listen in school is important for all kinds of learning, but it is especially important in music.

Young children find it hard to stop making their own sounds in order to listen to music, sound, or other people talking. The purpose of providing listening activities is to increase children's capacity to suspend making sounds in order to

- *Listen and Tell*—Invite children to close their eyes and listen to the sounds they hear, and then open them and describe what they heard.
- *Body Sounds*—Make sounds by snapping, clapping, clicking your tongue, or saying nonsense syllables and then invite children to imitate you.
- *What Was That?*—Ask children to guess what type of object or instrument was responsible for a sound you made behind a barrier.
- *Sound Containers*—Fill small containers with different materials like pennies, shells, or rice, and let

children shake them and guess what's inside. Make two of each type and ask children to match them.
- *Match the Beat*—Invite children to listen to the beat of a ticking clock, a metronome, a dripping faucet or drain pipe, the whirr of a fan, or a windshield wiper when you're on the bus and clap hands or nod heads to the beat.

listen. Simple games can build children's capacity to focus on sound and analyze what they have heard.

Moving to Music

Children don't naturally listen when you play recorded music for them. But they do naturally move. Moving to music is an important part of the music curriculum. As you select recorded music for children to dance and move to, you are helping them to listen to and understand music. It's useful to read more about creative movement activities to develop your repertoire of activities that combine music and movement.

Planning Music Curriculum

Because young children make music in their play, a critical part of the music curriculum is creating an environment for play and ensuring there is adequate time for children to use it. However, it is also important to plan music activities. You will plan music activities to introduce the group to new songs and then provide opportunities to practice; to help children learn about the elements of music and acquire the skills of a musician; to be sure that you are addressing a program goal or standard for music curriculum; and to involve music in an integrated curriculum study.

To help you in writing plans, Table 11.3 includes some common objectives for the preschool music curriculum.

Writing Music Plans

Since the day that her father came to school and sang with the class, Molly has been much happier in school. She and Ralph have become good friends. One day they play by spinning and spinning while Molly sings Ring Around the Rosie. *She trips several times and Ralph helps her up. Ralph does not sing, but he laughs and laughs when they both fall down. He begs Molly to sing it again and she happily complies. Spring and Jodi, their teachers, observe their play.*

TABLE 11.3   Some Typical Objectives for the Preschool Music Curriculum

Stage and Objectives	Singing	Composing and Improvising	Playing Instruments	Listening	Understanding Music Elements
Younger preschoolers *The ability to . . .*	• Learn short and simple songs with a distinct rhythm. • Sing with the group.	• Express feelings and ideas with song. • Express feelings and ideas with movement to music.	• Use simple instruments appropriately. • Distinguish the sounds of two dissimilar instruments.	• Express preferences for songs. • Listen for a sound or tune. • Notice feelings the music creates.	• Respond to musical elements in guided activities. • Explore individual music elements spontaneously. • Understand the terms *beat, tune.*
Older Preschoolers *The ability to . . .*	• Sing in a range from middle C or slightly lower, to C an octave higher. • Sing longer songs with more complex words and structure.	• Create a song or instrumental sequence that can be repeated. • Create ways to move to express the feelings and ideas in a song.	• Distinguish the sounds of two similar instruments. • Play classroom rhythm instruments in a group. • Control beat, tempo, and dynamics when using instruments. • Use chord and melody instruments carefully.	• Talk about preferences with personal reasons for choices (song is spooky). • Listen to a short piece of music presented by a live musician. • Recognize a favorite performer or group. • Recognize a tune when played or sung in a different way.	• Recognize and respond to suggestions related to musical elements (e.g., clap to the beat, wait for introduction, adjust pitch). • Understand the terms *beat, rhythm, tempo, rest, pitch, phrase, repetition.*

To plan music curriculum, you need to know the children both as individuals and as a group. Children like Molly are highly attuned to music (she has what Howard Gardner calls *musical intelligence*). Ralph is a physically capable child (having what Gardner calls *bodily-kinesethetic intelligence*). Because they know these children, Spring and Jodi can plan music activities both for Molly's skill and for Ralph's (and, of course, for the rest of their group).

Look at children's strengths. Molly has music skills—she sings in tune, makes up songs, and claps in time to music. Ralph has awareness of space and moves his body gracefully, but rarely sings.

Look at children's interests. Both Molly and Ralph love active play, and both have a burgeoning sense of humor. These strengths and interests guide their teachers in planning. They are also guided by their state standards and their program's goals.

Figure 11.6 shows an example of a plan Spring created for these children to build music skills and understanding.

FIGURE 11.6 Simple Music Activity Plan

The Hokey Pokey/Music

Objectives:	Respond to the musical element of *beat* by moving to the beat.
	Respond to the musical element of *form* by moving to the phrases in the song.
Standard:	Domain V (Music) Standard 2
What you need:	Large carpeted area
How to teach:	1. Invite seated children to "Do what the song tells you"–do actions with hands.
	2. Repeat a couple of times; then invite children to stand and sing the rest of the song and model actions.
	3. Invite the children to suggest other movements.
How to assess:	Children move body parts in and out of the circle in time to the beat and do hokey pokey motions following the phrases of the song.

Because she is an experienced teacher, Spring's short plan leaves out many details. It would not be enough of a guide for a beginning teacher. The detailed version that follows in Figure 11.7 gives you a better idea of what she planned to do.

Music in a Weekly Plan

As we have said before, we believe children need time both for self-directed play and teacher-guided group music daily. In the example included in Figure 11.8, you will see that songs with movement are repeated. In addition, a dance activity is offered. These activities allow children to develop music awareness and skills. Activities that involve music are highlighted.

Music in an Integrated Curriculum

Every integrated study can include music. In the *Study of Birds* sunburst in Figure 11.9, music is obvious in the songs. But music also was a part of family involvement activities, movement, literature activities, math activities, and even science as the class went on a listening walk to hear bird songs.

Every integrated study can include the following music activities:

- Songs related to the topic like *Baby Chicks Are Crying.*
- Movement activities that include songs or that involve moving to recorded music related to the study like the Chicken Dance.
- Children's literature song/storybooks related to the topic like *Fiddle I Fee.*
- Family involvement—inviting family members to share songs and recordings related to the topic.

Music for All Children

All young children need music. An infant playing with a rattle, a toddler dancing to the radio, a preschooler singing a made-up song, a kindergartner learning all the verses to the Rainbow Connection, or a child with a hearing impairment enjoying the vibration of the bass on the stereo speaker—all are participating in an important human endeavor.

FIGURE 11.7   Detailed Music Activity Plan

Activity:	**The Hokey Pokey** (a circle game)
	Music Curriculum Focus
WHO It's For:	This activity was planned for the *Striped Peacocks* (eight 3-year-olds).
Rationale:	Most of the *Peacocks* (especially Molly and Ralph) enjoy moving to music. Building the ability to sing and move to music is a goal for all the children, especially for Ralph.
Music Objectives:	*By participating in this activity the children will develop the ability to …*
	• Respond to the musical element of *beat* by moving in time to the beat.
	• Respond to musical element of *form* by moving as modeled in response to the phrases in the song.
Preschool Content Standard:	Domain V, Standard 2: Begin to learn about music elements and techniques.
Indicator:	Show awareness of musical elements.
HOW to Prepare	*What you need:*
	Large carpeted area
	Set up:
	Before the children come, push back tables
HOW to Teach	*Introduction:*
	As children come for circle time and get settled, begin a familiar fingerplay song that involves contrasting movement (*Open/Shut Them*); then say something like, "I have a new singing game to teach you."
	Teaching steps:
	1. Invite the children to "Do what the song tells you." (Do not ask them to stand.)
	2. Sing and do the actions: "You put your hands in, you put your hands out, you put your hands in and you shake them all about." (Don't worry about right and left.)
	3. Tell children that in the next part of the song: "Make your hands do a special dance" (show them and ask them to do it with you). Then sing *You Do the Hokey Pokey*.
	4. Repeat a couple of times, and when children seem comfortable, invite them to stand up.
	5. Sing the rest of the song and model the actions. Invite the children to "Do it with me."
	6. Repeat with other body parts. Encourage children to sing.
	Closure:
	At the end, invite the children to suggest other movements following the format of the song and comment, "Now you can do the Hokey Pokey."

HOW to Assess and Document

Objectives	Evidence of Learning Children might …	How to Document This Evidence
Respond to the musical element of *beat* by moving in time to the beat.	Clap hands to beat. Move body parts in and out of circle in time to beat.	Anecdotal observations, annotated photograph, or video recording
Respond to the musical element of *form* by moving as modeled in response to the phrases in the song.	Change motions as modeled.	Anecdotal observations, annotated photograph, or video recording

EVALUATION   (Things to remember for next time)

Children were not able to keep the circle shape and wanted to jump in the middle. Next time, practice being in and out of the circle first.

The music activities that we have described for typically developing preschoolers can also be the basis of music curriculum for preschoolers with special needs as well as primary age children.

FIGURE 11.8 A Week's Plan: Birds—Week #4

Objective: To help children understand that there are different kinds of birds with different characteristics.

	Monday	Tuesday	Wednesday	Thursday	Friday
Story	One Crow	Goose's Story	Daisy Comes Home	Nēnē	Baby Owl
Outdoor Activities **Purpose:** to help children develop …	**Hoop Jumping** Large motor coordination.	**Building a Brooding House** Concepts of shape and space.	**Hopping Like a Bird** Large motor strength and stamina.	**Building a Loft Perch** Concepts of shape and space.	**Building a Loft Cage** Concepts of shape and space.
Small Group 1 **Purpose:** to help children develop …	**Storyplaying Jacob's Story** Skill in dramatizing ideas.	*Fire Drill*	**Drawing Topo the Cockatiel** Ability to use art media to record ideas.	**Writing a Bird Book** Concepts of print.	**Campus 2nd Story Walk to View Birds** Awareness of birds' lives in the treetops.
Small Group 2 **Purpose:** to help children develop …	**Little Robin Red Breast Fingerplay Song** Ability to express ideas through language and music.		**One Little Bird Song Dramatization** Skill in singing and dramatizing ideas.	**Making Hard Boiled Eggs** Skill in singing and dramatizing ideas.	**Two Little Mynah Birds** The ability to recognize melody and form.
Indoor Special Activities **Purpose:** to help children develop …	**Life Drawing: Lovebirds** Ability to use art media to record ideas.	**Life Drawing: Lovebirds** Ability to use art media to record ideas.	**Feather Collage** Awareness of texture and shape in art.	**Egg Shell Collage** Skill in using space in art.	**Egg Shell Collage** Skill in using space in art.
Circle Time **Purpose:** to help children develop …	**Baby Chicks Are Crying Dramatization** The ability to express ideas and feelings through movement.	**Two Little Mynah Birds** The ability to recognize melody and form.	**Chicken Dance** Beginning dance skills and the ability to hear melodic patterns.	**Chicken Dance** Beginning dance skills and the ability to hear melodic patterns.	**Little Bird Action Song** The ability to express ideas and feelings through song and movement.

FIGURE 11.9 A Study of Birds Sunburst

A Study of Birds

Big Idea
There are lots of different birds with many colors, shapes, and sizes.

Big Idea
All birds have feathers and lay eggs to make baby birds.

Big Idea
Birds live in different places where they can find food, be safe, and raise their young.

Big Idea
Birds are part of people's lives: Some birds are pets, some give us food and feathers, some help plants grow.

Big Idea
Birds move in different ways.

Science
Comparing Love Birds and Chickens
Making Binoculars
Bird Watching
Chick Seriation Game
Raw Egg Exploration
Eggshell Exploration
Hatching Baby Quails
Feather Classification
Bird Watching
Listening Walk to Hear Bird Songs

Social Studies
Trip Books
Trip Predictions
Fertilizing the Garden with Chicken Manure
Planting Birdseed
Visit from Pet Birds and Their Owners
Naming Pet Quails
Bird Dramatic Play with Bird Hoods and Toys

Math
123 Birds Workjob
Counting Eggs Workjob
One Little Bird
Five Blue Pigeons
Bird Tally

Fine Motor Activities
123 Birds Workjob
Counting Eggs Workjob
Five Blue Pigeons
Bird Fingerplays
Feather Classification

Large Motor Activities
Bird Feeding
Little Bird Game
Walk Like a Crow

Language
Discussion:
What Do You Know About Birds?
Bird Naming
Bird Fingerplays
Bird Guessing Game
Bird Story Playing

Cooking
Egg Salad Sandwiches
Frittatas
Hard-Boiled Eggs

Literacy
Trip Books
Trip Predictions
Chick Journals
Names of the Birds Workjob
Bird Matching Workjob

Trips
Audubon Park
Zoo
Campus

Literature
See booklist
Prop Story Songs— baby chicks, little white duck, five little ducks
Bird Poems

Woodworking
Building …
• Birdhouse
• Bird Feeder
• Birdbath
• Quail Brooding House

Music/Movement/ Drama
Los Pollitos
Little Bird
Sassy Little Mynah Bird
Walking Like a Crow
Manu Lai Titi
5 Blue Pigeons
Little White Duck
Bird Movement
One Little Bird
Chicken Dance

Art
Eggshell Collage
Feather Collage
Feature Painting
Egg Tree
Bird Puppets
Bird Mobile
Bird Life Drawing
Bird Tissue Collage
Sculpting Birds
Egg Painting

Family Involvement
Trips
Sharing Pet Birds
Sharing Bird Songs/ Recordings
Family Bird Feeders
Bird Watching
Potluck

Children with Special Needs

Jena, a child with a speech impediment, is a 4-year-old in the Ducks Group. Although her disability is not visible, Jena's speech impediment (she stutters) impairs her ability to communicate with others. Jena avoids social play. She enjoys listening to stories, but other group time activities like discussions and fingerplays are difficult for her. But Jena loves to sing. Her stutter disappears when she is singing. The teachers make sure to have lots of singing throughout the curriculum.

Music can often provide a gift to a child with special needs. A child with limited vision or mobility may be able to participate in music activities in ways that are like the others in the class. Children with autism spectrum disorder may be moved by music when nothing else reaches them. Children with cognitive delays may respond to music in ways that are similar to typically developing children. Surprisingly, children like Jena who have speech delays are sometimes much more fluent when singing than talking (Sacks, 2008). Children with a hearing impairment may enjoy the physical vibrations of music even if they cannot hear all the notes.

How does music accomplish all this? Research suggests that the rhythms in music help regulate movement. It stimulates speech development and provides organization for cognitive and motor development. For all of these reasons, music has therapeutic as well as educational value. And if you have a child with special needs in your class, you need to have music.

Children in the Primary Grades

Musical challenges are enjoyed by 6-, 7-, and 8-year-old children. You can see this in the songs they choose and the activities they spontaneously undertake. At this age, children prefer longer and more complex songs like *Puff the Magic Dragon;* songs with less predictable words and structure like *Doodle-ee-doo;* call and response songs in which they sing only one part like *There's a Hole in the Bucket;* and songs with humor like *The Quartermaster's Store.* Because of their increased competence and self-confidence, they may take pride in practicing performing musical skits without the shyness and fear of criticism that will overtake them in middle childhood.

Primary school children have the capacity to accompany songs with the rhythm instruments that they formerly would have simply played with as noisemakers. And they can begin seriously playing instruments like the piano, ukulele, recorder, autoharp, guitar, or violin (instruments that are made in small sizes or are easy for small hands to play). They can begin to read simple musical notation.

In the early elementary years, children are ready to listen thoughtfully to recorded music from diverse genres. They will enjoy listening to a piece of music with a challenge ("Listen for the oboe making the sound of a cuckoo bird—try to count how many times the cuckoo calls."). And they will begin to have more distinct preferences for recorded music.

Final Thoughts

All young children need music. We all do. You have many gifts to give children. The ability to create and appreciate music and to express ideas and feelings with music is a treasure. To be able share this gift, you must nurture it in yourself. Take time for music, for the pleasure it brings, and the bond it gives you with children and with the rest of humanity.

Learning Outcomes

When you read this chapter, thoughtfully complete activities from the "To Learn More" section, and document this learning as suggested in the "For Your Portfolio" section, you will be making progress in the following *NAEYC Standards for Early Childhood Professional Preparation Programs* (2009):

Standard 1. Promoting Child Development and Learning

Students prepared in early childhood degree programs are grounded in a child development knowledge base. They use their understanding of young children's characteristics and needs and of the multiple interacting influences on children's development and learning to create environments that are healthy, respectful, supportive, and challenging for each child.

The key elements of standard 1 you will have learned about are . . .

1a: Knowing and understanding young children's characteristics and needs

1c: Using developmental knowledge to create healthy, respectful, supportive, and challenging learning environments

Standard 4. Using Developmentally Effective Approaches to Connect with Children and Families

Students prepared in early childhood degree programs understand that teaching and learning with young children is a complex enterprise, and its details vary depending on children's ages, characteristics, and the settings within which teaching and learning occur. They understand and use positive relationships and supportive interactions as the foundation for their work with young children and families. Students know, understand, and use a wide array of developmentally appropriate approaches, instructional strategies, and tools to connect with children and families and positively influence each child's development and learning.

The key elements of standard 4 you will have learned about are . . .

4a: Understanding positive relationships and supportive interactions as the foundation of their work with children

4b: Knowing and understanding effective strategies and tools for early education

4c: Using a broad repertoire of developmentally appropriate teaching/learning approaches

4d: Reflecting on their own practice to promote positive outcomes for each child

Standard 5. Using Content Knowledge to Build Meaningful Curriculum

Students prepared in early childhood degree programs use their knowledge of academic disciplines to design, implement, and evaluate experiences that promote positive development and learning for each and every young child. Students understand the importance of developmental domains and academic (or content) disciplines in an early childhood curriculum. They know the essential concepts, inquiry tools, and structure of content areas, including academic subjects, and can identify resources to deepen their understanding. Students use their own knowledge and other resources to design, implement, and evaluate meaningful, challenging curricula that promote comprehensive developmental and learning outcomes for every young child.

The key elements of standard 5 you will have learned about are . . .

5a: Understanding content knowledge and resources in academic disciplines

5b: Knowing and using the central concepts, inquiry tools, and structures of content areas or academic disciplines

5c: Using their own knowledge, appropriate early learning standards, and other resources to design, implement, and evaluate meaningful, challenging curricula for each child.

To Learn More

Observe a Program: For a morning, observe a program and see how the staff structures the environment and program to support children's musical development. Notice both the play opportunities and the planned group activities. Look at the plans and see how the planning reflects what you observed. Interview a teacher to learn how he or she thinks about music curriculum.

Observe a Child: For a morning, observe a child in a classroom, with a focus on the child's musical activity. Notice how the child engages with the planned activities and how he or she constructs his or her own opportunities for music learning. Notice the extent to which the child's activity and the planned curriculum seem to match. Observe to see how staff support the child's musical learning.

Observe a Master Teacher: Spend a morning with an early childhood educator who is experienced and has a curriculum leadership role in a program. (This teacher may be called the "lead," "head," or "mentor" teacher.) Then interview the educator about how he or she plans for and provides music curriculum.

Observe a Music Activity: Observe a teacher leading a planned music activity. Interview the teacher to find out the objectives for the activity. Reflect on any differences between what you saw and the focus of the plan.

Compare Two Programs: Observe music experiences in two early childhood programs. Compare the ways that the two address music curriculum—their similarities and differences. Reflect on which program seems to best support children's learning and why. What implications does this comparison have for your future work with young children?

Compare Two Ages: Observe two classrooms, one preschool and one for primary school children. Report on how each supports children's musical learning. Talk to the staff about how they make their curriculum choices. Notice how development influences curriculum choices.

Explore Resources: Read one of the books from the bibliography or one of the online resources listed here and write a review of it for your classmates.

Children's Music Network: www.cmnonline.org/index.htm A Web site with songs that you can listen to, lists of resources, Web links, and ideas for teachers, performers, songwriters, radio hosts, and parents.

Children's Music Web: www.childrensmusic.org/ A collection of resources for teachers, parents, and performers with articles for teachers many links to other Web sites.

Kididdles: www.kididdles.com/ Lyrics and brief recordings of 2000 children's songs designed to help you learn tunes.

KPR (Kids Public Radio): www.kidspublicradio.org/ Three, 24-hour program streams (lullabies, stories, and sing-along-songs) of good-quality children's music.

For Your Portfolio

Design a Music Environment: Design and draw a floor plan for a classroom and play yard that would promote children's music learning. Share your plan with an early childhood educator, discussing what you included and why. Ask for and consider the educator's feedback and suggestions. For your portfolio, include the floor plan and a reflection on what you learned by doing this project.

Plan and Implement a Music Activity: Observe a group of children for a morning, focusing on their music interest and skill. Based on what you observed, write and implement a music activity. Collect evidence of children's response in the form of anecdotal observations, photographs, or audio or video recordings. Reflect on how children responded and what they appear to have learned. What worked? What might you do differently next time?

How might you expand on this experience for children? For your portfolio, include the plan, a photograph, and a reflection on what you learned about yourself, children, planning, and teaching music.

Create a Music Learning Material: Design and make a music learning material to support the development of a particular child or group of children. Introduce it to the child or children and observe how it is used. Reflect on how the children responded and how you felt about what you did. What worked? What might you do differently next time? How might you expand on this experience for children? For your portfolio, include a photograph of a child using the material and a reflection on what you learned about yourself, children, learning materials, and teaching music.

Bibliography

Campbell, D. (2000). *The Mozart effect for children*. New York, NY: William Morrow.

Consortium of National Arts Education Associations. (1994). *National standards for arts education*. Reston, VA: MENC: The National Association for Music Education. www.menc.org

Edwards, L. C. (2010). *The creative arts: A process approach for teachers and children* (5th ed.). Upper Saddle River, NJ: Pearson.

Feierabend, J. M. (2006). *First steps in music for preschool and beyond*. Chicago, IL: GIA Publications.

Flowers, P. J., & Dunne-Sousa, D. (1990, Summer). Pitch-pattern accuracy, tonality, and vocal range in pre-school children's singing. *Journal of Research in Music Education, 38*(2), 102–114.

Greenberg, M. (1979). *Your children need music.* Englewood, NJ: Prentice-Hall.

Head Start Resource Center. (2010). *The Head Start child development and early learning framework: Promoting positive outcomes in early childhood programs serving children 3–5 years old.* Washington, DC: Office of Head Start, Administration for Children and Families, U.S. Department of Health and Human Services.

Kuhlman, K., & Schweinhart, L. J. (n.d.). *Timing in child development.* Ypsilanti, MI: HighScope. www.highscope.org/Research/Timing Paper/timingstudy.htm

Levitin, D. J. (2006). *This is your brain on music: The science of a human obsession.* New York, NY: Penguin (Dutton).

Levitin, D. J. (2008). *The world in six songs: How the musical brain created human nature.* New York, NY: Penguin (Plume).

Madaule, P. (1997, Spring). Music: An invitation to listening, language, and learning. *Early Childhood Connections: Journal for Music and Movement-Based Learning, 3*(2).

National Association for the Education of Young Children. (2009). *NAEYC standards for early childhood professional preparation programs.* www.naeyc.org/files/naeyc/file/positions/ProfPrepStandards09.pdf

The National Association of Music Educators (MENC). (1991). *MENC position statement on early childhood education.* Reston, VA: Author. www.menc.org/about/view/early-childhood-education-position-statement

Sacks, O. (2008). *Musicophilia: Tales of music and the brain* (Revised and Expanded edition). New York, NY: Knopf.

Thomas, A. E. (2008, Fall). Growing young musicians. *General Music Today, 22*(1), 13–18.

Weikart, P. S. (2003, September/October). Value for learning and living: Insights on the value of music and steady beat. *Child Care Information Exchange, 153,* 86–88.

Wright, S. (2003). *The arts, young children, and learning.* Boston, MA: Allyn and Bacon.

Zeitlin, P. (1982) *A song is a rainbow.* Glenview, IL: Scott Foresman.

MyEducationLab

Go to Topics 2: Child Development and Learning, and 9: Content Areas/Lessons and Activities in the MyEducationLab (www.myeducationlab.com) for *Meaningful Curriculum for Young Children,* where you can:

- Find learning outcomes for Child Development and Learning and Content Areas/Lessons and Activities along with the national standards that connect to these outcomes.
- Complete Assignments and Activities that can help you more deeply understand the chapter content.
- Apply and practice your understanding of the core teaching skills identified in the chapter with the Building Teaching Skills and Dispositions learning units.
- Listen to experts from the field in Professional Perspectives.

- Examine challenging situations and cases presented in the IRIS Center Resources.
- Check your comprehension on the content covered in the chapter with the Study Plan. Here you will be able to take a chapter quiz, receive feedback on your answers, and then access Review, Practice, and Enrichment activities to enhance your understanding of chapter content.

Go to the Course Resources section in MyEducationLab, where you can:

- Use the Online Lesson Plan Builder to practice lesson planning and integrating national and state standards into your planning.

If you can walk you can dance.
If you can talk you can sing.

PROVERB, ZIMBABWE

chapter twelve

CREATIVE MOVEMENT CURRICULUM
Creating with Body and Mind

Children move to play, to express feelings, and to communicate. Creative movement (sometimes called *creative dance*) is the early childhood subject area that helps children to develop understanding, skills, and dispositions that they will use later in dance and other physical fitness activities. When movement contains ideas and feelings that are expressed in individual ways, it is called *creative movement*.

Creative movement is different from, and not a substitute for, large muscle activity on the playground or large motor games and exercises. Although it is the forerunner of dance, it is different. In dance, a teacher formally instructs in specific ways of moving that are almost always accompanied by music. Creative movement is much more flexible and individual. It may or may not involve music, although it almost always involves the steady beat of a drum or other instrument. In a creative movement activity, children interpret and follow suggestions and are encouraged to find their own personal, creative, and innovative ways of moving.

Why Creative Movement?

*If I could **tell** you what I mean there would be no point in dancing.*

ISADORA DUNCAN

Young children are nearly always moving. As they move, they learn. Concepts such as *fast, slow, run, creep,* and *push* are experienced through movement. It would be impossible to keep children from moving. But why should creative expression through movement be a part of the early childhood curriculum?

The most important reason to include creative movement in your curriculum is that **creative movement gives children joy and satisfaction.** You need not be a child development expert to know this; you only need to observe. We believe that early childhood classrooms should be joyful places, and creative movement helps to make them joyful.

Creative movement provides a way for young children to express ideas and feelings. Expressing joy and sorrow and other feelings through movement is natural. It is a fundamental way that human beings communicate. Although children are learning to express themselves through language, in the early childhood years, the language of movement is easier and more direct. If you think of movement as a language for expressing ideas and feelings, the creative movement curriculum helps children to build the movement vocabulary for that language.

Creative movement teaches children new ways to use and practice physical skills. As you direct children in movement, you encourage them to make suggestions and express ideas in innovative ways. They gain awareness and control of their bodies. They develop basic dance skills that they may use in a variety of dancing activities ranging from creative dance to folk, jazz, street, or ballroom dancing.

Creative movement supports children's developing imagination and positive self-concept as they gain the ability to meet movement challenges. It is this focus on individual ways of moving that makes it *creative* movement.

Creative movement gives children new ways to think about themselves and the world. When children reenact a growing seed, an angry giant, or a floating cloud, they are both gaining aesthetic appreciation and constructing understanding.

To move with others in a group requires attention to the actions of others. Children who move in the same space with others must be aware of one another's needs and actions. Thus **creative movement enhances social development** as children learn to move with respect for the group and come to appreciate the creativity of others. They learn to take the role of follower and leader as you give each child a chance to direct the group. They learn to work with a partner as you challenge two children to *make a big shape together.*

Creative movement provides an avenue for physical activity. All children need physical activity to be healthy, but not all children enjoy rough-and-tumble play. If a child is reluctant to enter into other physical development activities, creative movement provides him or her with an alternative way to enjoy large motor activity and to build the strength, balance, and stamina that are gained through physical activity.

Last, and certainly not least, **creative movement is a way to develop understanding and skill in different curriculum areas.** A child responding to a teacher's suggestion to *bounce lightly on the balls of your feet* is developing vocabulary. A group of children marching *1-2-3-4, 1-2-3-4* have a concrete experience with number. When you play a section of Saint-Saens' *Danse Macabre* to inspire movement, you are giving children aesthetic and musical experiences. As you invite children to re-enact the life cycle of a butterfly, you are helping them to construct science understanding.

How Do Young Children Develop Skill in Creative Movement?

To participate in creative movement activities, young children must possess skill in several developmental areas. They need large motor skill, they need receptive language ability, and they must have social awareness. What you know about children's development in these three areas will help you to understand the creative movement curriculum.

Most children come to early childhood programs delighted to move. They are actively seeking ways to explore, express ideas, and develop physical competence. Children who are especially competent at and engaged by movement activities have what Howard Gardner calls high *bodily-kinesthetic intelligence,* the ability to control one's body and handle objects skillfully.

Learning to control movement is one of our first challenges as human beings. The sequence of physical development from lifting head to walking takes the bulk of the first year of life. By the time they reach the toddler years, children begin to "dance" with swaying bodies, bending knees, and swinging arms. Between the ages of 2 and 3, they respond physically to markedly rhythmic music and tend to persist at one type of movement throughout a movement session (Wright, 2003). Repetition of this sort helps children develop understanding and skill in both music and movement.

Three-year-olds have a great deal more of the physical control needed for creative movement and can gallop, run, hop briefly, and broad jump. They are spontaneous dancers and may begin to dance as soon as a lively recording is heard—at home, in the classroom, or at the local smoothie store. Three-year-olds begin to synchronize their movements to music or a steady drumbeat. They are able to understand and follow simple directions. Their ability to participate in group activities is much greater than it was when they were toddlers. They are learning to cooperate with their peers and enjoy repetitive, familiar movement activities.

Four-year-olds often dance and dramatize in play. Their responses to creative movement begin to be more symbolic. They have gained a great deal of balance and control, and can move their body parts in isolation. Four-year-olds can follow much more complex directions, can synchronize movement to music, and can respond quickly and skillfully to a change in directions. They are beginning to have the ability to understand their role as participants in group activities and can cooperate in these efforts, although they continue to have moments when it is difficult.

By the time children reach kindergarten and the primary grades, most have a well-developed ability to concentrate on movement activities. They can work cooperatively with others to use movement to represent ideas (for example, a nest of birds, a wave in the sea). They are able to make many suggestions for movement activities and can remember complex verbal explanations. At this age, children are sometimes shy about moving in front of others and may need time to trust that their movement expression will be accepted by both the teacher and their peers.

What Is Creative Movement Curriculum in Early Childhood?

Creative movement is more than children jumping around while music is playing. It can be thought of as a distinctive large motor activity in which the teacher guides children in developing physical skill and control while they express their feelings and ideas. The creative movement curriculum helps children to increase their aware-ness and understanding while they develop control, physical skills, and the disposi-tion to be physically active and expressive.

The Elements of Movement

Just as there are elements in art and music, there are elements of movement. Early childhood movement experts identify a number of different movement elements. These provide a framework to help you to plan and guide creative movement activities that help children to become confident, creative movers.

Body Awareness

In creative movement, the body is the medium of creative expression. Much of our teaching of creative movement is concerned with helping children to be aware of and able to control their bodies both when they are still and while they are moving. The ability to move one part of the body while keeping the rest still is called *body isolation* ("Make your arms dance while your feet rest"). This is a difficult skill for young chil-dren to develop. It is easier if you have children begin to learn these skills while seated.

Helping children to be aware of all of their body parts and where they are in space, along with where and how the body is moving is called *body awareness*. There are several aspects to body awareness. The most basic aspect is know-ing and naming body parts. Where your body is in a space is called *location* or *position*.

The movement element of *shape* has to do with the various shapes that the body can assume during movement. Body shapes send messages—such as slumping in sorrow or standing at atten-tion. As the relationship of body parts to each other changes (head on knees, hands behind back), so does body shape ("Make yourself small and round," "Make yourself tall and thin"). Movements also can have shape and size. A small low step is very different from a large, high marching step.

Traveling Movement

The ways we travel from one place to another are called *traveling* or *locomotor movements*. In creative movement activities, the physical development skills of walking, running, galloping, skipping, sliding, jumping, and hopping are applied in expressive ways. Children move through space at different speeds, with different degrees of force, and in ways that have smooth or jerky movement free or bound flow, each with its own distinct rhythm. If you ask children to travel in a happy way, in an angry way, or in a sad way, you are implicitly inviting them to try out different locomotor movements.

Body Gestures

The ways children move while staying in the same place are called *body gestures* or *non-locomotor movements*. Bending, stretching, twisting, rocking, swinging, bouncing, balancing, and transferring weight are all body gestures that you will have children use in creative movement activities. If you ask the children to "Bend forward and touch your toes" or "Sway like a tree being blown in the wind," you are inviting them to explore non-locomotor movement.

Space

Another element of creative movement is the place in which the movement occurs and the way bodies fill the environment. This element is called *space* (related to but different from the art element of space). There are several aspects of the element of space. Space involves *position* relative to the room, other people ("Find a place where you will have plenty of room to move without touching anyone or anything"), furniture, walls, and even to your own body (lie *on your back, kneel on the floor*). It includes *direction* (forward, backward, sideways) and *level* (high, middle, low). The places where the body travels in a creative movement activity are called *pathways.* Pathways can either lead across the floor (e.g., tiptoeing across the room) or can move a body part through space (e.g., drawing a circle in the air).

Space also can be thought about in terms of the space that is our own or *personal space* (space right around you, defined by your presence) and the space we share or *general space* (space used by the whole group that anyone can enter). Young children are just learning to differentiate between shared space and personal space. There is a cultural component to what feels comfortable and how much personal space you need.

Time

The element of *time* in movement concerns the duration and *tempo* (related to but different from the musical element of tempo) or speed of the movement. We want to help children to be able to have a range of controllable body tempo at their disposal. Young children have difficulty controlling speed and find slow controlled movement more difficult than quick movement.

Tempo, or time, is experienced through a contrast of fast and slow movements. Young children generally find it easier to move quickly since slow movements require greater concentration and body control. Slow movement is sustained, whereas fast movement can be jerky.

Rhythm

The element *rhythm,* like its musical equivalent, involves time. Movement rhythm involves the regular patterns of locomotor movement; the rhythm of a walk, a gallop, and a skip are each different. Rhythms can be *regular* (like a walking rhythm) or *syncopated* (like a galloping rhythm). When you play a repeating beat on a drum and invite children to "put the beat in your feet," you are giving them an experience with rhythm.

Force

The element that concerns the amount of energy that is brought to a particular motion is called *force.* Some movements, such as stamping heavily or punching into the air, require a lot of force. Others, such as tiptoeing or jumping lightly use less. Young children find strong, forceful movements very satisfying, but they also enjoy developing the control needed to move lightly. They learn about these differences through contrast (*fly like a butterfly, stomp like an elephant*).

Flow

The way force is controlled in movement is called *flow.* Flow determines whether movement is halting and jerky (called *bound flow*) or smooth and continuous (called *free flow*). Jumping and hopping are bound flow movements. Swaying and skating are free flow movements. Bound flow movement (especially quick bound flow movement) is generally easier for young children. Free flow movement requires greater concentration and control and so is usually more difficult.

Standards for Creative Movement Curriculum

What are the goals of the creative movement curriculum? Head Start and some states have standards for preschool creative movement curriculum; other states combine all the arts and have standards that do not differentiate art, music, and creative movement. A national consortium of arts education organizations has created dance standards for children in grades K–4.

Preschool Creative Movement Standards

The Head Start Child Development and Early Learning Framework for creative movement and dance is very simple and is tied to music. It lays out the expectations that children will express what is felt and heard in music through movement and dancing, and that they will move in time to different patterns of beat and rhythm in music. (See Figure 12.1.)

States tend to describe the expectation that children will participate in creative movement activities and learn to express ideas and feelings through movement. If your state has separate creative movement standards, they are likely to be similar to the following list.

Preschool programs provide opportunities for children to:

- participate in a variety of creative movement activities for enjoyment.
- demonstrate self-expression through creative movement.
- express interest in and begin to build a knowledge base in the arts including dance.
- respond to music through movement.

A Consortium of Music Educators (called the National Committee for Standards in the Arts) has developed dance curriculum standards for children in K–4 programs (see Figure 12.2). The standards for these grades are identical to those for K–12. However, the indicators (not included here) are differentiated for the primary grades and can be found at the National Association for Music Education (MENC) Web site: (www.menc.org/resources/view/national-standards-for-music-education/).

FIGURE 12.1 **Head Start Child Development and Early Learning Framework:**
Movement and Dance

The use of the body to move to music and express oneself.
- Expresses what is felt and heard in various musical tempos and styles.
- Moves to different patterns of beat and rhythm in music.
- Uses creative movement to express concepts, ideas, or feelings.

Source: Administration for Children and Families, Head Start Bureau, www.hsnrc.org/cdi/child-outcomes.cfm

FIGURE 12.2 National K–4 Standards for Arts Education: *Dance*

Standard 1: Identifying and demonstrating movement elements and skills in performing dance

Students:

- accurately demonstrate nonlocomotor/axial movements (such as bend, twist, stretch, swing)
- accurately demonstrate eight basic locomotor movements (such as walk, run, hop, jump, leap, gallop, slide, and skip), traveling forward, backward, sideward, diagonally, and turning
- create shapes at low, middle, and high levels
- demonstrate the ability to define and maintain personal space
- demonstrate movements in straight and curved pathways
- demonstrate accuracy in moving to a musical beat and responding to changes in tempo
- demonstrate kinesthetic awareness, concentration, and focus in performing movement skills
- attentively observe and accurately describe the action (such as skip, gallop) and movement elements (such as levels, directions) in a brief movement study

Standard 2: Understanding choreographic principles, processes, and structures

Students:

- create a sequence with a beginning, middle, and end, both with and without a rhythmic accompaniment; identify each of these parts of the sequence
- improvise, create, and perform dances based on their own ideas and concepts from other sources
- use improvisation to discover and invent movement and to solve movement problems
- create a dance phrase, accurately repeat it, and then vary it (making changes in the time, space, and/or force/energy)
- demonstrate the ability to work effectively alone and with a partner
- demonstrate the following partner skills: copying, leading and following, mirroring

Standard 3: Understanding dance as a way to create and communicate meaning

Students:

- observe and discuss how dance is different from other forms of human movement (such as sports, everyday gestures)
- take an active role in a class discussion about interpretations of and reactions to a dance
- present their own dances to peers and discuss their meanings with competence and confidence

Standard 4: Applying and demonstrating critical and creative thinking skills in dance

Students:

- explore, discover, and realize multiple solutions to a given movement problem; choose their favorite solution and discuss the reasons for that choice
- observe two dances and discuss how they are similar and different in terms of one of the elements of dance by observing body shapes, levels, pathways

Standard 5: Demonstrating and understanding dance in various cultures and historical periods

Students:

- perform folk dances from various cultures with competence and confidence
- learn and effectively share a dance from a resource in their own community; describe the cultural and/or historical context
- accurately answer questions about dance in a particular culture and time period (for example: In colonial America, why and in what settings did people dance? What did the dances look like?)

Standard 6: Making connections between dance and healthful living

Students:

- identify at least three personal goals to improve themselves as dancers
- explain how healthy practices (such as nutrition, safety) enhance their ability to dance, citing multiple examples

Standard 7: Making connections between dance and other disciplines

Students:

- create a dance project that reveals understanding of a concept or idea from another discipline (such as pattern in dance and science)
- respond to a dance using another art form; explain the connections between the dance and their response to it (such as stating how their paintings reflect the dance they saw)

Source: From *National Standards for Arts Education.* Copyright © 1994 by The National Association for Music Education (MENC). Used with permission.

Teaching Creative Movement

Since young children love to move, it is natural to include creative movement in your curriculum. Creative movement should be considered in the design of the program environment, included in the schedule, and addressed in your interactions with children. And of course, it should be part of your planning.

Creative Movement Through Play in a Planned Environment

Janae and Sasha are playing in the dramatic play area. Both are wearing long dresses, have their heads draped in scarves, and are wearing fancy shoes. Janae walks across the linoleum and discovers that there are taps on her shoes. "Listen!" She tells Sasha and she does a little dance as she explores the sounds the taps make. Steve, their teacher, observes this and puts on a lively piece of contemporary music (Diamonds on the Soles of Her Shoes by Paul Simon). Janae and Sasha and several other children begin a joyful dance. Steve pushes the tables back so Janae can continue on the linoleum. Soon everyone is dancing.

An environment for creative movement must be safe, and it must inspire creativity. The dance described above was inspired by props provided for play. It could not have occurred without an open space for movement. It would not have occurred if the teacher had not had appropriate music ready to play for the children. Nor would it have occurred if he had been unwilling to move the furniture or been concerned about noise or proper dance form.

Children need space to move. Uncluttered open spaces with clear boundaries are needed. Indoors, wood or low-pile carpeted floors provide the best

movement surface. Outdoors, a flat, grassy lawn without roots or dips is best to minimize tripping and falling.

If you are fortunate, you will have a dedicated large motor room available for creative movement. If creative movement activities must take place within your classroom, you will need to have a large, safe, open, inviting space. Some teachers design their rooms to include an open space for group meetings and creative movement. Others move tables and shelves when creative movement is planned. Outdoor space can also provide a good place for creative movement if the ground is even, weather permitting.

The ideal group size for creative movement is from 5 to 12 children, depending on the size of the space. If you must work with larger groups or if you have a very small space, you will need to have the children alternate between moving and being the audience.

The outdoors can be a wonderful place for creative movement. The shadows of trees, the songs of the birds, and the shifting of the wind can add new dimensions to moving. A large outdoor space also allows you to work with the whole group if your classroom is small. However, it may present challenges. Outdoors may not be a good option if others are using the outside play area, as your children may be enticed away by other children's activities. It will not work well if wind or traffic noise overshadows the sound of your voice or the music. Finally, outdoors may not be an option if the temperature, terrain, or precipitation makes it hard to comfortably move.

Creative Movement Equipment and Supplies

Besides having a safe space, two other things are essential for successful creative movement teaching. The first is a good hand-drum or tambourine. This will be your tool for signaling children. A hard beat will tell them to freeze. Soft tapping or jingling will let them know that a soft sustained movement is expected. Loud, slow, rhythmic sounds will tell them to stomp, and quick tapping or jingling will tell them to move quickly.

The other tool that you need is a device for playing recorded music aloud—a tape recorder, CD player, or MP3 player with speakers. A boom box powered by batteries will allow you to move your music outdoors. You'll need a collection of recorded instrumental music. Some should be quick and bouncy, like Mussorgsky's "Ballet of the Unhatched Chicks" from Pictures at an Exhibition. Others should be slow and contemplative like Smetana's Vltava (Moldau) from MaVlast (My Country). Every teacher should have a collection of different kinds of music to use with creative movement. If you have a functional old-fashioned record player and records, consider yourself fortunate. These allow you to stop and start recordings exactly where and when you want.

In addition to these two essential pieces of equipment, there are a variety of props that are helpful to have for your creative movement curriculum. These can be homemade, scrounged, or purchased. The In Practice box (Creative Movement Props and Alternatives) gives some ideas of props to use with young children.

A Schedule for Creative Movement

Regularly scheduled movement activities at least twice a week help children develop skill and build on previous experience. Plan movement sessions for group times or your regularly scheduled physical activity times. When movement activities occur only infrequently, children do not develop skills; in addition, children tend to be overstimulated by these activities because they are so rare.

Props to Purchase	Recycled, Homemade, or Scrounged Alternatives
Nylon juggling scarves	Reuse donated or thrift store scarves
Streamers or ribbon wands	Tie 3′ lengths of grosgrain ribbons to dollar store plastic bracelets
Heavy colored spots (called poly markers)	Sample carpet squares
Traffic cones and half cones	Recycle empty plastic gallon jugs (keep them stable by weighing them down with a few cups of kitty litter—wet it to make it solid)
Bean bags	Make bean bags with fabric scraps and rice or beans
Hula hoops	Make hoops with ¾″ or 1″ PVC pipe and pipe connectors
6′ lengths of good-quality braided rope	Dollar store jump ropes
Parachutes (designed for play not air safety)	Old sheets

Movement sessions for preschoolers can last for 10 to 20 minutes, or a shorter time for younger or less experienced children. If you observe that children are losing interest (you'll know because they'll stop participating in appropriate ways), you will want to change or end the movement session. As children become more familiar with movement activities, you may be able to extend movement sessions to half an hour. But as in all teaching, it's better to end an activity while children are still eager and interested than to keep going until they are bored and tired.

Your Role in Teaching Creative Movement

The ways in which you guide, participate, and interact with children can have a huge impact on their creative movement. In addition to providing a safe physical environment, you also need to provide an emotional climate in which it is safe to take risks.

Encouragement and stimulation inspire children to experiment in creative movement. Movement activities must match the level of physical and language development of the children. Successful movement experiences take thoughtful planning. An awareness of the goals of creative movement can guide you.

Basic rules for safety need to be established (no pushing, bumping, and so on) and an attitude of respect for individual interpretations and skill levels is essential. Most children will be delighted to participate in creative movement, but a few will hesitate. Children should never be forced to participate in a creative movement activity, nor should they be ridiculed or criticized for the way they move.

As children develop confidence and movement skills, they will become able to use movement to express creative ideas with little direction. In the beginning, however, you will need to provide a good deal of guidance. A few teaching principles will help.

Establish a signal. When you first begin creative movement with a group, establish a signal like a hard drumbeat to tell the children to stop (freeze). Practice stopping to this signal as a game until children understand it is an integral part of every movement activity. This will help you to maintain control of the group and assist children in focusing their movement.

Begin activities sitting down or standing still before inviting children to move freely around the room. This will help you to monitor how active children are going to be. Using your established signal, you can bring the children back to the seated or standing activity as needed.

Practice using personal and general space before you begin more complex activities. Encourage children to look around to see if they are filling the general space and avoiding other children's personal space. We like to use an image of a bubble that will pop if you intrude into another person's personal space.

Use contrasting movements. Alternate vigorous and quiet/ fast and slow/heavy and light/big and small activities. Learning about contrast is the way children develop understanding and control. In addition, it is an excellent way to keep children interested and focused on the activity.

Demonstrate the types of movement you want to encourage children to perform. Sometimes, in order to understand movement, children need to see it. You can demonstrate a movement yourself or invite an experienced child to demonstrate the movement: "Jessica, can you demonstrate the Hokey Pokey for the rest of us?"

Give children encouragement rather than praise ("You're gliding like swans!") and **offer a challenge if children's behavior is disruptive** ("Jump on one foot, jump low, make your hands jump").

When you have reached a planned or natural ending place, it is best to **finish the activity while it is still going well.** End sessions in a way that provides a transition to the next activity: "Tiptoe to the playground when I touch you on the shoulder."

Managing creative movement sessions can be challenging for beginners— both children and their teachers. While every group of children is different—some need very specific limits and others need lots of opportunity to explore—it is usually best to begin with short (15 minutes or less), simple, well-planned, and fairly structured activities and move on to more open activities later. Children who have had little experience with structured movement activities can become overexcited and uncontrolled, and this can be difficult to handle. As a beginner, you will be much more successful if you review your plans several times before attempting to implement a creative movement activity. If a movement session does not go well, do not blame the children or yourself. The learning that comes out of these experiences can be valuable for you as a teacher.

Creative Movement Activities

Creative movement activities are guided activities in which the teacher provides some stimulation and direction for movement. The younger the children, the simpler the activities must be. With a group of very young children, it might be as simple as jumping and stopping to the beat of a drum. As children become more experienced, they can be given more complex movement tasks. The general types of activities that we describe here are just a sample of what you can do.

Movement Songs

Simple movement songs and games (*I'm a Little Teapot, Hokey Pokey*) introduce children to the idea of moving to express ideas. These are especially useful for young and inexperienced children from whom you cannot expect sustained group interest.

Personal Space Activities

Activities can help children discover how to use all of their personal space—up high, down low, to the side, in back—as well as learn how to share the general space. Boundaries (for example, a chalked circle, a hoop, or a length of rope) can define the space for children to move within and around. Space may be filled in different ways while children stay in one place. Use images to motivate and encourage children to use space in diverse ways. Invite children to think about moving and filling space like balloons, fish, worms, trees,

374

bubbles, or birds. To help young children develop the idea of personal space, have them move in different ways while holding a hoop at waist height. The space within the hoop is their personal space, and their goal is to avoid touching other hoops.

Guided Movement

When you say the words *creative movement,* most experienced teachers think of guided movement. In a guided movement activity, the teacher gives children movement directions, usually while playing a drum or tambourine. Guided movement activities can be quite structured (as when children move parts of their bodies to the beat of a drum) or more open ended (as when children are invited to explore all the ways they can move to music with a scarf).

Movement elements and skills can provide a structure for guided creative movement. You can suggest that children move at different speeds and levels without touching or bumping anyone else. Contrast speed by asking children to move body parts at different tempos (raise your arms slowly, shake your hands quickly) or to move their whole body at different paces (run, creep, trot, slowly unbend, jump). Imagery of animals, plants, and machines can encourage exploration of speed, and the use of a drumbeat or music can help children learn to move to a particular tempo.

Activities that involve force can contrast heavy and light movement (stamping and then tiptoeing) and can involve isolated body parts or the whole body while in motion or stationary. Music can evoke heavy or light movements, as can images of animals and fantasy creatures (elephants, butterflies, bears, birds, monsters, fairies, giants, ghosts). You can also invite children to move a single body part in isolation ("Show you're happy with your foot!").

Children will respond with greater enthusiasm if you weave a story around your creative movement activity or invite them to represent something ("As I play my drum, slowly grow toward the sun and blossom like a flower"). Older preschoolers and primary school children enjoy choreographing a song or story. We find the work of Ann Barlin (Barlin, 1979; Barlin & Kalev, 1989) and Mimi Brodsky Chenfeld (Chenfeld, 2002) to be very useful in designing creative movement activities.

Moving to Music

One of the best ways to develop children's movement skills is to give them short, evocative pieces of music to listen and move to. Instrumental pieces like those suggested in the In Practice box (Music for Movement) suggest a particular type of movement. Begin by choosing two contrasting pieces. Play the opening bars of one and invite children to think of ways to move to the music. Once you decide as a group that it is tiptoeing or walking (or whatever) music, invite the group to move (remind them that when the music stops, their bodies should stop, too). When the first piece is done, repeat with a contrasting piece. On another occasion, try adding props.

Movement with People

Awareness of a *partner* or the other members of the *group* is a critical part of creative movement. It is difficult for children to be aware of other people, and this is one of the important skills that children are learning during creative movement activities. Moving with other people concerns space (facing one another, behind,

Music That Suggests Hopping/Jumping/Leaping		Music That Suggests Running	
"Ballet of the Unhatched Chicks" from *Pictures at an Exhibition* (Mussorgsky) "Leap Frog" from *Jeux D'Enfants* (Bizet) *Aragonaise* (Massenet) *Popcorn* (Hot Butter) *Zydeco Gris-Gris* (Beausoleil) "Russian Dance" from *Nutcracker Suite* (Tchaikovsky)		"The Ball" from *Jeux D'Enfants* (Bizet) "Catch Me" from *Scenes of Childhood* (Schumann) "Tag" from *Music for Children* (Prokofiev) *Flight of the Bumblebee* (Rimsky-Korsakov)	
Music That Suggests Walking	**Music That Suggests Creeping/Sneaking**	**Music That Suggests Sliding/Gliding**	
The Entertainer (Scott Joplin) *Gavotte* (Handel) *The Syncopated Clock* (Anderson)	"The Wolf" from *Peter and the Wolf* (Prokofiev) *In the Hall of the Mountain King* (Grieg) *The Sorcerer's Apprentice* (Dukas)	"Swans" and "Aquarium" from *Carnival of the Animals* (Saint-Saëns) "Arabian Dance" from *Nutcracker Suite* (Tchaikovsky)	
Music That Suggests Tiptoeing		**Music That Suggests Skipping/Galloping**	
"Chinese Dance" from *Nutcracker Suite* (Tchaikovsky) *Dance of the Little Swans* (Tchaikovsky) *Dance of the Hours* (Ponchielli)		"The Wild Horseman" from *Scenes of Childhood* (Schumann) *Comedian's Gallop* (Kabalevsky)	

side-by-side, etc.), similarity and difference, and time (simultaneous or separate, before or after). You can ask children to:

- copy or match a leader's movement.
- mirror (facing) or shadow (behind) a partner's movement.
- echo a leader's movement.
- move in unison.
- respond to another's movement.
- move or make a shape connected to another person.

Movement Activities Using Props

Many movement activities are enhanced by the use of props (see the In Practice box on Creative Movement Props and Alternatives). Most of these involve using the prop to help children to feel less inhibited and to enable them to focus on movement. Holding a scarf or streamer and moving it to music adds variety and helps children to interpret the tempo and force of a song or a piece of music ("Make your scarf dance to the music—the music is getting slower, so make your scarf dance slowly").

Using these movement props involves *object control skills*. Instead of propelling or striking objects (required when using balls), creative movement props require children to use the prop either as an extension of their bodies (scarves, streamers, ribbon wands) or as a challenge for moving around, with, or through (*hoops, parachutes, bean bags, poly spots, traffic cones, ropes*). Preschoolers are initially very excited by props and have difficulty using them productively. With experience and guidance, they can learn to use props in ways that enhance their creative movement expression.

Props like ropes, spots, hoops, or carpet squares help children to focus on space. Be sure there are enough for each participating child. Invite children to stand on a spot, rope, or in a hoop. Start a lively piece of music and ask children to walk, run, jump, or tiptoe around the spots or on the ropes in time to music. When the music stops, children should find another spot/hoop/rope to stand on/in.

Parachutes can be used as an aid to help children learn to move together. We like to use a parachute with a song. Walk or skip, keeping the parachute taut as you sing the song. Change directions with each new verse. Move the parachute up and down together to the rhythm of a song.

Creative Drama

With young children, creative movement and drama are closely tied to one another. The motivation for movement activities is often the suggestion to act like a character, animal, or object. Children naturally take on roles in their play and dramatize stories and scenes. With very young children, creative drama and movement are often part of the same activity. As you direct children in creative movement, you may alternate from directions that are exclusively related to body movement ("Bounce,") to directions that are related to a dramatic idea ("Bounce like a ball." "Hop like a rabbit."), to directions that are dramatic ideas as a part of a story or scenario ("The rabbit is hopping slowly now, he hears something. Quickly hop away to your burrow.").

Children's literature can offer motivation for creative movement and drama. A rabbit may become Peter Rabbit fleeing from Mr. MacGregor. Leo Lionni's story *Swimmy* intertwines the story of a fish with descriptions of the movements of sea creatures and serves as an excellent outline for a movement/drama session. Creative drama for young children involves their interpretations of story lines and ideas, not memorization of scripts, and should be outgrowths of children's ideas, not production efforts put on by staff for families. Some older children do become entranced by performance, however. With a skillful teacher, they can begin to extend their developing skills into performing dance and drama productions.

Choreographing a Song

A satisfying creative movement activity for older preschoolers and primary school children is to choreograph a song. This can grow quite naturally out of fingerplays and action songs. Essentially, it is an action song in which the children choose actions and move together to illustrate the lyrics.

Choose a song with strong imagery. As a group, decide on simple actions to accompany the song. Decide on a form for the group (e.g., everyone stands on a spot facing the center of the circle). Choose movements (steps) to go with each different phrase of the song, for example, rocking back and forth from one foot to another during the chorus. Children might want to use a prop like scarves to wave in special ways during the song. Finally, decide on a way to end the song— for example, everyone sits down on a spot.

Planning Creative Movement Curriculum

Because young children naturally express themselves through movement, creating an environment for play and ensuring that there is adequate time for children to use it is a critical part of the creative movement curriculum. However, it is also important to plan creative movement activities. You plan creative movement activities to help children learn to use movement expressively as a means of communication; to help children learn about the elements of movement and acquire skills they will use in dance; to be sure that you are addressing a program goal or standard for creative movement curriculum; and to involve creative movement in an integrated curriculum study.

To help you in writing plans, we have included some common objectives for the preschool creative movement curriculum in Table 12.1.

Writing Creative Movement Plans

It is morning activity time in the Fern Room (a class of 3- and 4-year-olds). Tayeden and Soullee are in the science area, looking at a chrysalis that has split. Out of it, the wings of a butterfly are starting to emerge. Soullee says, "Please come out butterfly." The children continue watching as the butterfly slowly emerges. Later that day, they watch as Melissa, their teacher, frees the butterfly. Melissa notices that while Soullee pretends to fly around the yard, Tayeden sits and watches her.

Successful creative movement activities take planning, especially when you are new to teaching. Soullee and Tayeden in the above vignette had a wonderful experience with the natural world. What could Melissa do to build on this interest and engage these children in creative movement?

To plan movement curriculum, you need to know the children both as individuals and as a group. Some children move easily and unselfconsciously. Others are awkward and feel uncomfortable moving in a group. Children's strengths and

TABLE 12.1 Objectives for Creative Movement

Individual Skills	Moving with a Group	Using Props	Understanding Movement Elements
• Move from place to place in a variety of ways. • Move in a controlled way while standing or sitting in one place. • Represent ideas and feelings through movement. • Move one part of the body while keeping the rest still.	• Move with awareness of others and the environment. • Respect the personal space of others. • Move in response to direction. • Identify empty and full spaces. • Move with a partner in a coordinated way. • Create movement "scenes" with group.	• Use simple props and appropriately (e.g., hops from hoop to hoop). • Use props appropriately and safely as a part of a group. • Use props in a structured, repetitive, or choreographed way.	• Demonstrate simple traveling movements (walk, run, hop) and body gestures. • Demonstrate concepts of personal and general space, speed, direction, level, tempo, force. • Move in different directions at different levels.

Caterpillar Metamorphosis Movement

Objectives: Represent ideas and feelings in movement, control tempo of movement, move at different levels.

Standard: Domain V (Creative Movement/Drama) Standard 1

What you need: Large carpeted area (push back tables), tambourine

How to teach:
1. Sing *Fuzzy, Fuzzy Caterpillar* by Patty Zeitlin.
2. Invite a child to move like a caterpillar.
3. Play tambourine and ask all children to move to the space and be a caterpillar.
4. Take children through stages—caterpillar, chrysalis, emerging, butterfly wings drying, butterfly flying.
5. Have children think of other things that grow and change and move like that thing to activity choice.

How to assess: Look for children wiggling slowly on ground, curling up and being still, standing on tiptoes using arms as wings. Document with photos and anecdotals.

interests should guide you in planning—along with your state's standards and your program's goals.

Figure 12.3 shows the plan Melissa created to take advantage of Soullee and Tayeden's interest and to build creative movement skills and understanding.

Because she is an experienced teacher, Melissa's short plan leaves out many details. It would not be enough of a guide for a beginning teacher. The detailed version in Figure 12.4, gives you a better idea of what she planned to do.

Creative Movement in a Weekly Plan

As we have said before, we believe that creative movement should be a regular feature in every week's plan for preschoolers. In the week's plan example included in Figure 12.5, you will see that there are songs with movement. In addition, parachute play (with a focus on moving as a group) is offered. These activities allow children to develop creative movement skills. Activities that involve creative movement are highlighted.

Creative Movement in an Integrated Study

Because creative movement is a way that children express their growing understanding, it is an important part of every integrated study. In *A Study of Myself and Others* sunburst in Figure 12.6, creative movement activities appear in the sections on creative movement, music, and physical development curriculum.

In addition, because an integrated study becomes a part of the life of the classroom, children naturally bring it into their creative movement. Children went to a "dance studio" as part of the curriculum where they could see themselves move in front of a wall of mirrors. When creative movement activities were planned, these experiences were often a part of creative expressions emerging from the children.

FIGURE 12.4   Detailed Creative Movement Activity Plan

Activity: **Creative Movement**	**Caterpillar Metamorphosis Movement** (a guided movement activity) **Curriculum Focus**
WHO It's For:	This activity was planned for the *Swimming Penguins* (ten 4-year-olds).
WHY This Activity **Rationale:**	Most of the *Swimming Penguins* (especially Soullee and Tayeden) are interested in the caterpillars that have been metamorphosing in the classroom. Building the ability to express ideas through movement is a goal for all the children, a strength for Soullee, and a challenge for Tayeden.
Objectives:	*By participating in this activity the children will develop the ability to …* • Represent ideas and feelings in movement. • Control the tempo of movement from slow to still to quick. • Move at different levels.
Preschool Content **Standard:**	Domain V, Standard 1: Create and express themselves through a variety of creative movement and drama experiences.
Indicators:	Participate in teacher-guided creative movement and drama activities; express ideas through movement and drama.
HOW to Prepare	*What you need:* large carpeted area, tambourine *Set up:* Before the children come, push back tables
HOW to Teach	*Introduction:* As children come for small-group time and get settled, sing the song *Fuzzy, Fuzzy Caterpillar* by Patty Zeitlin. *Teaching steps:* 1. Invite a child to move to the center of the carpet and be a caterpillar. 2. Tell children when the tambourine plays, they can all move to a space and be a caterpillar. 3. Play tambourine, take children through stages—caterpillar, making a chrysalis, chrysalis sleeping, butterfly emerging, wings drying, butterfly flying. 4. If children are engaged, repeat. *Closure:* Invite children to think of other things that grow and change— and move like that thing—(a child walking, a bird flying, a ladybug crawling) to activity choice.

HOW to Assess and Document

Objectives	Evidence of Learning Children might …	How to Document This Evidence
Represent ideas and feelings in movement.	Wiggle like a caterpillar. Use arms as wings and pretend to fly.	Anecdotal observations, annotated photograph, or video recording
Control the tempo of movement from slow to still to quick.	Move slowly as a caterpillar, curl up and be still when a chrysalis, move quickly when pretending to be a butterfly.	
Move at different levels.	Crawl on the ground and stand on tiptoes when flying.	

EVALUATION   (Things to remember for next time)

Set up a place for still sleeping caterpillars to stay. Dalton insisted that he was not ready to metamorphose and he was stepped on.

FIGURE 12.5   A Week's Plan: Myself and Others—Week #3

Objectives: To help children understand and describe their own characteristics and those of others; develop the ability to work with others in a group.

	Monday	Tuesday	Wednesday	Thursday	Friday
Story	*I Like Myself* (Beaumont)	*It's OK to be Different* (Parr)	*Abiyoyo* (Seeger)	*Ira Sleeps Over* (Waber)	*Ira Says Goodbye* (Waber)
Outdoor Activities **Purpose:** *to help children develop …*	**Giant Me Maps** Geographic awareness. Self-concept.	**Obstacle Course** Large motor strength and coordination.	**Obstacle Course** Large motor strength and coordination.	**Parachute Play** Ability to move with others in a group.	**Friend Mural Painting** Ability to work and communicate with a partner.
Small Group 1 **Purpose:** *to help children develop …*	**I Can Chart** Knowledge of self and others. Understanding of print.	**Me Story** Ability to use language to tell stories and learn about others.	**Writing Names with Unit Blocks** Ability to recognize and use symbols. Concepts of print.	**Favorites Graph** Awareness of ways to represent and compare quantity.	**Reading *Frog and Toad*** Ability to enjoy and understand books. Ability to listen with comprehension to spoken language.
Small Group 2 **Purpose:** *to help children develop …*	**I Can Discussion** A sense of self. Ability to participate in group discussion.	**Group Hollow Block Play** Ability to work together in groups. Understanding that friends help one another.	**Cooperative Block Building** Ability to work together in groups. Understanding that friends help one another.	**Making Banana Pudding** Health awareness and skill.	**What's Missing?** Vocabulary and memory.
Indoor Special Activities **Purpose:** *to help children develop …*	**Me and My Friends Game** Understanding of self and others. Positive peer relations.	**Giant Me Map** Geographic awareness. Self-concept.	**Construction Paper Collage** Skill in collage technique.	**Me Collage** Ability to express ideas using medium of collage.	**Me Collage** Ability to express ideas using medium of collage.
Circle Time **Purpose:** *to help children …*	**With My Own Two Hands** (repeated all week) Develop the ability to sing tunefully.	**Punchinello** Represent ideas and feelings through movement.	**Walk Around a Friend** Move with a partner in a coordinated way.	**Magic Rocks Growing Child** Represent ideas and feelings through movement.	**Punchinello** Represent ideas and feelings through movement.

Activities that support the creative movement curriculum are highlighted.

Creative Movement for All Children

Children with Special Needs

Alana, a child with spina bifida who uses a wheelchair, is a 4 1/2-year-old in the Rainbow Flowers Group. Alana participates eagerly in most preschool activities. She is well liked, and Zoe is her best friend. When it is time for creative movement, the teacher, Ginger, plays the drum and invites the children

FIGURE 12.6 A Study of Myself and Others Sunburst

A Study of Myself and Others

My Characteristics and Abilities

Big Idea
I am like other people—my body, my needs, my senses, my feelings.

Big Idea
I am unique—there is no one else with my body, preferences, or abilities.

My Friends

Big Idea
My friends are people I like—we care about each other and take care of each other.

Big Idea
I have friends at school—sometimes we like the same things, sometimes we like different things.

My Friends

Big Idea
Sometimes friends do things together—they cooperate and play.

Sometimes friends play with other people—they are still friends.

Big Idea
Friends help each other.

My Family

Big Idea
The people I love and live with are my family.

Big Idea
People in my family care about each other and take care of each other. I can help my family.

Big Idea
Sometimes we are happy and get along, sometimes we get mad at each other—we are still family.

Inquiry Curriculum

Social Studies
Giant Me Maps
Friends Comparison Chart
Hide a Friend
Me Story
Mother Child Art Game
Also all trips and family involvement

Science
X-rays on the Light Table
Baby/Child Comparison
Also all cooking activities

Math
Family Graph
Favorites Graph
Also all cooking activities

Communication Curriculum

Language
Me Poster Discussion
Family, Friends, Feelings Discussion
Friend Riddles
Family Clues

Literacy
Name Writing
Workjobs: Friend Sorting
Family Workjob
Me Puzzles
Journals: My Friend, My Family, Myself
Block Names

Literature
Hands Can
On the Day You Were Born
(see booklist)

Family Involvement
Story of the *Day You Were Born*
Potluck Lunch
Holiday Sharing

Trips
Visiting Family Members at Work
Visit to a Dance Studio

Creative Movement
Punchinello
Walk Around a Friend
The Family in the Dell
Hokey Pokey
Dancing to Favorite Music

Physical Development Curriculum

Cooking
Quesadillas for a Friend
English Muffin for a Friend
Family Favorites

Large Motor
Taking a Long Walk
Dressing Friends
Ball Sharing Game
Cooperative Balance Beam

Fine Motor
Cooperative Block Building
Friend Puzzles
Girl and Boy Puzzles

Sensory
Textured Playdough
Washing Baby Dolls

Arts Curriculum

Art
Me Collage
Round Collage
Self-Portraits
Family Portraits
Friend Portraits
Hands Can Painting
Friends Mural
Cooperative Golf Ball Painting

Music
Shake a Friend's Hand
I Am Here Today
Little Red Box
I Like You
Song Choosing
Container Drumming

to move around the movement area while the drum is beating. She reminds them to make sure not to bump into one another. Like Zoe, Alana sometimes forgets and Ginger reminds both girls to keep a big bubble of personal space around them. Ginger gives each child in the group a bean bag and challenges them to "Balance your bean bag on your head and move while I beat the drum slowly. If it falls, freeze until a friend can pick up your bean bag." Alana and Zoe both have to freeze when their bean bags fall off, and both giggle until someone picks them up and their movement activity continues.

Teachers are often surprised to learn that it is possible to include children with disabilities in virtually all activities. Just as you might accommodate your toddler at the family Thanksgiving table with a booster chair, a drop cloth, and smaller pieces of turkey, a child with disabilities can be included in the creative movement curriculum if you adjust your expectations, modify your environment, and alter your instructions. A child with a physical disability like Alana can move like the others in the class, though she might need to move *while* the drumbeats rather than *to* the beat of the drum. Similarly, like Ginger, you might need to remove barriers from the movement area in order to include all the children. You can use other strategies for other disabilities. For a child with a vision impairment, you might need to include more movement activities in which children work as partners. For a child with hearing loss, you might need to make your cues for movement visual and make sure you are within the child's line of sight. But all children, regardless of ability, can and should be included in the joy of creative movement.

Children in the Primary Grades

Primary school children have developed many skills and enjoy movement challenges like gymnastics and team sports. They have a strong sense of rhythm and a great deal of physical control. They can learn simple folk dances and gymnastics routines (make sure that they are not risking any injury as they attempt gymnastic exercises such as a forward roll or headstand, both of which can result in neck injuries). Since they enjoy working together, integrating music, drama, and movement for performance is an enjoyable way to use creative movement in the primary grades. At this age, children may be self-critical. For this reason, it is important to avoid adding pressure and to respect children who need time to get involved.

Final Thoughts

You have many gifts to share with children. Providing an opportunity for them to create, express ideas and feelings, and appreciate movement is one of them. You give this gift by planning regular opportunities for creative movement, by designing a learning environment with movement in mind, and through sensitivity to children's feelings and relationships. As you do these things, you support one of the most natural of ways for children to express their creativity and help them to begin a life in which movement is a joyful part of their every day lives.

Learning Outcomes

When you read this chapter, thoughtfully complete activities from the "To Learn More" section, and document this learning as suggested in the "For Your Portfolio" section, you will be making progress in the following *NAEYC Standards for Early Childhood Professional Preparation Programs* (2009):

Standard 1. Promoting Child Development and Learning

Students prepared in early childhood degree programs are grounded in a child development knowledge base. They use their understanding of young children's characteristics and needs and of the multiple interacting influences on children's development and learning to create environments that are healthy, respectful, supportive, and challenging for each child.

The key elements of standard 1 you will have learned about are . . .

1a: Knowing and understanding young children's characteristics and needs

1c: Using developmental knowledge to create healthy, respectful, supportive, and challenging learning environments

Standard 4. Using Developmentally Effective Approaches to Connect with Children and Families

Students prepared in early childhood degree programs understand that teaching and learning with young children is a complex enterprise, and its details vary depending on children's ages, characteristics, and the settings within which teaching and learning occur. They understand and use positive relationships and supportive interactions as the foundation for their work with young children and families. Students know, understand, and use a wide array of developmentally appropriate approaches, instructional strategies, and tools to connect with children and families and positively influence each child's development and learning.

The key elements of standard 4 you will have learned about are . . .

4a: Understanding positive relationships and supportive interactions as the foundation of their work with children

4b: Knowing and understanding effective strategies and tools for early education

4c: Using a broad repertoire of developmentally appropriate teaching/learning approaches

4d: Reflecting on their own practice to promote positive outcomes for each child

Standard 5. Using Content Knowledge to Build Meaningful Curriculum

Students prepared in early childhood degree programs use their knowledge of academic disciplines to design, implement, and evaluate experiences that promote positive development and learning for each and every young child. Students understand the importance of developmental domains and academic (or content) disciplines in an early childhood curriculum. They know the essential concepts, inquiry tools, and structure of content areas, including academic subjects, and can identify resources to deepen their understanding. Students use their own knowledge and other resources to design, implement, and evaluate meaningful, challenging curricula that promote comprehensive developmental and learning outcomes for every young child.

The key elements of standard 5 you will have learned about are . . .

5a: Understanding content knowledge and resources in academic disciplines

5b: Knowing and using the central concepts, inquiry tools, and structures of content areas or academic disciplines

5c: Using their own knowledge, appropriate early learning standards, and other resources to design, implement, and evaluate meaningful, challenging curricula for each child.

To Learn More

Observe a Program: For a morning, observe a program and see how the staff includes creative movement opportunities. Notice both the play opportunities and the planned group activities. Look at the plans and see how the planning reflects what you observed. Interview a teacher to learn how he or she thinks about creative movement curriculum.

Observe a Child: For a morning, observe a child in a classroom, with a focus on expressive movement. Notice how the child engages with any planned creative movement activities and how he or she constructs his or her own opportunities for moving expressively. Notice the extent to which the child's activity and the planned curriculum seem to match. Observe to see how staff support the child's growing creative movement ability.

Observe a Creative Movement Teacher: Spend a morning with an educator who is experienced in creative movement. S/he may be a classroom teacher or a movement specialist in a preschool, elementary school, or a teacher in a dance or gymnastics program. Then interview the educator about how he or she plans for and provides creative movement curriculum to children of different ages.

Observe a Creative Movement Activity: Observe a teacher leading a planned creative movement activity. Interview the teacher to find out the objectives for the activity. Reflect on any differences between what you saw and the focus of the plan.

Compare Two Programs: Observe creative movement in two early childhood programs. Compare the ways that the two address creative movement curriculum—their similarities and differences. Reflect on which program seems to best support children's learning and why. What implications does this comparison have for your future work with young children?

Compare Two Ages: Observe two classrooms, one preschool and one for primary school children. Report on how each includes creative movement in the curriculum. Talk to the staff about how they make their curriculum choices. Notice how development influences curriculum choices.

Explore Resources: Read one of the books from the bibliography or one of the online resources listed here and write a review of it for your classmates.

The American Orff-Schulwerk Association: www.aosa.org/

Cener for Movement Education and Research: www.movement-education.org/

Creative Dance Center: www.creativedance.org/

Dance and the Child International USA: www.daciusa.com/

Early Childhood Music and Movement Association: www.ecmma.org/

National Dance Education Organization (NDEO): www.ndeo.org/

For Your Portfolio

Design a Classroom for Creative Movement: Design and draw a floor plan for a classroom and play yard that would support creative movement. Share your plan with an early childhood educator, discussing what you included and why. Ask for and consider the educator's feedback and suggestions. Set up a real classroom or play yard utilizing as many of your ideas as possible and use it. For your portfolio, include the floor plan, photographs or video of children, and a reflection on what you learned by doing this project.

Plan and Implement a Creative Movement Activity: Observe a group of children for a morning, focusing on their movement interest and skill. Based on what you observed, write and implement a creative movement activity. Collect evidence of children's responses in the form of anecdotal observations, photographs, or video recordings. Reflect on how children responded and what they appear to have learned. What worked? What might you do differently next time? How might you expand on this experience for children? For your portfolio, include the plan, a photograph, and a reflection on what you learned about yourself, children, planning, and teaching.

Find or Create a Creative Movement Prop: Use the prop with a particular child or group of children. Introduce it to the child or children and teach with it. Reflect on how the children responded and how you felt about what you did. What worked? What might you do differently next time? How might you expand on this experience for children? For your portfolio, include a photograph of a child using the material and a reflection on what you learned about yourself, children, learning materials, and teaching.

Bibliography

Barlin, A. L. (1979). *Teaching your wings to fly*. Santa Monica, CA: Goodyear Publishing Co.

Barlin, A. L., & Kalev, N. (1989). *Hello toes! Movement games for young children*. Pennington, NJ: Dance Horizons, Princeton Book Co.

Chenfeld, M. B. (2002). *Creative experiences for young children* (3rd ed.). New York, NY: Heinneman.

Edwards, C. (2009). *The creative arts: A process approach for teachers and children* (5th ed.). Upper Saddle River, NJ: Pearson.

Edwards, L. C., Bayless, K. M., & Ramsey, M. E. (2009). *Music and movement: A way of life for the young child* (6th ed.). Upper Saddle River, NJ: Pearson.

Feeney, S., Moravcik, E., & Nolte, S. (2013). *Who am I in the lives of children?* (9th ed.). Upper Saddle River, NJ: Pearson.

Fraser, D. L. (1991). *Playdancing.* Pennington, NJ: Dance Horizons, Princeton Book Co.

Gardner, H. (1989). *To Open Minds.* New York, NY: Basic Books.

Head Start Resource Center. (2010). *The Head Start Child development and early learning framework: Promoting positive outcomes in early childhood programs serving children 3–5 years old.* Washington, DC: Office of Head Start, Administration for Children and Families, U.S. Department of Health and Human Services.

Isenberg, J. P., & Jalongo, M. (2000). *Creative expression and play in the early childhood curriculum* (3rd ed.). Upper Saddle River, NJ: Pearson.

Mitchell, A., & David, J. (Eds.). (1992). *Explorations with young children.* Mt. Rainier, MD: Gryphon House.

Pica, R. (2009). *Experiences in music & movement: Birth to age 8* (4th ed.) Florence, KY: Wadsworth Publishing.

Purcell, T. (1994). *Teaching children dance: Becoming a master teacher.* Champaign, IL: Human Kinetics.

Rowen, B. (1982). *Learning through movement: Activities for the preschool and elementary school grades.* New York, NY: Teachers College Press.

Rowen, B. (1994). *Dance and grow: Developmental activities for three- through eight-year-olds.* Pennington, NJ: Dance Horizons.

Sullivan, M. (1982). *Feeling strong, feeling free: Movement exploration for young children.* Washington, DC: NAEYC.

Wright, S. (2003). *The arts, young children, and learning.* Boston, MA: Allyn and Bacon.

MyEducationLab

Go to Topics 2: Child Development and Learning, and 9: Content Areas/Lessons and Activities in the MyEducationLab (www.myeducationlab.com) for *Meaningful Curriculum for Young Children,* where you can:

- Find learning outcomes for Child Development and Learning and Content Areas/Lessons and Activities along with the national standards that connect to these outcomes.
- Complete Assignments and Activities that can help you more deeply understand the chapter content.
- Apply and practice your understanding of the core teaching skills identified in the chapter with the Building Teaching Skills and Dispositions learning units.
- Listen to experts from the field in Professional perspectives.

- Examine challenging situations and cases presented in the IRIS Center Resources.
- Check your comprehension on the content covered in the chapter with the Study Plan. Here you will be able to take a chapter quiz, receive feedback on your answers, and then access Review, Practice, and Enrichment activities to enhance your understanding of chapter content.

Go to the Course Resources section in MyEducationLab, where you can:

- Use the Online Lesson Plan Builder to practice lesson planning and integrating national and State standards into your planning.

PART 5
Inquiry Curriculum

The universe is the child's curriculum.

MARIA MONTESSORI

In this section, we focus on how the curriculum can be designed to support children's growing understanding of the world in which they live. We discuss inquiry processes that are the building blocks for children's construction of knowledge and how these contribute to concept development. We will focus on 3 subject areas that are closely connected with cognitive development: math, science, and social studies. Although the primary focus of these subjects is cognitive development, the social studies component relates, in large part, to social and emotional development as well.

Young children have a compelling curiosity to figure out why and how the world works. They learn by doing. From their earliest months, they observe phenomena, discover relationships, search for answers, and communicate their discoveries. They construct understanding as they explore, experiment, and act upon their environment. Through play, they acquire and order knowledge. Children *inquire* (seek information), construct understanding, and develop concepts as they play and participate in all curriculum activities. However, experiences in mathematics, science, and social studies are uniquely suited to the development of thinking and problem solving, and are the areas of the curriculum in which inquiry is a primary emphasis. The above quote from Dr. Maria Montessori underlines children's interest in learning about the world—what these subject areas help them to do.

If you remember math, science, and social studies education as memorizing facts to recall for a test, you may question whether these subjects are appropriate for young children. If so, you will be pleased to know that learning "facts" is not the purpose of the inquiry curriculum in early childhood education. Instead, the goals are to support children's natural curiosity and inherent sense of wonder, to inquire and solve problems, and to construct understanding of the world.

Giving children information is not your primary role in the inquiry curriculum; indeed, it is not your primary role in early childhood education. Instead, you help children construct understanding by providing the necessary raw materials: time, space, equipment, and experiences. You encourage and support them in discovering for themselves.

Inquiry does not mean learning right answers. It means to ask, discover, think, take risks, make mistakes, and learn from them. When adults give children many opportunities to explore these topics, they begin to understand that it is desirable to think creatively about problems, acceptable not to have an answer, and okay to give the "wrong" answers.

Reflect on a time when you were curious . . .

Think of a time when you were really curious about learning something. What made it interesting? What did you do to find out more about it? Do you still remember what you learned? How do you use it?

A Developmental Perspective

The way children's thinking changes over time is a fascinating area of child development. The work of Jean Piaget and his followers is enlightening because of their careful observations of the characteristic ways that children think and develop concepts. The work of Lev Vygotsky complements Piaget's thinking because of Vygotsky's focus on how the "social context" (teachers, parents, and other children) contributes to children's thinking and learning.

Piaget observed that children's thinking is very different from the logical thinking of adults and is reliant on direct, repeated sensory experiences. As children have these experiences, they **construct** their own knowledge.

Piaget's work has helped educators to understand that children's cognitive development proceeds through stages, just like their physical development. It is as foolish to attempt to rush a child into thinking like an adult as it would be to attempt to teach a crawling infant to high jump. While cognitive development cannot be rushed, research suggests that it can be impaired. Intellectual stimulation is required in order for children to learn to think and reason (Healy, 1992).

Piaget described 3 kinds of knowledge. **Physical knowledge,** the knowledge of external reality, is the understanding that is gained from doing things or acting on the physical world. For example, by holding and playing with a playground ball, children experience and learn about its properties—its texture, its shape, its weight and squishiness, and its tendency to roll away and bounce.

Logico-mathematical knowledge is the knowledge of logical relationships. Children observe, compare, and think. For example, children will observe the relationship between a tennis ball and a playground ball. Both have similar shapes and roll and bounce. There are also differences observed in size, color, texture, and weight. Logico-mathematical knowledge requires direct experience, but is based on the internal process of reflection on what is experienced. Through the experience of playing with many balls, a child develops the idea of *ball* as a single category based on shared characteristics. Logico-mathematical knowledge is dependent on one's own observation, experience, and reflection; it is not arbitrary or dependent on others, and it cannot be taught.

The last kind of knowledge is **social knowledge,** which depends on what is learned from others and not on direct experience of objects or events. It is based on what people decide. For example, children learn that spherical objects that you throw and play with are called *balls*. They learn that balls are used to play games and that different kinds of balls are used for different games.

All 3 kinds of knowledge are important. However, in traditional educational settings, teachers have often taught math, science, and social studies as social knowledge without providing experiences that allow children to develop physical or logico-mathematical knowledge.

Piaget's description of cognitive development as constructed knowledge suggests that in order for children to really understand math, science, and social studies, they must have opportunities to explore and act on the real world to establish relationships and construct their own knowledge.

Like Piaget, Vygotsky believed that children are active participants in their own learning and that they construct their knowledge and understanding. However, unlike Piaget, who believed that children's development is bound by their maturational stage, Vygotsky suggested that children's learning is shaped by their social experiences and by interactions with and expectations from peers, older children, and adults.

For Vygotsky, *social context* affects both *how* children think and *what* they think about (Bodrova & Leong 2007). Social context is everything in the child's environment that is influenced by culture. The circumstances of the family, the values of the school, and the geographic location of the community all influence both what children think about and the ways that their thinking is structured and focused. For example, children raised in families where spoken language is valued as the primary way to communicate will understand and organize experiences and information differently than a child from a family in which non-verbal communication is more acceptable. A significant role of culture is to pass knowledge from one generation to the next. Vygotsky believed that children do not construct all knowledge and understanding independently, but instead are influenced by interactions with family members, peers, teachers, and others.

In Vygotsky's view, the development of language allows children to organize and integrate experiences and develop concepts, thus making language central for thinking. Communication with others is vital because children develop language in relationships with more competent speakers (adults and older children). While Piaget believed that cognitive development creates language, Vygotsky proposed that language is used by children as a means for developing thoughts and creating understanding.

Vygotsky believed that every function in development occurs first at the social level and then at the individual level. Children develop through what he referred to as the *zone of proximal development,* the range of behaviors between what a child can accomplish independently and what can be done with help. In *Thought and Language,* Vygotsky wrote, "What the child can do in cooperation today he can do alone tomorrow" (1962). In this view, adults support learning by providing a small amount of assistance, a *scaffold,* to allow children to successfully complete a task. As the child becomes more competent, less assistance is offered until the child can do it alone.

Concept Development

Through activity, children develop concepts to help make sense of experience. A concept is a mental image or language picture that is communicated in a single word or combination of words—it has a general, not a specific meaning. As a child repeatedly experiences the characteristics of an object, animal, person, or event, and mentally combines and organizes them, he or she is *constructing* a concept. For example, an infant may have constructed the concept *door* based on many repeated experiences, including: a slam, mother returning through this spot, the way to get where you want to go, pinched fingers, a light source at night, and the barrier to what is desired. Concepts are generalized as children recognize the common attributes of objects, people, ideas, and experiences. In the door example, the initial concept of *door* may only refer to the door of the bedroom. As many doors are experienced, the concept is generalized and different doors are recognized: the door of the family car, of grandma's house, the automatic door at the supermarket, and finally doors in general. Although the doors differ greatly, the common characteristics are recognized and the concept is established.

A child's ability to understand and develop a concept is dependent on cognitive maturation and the availability of relevant experiences, as well as scaffolding by adults and other children. Concepts differ in how difficult they are for children to understand. Whether or not a concept is likely to be understood is related to its degree of abstraction and complexity.

Concepts can be thought of as existing on a continuum from concrete to abstract. The *concreteness* of a concept refers to whether it can be directly experienced or observed. Concrete concepts are accessible to children. They can be experienced through the senses—seen, heard, held, felt, touched, tasted. Concepts that depend on information outside of direct experience are abstract and cannot be completely understood by a young child regardless of how hard an adult may try to provide the experience through language, books, or pictures. This makes times, events, and places that cannot be directly experienced in some way (e.g., a trip to the moon, World War II) and abstract concepts (e.g., social justice, liberty) mostly meaningless to young children.

The *complexity* of a concept, the amount of information needed to define it, is the second quality that affects a young child's ability to understand. Children acquire concepts of low complexity more quickly than those of high complexity. Some concepts are available to children through direct experience, but involve many interrelated ideas. These cannot be understood since young children's capacity for creating and retaining connections between such ideas has not yet developed. The concept of *wind* is both relatively simple and concrete, defined primarily by one's experience of it against the skin and its ability to move objects about. The concept of a weather system, however, is complex and requires the grasp of numerous other supporting concepts including evaporation, wind patterns, cloud formation, low- and high-pressure

Reflect on a time when you made a discovery . . .

Think of a time when you discovered something. What did you discover? How did you discover it? Do you still remember what you learned? How did you feel when you discovered it?

areas, and precipitation. Young children will not understand the phenomena of a weather system because it requires attending to a variety of attributes simultaneously. Providing experiences with some of the components of weather will, however, lay a foundation for later understanding of the complex concept.

Inquiry Processes

Inquiry for a young child involves many opportunities to explore and experiment. The processes a child uses to learn about the world and construct concepts are called *inquiry processes*. An inquiring child uses the senses to gain information that will contribute to the development of concepts. Curriculum specialists identify between 10 and 15 distinct inquiry processes; the following are those that best apply to young children:

- **Exploring.** Using the senses to observe, investigate, and manipulate
- **Identifying.** Naming and describing what is experienced
- **Classifying.** Grouping objects or experiences by their common characteristics
- **Comparing and contrasting.** Observing similarities and differences between objects or experiences
- **Hypothesizing.** Using the data from experiences to make guesses (hypotheses) about what might happen
- **Generalizing.** Applying previous experience to new events

Supportive comments about children's discoveries and explorations encourage further inquiry and model an inquiring mind. They help children to form concepts, but do not hand them preformed ideas.

Communication That Supports Inquiry

Talking with children as they explore and discover is one of the most important things you will do to help them learn to think. Skilled educators target their comments, questions, and activities to support the natural curiosity of children. You can make statements about your own wonder and curiosity. Supportive comments on the discoveries and explorations of children encourage further inquiry. Questions help children to notice detail, make comparisons, and come to conclusions. For example, if a group of children are exploring what happens when they narrow a faucet with a finger, making the water spray out, you might comment: "I wonder what makes that happen? You found a way to change the water flow. Can you make it come out slower (faster)? What do you have to do to change it? Why do you think that happens?" As Vygotsky suggested, such questions encourage children to organize and integrate experiences and help them to develop concepts.

You can express a sense of curiosity about and appreciation of the world in statements like, "I wonder why the clouds are moving so quickly?" "Look at how different each shell is." "The baskets all nest together the little ones inside the big ones." "I wonder why cats purr." "What do you think would happen if people purred?" "The mother bear is looking after her cubs—every mother seems to do that." "I can feel the rabbit's heart is beating quickly and hard—Why do you suppose that's happening?" Statements like these model an inquiring mind and help children to form concepts without handing them pre-formed ideas.

Giving information is not your most important role. For example, we once observed a child who found a praying mantis and eagerly asked his teacher what it ate so that it could be kept alive. The teacher explained that she did not know, but asked, "How can we find out?" This resourceful 4-year-old questioned other adults, looked through a book about insects in the science area, and found a photograph of a praying mantis. He took it to his teacher and she read to the group about the insect. They proceeded to offer the praying mantis ants and beetles, and discovered its preferred foods. Had the teacher simply said, "It eats bugs," the learning would have been much less meaningful to the child.

Open-ended questions encourage children to think. They say to the child, "Tell me more." Questions are open when they can be answered in a number of different ways, and have more than one correct answer. You can develop skill in asking open-ended questions by practicing until you can ask them with comfort. The following are the beginning phrases of some open-ended questions.

What would happen if . . . ?
What do you notice? (see, hear, feel, smell)
How are these the same? (different)
What do you think . . . ?
How do you know . . . ?
How could we find out . . . ?

A closed question has only one correct or acceptable answer, for example, "What color is it?" "What is the name of this shape?" Closed questions can help you to learn whether children have acquired a concept or piece of information, but they do not stimulate inquiry, and sometimes they squelch it. In most classrooms, educators use a mixture of open-ended and closed questions. The kind of mix is influenced by values, objectives, and the nature of the particular situation. Awareness of the purpose of each type of question can help you to make conscious choices about which to use. If you wish to stimulate children to inquire, you will ask many open-ended questions.

To help children think flexibly, it is useful to ask questions that have many possibilities. Jane Healy, in her book *Is Your Bed Still There When You Close The Door?* (Healy, 1992), suggests many creative thinking questions that adults can ask children such as: "What different things could you do with a balloon?" "If you had a pair of magic wings where would you fly?" "What would happen if everything was yellow?"

The silence that you allow between statements or questions is also an important factor in how children respond. Researchers have found that 3 to 5 seconds is the average amount of silence that occurs between adult questions and the child's response or a follow-up comment. They found that if the adult waits only 1 or 2 seconds, one-word responses are most frequent. If the wait lasts for several seconds longer, children respond with whole sentences and complex thoughts that represent more creativity and increased speculation (Brualdi, 1998; Good & Brophy, 2000; Stahl, 1994).

Try It Out!

Try asking a child some open-ended questions. Notice what happens when you use this approach? How is it different from other kinds of interactions? What did you learn from the experience?

Bibliography

Bodrova, E., & Leong, D. J. (2007). *Tools of the mind: The Vygotskian approach to early childhood education* (2nd ed.). Upper Saddle River, NJ: Pearson.

Brualdi, A. C. (1998). Classroom questions. *Practical Assessment, Research & Evaluation*, 6(6). http://PAREonline.net/getvn.asp

Good, T. L., & Brophy, J. E. (2000). *Looking in classrooms*. New York, NY: Longman.

Healy, J. (1992). *Is your bed still there when you close the door?* New York, NY: Doubleday.

Stahl, R. J. (1994). *Using "think-time" and "wait-time" skillfully in the classroom*. ERIC Digest. (ERIC Identifier: ED370885) Bloomington, IN: ERIC Clearinghouse for Social Studies/Social Science Education.

A mathematician, like a painter or a poet, is a maker of patterns.

G. H. HARDY

chapter thirteen

MATH CURRICULUM
Discovering Patterns and Solving Problems

Mathematics is a way of structuring experience to form ideas about the quantitative, logical, and spatial relationships between things, people, and events. Like many people, you may think of mathematics as comprising numbers and the things we do with numbers––a set of useful techniques for counting, measuring, and accounting. The word may cause you to think of the complexities of geometry, algebra, trigonometry, statistics, or calculus. You may feel intimidated or fearful at the very idea of mathematics (a common fear of math known as *math anxiety,* similar to stage fright). Indeed, like one of the authors, you may have been attracted to early childhood education in part because you thought you wouldn't need to study math in order to teach young children.

If this is how you feel, you may be surprised to learn that teachers of young children do teach math, and the math they teach is far more than numbers, equations, or a set of rules and procedures for counting and measuring. In fact, although numbers are useful symbols, much of math is not about numbers. Instead, math can be viewed as a way of thinking, the science of patterns of number, shape, space, reasoning, chance, and motion.

In this chapter, we hope to help you to understand what math in early childhood education is and why it is important. We will acquaint you with some concrete and appropriate ways to bring math into your early childhood program. If you have math anxiety we hope to help you to feel comfortable with your role as a teacher of mathematics.

Why Math?

Math is important in early childhood education because the conceptual under-pinnings of later math skills are based on many years of concrete experiences that may not seem to relate to mathematics. Math concepts and the language used to express them (*more* and *fewer, far* and *near, similar* and *different, short* and *tall, now* and *later, first* and *last, over* and *under*) are essential for later mastery of complex mathematics and are learned in early childhood. As an early childhood teacher, you are starting children on the journey to *numeracy,* a term similar to *literacy* that describes the ability to reason with numbers and other math concepts; confidence and competence with numbers and measures; an inclination and ability to solve quantitative or spatial problems; understand-ing of ways in which data are gathered and presented; and the application of math to everyday tasks.

Look around you—*math is everywhere.* You see numerals on each page of this book, on your phone, on the watch on your wrist, and on the keyboard of your computer. You can see math in the shapes of the furniture and the proportions of the room in which you are sitting, in the engineering of the light bulb that illuminates the page, and in the shape of the flower you see outside the window. Math is part of your world, part of your life, and part of your culture. So, of course, you want children, from an early age, to feel at home in that world.

Math is useful. The utility of arithmetic (numbers and computation) is obvi-ous, even to those of us who feel math anxiety. It helps us to answer practical questions: How many chairs do we need at the table? How many cookies can each of us have? How much baking soda do I need if I double the recipe? How many more points do I need to earn an A in this class? Almost every area of your life requires some arithmetic. And you probably have a calculator that helps you figure out the answers to questions like these.

Even without a calculator you have *number sense,* the ability to "recognize that something has changed in a small collection when, without . . . direct knowl-edge, an object has been removed or added" (Dantzig, 1954, as cited in Devlin, 2003). Devlin (2003) reports that even newborn babies attend to numerical dif-ferences in images and sounds (that is, they pay attention when the number of items in a picture or the number of syllables in a series of words changes—they can tell that 3 is more than 2 or 1). If you give the cashier a $20 bill for an item that costs $9.95 and expect about $10 in change, you have number sense.

The more you understand math, the more you will notice math in your classroom. You will discover that an interest in mathematics is common in young children. A toddler determinedly working to fit together a set of nesting cups is doing math. A preschooler painting a symmetrical painting at the easel is doing math. And a kindergartner guessing who has the most marbles is doing math.

Understanding How Young Children Learn Math

Young children begin learning math concepts informally at home and in the world around them. The development of mathematical thinking entails a long process that consists of far more than learning how to count and calculate. Math concepts evolve as children mature and have many real-life experiences. In other words, math concepts are constructed.

The work of Piaget and others has led to an investigation of the kinds of math concepts children can construct and the ways they do this best. Traditionally, beginning math curriculum has often been taught as "social knowledge" through repetitious drill and the memorization of rules and number facts. Instead, young children need opportunities to actively manipulate materials that help them to construct ideas about number, space, and logical relationships.

The discovery of what young children are capable of learning has led to a rethinking of the traditional content of math curriculum. Today, math education for young children is designed to help them to learn to think logically and flexibly, and to creatively solve problems found in daily life.

Children are discovering math concepts in the course of the ordinary activities and routines of classroom living. They are coming to think of themselves as part of a community of people who use number to order and communicate about their world. You will notice this happening when you observe young children pretending to use number as they label distance, quantity, and ages ("My doll is twenteen." "It's thirty-fifty miles." "I can eat infinity ice-cream.").

What Is Math Curriculum in Early Childhood?

Math for young children involves content that is varied, rich, and meaningful, filled with interesting concepts and useful purposes. It is an active process. Doing math (as opposed to knowing math facts) involves solving problems, making connections, reasoning, representing ideas, and communicating with others.

Math Processes

Problem Solving

One of the most important math processes is solving problems. All young children strive to solve problems. However, they are not born with the ability to do so. They learn this skill at home and in school. Some children have effective problem-solving skills. They focus their attention, try alternatives, make hypotheses, take risks, and persevere when they encounter barriers. Others do not, and one of your teaching tasks will be to help them acquire these skills.

You will help children become math problem solvers when you provide materials to be explored (e.g., collections of materials to be sorted) and math problems to be solved (e.g., by deliberately having too few materials so that children have to figure out how to divide them).

Reasoning

Reasoning means drawing logical conclusions. Young children engage in mathematical reasoning when they apply something they know to solve a math-related problem. When you ask questions that challenge them to explain their thinking ("How do you know we'll need 3 more?") or justify their solutions to problems ("Why does the starfish belong with the scallop shells and not the cone shells?"), you are helping them to develop reasoning skill.

Communicating

Today, teachers of mathematics consider it critical for children to be able to communicate about math ideas. They can begin to develop the ability to communicate mathematical ideas in early childhood programs.

What does this mean? There are many ways to communicate math ideas. As you talk with children about math ideas, you are helping them learn to communicate verbally. However, preschool children are often better at showing than telling, so you will also help them learn how to show their math ideas. When you ask Lidia to "point to the 3 bowls for the 3 bears," you are helping her learn to communicate a math idea. You can also invite children to draw, paint, and even symbolize mathematical ideas physically.

Connecting

Young children come to school using math to solve problems. Unfortunately, as they "learn math" in primary school, they often give up their intuitive math sense. Memorized math rules are substituted. By using manipulative materials in preschool settings and employing math language to talk with children about what they are doing ("Oh, you took away 4 of the cubes. You subtracted them; how many do you have left?" "You classified the shells—how would you describe this group?"), you can help them to connect informal math with the formal math they will be learning in the future.

Representing

Children can represent their growing math knowledge by organizing and recording ideas on graphs, with tallies, in diagrams, on maps, and in drawings and photographs. When you help children to make representations and then use them to communicate with others ("Here's the graph of the Caterpillars' pets. How can you tell that most of us have dogs?"), to remember what has taken place ("This map shows how far we walked today"), or to plan for the future ("This chart tallies our vote to make grilled cheese sandwiches next week"), you are helping them to understand the power of mathematical ideas.

Math Content

What is the math content of the early childhood curriculum? What is the foundation that young children need to help them to make sense of the physical and social world and to master abstract mathematical concepts later in their school careers? If math in early childhood isn't just rote counting and naming shapes, what is it?

Underlying the early childhood math curriculum are some foundational math concepts: matching, classification, comparison, and ordering. These must be acquired before children are ready to learn concepts related to the 5 math areas addressed in Common Core State Standards for Mathematics (see Figure 13.2 on pages 406–407): counting and cardinality, operations and algebraic thinking, number and operations in base ten, measurement and data, and geometry.

The Foundational Concepts: Matching, Sorting and Classifying, Ordering and Seriation

Children begin learning the concepts that underlie math understanding in the first months of life as they hold and play with objects. Learning these foundational skills and concepts continues in your preschool classroom.

Matching

Matching is the foundational skill for understanding one-to-one correspondence. When each child in your class is given a cracker, as each foot is given a shoe, children are experiencing one-to-one correspondence. Understanding one-to-one correspondence is the basis for understanding number.

In the preschool years, children begin to develop skill in several kinds of matching tasks, including matching identical items (e.g., pairs of shoes), matching different items (e.g., one napkin for each plate), and matching groups or "sets" of identical items one to one.

Sorting and Classifying

One of the ways we organize and understand daily life is by classifying. Classification entails sorting or grouping people, objects, ideas, or events by shared characteristics. As children come to understand that they can group things based on the ways they are alike, they have developed the basic concept of *classification*. When they exclude them based on the ways that they are different (negation, or "not like"), they are *comparing*. As they become more sophisticated and flexible in the categories they use, children are developing more profound understanding of classification. They are learning to classify things according to common attributes when they hang up all the dresses; place all the dishes in the cupboard; put all the large beads in a basket and all the small beads in a can; and sort buttons by size, shape, color, or number of holes. When all the children with Spiderman T-shirts want to sit together, they are demonstrating the ability to classify.

Ordering and Seriation

When objects are ordered in a sequence based on a difference in the degree of some quality such as length, weight, texture, or shading, they are arranged in a series or *seriated*. Children gain experience in seriating when they arrange things in their environment, for example, themselves from shortest to tallest, balls from smallest to largest, or a set of color chips from palest to darkest. When they seriate and then match 2 groups (e.g., arranging flowers from largest to smallest and matching them with similarly sized vases), they are performing *double seriation*.

The concept of ordering is important because, like matching, it is foundational to understanding number. The sequence of number is an ordered, or seriated sequence, with each number being one more than the last.

Number and Operations

What could be simpler than number? 1-2-3-4-5. It seems like it should be easy. However, number involves several complex, related ideas that concern quantity and order.

There are many misconceptions about what number is in the early childhood years. Having the ability to count and having an understanding of number are not the same thing. Being able to count reflects a child's ability to memorize and mimic certain behaviors (touching and saying a number). It is a rote activity unless a child has a concept of number (one-ness, two-ness, three-ness, and so on). Only then does a child understand that the name represents a specific quantity. A parent of our acquaintance proudly told us that her 4-year-old "knew" numbers up to 20. Indeed, the child could recite the words *one, two, three,* and so forth in proper order. However, when asked, she could not point to a stack of 6 blocks from among several piles of 6 or less. Despite her rote counting skill, she clearly demonstrated that "six-ness" was not a concept she had acquired. It's easy to understand how confusing number must be when we think of the many ways adults use number words ("You can have 3 crackers." "Mommy will come get you at 3." "You can go on the big slide when you are 3.").

Number—Not Just Counting

Children only gradually come to really understand number despite rather easily learning to count using number names in the correct order. They use counting as a *reliable* (i.e., consistently accurate) tool when underlying number concepts are in place—usually around the age of 7. Young children learn about number by exploring and describing arrangements and combinations of objects. It is important that children have repeated opportunities to use many kinds of objects both in play and in practical life situations so they can manipulate and talk about number. This will help them begin to understand that number is unrelated to specific objects and instead is a tool to describe and understand many aspects of the world.

Children do not understand number until they understand the following:

- There is a one-to-one correspondence between each number name and an object in the set being counted.
- A number name applies not only to the last object named, but also to the entire set of objects.
- Other number names mean more or less than the one being considered.
- Number is the same regardless of the objects that are counted (a group of 3 elephants and a group of 3 mice have the same number, even though the elephants are much larger).
- The physical arrangement of the objects does not influence how many there are.

One-to-one correspondence is a precursor of counting and understanding of number. Children must first learn that objects matched one for one (for example: a mat for each person) share the same quantity before they can understand number.

Quantity or "amount" is what we usually think of when we refer to number. A set of objects has a certain quantity that is unchanging and unrelated to the physical act of touching and naming (*1-2-3*) the objects. This characteristic is also referred to as *cardinal* number, or *many-ness*. Children can learn to *compare* quantity and determine if a group (or set) of objects has more, less, fewer, or the same number, even without counting.

Order of objects or events (first, second, third, etc.) is another way children come to understand number. This concept is sometimes called *ordinal* number. When you talk about which ingredient in a recipe comes *first*, or when a child complains that she doesn't want to be *last*, ordinal number is being used.

Numerals, like letters, are symbols that give us information. A numeral is not the same as a number, just as the printed letters "i-c-e-c-r-e-a-m" are not the same as an ice-cream cone (or even a picture of one). Children learn about numerals as labels (Room 3 is our room) that are sometimes called *nominals.* As they reach the primary grades and develop understanding of number concepts, they can begin to use numerals as symbols for quantity and order.

Numeral recognition is a visual perceptual task. Until children develop the number concept and understand that the word represents the concept, they are not able to understand the meaning of a numeral *even when they know its name.* Numerals and their names are social knowledge—useful for communicating once the underlying concept is in place. Although young children may appear to be reading numerals, a closer look at their understanding will often demonstrate that they are naming the shape of the numeral rather than understanding the number concept.

Does this mean you should ignore numerals? No! Just as literacy begins with play with letters in print, so numeracy includes play with numerals. Similarly, an environment that includes numerals—for example, used in recipe charts, on the phone in the dramatic play area, or on a sign indicating the number of children an area can accommodate—gives children important experiences of how numerals are used in our society.

Operations

In math, an **operation** is an action, or procedure, that produces a number value. The study of numerical operations is called *arithmetic.* Counting, addition, subtraction, multiplication, and division are all operations. In preschool programs, we give children experiences with a few basic operations using small numbers.

Counting (the operation of adding one more to a series) requires several abilities. It requires the memorization of a sequence of number names that always are used in the same order (called the *stable order rule*). To count, children must be able to recognize and use the patterns involved in counting numbers greater than 9. Once the names for the numbers from 1–9 have been memorized, the "teens" and the names for the "decades" (10, 20, 30, etc.) are learned. Since the pattern differs, these numbers are harder to learn. To use counting, the number names must be linked through one-to-one correspondence to objects. To count correctly, children have to keep track of the items that have been included so as not to count them more than once. They must be able to count the same group of objects more than once and realize that each time they must end up with the same number. So counting, that simplest of operations, is actually quite complex.

Part-part-whole relationships is a fundamental concept needed for understanding number and a requirement for understanding operations. When a child notes that 2 fingers on one hand and 3 on another is 5 just as 5 fingers on one hand is 5, she is showing that she understands part-part-whole relationships.

In **change operations,** objects are *added to* or *taken away* from a group. Children go through stages in solving change-operation problems (Copley, 2000). Initially, they count all objects (if a child has 3 blocks and is given 2 more, he counts them all "1-2-3-4-5—now I have 5!"). With greater experience they "count on" (if a child has 3 blocks and is given 2 more, he counts "4-5—now I have 5!"). Finally, children perform the arithmetic in their heads (if a child has 3 blocks and is given 2 more, he looks at them without counting and says "now I have 5!"). When a child is able to instantly recognize the quantity of items in a group of 2, 3, 4, 5, or 6 without counting, he or she is said to be *thinking in groups*.

Patterns

Children's lives are full of patterns. If each night they take a bath, use the toilet, brush their teeth, put on pajamas, and hear a story, they are following a pattern. If they play the *Hokey Pokey* at circle time, they are following a pattern. There are patterns in quilts, in toys and books, in songs, in traffic lights, and in packages. Patterns are an important part of math. Our number system is a pattern. Math problems are often solved by looking for patterns. Patterns form the foundation for algebraic thinking.

Patterns can involve number, shapes, sounds, words, and attributes like color. They abound in a preschool classroom. When children create bead necklaces with

alternating colors, arrange parquetry blocks, or sing the chorus after every verse of a song, they are experiencing patterns.

There are 3 general types of patterns. In a *repeating pattern,* a core element repeats (like the chorus of a song). In a *growing pattern,* the core element is used to create larger elements (like the blocks in a block structure or the words to the song *The Green Grass Grew All Around*). In a *relationship pattern,* a connection is made between two sets (if you have 1 red marker in one box of markers you have 2 red markers in two boxes). Young children can learn to *recognize* patterns, you can ask them to *describe* patterns, they can *extend* an existing pattern, and they can *create* their own patterns.

Measurement

Measurement is the process of comparing size, volume, distance, weight, or quantity to a standard. Adults use numerically expressed standards such as meters, ounces, or dollars. Measurement is a very practical part of math that we informally use with children all the time. ("We need 3 cups of flour in this playdough." "I bet you grew 2 inches last month." "We need another foot of ribbon.")

Measurement for children involves making comparisons of things in the immediate environment. They discover the concept of measurement when they experiment to find how many unit blocks equal the width of the carpet, count how many cups of water fill a large container at the water table, or compare their height to the heights of their friends and teachers. Children need experience comparing *length, mass* (heavy/light), *capacity,* and *temperature.* Older children will also begin to use *money*—another, more abstract, standard.

We also measure *time.* As children notice the sequence of events in their daily lives, they are learning about time. For example, lunch is always followed by rest time, and a story about zoo animals is read before a visit. Duration is another time-related concept. Children begin to understand duration as they notice such

things as outdoor play lasting a long time in comparison to stor~
lasts for a short period.

Geometry and Spatial Sense

Geometry is the part of math concerned with questions of size, shape, relative position of figures, and the properties of space. It is more than learning the names of a
few regular shapes, although this is how it is taught in many preschool classrooms.

Space

Concepts of *space* have to do with the way objects relate to others based on
position, direction, arrangement, and distance (or proximity). Children develop
these ideas as they observe spatial relationships between people and objects.
The concept of *position* may be developed when children engage in day-to-day
activities such as putting away the blocks, with the long ones on the *bottom* shelf
and the short ones on the shelf *above,* and the block people in the basket *next
to* the trucks. The concept of *direction* may be discovered as a child first drives a
tricycle forward and then backward. When a child kicks a ball to a nearby child
and then to a faraway child, the concept of *distance* is being explored.

Shape

Shape or geometry refers to 2- and 3-dimensional objects and their properties.
It is easy to think of shape as simply referring to the Euclidean shape names we
know well (*circle, triangle, rectangle, square,* and so on). Shape also involves
how shapes are constructed (for example, 2 C-shaped blocks can be put together
to create a circle), topological characteristics such as whether a shape is open or
closed (a C is an open shape and an O is a closed shape), and how the appearance of shapes changes based on how we look at them (for example, the table
top may look thin from the side and round from above) and how shapes can
be manipulated while retaining their characteristics (a round ball of clay retains
some of its roundness even when squashed flat into a pancake). Geometry in
early childhood education is a real-world experience. Children can identify how
objects are similar and different in shapes and properties. As they manipulate
blocks, puzzles, clay, games, and toys, they are learning about geometry.

Young children notice shape long before they come to preschool. By the age of
5 or 6, they can recognize and name shapes (*triangle, circle, square,* etc.) in diverse
circumstances (the steering wheel is a circle, the tire is a circle, the ball is a circle).
But initially, they cannot think about and name the attributes of shapes. As they get
older and have more experience, they begin to be able to understand the characteristics of shapes (e.g., a triangle has 3 sides). While it is appropriate to use shape
names when you are discussing shapes with children—"Would you bring me some
triangle blocks for the roof of my building?" or "We have circle-shaped paper to paint
on today," it is not necessary or appropriate to focus your curriculum on learning
shapes. Instead, you can remember that children are learning about shape as they
experience form in relation to their world through such activities as building with
blocks, painting, working with clay, and playing with manipulative toys and puzzles.

Data Analysis and Probability

Data analysis means collecting, sorting, representing, analyzing, and interpreting information. In preschool and kindergarten classrooms, you might see data
analysis in a chart listing all the places that children have found bugs. Or you
might see it more formally in a graph comparing the number of children in the
class who are 5 and the number who are 6.

Data display and analysis is an important part of a meaningful integrated study with young children. Encouraging children to ask questions about a topic and deciding how to record and display the answers gives seriousness of purpose to young children's investigations and honors their discoveries.

Probability is the measure of how likely it is that an event will occur. In preschool and kindergarten programs, probability is an informal and very basic activity. You are giving children experiences with probability when you use words like *impossible, maybe, likely,* and *for certain* when discussing class routines ("What are we likely to do after lunch?") and community events ("Do you think it's possible that a parade will come down our street?").

Standards for Math Curriculum

Although there are no national standards for math in preschool programs, Head Start (see Figure 13.1) and almost all states have standards for math curriculum. The National Governors Association Center for Best Practices (NGA Center) and the Council of Chief State School Officers (CCSSO) have developed standards for children in K–2 programs (see Figure 13.2). Content standards and guidelines can help you to identify goals and objectives for the math curriculum. These, in turn, will help you to select activities that will help children acquire knowledge and skills. Since these standards address the learning of 5- through 8-year-olds, they include much that is not appropriate for teaching most 3- to 5-year-olds. Head Start and state preschool content standards lay out the expectation that teachers provide opportunities for development and/or that children develop certain skills. All of them address:

- understanding of number and the development of number sense.
- development of spatial sense and understanding of simple geometry.
- the ability to recognize and create patterns.
- beginning ability to measure.

In addition, many states also have standards for ordering, data recording, and problem solving. The amount of detail prescribed in the standards for different states varies. Some have very general statements, whereas others provide many details about the skills and concepts children should learn and the teaching methods to be used. If you compare the Head Start standards for 3- and 4-year-olds (Figure 13.1) with the Common Core State standards for children in kindergarten through grade 2 (Figure 13.2), you will note that there is much more content and more specific details in the Common Core State standards. However, both address numbers and operations, patterns (algebra) and measurement, and geometry.

Your program's goals may be based on state or national standards, or they may have been developed independently by your staff or a curriculum specialist. However, it is likely that they will include some version of these standards.

Teaching Math

Teaching math begins when you create a classroom climate in which inquiry, questioning, and exploring are not only accepted, but also expected. The following

FIGURE 13.1 Head Start Child Development and Early Learning Framework: *Mathematics Knowledge and Skills*

Number Concepts and Quantities

The understanding that numbers represent quantities and have ordinal properties (number words represent a rank order, particular size, or position in a list).

- Recognizes numbers and quantities in the everyday environment.
- Recites numbers in the correct order and understands that numbers come "before" or "after" one another.
- Associates quantities and the names of numbers with written numerals.
- Uses one-to-one counting and subitizing (identifying the number of objects without counting) to determine quantity.
- Uses the number name of the last object counted to represent the number of objects in the set.

Number Relationships and Operations

The use of numbers to describe relationships and solve problems.

- Uses a range of strategies, such as counting, subitizing, or matching, to compare quantity in two sets of objects and describes the comparison with terms, such as *more, less, greater than, fewer,* or *equal to*.
- Recognizes that numbers (or sets of objects) can be combined or separated to make another number through the grouping of objects.
- Identifies the new number created when numbers are combined or separated.

Geometry and Spatial Sense

The understanding of shapes, their properties, and how objects are related to one another.

- Recognizes and names common shapes, their parts, and attributes.
- Combines and separates shapes to make other shapes.
- Compares objects in size and shape.
- Understands directionality, order, and position of objects, such as *up, down, in front, behind*.

Patterns

The recognition of patterns, sequencing, and critical thinking skills necessary to predict and classify objects in a pattern.

- Sorts, classifies, and serializes (puts in a pattern) objects using attributes, such as color, shape, or size.
- Recognizes, duplicates, and extends simple patterns.
- Creates patterns through the repetition of a unit.

Measurement and Comparison

The understanding of attributes and relative properties of objects as related to size, capacity, and area.

- Compares objects using attributes of length, weight and size (*bigger, longer, taller, heavier*).
- Orders objects by size or length.
- Uses nonstandard and standard techniques and tools to measure and compare.

Source: Administration for Children and Families, Head Start Bureau, www.hsnrc.org/cdi/child-outcomes.cfm

principles for teaching math in preschool are based on the principles created by the National Council of Teachers of Mathematics.

1. **Support math learning and problem solving in all children.** It is common for teachers to have very different expectations about the problem-solving abilities of girls and boys. Be sure to nurture confidence, enthusiasm, and interest in math and problem solving for all children.

FIGURE 13.2 Overview of Common Core State Standards for Mathematics K–2

Mathematical Practices K–2

1. Make sense of problems and persevere in solving them.
2. Reason abstractly and quantitatively.
3. Construct viable arguments and critique the reasoning of others.
4. Model with mathematics.
5. Use appropriate tools strategically.
6. Attend to precision.
7. Look for and make use of structure.
8. Look for and express regularity in repeated reasoning.

Kindergarten

Counting and Cardinality

- Know number names and the count sequence.
- Count to tell the number of objects.
- Compare numbers.

Operations and Algebraic Thinking

- Understand addition as putting together and adding to, and understand subtraction as taking apart and taking from.

Number and Operations in Base Ten

- Work with numbers 11–19 to gain foundations for place value.

Measurement and Data

- Describe and compare measurable attributes.
- Classify objects and count the number of objects in categories.

Geometry

- Identify and describe shapes.
- Analyze, compare, create, and compose shapes.

Grade 1

Operations and Algebraic Thinking

- Represent and solve problems involving addition and subtraction.
- Understand and apply properties of operations and the relationship between addition and subtraction.
- Add and subtract within 20.
- Work with addition and subtraction equations.

Number and Operations in Base Ten

- Extend the counting sequence.
- Understand place value.
- Use place value understanding and properties of operations to add and subtract.

Measurement and Data

- Measure lengths indirectly and by iterating length units.
- Tell and write time.
- Represent and interpret data.

Geometry

- Reason with shapes and their attributes.

(continued)

Grade 2

Operations and Algebraic Thinking

- Represent and solve problems involving addition and subtraction.
- Add and subtract within 20.
- Work with equal groups of objects to gain foundations for multiplication.

Number and Operations in Base Ten

- Understand place value.
- Use place value understanding and properties of operations to add and subtract.

Measurement and Data

- Measure and estimate lengths in standard units.
- Relate addition and subtraction to length.
- Work with time and money.
- Represent and interpret data.

Geometry

- Reason with shapes and their attributes.

2. **Take advantage of everyday opportunities for problem solving.** Rather than correcting children's mistakes or handing them solutions to problems, use these occasions as teaching moments.

3. **Make math concrete and manipulative.** Avoid sedentary and abstract activities like worksheets. Instead provide real experiences with manipulative toys and real objects.

4. **Integrate math into other curriculum areas.** Math is part of everything. You teach math best when you do not isolate it, but recognize and include it in all subject areas.

5. **Begin with simple concepts before moving to more complex concepts.** Young children learn math best when we build on simple concepts that are within their grasp. Always start simple.

Try It Out!

Think of 2 ways that you could introduce mathematical ideas as you work with 3-year-olds who are fingerpainting.

Math Learning Through Play in a Planned Environment

As children play in a planned environment, they have many opportunities to manipulate objects, including those created as "math" teaching equipment (like Unifix cubes or Cuisenaire rods) and other equipment that lends itself to the development of mathematical concepts (like blocks and button collections). They also learn about math in their play with their peers. With other children they will be

challenged ("You got more than me!" or "I don't want to be second!"), and they will need to work out mathematical problems in very meaningful and very concrete ways.

In addition to all of the places that math learning will incidentally occur in your classroom, 2 centers are particularly focused on mathematical learning. The manipulative toys center includes a great deal of math learning. If you have space in your classroom, you can create a special math center that includes some of the materials from the manipulative toys area. The block area also involves a great deal of math learning.

A Math Center

Sheltered space, well-organized shelves, and a clear work area with table and chairs or carpet and mats give the necessary structure for an area where children can focus on math. At the heart of a math center are *math materials*. These can include:

- **Math manipulatives** like Unifix cubes, attribute blocks, parquetry blocks, Cuisenaire rods, geoboards, pegboards, and colored 1-inch cubes. These open-ended toys can be used in many different ways, including building understanding of one-to-one correspondence, counting, comparing, measuring, patterning, and developing geometric awareness. All are specifically designed to give experience with math concepts. It is useful to learn about them by reading manufacturers' brochures and Web sites, and books like Juanita Copley's *The Young Child and Mathematics*.

- **Math games,** both manufactured and teacher-made (often called *workjobs*), can address a wide variety of math skills. Unlike math manipulative toys, these are close ended (designed to be used in a specific way) and are often self-correcting so that children can tell easily if they have succeeded in solving the problem the material presents. Mary Barrata-Lorton's books *Workjobs, Workjobs II,* and *Math Their Way* give many suggestions for math games you can make. Many teachers prepare math workjobs that address the content of an integrated study as well as targeted math concepts (e.g., a game in which children fill numbered baskets with the appropriate numbers of cat and dog counters for a study of pets, or a game in which children match a plastic insect to its outline to develop spatial awareness during a study of insects).

- **Puzzles and fit-together toys** like stacking cups and the arcobaleno puzzle, pictured on page 402, are close ended, designed to be taken apart and put together in one or two ways. They give children geometric and spatial experience in addition to presenting problems to be solved.

- **Sorting collections** (buttons, rocks, keys, shells, caps) and sorting trays give children the opportunity to match, sort, classify, and seriate. A set of sorting materials will have many objects that are similar but that vary so that children must consider each item before sorting it. As with teacher-made workjobs, sorting collections can be targeted to a topic of study; for example, children can sort feathers during a study of birds.

Counters are objects to use to count, graph, and pattern. Generally, counters are small, so that a handful can be held by a young child. Educational supply houses produce counters in a range of shapes and colors. It's possible to find counters to relate to almost any curriculum study—dogs, cats, vehicles, bugs, or birds. Found and recycled items like bottle caps, pebbles, and florist's marbles can also be used as counters.

Measurement tools like rulers, tape measures, measuring cups and spoons, timers, balances, and kitchen scales give children the opportunity to explore standard measurement units. By providing string and strips of heavy cardboard that can be cut to the length of an arm or finger, you can encourage children to use non-standard measurement.

Montessori math and sensorial materials like number rods, golden beads, the pink tower, the broad stair, and knobbed and knobless cylinders present many manipulative math experiences and can be housed in a math center. Like math manipulatives, these were devised with specific concepts/skills in mind, and it is valuable to read about their intended uses. Books like Hainstock's *Teaching Montessori in the Home* or Gettman's *Basic Montessori Learning* can help you to understand these pieces of equipment.

Math-oriented picture books like Pat Hutchins's *The Doorbell Rang,* and Eric Carle's *The Very Hungry Caterpillar* can be included in a math center. A children's librarian can recommend many more to you. Often teachers like to pair a math picture book with a math manipulative material to give a concrete experience (e.g., a set of 12 felt cookies, paper plates, and a cookie sheet to go with *The Doorbell Rang*).

Display spaces for math-related group work, such as graphs, and math-oriented prints and posters are an important aspect of a math center. For example, displays can be targeted to an integrated study. In one class that was studying bread, a graph of the types of bread that different children ate in their homes was posted. In another class that was studying families, photo displays of different sizes of families were displayed.

If you have sheltered space, a computer with **math-related programs** and chairs for at least 2 children can be housed in the math area. Because these are much more abstract than "hands-on" math materials, it is important not to sacrifice the space required for math manipulatives to place a computer in the math area. "Screen time" is no substitute for real experience.

The Unit Block Area

Unit blocks provide math learning experiences as well as help children develop motor coordination and strength, imagination, and social skills. In the block area, children learn about mathematical relationships, equivalencies measurement, ratio, and problem solving. The different sizes and shapes of unit blocks are based on a unit block that is $5\frac{1}{2}'' \times 2\frac{3}{4}'' \times 1\frac{3}{8}''$. Other blocks are exactly proportioned (half, quarter, double, quadruple, etc.) so that as children play, they experience mathematical relationships and develop concepts of equivalence and symmetry.

To effectively develop math concepts, a unit block area requires a set of hardwood unit blocks—at least a basic set (100–150 blocks in 14–20 shapes), sometimes called a *nursery,* or *preschool set.* Older children benefit from a larger and more complex set that includes 200 to 700 blocks in 20 to 25 shapes (sometimes called a *school* or *classroom set*). It is useful to know about the stages of block play (see Figure 13.3) so that you can better understand how blocks may be used by the children you teach.

Much of the mathematical learning in block play is lost if blocks are stored without organization in a box or bin. Instead, blocks should be stored on low, open shelves in which each type of block has its own individual place. Blocks with similar qualities should be stored near each other, placed so that children can easily see how they differ (e.g., lengthwise for long blocks so that the differences in length are evident). Each shelf should be clearly marked with an outline to enable children to find the blocks they need for their constructions and put

FIGURE 13.3   Stages of Block Building

Stage 1:

Blocks are carried around but are not used for construction (very young children under 2 years of age).

Stage 2: *Building Begins*

At approximately age 2 or 3, children mostly make rows, either horizontal (on the floor) or vertical (stacking).

Stage 3: *Bridging*

Children create a bridge (or portal) by using two blocks to support a third. In architecture this is known as the post-and-lintel system.

Stage 4: *Enclosures*

Four or more blocks are placed in such a way that they enclose a space.

Stage 5: *Patterns and Symmetry*

When facility with blocks is acquired, patterns and symmetry are observed. Buildings are generally not named (ages 3–4).

Stage 6: *Naming of Structures*

With names that relate to function of the building (ages 4–5). Before this stage, children may have named their structures, but not necessarily based on the function of the building.

Stage 7: *Reproducing Structures*

Beginning at age 5, buildings often reproduce actual structures they know like cities, cars, airplanes, and houses. They also use block structures as part of dramatic play.

Source: Johnson, James E., Christie, James F., Wardle, Francis, *Play, Development and Early Education*, 1st Edition, © 2005, pp. 237–238. Reprinted with permission of Pearson Education, Inc. Upper Saddle River, NJ.

them back in the appropriate places (we recommend using solid colored contact paper to create the outline). In our own classrooms we print the mathematical name for the block (1/2 units, double units, etc.) directly on the outline to remind adults to use these descriptions.

Math Everywhere

Math learning takes place throughout an early childhood learning environment. Setting plates on the table in the dramatic play area develops one-to-one-correspondence. Reading a counting book in the library teaches about number. At the sensory table, filling a bucket with water or sand gives experience with volume. Putting together a puzzle builds concepts of space. Dividing a ball of clay into 2 pieces and then rejoining them in the art center is a math experience. Computer programs that involve number, shape, and space are developing math concepts. Games, manipulative toys, outdoor exploration where spatial concepts like *top/bottom, in/out, up/down* are experienced all teach mathematical concepts.

These are only a sample of the potential of the early childhood program environment for supporting math learning. Look closely at how the learning environment of the center in which you work supports children's construction of math concepts so you can better evaluate what you might do to expand and enrich children's learning opportunities.

A Schedule for Math Learning

Young children develop many math concepts through play. For this reason, math, like every other curriculum area, requires that children have uninterrupted blocks of time for math discovery through play throughout the day. In addition, they learn concepts through carefully planned math activities. So, regularly scheduled time for small groups to gather and explore math concepts is also important.

Significant blocks of time for both indoor and outdoor play (45 minutes to an hour) are essential for math. When you are able to explain to parents, administrators, and co-workers that this play time contributes to children's learning of academic subjects like math, you may find that you gain more support for allowing children the freedom for meaningful discovery through play.

Because young children have limited tolerance for sedentary group experiences, it is important to plan carefully for short (10–20 minute) small-group times to introduce math concepts. The time that you meet with small groups to explore math needs to be frequent, active, playful, and filled with interesting and meaningful math experiences.

In addition, children learn about math as they handle the routines of the day. When each child has one cracker and rests on one mat, one-to-one correspondence is experienced. As they learn the sequence of the daily schedule, learn to pour half a glass of milk, or cut their apples in 2 parts, they are using math.

Your Role in the Math Curriculum

Teaching math in the early childhood years involves recognizing children's math interests and understanding, providing math experiences, and supporting children as they construct math concepts for themselves. It is important to be aware of when and how mathematics is meaningful to children. A child who is comparing and arranging the dishes in the dramatic play area and setting the table for the other children is using ideas of classification and quantity, and providing you with important information. Based on your observations of children, you can add additional activities and ask stimulating questions that will provide opportunities to help them learn.

Using math ideas in daily conversation will help children to become aware of math concepts. The questions that you ask can help preschool children by encouraging them to question, to think about math, and to share ideas with one another. Ask questions that encourage mathematical thinking and problem solving: "Which beads do you think belong together? Why?" "Can you find me a doll that is smaller than this one but larger than this one?" "Can you cover the mat with blocks? What kind will you use? Why?" "How many cubes do you think will fit along the side of the box? Would you like your cracker whole or in 2 pieces?" "What shall we put next in our pattern?" "How could we find out who's tallest?" "Tell Darius how you know it's a square."

When questions are respectful and are a part of playful interactions with children, they are likely to respond positively. However, it's important to be prepared to forego or refocus questioning when children do not appear interested.

Math Anxiety and You

As we have mentioned, math anxiety is common. If you experience math anxiety, you may be at risk of passing your anxiety on to children. However, there are several things you can do if you feel frustrated or helpless about your ability to do math.

Reflect on how math was taught in your schools . . .

How was math taught in the schools of your childhood? What do you remember most vividly? Did these experiences influence what you have done as an adult? How do you use what you learned in your life today?

First, be aware of the competent way you use math to manage your life. You use math to shop, cook, pay your bills, do the laundry, and manage hundreds of tasks each day. You estimate, count, use a calculator, drive, catch a bus, ride a bike, or walk to get yourself to different places each day. By acknowledging your own competence, you may feel less frightened, panicked, and humiliated.

Second, realize that you may have been taught to expect to do poorly at math by society, family members, or teachers. If powerful people tell you things, you tend to believe them. And if you believe you're bad at math, you probably have been telling yourself the same thing for years. You won't overcome this negativity overnight. But you can start believing that you are better at math than you thought.

Finally, know that since you really are much more competent than you previously believed, you *can* bring math to children. You have a wonderful opportunity to use math as you *learn* with children, *play* with them, and *laugh* with them. By doing so, you will be teaching and enjoying both math and the children, and all will benefit.

Math Activities

There are multitudes of appropriate math activities, far more than we could describe in this book. There are also a few inappropriate math activities for preschool and kindergarten children that are largely abstract and symbolic, and do not draw on children's lives as a source of content. Worksheets and calendar are the most common examples of inappropriate math activities.

Good teachers of young children create a math-rich environment and are attuned to children's math interests. In addition, they have a repertoire of appropriate math activities. Like other good teachers, you will develop your own repertoire as you read books, observe other teachers, and follow the interests of the children themselves. The categories of activities presented here are designed to help you to think about ways you can appropriately teach math to young children.

Manipulatives

Playing with math manipulatives is perhaps the most fundamental math activity. Virtually all of the concepts appropriate for helping young children learn math in preschool can be taught as you interact with children using math manipulatives. Often this teaching is spontaneous: You observe children playing with the material and then pose an appropriate question or task. Having knowledge of children and sensitivity to what their play means as well as understanding the potential of the material will help you to do this well. We encourage you to spend time watching children at play with math manipulatives to build your own skill at identifying their growing math understanding. Playing with the materials yourself is another way to develop understanding of math manipulatives.

You can plan activities using math manipulatives. Select a concept based on standards and the interests of your children. Choose an appropriate math manipulative. Then plan for an intriguing task that will help children to acquire the targeted concept.

Games/Workjobs

Simple games can help children to understand math concepts. A few board games (*Chutes and Ladders, Candy Land,* and *Hi Ho Cherry-O*) and a few card games (*Go Fish, Old Maid*) can be played with preschoolers. Because these games emphasize winners and losers, they can be difficult for some children to play and may be viewed as inappropriate by families from cultures that emphasize cooperation. Create math workjobs and games that are cooperative, or re-focus traditional board and card games to de-emphasize winning and losing (e.g., not focusing on the winner and instead counting the number of spins until everyone is home, or trades until all the cards are paired up).

Large motor games also can develop mathematical concepts. When you play a game like *Fire on the Mountain* in which each firefighter is paired with one tree, children are experiencing one-to-one correspondence. And when children make a circle to play *Go in and Out the Window,* they are learning about spatial relationships.

Graphing and Charting

Graphs are diagrams that show relationships between varying quantities. Charts provide a way to visually organize a group of related facts in the form of a diagram or list. Both graphs and charts are useful in recording preschool children's math discoveries, and are most appropriate for children 4 years of age and older. When you ask children to name the different kinds of bugs they have found, write this list on a sheet of poster paper, post it in the classroom, and add to it as new bugs are discovered, you are making a data chart (see Figure 13.4).

When you create a list comparing the number of children who are 5 to the number of children who are 4, you have created a graph. A graph allows you to quickly compare quantity (see Figure 13.5).

FIGURE 13.4 **Bugs on the Playground Chart**

Bugs we have seen on the playground
Ladybug
Painted Lady Butterfly
Cockroach
Fly
Mosquito
Bumble Bee
Roly Poly
Millipede
Praying Mantis

FIGURE 13.5 Example of a Graph

	We Are 5	We Are 4
1	Matthew	Holly
2	Ira	Lili
3	Lani	Shey
4	David	Aidan
5		Tiana
6		Estella

FIGURE 13.6 Pictorial Recipe

You demonstrate the utility of charts and graphs by hanging them in the classroom and referring to them regularly. When left to hang as decorations that are never used again, they are less useful.

Cooking

Even the simplest cooking involves math. Cooks need to make enough so that everyone can eat. Containers must be filled (to the top or halfway). You make sure that the whole top of the pizza, cake, etc. is covered. Ingredients are counted or measured. Cooked foods are timed, and temperature is measured. By creating pictorial recipes that enable children to SEE the recipe (see Figure 13.6), you can make the math in cooking visible.

Riddles and Clues

Young children love a challenge! Simple riddles (sometimes called *clues*) are problem-solving exercises that can help children to focus on math concepts.

"I'm thinking of a shape that's round that has no corners. Can you guess what shape I'm thinking of?" "I'm thinking of how many cookies I'd have if I had 2 and I gave 1 to my friend." Coming up with the answers to "riddles" like this is fun for children when they feel successful. That means your job is to guess what kind of mental problem solving will be just within the reach of your children. It's not fun to feel incompetent or humiliated, so be sure that when you ask riddles or give clues, you give ones that children are capable of figuring out. Start simply and make the riddles more complex in response to children's ability.

Fingerplays and Songs

Many fingerplays and children's songs involve simple counting-on or taking away operations. Because they involve action or singing, these activities tap into alternative ways of learning and knowing. They help children who have different kinds of intelligence to be successful at math. While you are learning to be a teacher, it's a good time to start gathering a collection of math fingerplays and songs that you can share with children.

Books

Your local library has a selection of children's books that involve math. Many of these are counting books. Counting books usually show numbers from 1 to 10 (though many go beyond). And the items counted are incredibly varied: African animals (*Bringing the Rain to the Kapiti Plain*), fruit (*The Very Hungry Caterpillar*), farm animals (*Barn Cat*), visitors (*One was Johnny*). All include images of different quantities of items paired with the numeral.

Other books demonstrate additional math concepts such as Pat Hutchins's *The Doorbell Rang* (part-part-whole relationships), Dr. Seuss's *Green Eggs and Ham* (spatial concepts), Raymond Briggs's *Jim and the Beanstalk* (measurement), Rosemary Wells's *Bunny Money* (money).

Art

Like cooking, art by its very nature involves math. Spatial relationships, patterns, and symmetry are present in almost every work of art. As you talk with children about their artwork, you can make their inherent math concepts come alive— "You filled your paper with dots." "There's a circle at the top and another at the bottom." "I see 3 people in this painting."

Planning Math Curriculum

Children are natural mathematicians, and their interest is the launching place for your math curriculum. As you have learned, math includes lots of things that we often don't consider when we think about math in early childhood (matching, classification, comparison, ordering, patterns, measurement, data analysis, and probability) as well as those we do think of (number and shape). These big concepts provide you with a framework for thinking about the kinds of experiences that you will provide. In the classroom environment, you provide the basic tools for math exploration. Your ability to recognize math learning in children and to join in by asking good questions and sharing their enthusiasm is another critical element. You also need to have knowledge of the strategies that can best help children learn math, and you need to know what educators have identified as important math learning for young children.

Writing Plans for Math

During a study of Gardens, the children brought boots to wear while garden-ing. Holly had purple boots. David had black boots. "My boots are bigger than yours!" David declared. "No they're not! Mine are bigger!" Holly argued. Holly and David stood side by side and looked at their boots—you couldn't tell which were bigger by looking.

"How can we find out which are bigger?" Emiko, the teacher, asked. Holly sat down on the grass and pulled off one boot. She held it up to David. Emiko said to David, "It looks like Holly wants to compare your boot to her boot to see if you can tell which is bigger." David sat down and pulled off his boot. They put the boots sole to sole. The purple boot's toe stretched beyond the toe of the black boot. "Look!" David said, standing the two boots next to each other. David's black boot was an inch taller than Holly's. "Mine is bigger!" Holly moved her hand smoothly from the top of the purple boot to the top of the black boot, "Nope! They're the same." The children pulled their boots back on and ran back to the garden.

Planning for math begins by paying attention to children and being aware of the math questions that intrigue them. Emiko began this process by observing Holly and David in their play and noticing that their quarrel was an opportunity for math learning. Rather than solving their problem or dismissing their concern, she asked an important inquiry question—*How can we find out?* The question encouraged a math solution, and Emiko introduced math language (*compare, bigger*). The children *compared* the boots, but neither child was convinced by the comparison. Then the children's interest in the math problem was overshadowed by their interest in the garden.

This situation gave Emiko insight into the children's understanding of concepts concerning *comparison* and *measurement*. It also helped her to see their interests (*measurement of meaningful objects*) and their strengths (*beginning ability to understand the measurable attributes of objects, compare objects according to these attributes,* and *measure*). So Emiko planned the activity shown in Figure 13.7 to build on these interests and strengths.

Because she is an experienced teacher, Emiko's short plan leaves out many details. It would not be enough of a guide for a beginning teacher. The detailed version in Figure 13.8 gives you a better idea of what she planned to do.

FIGURE 13.7 Simple Math Activity Plan

Comparing and Measuring Garden Boots

Objectives:	Compare measurable attributes, develop vocabulary of comparison, measure using non-standard units.
Standard:	HPCS Domain IV (Math) Standard 4
What you need:	Children's and teacher's garden boots, sidewalk chalk, unit and half-unit blocks, chart paper with questions "Which boot is tallest?" "Which boot is shortest?" and pens
How to teach:	1. Ask each child to get one of their garden boots and line up all of the boots from tallest to shortest.
	2. Fill in the chart paper.
	3. Have children stack blocks by the boots, count, and add information to the chart.
	4. Read the chart back to the children
How to assess:	Look for children measuring and comparing other things, or using blocks to measure.

FIGURE 13.8   Detailed Math Activity Plan

Activity:	**Comparing and Measuring Garden Boots** (a structured small-group examination of size)
Curriculum Area:	Math
WHO It's For:	This activity was planned for David, Holly, and the Lion Giggles (eight children in the 4-year-old group)
WHY This Activity Rationale:	Holly and David were arguing about whose garden boots were bigger. They tried several measurement strategies, but were not able to apply them in a consistent or meaningful way.
Math Objectives:	*By participating in this activity the children will…*

- Develop awareness of and compare measurable attributes.
- Develop vocabulary of comparison: length (longer/shorter, shorter/taller), size (bigger/smaller), weight (heavier/lighter).
- Learn to measure using non-standard units.

Concepts to Begin to Develop:

- Comparison: objects can be compared by size (length, width, height)
- Measurement: comparing objects to a standard

Preschool Content Standard(s): Domain IV (Cognitive) Math Standard 4: Develop and use measurement concepts.

Indicator: Measure using standard and non-standard units

HOW to Prepare

What you need:

- 15 to 20 minutes at small-group time outside on the sidewalk
- Children's and teacher's garden boots
- Sidewalk chalk
- A basket or box with 10 unit and 5 half-unit blocks
- Chart paper posted on the outside easel and pens

Set up:
On a piece of chart paper, write and illustrate the questions.
Which boot is tallest?

Which boot is tallest?   Which boot is shortest?

HOW to Teach

Introduction:
Meet the Lion Giggles outside for small group. Show them a teacher boot. Say something like, "Holly and David were comparing their boots and I wanted to compare everyone's boots to find out how big they are." Ask each child to get one of their own garden boots from the boot shelf

Teaching steps:

1. Invite children to look at the boots. Ask if they would like to include the teacher's boot or leave it out. Invite children to line up the boots from tallest to shortest.

2. With the children, fill in the answer to the questions.

Whose boot is tallest?   Whose boot is shortest?
David's boot is tallest.   Cielo's boot is shortest.

3. Say something like, "I brought these blocks so that we could measure how many blocks tall the boots are." With the children, stack the blocks, count, and add the information to the chart.

David's boot is 2½ blocks tall.   Cielo's boot is 2 blocks tall.

(continued)

FIGURE 13.8 Detailed Math Activity Plan (continued)

4. If children are still attentive, invite children to do one of the following:

   a. Measure their own boot with blocks and add the information to the chart.

   b. Determine the longest boot: "I wonder which boot has the longest sole." (Hold up a boot sole side up.) Draw a base line on the sidewalk, set the heel of each boot against it and draw a toe line. Add this information to the chart. (Alternatively, ask the children if they can think of a way to find out this information and use their method.)

   c. Measure the teacher's boot and add it to the chart.

   d. Use a boot as a measure and find out how many boots' long things are (e.g., the table, the door, the sidewalk from the door to the sandbox).

Consideration:

If children seem to be sad or angry that their boots were not acknowledged, have each child explain one thing that their boot is "most of" (e.g., whose boot is greenest, spottiest, dirtiest) and add to the chart.

Closure:

Once the boots have been measured and the data recorded, read the chart back to the children. Say something like, "Thank you for helping me figure out which boot(s) were the tallest and longest." Ask children to select where they would like to play next. Offer the sidewalk chalk and blocks to children who would like to measure how long other things are.

HOW to Assess and Document

Objectives	Evidence of Learning Children might …	How to Document This Evidence
Develop awareness of and compare measurable attributes.	Attempt to measure the length or height of other things (or suggest that we measure the width or weight of the boots).	Anecdotal records, photos of children lining up boots, chart with children's discoveries
Develop vocabulary of comparison: length (longer/shorter, shorter/taller), size (bigger–smaller), weight (heavier–lighter).	Say things like "David's boot is taller but Holly's boot is longer" and "The teacher's boot is the biggest."	
Learn to measure using non-standard units.	Use blocks (or other items) to measure how long the boots are.	Photos of children using blocks or other items to measure

Math in a Weekly Plan

Math learning is a part of many of the activities that occur spontaneously in children's self-selected play, so, as we have said before, they need blocks of time for unstructured play. Math can be planned as part of the daily teacher-guided activities. In the example included in Figure 13.9, you will see that small-group activities include math content each day while also addressing music, language, and movement goals. In addition, math learning is identified in stories, sensory activities, and large-group activities. Activities that involve math are highlighted.

Math in an Integrated Study

An integrated study abounds in opportunities to include math. This can be easily seen in the *Pets* sunburst in Figure 13.10. Some planned activities were specifically designed as math activities, but many others also indirectly involved math ideas.

FIGURE 13.9 **A Week's Plan: Pets—Week #2**

Objectives: To help children understand that pets are animals that live with families; build physical, communication, creative, and inquiry skills and understanding.

	Monday	Tuesday	Wednesday	Thursday	Friday
Story	*Fun Dog, Sun Dog* (Heiligman)	*Move Over, Rover* (Beaumont)	*I Have a Pet!* (Halpern)	*The Perfect Pet* (Palatini)	*Pet Show* (Keats)
Outdoor Activities **Purpose:** *to help children to…*	**Goop in the Water Table** Increase sensory awareness. Develop strength and coordination of small muscles. Develop concepts of shape and space.	**Parachute Play** Develop strength and coordination of large muscles. Develop ability to work together in groups.	**Parachute Play** Develop strength and coordination of large muscles. Develop ability to work together in groups.	**Goop in the Water Table** Increase sensory awareness. Develop strength and coordination of small muscles. Develop concepts of shape and space.	**Goop in the Water Table** Increase sensory awareness. Develop strength and coordination of small muscles. Develop concepts of shape and space.
Small Group 1 Caterpillars **Purpose:** *to help children to…*	**Visiting Dog: Observation and Drawing** Learn about characteristics of living things. Engage in scientific inquiry.	**Journal: My Favorite Pet** Acquire concepts of print. Develop interest in writing.	**KWL Chart:** What do you know about pets? What do you want to learn about pets? Begin to view themselves as serious learners. Acquire concepts of print. (assessment activity)	**Brainstorm and Vote:** What new pet shall we get for our classroom? What would it need? Understand what people need to do to work and live together in groups. Acquire numeracy concepts and understanding of the utility of number.	**Write a Recipe for Grilled Cheese Sandwiches** Acquire numeracy concepts and understanding of the utility of number. Acquire concepts of print.
Small Group 2 Peacocks **Purpose:** *to help children to…*	**Fingerplays: Five Little Puppies, My Little Kitty** Learn about numbers, numerical representation, and simple numerical operations. Listen with comprehension to a variety of spoken forms of language.	**Walk Around the Chair: Pets** Learn about movement elements and techniques. Acquire spatial concepts.	**Fingerplays: Five Little Puppies, My Little Kitty** Learn about numbers, numerical representation, and simple numerical operations. Listen with comprehension to a variety of spoken forms of language.	**Walk Around the Chair: Pets** Learn about movement elements and techniques. Acquire spatial concepts.	**Puppet Pets** Acquire increasingly rich vocabulary and sentence structure. Use language in a variety of ways.

(continued)

419

FIGURE 13.9 A Week's Plan: Pets—Week #2 (continued)

	Monday	Tuesday	Wednesday	Thursday	Friday
Indoor Special Activities **Purpose:** *to help children to …*	**Fabric Collage** Create and express ideas through art. Learn about art elements and techniques.	**Sand Collage** Learn about art elements and techniques. Develop eye and hand coordination. Develop appreciation for natural beauty.	**Sand Collage** Learn about art elements and techniques. Develop eye and hand coordination. Develop appreciation for natural beauty.	**Fabric Collage** Create and express ideas through art. Learn about art elements and techniques.	**Cooking Grilled Cheese Sandwiches** Learn about numbers, numerical representation, and simple numerical operations. Develop awareness of nutritious foods and food safety. Develop a sense of competence. Learn how food changes when heated.
Circle Time **Purpose:** *to help children to …*	**Pet Clues** Listen with comprehension to spoken language. Practice problem solving.	**Pet Clues** Listen with comprehension to spoken language. Practice problem solving.	**New Song: The Pets** Learn about music elements and techniques. Express ideas through music.	**New Song: I Met a Little Dog** Learn about music elements and techniques. Express ideas through music.	**Walk Around the Chair: Pets** Learn about movement elements and techniques. Acquire spatial concepts.

Every integrated study can include the following math activities:

- Math workjobs/games related to the topic (in this case the Pets on Dots Game, the Adult/Baby Pet Matching Workjob, and the Puppy Sequencing Workjob)
- Graphs representing something quantitative that children learned (in this study, the Pet Graph)
- Fingerplays and songs (either existing or made up by the teacher) related to the content (in this case, *My Little Kitty, Five Little Puppies,* and *How Much Is That Doggie in the Window?*)
- Children's literature related to the topic and to math

Math for All Children

It's easy to see that typically developing preschoolers and primary school children can learn about math. It may be harder to envision how math can be presented to children with special needs.

Children with Special Needs

Christopher enters the classroom each morning bouncing. He runs and runs and runs. Christopher has difficulty sitting still, difficulty listening, and difficulty participating in the classroom. Christopher has ADHD—attention deficit hyperactivity disorder.

FIGURE 13.10   A Study of Pets Sunburst

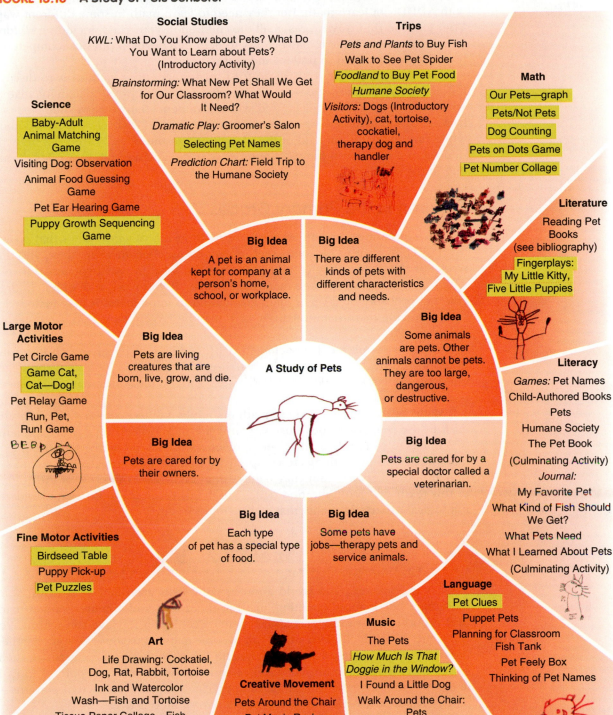

Social Studies

KWL: What Do You Know about Pets? What Do You Want to Learn about Pets? (Introductory Activity)

Brainstorming: What New Pet Shall We Get for Our Classroom? What Would It Need?

Dramatic Play: Groomer's Salon

Selecting Pet Names

Prediction Chart: Field Trip to the Humane Society

Science

Baby-Adult Animal Matching Game

Visiting Dog: Observation

Animal Food Guessing Game

Pet Ear Hearing Game

Puppy Growth Sequencing Game

Trips

Pets and Plants to Buy Fish

Walk to See Pet Spider

Foodland to Buy Pet Food

Humane Society

Visitors: Dogs (Introductory Activity), cat, tortoise, cockatiel, therapy dog and handler

Math

Our Pets—graph

Pets/Not Pets

Dog Counting

Pets on Dots Game

Pet Number Collage

Literature

Reading Pet Books (see bibliography)

Fingerplays: My Little Kitty, Five Little Puppies

Large Motor Activities

Pet Circle Game

Game Cat, Cat—Dog!

Pet Relay Game

Run, Pet, Run! Game

Literacy

Games: Pet Names

Child-Authored Books

Pets

Humane Society

The Pet Book

(Culminating Activity)

Journal:

My Favorite Pet

What Kind of Fish Should We Get?

What Pets Need

What I Learned About Pets

(Culminating Activity)

Fine Motor Activities

Birdseed Table

Puppy Pick-up

Pet Puzzles

Language

Pet Clues

Puppet Pets

Planning for Classroom Fish Tank

Pet Feely Box

Thinking of Pet Names

Art

Life Drawing: Cockatiel, Dog, Rat, Rabbit, Tortoise

Ink and Watercolor Wash—Fish and Tortoise

Tissue Paper Collage—Fish

Life Painting Cockatiels, Fish, Pet Mural (Culminating Activity)

Creative Movement

Pets Around the Chair

Pet Magic Rocks

Fish (Creative Movement)

Little Bird, Little Bird

Dog Movement

Moving Like a Pet

Music

The Pets

How Much Is That Doggie in the Window?

I Found a Little Dog

Walk Around the Chair: Pets

Little Bird, Little Bird

Did You Ever See the Fishes?

Bingo

The Pets in the House

Creating a Pet Song (Culminating Activity)

Big Idea
A pet is an animal kept for company at a person's home, school, or workplace.

Big Idea
There are different kinds of pets with different characteristics and needs.

Big Idea
Some animals are pets. Other animals cannot be pets. They are too large, dangerous, or destructive.

Big Idea
Pets are living creatures that are born, live, grow, and die.

A Study of Pets

Big Idea
Pets are cared for by their owners.

Big Idea
Pets are cared for by a special doctor called a veterinarian.

Big Idea
Each type of pet has a special type of food.

Big Idea
Some pets have jobs—therapy pets and service animals.

You may know children like Christopher; you may have been one. Children with ADHD can learn math. But they need to learn math in some different ways. Your job is to find ways to reach all the children in your class, including children like Christopher. While it may be easy to help him develop physical competence, how do you help him to understand math?

The first thing that you will do for Christopher (or any child) is to discover his strengths and interests. Since Christopher is great at physical activity, math in your classroom must be integrated with movement. Balls thrown into boxes or baskets can be counted. Spatial concepts like *far* and *near* can be talked about while running from one end of the playground to the other. Three can be experienced as a number of jumps, a number of hops, and a number of piles of sand dug in the sandbox.

Children in the Primary Grades

Older children are eager to learn to use math in the practical ways that grown-ups do. They want to be competent in making number, measurement, and time work for them, and they continue to need the base in real experience in play with sand, water, blocks, and manipulative toys. If you work with older children, you will probably be given a math curriculum to implement. It may include lessons involving math manipulatives, or it may be largely based on symbolic and abstract skills.

You can supplement a packaged math curriculum by giving children lots of opportunities to use math in real life. For example, you can cook with children. In cooking, children will use standard measurement and note its usefulness.

Make sure to continue to use math manipulatives to make math real for children in the primary grades. Just as younger children need repeated experience of 3 things to comprehend three-ness, older children need many opportunities to manipulate sets of 12 things to comprehend that 12 really breaks down into sets of 3 and 4. Otherwise, they may believe until adulthood (like one of the authors of this text!) that multiplication tables are magic formulas to be memorized and not logical aspects of reality that can be understood.

Final Thoughts

Math *is* everywhere. The world and our daily lives are filled with math. Much more than being about counting, math is about life. And you are good at math. Feel proud of your math accomplishments. Feel joy in it. Have fun with it. You can share this with children—they can become math conscious. As you give them the concrete experiences upon which math is based, they can come to see themselves as individuals who use number and measurement as important tools in daily life. All it takes is an attitude of appreciation for the science of patterns—a part of children's world and yours, and a part of all our lives.

Learning Outcomes

When you read this chapter, thoughtfully complete activities from the "To Learn More" section, and document this learning as suggested in the "For Your Portfolio" section, you will be making progress in the following *NAEYC Standards for Early Childhood Professional Preparation Programs* (2009):

Standard 1. Promoting Child Development and Learning

Students prepared in early childhood degree programs are grounded in a child development knowledge base. They use their understanding of young children's characteristics and needs and of the multiple interacting influences on children's development and learning to create environments that are healthy, respectful, supportive, and challenging for each child.

The key elements of standard 1 you will have learned about are . . .

1a: Knowing and understanding young children's characteristics and needs

1c: Using developmental knowledge to create healthy, respectful, supportive, and challenging learning environments

Standard 4. Using Developmentally Effective Approaches to Connect with Children and Families

Students prepared in early childhood degree programs understand that teaching and learning with young children is a complex enterprise, and its details vary depending on children's ages, characteristics, and the settings within which teaching and learning occur. They understand and use positive relationships and supportive interactions as the foundation for their work with young children and families. Students know, understand, and use a wide array of developmentally appropriate approaches, instructional strategies, and tools to connect with children and families and positively influence each child's development and learning.

The key elements of standard 4 you will have learned about are . . .

4a: Understanding positive relationships and supportive interactions as the foundation of their work with children

4b: Knowing and understanding effective strategies and tools for early education

4c: Using a broad repertoire of developmentally appropriate teaching/learning approaches

4d: Reflecting on their own practice to promote positive outcomes for each child

Standard 5. Using Content Knowledge to Build Meaningful Curriculum

Students prepared in early childhood degree programs use their knowledge of academic disciplines to design, implement, and evaluate experiences that promote positive development and learning for each and every young child. Students understand the importance of developmental domains and academic (or content) disciplines in an early childhood curriculum. They know the essential concepts, inquiry tools, and structure of content areas, including academic subjects, and can identify resources to deepen their understanding. Students use their own knowledge and other resources to design, implement, and evaluate meaningful, challenging curricula that promote comprehensive developmental and learning outcomes for every young child.

The key elements of standard 5 you will have learned about are . . .

5a: Understanding content knowledge and resources in academic disciplines

5b: Knowing and using the central concepts, inquiry tools, and structures of content areas or academic disciplines

5c: Using their own knowledge, appropriate early learning standards, and other resources to design, implement, and evaluate meaningful, challenging curricula for each child.

To Learn More

Observe a Program: For a morning, observe a program and see how the staff structures the environment and program to support children's development in math. Look at the plans and see how the planning reflects what you observed. Interview a teacher to learn how he or she thinks about math.

Observe a Child: For a morning, observe a child in a classroom, with a focus on the child's activity in math. Notice how the child engages with the experiences offered and how he or she constructs his or her own opportunities for learning. Notice the extent to which the child's learning experiences and the planned curriculum seem to match. Observe to see how staff support the child's math learning in this area.

Observe a Master Teacher: Spend a morning with an early childhood educator who is experienced and has a curriculum leadership role in a program. (This teacher may be called the "lead," "head," or "mentor" teacher.) Then interview the educator about how he or she plans for and provides math curriculum.

Observe a Math Activity: Observe a teacher leading a planned math activity. Identify the math content. Interview the teacher to find out the objectives for the activity. Reflect on any differences between what you saw and the focus of the plan.

Compare Two Programs: Observe math in two early childhood programs. Compare the ways that the two address math—their similarities and differences. Reflect on which program seems to best support children's learning and why. What implications does this comparison have for your future work with young children?

Compare Two Ages: Observe two classrooms, one preschool and one for primary school children. Report on how each supports children's math learning. Talk to the staff about how they make their curriculum choices in this area. Notice how development influences curriculum choices.

Explore Resources: Read one of the books from the bibliography and write a review of it for your classmates. Look at several online resources and summarize their contents:

Common Core State Standards for Mathematics: corestandards.org/assets/CCSSI_Math%20Standards.pdf

The National Council of Teachers of Mathematics: www.nctm.org

Illuminations NCTM lesson plans: illuminations.nctm.org

Montessori Mathematics Introduction: www.infomontessori.com/mathematics/introduction

NAEYC Position statement on Early Childhood Mathematics: Promoting Good Beginnings: www.naeyc.org/positionstatements/mathematics

For Your Portfolio

Design a Math Center: Design and draw a floor plan for an ideal math center for preschoolers. Share your plan with an early childhood educator, discussing what you included and why. Ask for and consider the educator's feedback and suggestions. Set up a math center in a real classroom utilizing as many of your ideas as possible and let children use it. For your portfolio, include the floor plan, photographs of children using the center, and a reflection on what you learned by doing this project.

Plan and Implement a Math Activity: Observe a group of children for a morning, focusing on the ways they express mathematical understanding. Based on what you observed, write and implement a math activity. Collect evidence of children's responses in the form of anecdotal observations, work samples, photographs, or video recordings. Reflect on how children responded and what

they appear to have learned. What worked? What might you do differently next time? How might you expand on this experience for children? For your portfolio, include the plan, a work sample or photograph, and a reflection on what you learned about yourself, children, planning, and teaching.

Create a Math Learning Material: Design and make a math learning material to support the development of a particular child or group of children. Introduce it to the child or children and observe how it is used. Reflect on how the children responded and how you felt about what you did. What worked? What might you do differently next time? How might you expand on this experience for children? For your portfolio, include a photograph of a child using the material and a reflection on what you learned about yourself, children, learning materials, and teaching.

Bibliography

Bullard, J. (2010). *Creating environments for learning, birth to eight*. Upper Saddle River, NJ: Pearson.

Copley, J. V. (2000). *The young child and mathematics*. Washington, DC: NAEYC.

Devlin, K. (2000). *The math gene: How mathematical thinking evolved and why numbers are like gossip*. New York, NY: Basic Books.

Devlin, K. (2003). *Mathematics: The science of patterns*. New York, NY: Henry Holt & Co.

Feeney, S., Moravcik, E., & Nolte, S. (2013). *Who am I in the lives of children?* (9th ed.). Upper Saddle River, NJ: Pearson.

Geist, E. (2009). *Children are born mathematicians: Supporting mathematical development, birth to age 8*. Upper Saddle River, NJ: Pearson.

Head Start Resource Center. (2010). *The Head Start Child development and early learning framework: Promoting positive outcomes in early childhood programs serving children 3–5 years old*. Washington, DC: Office of Head Start, Administration for Children and Families, U.S. Department of Health and Human Services.

Johnson, J. E., Christie, J. F., & Wardle, F. (2005). *Play, development and early education*. Upper Saddle River, NJ: Pearson.

Koralek, D. (Ed.). (2003). *Spotlight on young children and math*. Washington, DC: NAEYC.

Mitchell, A., & David, J. (Eds.). (1992). *Explorations with young children: A curriculum guide from the Bank Street College of Education*. Beltsville, MD: Gryphon House.

National Association for the Education of Young Children. (2009). *NAEYC standards for early childhood professional preparation programs*. www.naeyc.org/files/naeyc/file/positions/ProfPrepStandards09.pdf

National Council of Teachers of Mathematics. (2000). *Principles and standards for school mathematics*. Reston, VA: Author.

National Governors Association Center for Best Practices and Council of Chief State School Officers. (2010). *Common core state standards for mathematics*. Washington, DC: Author.

Smith, S. S. (2009). *Early childhood mathematics* (4th ed.). Upper Saddle River, NJ: Pearson.

MyEducationLab

Go to Topics 2: Child Development and Learning, and 9: Content Areas/Lessons and Activities in the MyEducationLab (www.myeducationlab.com) for *Meaningful Curriculum for Young Children,* where you can:

- Find learning outcomes for Child Development and Learning and Content Areas/Lessons and Activities along with the national standards that connect to these outcomes.
- Complete Assignments and Activities that can help you more deeply understand the chapter content.
- Apply and practice your understanding of the core teaching skills identified in the chapter with the Building Teaching Skills and Dispositions learning units.
- Listen to experts from the field in Professional Perspectives.

- Examine challenging situations and cases presented in the IRIS Center Resources.
- Check your comprehension on the content covered in the chapter with the Study Plan. Here you will be able to take a chapter quiz, receive feedback on your answers, and then access Review, Practice, and Enrichment activities to enhance your understanding of chapter content.

Go to the Course Resources section in MyEducationLab, where you can:

- Use the Online Lesson Plan Builder to practice lesson planning and integrating national and state standards into your planning.

It is little short of a miracle that modern methods of instruction have not already completely strangled the holy curiosity of inquiry, because what this delicate little plant needs most, apart from initial stimulation, is freedom, without that it is surely destroyed.

ALBERT EINSTEIN

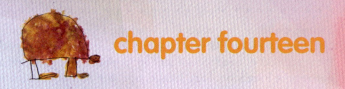

SCIENCE CURRICULUM

Discovering the Natural World

What comes to your mind when you think of science? Some people think of a collection of formulas and facts to be memorized from a textbook. Others think of concepts that are complex and hard to understand, known to scientists, but not to ordinary people. Still others see science as serious, boring, and unrelated to real life. If your view is like any of these, you may wonder why we have included a chapter on science in a book on early childhood curriculum.

Of course, we have included it because science is *not* a collection of difficult, boring facts to be memorized. Science *is* a process of exploration and experimentation, of questioning and learning. Although science involves logic and information, scientists do not view their subject as a collection of static facts. They define science more by the questions they pose than by the answers they know. Scientists know that science is always in a state of flux, always growing and changing, always a process of discovery. It involves observing, testing, and predicting.

Scientists pursue solutions to scientific problems in much the same way that young children play—actively, enthusiastically, and creatively. There is a true kinship between a child at play and a scientist in the midst of inquiry. You will observe this similarity when you watch a child intently involved in exploration and hear this when you talk with a scientist about his or her research. Both are doing things, trying things out, taking joyful risks. For this reason, educators sometimes refer to *science* as "*sciencing*"—a verb rather than a noun—an active process. It is this view of science that we want you to be able to share with children.

Touch a scientist and you touch a child.

RAY BRADBURY

Why Science?

Young children are natural scientists. They have a compelling curiosity to figure out why and how the world works. Their scientific exploration does not wait until they are old enough to sit still for a science lesson, or are competent enough to manage a Pyrex beaker. This is true for an infant who is learning about physiology as she first discovers her toe and physics as she drops a bottle from her high chair. It is also true for a third grader who is carefully observing and drawing the parts of a wildflower.

If you associate science with memorizing facts to recall for a test, you will be pleased to know that learning "facts" is not the main purpose of the science curriculum in early childhood education. Instead, its goals are to support children's natural curiosity and inherent sense of wonder, to help them learn to think flexibly, to inquire and solve problems, and to construct understanding of the world. In other words, the goal is to help children acquire the attitudes and dispositions of scientists—to feel confident and curious, and to wonder, explore, and ask questions.

Understanding How Young Children Learn Science

Young children learn science actively through real experiences, as they touch, manipulate, see, hear, smell, and taste real things. They learn science as they play, explore, think, interact with others, and express their growing understanding in diverse ways. Active science experiences help children to *discover* and *construct* concepts.

Discovery is rewarding. Brain research tells us that interesting and pleasurable experiences engage the brain—unlike repetitive tasks like memorizing facts or completing worksheets (Cliatt & Shaw, 1991). Because of this, active engagement is essential for science learning. When children are engaged in exploration, they are learning in a way that is satisfying. This is not merely a philosophical approach that favors child-centered learning; it is the way all young children learn science.

But young children, like adults and older children, are individuals. While there are many similarities in how they learn, there are individual differences. One child may explore an object with all of her senses, eagerly touching, shaking, turning over, or smelling it. Another may prefer to observe from a distance, and describe or draw a picture of what he saw. Some children show a particular interest in science. They have heightened sensitivity to the patterns and variations in nature and easily learn the characteristics of objects and species. These children have a high degree of what Howard Gardner calls *naturalist intelligence* (Gardner, 1999; Wilson, 1998).

Some of the things you already know about how young children think will help you to understand how they learn science—and consequently will affect how you teach science.

Katie, age 3, is sorting a basket of shells. She places 2 smooth spotted cowry shells together. A second later she adds a spotted cone shell to the cowry shells. Then she adds a striped cone shell to the mix. Soon all the shells are piled together.

Young children focus on one aspect of an object or phenomenon at a time. As Katie considered each shell, she seemed to notice a different aspect of "shell-ness" and forget the previous one. If you have ever watched a child like Katie sorting, you may have observed this. This is characteristic of the way young children think. It is one of the reasons they need multiple experiences with the same concepts. Katie will sort shells many times before she can see what makes all the cowry shells the same. She is demonstrating that there are many ways of defining categories, a powerful way that scientists analyze their data (called *multivariate analysis*) and search for hidden patterns.

Four-year-olds Tommy and Leah are playing with clay. Each starts with a tennis ball-sized chunk of clay. Both children cheerfully pound and roll their clay. Leah carefully rolls her ball of clay into a long, long log. Tommy looks and protests—"She has more than me." Tommy's teacher takes Tommy's ball and shows him how she can make it into a log the same length as Leah's. She then rolls the clay back into a ball and hands it back to Tommy. Again Tommy protests—"She has more than me!"

How could Tommy have made such a mistake? Why didn't the demonstration help him understand? Tommy didn't make this mistake because he is naïve or slow to learn. The mistake (he was unable to *conserve;* that is, he could not see that the quantity did not change when the shape changed) was made because Tommy is a 4-year-old. His mistake reflects a fundamental characteristic of young children's thinking.

Young children are deceived by appearances. Since the log of clay *looks* bigger to Tommy, he believes it *is* bigger. He *knows* it is; his eyes tell him so. It will take many, many experiences, much time, and a shift in thinking (probably when Tommy nears the age of 7) before this changes. Demonstrations like the one his teacher made are unlikely to change his perception.

Doing science (*sciencing!)* depends on sensory input—hearing, smelling, seeing, touching, moving, tasting. Therefore, sensory experience should be at the core of the early childhood science curriculum. Looking and listening are generally considered acceptable ways for children to find out about the world. While these are valuable, they should not be encouraged to the exclusion of taste, touch, smell, and physical manipulation.

> **Try It Out!**
> Play with young children by placing an identical quantity of water in different sizes of containers or by rolling identical-size balls of dough into different shapes. As you do, see if they seem to understand how quantities stay the same when appearances change.

What Is Science Curriculum in Early Childhood?

What should you focus on when you teach young children science? Science is a large field involving every aspect of life, with a virtually limitless number of concepts to learn. You cannot, in a year or even two, begin to teach children all about science. You may feel overwhelmed at the prospect of figuring out what constitutes early childhood science.

It is easier and less intimidating to consider teaching science when you realize that the most important thing you can do is to build children's ability and disposition to inquire. To do scientific inquiry, children need underlying skills. These include the ability to:

- Ask questions about objects, organisms, and events in their environment
- Plan and conduct a simple investigation of an object, organism, or event in their environment
- Use simple equipment and tools to gather data (information) and extend their senses
- Make use of data to construct reasonable explanations
- Communicate investigations and explanations (National Research Council, 1996)

In addition to helping children learn how to inquire (i.e., how to learn), you will also help them to investigate science concepts in three broad categories: life science, physical science, and earth science.

Life Science

Shey finds a praying mantis on the playground. Together with his teacher, he puts it in a plastic jar. He spends the larger part of the morning watching it slowly march from one end of a branch to the other. He studies it with fascination, and then asks the teacher, "What will my praying mantis eat?"

Children are curious about the living things that share their environment. They want to know what they are, how they live, what they need, how they move, and what their life cycle is like. They are curious about *life science*. Life science involves the structures, origins, growth, and reproduction of plants and animals. Another word for life science is *biology*.

The raw materials of life science abound in and around most classrooms. Starting with their own bodies, children are learning about life science. They are learning biology when they notice their own breath, movement, sensation, and digestion. As they observe the transformation of a caterpillar into a butterfly, the seed into a plant, or the flight of a bird, they are having concrete experiences with life science.

While there are many things to learn about life science, we find it useful to identify a few simple concepts that we teach in of this area of science. Figure 14.1 provides a guide to some basic life science concepts that you will help children acquire. These serve as a starting place. As you know, there is **much** more to know and learn about plants and animals. You can use these extremely simple concepts to talk with children about what they are observing about living things.

Physical Science

Desiree rolls a marble down the marble runway. She watches with delight as the marble spins its way around and around and then flies out of a tube and lands a foot away from the runway toy. She laughs and announces, "My marble can fly!"

The study of the properties of objects, materials, and energy and the interactions between them is called *physical science*. All young children, like Desiree in the vignette above, observe physical properties. They experiment with how objects react to force. They test how they can make them move and interact.

FIGURE 14.1 Life Science Concepts

Chapter Fourteen
Science Curriculum

- Plants and animals (including people) are living beings.
- There are many different kinds of plants and animals.
- Each kind of plant and animal has particular characteristics: appearance, needs, and behavior.
- Some plants or animals are similar to one another; some are very different.
- All plants and animals have needs for particular food and habitats.
- Plants and animals rely on other plants or animals for their food.
- All plants and animals grow and change—they have a life cycle with a beginning and an end.
- Every plant and animal creates young that are similar to their parents.
- Plants and animals change the environment in which they live.

They experience the energy of heat and light. They mix and pour substances in their play. As they do so, they are learning about *physics* (energy, motion, and force) and *chemistry* (the composition, properties, and transformation of matter). Concepts basic to physics and chemistry are experienced and explored by young children in the course of daily activity. Their curiosity is aroused when these have personal impact.

When children explore objects and act to create or alter speed, leverage, and balance, they are involved in physical knowledge activities and they are experiencing physics. When they act to make substances change by combining, heating, or cooling, they experience chemistry. Physical science for young children involves the exploration of the commonplace.

Physical science activities are uniquely appropriate to young children because they involve action and observation. Children first become aware of the physical properties of the world through their exploratory play. A ball rolls across the floor. An unbalanced pile of blocks collapses. A rock dropped into a pond makes rings of ripples. The playdough disintegrates when left in the water play table. The oil separates from the rest of the salad dressing. The glass of milk left in the sun curdles. The ice in the water table melts. These are children's first science experiments. Many repeated experiences such as these help children to generalize from their observations and make predictions. This process of generalization and prediction lies at the very heart of science.

Like life science, there are many things to learn about physical science. A few simple concepts (shown in Figure 14.2) may be helpful to you in teaching physical science. As you know, there is *much* more to know and learn, but these concepts will help you to talk with children about what they are observing.

Earth Science

Taylor sits under the shade of a big tree in the yard. He is digging a hole. He digs and digs and carefully examines each rock, root, and snail shell that he unearths in his digging. Then he gets a bucket of water and pours it in his hole and watches the water bubble and gradually seep into the ground.

The study of the earth, sky, and oceans is called *earth science*. Children, like Taylor in the above vignette, experience earth sciences when they observe, explore, and wonder about the common features of the earth, sky, and ocean such as sand, dirt, water, and rocks, and natural phenomena like shadows,

FIGURE 14.2   Physical Science Concepts

- Everything has properties or qualities
  - All objects have a size, weight, color, and temperature.
  - Everything has a state—solid, liquid, or gas—which can change with temperature or pressure.
- Force
  - Force (push and pull) causes things to move—to stop and start.
  - Gravity is the force of the earth—it pulls objects toward it.
  - Friction is the force that stops the movement of two touching things.
  - Magnetism is a force that attracts (pulls) or repulses (pushes) materials like iron toward or away from a magnet (an object with a strong magnetic field) from a distance.
  - A machine is a device that changes the direction or strength of force. Machines help people use force to do work. Wheels, levers, ramps, pulleys, and screws are all machines.
- Energy
  - Light is a type of energy. It moves in a straight line. Shadows are created when the path of light is blocked. White light is made up of different colors. When white light shines through a prism, it splits into different colors, becoming a rainbow.
  - Heat is a form of energy—it changes things from cold to hot.
  - Electricity is a form of energy that can make light or heat and run machines.
  - Objects that are moving have kinetic energy.

sunsets, frost, and streams. There are a host of earth sciences, including *geology* (the study of the origin, history, and structure of the earth), *meteorology* (the study of weather), *oceanography* (the study of the ocean) and *astronomy* (the study of celestial bodies outside of the earth's atmosphere).

Basic concepts of earth science are experienced and explored by young children in the course of daily activity. When children ask questions like: "Where does the sand come from?" "What made the mountains?" "Where did the sun go?" and "Where did the snow come from?" you will know that they are curious about this aspect of science.

Children's curiosity is aroused by these subjects when they have personal meaning. As they walk over hills and look at the layers of rock formations, they are experiencing geology. If they pound sandstone into bits, they are making geologic experiments. When they observe the moon hanging in the sky above the playground in the morning, they are observing astronomical phenomena. When they guess that dark clouds in the sky hold rain, they are making meteorological predictions. Young children's concepts of earth sciences are limited to what they can see and experience. Children will be curious about these phenomena, and in school they can have a place to talk, write, and read about them.

We are dependent on the resources of the earth for survival, and, consequently, we have responsibility for using them with care. We are teaching *ecology* when we help children to understand that animals and people need clean air and water and a safe, healthy environment, and that they can participate in taking care of the environment. Because of its critical importance, ecology is increasingly a part of the curriculum. You teach it as you read, observe, and talk about people's effect on the environment (for example, noticing where people have trodden the grass away, or where they have planted a garden), when you observe how garbage is collected and disposed of, when you notice the effects of litter, and as you observe the impact of people on animals and plants in your environment.

FIGURE 14.3   Earth Science Concepts

Rocks, Dirt, and Water

- The earth is made of rocks (minerals), dirt (broken down plant/animal matter) and water.
- Rocks, dirt, and water are not alive.
- Rocks, dirt, and water have different properties—appearance, color, texture, solidity, temperature, reactions to heat, cold, pressure, and moisture.
- Rocks, dirt, and water can exist in different states, e.g., solid, liquid, gas.

Earth Features

- The earth has different features: mountains/hills/plains/islands/volcanoes, rivers/streams/lakes/oceans.
- The earth's features can change. Changes can be natural (e.g., erosion, tides, earthquakes, volcanic eruptions) or caused by human beings (e.g., pollution, mining, dams).

Weather and Seasons

- The earth has seasons and different kinds of climate and weather.
- Seasons mean changes in temperature, precipitation, and the length of day and night, which are different in different places.
- Weather is the day-to-day temperature, wind, and precipitation in a particular place.
- Climate is the usual weather in a particular place over long periods of time.

Sun, Moon, and Stars

- The sun is a star close to the earth that provides heat and light.
- The earth moves around the sun.
- The sun causes earth's climate and weather.
- The moon moves around the Earth.
- Moonshine is the sun's reflection. As different parts face the sun they are lit up so it seems to have different shapes.
- A star is a ball of very hot gas in space.
- Stars look like shiny dots because they are far away.

A visit to the zoo provides children with the opportunity to see animals that are in danger of extinction and to learn about the kinds of habitats they need and how they are threatened are also lessons in ecology.

While there are many things to learn about the earth and atmosphere, a few simple concepts can guide your teaching. Figure 14.3 gives you a guide to some basic earth science concepts. While there is *much* more to know and learn about the earth and sky, these can serve as a starting place to help you to talk with children about what they observe.

Standards for Science Curriculum

What should you try to accomplish in the science curriculum? What goals should you have for young children? Content standards and guidelines developed by national organizations, states, and individual programs can help you to identify goals for the science curriculum. These, in turn, help you to select activities.

FIGURE 14.4   Head Start Child Development and Early Learning Framework: *Science Knowledge and Skills*

Scientific Skills and Methods

The skills to observe and collect information and use it to ask questions, predict, explain, and draw conclusions.

- Uses senses and tools, including technology, to gather information, investigate materials, and observe processes and relationships.
- Observes and discusses common properties, differences, and comparisons among objects.
- Participates in simple investigations to form hypotheses, gather observations, draw conclusions, and form generalizations.
- Develops growing abilities to collect, describe, and record information through a variety of means, including discussion, drawings, maps, and charts.
- Collects, describes, and records information through discussions, drawings, maps, and charts.

Conceptual Knowledge of the Natural and Physical World

The acquisition of concepts and facts related to the natural and physical world and the understanding of naturally-occurring relationships.

- Observes, describes, and discusses living things and natural processes.
- Observes, describes, and discusses properties of materials and transformation of substances.

Source: Administration for Children and Families, Head Start Bureau, www.hsnrc.org/cdi/child-outcomes.cfm

The National Committee on Science Education Standards and Assessment of the National Research Council has developed standards for children in K–4 programs (Figure 14.5). While there are no national standards for science in preschool programs, Head Start (Figure 14.4) and almost all states have standards for science curriculum. These standards lay out the expectation that teachers provide opportunities for development and/or that children develop certain skills. Almost all of them address:

- the development of inquiry skills (sometimes called *scientific skills*).
- the acquisition of knowledge of physical science, earth (and space) science, and life science. Some also address technology and health.

The amount of detail prescribed in the standards for different states varies. Some have very general statements, whereas others provide many details about the skills and concepts that children should learn. As you can see from the preschool standards for Head Start (Figure 14.4) and the national standards for children in kindergarten and primary school (Figure 14.5), there is greater specificity of content in the standards for older children. However, the focus on the development of inquiry skills and learning about science that is personally meaningful is consistent.

Your program's goals may be based on state or national standards, or they may have been developed independently by your staff or a curriculum specialist. However, it is likely that they will include some version of these goals.

Teaching Science

Teaching science involves creating an environment for science learning, incorporating opportunities for science experiences in the daily schedule, and supporting science through your behavior and interactions with children. And of course, it involves planning science experiences.

FIGURE 14.5 National Science Content Standards: K–4

Content Standard A: Science as Inquiry

As a result of activities in grades K–4, all students should develop

- Abilities necessary to do scientific inquiry
- Understanding about scientific inquiry

Content Standard B: Physical Science

As a result of activities in grades K–4, all students should develop

- Properties of objects and materials
- Position and motion of objects
- Light, heat, electricity, and magnetism

Content Standard C: Life Science

As a result of activities in grades K–4, all students should develop

- The characteristics of organisms
- Life cycles of organisms
- Organisms and environments

Content Standard D: Earth and Space Science

As a result of activities in grades K–4, all students should develop

- Properties of earth materials
- Objects in the sky
- Changes in earth and sky

Content Standard E: Science and Technology

As a result of activities in grades K–4, all students should develop

- Abilities of technological design
- Understanding about science and technology
- Abilities to distinguish between natural objects and objects made by humans

Content Standard F: Science in Personal and Social Perspectives

As a result of activities in grades K–4, all students should develop

- Personal health
- Characteristics and changes in populations
- Types of resources
- Changes in environments
- Science and technology in local challenges

Content Standard G: History and Nature of Science

As a result of activities in grades K–4, all students should develop

- Science as a human endeavor

Source: Reprinted with permission from *National Science Education Standards*, 1996 by the National Academy of Sciences. Courtesy of the National Academies Press, Washington, D.C.

Science Learning Through Play in a Planned Environment

The learning environment will affect the scope and variety of the science curriculum that you can offer. While science can happen throughout the learning environment, a science discovery area and an outdoor play area provide a laboratory for science experiences.

The Discovery Center

Classroom areas for scientific exploration are often called *science centers*. We prefer the term *discovery center* since this suggests that the center is a laboratory where discoveries of many different kinds can occur and because the term *discovery* is one that children understand. In the discovery center, children can make observations, explore phenomena, research things that interest them, share data, and actively attempt to solve problems.

Arrange your discovery center in a place in the classroom that has access to electricity and water. Define the space with low, open shelves for storage and a low table or counter for investigation, observation, and recording data. Set tables for displays against a taller shelf or wall. Bulletin boards for displaying posters and data are another important part of the discovery center. A light table can be used for science explorations.

Things to investigate such as machinery to disassemble, projects such as an aquarium or a terrarium, ant farms, sorting collections, and plants are the heart of an active discovery center. Learning materials such as a sink and float game, and picture collections for sorting and describing may be stored and used in the science area. To be effective, these need to reflect children's interests. They need to be maintained, kept clean, and monitored. A dusty collection of broken shells and dried up leaves will not inspire children to investigate.

Tools for investigation should be stored in or near the discovery center: sorting trays, plastic tubs and pitchers, jars or aquaria, insect and animal cages, airtight containers for storage, balances, scales, measuring cups and spoons, and magnifying glasses. Photographs and posters that illustrate science concepts as well as graphs and charts that show children's discoveries can be displayed on bulletin boards. Books related to investigations should be available, such as a resource book on insects next to a cage with a praying mantis. If space and resources permit, a computer with an Internet connection or an encyclopedia in the discovery area provide ways for children and teachers to research science questions as they arise. Table 14.1 provides some ideas for equipping your discovery area.

TABLE 14.1 Equipping a Discovery Area

Space	Furnishings	Things to Investigate	Tools for Investigation	Display	Prepared Learning Materials	Resources
Defined, sheltered space Good lighting—natural if possible Access to electricity and water	One or two open shelves and low tables Bookshelf Light table	Animals and plants Machinery Artifacts (e.g., shells, stones)	Sorting trays Plastic tubs and pitchers Jars or aquaria, insect, and animal cages Airtight containers for storage Balances Scales Measuring cups and spoons Magnifying glasses Tongs and tweezers Eyedroppers	Bulletin boards Picture collections Photographs and posters that illustrate science concepts Graphs/charts of children's discoveries	Science-related games Sorting collections	Books An encyclopedia A computer with an Internet connection

The Outdoor Environment

Regularly scheduled opportunities to experience the natural world are vital to ensure a rich and meaningful science curriculum. An outdoor environment needs plants, dirt, trees, grass, and the creatures that inhabit them. The yard is a good place for science activities such as planting a garden, mounting a bird feeder, or housing a pet. As children explore slides, swings, balls, and trikes, they are experiencing physics concepts relating to force, gravity, leverage, and friction.

If your outside play area is a rooftop or parking lot, it is critical for science learning to make sure it includes nature by adding potted plants, garden boxes, pets, and sand tables (to fill with sand, water, or dirt). Regular walks to parks can supplement but not substitute for daily experience with nature in the playground.

Many appropriate and worthwhile science experiences require moving beyond the walls of the early childhood program. Science learning trips can be as simple as a nature walk in the neighborhood or can involve visits to locations like the zoo, aquarium, wildlife preserve, farm, museum of natural science, forest, seashore, or mountains. Whether your trips are nearby and spontaneous or more distant and carefully planned, they will promote more science learning if there is enough time for children to learn by discovery. This is facilitated by allowing small groups of children to visit sites where they can explore and discuss experiences in an unhurried fashion.

Science Everywhere

The discovery center and outdoor playground provide the most obvious locations for science learning. But you will do a better job of teaching science if you learn to recognize the science that happens throughout the classroom.

In the *art area,* children learn about color and the ways that colors change as they mix. They experience chemistry as they make playdough. They gain concrete knowledge of processes like evaporation as clay and paint dry. At the *sensory table,* they develop observation skills. They learn about the properties of matter—the nature of water, dirt, sand, ice, and combined materials like cornstarch goop. The *block area* provides a physics laboratory where children learn about balance, friction, and gravity. For reference and recreation, science books should be a part of every classroom *library.* Simple machines can be created with manipulative toys, and many puzzles and games help children learn science concepts in the *manipulative toys area*.

A Schedule for Science Learning

Since young children develop many science concepts through play, children need blocks of time for discovery throughout the day. In addition, they learn concepts through carefully planned science activities. So, regularly scheduled time for small groups to gather and explore science questions is also important.

Significant blocks of time for both indoor and outdoor play (45 minutes to an hour) are essential for science. When you are able to explain to parents, administrators, and co-workers that this play time contributes to children's learning of academic subjects like science you may find that you gain more support for allowing children the freedom for meaningful discovery through play.

Because young children have limited tolerance for sedentary group experiences, it is important to plan carefully for short (10–20 minute) small-group times to introduce science concepts and provide for science discovery. The time that you meet with small groups around science topics needs to be frequent, active, and filled with interesting and meaningful real science experiences (not listening to the teacher or other children talk, or watching a video).

Your Role in the Science Curriculum

The Tom Towels (a group of 4-year olds) took a walk around their school past an empty lot. Along the way, they found an animal skeleton along the side of the road. They were fascinated and curious. Their teacher, Mary Ann (who had brought several plastic bags along on the trip), gathered the bones and took them back to the classroom for further exploration. Renee (another teacher) responded to their find with repulsion. Fortunately, the group was not deterred and they spent several days examining, reassembling the skeleton, counting the bones and teeth, hypothesizing that it had been a dinosaur, and finally figuring out that it had been a dog.

Your main role in science education is the preservation and encouragement of the natural curiosity of children. To maintain children's attitude of playfulness toward science, you need to view their difficult questions as an opportunity to model the attitudes of the scientist: curiosity, questioning, openness to exploration, and problem solving. Together, you will work to figure out how to learn the answers to questions through observation, research, or experimentation.

Your own spirit of scientific inquiry will affect what is learned and the attitudes that children develop about science. While it is not necessary to have a degree in physics to offer science experiences in your classroom you do need to appreciate the value of science and be open to subject matter that is of interest to young children. And you need to be able to make mistakes and learn from them.

Young children **are** scientists—people engaged in systematic activity to acquire knowledge about the world. So to teach science, you also must become a scientist. What do scientists do? Scientists do not have all the answers. Instead, they try to understand natural phenomena. They observe, they question, they gather and compare data, and they do research. They are learning all the time. That is what good teachers do, too.

Science Activities

What are science activities? Many planned and unplanned activities help children learn about science. To plan a science curriculum for your children, it helps to have a repertoire of activities that you can adapt for your setting and for the science interests of the children in your class.

Exploring and Observing

All science involves observation—attentive noticing. When you provide children with real objects, animals, plants, and phenomena, and encourage them to observe with all of their senses, you are providing them with a science *experience.* Exploration and observation often happen spontaneously as children play outdoors and with materials like water, blocks, and sand.

You can also plan for exploration and observation in activities. When you provide materials to be explored and tools to enhance observation with science concepts in mind, you are planning for science exploration. When you provide the children with magnifying glasses and ask them to look carefully at a bug, you are providing a planned science observation activity. You can plan for observation and exploration in life, physical, and earth sciences.

Comparing and Classifying

As children interact with materials, they compare them. Teachers who understand science can help children do this by purposefully providing similar things to be compared. In the vignette with Katie and the shells on page 428, the teacher had planned an experience in comparison and classification. In addition to simply providing materials, you can enhance comparison and classification activities by asking children to talk about their comparisons ("How are these shells the same?"). As you work with children in groups, you can ask them to tell one another about their classifications ("Hannah, can you show Julian which shells you think belong together?").

Questioning, Hypothesizing, and Investigating Theories

Children have many questions about the world, but they don't always ask them out loud. One of your most important jobs as a teacher of science is to notice children and help them to begin to ask questions. As you help them give voice to their questions, you can also assist them in beginning to hypothesize. A simple word for a hypothesis is *guess*. As children attempt to predict what happens in a wide range of circumstances, their hypotheses evolve into *theories*—ideas about how something works.

Children have many theories about how the world works. Scientists (and children) use hypotheses and testing to develop theories. By talking with children and really listening to them, you may get to hear what those theories are. "A dead bird will revive if we give it water." "Seeds will grow if we dig them up and look at them." "A ball can bounce over a house." Children's questions and theories can be the basis for planned *investigations*.

Perhaps in remembrance of their own high school science labs, teachers sometimes plan science investigations before children have theories, or even questions. They call them *experiments*. In truth, if children have no questions or theories, these are neither experiments nor investigations. Instead, they are *demonstrations*. Demonstrations can serve to pique children's interests. Because they are based on adult questions and ideas about what is interesting, they often fail to engage young children. Instead, plan investigations of phenomena that you observe children being curious about. The results will be more rewarding for all concerned.

Recording and Organizing Data

Tyler, age 4 1/2, discovers an iridescent green bug on the playground. He is captivated by the insect and carries it to his teacher. The teacher finds a clear plastic bug bottle to hold it. They examine it carefully. Robin, the teacher, leaves the bug bottle on the table in the discovery area. Tyler gets colored pencils and paper and carefully observes and draws the bug.

As children observe, investigate, and learn about the world, they can begin to record their findings. Recording and organizing data is an important part of science. It is the way that scientists reflect on and make sense of what they have observed. There are several ways to record and organize data.

Graphing

A graph is used to compare the relative quantity of objects or phenomena. When the 4-year-olds in the previous vignette wanted to find out what type of bug was most often found in the grass of the playground, they gathered, counted, and then recorded the number of bugs collected in 10 minutes. Their teacher used a simple bar graph to make the comparison (the answer: roly-poly bugs).

Charting

A chart is a way to make a record of diverse pieces of data. When teachers make a poster-sized written record of what children observe and describe, it is called *charting.* This information can be added to and used to compare with other data sources.

Journaling

When there is an ongoing project that takes place over time such as growing a garden, hatching chicken eggs, or watching caterpillars transform into butterflies, a journal is a good way for children to record data. Each day the children dictate to the teacher and/or draw what they observe. Photos can be added to this documentation. This serves as a daily diary of scientific investigation.

Art

Although young children cannot yet write, their art drawings, paintings, collage and sculpture (such as the drawing that Tyler made) can serve as important documentation. And creating art helps children to be good observers, as you can see from the children's art we have included in this book.

Planning Science Curriculum

Children's natural curiosity is the beginning place for your science curriculum, but it is not the end. The framework of life science, physical science, and earth science provides you with a way to think about the kinds of experiences that you will provide. The environment you create can provide the inspiration for science. Your ability to feel and share curiosity and enthusiasm for science is another critical element. Finally, you need to have knowledge. You need to know some science—and you do. You are an educated adult. Through your own schooling and by living for two or more decades, you have learned a lot about science. As you become a teacher of science, you will use what you have learned so you can become a guide for children and a fellow learner. You need not be a scientist or an expert. However, you do need to have a scientist's perspective—that the world is infinitely interesting, that science is about questions (not answers), and that it is possible and worth the effort to learn about science.

You also need to have knowledge of the strategies that can best help children learn science. And you need to know what educators have identified as important science learning for young children.

Using Science as the Core of an Integrated Study

Perhaps the best, and most natural, way for young children to learn about science is through an integrated study. Literature, art, music, math, literacy, language, social studies, creative movement—all can be used well and with integrity to help young children learn about a science topic. Furthermore, science is one of the two best curriculum areas (the other is social studies) that can be used to focus integrated curriculum.

The sunburst included in this chapter on the topic *Bugs* is a science topic. All of the activities that were planned for this study directly or indirectly were related to science. For example, the activity named Comparing Eric Carle Bugs and Real Bugs involved matching and comparing photographs of bugs with the tissue paper collage images of bugs created by Eric Carle. This activity was a literature extension with science content. And each of the activities listed in Figure 14.6 is similarly a science activity regardless of the other subject matter. For this reason none of the activities are highlighted. All are science.

Writing Activity Plans for Science

Tyler's discovery of the iridescent green bug on the playground led to many questions and discoveries. Children noticed its almost square shape and its long antennae. Tyler noted that his hand that had held the bug smelled "funny." Other children asked, "What kind of bug is it?" Tyler asked, "What does it eat?" Soullee wondered, "Will it bite?" "I don't know" Robin, the teacher, responded, "I wonder how we could find out."

You begin planning for science by providing raw materials and paying attention to children. Robin began this process by giving children time and a place in which to find insects, providing the equipment to study them, and joining with the children in examining the beautiful bug. She knew that simply providing an answer to their questions was not the best way to help children learn about science or to teach them about insects. But the children were interested, so she needed to capitalize on this "teachable moment."

The most important thing Robin did was build children's ability and disposition to inquire. The first of the National Science Education Standards for young children is ". . . all children should develop abilities to do scientific inquiry." Similarly, the first of the Head Start Child Outcomes is ". . . provide children with experience with scientific skills and methods." To do scientific inquiry, children need to be able to:

- Ask questions about objects, organisms, and events in the environment
- Plan and conduct a simple investigation
- Employ simple equipment and tools to gather data and extend the senses
- Use data to construct a reasonable explanation
- Communicate investigations and explanations. (National Research Council, 1996)

To build on the children's interests and to help them to do scientific inquiry, Robin planned the activity shown in Figure 14.7.

Because she is an experienced teacher, Robin's short plan leaves out many details. It might not be enough of a guide for a beginning teacher. The longer, more elaborate version in Figure 14.8 gives you a better idea of what Robin planned to do.

FIGURE 14.6 Bugs Activity Sunburst

Science
Bug Feely Box
I'm a Mixed-Up Bug Workjob
Pretend Pollinators
Collecting Bugs
Planting a Butterfly Garden
What Do You
Know About Bugs?
KWL Chart
What Have We
Learned About Bugs?

Trips and Resource Visitors
Campus Walks
Hike Aiea Loop Trail
Waimea Falls Cultural Park
Pearl City Urban Garden
Entomologist Visit
Beekeeper Visit
Bug Sharing by Families

Social Studies
Aiea Loop Trail Prediction
Chart and Follow-Up

Blocks
Build a Bug in Blocks

Math
Bug Graph
Hungry
Ladybugs
Workjob

Large Motor
Bug Hunt
Move Like a Bug
Bug Run
Bug House Woodworking
Cricket Hoop Jumping
Giant Bug Puzzles
Tunnel of Bugs
Cricket Jumping

Big Idea
"Bugs" are different from
one another.
• They look different.
• They eat different things
• They live in different places.
• They move different ways.
• Some live alone, others live
with other bugs.
• Some make sounds;
others don't.

Big Idea
"Bugs" have ways to
protect themselves.

Big Idea
There are lots of
kinds of "bugs."
• They live almost
everywhere.

Big Idea
All "bugs" have
important jobs.
• Some pollinate flowers.
• Some help break down
garbage and turn it into dirt.
• Some are food for birds
and other animals.

**A Study of
"Bugs"
(insects, spiders,
and other terrestrial
invertebrates)**

Language
Bug Clues
Fingerplays: The
Beehive
The Caterpillar
Where Do We Find
Bugs? Discussion
Insect and Spider Card
Game

Cooking and Tasting
Honey Tasting
Honey Balls

Big Idea
"Bugs" have special bodies.
• Insects' bodies have 3
parts, 6 legs, antennae, and
special eyes. They have no
bones (they have an
exoskeleton).
• Spiders' bodies have 2
parts, 8 legs, they have
an exoskeleton, they
can have 2, 4, 6, 8 or
no eyes.

Big Idea
Most "bugs" hatch
from eggs.
• Then their bodies
change from larva to
adults.

Big Idea
A few "bugs" can
hurt people.
• They bite or sting.
• They can spread germs.
• They can damage homes
and plants.

Big Idea
Some "bugs" help people.
• They make things we use.
• They pollinate food plants and
flowers.
• They eat bugs that harm us.

Art
Caterpillar Drawing
Sculpting Clay Bugs
Bug Life Drawing
Cricket Life Drawing
3-D Bug Collage

Music
Little Bug, Little Bug
Fuzzy Fuzzy
Caterpillar
First Comes a Butterfly
Eency Weency Spider
Shoo Fly
Lady Bug (Frank Leto)
Bugs, Bugs, Bugs

**Movement and
Drama**
Pretend Pollinators
Not So Magic Rocks
Bugs Around the Chair
Moving Like Bugs
Bumblebee Buzz
Creating a Ladybug Puppet
Story
Bug Story to Dramatize

Literature
See booklist
Literature Extensions:
The Very Hungry
Caterpillar
Flannelboard Story
Comparing
Eric Carle Bugs and Real Bugs
Matching Game
Grouchy Ladybug Flannelboard
Story

Literacy
Caterpillar Book
What Do You Know About Bugs
KWL Chart
Where Do We Find Bugs? Discussion
and Chart
Cricket Discussion and Language
Experience Chart
Hike Book
My Favorite Bug Book

FIGURE 14.7   Simple Science Activity Plan

Observing a Bug

Objectives:	Develop children's ability to plan and conduct a simple investigation, gather data, name and understand some characteristics of insects
Standard:	HPCS Domain IV, Science Standards 2 and 4
What you need:	Green bugs in plastic jars, magnifying glasses, chart paper (1 with questions, 2 blank), pen, books on insects (e.g., Hawaiian Insects and Their Kin)
How to teach:	1. Meet in Discovery Area and explain, "We can figure out some answers to our questions."
	2. Invite children to use magnifying glasses and describe what they see—write words.
	3. Ask children to look at parts of the bug.
	4. Distribute books to look for a similar bug to compare to our bug.
	5. Write answers with questions on chart.
How to assess:	Look/Listen for children talking about insects, asking questions, using magnifying glass, comparing photos, drawing observations. Document with photos, work samples, and anecdotals.

FIGURE 14.8   Detailed Science Activity Plan

Activity:	**Observing a Bug** (a small-group observation and data recording activity)
Curriculum Area:	Science
WHO It's For:	This activity was planned for Tyler and the Airplanes (the 4-year-old group).
WHY This Activity Rationale:	Tyler discovered an iridescent green bug on the playground. He and the other Airplanes were intrigued by it, observed it, and had many questions about it. They wanted to know what kind of bug it is, what it eats, and if it bites people. This activity is designed to help the children learn to gather data that will be helpful to them in finding the answer to their questions.
Science Objectives:	*By participating in this activity the children will…*
	○ Plan and conduct a simple investigation.
	○ Learn to gather data.
	○ Begin to understand the characteristics of insects.
	○ Develop the disposition to do scientific inquiry.
Concepts to Begin to Develop:	○ Each kind of plant and animal has particular characteristics: appearance, needs, and behavior.
	• Insects have special bodies—they have hard shells (exoskeletons), 6 legs, and antennae.
	• Insects have ways to protect themselves.
Preschool Content Standard(s):	Domain IV, Science Standard 2: Engage in scientific inquiry.
Indicators:	Ask scientific questions. Use observations in making predictions. Use materials appropriate for problem solving and exploration of the physical world, including equipment. Engage in discussions and/or document in drawing/writing what is learned through exploration.
Standard 4:	Explore characteristics of living things.
Indicators:	Explore the nature of life through observation of and interaction. Notice similarities, differences, and categories of animals, as well as appearances, behaviors, and habitats.

(continued)

FIGURE 14.8   Detailed Science Activity Plan (continued)

***HOW* to Prepare**	*What you need:* ○ 15–20 min at small-group time in the Discovery Area ○ One or more of the green bugs found on the playground in a clear container. If more than one bug is available, put them in two containers. ○ Table and 5 chairs ○ Several magnifying glasses ○ 2 pieces of chart paper and pen ○ Books on insects: *Hawaiian Insects and Their Kin* by Howarth and Mull, *Common Insects of Hawaii* by Fullaway and Krauss, *Insects: Hawaii Nature Study Project* by CRDG, *All Color Book of Insects* by Michael Tweedie *Set up:* On one piece of chart paper, write the children's questions. What kind of bug is it? What does it eat? Will it bite? On the other piece of chart paper write: Things We Noticed About Our Bug
***HOW* to Teach**	*Introduction:* Meet in the Discovery Area. Bring out the bug(s) and explain that you hope we might figure out some of the answers to our questions about the green bug. Say something like, "I thought if we wrote down everything we notice about the bug, we might look in these books about bugs and see if there is a bug like it. The book might tell us more about bugs like the one we found." *Teaching steps:* 1. Invite children to look at the bug and describe what they see. Offer magnifying glasses so they can look more closely (may need to help children hold magnifying glass at correct distance). As they describe what they see, write their words very quickly on chart paper. 2. Ask children to look at specific parts of the bug (e.g., "What's on its head?" "How many legs does it have?" "What can you see on its underside?") and write their answers on the chart. 3. Distribute books to children who are still attentive. Invite them to look for a picture of a bug that is similar to our bug. Note that we will read about it and find out if it is similar to our bug. (Invite others to go play and come back later if they would like to hear what we learn.) 4. As children find photos, read about those insects and compare them to our bug. If the bug has been identified, write the answers on the chart paper that contains the questions. *Closure:* Once the bug has been identified, suggest that they share what they have learned with others at meeting time. Note that they can share the book with the pictures and the charts. Invite children to continue to look at the bug (and draw it if they so desire) or play elsewhere.

HOW to Assess and Document

What to look for to identify if the objectives were met and how to document.

Objectives	Evidence of Learning Children might …	How to Document This Evidence
• Develop a disposition to do scientific inquiry.	Ask questions about bugs or other living things or phenomena.	Anecdotal records
• Plan and conduct a simple investigation.	Use magnifying glass to look at bugs. Look through books and compare photos.	
• Learn to gather data.	Draw or otherwise want to record observations of the bug.	Work samples
• Begin to understand the characteristics of insects.	Talk about characteristics of insects or identify insects by saying things like: "It has antennae like the green bug."	Anecdotal records

Science in a Weekly Plan

As we have said before, young children develop many science concepts through play, so they need blocks of time for discovery through play throughout the day as well as in thoughtfully planned, teacher-guided small groups during which science is explored. Although the entire topic in Figure 14.9 relates to science,

FIGURE 14.9 A Week's Plan: A Study of Bugs—Week #6

Objectives: To help children to understand the characteristics of bugs—body structure, movement, color, size, etc. and become aware that some people have jobs teaching and learning about bugs.

	Monday	Tuesday	Wednesday	Thursday	Friday
Story 2–3 stories are read, children choose the 2nd and 3rd story	*It's a Good Thing There Are Insects* (Fowler)	*In the Tall, Tall Grass* (Fleming)	*Bugs for Lunch* (Facklam)	*I Love Bugs!* (Philemon)	*Maggie and the Pirate* (Keats)
Outdoor Activities **Purpose:** to help children to …	**Cornstarch Goop** Increase sensory awareness. Explore physical properties of substances.	**Obstacle Course** Develop large muscle strength and coordination.	**Fingerpainting** Increase sensory awareness. Explore art elements and techniques.	**Mud Painting** Increase sensory awareness. Explore art elements and techniques.	**Cricket Observation and Jumping** Understand some of the ways bugs move. Develop large muscle strength and coordination.
Small Group 1 Butterflies (4-year-olds) **Purpose:** to help children to …	**Entomologist Visit** Both groups will participate as Entomologists Steve and Anita M. show and teach us about a variety of real bugs. Solidify knowledge of the characteristics of insects— three body parts, a hard outer skeleton, six legs, antennae, and special eyes. Understand that some people have jobs teaching and learning about bugs.	**Read Story:** *You Can Be a Woman Entomologist* (Underwood) Understand and appreciate books. Learn about the work of an entomologist.	**Create a** *Book About Bugs* Understand that books are created by people. Express understanding through drawing and print.	**Read** *Book About Bugs* **Created Yesterday** Understand that books are created by people. Consolidate knowledge of bugs.	**Cricket Life Drawing** Increase observation skills and understanding of the characteristics of insects. Acquire ability to express ideas and feelings through art.
Small Group 2 Airplanes (3-year-olds) **Purpose:** to help children to …		**Create a Story with Bug Puppets** Express ideas through creative drama.	**Leaf Collage** Create using diverse art media and techniques.	**Read Book and Act Out** *In the Tall Tall Grass* (Fleming) Develop new vocabulary and appreciation for books. Express ideas through creative drama.	**Bug Feely Box** (using plastic bugs) Increase sensory observation skills. Develop vocabulary and speaking skill.

(continued)

FIGURE 14.9 A Week's Plan: A Study of Bugs—Week #6 (continued)

	Monday	Tuesday	Wednesday	Thursday	Friday
Indoor Activities (In addition to learning centers, one "special activity" is planned.) **Purpose:** to help children to …	Clay Sculpture Learn to use clay as a medium of expression. Learn about art elements and techniques.	**Cooking Grilled Cheese Sandwiches** Acquire self-help skills. Develop a disposition to eat wholesome food.	Ink and Watercolor Wash Create and express ideas and feelings using art media. Begin to learn about art elements and techniques.	3D Bug Construction — construct Create and express ideas and feelings using art media. Understand that bugs have special bodies. Begin to learn about art elements and techniques.	
Circle Time **Purpose:** to help children to…	Sing: *Shoo Fly* using rhythm instruments Learn to create and express ideas in song and with instruments.	Sing *Lady Bug Lady Bug* (song with actions) Express ideas through music and movement.	Sing and Play *Little Bug Fly Thru My Window* Create and express ideas through music and movement. Begin to learn about movement elements and techniques. Acquire awareness of ways that insects move.		Sing/Play *See How I'm Jumping* Develop awareness of music and movement elements. Acquire skill in controlling different locomotor motions.

Ongoing Activities available all week: Drawing, easel painting, hollow blocks and crates, play structure, sand play, trikes, experiencing nature unit blocks, pretend play, puzzles, light table, reading books and writing, games.

the example included here has only a few specific science activities. However, several of the art, music, literature, and movement experiences also help children develop science understanding.

Science for All Children

Once you understand what constitutes science for young children you will realize that all young children are scientists. An infant repeatedly tossing a toy on the floor, a toddler crouched on the sidewalk watching the ants crawl out of a crack, a preschooler dropping his grapes in his milk, a kindergartner taking apart an old piece of machinery, and a child with vision impairment bringing a leaf up to her nose are all learning about the world—they are doing science. The science activities that we have described for typically developing preschoolers can also be the basis of science curriculum for preschoolers with special needs as well as primary age children.

Children with Special Needs

Paul, a child with a visual impairment, is a 3-year-old in the Peacocks Group. Paul wears glasses, but his vision is quite limited. Although he plays with other children, he avoids active play. He enjoys listening to stories, playing with sensory materials, and building with blocks. Like many 3-year-olds, he has not yet made a friend at school. And like many 3-year-olds, he is not very attentive to teacher-led activities. The teachers in Paul's class have just embarked on a study of bugs.

How does a child like Paul develop an understanding of science? What should his teachers do to help him learn about a world he cannot see well? How can they help him learn about bugs?

It's important when teaching a child like Paul (or any child) to discover his strengths and interests. Paul seems to learn about the world best by touching and listening. So the first teaching task is to create learning activities that capitalize on these interests and abilities. Storytelling activities, songs, sensory activities, and art activities with a strong sensory component were his teachers' first choices. How did Paul's teachers help him learn about bugs? They brought safe, real bugs into the classroom. Paul delighted in listening to the crickets, in holding caterpillars and millipedes, in listening to the loud buzz of the carpenter bee in the bug house. He enjoyed the many Eric Carle stories about bugs and he could see the bright, big illustrations as well as enjoy the sounds and tactile elements in many of the stories. His teachers rigged a camera to a video monitor so that all the children could enjoy an enlarged view of the classroom bugs. With just a little reflection they were able to bring science to Paul.

Children in the Primary Grades

Primary children, too, learn best when science continues to be a form of play. This is quite different from a traditional model where children may do "hands-on" experiments only to duplicate the results in the textbook rather than to explore and find out what was really going on. Wassermann and Ivany, in their lovely book on science curriculum *Teaching Elementary Science: Who's Afraid of Spiders?* (1996), describe what they refer to as the *Play-Debrief-Replay* model for teaching sciencing. In this method, the teacher sets up a science play center with materials to explore. Children "play," and explore the materials freely; "debrief," and discuss what they have done with a teacher who assists them in reflecting on what they have observed; and then "replay," and try it again with the same materials. As you model an inquiring and respectful attitude toward the world, you help children to think like scientists. Science, rather than being scary or mysterious, is everyday, accessible, infinitely interesting, and definitely worth knowing.

Final Thoughts

Young children *are* natural scientists. Their openness, inquisitiveness, playfulness, and willingness to take risks to learn are the essence of what science is and what scientists should be. As a teacher of young children, you are privileged to be able to join with them on the adventure of a lifetime, learning about our world.

There are endless scientific problems to be solved in the world. And solving them is critical to human survival, to your survival. The scientists who will discover the cure for cancer, the solution to global warming, an end to aging, or a way to end pollution may be young children in your classroom tomorrow. As you help them to be curious, appreciate nature, develop a disposition to experiment, explore, and think of innovative answers, you are contributing to the future of the world. They need you to be a wonderful science teacher—we all do.

Learning Outcomes

When you read this chapter, thoughtfully complete activities from the "To Learn More" section, and document this learning as suggested in the "For Your Portfolio" section, you will be making progress in the following *NAEYC Standards for Early Childhood Professional Preparation Programs* (2009):

Standard 1. Promoting Child Development and Learning

Students prepared in early childhood degree programs are grounded in a child development knowledge base. They use their understanding of young children's characteristics and needs and of the multiple interacting influences on children's development and learning to create environments that are healthy, respectful, supportive, and challenging for each child.

The key elements of standard 1 you will have learned about are . . .

1a: Knowing and understanding young children's characteristics and needs

1c: Using developmental knowledge to create healthy, respectful, supportive, and challenging learning environments

Standard 4. Using Developmentally Effective Approaches to Connect with Children and Families

Students prepared in early childhood degree programs understand that teaching and learning with young children is a complex enterprise, and its details vary depending on children's ages, characteristics, and the settings within which teaching and learning occur. They understand and use positive relationships and supportive interactions as the foundation for their work with young children and families. Students know, understand, and use a wide array of developmentally appropriate approaches, instructional strategies, and tools to connect with children and families and positively influence each child's development and learning.

The key elements of standard 4 you will have learned about are . . .

4a: Understanding positive relationships and supportive interactions as the foundation of their work with children

4b: Knowing and understanding effective strategies and tools for early education

4c: Using a broad repertoire of developmentally appropriate teaching/learning approaches

4d: Reflecting on their own practice to promote positive outcomes for each child

Standard 5. Using Content Knowledge to Build Meaningful Curriculum

Students prepared in early childhood degree programs use their knowledge of academic disciplines to design, implement, and evaluate experiences that promote positive development and learning for each and every young child. Students understand the importance of developmental domains and academic (or content) disciplines in an early childhood curriculum. They know the essential concepts, inquiry tools, and structure of content areas, including academic subjects, and can identify resources to deepen their understanding. Students use their own knowledge and other resources to design, implement, and evaluate meaningful, challenging curricula that promote comprehensive developmental and learning outcomes for every young child.

The key elements of standard 5 you will have learned about are . . .

5a: Understanding content knowledge and resources in academic disciplines

5b: Knowing and using the central concepts, inquiry tools, and structures of content areas or academic disciplines

5c: Using their own knowledge, appropriate early learning standards, and other resources to design, implement, and evaluate meaningful, challenging curricula for each child.

To Learn More

Observe a Program: For a morning, observe a program and see how the staff structures the environment and program to support children's science learning. Notice both the play opportunities and the planned group activities. Look at the plans and see how the planning reflects what you observed. Interview a teacher to learn how he or she thinks about science curriculum.

Observe a Child: For a morning, observe a child in a classroom, with a focus on the child's science exploration. Notice how the child engages with the planned activities and how he or she constructs his or her own opportunities for learning. Notice the extent to which the child's activity and the planned curriculum seem to match. Observe to see how staff support the child's science learning.

Observe a Master Teacher: Spend a morning with an early childhood educator who is experienced and has a curriculum leadership role in a program. (This teacher may be called the "lead," "head," or "mentor" teacher.) Then interview the educator about how he or she plans for and provides science curriculum.

Observe a Science Activity: Observe a teacher leading a planned science activity. Interview the teacher to find out the objectives for the activity. Reflect on any differences between what you saw and the focus of the plan.

Compare Two Programs: Observe science experiences in two early childhood programs. Compare the ways that the two address science curriculum—their similarities and differences. Reflect on which program seems to best support children's learning and why. What implications does this comparison have for your future work with young children?

Compare Two Ages: Observe two classrooms, one preschool and one for primary school children. Report on how each supports children's science learning. Talk to the staff about how they make their curriculum choices. Notice how development influences curriculum choices.

Explore Resources: Read one of the books from the bibliography or several of the online resources listed here and write a review for your classmates.

American Association for the Advancement of Science: www.aaas.org/

National Center for Science in Early Education: www.cnsm.csulb.edu/depts/scied/NCSEC/

National Science Teachers Association: www.nsta.org/elementaryschool

National Wildlife Federation: www.nwf.org/kids

PBS Teachers PreK Science & Tech: pbs.org/teachers/classroom/prek/science-tech/resources/

For Your Portfolio

Design a Discovery (Science) Area: Design and draw a floor plan for a discovery (science) area that would promote children's science exploration and learning. Share your plan with an early childhood educator, discussing what you included and why. Ask for and consider the educator's feedback and suggestions. Set up a discovery area in a real classroom utilizing as many of your ideas as possible and let children use it. For your portfolio, include the floor plan, photographs or video of children using the area, and a reflection on what you learned by doing this project.

Plan and Implement a Science Activity: Observe a group of children for a morning, focusing on their science interest and skill. Based on what you observed, write and implement a science activity. Collect evidence of children's responses in the form of anecdotal observations, photographs, or video recordings. Reflect on how children responded and what they appear to have learned. What worked? What might you do differently next time? How might you expand on this experience for children? For your portfolio, include the plan, a photograph, and a reflection on what you learned about yourself, children, planning, and teaching.

Create a Science Learning Material: Design and make a science game or other learning material to support the development of a particular child or group of children. Introduce it to the child or children and observe how it is used. Reflect on how the children responded and how you felt about what you did. What worked? What might you do differently next time? How might you expand on this experience for children? For your portfolio, include a photograph of a child using the material and a reflection on what you learned about yourself, children, learning materials, and teaching.

Bibliography

Cliatt, M. J. P., & Shaw, J. M. (1991). *Helping children explore science: A sourcebook for teachers of young children.* Upper Saddle River, NJ: Pearson.

Davis, G. A., & Keller, J. D. (2009). *Exploring science and mathematics in a child's world.* Upper Saddle River, NJ: Pearson.

Elkind, D. (1999). *Educating young children in math, science, and technology.* In Project 2061 www .project2061.org/. Washington, DC: American Association for the Advancement of Science.

Feeney, S., Moravcik, E., & Nolte, S. (2013). *Who am I in the lives of children?* (9th ed.). Upper Saddle River, NJ: Pearson.

Gardner, H. (1999). *Intelligence reframed: Multiple intelligences for the 21st century.* New York, NY: Basic Books.

Gelman, S. A. (1999). *Concept development in preschool children.* In Project 2061 www.project2061.org/. Washington, DC: American Association for the Advancement of Science.

Harlan, J. D., & Rivkin, M. S. (2011). *Science experiences for the early childhood years: An integrated affective approach* (10th ed.). Upper Saddle River, NJ: Pearson.

Head Start Resource Center. (2010). *The Head Start Child development and early learning framework: Promoting positive outcomes in early childhood programs serving children 3–5 years old.* Washington, DC: Office of Head Start, Administration for Children and Families, U.S. Department of Health and Human Services.

Lind, K. (1999). *Science in early childhood: Developing and acquiring fundamental concepts and skills.* In Project 2061 www.project2061.org/. Washington, DC: American Association for the Advancement of Science.

Lind, K. (2000). *Exploring science in early childhood education* (3rd ed.). Clifton Park, NY: Delmar.

Louv, R. (2006). *The last child in the woods.* Chapel Hill, NC: Algonquin Books.

National Association for the Education of Young Children. (2009). *NAEYC standards for early childhood professional preparation programs.* www.naeyc.org/files/naeyc/file/positions/ProfPrepStandards09.pdf

National Research Council. (1996). *National science education standards.* Washington, DC: The National Academy Press.

Seefeldt, C., & Galper, A. (2007). *Science: Active experiences for active children.* Upper Saddle River, NJ: Pearson.

Wasserman, S., & Ivany, J. W. G. (1996). *The new teaching elementary science: Who's afraid of spiders?* (2nd ed.). New York, NY: Teachers College Press.

Wilson, L. O. (1998). *Journeys: Inside out, outside in.* Carmel, NY: Zephyr Press.

MyEducationLab

Go to Topics 2: Child Development and Learning, and 9: Content Areas/Lessons and Activities in the MyEducationLab (www.myeducationlab.com) for *Meaningful Curriculum for Young Children,* where you can:

- Find learning outcomes for Child Development and Learning and Content Areas/Lessons and Activities along with the national standards that connect to these outcomes.
- Complete Assignments and Activities that can help you more deeply understand the chapter content.
- Apply and practice your understanding of the core teaching skills identified in the chapter with the Building Teaching Skills and Dispositions learning units.
- Listen to experts from the field in Professional Perspectives.

- Examine challenging situations and cases presented in the IRIS Center Resources.
- Check your comprehension on the content covered in the chapter with the Study Plan. Here you will be able to take a chapter quiz, receive feedback on your answers, and then access Review, Practice, and Enrichment activities to enhance your understanding of chapter content.

Go to the Course Resources section in MyEducationLab, where you can:

- Use the Online Lesson Plan Builder to practice lesson planning and integrating national and state standards into your planning.

If you don't understand yourself you don't understand anybody else.

NIKKI GIOVANNI

chapter fifteen

SOCIAL STUDIES CURRICULUM
Discovering the Social World

Social studies concerns relationships among people as well as the interconnections between people and the world in which they live. You may feel a little confused about social studies because it includes a number of different fields and is taught in a great variety of ways. While you almost certainly experienced social studies in your early school experiences, you may not have heard the term *social studies* until you were well out of early childhood.

If you think of social studies as interesting and exciting, then your teachers presented it in worthwhile and memorable ways and you are probably looking forward to reading this chapter. If, on the other hand, you think of social studies as a dull subject requiring the memorization of dates, names, and places, you are probably wondering why it is included in a book on early childhood curriculum. You may be dreading reading this chapter.

Why Social Studies?

Young children are social scientists from the beginnings of their lives. Like all human beings, they are interested in other people. Even the youngest children are psychologists, intently studying the behavior of the people who share their homes, schools, and communities. They are anthropologists learning about the customs of their family, culture, and society. They are sociologists noting how adults and children in groups interact with one another in their community, school, church, and neighborhood. They are political scientists seeking to understand the rules and power of their classroom, playground, and home. They are geographers experiencing night and day, weather and seasons, dirt and water, hills, yards, and streams. They are economists learning about the value of re-sources in their homes and classrooms and experiencing the laws of supply and demand with toys and cookies. Children do not wait to learn social studies until they are old enough to attend a lecture or read a study. They are learning about social studies from the time they are born.

When appropriately taught to young children, social studies has a great deal of content that is important and worth knowing for young children. Learning this content can help children to:

- appreciate and respect themselves, other people, their culture, and their environment.
- deal with some of the important issues in their lives.
- develop a sense of belonging to and responsibility for their family, community, and environment.
- recognize some of the significant patterns that shape people's lives and the world.
- explore, understand, and experience aspects of the world that lay the foundation for later comprehension of the social sciences.
- develop skills in a range of subject areas.

The content and teaching methods for social studies are more diverse than those for any other subject area. This is true not only because social studies includes many different subject areas, but also because it is the place in the curriculum that most reflects the concerns of teachers, families, and community. More than any other subject area, social studies provides a way to communicate values that people think are important and want children to learn.

Understanding How Young Children Learn Social Studies

Young children have a very global, undifferentiated idea about themselves, other people, and the world. The ways in which they understand people and the world are important for you to be aware of as you learn to teach social studies.

Preschool and kindergarten children recognize thoughts and feelings within themselves and others. They can see that others' views and feelings might be different from their own and that two people might react differently to the same situation.

Young children begin to identify ethnic and racial distinctions very early in life. They are aware of racial differences and are beginning to develop positive and negative attitudes about these differences. Racial awareness develops as they observe attributes such as skin color, hair, and facial features. Since their thinking is still based on perception and not on logic, they may believe that skin color is caused by external sources such as dirt, paint, or exposure to the sun. They do not understand that race is permanent and determined by heritage. It is not uncommon for a young child to believe that a person is Japanese when wearing a kimono, or Native American when sun tanned.

Similarly, preschool and kindergarten children understand that being a boy or a girl is unique and mutually exclusive, but they may not understand that gender identity is unchanging and based on anatomy. Often they will look at clothes or the length of a person's hair to determine if that person is a boy or a girl. For

MyEducationLab

Visit the MyEducationLab for *Meaningful Curriculum for Young Children* to enhance your understanding of chapter concepts with a personalized Study Plan. You'll also have the opportunity to hone your teaching skills through video-based Assignments and Activities, IRIS Center Resources, and Building Teaching Skills and Disposition lessons.

example, a teacher we know who had cut her hair short was asked, "Are you a boy?" by one of the children in her class. When the teacher asked if girls could have short hair and boys could have long hair, a child responded, "My Daddy used to be a girl. He had a ponytail."

Young children's attitudes are heavily influenced by the adults in their lives. Early experiences at home, in school, and in the community establish predispositions toward one's own group that tend to continue throughout life. Child development research demonstrates that by the age of 10, these attitudes are formed and are very resistant to change. Because of this, early childhood is the appropriate time to develop understanding and appreciation of others.

The things you know about how young children learn in general are very relevant to the way they learn social studies. The way young children learn social studies may not seem as obvious as how they learn science or math, so we have included a brief look at how principles of learning apply to social studies.

Principle #1: Children learn by doing. Like math and science concepts, social studies concepts are learned best when they are directly experienced. Knowledge of social aspects of the world (like physical knowledge) must be constructed by children from the materials and experiences that are available to them. Planning to provide direct experiences with social studies requires a little more thought than the more obvious strategies of setting out math manipulatives or creating a science corner. But because social studies topics are vital and meaningful, the extra thought and planning are very rewarding.

Principle #2: Children learn best when they have many direct experiences with the world around them. In social studies, direct experiences involve taking children into the world or bringing the world to them. Real experiences like taking field trips and having class visitors are essential for social studies learning. Since you can't provide direct experiences with all people, places, and historical times, well-chosen exploration of artifacts can offer a meaningful (if not hands-on) experience of unfamiliar people and places.

Principle #3: Children need to reflect and re-enact their experiences in order to develop concepts and understand relationships. Meaningful social studies experiences such as taking a neighborhood walk or visiting a bakery or ice-cream store provide many opportunities for children to demonstrate their understanding through reenacting their experiences. A group of children who have been on these trips can, among other things, discuss what they saw, record their observations on graphs, make maps, create drawings or paintings of what they observed, construct it with blocks, and write a book or sing a song about what they learned. This processing is an essential part of children's learning about social studies.

Principle #4: Children formulate concepts over time and through repeated experiences. Even a concept that appears to be simple (such as "family") needs to be constructed. To construct a concept, children need many experiences over time (for example, by experiencing many different families with different compositions and varying roles).

Principle #5: Each child learns in a unique way and at an individual pace. Because children don't all learn the same way, social studies must be taught to children in diverse ways. One child might best learn a concept by reading a book, another by singing a song, and others by acting it out. Effective teachers present social studies concepts in diverse ways, knowing that children learn best when they can choose activities that are appropriate and meaningful to them.

Principle #6: Children learn best when adults provide support to help them to become more capable. Since social studies includes a number of different disciplines and can be learned in many ways, there are numerous ways adults can support children's developing understandings. Providing meaningful experiences in the world, giving children many opportunities to re-enact their experiences, and asking just the right question at the right time to help a child to grasp a concept are some of the most important ways to support learning relating to people and relationships.

Principle #7: Children learn best when there is communication and consistency between home and school. Because young children first experience social science concepts in their homes, social studies teaching requires a partnership between the family and the teacher. When you involve families in social studies curriculum, you make it meaningful. When families contribute artifacts to be explored, serve as resource visitors who share skills and knowledge, or simply come on a field trip, they are better able to help children understand the link between what they are learning in school and what they are experiencing in their lives.

What Is Social Studies Curriculum in Early Childhood?

Social studies is an umbrella term that can include a number of different fields. The following social science disciplines can be included in social studies curriculum for young children.

Psychology is the study of mind, emotions, and behavior. Psychologists deal with patterns that predict and explain individual behavior. Experiences in early childhood classrooms that lay the foundation for understanding of psychology include activities that help children to gain awareness of self and others as well as their own strengths, weaknesses, feelings, and reactions.

Sociology is the study of how human society functions—its development, institutions, and organization. Sociologists study human activity and try to find explanations for why people do what they do. In early childhood, children can study the ways people live together in families, schools, and communities. They can explore the roles and responsibilities people have and the ways decisions and rules are made. This can help children understand that while people may do things in different ways, they have the same basic needs and share a common humanity. Children can come to appreciate that all people in families have similar needs and ways of looking after one another. They also can begin to view themselves as responsible members of the social groups in which they live.

Cultural anthropology is the study of the way people live in different cultures. Cultural anthropologists explore the common features of people's lives, including family patterns, language, food, shelter, and clothing. For children, cultural anthropology involves understanding themselves and becoming aware of others. Since culture shapes many things about families, young children learn about cultural anthropology as they explore family patterns, rituals, and celebrations. Social studies in early childhood can help children learn that although people speak and do things in different ways, they have the same basic needs and share a common humanity.

Economics is the study of how people acquire, share, and use the things they want and need. Economists study how society distributes resources, such as land, labor, raw materials, and machinery, to produce goods and services. Children can begin to learn some economics concepts like work, exchange, production, and consumption. This content should relate to events in their everyday lives like buying, selling, and trading, and where the things they buy and use are made.

Political science is the study of government and political institutions, how people are governed, and how people use power to make and enforce decisions. Political scientists look at how people allocate and transfer power, and study the different roles and systems that people have devised to govern their societies. Young children can learn political science concepts like authority and rules, citizenship, and democratic decision making. As they experience how decisions and rules are made in the classroom, you have the opportunity to help them understand the principles of how to live in a democracy.

Geography is the study of the earth's surface, its natural features, climate, resources, population, and the effects of human activity. Geographers look at places and maps and seek explanations for what they see. They look for patterns in the arrangement and distribution of cities, economics, politics, peoples, transportation, and other phenomena. As you take trips into the world beyond the school walls and represent what you have seen through maps, photographs, and drawings, children are studying geography. Children are natural geographers when they explore and try to understand their environment. The attributes of different environments can be experienced through the senses. Children revel in the textures, the smells, the sounds, the sights, and the tastes of a place. They are fascinated by weather and seasons. A globe or a map may inspire children to talk excitedly about places they have visited, what they saw, and what they did.

History is the study of the events that make up the past. Historians learn about, record, and tell others about what happened in the past. An understanding of history is developed as children observe and talk about changes in themselves, in their families and other people, and in places. They can learn about the history of themselves and their own family. This is an appropriate way for children to learn about history. They can learn about the history of their own family through experiences like having their family members write the story of their own birth or arrival in the family. They can become aware of history as they observe changes in their own school and neighborhood.

Ecology is the study of the interaction and relationships between living things and their environment. Young children can learn how their lives are affected by the place in which they live as well as how the place where they live is affected by people. It is not too early for children to become aware of our dependence on the environment, or to learn in simple terms about issues affecting the environment and our role in caring for it.

Approaches to Early Childhood Social Studies

Over the years, a number of different approaches to teaching social studies have evolved that you may observe in early childhood programs.

- **Classroom jobs** help children to understand that they are a part of a community in which people have responsibilities (sociology).
- **Creating classroom rules** helps children to understand authority and the democratic process (political science).

- **Keeping a classroom journal or diary** helps children to understand that the past influences the present (history).

Daily Classroom Life

Although it is not a formal curriculum approach, by far the most common way that children learn about social studies is by experiencing day-to-day interactions in the classroom. Helping children learn to share, talk about their feelings, and develop other social skills in early childhood classrooms are informal ways of teaching social studies. When viewed through this lens it becomes clear that social studies curriculum is being taught all the time.

With just a little more thought and planning, the informal social studies curriculum can be made more intentional and visible. The In Practice box gives you a few ideas for ways to think about using classroom routines as social studies activities.

Holidays

Walk into almost any preschool or elementary school classroom during the week(s) before a holiday and you will see walls festooned with decorations. You probably remember holiday celebrations in your own schooling. Holiday activities may have brought change and excitement to your elementary school days.

In many programs, the celebration of holidays is the main way in which social studies is taught in spite of the fact that holidays are rarely included in formal early childhood social studies curricula. Unfortunately, the use of holidays as part of the social studies curriculum has inherent problems.

The first problem involves the religious nature of many holidays. In a homogeneous society or a religious school, holidays can be taught as a part of a shared culture or belief system. However, in our diverse society, we do not all come from the same culture or share the same beliefs. So, the foundational religious beliefs that form the basis of many holidays are removed from the ways they are celebrated in publicly funded schools. This removal also eliminates the kernel of social studies content (learning about how different groups of people live and what they believe). As a result, the celebration activities, devoid of their original content, often turn into a cycle of look-alike craft activities rather than a meaningful study of culture and celebration.

If you came from a family with different beliefs from the majority, then holiday activities may have made you feel isolated, sad, or even ashamed when holidays were celebrated in school. This contradicts the early childhood social studies curriculum goal of helping children learn to appreciate and respect themselves and others.

The second problem with holiday activities as social studies curriculum is that they fail to provide meaningful learning about diverse people and cultures.

For example, typical St. Patrick's Day activities like coloring green shamrocks, drinking green milk, and cutting out pictures of leprechauns have little to do with Ireland or the cultural heritage of either Catholics or the Irish. If you reflect on school holiday activities, you may realize that many of them are similarly stereotyped and lacking in meaningful learning or social science content. And while there is definitely interesting social studies involved in every holiday (e.g., the historical reasons why a religious holiday in Ireland became an occasion for parades and community festivities in the United States), these are often not appropriate or meaningful to young children.

Particular problems are attached to the idealized and historically inaccurate picture of the first American Thanksgiving typically presented in school. It is important for you to understand that for many Native Americans, the traditional "Thanksgiving" holiday is a day of sorrow and shame. The sorrow is for the fallen members of the Wampanoag tribe (and all Native Americans) who were decimated by disease and mistreatment. The shame is for a country that honors people (the Pilgrims) who used religion to condone murder, treachery, and slavery. Dressing children up as Pilgrims and Indians is a particularly inappropriate and ineffective way to teach them about gratitude and the joy of a good harvest.

Culture

In many schools, sometimes in conjunction with holiday celebrations, teachers focus on the study of a particular culture ("We are studying Japan, Mexico, China, American Indians"). Like holiday curriculum, this approach often leads to superficial learning, what Louise Derman-Sparks (Derman-Sparks, 1989) refers to as *tourist curriculum* (an educational approach that "drops in" on strange, exotic people to see their holidays and taste their foods, and then returns to the "real" world of "regular" life). Tourist curriculum communicates that the dominant way of life is "normal" or "right," and that "other" cultural groups are less real and important than the dominant groups.

Ethnicity, a term often used in conjunction with culture, has to do with people's heritage and national origins. For most people, culture and ethnicity are linked. A child may be a member of a visible ethnic minority—African American, Hispanic American, Native American, Asian American; or a member of a group whose ethnic identity is based on national origin and largely defined by common culture—Polish American, Irish American, or Italian American.

You may find yourself pressured to decorate your classroom with multicultural paraphernalia in a mistaken attempt to address standards concerning cultural diversity. It is important to remember that the study of culture can be meaningful to young children only if it provides accurate and respectful information about the group being studied; if it portrays them as they live today as well as historically; and if it depicts everyday activities as well as activities that relate to cultural celebrations. The In Practice box on page 460 suggests a few ways to authentically add cultural diversity to your classroom.

Start with the diversity within your classroom and community and invite knowledgeable sources to share languages, songs, stories, foods, and customs that they use in their everyday lives.

ASK families to tell you about their customs and beliefs *before* you plan a celebration or cultural study. INVITE families to be cultural resources for your class.

If you know another language, use it. If not, learn a few words in a different language and use them. For example, "Today I'm going to use Spanish numbers—you can count with me—*uno, dos, tres, cuatro, cinco! Dos* children can paint at the easel."

Include good-quality children's literature from different cultures in your library. Kane/Miller books (www.kanemiller.com/) offer a good selection of award-winning children's literature from around the world.

Display artwork from diverse cultures in your classroom. For example, pair a painting of water lilies by Monet with a Japanese Ukiyo-e print of cherry blossoms.

Sing songs in diverse languages. Children enjoy and quickly pick up the words to simple songs. Start with songs you know (e.g., *Frère Jacques*) and then learn a few new ones.

Expanding Horizons

Starting in the 1930s, educators began to organize elementary school social studies curriculum by what is known as the *expanding horizons* approach. This approach begins with the child, family, and neighborhood in kindergarten and primary school, and includes other topics as children enter the upper elementary grades (the state, nation, neighboring countries). If you remember learning about community helpers in preschool or kindergarten, it's likely that your teacher was using some variation on the expanding horizons approach to social studies.

The expanding horizons approach reflects an era in which children were isolated in their family and community. Today, even though this approach is often denounced as being limited and narcissistic (focused on "me"), it is still the basis of most elementary school K–6 social studies texts. Because of immigration, technology, travel, and media, young children experience a much broader world today. They meet people and know about places that are far more diverse than they were exposed to in the past. It seems certain that this will continue. It still makes sense to have young children begin learning social studies through subjects that are of interest and that can be directly experienced like family and neighborhood. However, it is important to enhance this foundation with experiences that help them to understand and appreciate people from other places and other cultures.

Social and Political Issues

Today, there is a good deal of interest in teaching young children about issues that have an impact on people's lives, including such topics as racial and cultural differences, global warming (often presented in books about the rainforest), bias and prejudice, stereotyping, rules and laws, cooperation and conflict resolution, aging, caretaking and compassion, disabilities, and how we get goods and services. These topics are unquestionably important. They will influence the future of the world! They are especially important to young adults and older children who are starting to view themselves as the inheritors of the world we will leave behind. Teaching these topics may help children become responsible citizens— an important goal of social studies. When used as social studies curriculum in early childhood, however, we believe these topics often have limitations. Because they are often part of an adult agenda, it can be hard to make social and political issues relevant to young children's lives. As a result, they may not help children to learn underlying social science skills and concepts. Since children can do very little about racism and global warming, including these topics in the early childhood curriculum may make children feel powerless. Rather than trying to teach children directly about social and political issues, it is useful to think about how these topics can be presented in ways that are more meaningful to young children.

You can address many issues as a part of your daily life in the classroom. Children learn about power and rules by the way we treat them. They learn about acceptance and bias from us. They learn about environmental responsibility by caring for their own school and neighborhood. You can help children by being a model of a responsible, strong, competent, compassionate, active person. Your own feelings about age, race, class, handicapping conditions, and sex roles will be communicated to children—so it is important to give positive, affirming, anti-biased messages. You can make sure that books, puzzles, pictures, and other educational materials present a similarly nonbiased view. Creating a compost bin in the yard teaches children more about conserving resources than watching a video on saving the rainforest. It is important to learn to talk thoughtfully and openly to children when social and political subjects come up and to think ahead about some of the things that you might say to help extend their understanding of issues that concern them.

The Bank Street Approach

Since its inception in 1916, Bank Street Children's School in New York City has used social studies as the core of its curriculum. The life of the classroom itself is considered implicit social studies, so its organization and management is given a great deal of consideration. All curriculum areas are integrated around in-depth studies of social science topics. Children are given opportunities to work both independently and collaboratively. And trips into the community are considered a central part of this learning. The Bank Street approach is similar to the expanding horizons approach because topics that are most directly related to self and family are usually addressed in preschool and kindergarten.

Do you remember studying something in your community for a period of several weeks or months? Did you take many trips into your community to have real experiences with these topics? Did you get to recreate a store and sell products in it, or visit a Mexican restaurant and then learn how to grind corn to make tortillas? If so, your teacher and school were probably using or had been influenced by the Bank Street approach.

This approach is still the core of the curriculum at Bank Street Children's School in New York City and it is used by many teachers who have studied there over the years or been introduced to this approach in courses or workshops. It is an approach that we have regularly taught in our college classes.

"Who Am I?" Questions

For a number of years, two of the authors of this book (Stephanie and Eva) have based social studies curriculum on a framework that uses the question "Who Am I?" to relate social studies learning directly to young children's lives (Feeney & Moravcik, 1995). We have found that this approach works well for teaching social studies because it combines study of social science subject areas with some recurring themes in young children's lives. Over the years, we have found that when this approach is thoughtfully used, it engages children intellectually and emotionally and teaches them many worthwhile things about people and relationships.

This approach has some elements of the expanding horizons approach and is also related in terms of goals and methods to the Bank Street approach. It differs from them in the use of four specific questions as an organizing framework. Like the expanding horizons approach, it begins with the child, family, and neighborhood, but it also addresses the topic of self and exploration of environments.

Four different aspects of the question "Who Am I?" provide the core of the social studies curriculum:

Who Am I as an Individual? (SELF)

Who Am I as a member of a FAMILY?

Who Am I as a member of a COMMUNITY?

Who Am I as a person who lives in an ENVIRONMENT?

Social studies experiences based on these questions address issues in children's lives and contribute to children's understanding and appreciation of the social aspects of the world in which they live.

Standards for Social Studies Curriculum

Content standards and guidelines developed by the National Council for the Social Studies, Head Start, states, and individual programs can help you learn about appropriate social studies content. They also can help you identify goals and objectives for the social studies curriculum. These, in turn, will help you to select activities that will help children to acquire knowledge and skills.

There are no national standards for social studies in preschool programs. However, **Head Start** (see Figure 15.1) and some states do have standards for preschool social studies curriculum. There is some consistency within these standards. Almost all include standards for history, economics, geography, and political science (sometimes called civics or citizenship). Some frame these relative to family, community, and environment. A few also describe standards related to ecology and psychology.

The National Council for the Social Studies has identified 10 teaching **"strands"** for K-12 programs (see Figure 15.2). Since these standards address the learning of older children, they include much that is not appropriate for teaching most 3- to 5-years-olds. These standards lay out expectations for teachers to provide children with opportunities to develop social studies understanding or concepts. Although they vary from state to state (and no

FIGURE 15.1 Head Start Child Development and Early Learning Framework: *Social Studies*

Self, Family, and Community

The understanding of one's relationship to the family and community, roles in the family and community, and respect for diversity.

- Identifies personal and family structure.
- Understands similarities and respects differences among people.
- Recognizes a variety of jobs and the work associated with them.
- Understands the reasons for rules in the home and classroom and for laws in the community.
- Describes or draws aspects of the geography of the classroom, home, and community.

People and the Environment

The understanding of the relationship between people and the environment in which they live.

- Recognizes aspects of the environment, such as roads, buildings, trees, gardens, bodies of water, or land formations.
- Recognizes that people share the environment with other people, animals, and plants.
- Understands that people can take care of the environment through activities, such as recycling.

History and Events

The understanding that events happened in the past and how these events relate to one's self, family, and community.

- Differentiates between past, present, and future.
- Recognizes events that happened in the past, such as family or personal history.
- Understands how people live and what they do changes over time.

Source: Administration for Childern and Families, Head Start Bureau, www.hsnrc.org/cdi/child-outcomes.cfm

FIGURE 15.2 Framework of Social Studies Themes for K–12 Social Studies Programs

I. **Culture:** Social studies programs should include experiences that provide for the study of culture and cultural diversity.

II. **Time, Continuity, and Change:** Social studies programs should include experiences that provide for the study of the past and its legacy.

III. **People, Places, and Environments:** Social studies programs should include experiences that provide for the study of people, places, and environments.

IV. **Individual Development and Identity:** Social studies programs should include experiences that provide for the study of individual development and identity.

V. **Individuals, Groups, and Institutions:** Social studies programs should include experiences that provide for the study of interactions among individuals, groups, and institutions.

VI. **Power, Authority, and Governance:** Social studies programs should include experiences that provide for the study of how people create, interact with, and change structures of power, authority, and governance.

VII. **Production, Distribution, and Consumption:** Social studies programs should include experiences that provide for the study of how people organize for the production, distribution, and consumption of goods and services.

VIII. **Science, Technology, and Society:** Social studies programs should include experiences that provide for the study of relationships among science, technology, and society.

IX. **Global Connections:** Social studies programs should include experiences that provide for the study of global connections and interdependence.

X. **Civic Ideals and Practices:** Social studies programs should include experiences that provide for the study of the ideals, principles, and practices of citizenship in a democratic republic.

Source: From *National Curriculum Standards for Social Studies: A Framework for Teaching, Learning, and Assessment,* by National Council for the Social Studies, 2010, Silver Spring, MD: National Council for the Social Studies.

state includes all), you can expect to find standards that ask you to provide opportunities for children to develop some of the following concepts:

1. History concepts
   - Things, people, and places change over time.
   - Past events relate to present and future activities.
   - Events and routines occur in a regular and predictable order.
   - There is language to describe time (e.g., day, night, yesterday, today, tomorrow).
   - Each of us has a personal and family history.

2. Geography concepts
   - Different places relate to one another in terms of their location.
   - Places have geographic features and characteristics.
   - Geographic location has an impact on daily life.
   - A map is a picture of a place using a "bird's-eye" view. People construct and use maps to understand places.

3. Political science/sociology (civics) concepts
   - People need to work to live together in groups.
   - People need to communicate, share, cooperate, and participate as members of a community.
   - Family and community members have roles, jobs, rules, and relationships.
   - The democratic process allows people in groups to cooperatively and fairly make decisions for the good of individuals and the community as a whole.

4. Economics concepts
   - People have many needs and wants.
   - People depend upon one another for the things (goods) and help (services) they need.
   - People do work outside and inside their homes.
   - People work together to grow, produce, distribute, and consume goods and services that meet their wants and needs.
   - A community benefits from many different people working in many different ways.
   - Money makes it easier to trade, borrow, save, and compare goods and services.

5. Ecology concepts
   - There is a relationship between humans and the environment.
   - People depend on the natural resources found in their environment.
   - People have a responsibility to take care of the resources in their environment.

6. Psychology concepts
   - People are alike in some ways and different in some ways.
   - Feelings can be identified and expressed.
   - Many different things influence people's thinking and behavior.

7. Cultural anthropology concepts
   - People belong to/come from different cultures.
   - There are similarities and differences between people from diverse backgrounds.

In addition, many also have standards related to school behaviors such as the ability to play in groups, share, take turns, attend, and focus. Your program's goals may be based on state or national standards, or they may have been developed independently by your staff or a curriculum specialist. However, it is likely that they will include some version of these standards.

Teaching Social Studies

Children, their cultures, and the world beyond the classroom are at the center of social studies curriculum. Perhaps more than any other curriculum area, the social studies you teach will be unique to your classroom. It will reflect your group of children, their families, and their cultures, along with your community and your geography. The world beyond the school walls will profoundly influence what social studies content you will pursue. If you work in a city, you will have a different social studies curriculum than if you work in the country. Whether your program is near the ocean, on the prairie, or in the mountains will deeply influence your social studies teaching.

It takes thoughtful planning based on knowledge of child development to weave social studies topics into meaningful learning experiences for young children. Basic strategies include direct experiences in the classroom and the area around your school, follow up on experiences, and good questions. It is important to be awake to the social studies learning possibilities inherent in the children's lives, their families, your program, and the community.

Social Studies Learning Through Play in a Planned Environment

Children learn about social studies as you select what you bring into the environment. A classroom that is clean, well organized, and aesthetically pleasing, and that reflects the cultures in your classroom is both an expression of your respect for children and their families and a powerful social studies teaching tool.

Like other inquiry subjects, social studies can best be implemented in a classroom that is arranged in learning centers or areas designed for particular activities. The block and dramatic play areas are important places for children to act upon themes from the social studies. Writing and art areas in which children can record and report their experiences are important to social studies, as is a library well stocked with many carefully selected books that will enhance and extend social studies themes.

The Dramatic Play Area

The dramatic play area allows children to naturally integrate their growing understanding of social studies. In it they demonstrate their understanding and skills in daily living. In the dramatic play center, children "make believe," often imitating the actions of the very important adults in their lives. As children act out roles, they develop language, organize their previous experiences, practice cooperating with others, and develop the ability to use symbols to represent real objects and events. (This ability is directly related to the ability to symbolize that is required for reading and writing.)

A dramatic play area requires sheltered space and simple, child-sized furniture, typically including a stove, a sink, and a table with chairs for 2 to 4 children. Dolls, diverse clothing, and props representing a variety of ages, genders, cultures, and careers give children the opportunity for elaborate dramatic play that reflects their understanding of social studies. In order to expand their knowledge, you may have to seek out props for the dramatic play area that reflect diversity of age, sex-role, ability, and ethnic origin. Common objects of daily life such as kitchenware, books, furnishings, and tools also form a part of the equipment of the dramatic play area. Open shelves with bins or baskets, or hooks on the wall, provide storage for dramatic play clothing and props. Arrange materials so they are easy to find. Make picture labels for storage shelves for materials that you will always have out.

The dramatic play area is often organized into a "home" environment emphasizing behaviors that reflect daily living. Children may expand upon this theme, as may teachers when they rearrange or expand this area to reflect many different aspects of the social environment. We have seen dramatic play areas converted into doctor's offices, restaurants, campsites, and bunkhouses.

Since it is not possible or desirable to have all the props available at all times, it is especially important to organize and rotate props in the dramatic play area. You can respond to children's social studies learning by adding appropriate materials when you observe a new interest developing or when you begin a new topic of study—for example, contributing fire hats, a rain slicker, boots, and a length of hose when the children are pretending to be firefighters. To prevent clutter, props can be stored in sturdy, attractive, lidded boxes organized by occupation, situation, or role.

The Block Area

The block area is a particularly important place for children to act upon ideas from the social studies. Unit blocks and hollow blocks are raw materials that children can use to recreate their experiences and represent social studies ideas. First mapping experiences are a natural outgrowth of block play.

You can enhance and extend unit block play to develop social studies concepts by adding toy vehicles, diverse human and animal figures, and other props (a doll house, carpet or fabric squares, stones, and sanded, smooth pieces of wood), and encouraging children to make their own props using materials available in the art area. Children's block building demonstrates their growing social studies understanding and helps them to acquire concepts and skills.

Hollow blocks give children the opportunity to construct a world they can physically enter. Like dramatic play, hollow block play helps children to act out roles, organize experiences, cooperate with others, and use symbols to represent real objects and events. If possible, place hollow blocks near or in the dramatic play area so that children can use them to create the buildings, vehicles, and furnishings they need to extend their social studies dramatic play.

Social Studies Everywhere

Changes in the learning environment are a signal to children and families that a new topic of study is about to begin. New pictures on the wall, accessories in the dramatic play and block areas, books in the library corner, and displays all provide stimulus for observations, questions, and exploration by the children. The school supply room, local school supply or toy store, bookstores, the local thrift shop, school and neighborhood libraries, and your own closet are good places to find social studies resources for the learning environment. The children's families may also be able to help you find materials you need.

Begin by collecting pictures, posters, and maps to display on walls or bulletin boards. Leave some empty display space for the work that children will create. Materials can also be displayed on shelf tops and in display areas. Group projects such as murals and sculpture can be given large display spaces. Some teachers use a single bulletin board or display area to attractively exhibit one type of work such as maps that children have drawn, while others set aside space for each child's work. You can convey a clear understanding of what is being studied to parents and other classroom visitors by including a brief statement explaining each display.

A Schedule for Social Studies

Since young children develop many social studies concepts through play, it is especially important within the social studies curriculum to schedule large blocks of time for self-selected activity. In addition, children will learn concepts through thoughtfully planned, focused social studies group activities.

Your Role in Teaching Social Studies

In the broadest sense, social studies is learned through everything children experience in school. They do not come to accept and appreciate themselves, others, and the environment solely through planned social studies curriculum, nor do they learn to get along with people because of it. The quality of your relationships with children and families is the foundation upon which social studies curriculum is based. Therefore, in addition to curriculum, it is important to provide a positive social climate—letting children know that they are worthwhile and respected, helping children learn to handle problems in constructive ways, honoring families' cultures, and communicating with families and involving them in the classroom.

Conflict is an inevitable aspect of group life and can offer social studies "teachable moments." It is important to learn to view conflict as an opportunity to help children learn that people can disagree, that this does not have to damage relationships, and that people who disagree can work together to find a solution or to handle differences productively.

One of the most critical social studies teaching tasks is to ask questions that stimulate children's thinking and help them to synthesize what they know. An open-ended, appropriately timed question can help children to create their own understanding. Recognizing the "teachable moment" and asking questions like this is a skill that takes time and practice to develop.

Social Studies Activities

Social studies can be approached in many and diverse ways. Virtually any curriculum activity can be geared to social studies learning. Art, music, cooking, graphing, storytelling, and creative dramatics can be integrated with social studies. However, there are 5 activities that we think of as primarily involving social studies curriculum: learning trips, mapping, resource visitors, block building, and dramatic play.

Learning trips, taking children into the community/environment to have real experience with a social science topic, is the most important social studies activity. It would be difficult, and a little silly, to teach about the community without ever venturing into it or to study geographic features without ever going to look at them. Whether you go on a trip to the shops located on your street or take a bus trip to a farm, you can use the environment beyond the program walls to provide early experiences with economics, anthropology, geography, sociology, and history.

Because of the expense and effort involved, it is not uncommon for learning trips to be viewed as whole-school "treats" or

Plan the Trip. The first step is to visit a site to determine its suitability for a class visit. Ask yourself the following questions:

- What are the learning possibilities for my group of young children at this site?
- Will this trip further children's understanding?
- Will this site challenge children's thinking?
- Will the people at the site welcome children and support their learning?
- Can the trip be completed in a realistic amount of time for my group?
- Does the cost of the trip balance its learning possibilities?

Plan short, simple trips based on an aspect of the topic being studied. The most effective trips involve small groups, since children need the opportunity to talk with an adult about the trip while it is happening. If the entire class must go, make sure additional adults come along. Begin with brief trips in your building and the surrounding neighborhood. Revisit sites to help children understand more. Returning gives an opportunity to make new discoveries.

Before the Trip. Lead a focused discussion. Record children's ideas on an *inventory chart* to show what they already know. Ask questions like: "What do you know about the place we are visiting?" and "What would you like to learn?" Ask children to predict what they will observe and learn on the upcoming trip and list their ideas on a *prediction chart.*

During the Trip. Use tripboards (homemade or commercial clipboards). Tripboards are children's introduction to the scientist's practice of making field notes to record observations and organize information gathered on the trip. Create tripboard sheets with questions or tasks linked to the trip that match the developmental stage and abilities of children. Four-year-olds might be asked to draw a picture of flowers seen in a garden. Children who can write might be asked to use a checklist to identify items at the store or tally the numbers and kinds of uniforms at the airport. **Ask open questions.** Pay attention to what children notice and write down what they are curious about. If possible, take pictures on the trip. If you go with a large group, divide up and provide all adults with a sheet of information and suggestions for questions they might ask children.

After the Trip. Follow-up activities help children learn. Use completed tripboard sheets as references. Prediction and inventory charts can be reviewed to validate what was true. Things that were not predicted can be added. *Group stories can be* based on the trip to emphasize the sequence of events. Summarize with questions such as: "What did we do?" "What did we see?" "What do you know about now that you didn't know before we took our trip?" Tripboard sheets can be used as pages for *trip books.*

Children can use *blocks* to recreate a place they visited. Bring builders together to review tripboards and plan work based on that information. Photograph or sketch structures and file them in portfolios. In *dramatic play* children may assume roles based on people they met. Relevant props can be introduced. A brief discussion may serve as the initial point for dramatic play. Other follow-up projects can include writing, art, math, science, and food and cooking activities.

outings that have little or nothing to do with the curriculum. Instead, learning trips are most productive when they have a specific purpose and involve small groups of children. It is useful to think of them as "field work." Just as an anthropologist might take a trip to a village to learn about the customs of the villagers, so, too, our children are social scientists going into the field to learn about some aspect of social studies. The In Practice box provides you with some useful guidelines for planning social studies learning trips.

Maps are symbolic representations that show objects or places from a bird's-eye perspective. Although we do not teach children formal map skills, introductory mapping activities lay the foundation for children's understanding of maps.

Life Size or "Outline" Maps Trace around a body part like a hand to show how a record of a 3-dimensional object can be made.

Block Maps Have children construct a map of familiar place (the classroom, the yard, the block, their home) using blocks as a 3-dimensional medium.

Scale Maps with Tracing Arrange symbolic materials like doll house furniture or blocks to show a familiar space. Once the space has been mapped, trace the items with a pencil onto paper, creating a map.

Scale Maps Without Tracing (the next level of mapping) Make simple maps of familiar areas without the inter-mediate step of using blocks/props. Begin with a small, familiar space (e.g., the pretend area, the garden) and map while actually looking at the space. Gradually move on to mapping larger spaces and mapping from memory.

Even very young children enjoy looking at maps and globes, and these should be present in your classroom. By observing adults use maps and pretending to read maps, children come to understand that maps give useful information about locations and landmarks. Map-making activities build on children's direct experience and gradually increase in complexity. In mapping, start with what is concrete and of high interest: their own bodies and their immediate environment, as shown in the In Practice box.

Social studies is about people and their relationship to one another and the world. So it makes sense that inviting *resource visitors* into the classroom to provide children with experiences related to particular topics is a good way to help children learn social studies.

It is very important to prepare both the visitor and the children for the classroom visit. Visitors need to understand the learning styles and abilities of your group of children. They need to provide things for children to see and touch. Prepare any visitor in advance for the short attention span of children and help them to limit passive, "listening-only" activities. Some examples of appropriate social studies visitors that we have seen include: a very pregnant mom who allowed children to feel the baby kick and listen to its heartbeat, an entomologist who showed a simple slide show and brought live bugs for children to observe and touch, a trainer who brought an assistance dog for children to meet, a cultural representative who taught children a song and demonstrated the making (and eating) of a special food.

Block building and *dramatic play* (both self and teacher initiated) are two of the most important learning experiences in the social studies curriculum. These activities enable children to recreate their experiences and build concepts. To initiate social studies-related block building or dramatic play with a particular focus in mind, begin by inviting children to join you in the area (e.g., "I want to make a restaurant in the pretend area today."/"I want to build a fire station in blocks"), asking them to help you structure the play ("What will we need? Where shall we put it?"), and then asking them to take on roles ("Who wants to be the cook/waiter/customer?"/"Which figure is the fire chief? Who's going to hold him/her?"). Finally, invite children to create and act out a scenario by playing *with* them ("We have apple pie as our special today—may I take your order?" "Chef, we need two apple pies and a bowl of soup for table 1"/"Ding-ding-ding someone pulled the fire alarm—let's drive the fire engine to the fire—oops we need a house to catch on fire").

Planning Social Studies Curriculum

Social studies is not only best taught *through* integrated curriculum, but also is best used *as* the foundation of an integrated curriculum study. For this reason, we begin our discussion of planning social studies curriculum an integrated study.

Using Social Studies as the Core of an Integrated Study

Because social studies is so broad and can be approached in so many different ways, it is one of the two best subjects (the other is science) for organizing and integrating curriculum. Food preparation, visits from resource people, songs, dances, artifacts (from a family, culture, or place), books, and trips related to a topic all contribute to concept development in the social sciences. Follow-up activities can occur in every area of the curriculum. Children gain deeper understanding when they recreate and re-experience concepts in blocks, dramatic play, art work, graphs, child-authored books, songs, and games.

Planning an appropriate social science study, like planning for any curriculum, takes an artful blend of what you know about the children you teach, what you know about children in general, and what you know about the subject area.

> In the hollow block area, Kane, Gabriel, James, and Sol are playing ice-cream store. They have been doing this each day for over a week. Each day, their play has become more elaborate. Today, they tape together cones of paper and fill them with wadded paper towels. They make a sign showing an ice-cream cone and the number 5. Then, they await the customers, calling out, "Ice cream for sale 50 cents a cone." Margaret, their teacher, orders a cone of mint chocolate chip and pays for her purchase with a slip of paper on which she has written the number 8. Hurriedly, Gabriel runs to the writing center and cuts more slips of paper. He returns and gives Margaret her change—two tiny slips of paper.

A parent or an inexperienced teacher might think . . . "how cute!" or "how funny!" But an experienced teacher who understands children and curriculum thinks "social studies!" What does the above scenario have to do with social studies? It is an example of the way that children show you what they are striving to understand about the ways people live together in groups. It shows that these children are building concepts of:

- Economics (goods and services are supplied and paid for)
- Sociology (people work with one another to get the things they need)
- Psychology (different people like different things)

Margaret might have decided to embark on a study of ice cream. It would have been fun, the parents would have enjoyed it, and the children might have learned about the science of making ice cream. Everyone would have loved the sensory delights of eating a lot of ice cream. However, Margaret had a broader vision for her class. She decided to focus her curriculum on *Stores*.

The sunburst of an integrated study of *Stores* (a social studies topic) shown in Figure 15.3 demonstrates the many ways that a social studies topic can be used to integrate curriculum. Because this entire study involves social studies, we have not highlighted any specific activities as social studies (though you will note that there is a social studies section of the sunburst).

FIGURE 15.3   A Study of Stores Sunburst

Social Studies
KWL: What Do You Know About Stores?/What Do You Want to Learn?
Store Prediction Chart and Validation
Making and Selling Lemonade
Mapping Our Trips to Stores
Meet the People Who Work in the Stores
Shopping Sequence Game

Fine Motor
Using Tools from the Hardware Store
"Ice Cream" Tong Transfer Game

Large Motor
Bus Stop Game
Delivery Van Game
Garbage Trucks

Blocks
Stores Floor Map
Creating Stores with Hollow Blocks

Pretend Play
Transforming the Pretend Area into Stores: Grocery Store, Bookstore, Clothing Store, Ice-Cream Stand
Need grocery carts, empty shelves, empty containers, cash register, "money," pretend food, pretend ice-cream cones, and pom-poms

Woodworking
Building a Lemonade Stand

Science/Sensory
Making Ice Cream
Scoops and "Cones" in the Sand Table with Wet Sand

Creative Movement
Five Currant Buns
Magic Rocks with Store Motif

Art
Ice-Cream Cone Collage
Lemon Printing
Making Watercolor Bookmarks to Sell at the Bake Sale
Grocery Label Collage

Trips
Ice-Cream Store
Hardware Store
Grocery Store
Department Store
Bookstore
Chinatown Market

Math
How Much Should We Charge for Lemonade?
Bus Money Game
Making Play Money for the Store
What Can We Buy at the Bookstore?
Lemonade Sequencing Game

Big Idea
Stores are set up so customers can get what they want to buy and so that the store can take money and give change. There is equipment to organize, display, and keep things that are for sale and other needed things.

Big Idea
There are different stores where you buy things that you want and need.

Big Idea
Parts of a store are used by customers and other parts are used by employees.

Big Idea
A store is a place where people pay to get goods (things) or services (help).

A Study of Stores

Big Idea
Stores get things they sell from other places (factories, farms, etc.).

Big Idea
Shopping is a process: You decide what to buy, you pay for it, you get what you paid for, and leave the store.

Big Idea
Lots of people have jobs in stores. They use different equipment to do their different jobs.

Literature
Bunny Money Game (see booklist)
To Market To Market Flannelboard Story

Literacy
Stores Book
Grocery Store Lotto
Ice-Cream Store Book
Lemonade Book
Catalogue Shopping
Shopping Lists
Store Matching Game

Language
Echo Game with Store Words
Store Guessing Game
Ice-Cream Flavors Game
Shopping Bag Game

Music
Lemonade Song
I Had a Little Lemon Tree
Sammy
Come On Let's Go to Market
A Shopping We Will Go
Wheels on the Bus
There Are Many Kinds of Stores
The Muffin Man
Quartermaster's Store

Cooking/Sensory
Ice Cream
Lemonade
Mashed Potatoes
Hard-boiled Eggs
Noodles from Chinatown
Stir Fry
Spaghetti

Writing Activity Plans for Social Studies

As they go to visit different stores (Dave's Ice Cream, Home Depot, Foodland, Holiday Mart, The Bookstore) in the nearby community, Margaret takes pictures of the storefronts, the cash registers, the loading docks, and the managers, and gathers items with each store's logo. She makes a set of cards for each store along with picture cards of representative items sold. She turns these into a matching game: Match the logo, goods, and feature to the store (small boxes with the picture of the store on the front). The children instantly love the game. They are especially delighted by the fact that they can use the store boxes in the block area to recreate the route that they follow as they walk to the stores. The game leads to many spontaneous discussions about stores and the things they sell and the things that they need.

Having identified *Stores* as the focus of her social studies curriculum, Margaret decided that she wanted to create an activity to help her class understand that even though each of the stores is different, in some ways, all stores are alike. Margaret realized that her activity related to the social science area of economics and one of her state's social studies content standards—Social Studies Standard Four: *Explore how people depend upon one another for the things (goods) and help (services) they need* (School Readiness Task Force, Hawaii Good Beginnings Interdepartmental Council, 2004).

Like Margaret, when you begin planning for social studies, you will start thinking about and paying attention to children. Margaret began this activity by understanding children in general and by paying attention to the children she teaches. Social studies begins with the children, their families, their community, and their environment.

Now Margaret can help children start to make connections. She decided that she wanted to help children learn that all people depend on one another in their community. Margaret planned the activity described in Figure 15.4 as well as many other activities.

Because she is an experienced teacher, Margaret's short plan leaves out many details. It might not be enough of a guide for a beginning teacher. The longer, more elaborate version in Figure 15.5 gives you a better idea of what Margaret planned to do.

FIGURE 15.4 Simple Social Studies Activity Plan

Neighborhood Stores Matching Game

Objectives:	Identify some of the ways in which stores are alike and ways in which they are different.
Standard:	HPCS Domain IV, Standard 4
What you need:	Store Matching Game with 5 stores
How to teach:	1. Demonstrate how to play the game—2 sets only.
	2. Put out 3 sets of cards. Watch children as they play the game—encourage them to notice similarities between the stores.
	3. Comment as children work that each of the stores has a cash register, shelves, tables, front window, and loading dock.
	4. Comment that "We need the X store so we can get the X we need."
How to assess:	Listen for children commenting on similarities/differences.

FIGURE 15.5   Detailed Social Studies Activity Plan

Activity:	**Neighborhood Stores Matching Game** (a workjob for children to do on their own or with others)
Curriculum Area:	Social Studies
WHO It's For:	The Sprouts (the 4-year-old group)
Rationale:	The Sprouts were interested in ways that each of the stores we visited was different. This game is designed to help them see how the stores are the same.
Social Studies Objectives:	*By participating in this activity the children will …* • Identify some ways that stores are similar and different. • Describe some characteristics of stores. • Develop skill in observing and matching.
Concepts to Begin to Develop:	• Stores are set up so customers can get what they want to buy. • All stores need a place to take money and give change. • Stores have equipment to organize, display, and keep things that are for sale and other needed things.
Preschool Content Standard(s):	Domain IV, Social Studies Standard 4: Explore how people depend upon one another for the things (goods) and help (services) they need (economics).
Indicators:	Talk about similarities between stores, match types of goods to types of stores
HOW **to Prepare**	*What you need:* Stores matching game: • Pictures of each store (front, cash register, shelves, loading dock, employees) • Pictures of 3 things sold at each store • 5 small boxes with lids (about 4" deep) • 7 cards for each box (5 colors, 35 total) sized to fit inside • Contact paper *Set up:* • Glue a photo of the storefront to the front of each box (cover with contact paper). Glue the appropriate logo to the bottom of each box. • Make a set of 7 cards to fit inside each box. Glue appropriate logo on the back of each card. Laminate the cards.
HOW to **Teach**	*Introduction:* Set out 2 of the boxes and 2 sets of cards. At group time, invite children to name the stores. Show 2 of the cards (1 with goods and 1 with a photo of a store furnishing). Ask a child to try to match the cards to the store. Show the logo as a way to self-check. Explain that the game will be available to play and where it will be. *Teaching steps:* 1. Put out 2 sets of cards/store boxes for each child who wishes to play. Allow children to try the game independently. If they need help, suggest that they ask another child. 2. Stay near to make sure that children are able to use the game appropriately and to support as needed. 3. Once children have the idea, talk with individuals about the game—say something like "I notice that each of your stores has a cash register, shelves, tables, front window, loading dock, and things to sell." 4. If a child finds the game too easy, add the third store to the mix. For a real challenge, invite one child to sort all 5 stores' cards. *Closure:* Once a child has completed the game, comment "We need the X store so we can get X when we need it." Or ask a question: "If I needed milk, which store should I go to?" "How are the ice-cream store and the grocery store alike? How are they different?" Invite a child to tell another child that the space is free. Encourage children to teach one another how to play.

(continued)

FIGURE 15.5 Detailed Social Studies Activity Plan (continued)

HOW to Assess and Document

What to look for to identify if the objectives were met and how to document.

Objectives	Evidence of Learning Children might …	How to Document This Evidence
• Identify some ways that stores are similar and different.	Sort pictures of store fixtures and comment "This is the same as the ice-cream store" or "Only the hardware store can have hammers."	Anecdotal records—audio recording of child's comments
• Describe some characteristics of stores.	Say something about what stores are like—e.g., "All stores have …"	
• Develop skill in observing and matching.	Match photos of objects to stores correctly.	

EVALUATION   The boxes became block props! A good activity in itself, so two sets of boxes needed.

Social Studies in a Weekly Plan

Since young children develop many social studies concepts through play, they need blocks of time for discovery through play throughout the day, as well as thoughtfully planned, teacher-guided small groups during which social studies concepts can be explored. Although the entire topic of *Stores* relates to social studies, the example included in Figure 15.6 has only a few specific social studies activities that are highlighted in the plan. However, several of the art, music, literature, and movement experiences also help children develop social studies understanding.

Social Studies for All Children

Now that you know what makes up social studies for young children, you are probably much more aware of the many ways that you can bring this subject to all young children. Regardless of age or ability, all young children are learning about people and the ways in which people influence and are influenced by the social world in which they live. The social studies activities that we have described for typically developing preschoolers can also be the basis of curriculum for preschoolers with special needs as well as primary age children.

Children with Special Needs

Torie, a 4 1/2-year-old in the Sprouts class, is similar to the other children. She loves to dress up and pretend and is deeply attached to the "squishy" baby (a very soft rag doll). She sings clearly and on key. She dances to any music with a lively beat. She is fearless when something new or different is offered to the class. However, Torie isn't able to do some things that most of the others can do. She can't guess a simple riddle. When Margaret asks the children, "What's something white that you drink?" Torie says, "A giraffe." She's not yet able to ride a trike, though most of the children have been riding trikes since the beginning of the year. Torie has yet to name her scribbles when she draws or paints. She cannot find her name when it is written on her cubby or on a piece of paper. Torie is developmentally delayed.

FIGURE 15.6 A Week's Plan: A Study of Stores—Week #3

Objectives: To help children to understand there are different stores where you buy things that you want and need; and stores have similarities in the ways they are set up and the ways they are used by customers and the people who work in the store.

	Monday	Tuesday	Wednesday	Thursday	Friday
Story	*A Dollar for Penny* (Allen)	*Ice Cream* (Cooper)	*The Cookie Store Cat* (Rylant)	*The Supermarket Mice* (Gordon)	*Ice-Cream Cones for Sale* (Greenstein)
Outdoor Activities **Purpose:** *to help children to…*	**Rubbish Pick-Up With Trikes** Develop understanding of the ways people in communities work together. Develop large motor strength and stamina.		**Fire on the Mountain Game** Develop large motor control and coordination.	**Sorting Recyclables**	
Small Group 1 **Butterflies (4's—Cats)** **Purpose:** *to help children to…*	**KWL Chart—What Do You Know About Stores?** Think about stores and their importance. Understand some of the common features of stores.	**Ice-Cream Store Prediction Chart** Prepare for trip. Think about stores and what stores are like. Acquire understanding of print.	**Ice-Cream Store Trip (City Bus)** Understand some of the common features of stores. Become aware of how money is used to buy things we want and need.	**Validate Ice-Cream Store Prediction Chart** Understand some of the common features of stores. Understand the purpose of print.	**Planning a Pretend Area Store** Understand some of the common features of stores.
Small Group 2 **Airplanes (3's—Butterflies)** **Purpose:** *to help children to…*	**Read Carl Goes Shopping** Develop understanding of story structure. Understand some of the common features of stores.	**Store Riddles** Think about stores and their importance. Acquire oral language skill.	**Making Ice-Cream (while the Cats are away)** Become aware that substances change in response to changes in temperature. Understand that goods including food are manufactured by people.	**Ice-Cream Store Trip (city bus)** Understand some of the common features of stores. Become aware of how money is used to buy things we want and need.	**Trip Discussion** Acquire ability to participate in group discussion. Understand some of the common features of stores.
Indoor Special Activities **Purposes:** *to help children to…*	**Liquid Watercolors** Develop skill in using watercolor medium. Learn about art element—color. Express ideas and feelings through art.		**Cone and Circle Collage** Express ideas through collage medium.	**Making Ice Cream** (*while the Butterflies are away*) Become aware that substances change in response to changes in temperature. Understand that goods, including food, are manufactured by people.	**Cone and Circle Collage** Express ideas through collage medium.
Circle Time **Purpose:** *to help children to…*	*Oh Do You Know the Muffin Man?* Acquire the ability to sing tunefully.	*Five Currant Buns Singing Game* Develop understanding of one-to-one correspondence. Acquire the ability to express ideas through song.		*Oh Do You Know the Ice-Cream Man?* Acquire the ability to improvise songs.	

It is not unusual to have children like Torie in a preschool class. Children with developmental delays may or may not be identified in preschool. But they are there. How do you make social studies meaningful to a child like Torie? Is it even important to do so? Torie, like all of the children in your class, is entitled to your best efforts as a teacher. And like all the other children, there are many things that she can learn about social studies.

Since Torie enjoys music and dance, one thing you can do is help her to learn simple songs from different cultures. As you do so, you can talk about how people everywhere like to sing. Since she enjoys pretend play, you can encourage her to show how a waitress takes your order, or how someone cooks dinner. Physically experiencing social studies concepts will help Torie learn them. And though she may not be able to articulate these concepts, they are becoming part of her.

Children in the Primary Grades

If you teach kindergarten or primary school, social studies can be the core of your curriculum in many meaningful ways. The children in your class can use the tools of the social scientist. They can read and record information in a systematic and thoughtful way. You can involve them in planning, and they can help to decide the direction and focus of a study.

At this age, you can ask children to work in teams to investigate an aspect of a study or create explorations for the rest of the class. For example, we have seen children investigate and set up a supply store in dramatic play, build models of buildings, create real and imaginary maps, and write and illustrate books. These children used both the tools of the social scientist and their play to learn more about subjects that were interesting and meaningful to them.

Final Thoughts

Exploring how people relate to one another and the world and reconstructing what they know are the processes by which young children learn social studies. They learn by doing, observing, and interacting. Through play, they will reconstruct and order this knowledge. As an early childhood educator, you will guide children on this voyage of discovery and help them to understand the social world in which they live. As you do so, you support their natural curiosity, develop their love of learning, and help them to be the thinkers and problem solvers of the future.

Learning Outcomes

When you read this chapter, thoughtfully complete activities from the "To Learn More" section, and document this learning as suggested in the "For Your Portfolio" section, you will be making progress in the following *NAEYC Standards for Early Childhood Professional Preparation Programs* (2009):

Standard 1. Promoting Child Development and Learning

Students prepared in early childhood degree programs are grounded in a child development knowledge base. They use their understanding of young children's characteristics and needs and of the multiple interacting influences on children's development and learning to create environments that are healthy, respectful, supportive, and challenging for each child.

The key elements of standard 1 you will have learned about are . . .

1a: Knowing and understanding young children's characteristics and needs

1b: Using developmental knowledge to create healthy, respectful, supportive, and challenging learning environments

Standard 4. Using Developmentally Effective Approaches to Connect with Children and Families

Students prepared in early childhood degree programs understand that teaching and learning with young children is a complex enterprise, and its details vary depending on children's ages, characteristics, and the settings within which teaching and learning occur. They understand and use positive relationships and supportive interactions as the foundation for their work with young children and families. Students know, understand, and use a wide array of developmentally appropriate approaches, instructional strategies, and tools to connect with children and families and positively influence each child's development and learning.

The key elements of standard 4 you will have learned about are. . .

4a: Understanding positive relationships and supportive interactions as the foundation of their work with children

4b: Knowing and understanding effective strategies and tools for early education

4c: Using a broad repertoire of developmentally appropriate teaching/learning approaches

4d: Reflecting on their own practice to promote positive outcomes for each child

Standard 5. Using Content Knowledge to Build Meaningful Curriculum

Students prepared in early childhood degree programs use their knowledge of academic disciplines to design, implement, and evaluate experiences that promote positive development and learning for each and every young child. Students understand the importance of developmental domains and academic (or content) disciplines in an early childhood curriculum. They know the essential concepts, inquiry tools, and structure of content areas, including academic subjects, and can identify resources to deepen their understanding. Students use their own knowledge and other resources to design, implement, and evaluate meaningful, challenging curricula that promote comprehensive developmental and learning outcomes for every young child.

The key elements of standard 5 you will have learned about are. . .

5a: Understanding content knowledge and resources in academic disciplines

5b: Knowing and using the central concepts, inquiry tools, and structures of content areas or academic disciplines

5c: Using their own knowledge, appropriate early learning standards, and other resources to design, implement, and evaluate meaningful, challenging curricula for each child.

To Learn More

Observe a Program: For a morning, observe a program and see how the staff structures the environment and program to support children's understanding of social studies. Notice both the play opportunities and the planned group activities. Look at the plans and see how the planning reflects what you observed. Interview a teacher to learn how he or she thinks about social studies curriculum.

Observe a Child: For a morning, observe a child in a classroom, with a focus on the child's social studies learning. Notice how the child engages with the planned activities and how he or she constructs his or her own opportunities for learning. Notice the extent to which the child's activity and the planned curriculum seem to match. Observe to see how staff support the child's social studies learning.

Observe a Master Teacher: Spend a morning with an early childhood educator who is experienced and has a curriculum leadership role in a program. (This teacher may be called the "lead," "head," or "mentor" teacher.) Then interview the educator about how he or she plans for and provides social studies curriculum.

Observe a Social Studies Activity: Observe a teacher leading a planned social studies activity. Interview the teacher to find out the objectives for the activity. Reflect on any differences between what you saw and the focus of the plan.

Compare Two Programs: Observe social studies experiences in two early childhood programs. Compare the ways that the two address social studies curriculum—their similarities and differences. Reflect on which program seems to best support children's learning and why. What implications does this comparison have for your future work with young children?

Compare Two Ages: Observe two classrooms, one preschool and one for primary school children. Report on how each supports children's social studies learning. Talk to the staff about how they make their curriculum choices. Notice how development influences curriculum choices.

Explore Resources: Read one of the books from the bibliography or one of the online resources listed here and write a review of it for your classmates.

Social Studies for Early Childhood and Elementary School Children: Preparing for the 21st Century: www.socialstudies .org/positions/elementary

Bank Street Social Studies Social Studies and Geography (1934) by Lucy Sprague Mitchell: www.bankstreet.edu/ library/ssgeo.html and Social Studies in the Lower School: www.bankstreet.edu/sfc/socialstudies_lower.html

Educators for Social Responsibilities: http://esrnational.org

Teaching Tolerance: www.tolerance.org/

For Your Portfolio

Design a Social Studies Exploration Center: Design and draw a floor plan for a classroom center that would promote children's social studies learning (this might be a dramatic play area or an area where you share books, games, maps, and artifacts). Share your plan with an early childhood educator, discussing what you included and why. Ask for and consider the educator's feedback and suggestions. Set up a center in a real classroom utilizing as many of your ideas as possible and let children use it. For your portfolio, include the floor plan, photographs or video of children using the area, and a reflection on what you learned by doing this project.

Design a Dramatic Play Center: Design and draw a floor plan for a dramatic play center that would promote children's understanding of one or more social studies concepts. Share your plan with an early childhood educator, discussing what you included and why. Ask for and consider the educator's feedback and suggestions. Set up a dramatic play center in a real classroom utilizing as many of your ideas as possible and let children use it. For your portfolio, include the floor plan, photographs or video of children using the center, and a reflection on what you learned by doing this project.

Plan and Implement an Integrated Social Studies Exploration: Observe a group of children focusing on their social studies interest. Based on what you observed, design and implement a simple social studies exploration that integrates several areas (e.g., go to a bakery, come back and draw about and write about the trip, recreate it in dramatic play). Collect evidence of children's responses in the form of anecdotal observations, photographs, or video recordings. Reflect on how children responded and what they appear to have learned. What worked? What might you do differently next time? How might you expand on this experience for children? For your portfolio, include your plans, a photograph, and a reflection on what you learned about yourself, children, planning, and teaching.

Create a Social Studies Game: Design and make a social studies game to support the development of a social studies concept. Introduce it to children and observe how it is used. Reflect on how the children responded and how you felt about what you did. What worked? What might you do differently next time? How might you expand on this experience for children? For your portfolio, include a photograph of a child using the material and a reflection on what you learned about yourself, children, learning materials, and teaching.

Bibliography

Bredekamp, S. (2011). *Effective practices in early childhood education: Building a foundation.* Upper Saddle River, NJ: Pearson.

Derman-Sparks, L., & A.B.C. Task Force. (1989). *Anti-bias curriculum: Tools for empowering young children.* Washington, DC: NAEYC.

DeVries, R., & Kohlberg, L. (1990). *Constructivist early education: Overview and comparison with other programs.* Washington, DC: NAEYC.

Edwards, C. P. (1986). *Social and moral development in young children.* New York, NY: Teachers College Press.

Feeney, S., & Moravcik, E. (1995). *Discovering me and my world.* Circle Pines, MN: American Guidance Service.

Feeney, S., Moravcik, E., & Nolte, S. (2013). *Who am I in the lives of children?* (9th ed.). Upper Saddle River, NJ: Pearson.

Forman, G., & Kushchner, D. S. (1977). *The child's construction of knowledge.* Monterey, CA: Brooks/Cole Publishing Co.

Head Start Resource Center. (2010). *The Head Start Child development and early learning framework: Promoting positive outcomes in early childhood programs serving children 3–5 years old.* Washington, DC: Office of Head Start, Administration for Children and Families, U.S. Department of Health and Human Services.

Hirsch, E. (1984). *The block book.* Washington, DC: NAEYC.

Hopkins, S., & Winters, J. (1990). *Discover the world: Empowering children to value themselves, others and the earth.* Philadelphia, PA: New Society Publishers. (In Cooperation with Concerned Educators Allied for a Safe Environment.)

Johnson, J. E., Christie, J. F., & Wardle, F. (2005). *Play and early childhood development* (3rd ed.). Upper Saddle River, NJ: Pearson.

Judson, S. (Ed.). (1984). *A manual on nonviolence and children.* Philadelphia, PA: New Society Publishers.

Kendall, F. E. (1983). *Diversity in the classroom: A multicultural approach to the education of young children.* New York, NY: Teachers College Press.

Levin, D. E. (2003). *Teaching young children in violent times: Building a peaceable classroom* (2nd ed.). Cambridge, MA: Educators for Social Responsibility and Washington, DC: NAEYC.

Levin, D. E., & Carlsson-Paige, N. (2006). *The war play dilemma: What every parent and teacher needs to know* (2nd ed.). New York, NY: Teachers College Press.

Mitchell, A., & David, J. (Eds.). (1992). *Explorations with young children.* Mt. Rainier, MD: Gryphon House.

Mitchell, L. S. (1934). *Young geographers.* New York, NY: John Day Co.

National Association for the Education of Young Children. (2009). *NAEYC standards for early childhood professional preparation programs.* www.naeyc.org/files/naeyc/file/positions/ProfPrepStandards09.pdf

National Council for the Social Studies (NCSS). (2010). *National curriculum standards for social studies: A framework for teaching, learning, and assessment.* Silver Spring, MD: NCSS.

Neugebauer, B. (Ed.). (1987). *Alike and different: Exploring our humanity with young children.* Redmond, WA: Exchange Press.

Neugebauer, B. (Ed.). (1989). *The wonder of it: Exploring how the world works.* Redmond, WA: Exchange Press.

School Readiness Task Force, Hawaii Good Beginnings Interdepartmental Council. (2004). *Hawaii Preschool Content Standards.* Honolulu, HI: Good Beginnings Alliance.

Seefeldt, C. (Ed.). (1992). *The early childhood curriculum: A review of current research.* Early Childhood Education Series. New York, NY: Teachers College Press.

Seefeldt, C., Castle, A., & Falconer, R. (2010). *Social studies for the preschool/primary child* (8th ed.). Upper Saddle River, NJ: Pearson.

Seefeldt, C., & Galper, A. (2006). *Active experiences for active children: Social studies.* Upper Saddle River, NJ: Pearson.

Sunal, C. (1990). *Early childhood social studies.* Columbus, OH: Merrill.

Wichert, S. (1989). *Keeping the peace: Practicing cooperation and conflict resolution with preschoolers.* Philadelphia, PA: New Society Publishers.

MyEducationLab

Go to Topics 2: Child Development and Learning, 9: Content Areas/Lessons and Activities, and 12: Guiding Children in the MyEducationLab (www.myeducationlab.com) for *Meaningful Curriculum for Young Children,* where you can:

- Find learning outcomes for Child Development, Learning and Content Areas/Lessons and Activities, and Guiding Children along with the national standards that connect to these outcomes.
- Complete Assignments and Activities that can help you more deeply understand the chapter content.
- Apply and practice your understanding of the core teaching skills identified in the chapter with the Building Teaching Skills and Dispositions learning units.

- Examine challenging situations and cases presented in the IRIS Center Resources.
- Check your comprehension on the content covered in the chapter with the Study Plan. Here you will be able to take a chapter quiz, receive feedback on your answers, and then access Review, Practice, and Enrichment activities to enhance your understanding of chapter content.

Go to the Course Resources section in MyEducationLab, where you can:

- Use the Online Lesson Plan Builder to practice lesson planning and integrating national and state standards into your planning.

Appendix A

Planning Forms

Curriculum Focus: Objectives:					
Week of:	Monday	Tuesday	Wednesday	Thursday	Friday
Story					
Outdoor Activities **Purpose:** *to help children ...*					
Small Group 1 **Purpose:** *to help children ...*					
Small Group 2 **Purpose:** *to help children ...*					
Indoor Special Activities **Purpose:** *to help children ...*					
Circle Time **Purpose:** *to help children ...*					

Activity Plan Form—Detailed

Primary Curriculum Area:

Activity name, type, and brief description:

***WHO* It's For:**

Children (who this activity is planned for)

***WHY* This Activity**

Rationale: (why you have chosen this activity for these children at this time)

Objectives: *By participating in this activity the children will ...*

Standard(s): (state or national)

***HOW* to Prepare** *What you need:*
(materials, equipment, space, time)

Set up:

***HOW* to Teach** *Introduction:*

(how to begin so children will be interested and know what to do)

Teaching steps:

(what to do and say step by step to provide the experiences that will teach children the concepts, develop the skills, build the attitudes or dispositions that are described in the objectives)

Closure:

(what you will do or say to reinforce/support what children have learned and help them make a transition to another activity)

***HOW* to Assess and Document**

What to look for to identify if the objectives were met and how to document.

Objectives	Evidence of Learning Children might ...	How to Document This Evidence
Objectives from the first part of the plan	Things a child might do or say during the activity if objectives were met Things a child might do or say later during play, routines, or other activities if objectives were met	Observations, work samples, photographs, etc.

Activity Plan Form—Simple

Activity Name/Curriculum Area:

Objective:

Standard:

What you need:

How to teach:

How to assess:

Rationale, Goals, and Big Ideas for a Study of _____

_____

Date: _____

Rationale

I observed _____

_____

I have selected the topic _____

because _____

_____

Goals of the Study

1. To provide a focus for curriculum.

2. To help children learn about _____, its/their properties, uses, and value.

3. To help children appreciate the role of _____ in their lives.

4. To build a sense of curiosity and a disposition to learn.

5. To help children to learn to use inquiry processes.

6. To provide content for learning in all domains: physical, cognitive, social-emotional, creative.

Big Ideas

1.

2.

3.

4.

Web for Brainstorming Activities to Go with an Integrated Study

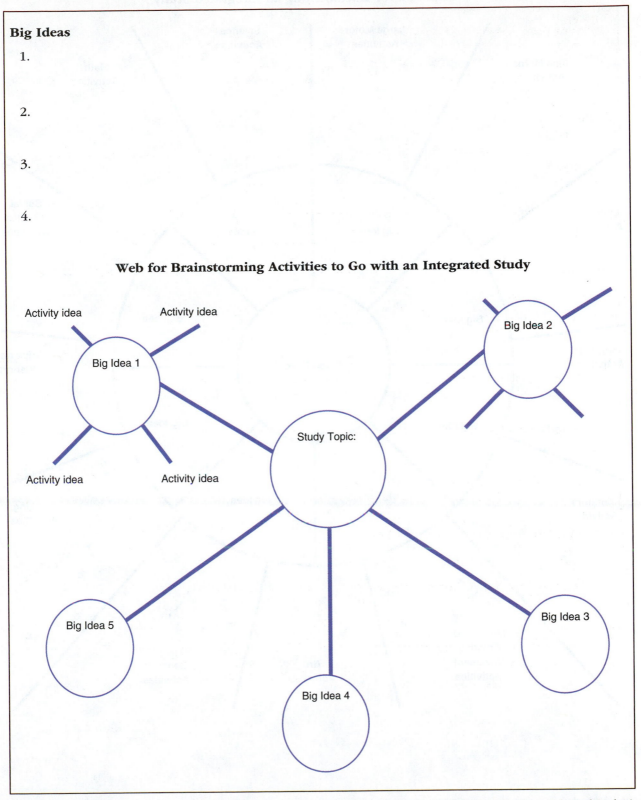

Sunburst for Documenting an Integrated Study

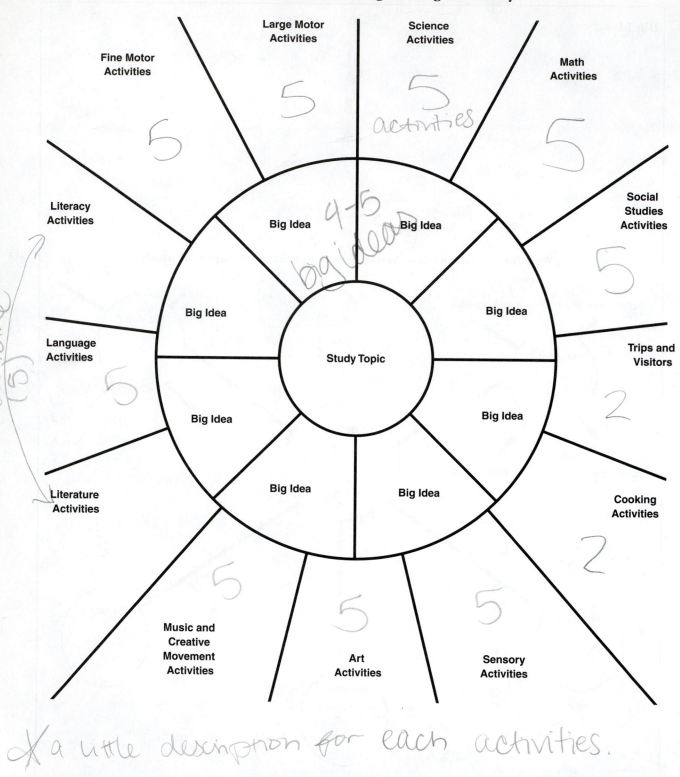

Fine Motor Activities

Large Motor Activities

Science Activities

Math Activities

Literacy Activities

Social Studies Activities

Language Activities

Trips and Visitors

Literature Activities

Cooking Activities

Music and Creative Movement Activities

Art Activities

Sensory Activities

Big Idea

Study Topic

5

5

activities

9-5 big ideas

5

5

5

combine (5)

2

2

5

5

5

X a little description for each activities.

Appendix B

Hawai'i Preschool Content Standards
Curriculum Guidelines for Programs for Four-Year-Olds

Author note: The Hawai'i Preschool Content Standards are included here as an example of curriculum content standards. These standards, adopted by the Hawai'i Good Beginnings Interdepartmental Council and the Hawai'i School Readiness Task Force, were designed as a tool to assist teachers of four year olds in developing meaningful learning experiences for young children. Like all appropriate content standards, they are not meant to be assessment measures but instead intended for use as a guide to planning curriculum. Similar standards have been adopted by all states. Throughout this book we have given examples of national standards that can be applied when developing learning experiences for young children.

We have used the Hawai'i Preschool Content Standards as a guideline when developing the Simple Activity Plans and the Detailed Activity Plans in most chapters of this book. We include them here as a reference so that you can see examples of how to use preschool content standards when creating learning experiences for young children.

DOMAIN I: PHYSICAL DEVELOPMENT, HEALTH AND SAFETY

Standard 1: Develop health awareness and skills.
Standard 2: Learn and follow basic safety rules.
Standard 3: Acquire basic self-help skills.
Standard 4: Develop strength and coordination of small muscles.
Standard 5: Develop strength and coordination of large muscles.

DOMAIN II: PERSONAL AND SOCIAL DEVELOPMENT

Standard 1: Understand and express feelings appropriately.
Standard 2: Begin to develop a sense of self.
Standard 3: Develop social skills and positive peer and adult relationships.
Standard 4: Develop a positive and open approach to learning.
Standard 5: Acquire behaviors and skills expected in school.

DOMAIN III: COMMUNICATION, LANGUAGE DEVELOPMENT AND LITERACY

Communication: Speaking and Listening
Standard 1: Use language in a variety of ways.
Standard 2: Listen with comprehension to a variety of spoken forms of language.

Language Acquisition
Standard 3: Acquire increasingly rich vocabulary and sentence structure.

Emergent Reading and Writing
Standard 4: Recognize and use symbols.
Standard 5: Enjoy and understand books.
Standard 6: Show interest in writing.
Standard 7: Acquire concepts of print.
Standard 8: Acquire emergent literacy skills while exploring print in books and the environment.

DOMAIN IV: COGNITIVE DEVELOPMENT

Symbolic Play
Standard 1: Represent fantasy and real-life experiences through pretend play.
Standard 2: Engage in sustained symbolic play with other children.

Mathematics

Standard 1: Learn about numbers, numerical representation, and simple numerical operations.

Standard 2: Recognize and create patterns and become aware of relationships.

Standard 3: Develop concepts of shape and space.

Standard 4: Develop and use measurement concepts.

Standard 5: Represent and interpret data.

Science

Standard 1: Increase sensory awareness.

Standard 2: Engage in scientific inquiry.

Standard 3: Explore physical properties of the world.

Standard 4: Explore characteristics of living things.

Standard 5: Learn about earth and sky.

Standard 6: Have a variety of educational experiences that involve technology.

Social Studies

Standard 1: Learn about themselves and other people.

Standard 2: Appreciate their own and other cultures.

Standard 3: Become aware of how things, people, and places change over time.

Standard 4: Explore how people depend upon one another for the things (goods) and help (services) they need.

Standard 5: Understand what people need to do to work and live together in groups.

Standard 6: Develop geographic awareness

Standard 7: Develop awareness of the natural environment and how it can be protected.

DOMAIN V: CREATIVE DEVELOPMENT

Visual Art

Standard 1: Create and express themselves through a variety of art experiences.

Standard 2: Begin to learn about art elements and techniques.

Music

Standard 1: Create and express themselves through a variety of music experiences.

Standard 2: Begin to learn about music elements and techniques.

Creative Movement and Drama

Standard 1: Create and express themselves through a variety of creative movement and drama experiences.

Standard 2: Begin to learn about movement elements and techniques.

Aesthetic Appreciation

Standard 1: Develop appreciation for natural and cultural beauty and for visual and performing arts.

Index